Effective Methods
for Software Testing

Third Edition

Effective Methods
for Software Testing
Third Edition

William E. Perry

WILEY

Wiley Publishing, Inc.

Effective Methods for Software Testing, Third Edition
Published by
Wiley Publishing, Inc.
10475 Crosspoint Boulevard
Indianapolis, IN 46256
www.wiley.com

ISBN-13: 978-0-7645-9837-1
ISBN-10: 0-7645-9837-6

Manufactured in the United States of America

10 9 8 7 6 5 4 3 2 1

3MA/QV/QU/QW/IN

For general information on our other products and services or to obtain technical support, please contact our Customer Care Department within the U.S. at (800) 762-2974, outside the U.S. at (317) 572-3993 or fax (317) 572-4002.

Library of Congress Control Number: 2005036216

This book is dedicated to my wife Cynthia, who for many years has been "testing" my ability to live in accordance with our marriage vows. She taught me that testing is a lifelong process, that testing is necessary to ensure that you are meeting your objectives, and that testing can be fun if it is performed correctly. Thank you, Cynthia. What you have taught me is incorporated into many of the concepts in this book.

About the Author

William E. Perry holds degrees from Clarkson University, University of Rochester, and Rochester Institute of Technology. Bill also holds the following professional certifications: CPA (Certified Public Accountant), CIA (Certified Internal Auditor), CISA (Certified Information Services Auditor), CSQA (Certified Software Quality Analyst), and CSTE (Certified Software Tester). He has been an examiner for the Malcolm Baldrige National Quality Award, and served on standards committees for NIST (National Institute of Standards and Technology), IEEE (Institute of Electrical and Electronics Engineers), AICPA (American Institute of Certified Public Accountants) and ISACA (Information Systems Audit and Control Association).

In 1980, Bill founded the Quality Assurance Institute (QAI), a professional association for testers. QAI offers professional certification for Quality Assurance, Software Testing, Software Project Leaders and Business Analyst Professional. More than 27,000 individuals have been certified since the inception of the program.

Bill has authored more than 50 books, many published by John Wiley & Sons. He recently founded the Internal Control Institute (ICI). ICI and St. Petersburg College recently formed the Internal Control Center of Excellence to share best internal control practices, hold conferences on emerging internal control practices, and to offer e-learning courses and a professional certification in internal control.

Credits

Executive Editor
Robert Elliott

Production Editor
Felicia Robinson

Editorial Manager
Mary Beth Wakefield

Production Manager
Tim Tate

Vice President and Executive Group Publisher
Richard Swadley

Vice President and Executive Publisher
Joseph B. Wikert

Project Coordinator
Michael Kruzil

Graphics and Production Specialists
Carrie Foster
Mary J. Gillot
Lauren Goddard
Denny Hager
Joyce Haughyey
Stephanie D. Jumper
Rashell Smith

Quality Control Technicians
John Greenough
Brian H. Walls

Proofreading and Indexing
Techbooks

Contents

Introduction   **xxv**

Part I   **Assessing Testing Capabilities and Competencies**   **1**

Chapter 1   **Assessing Capabilities, Staff Competency, and User
                Satisfaction**   **3**
                The Three-Step Process to Becoming a World-Class Testing
                   Organization   3
                Step 1: Define a World-Class Software Testing Model   5
                   Customizing the World-Class Model for Your Organization   7
                Step 2: Develop Baselines for Your Organization   8
                   Assessment 1: Assessing the Test Environment   8
                      Implementation Procedures   9
                      Verifying the Assessment   13
                   Assessment 2: Assessing the Capabilities of Your Existing
                      Test Processes   13
                   Assessment 3: Assessing the Competency of Your Testers   14
                      Implementation Procedures   14
                      Verifying the Assessment   16
                Step 3: Develop an Improvement Plan   16
                Summary   18

Part II   **Building a Software Testing Environment**   **35**

Chapter 2   **Creating an Environment Supportive of Software Testing**   **37**
                Minimizing Risks   38
                   Risk Appetite for Software Quality   38
                   Risks Associated with Implementing Specifications   39
                      Faulty Software Design   39
                      Data Problems   39

Risks Associated with Not Meeting Customer Needs   40
Developing a Role for Software Testers   43
Writing a Policy for Software Testing   45
Criteria for a Testing Policy   45
Methods for Establishing a Testing Policy   46
Economics of Testing   47
Testing—An Organizational Issue   50
Management Support for Software Testing   50
Building a Structured Approach to Software Testing   51
Requirements   54
Design   54
Program   55
Test   55
Installation   55
Maintenance   55
Developing a Test Strategy   56
Use Work Paper 2-1   58
Use Work Paper 2-2   58
Summary   60

Chapter 3   Building the Software Testing Process   63
Software Testing Guidelines   63
Guideline #1: Testing Should Reduce Software Development
    Risk   64
Guideline #2: Testing Should Be Performed Effectively   65
Guideline #3: Testing Should Uncover Defects   65
Defects Versus Failures   65
Why Are Defects Hard to Find?   66
Guideline #4: Testing Should Be Performed Using Business
    Logic   67
Guideline #5: Testing Should Occur Throughout the
    Development Life Cycle   68
Guideline #6: Testing Should Test Both Function and Structure   69
Why Use Both Testing Methods?   69
Structural and Functional Tests Using Verification and
    Validation Techniques   69
Workbench Concept   71
Testing That Parallels the Software Development Process 72
Customizing the Software-Testing Process   74
Determining the Test Strategy Objectives   74
Determining the Type of Development Project   75
Determining the Type of Software System   76
Determining the Project Scope   77
Identifying the Software Risks   77
Determining When Testing Should Occur   79
Defining the System Test Plan Standard   79

	Defining the Unit Test Plan Standard	83
	Converting Testing Strategy to Testing Tactics	83
	Process Preparation Checklist	86
	Summary	86
Chapter 4	**Selecting and Installing Software Testing Tools**	**103**
	Integrating Tools into the Tester's Work Processes	103
	Tools Available for Testing Software	104
	Selecting and Using Test Tools	108
	Matching the Tool to Its Use	109
	Selecting a Tool Appropriate to Its Life Cycle Phase	109
	Matching the Tool to the Tester's Skill Level	111
	Selecting an Affordable Tool	114
	Training Testers in Tool Usage	116
	Appointing Tool Managers	117
	Prerequisites to Creating a Tool Manager Position	118
	Selecting a Tool Manager	118
	Assigning the Tool Manager Duties	119
	Limiting the Tool Manager's Tenure	120
	Summary	120
Chapter 5	**Building Software Tester Competency**	**125**
	What Is a Common Body of Knowledge?	125
	Who Is Responsible for the Software Tester's Competency?	126
	How Is Personal Competency Used in Job Performance?	126
	Using the 2006 CSTE CBOK	127
	Developing a Training Curriculum	128
	Using the CBOK to Build an Effective Testing Team	129
	Summary	131
Part III	**The Seven-Step Testing Process**	**151**
Chapter 6	**Overview of the Software Testing Process**	**153**
	Advantages of Following a Process	153
	The Cost of Computer Testing	154
	Quantifying the Cost of Removing Defects	155
	Reducing the Cost of Testing	156
	The Seven-Step Software Testing Process	156
	Objectives of the Seven-Step Process	159
	Customizing the Seven-Step Process	160
	Managing the Seven-Step Process	161
	Using the Tester's Workbench with the Seven-Step Process	162
	Workbench Skills	163
	Summary	164
Chapter 7	**Step 1: Organizing for Testing**	**165**
	Objective	165
	Workbench	166
	Input	167

Do Procedures	167
Task 1: Appoint the Test Manager	167
Task 2: Define the Scope of Testing	168
Task 3: Appoint the Test Team	168
Internal Team Approach	169
External Team Approach	170
Non-IT Team Approach	170
Combination Team Approach	170
Task 4: Verify the Development Documentation	171
Development Phases	171
Measuring Project Documentation Needs	174
Determining What Documents Must Be Produced	175
Determining the Completeness of Individual Documents	179
Determining Documentation Timeliness	180
Task 5: Validate the Test Estimate and Project Status	
Reporting Process	181
Validating the Test Estimate	182
Testing the Validity of the Software Cost Estimate	185
Calculating the Project Status Using a Point System	189
Check Procedures	200
Output	200
Summary	200

Chapter 8   Step 2: Developing the Test Plan   209

Overview	209
Objective	210
Concerns	210
Workbench	211
Input	212
Do Procedures	212
Task 1: Profile the Software Project	212
Conducting a Walkthrough of the Customer/User Area	212
Developing a Profile of the Software Project	213
Task 2: Understand the Project Risks	215
Task 3: Select a Testing Technique	222
Structural System Testing Techniques	223
Functional System Testing Techniques	229
Task 4: Plan Unit Testing and Analysis	235
Functional Testing and Analysis	236
Structural Testing and Analysis	238
Error-Oriented Testing and Analysis	240
Managerial Aspects of Unit Testing and Analysis	243
Task 5: Build the Test Plan	244
Setting Test Objectives	245
Developing a Test Matrix	245
Defining Test Administration	250
Writing the Test Plan	251

Task 6: Inspect the Test Plan	254
Inspection Concerns	255
Products/Deliverables to Inspect	256
Formal Inspection Roles	256
Formal Inspection Defect Classification	258
Inspection Procedures	259
Check Procedures	262
Output	262
Guidelines	262
Summary	263

Chapter 9	**Step 3: Verification Testing**	**291**
	Overview	292
	Objective	293
	Concerns	294
	Workbench	294
	Input	296
	The Requirements Phase	296
	The Design Phase	296
	The Programming Phase	297
	Do Procedures	298
	Task 1: Test During the Requirements Phase	298
	Requirements Phase Test Factors	299
	Preparing a Risk Matrix	302
	Performing a Test Factor Analysis	310
	Conducting a Requirements Walkthrough	312
	Performing Requirements Tracing	314
	Ensuring Requirements Are Testable	315
	Task 2: Test During the Design Phase	316
	Scoring Success Factors	316
	Analyzing Test Factors	318
	Conducting a Design Review	320
	Inspecting Design Deliverables	322
	Task 3: Test During the Programming Phase	323
	Desk Debugging the Program	325
	Performing Programming Phase Test Factor Analysis	326
	Conducting a Peer Review	328
	Check Procedures	330
	Output	331
	Guidelines	331
	Summary	332

Chapter 10	**Step 4: Validation Testing**	**409**
	Overview	409
	Objective	410
	Concerns	410
	Workbench	410
	Input	411

Do Procedures   412
    Task 1: Build the Test Data   412
        Sources of Test Data/Test Scripts   412
        Testing File Design   413
        Defining Design Goals   414
        Entering Test Data   414
        Applying Test Files Against Programs That Update
            Master Records   414
        Creating and Using Test Data   415
        Payroll Application Example   416
        Creating Test Data for Stress/Load Testing   430
        Creating Test Scripts   430
    Task 2: Execute Tests   434
    Task 3: Record Test Results   436
        Documenting the Deviation   437
        Documenting the Effect   438
        Documenting the Cause   438
Check Procedures   439
Output   439
Guidelines   439
Summary   440

Chapter 11   Step 5: Analyzing and Reporting Test Results   459
Overview   459
Concerns   460
Workbench   460
Input   461
    Test Plan and Project Plan   461
    Expected Processing Results   461
    Data Collected during Testing   461
        Test Results Data   462
        Test Transactions, Test Suites, and Test Events   462
        Defects   462
        Efficiency   463
    Storing Data Collected During Testing   463
Do Procedures   463
    Task 1: Report Software Status   464
        Establishing a Measurement Team   465
        Creating an Inventory of Existing Project Measurements   465
        Developing a Consistent Set of Project Metrics   466
        Defining Process Requirements   466
        Developing and Implementing the Process   466
        Monitoring the Process   466
    Task 2: Report Interim Test Results   470
        Function/Test Matrix   470
        Functional Testing Status Report   471
        Functions Working Timeline Report   472
        Expected Versus Actual Defects Uncovered Timeline Report 472

Defects Uncovered Versus Corrected Gap Timeline Report	473
Average Age of Uncorrected Defects by Type Report	475
Defect Distribution Report	475
Normalized Defect Distribution Report	476
Testing Action Report	477
Interim Test Report	478
Task 3: Report Final Test Results	478
Individual Project Test Report	480
Integration Test Report	480
System Test Report	480
Acceptance Test Report	482
Check Procedures	482
Output	482
Guidelines	482
Summary	483

Chapter 12 **Step 6: Acceptance and Operational Testing** **491**

Overview	491
Objective	492
Concerns	493
Workbench	494
Input Procedures	495
Task 1: Acceptance Testing	496
Defining the Acceptance Criteria	497
Developing an Acceptance Plan	498
Executing the Acceptance Plan	499
Developing Test Cases (Use Cases) Based on How Software Will Be Used	500
Task 2: Pre-Operational Testing	503
Testing New Software Installation	509
Testing the Changed Software Version	509
Monitoring Production	512
Documenting Problems	513
Task 3: Post-Operational Testing	513
Developing and Updating the Test Plan	514
Developing and Updating the Test Data	515
Testing the Control Change Process	517
Conducting Testing	518
Developing and Updating Training Material	518
Check Procedures	522
Output	522
Is the Automated Application Acceptable?	522
Automated Application Segment Failure Notification	523
Is the Manual Segment Acceptable?	523
Training Failure Notification Form	524
Guidelines	524
Summary	525

Chapter 13 Step 7: Post-Implementation Analysis   **571**
       Overview   571
       Concerns   572
       Workbench   572
       Input   574
       Do Procedures   574
         Task 1: Establish Assessment Objectives   574
         Task 2: Identify What to Measure   575
         Task 3: Assign Measurement Responsibility   575
         Task 4: Select Evaluation Approach   575
         Task 5: Identify Needed Facts   576
         Task 6: Collect Evaluation Data   577
         Task 7: Assess the Effectiveness of Testing   577
           Using Testing Metrics   577
       Check Procedures   580
       Output   580
       Guidelines   581
       Summary   581

Part IV   Incorporating Specialized Testing Responsibilities   **583**

Chapter 14 Software Development Methodologies   **585**
       How Much Testing Is Enough?   585
         Software Development Methodologies   586
           Overview   586
           Methodology Types   587
           Software Development Life Cycle   588
         Defining Requirements   592
           Categories   592
           Attributes   593
         Methodology Maturity   596
         Competencies Required   598
         Staff Experience   600
         Configuration-Management Controls   600
           Basic CM Requirements   600
           Planning   602
           Data Distribution and Access   602
           CM Administration   602
         Configuration Identification   603
         Configuration Control   605
       Measuring the Impact of the Software Development Process   605
       Summary   606

Chapter 15 Testing Client/Server Systems   **611**
       Overview   611
       Concerns   612
       Workbench   613
       Input   614

Do Procedures   614
    Task 1: Assess Readiness   614
        Software Development Process Maturity Levels   615
        Conducting the Client/Server Readiness Assessment   621
        Preparing a Client/Server Readiness Footprint Chart   621
    Task 2: Assess Key Components   622
    Task 3: Assess Client Needs   622
Check Procedures   624
Output   624
Guidelines   624
Summary   624

Chapter 16   Rapid Application Development Testing   633
Overview   633
Objective   634
Concerns   634
    Testing Iterations   634
    Testing Components   635
    Testing Performance   635
    Recording Test Information   635
Workbench   635
Input   636
Do Procedures   636
    Testing Within Iterative RAD   636
    Spiral Testing   638
    Task 1: Determine Appropriateness of RAD   639
    Task 2: Test Planning Iterations   640
    Task 3: Test Subsequent Planning Iterations   640
    Task 4: Test the Final Planning Iteration   642
Check Procedures   642
Output   643
Guidelines   643
Summary   643

Chapter 17   Testing Internal Controls   655
Overview   655
Internal Controls   657
    Control Objectives   657
    Preventive Controls   658
        Source-Data Authorization   658
        Data Input   659
        Source-Data Preparation   659
        Turnaround Documents   659
        Prenumbered Forms   659
        Input Validation   659
        File Auto-Updating   661
        Processing Controls   661

Detective Controls   662
    Data Transmission   663
    Control Register   663
    Control Totals   664
    Documenting and Testing   664
    Output Checks   664
Corrective Controls   665
    Error Detection and Resubmission 665
    Audit Trails   665
Cost/Benefit Analysis   666
Assessing Internal Controls   666
Task 1: Understand the System Being Tested   666
Task 2: Identify Risks   668
Task 3: Review Application Controls   668
Task 4: Test Application Controls   668
    Testing Without Computer Processing   669
    Testing with Computer Processing   669
    Transaction Flow Testing   672
    Objectives of Internal Accounting Controls 673
    Results of Testing   677
Task 5: Document Control Strengths and Weaknesses   677
Quality Control Checklist   678
Summary   678

Chapter 18 Testing COTS and Contracted Software   685
Overview   686
COTS Software Advantages, Disadvantages, and Risks   686
COTS Versus Contracted Software   686
COTS Advantages   687
COTS Disadvantages   687
Implementation Risks   688
Testing COTS Software   689
Testing Contracted Software   690
Objective   691
Concerns   691
Workbench   692
Input   693
Do Procedures   693
Task 1: Test Business Fit   693
    Step 1: Testing Needs Specification   693
    Step 2: Testing CSFs   695
Task 2: Test Operational Fit   696
    Step 1: Test Compatibility   697
    Step 2: Integrate the Software into Existing Work Flows   698
    Step 3: Demonstrate the Software in Action   700
Task 3: Test People Fit   701

	Task 4: Acceptance-Test the Software Process	702
	Step 1: Create Functional Test Conditions	702
	Step 2: Create Structural Test Conditions	703
	Modifying the Testing Process for Contracted Software	704
	Check Procedures	705
	Output	705
	Guidelines	706
	Summary	706
Chapter 19	**Testing in a Multiplatform Environment**	**717**
	Overview	717
	Objective	718
	Concerns	718
	Background on Testing in a Multiplatform Environment	718
	Workbench	719
	Input	720
	Do Procedures	721
	Task 1: Define Platform Configuration Concerns	721
	Task 2: List Needed Platform Configurations	723
	Task 3: Assess Test Room Configurations	723
	Task 4: List Structural Components Affected by the Platform(s)	723
	Task 5: List Interfaces the Platform Affects	725
	Task 6: Execute the Tests	726
	Check Procedures	726
	Output	726
	Guidelines	726
	Summary	727
Chapter 20	**Testing Software System Security**	**733**
	Overview	733
	Objective	734
	Concerns	734
	Workbench	734
	Input	735
	Where Vulnerabilities Occur	735
	Functional Vulnerabilities	736
	Vulnerable Areas	737
	Accidental Versus Intentional Losses	738
	Do Procedures	739
	Task 1: Establish a Security Baseline	739
	Why Baselines Are Necessary	740
	Creating Baselines	740
	Using Baselines	749
	Task 2: Build a Penetration-Point Matrix	751
	Controlling People by Controlling Activities	751
	Selecting Security Activities	752
	Controlling Business Transactions	755

Characteristics of Security Penetration	756
Building a Penetration-Point Matrix	757
Task 3: Analyze the Results of Security Testing	760
Evaluating the Adequacy of Security	761
Check Procedures	762
Output	762
Guidelines	762
Summary	762

Chapter 21   Testing a Data Warehouse — **765**

Overview	765
Concerns	765
Workbench	766
Input	767
Do Procedures	768
Task 1: Measure the Magnitude of Data Warehouse Concerns	768
Task 2: Identify Data Warehouse Activity Processes to Test	769
Organizational Process	769
Data Documentation Process	769
System Development Process	770
Access Control Process	771
Data Integrity Process	771
Operations Process	772
Backup/Recovery Process	773
Performing Task 2	774
Task 3: Test the Adequacy of Data Warehouse Activity Processes	774
Check Procedures	780
Output	780
Guidelines	780
Summary	780

Chapter 22   Testing Web-Based Systems — **799**

Overview	799
Concerns	800
Workbench	800
Input	801
Do Procedures	802
Task 1: Select Web-Based Risks to Include in the Test Plan	802
Security Concerns	803
Performance Concerns	803
Correctness Concerns	804
Compatibility Concerns	804
Reliability Concerns	806
Data Integrity Concerns	806
Usability Concerns	806
Recoverability Concerns	807

Task 2: Select Web-Based Tests   807
    Unit or Component   807
    Integration   807
    System   807
    User Acceptance   808
    Performance   808
    Load/Stress   808
    Regression   808
    Usability   808
    Compatibility   808
Task 3: Select Web-Based Test Tools   809
Task 4: Test Web-Based Systems   809
Check Procedures   809
Output   810
Guidelines   810
Summary   811

Part V   **Building Agility into the Testing Process**   **817**

Chapter 23 **Using Agile Methods to Improve Software Testing** **819**
The Importance of Agility   819
Building an Agile Testing Process   820
Agility Inhibitors   821
Is Improvement Necessary?   822
Compressing Time   823
    Challenges   824
    Solutions   825
    Measuring Readiness   826
    The Seven-Step Process   826
Summary   827

Chapter 24 **Building Agility into the Testing Process** **831**
Step 1: Measure Software Process Variability   831
    Timelines   832
    Process Steps   833
        Workbenches   833
        Time-Compression Workbenches 834
        Reducing Variability   835
        Developing Timelines   836
    Improvement Shopping List   841
    Quality Control Checklist   841
    Conclusion   842
Step 2: Maximize Best Practices   842
    Tester Agility   842
        Software Testing Relationships 843
        Tradeoffs   845
        Capability Chart   847
        Measuring Effectiveness and Efficiency 848

Improvement Shopping List   856
Quality Control Checklist   856
Conclusion   857
Step 3: Build on Strength, Minimize Weakness   857
Effective Testing Processes   857
Poor Testing Processes   860
Improvement Shopping List   860
Quality Control Checklist   860
Conclusion   861
Step 4: Identify and Address Improvement Barriers   861
The Stakeholder Perspective   861
Stakeholder Involvement   863
Performing Stakeholder Analysis   863
Red-Flag/Hot-Button Barriers   864
Staff-Competency Barriers   865
Administrative/Organizational Barriers   865
Determining the Root Cause of Barriers/Obstacles   866
Addressing the Root Cause of Barriers/Obstacles   867
Quality Control Checklist   869
Conclusion   869
Step 5: Identify and Address Cultural and Communication
Barriers   869
Management Cultures   870
Culture 1: Manage People   871
Culture 2: Manage by Process   873
Culture 3: Manage Competencies   874
Culture 4: Manage by Fact   876
Culture 5: Manage Business Innovation   878
Cultural Barriers   879
Identifying the Current Management Culture   879
Identifying the Barriers Posed by the Culture   879
Determining What Can Be Done in the Current Culture   879
Determining the Desired Culture for Time Compression   879
Determining How to Address Culture Barriers   880
Open and Effective Communication   880
Lines of Communication   881
Information/Communication Barriers   882
Effective Communication   882
Quality Control Checklist   884
Conclusion   885
Step 6: Identify Implementable Improvements   885
What Is an Implementable?   885
Identifying Implementables via Time Compression   886
Prioritizing Implementables   888
Documenting Approaches   890
Quality Control Checklist   890
Conclusion   890

Step 7: Develop and Execute an Implementation Plan . 891
Planning 891
Implementing Ideas 891
Requisite Resources 893
Quality Control Checklist 894
Conclusion 894
Summary 895

Index **929**

Introduction

Most books about software testing explain "what" to do. This book, on the other hand, takes more of a "how-to" approach. It provides the procedures, templates, checklists, and assessment questionnaires necessary to conduct effective and efficient software testing.

The book is divided into five parts, as follows:

- **Part One: Assessing Testing Capabilities and Competencies.** It is difficult to make any significant change until you know where you are. A baseline tells not only where you are, but lets you measure your progress as your testing strategies and techniques improve. Part One provides three baseline assessments: the capabilities of your software testing group, the competencies of your individual testers, and the effectiveness of your test processes.

- **Part Two: Building a Software Testing Environment.** Software testers are most effective when they work in an environment that encourages and supports well-established testing policies and procedures. The environment includes the procedures and tools for testing, as well as the support and encouragement of management. Part Two begins by describing how to build an environment conducive to testing, and then expands the discussion by describing how to develop a testing process, select testing tools, and build the competency of your testers.

- **Part Three: The Seven-Step Testing Process.** Part Three comprises the core material in the book. It defines a world-class software testing process, from its initiation through testing changes made to operational software systems. This material can be used two ways. First, it contains sufficient procedures and templates so that an organization can use the process as their own. Of course, most organizations inevitably will make some changes to accommodate local vocabulary, specific needs, and customs. This customization process, the seven-step process in this book becomes "owned" by the software testers.

- **Part Four: Incorporating Specialized Testing Responsibilities.** The seven-step testing process is a generic process that almost all software testing organizations can use. However, the mission of software testers may incorporate specialized activities, such as testing security. Rather than incorporating these specialized testing activities directly into the seven-step process, they are presented as individual, specialized activities. As appropriate, they can be incorporated into the seven-step process.

- **Part Five: Building Agility into the Testing Process.** Part Five, which draws on what you've learned earlier in the book, is designed to help you identify the strengths and weaknesses of your current software testing process, and then modify it to become more usable or agile.

Getting the Most Out of This Book

This book is not designed to be read like a novel, from beginning to end, nor is it filled with human interest stories about testers. The book focuses on how to conduct software testing. It is designed to help you improve your testing competencies and processes. The self-assessments in Part One will help you identify which parts of the book you need to read first.

The following guidelines will help you maximize the benefit from this book:

- **Establish a baseline of current performance.** Part One of this book (and Chapter 5) contains four self-assessments for establishing baselines. You need to know where you are so that you can develop a good plan for moving forward.

- **Define the software testing organization you would like to have.** It has been said that if you do not know where you're going, all roads lead there. Too many software testing groups just add new testing programs, processes, and tools without knowing if they will integrate effectively.

- **Develop a plan for moving from your baseline to your goal.** Few organizations can quickly and effectively install an entirely new software testing process. Gradual change is normally much better than radical change. Therefore, identify the gaps between where you are and where you want to be. Determine which of those gaps if closed would provide the greatest benefit to your organization. That becomes the part of the plan you implement first. Over time you will move the entire testing process from your current baseline to your desired goal.

For additional information on software testing conferences and training programs, visit www.taiworldwide.org. For information on software testing certifications, visit www.softwarecertifications.org.

What's New in the Third Edition

The core of this book is the step-by-step process for testing software. This edition has simplified that process from 11 steps to 7 steps.

A major addition to this edition is the self-assessment in Chapter 5, which testers can use to identify their strengths and weaknesses and then build a personal improvement plan. The self-assessment is based on the Common Body of Knowledge (CBOK) for the Certified Software Tester (CSTE).

Other significant additions include

- A new chapter on testing internal control

- An expanded chapter on testing security

- A new chapter on adapting testing to the developmental methodology used to build the software

- Two new chapters on how to incorporate agile methods into the testing process

What's on the CD

This book includes a CD that contains the work papers and quality control checklists to help you implement the software testing process.

To use the CD, first you need to select a software testing activity that you want to implement in your organization—for example, test planning. Then, from the chapter on test planning, identify those work papers and checklists that you believe would be beneficial to your organization. You can extract those work papers and checklists from the CD and begin a customization process. For example, you can include the name of your organization, add or delete portions of the work papers, and change the terminology to be consistent with your organization.

After you have used the work papers for conducting a software test, you should bundle the work papers into a case study for new testers. If they use the book to learn the basics of software testing and then can cross reference what they have learned to examples of how the work papers are actually used in software testing, learning should be accelerated.

Effective Methods for Software Testing

Third Edition

PART One

Assessing Testing Capabilities and Competencies

CHAPTER 1

Assessing Capabilities, Staff Competency, and User Satisfaction

It has been said, "If you do not know where you are going, all roads lead there." Traditionally, many IT organizations annually develop a list of improvements to incorporate into their operations without establishing a goal. Using this approach, the IT organization can declare "victory" any time it wants.

This chapter will help you understand the importance of following a well-defined process for becoming a world-class software testing organization. This chapter will help you define your strengths and deficiencies, your staff competencies and deficiencies, and areas of user dissatisfaction.

The objective of this chapter is threefold: to define a world-class software testing model, to provide a self-assessment process for your software testing organization to measure yourself against the world-class model, and to provide some planning considerations for moving to a world-class level.

The Three-Step Process to Becoming a World-Class Testing Organization

The roadmap to become a world-class software testing organization is a simple three-step process, as follows:

1. Define or adopt a world-class software testing model.

2. Determine your organization's current level of software testing capabilities, competencies, and user satisfaction.

3. Develop and implement a plan to upgrade from your current capabilities, competencies, and user satisfaction to those in the world-class software testing model.

This three-step process requires you to compare your current capabilities, competencies, and user satisfaction against those of the world-class software testing model. This assessment will enable you to develop a baseline of your organization's performance. The plan that you develop will, over time, move that baseline from its current level of performance to a world-class level. Understanding the model for a world-class software testing organization and then comparing your organization will provide you with a plan for using the remainder of the material in this book.

Software testing is an integral part of the software-development process, which comprises the following four components (see Figure 1-1):

1. **Plan (P): Devise a plan.** Define your objective and determine the strategy and supporting methods to achieve it. You should base the plan on an assessment of your current situation, and the strategy should clearly focus on the strategic initiatives/key units that will drive your improvement plan.

2. **Do (D): Execute the plan.** Create the conditions and perform the necessary training to execute the plan. Make sure everyone thoroughly understands the objectives and the plan. Teach workers the procedures and skills they need to fulfill the plan and thoroughly understand the job. Then perform the work according to these procedures.

3. **Check (C): Check the results.** Check to determine whether work is progressing according to the plan and whether the expected results are being obtained. Check for performance of the set procedures, changes in conditions, or abnormalities that may appear. As often as possible, compare the results of the work with the objectives.

4. **Act (A): Take the necessary action.** If your checkup reveals that the work is not being performed according to the plan or that results are not what you anticipated, devise measures to take appropriate actions.

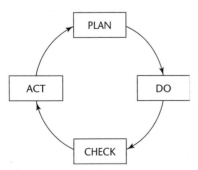

Figure 1-1   The four components of the software-development process.

Testing involves only the "check" component of the plan-do-check-act (PDCA) cycle. The software development team is responsible for the three remaining components. The development team plans the project and builds the software (the "do" component); the testers check to determine that the software meets the needs of the customers and users. If it does not, the testers report defects to the development team. It is the development team that makes the determination as to whether the uncovered defects are to be corrected.

The role of testing is to fulfill the check responsibilities assigned to the testers; it is not to determine whether software can be placed into production. That is the responsibility of the customers, users, and development team.

Step 1: Define a World-Class Software Testing Model

There is no generally accepted model for a world-class software testing organization. However, analyzing the best testing organizations among the more than 1,000 IT organizations affiliated with the Quality Assurance Institute (QAI) enabled QAI to identify the attributes of the best software testing organizations (see Figure 1-2). Organizations that follow this model report more effective and efficient testing than those that do not.

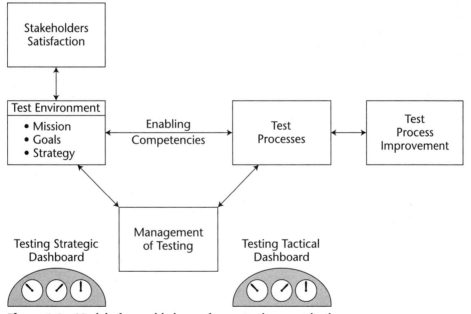

Figure 1-2   Model of a world-class software testing organization.

The world-class software testing model includes

- **Test environment.** The conditions that management has put into place that both enable and constrain how testing is performed. The test environment includes management support, resources, work processes, tools, motivation, and so forth.

- **Process to test a single software project.** The standards and procedures testers use to test.

- **Tester competency.** The skill sets needed to test software in a test environment. The three self-assessments that follow are for the above three attributes of a world-class software testing organization.

NOTE The three self-assessments in this chapter correspond to the preceding three attributes of a world-class software testing organization.

The world-class model of a software testing organization focuses on stakeholder satisfaction. This assumes a greater role for a world-class software testing organization than just testing against documented software requirements. Chapter 2 defines the many roles that software testing can adopt; however, those roles include much more than testing documented software requirements. They include testing for quality factors such as ease of use, meeting testing schedules and budgets, and minimizing the risks involved with any software project.

According to the world-class model, the following parties have a vested interest in software testing:

- **Software customer.** The party or department that contracts for the software to be developed.

- **Software user.** The individual or group that will use the software once it is placed into production. (Note: This may be the customer or it may be parties other than the customer.)

- **Software developer.** The individual or group that receives the requirements from the software user or assists in writing them, designing, building, and maintaining the software, as needed.

- **Development tester.** The individual or group that performs the test function within the software development group.

- **IT management.** The individual or group with responsibility for fulfilling the information technology mission. Testing supports fulfilling that mission.

- **Senior management.** The CEO of the organization and other senior executives who are responsible for fulfilling the organization mission. Information technology is an activity that supports fulfilling that mission.

- **Auditor.** The individual or group responsible for evaluating the effectiveness, efficiency, and adequacy of controls in the information technology area. Testing is considered a control by the audit function.

- **Project manager.** The individual responsible for managing the building, maintaining, and/or implementing of software.

The test mission, strategy, and environment must be focused on stakeholder satisfaction. The mission defines the testing objectives; the strategy defines how the mission will be accomplished; and the environment provides the culture, processes, and tools that are conducive to effective and efficient software testing.

The test processes are those step-by-step procedures that the testers will follow to accomplish their assigned tasks. Test processes executed by trained and competent testers enable those testers to accomplish the defined test mission.

The test processes need to be improved continually for two reasons: to make them more effective and efficient to use, and to incorporate updated approaches into testing new technologies and software development methodologies.

The responsibility for ensuring that the execution of the test processes meets the defined test mission lies with management. Management must ensure that testers are following and can accomplish the test plan, and that the plan will, in fact, accomplish the test objectives. If not, management should modify the plan to meet those objectives.

Management and testers need tools to enable them to fulfill their responsibilities. Two very important tools are the testing strategic dashboard and the testing tactical dashboard. The *testing strategic dashboard* includes key indicators such as user satisfaction, staff competency, and the percent of tests completed. The *testing tactical dashboard* includes test indicators such as the number of requirements tested and percent correct, defects uncovered, defects corrected and uncorrected, and the schedule and budget status.

Management must ensure that if you meet the testing tactical key indicators, you will, in fact, meet the objectives defined by the strategic key indicators.

Customizing the World-Class Model for Your Organization

You can customize the world-class model for software testing by defining the attributes of each of its components (refer to Figure 1-2). The material in this book explains the attributes of all the components: stakeholder satisfaction, test mission, test management and enabling competencies are discussed in Part 2. The test processes are explained in Parts 3 and 4. Test process improvement is described in Part 5 of this book.

As you read those parts of the book, you can customize those attributes based on the mission of your organization. For example, in describing a tester's competency, skill sets for testing COTS software and outsourced software will be listed. However, if your organization does not use COTS software or does not outsource the development of software, you would not need those skills in your testing staff. Likewise, if your testers are not responsible for testing security, you would not need a test processes for testing security.

The three self-assessments included in this chapter are based on the model in Figure 1-2. However, it is recognized that few testing organizations need all these testing capabilities and competencies. Therefore, you need to develop the model that is suited to your test mission.

Step 2: Develop Baselines for Your Organization

This section presents the following three self-assessment categories to enable you to compare your testing organization against the world-class model:

1. **Assessing the test environment.** This includes user satisfaction, management support, environment, planning, tools, test processes, measurement, quality control, and training.

2. **Assessing the process for testing individual software projects.** This category of assessment will assess your testing process against the seven-step process for testing individual software projects presented in Part 3 of this book.

3. **Assessing the competencies of software testers.** This self-assessment will be based on the 2006 Common Body of Knowledge (CBOK) developed by the Certification Board of the Software Certifications Organization. Each of the recommended ten competencies for software tester will be assessed. A more detailed assessment to be used in individuals to compare their specific test competencies against the 2006 CBOK is provided in Chapter 5.

Assessment 1: Assessing the Test Environment

During the past 25 years, the Quality Assurance Institute (QAI) has been studying what makes software testing organizations successful. As a result, QAI has identified the following eight criteria:

Test environment planning

Management support

Use of test processes

Test tools

Quality control

Test measurement

User satisfaction

Test training

When these eight criteria are in place and working, the result is normally a world-class testing organization.

The assessment process developed by QAI has five items to address within each of the eight criteria. The more of those items that are in place and working, the more likely that criteria will contribute to world-class testing. Figure 1-3 shows a cause-effect diagram indicating the areas to address, called *drivers*, which results in a world-class testing organization.

DRIVERS OF WORLD-CLASS TESTING   DESIRED RESULTS

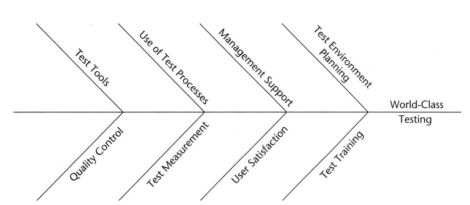

Figure 1-3   Overview of the testing environment.

Software testing organizations can use the results of this assessment in any one of the following three ways:

1. To determine their current testing environmental status versus the environment of a world-class testing organization. The responses to the items address will indicate an organization's strengths and weaknesses compared to the environment of a world-class testing organization.

2. To develop the goal/objectives to accomplish becoming a world-class testing organization. QAI's world-class criteria indicate a profile of the environment of a world-class testing organization. Achieving those objectives can lead you to become a more effective software testing organization.

3. To develop an improvement plan.

By doing the assessment, you will develop a Footprint Chart that shows where improvement is needed. Those criteria in which you are deficient become the means for improving the environment of your software testing organization.

Implementation Procedures

This practice involves the following four tasks:

- Build the assessment team.
- Complete the assessment questionnaires.
- Build the footprint chart.
- Assess the results.

Building the Assessment Team

The assessment team should combine people who in totality possess the knowledge of how your organization manages software testing. Before the team is established, the areas to address should be reviewed to determine the makeup of the team. It is recommended that a matrix be prepared with the seven assessment criteria on one dimension and the recommended assessment team on the other. The matrix should indicate which assessment team member is knowledgeable about each of the seven assessment criteria.

Once all seven criteria have been associated with an assessment team member, it can be concluded that the team is adequate to perform the assessment.

Completing the Assessment Questionnaire

The assessment questionnaire in Work Paper 1-1 consists of eight categories, with five items to address for each category. A Yes or No response should be made, as follows:

- A Yes response means all of the following:
    - Criteria items are documented and in place.
    - Criteria items are understood by testers.
    - Criteria items are widely used, where applicable.
    - Criteria items have produced some possible results.

- A No response means any of the following:
    - No formal item in place.
    - Criteria items are applied differently for different test situations.
    - No consistency as to when used or used very seldom.
    - No tangible results were produced.

The assessment team should read aloud each item and then discuss how that item is addressed in their testing environment. The results should be recorded on Work Paper 1-1. The assessment team may also wish to record comments that clarify the response and/or to provide insight in how that area may be improved.

Building the Footprint Chart

For this task, you should transcribe the results of Work Paper 1-1 onto Work Paper 1-2. To do so, total the number of Yes responses for each criterion. Then place a dot on Work Paper 1-2 on the line representing the number of Yes responses. For example, if you have three Yes responses for test training, you should place a dot on the test training line at the intersection of the line representing three Yes responses. A dot should be marked on the line representing all seven criteria for the number of Yes responses. Then connect the dots with a line, resulting in what is called a "footprint" of the status of your testing environment versus the environment of a world-class testing organization.

Assessing the Results

You should make the following two assessments regarding the footprint developed on the Work Paper 1-2:

1. **Assess the status of each criteria versus what that criteria should be in the world-class testing environment.** To do this, you need to look at the number of Yes responses you have recorded for each criterion versus a world-class organization, which would have five Yes responses. For example, three Yes responses for test training would indicate that improvements could be made in your test training process. The two items that received No responses are indications of where improvements are needed to move your test training activities to a world-class level.

2. **Interpret your testing environment footprint chart.** The footprint in your Work Paper 1-2 provides an overview of your testing environment. Given the footprint, your assessment team should attempt to draw some conclusions about your testing environment. Three examples are given to help in drawing these conclusions, as shown in Figures 1-4, 1-5, and 1-6.

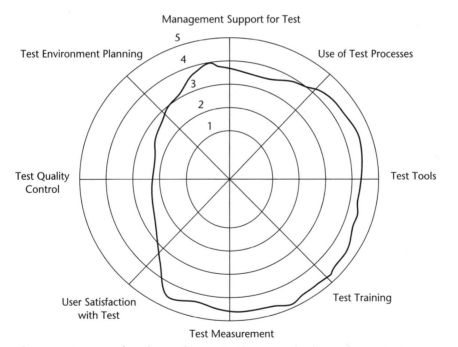

Figure 1-4 Example of a software testing organization using a test as a part of development.

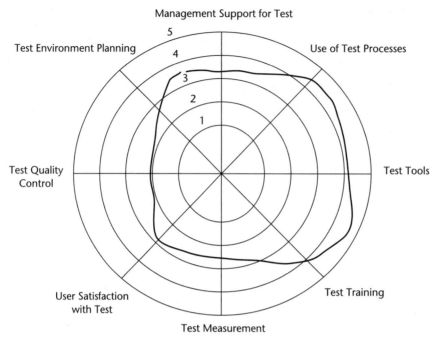

Figure 1-5   Example of a testing organization using, but not enforcing, the test process.

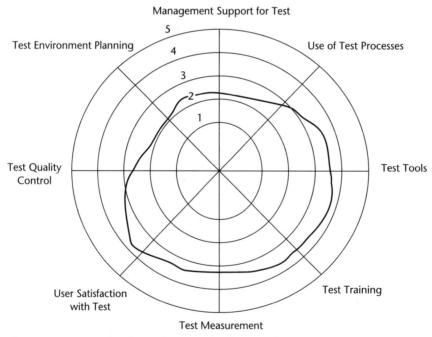

Figure 1-6   Example of a testing organization practicing testing as an art.

Verifying the Assessment

The following list of questions, if responded to positively, would indicate that the assessment has been performed correctly:

1. Does the assessment team comprise the knowledge needed to answer all of the items to address within the seven criteria?

2. Are the individual assessors free from any bias that would cause them not to provide proper responses to the items to address?

3. Was there general consensus among the assessment team to the response for each item to address?

4. Are the items to address appropriate for your testing organization?

5. Have the items to address been properly totaled and posted to the Footprint Chart Work Paper?

6. Does the assessment team believe the Footprint Chart is representative of your testing environment?

7. Does your assessment team believe that if they improve the items to address, which have No responses, the testing organization will become more effective?

8. Does your organization believe that the overall assessment made is representative of your environment?

Assessment 2: Assessing the Capabilities of Your Existing Test Processes

To assess the capabilities of your existing test processes, follow the same procedure that you used to assess your test environment. Note that you should use the same team for both assessments. The only change you will need is to substitute self-assessment questionnaires in assessing the test environment process with the self-assessment questionnaires for assessing the test processes included in this section.

The assessment of test processes will be divided into the following seven categories:

Preparing for a software testing project

Conducting test planning

Executing the test plan

Conducting acceptance testing

Analyzing test results and preparing reports

Testing the installation of software

Post-test analysis

Note that these seven categories of test processes correspond to a seven-step software testing process presented in Part 3 of this book. Thus, each assessment will help you determine your strengths and weaknesses in each of the seven steps of the proposed software testing process.

To conduct this self-assessment, answer the questionnaire in Work Paper 1-3 and post your results to Work Paper 1-4, as described in the preceding section.

Assessment 3: Assessing the Competency of Your Testers

This practice will enable you to assess your testing competencies against the ten skill categories in the Common Body of Knowledge (CBOK) for the Certified Software Tester (CSTE) certificate. At the conclusion of the assessment, you will develop a Footprint Chart that shows your competencies against the skill categories needed to become a CSTE. You can use the results to design a program for improving your personal test competencies.

Figure 1-7 shows a cause-effect diagram indicating the areas of competency assessment. In the diagram these are called the drivers that result in becoming a fully competent software tester. The drivers are, in fact, the ten CBOK skill categories.

Implementation Procedures

This practice involves performing the following four tasks:

1. Understand the CSTE CBOK.
2. Complete the assessment questionnaires.
3. Build the footprint chart.
4. Assess the results.

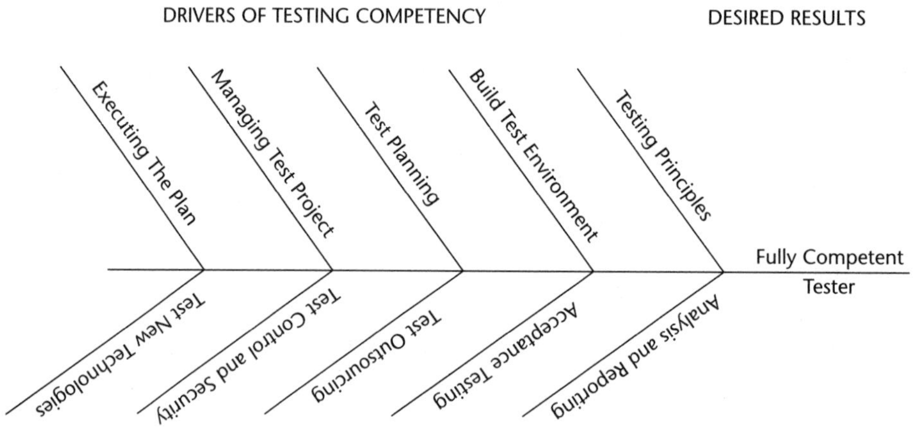

Figure 1-7   Test competency cause-effect diagram.

Understanding the CSTE CBOK

Before you can effectively evaluate your software test competencies, you need to understand the 2006 CSTE CBOK. The final version of the 2006 CSTE CBOK is available through the Software Certification Organization. The discussion draft version of the 2006 CSTE CBOK is included in Chapter 5 as a detailed skill-assessment questionnaire. This step requires you to read through the CBOK and to obtain clarifications of the material as necessary. The best source for these clarifications is the CSTE CBOK study guide, which is available from the Quality Assurance Institute (`www.QAIworldwide.org`).

Completing the Assessment Questionnaires

The assessment questionnaire in Work Paper 1-5 contains ten knowledge categories with 5 items in each category, for a total of 50 items to assess. For each item, a Yes or No response should be made. The meanings of the Yes and No responses are as follows:

- A Yes response means all of the following:
    - You have had formal training, experience, or self-study supporting this skill item.
    - You have actively used the skill in your personal or work life.
    - You have accomplished some positive result using this skill item.
- A No response means any of the following:
    - You do not understand the theory and concepts supporting the skill item.
    - You have never used the skill item in a personal or work situation.
    - You have used the skill item but you have never achieved any positive results.

Prior to answering each question, you should think through the meaning of the question. This may require referring back to the CSTE study guide. Using the Yes/No response criteria, you need to come to a consensus on whether a Yes/No response should be indicated for the skill item. The result of your assessment should be recorded on the appropriate questionnaire.

You need to progress sequentially through the self-assessment questionnaires. Note that you may wish to make notes on the questionnaire to clarify your response or to indicate ideas on how you could improve your competency in that skill item.

Building the Footprint Chart

To build the footprint chart, transcribe the results of Work Paper 1-5 onto Work Paper 1-6. To do so, total the number of Yes responses for each of the ten knowledge categories. Then place a dot on Work Paper 1-6 on the lines corresponding to the knowledge category. For example, if you have three Yes responses for the Test Planning category, you should place a dot on the Test Planning line at the intersection of the line representing the three Yes responses. After you have placed all ten dots, draw a line to connect them. This line, called a *footprint*, represents the status of your testing competencies versus those specified in the CSTE CBOK.

Assessing the Results

You should make the following two assessments regarding the footprint you developed on Work Paper 1-6:

1. **Compare your results for each knowledge category versus what the knowledge category should be as indicated in the CSTE CBOK.** Any rating less than five Yes responses indicates a potential area of improvement in that knowledge category. An analysis of the CBOK knowledge categories will be helpful in determining where to focus improvement, as will studying the CSTE guide to identify areas for potential improvement.

2. **Compare your testing competencies against your current job responsibilities.** The footprint provides an overview of your current competencies. Using your current job description, develop another footprint, which you believe is needed to achieve your current job responsibilities. Any deficiencies should be your first objective for improvement; your second for improvement would be to achieve the skill competencies needed to become a CSTE.

Verifying the Assessment

A positive response to the following questions indicates that you have correctly performed the competency assessment: (Note: Any negative response to the following five questions would reduce the value in using this self-assessment to measure an individual tester's competency.)

1. Do you have enough knowledge of the CSTE CBOK to understand the assessment questions?

2. Do you understand the skills required for each of the 50 assessment items in the questionnaires?

3. Do you understand the Yes and No response criteria, and have you used them in developing the competency assessment?

4. Do you believe the 50 assessment items fairly represent the competencies needed to be fully effective in software testing?

5. Do you believe that the 2006 CSTE CBOK used for this assessment is representative of your personal testing competencies?

Step 3: Develop an Improvement Plan

The objective of the action plan is to move software testing from where it is (the baseline) to where it should be (the goal). There is no one way to develop this plan. Some organizations want to implement the plan so it is on a "pay as you go basis." Other organizations are willing to invest in developing a significantly improved test process knowing that the payback will come after the process is developed and deployed.

The practices outlined in this book correspond to the three self-assessment footprints. If your organization is deficient in one or more components of the footprints, refer to the related chapter in this book that will help you develop your improvement plan, as shown in the following table:

ASSESSMENT NUMBER	ASSESSMENT CRITERIA	CHAPTER
1	Test environment assessment:	
	Test Environment Planning	2
	Management Support	2
	User Satisfaction	2
	Use of Process	3
	Test Tools	4
	Test Training	5
	Test Measurements	11
	Test Quality Control	2, 23, 24
2	Test Process Assessment:	
	Preparing for a Software testing Project	6
	Test Planning General	6, 7, 8
	Planning for specialized areas:	
	The Impact of Software Developmental Methodology When Testing	14
	Testing Client/Server Systems	15
	Testing Rapid Application Development	16
	Testing the Adequacy of Internal Control	17
	Testing Off-the-Shelf Software	18
	Testing in a Multi-Platform Environment	19
	Testing Security	20
	Testing a Data Warehouse	21
	Testing Web-based Systems	22

(continues)

ASSESSMENT NUMBER	ASSESSMENT CRITERIA	CHAPTER
	Test Execution	9, 10
	Acceptance Testing	12
	Test Analysis and Reporting	11
	Testing Software Installation	12
	Post Test Analysis	13
	Improving the test processes	23, 24
3	CSTE Knowledge Category	
	1 Software Testing Principles and Concepts	2 to 24
	2 Building the Test Environment	2 to 5
	3 Managing the Test Project	6, 7
	4 Test Planning	8
	5 Executing the Test Plan	9, 10
	6 Test Analysis and Reporting	11
	7 User Acceptance Testing	12
	8 Testing Software Developed by Outside Organizations	18
	9 Testing Software Controls and the Adequacy of Security Procedures	17, 20
	10 Testing New Technologies	14, 15, 16, 19, 21, 22

Summary

This chapter described how to assess your software testing processes and the competency of your testers. The chapter also briefly addressed specialized testing responsibilities and the need to improve your testing process and/or make your testing process more agile.

The chapter was built around a simple, three-step improvement process: determining your desired software testing performance, measuring your current performance against that performance goal, and developing a plan to move from where you are to a world-class testing organization.

WORK PAPER 1-1   Self-Assessment on Software Testing Environment

ITEMS TO ADDRESS ON TEST ENVIRONMENT PLANNING	YES	NO	COMMENTS
1. Does your IT organization have a policy on software testing?			
2. Does your software testing organization have a test strategy?			
3. Does your software testing organization have software processes and tools to support that testing strategy?			
4. Does your software testing approach include both erification and validation testing (i.e., testing the software in both a static and executable mode)?			
5. Does your testing strategy address the various roles that testing can assume, and determine which of those roles will be incorporated into your organization's testing strategy (e.g., testing user needs in addition to software specifications)?			
ITEMS TO ADDRESS ON MANAGEMENT SUPPORT	**YES**	**NO**	**COMMENTS**
1. Does management provide the resources necessary (including calendar time) to adequately train, plan, conduct, and evaluate results for software testing assignments?			
2. Are testers involved from the inception through termination of software projects to ensure that testing concerns are continuously addressed?			
3. Does management allocate as many resources to the test processes and tools as it does to the development process and tools?			
4. Does management spend as much time on test planning and test execution as it does on development planning and development execution?			
5. Is management knowledgeable and sufficiently trained in test theory, processes, and tools to effectively manage test planning and execution, and understand and effectively act on test results?			

(continues)

WORK PAPER 1-1 *(continued)*

ITEMS TO ADDRESS ON THE USE OF TEST PROCESSES	YES	NO	COMMENTS
1. Do testers follow processes to plan tests, prepare test data, execute tests, and develop and report test results?			
2. Can testers correctly interpret documented test processes so that the test procedures can be followed as intended?			
3. Do the processes provided for testing cover all the activities that are needed to perform effective testing?			
4. Has a plan been developed and put in place to mature the test processes so that they become more effective and efficient and are performed on time?			
5. Do the owners/users of the test processes (the testers) build the processes used for testing?			

ITEMS TO ADDRESS ON TEST TOOLS	YES	NO	COMMENTS
1. Do testers use an automated tool to generate and reuse test data?			
2. Are test tools selected in a logical manner?			
3. Can testers use test tools only after they have received adequate training in how to use them?			
4. Is test tool usage specified in the test plan?			
5. Has a process for obtaining assistance in using test tools been established, and does it provide testers with the needed instructional information?			

WORK PAPER 1-1   *(continued)*

ITEMS TO ADDRESS ON TEST TRAINING	YES	NO	COMMENTS
1. Does a career training plan for testers exist, and is it in use to develop a tester from an unskilled state to a master tester state?			
2. Are testers adequately trained in test processes before using those processes for testing?			
3. Are testers trained in the theory of testing, risk analysis, the various approaches to testing, and so forth so that they understand "why" they perform certain test tasks?			
4. Are testers trained in statistics so that they understand the level of confidence they can provide a user by different test approaches and how to interpret test results?			
5. Are testers trained in how to measure process performance, and do they use the results of that measurement to improve the test processes?			
ITEMS TO ADDRESS ON USER SATISFACTION	**YES**	**NO**	**COMMENTS**
1. Do users get the information they need to track test progress and assess results prior to placing software into production?			
2. Are surveys conducted to determine user satisfaction with test planning, test execution, test results, communications, and so forth?			
3. Do users participate in tests that determine whether the software is acceptable for use?			
4. Are users presented with a plan for testing, and do they "approve" (i.e., agree) that if that plan is followed, they will consider testing to be satisfactory?			
5. Are the user support activities (such as data entry, output usage, terminal usage, manual usage, and so forth) validated as part of testing?			

(continues)

WORK PAPER 1-1 *(continued)*

	ITEMS TO ADDRESS TO TEST MEASUREMENT	YES	NO	COMMENTS
1.	Does a set of test measures and metrics exist, and are they used to measure the efficiency and effectiveness of software testing?			
2.	Has a measurement process been installed to measure the efficiency of the test processes?			
3.	Is compliance to the budget and schedule measured and variances addressed effectively?			
4.	Is tool usage measured to assess the contribution received from automated testing?			
5.	Is the percentage of defects removed versus the total defects eventually attributable to a development phase measured?			
	ITEMS TO ADDRESS TO TEST QUALITY CONTROL	YES	NO	COMMENTS
1.	Are defects made by testers during testing recorded and effectively addressed?			
2.	Is the test plan reviewed/inspected during/after completion by peers for adequacy and compliance to test standards?			
3.	Does the test plan include the procedures that will be used to verify that the plan is executed in accordance with the plan?			
4.	Are regular reports prepared that show the full status of testing individual software systems?			
5.	Are the individual quality control reports periodically summarized to show the efficiency and effectiveness of testing in the entire information services organization?			

WORK PAPER 1-2   Test Environment Assessment Footprint Chart

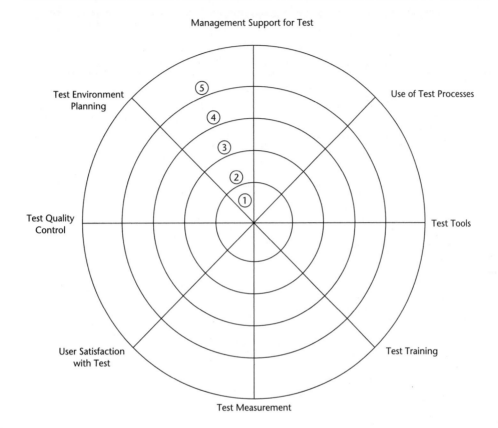

WORK PAPER 1-3   Self-Assessment on Test Processes

ITEMS TO ADDRESS ON PREPARING FOR A SOFTWARE TESTING PROJECT	YES	NO	COMMENTS
1. Have the objectives and requirements for this software system being developed been defined?			
2. Are the requirements testable?			
3. Have adequate time and resources been allotted for both development and testing?			
4. Has the process to be used for testing software been defined?			
5. Are the testers familiar with the methodology that will be used to develop the software?			
ITEMS TO ADDRESS ON TEST PLANNING	**YES**	**NO**	**COMMENTS**
1. Have the risks associated with the software been defined?			
2. Have the test objectives been defined?			
3. Do the testers have a well-structured process to follow to develop the test plan?			
4. Have the constraints that will be imposed on testing been defined?			
5. Does the test plan include a matrix that relates the test objectives to the tests that will be conducted?			
ITEMS TO ADDRESS ON TEST EXECUTION	**YES**	**NO**	**COMMENTS**
1. Is there a process to follow to design test data?			
2. Will verification testing be performed during the requirements phase of development?			
3. Will verification testing be performed during the design and build phases of development?			
4. Is a process in place to record and track defects?			
5. Will test execution be performed in accordance with a plan included in the test plan?			

WORK PAPER 1-3 *(continued)*

ITEMS TO ADDRESS ON ACCEPTANCE TESTING	YES	NO	COMMENTS
1. Have the users defined acceptance criteria?			
2. Do the users have a planning process to follow in developing an acceptance test plan?			
3. Do the users have the competencies needed to conduct acceptance testing? (Note that the competencies may include professional software testers involved in acceptance testing)			
4. Will acceptance testing simulate real-world processing conditions?			
5. Prior to acceptance testing, has the user determined the actions that will be taken based on the software meeting or not meeting the acceptance test criteria?			
ITEMS TO ADDRESS ON TEST ANALYSIS AND REPORTING	**YES**	**NO**	**COMMENTS**
1. Will test reporting be tied to the testing plan as defined in the test plan?			
2. Will test reporting follow the test plan's reporting standards?			
3. Will both interim and final test reports be issued?			
4. Will reporting report back on status of the function/test matrix included in the test plan?			
5. Will the test report include an analysis and recommendation by the software test team?			

(continues)

WORK PAPER 1-3 *(continued)*

ITEMS TO ADDRESS ON TESTINGSOFTWARE INSTALLATION	YES	NO	COMMENTS
1. Does a software configuration plan exist and is that plan effective and operational?			
2. Does version control exist as part of the software configuration management plan?			
3. Does the installation plan include the appropriate training and use of personnel?			
4. Have all the interfaces to other software systems been identified and addressed in the installation process?			
5. Will the installed software be tested to ensure its correct prior to moving to an operational status?			
ITEMS TO ADDRESS ON POST-TEST ANALYSIS	YES	NO	COMMENTS
1. Will an analysis of the testing process be conducted after the software is placed into an operational status?			
2. Will that analysis include the operational results of the software?			
3. Will that analysis identify good and bad testing practices?			
4. Does that analysis include a set-up matrix that will be used to quantitatively assess the effectiveness of testing?			
5. Is there a process to incorporate the results of a post-test analysis into a process to improve the software testing process?			

WORK PAPER 1-4   Test Process Assessment Footprint Chart

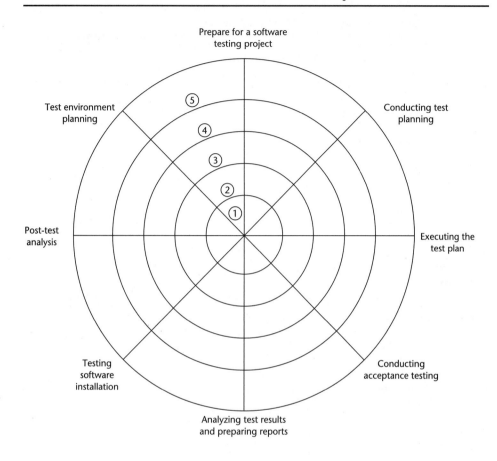

WORK PAPER 1-5   Self-Assessment on Tester Competency

ITEMS TO ADDRESS FOR SOFTWARE TESTING PRINCIPLES AND CONCEPTS	YES	NO	COMMENTS
1. Are you familiar with the technical terms used to describe various testing techniques, tools, principles, concepts and activities?			
2. Do you have knowledge of the different levels of testing, such as unit testing?			
3. Do you have an understanding of the multiple roles of software testers, including testing against specifications and testing to meet users' needs?			
4. Do you understand the "V" concept of testing?			
5. Do you understand the tester's workbench, meaning that you understand the process by which the testing task is performed?			
ITEMS TO ADDRESS FOR BUILDING THE TEST ENVIRONMENT	**YES**	**NO**	**COMMENTS**
1. Do you understand the concepts of policies, standards and procedures and their integration into test processes?			
2. Do you understand how to select processes for performing the test activities?			
3. Do you understand how to adapt a test environment to different software development methodologies?			
4. Do you understand a process for acquiring and deploying test tools?			
5. Do you understand what management must do in order to create a work environment in which testers are motivated to do the right thing in an efficient and effective manner?			

WORK PAPER 1-5   *(continued)*

ITEM TO ADDRESS FOR MANAGING THE TEST PROJECT	YES	NO	COMMENTS
1. Do you possess the necessary communication skills to effectively manage a test project?			
2. Do you possess the personal effectiveness skills, such as negotiation, to effectively manage the test project?			
3. Do you have the test administration skills, such as budgeting and scheduling, to effectively administer the test project?			
4. Do you have the skills to ensure that the test plan and processes used in the project will be in line with the organizational goals, user business objectives, release cycles, and different development for methodologies?			
5. Do you have the skills needed to develop working relationships with users and other stakeholders in the testing process?			
ITEMS TO ADDRESS FOR TEST PLANNING	**YES**	**NO**	**COMMENTS**
1. Do you understand the methods for performing risk analysis?			
2. Do you know how to estimate the magnitude of risks?			
3. Do you know how to develop a test plan that meets industry test plan standards?			
4. Are you competent in software configuration management, change management, and version control?			
5. Can you develop test objectives and acceptance criteria for a project being tested?			

(continues)

WORK PAPER 1-5 *(continued)*

ITEMS TO ADDRESS FOR EXECUTING THE TEST PLAN	YES	NO	COMMENTS
1. Do you have the skills necessary to design test data and test scripts?			
2. Can you develop a test cycle strategy that will determine the number of test cycles to be conducted and what type of testing will occur during these cycles?			
3. Do you know the type of information that must be recorded to effectively document test results?			
4. Do you understand the process that testers should follow in recording and monitoring the resolution of defects?			
5. Do you understand what is necessary to test changes introduced to software testing after you have started testing?			

ITEMS TO ADDRESS FOR TEST ANALYSIS AND REPORTING	YES	NO	COMMENTS
1. Do you understand the difference between a measure and a metric?			
2. Do you know how to report results of testing that is consistent with the IT industry test reporting standards?			
3. Are you familiar with, and can you calculate the more common metrics used in testing, such as defect removal efficiency?			
4. Do you know the type of information that must be gathered during testing to enable test reports to provide the information projects need to assess their readiness to be placed into operation, such as code coverage and requirements coverage?			
5. Do you have a knowledge of the tools needed to develop effective test reports, such as statistical analytical tools?			

WORK PAPER 1-5 *(continued)*

ITEMS TO ADDRESS FOR USER ACCEPTANCE TESTING	YES	NO	COMMENTS
1. Do you understand the differences between the system test and acceptance test?			
2. Can you create "use case" test conditions?			
3. Do you understand that the user's role and the software tester's role in acceptance testing?			
4. Can you develop, in conjunction with users, an acceptance test plan that is consistent with the industry standards for acceptance test plan?			
5. Do you know how to develop user acceptance criteria that are verifiable?			
ITEMS TO ADDRESS FOR TESTING SOFTWARE DEVELOPED BY OUTSIDE ORGANIZATIONS	**YES**	**NO**	**COMMENTS**
1. Do you know the difference between software developed in-house and software developed by outside organizations?			
2. Are you familiar with the process that would enable you to effectively test commercial off-the-shelf (COTS) software?			
3. Are you knowledgeable in a process that would enable you to assess the software testing capabilities of an outside organization being considered for outsourcing?			
4. Are you knowledgeable in the process that would enable you to test new versions of software acquired from outside organizations?			
5. Do you know the risks/concerns associated with acquiring COTS software?			

(continues)

WORK PAPER 1-5 *(continued)*

ITEMS TO ADDRESS FOR TESTING SOFTWARE CONTROLS AND THE ADEQUACY OF SECURITY PROCEDURES	YES	NO	COMMENTS
1. Are you knowledgeable in the vocabulary of internal control and security?			
2. Are you knowledgeable in the industry-accepted model for internal control?			
3. Are you knowledgeable in how to test systems of internal control in software business applications?			
4. Do you understand the relationship between risk and control?			
5. Are you knowledgeable in how to test the adequacy of security in a business application software system?			
ITEMS TO ADDRESS FOR TESTING NEW TECHNOLOGIES	YES	NO	COMMENTS
1. Do you understand how to test new application architecture?			
2. Do you know how to test new application business models?			
3. Do you know how to test new communication methods?			
4. Do you know how to test new hardware technologies?			
5. Do you know how to evaluate the effective integration of new technologies into an organization's IT policies and procedures?			

WORK PAPER 1-6   Test Process Assessment Footprint Chart

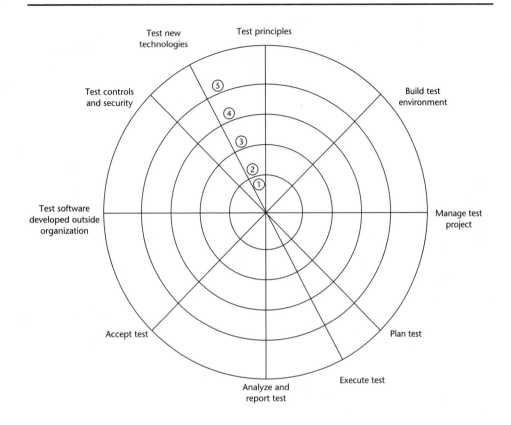

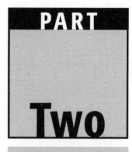

Building a Software
Testing Environment

CHAPTER 2

Creating an Environment Supportive of Software Testing

Senior IT management is responsible for creating an environment in which software testing is effective and efficient. Only management can create that type of environment. If such an environment does not exist, the probability of dissatisfying project personnel and software users is high.

Management controls all the attributes of the environment. They determine the business that the organization performs, the physical location of the organization, the layout of the office for testers, which hardware and operating system software will be used, and which software projects will be developed. In addition, management hires the testers, determines the type of training they will receive, and approves the testing processes and tools. How testers are motivated, rewarded, and satisfied with their work tasks is also under management's control.

This chapter focuses on management's role in creating an environment conducive to software testing by addressing the following topics:

- Management's risk appetite for ineffective software

- The role management assigns to testing

- The policy for testing

- The type of support management provides for software testing

- The resources allocated for testing

- The processes and tools that will be used for testing

Minimizing Risks

The primary objective of software testing is to minimize operational risk by identifying defects prior to the software being placed into operation.

Risk Appetite for Software Quality

A *risk appetite* is the amount of risk that management is willing to take so that the software placed into operations will be risk-free. Figure 2-1 illustrates the two gaps that can cause customers and users to be dissatisfied: a specifications gap and a needs gap.

The IT project group defines the specifications for building software. The project objective is to implement the specifications as documented by the IT project group and agreed to by the customer/user. If they fail to deliver the specifications, or deliver them in an incomplete and inaccurate manner, a specifications gap results.

The second gap is a needs gap. This is the gap between what the customer of the software needs and what was delivered. If the customer needs and the software specifications were the same, there would be only one gap. However, because the process to gather the software requirements is often defective, there are, in fact, two gaps.

Management's risk appetite is the amount of gap that they are willing to accept. Reasons that the gap might exist include tight schedules, limited budgets, inadequate development and testing staff, and work processes that are prone to defects.

Software testers are a means that management can use to close both of these gaps. The testers can determine whether the delivered software meets the specifications. The testers can also determine whether both the specified and delivered software will meet customer needs.

The testing environment to a large degree will enable software testers to perform a role that will both identify early in the project potential gaps, and during the project determine the magnitude of those gaps. However, to do this, management must create an environment that enables the testers to fulfill these responsibilities.

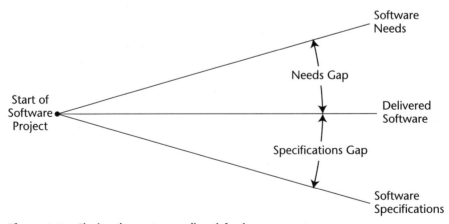

Figure 2-1   Closing the customer dissatisfaction gap.

Risks Associated with Implementing Specifications

There are many risks that, if not properly controlled, will result in missing, incomplete, inaccurate specifications. The risk factors that can cause specifications not to be implemented as specified include:

- **Inadequate schedule and budget.** If the testers do not have adequate time or resources, they will not be able to test all the implemented specifications.

- **Inadequate test processes.** If the test processes are defective, the testers will create defects as they conduct testing. Thus, even though they have performed the process as specified, they will not be able to accomplish the tasks those test processes were designed to achieve.

- **Inadequate competency.** Testers who do not know the basics of testing, who do not know how to use the test processes provided them, and who are inadequately trained in the use of testing tools and techniques will not be able to accomplish test objectives.

Faulty Software Design

The software problems that most commonly cause bad design decisions include:

- **Designing software with incomplete or erroneous decision-making criteria.** Actions have been incorrect because the decision-making logic omitted factors that should have been included. In other cases, decision-making criteria included in the software were inappropriate, either at the time of design or later, because of changed circumstances.

- **Failing to program the software as intended by the customer (user) or designer.** This results in logic errors, often referred to as programming errors.

- **Omitting needed edit checks for determining completeness of output data.** Critical data elements have been left blank on many input documents, and because no checks were included, the applications processed the transactions with incomplete data.

Data Problems

Common data input problems include:

- **Incomplete data.** Some input documents prepared by people omitted entries in data elements that were critical to the application but were processed anyway. The documents were not rejected when incomplete data was being used. In other instances, data needed by the application that should have become part of information technology (IT) files was not put into the system.

- **Incorrect data.** People have often unintentionally introduced incorrect data into the IT system.

- **Obsolete data.** Data in the IT files became obsolete because of new circumstances. The new data may have been available but was not entered into the computer.

Risks Associated with Not Meeting Customer Needs

Meeting customers' needs must be differentiated from implementing the documented software specifications. One of the major problems in meeting needs is that the process for documenting needs by the IT project leader is defective.

Let's look at an example of how implementing the specification correctly will not meet the customer's needs. Let's assume we built an order entry system in which someone can order the product wanted and the quantity of that product. That sounds like a relatively simple specification to implement. However, associated with that is a user need that each order represents what the customer actually wants. Suppose they wanted Y but ordered X. The specification would be met, but the wrong product would be shipped. If the order entry specification also stated that the IT customer wanted 98 percent of the orders to represent what their customer actually wanted, meeting customer expectations would be better defined. Without that qualifier the customer would expect 100 percent correct orders.

In this book, these qualifiers will be called "test factors." In other publications, they have been referred to as quality factors and quality attributes. We will describe these test factors which become software risks.

While the test factors themselves are not risks, they are attributes of the software that, if they are wanted, pose a risk to the success of the software, and thus constitute a business risk. For example, if the software is not easy to use, the resulting processing may be incorrect. The test process should use those test factors during test planning. The definition of the test factors enables the test process to be logically constructed like other parts of information services.

When stated in a positive manner, the test risks become the factors that need to be considered in the development of the test strategy. See Figure 2-2 for factors and examples. The following list briefly describes the test factors:

- **Correctness.** Assurance that the data entered, processed, and outputted by the application system is accurate and complete. Accuracy and completeness are achieved through controls over transactions and data elements, which should commence when a transaction is originated and conclude when the transaction data has been used for its intended purpose.

- **File integrity.** Assurance that the data entered into the application system will be returned unaltered. The file integrity procedures ensure that the right file is used and that the data on the file and the sequence in which the data is stored and retrieved is correct.

- **Authorization.** Assurance that data is processed in accordance with the intents of management. In an application system, there is both general and specific authorization for the processing of transactions. General authorization governs the authority to conduct different types of business, whereas specific authorization provides the authority to perform a specific act.

- **Audit trail.** The capability to substantiate the processing that has occurred. The processing of data can be supported through the retention of sufficient evidential matter to substantiate the accuracy, completeness, timeliness, and authorization of data. The process of saving the supporting evidential matter is frequently called an audit trail.

- **Continuity of processing.** The ability to sustain processing in the event problems occur. Continuity of processing ensures that the necessary procedures and backup information are available to recover operations should integrity be lost. Continuity of processing includes the timeliness of recovery operations and the ability to maintain processing periods when the computer is inoperable.

- **Service levels.** Assurance that the desired results will be available within a time frame acceptable to the user. To achieve the desired service level, it is necessary to match user requirements with available resources. Resources include input/output capabilities, communication facilities, processing, and systems software capabilities.

- **Access control.** Assurance that the application system resources will be protected against accidental and intentional modification, destruction, misuse, and disclosure. The security procedure is the totality of the steps taken to ensure the integrity of application data and programs from unintentional and unauthorized acts.

- **Compliance.** Assurance that the system is designed in accordance with organizational strategy, policies, procedures, and standards. These requirements need to be identified, implemented, and maintained in conjunction with other application requirements.

- **Reliability.** Assurance that the application will perform its intended function with the required precision over an extended period of time. The correctness of processing deals with the ability of the system to process valid transactions correctly, while reliability relates to the system's being able to perform correctly over an extended period of time when placed into production.

- **Ease of use.** The extent of effort required to learn, operate, prepare input for, and interpret output from the system. This test factor deals with the usability of the system to the people interfacing with the application system.

- **Maintainability.** The effort required to locate and fix an error in an operational system. Error is used in the broad context to mean both a defect in the system and a misinterpretation of user requirements.

- **Portability.** The effort required to transfer a program from one hardware configuration and/or software system environment to another. The effort includes data conversion, program changes, operating system, and documentation changes.

- **Coupling.** The effort required to interconnect components within an application system and with all other application systems in their processing environment.

- **Performance.** The amount of computing resources and code a system requires to perform its stated functions. Performance includes both the manual and automated segments involved in fulfilling system functions.

- **Ease of operation.** The amount of effort required to integrate the system into the operating environment and then to operate the application system. The procedures can be both manual and automated.

TEST FACTOR	EXAMPLE
Correctness	Assurance that: • Products are priced correctly on invoices • Gross pay is properly calculated • Inventory-on-hand balances are correctly accumulated
Authorization	Assurance that: • Price overrides are authorized by management • Credits for product returns have been approved by management • Employee overtime pay is authorized by the employee's supervisor
File integrity	Assurance that: • The amounts in the detail records of a file support the control totals • Customer addresses are correct • Employee pay rates are correct
Audit trail	Assurance that: • Employee gross pay can be substantiated by supporting documentation • Sales tax paid to a specific state can be substantiated by the supporting invoices • Payments made to vendors can be substantiated should the vendor disavow receiving the payment
Continuity of processing	Assurance that: • Banking transactions can continue if computer becomes inoperational • Recovery of an online system can occur within the predetermined tolerances
Service levels	Assurance that: • Response time in an online system is within the time span tolerance • Application workload can be completed in accordance with the application schedule • Changes to the system can be incorporated within the agreed upon schedule
Access control	Assurance that: • Programmers will not be given access to data • Access will be restricted to predetermined system resources • Automated access mechanisms will be current
Compliance	Assurance that: • Information services standards are complied with • System development strategy is followed • System is developed in accordance with budgets and schedules

Figure 2-2   Test factor examples.

TEST FACTOR	EXAMPLE
Reliability	Assurance that: • Users can enter the correct information on a day-to-day basis • Errors can be correctly reprocessed • Appropriate action will be taken on system reports
Ease of use	Assurance that: • Input forms minimize input errors • Flow of work will be optimized in order to process work quickly • Reporting procedures will be written in easy-to-understand terminology
Maintainable	Assurance that: • Program documentation will be up-to-date • Program segments will point to other segments that need to be changed concurrently with that segment • Segments of programs will be identified with appropriate identifiers
Portable	Assurance that: • Computer program will only use common language features • System will be hardware independent • System will be independent of system software special features
Coupling	Assurance that: • Segments in one application requiring concurrent changes in other applications will be properly identified • Common documentation will be up-to-date • Changes will be coordinated
Performance	Assurance that: • System is completed within time and budget constraints • System achieves performance acceptance criteria • Hardware and software usage is optimized
Ease of operations	Assurance that: • Operation documentation is up-to-date • Operators are trained in any special application operating procedures • Correct version of programs run in production

Figure 2-2   *(continued)*

Developing a Role for Software Testers

Previously, this chapter recognized two customer dissatisfaction gaps, or two classes of risk-associated implementing software. Also discussed were many of the specific risks associated with these two gaps.

Management needs to evaluate these risks and determine their level of risk appetite. For example, is management willing to accept the risk of unmaintainable software? If not, management should take action to minimize that risk. An obvious action is to develop maintenance standards. Another obvious action is to test the software to ensure its maintainability. Implicit in this example is a definition of maintainability. Does it mean that with unlimited effort, the software can be changed? Or, does it mean a change to an internal table can be done within one hour, a minor specification change can be done within four hours, and so forth?

The role of all software testing groups is to validate whether the documented specifications have been implemented as specified. Additional roles that might be assigned to software testers include the following:

- **Testing for all or part of the test factors.** When establishing the software testing role, management will want to accept some test factors for incorporating into the software tester's role such as testing for ease of use, and exclude others such as operational performance of the software. In other words, management may decide they can live with inefficient software but cannot live with difficult to use processes.

- **Ensuring that the documented specifications meet the true needs of the customer.** Testers can attempt to verify that the documented specifications are in fact the true needs of the customer. For example, they might initiate a requirements review as a means of verifying the completeness of the defined specifications.

- **Improving the software testing process.** Testers can use the analysis of their testing to identify ways to improve testing.

- **Improving the developmental test process.** Testers can use their experience in testing to make recommendations on how the software development process could be improved.

- **Participating in acceptance testing.** Testers can use their software testing expertise to help the users of the software systems develop and implement acceptance testing plans that will determine whether the completed software meets the operational needs of the users.

- **Recommending changes to the software system.** In developing and conducting software tests, testers may identify better ways of implementing the documented specifications.

- **Evaluating the adequacy of the system of controls within the software system.** There are two components of a software system: the component that does the specified work and the component that checks that the specified work was performed correctly. The latter component is referred to as the "system of internal control within the software system." Testers can evaluate whether those controls are adequate to reduce the risks for which they were designed to minimize.

Management needs to clearly establish the role for software testers in their IT organization. Some IT managers want a limited role for software testers, whereas others want an expanded role. Also included in a decision of the role of software testers is whether they will be independent of the developmental project or part of the developmental project.

Writing a Policy for Software Testing

A software testing policy serves two purposes. First, it is the basis for defining what software testers will include in the test processes. Second, it explains to outside parties, such as organizational management, IT customers and users, as well as project personnel, the role and responsibilities of software testing.

Criteria for a Testing Policy

A testing policy is management's definition of testing for a department (see Figure 2-3). A testing policy involves the following four criteria:

- **Definition of testing.** A brief but clear definition of testing.
- **Testing system.** The method through which testing will be achieved and enforced.
- **Evaluation.** How information services management will measure and evaluate testing.
- **Standards.** The standards against which testing will be measured.

Good testing does not just happen, it must be planned; and a testing policy should be the cornerstone of that plan. Figure 2-3 is a simplistic testing policy that an IT department could adopt. A good practice is for management to establish the testing policy for the IT department, have all members of IT management sign that policy as their endorsement and intention to enforce that testing policy, and then prominently display that endorsed policy where everyone in the IT department can see it.

IT management normally assumes that their staff understands the testing function and what management wants from testing. Exactly the opposite is typically true. Testing often is not clearly defined, nor is management's intent made known regarding their desire for the type and extent of testing.

IT departments frequently adopt testing tools such as a test data generator, make the system programmer/analyst aware of those testing tools, and then leave it to the discretion of the staff how testing is to occur and to what extent. In fact, many "anti-testing" messages may be indirectly transmitted from management to staff. For example, pressure to get projects done on time and within budget is an anti-testing message from management. The message says, "I don't care how you get the system done, but get it done on time and within budget," which translates to the average systems analyst/programmer as "Get it in on time even if it isn't tested."

TESTING POLICY
ABC INFORMATION TECHNOLOGY DEPARTMENT

TESTING DEFINITION

Determine the validity of the computer solution to a business problem.

TESTING SYSTEM

Develop and execute a test plan in accordance with departmental procedures
and user requirements.

MEASUREMENT OF TESTING

Calculate the cost of correcting defects not discovered during testing.

TESTING STANDARDS

Allow only one defect per 250 executable program statements.

Philip Jones

George Wilson

Elizabeth Charney

Max Hartman

Figure 2-3   Testing policy.

Methods for Establishing a Testing Policy

The following three methods can be used to establish a testing policy:

1. **Management directive.** One or more senior IT managers write the policy. They determine what they want from testing, document that into a policy, and issue it to the department. This is an economical and effective method to write a testing policy; the potential disadvantage is that it is not an organizational policy, but rather the policy of IT management.

2. **Information services consensus policy.** IT management convenes a group of the more senior and respected individuals in the department to jointly develop a policy. While senior management must have the responsibility for accepting and issuing the policy, the development of the policy is representative of the thinking of all the IT department, rather than just senior management. The advantage of this approach is that it involves the key members of the IT department. Because of this participation, staff is encouraged to follow the policy. The disadvantage is that it is an IT policy and not an organizational policy.

3. **Users' meeting.** Key members of user management meet in conjunction with the IT department to jointly develop a testing policy. Again, IT management has the final responsibility for the policy, but the actual policy is developed using people from all major areas of the organization. The advantage of this approach is that it is a true organizational policy and involves all of those areas with an interest in testing. The disadvantage is that it takes time to follow this approach, and a policy might be developed that the IT department is obligated to accept because it is a consensus policy and not the type of policy that IT itself would have written.

Testing is an organizational responsibility. It is the recommendation of the author that a user committee be convened to develop a testing policy. This meeting serves the following purposes:

- It permits all involved parties to participate in the development of a testing policy.
- It is an educational process where users understand the options and costs associated with testing.
- It clearly establishes for all involved departments that testing is an organizational responsibility and not just an IT responsibility.

Economics of Testing

One information services manager described testing in the following manner: "Too little testing is a crime, but too much testing is a sin." The risk of under-testing is directly translated into system defects present in the production environment. The risk of over-testing is the unnecessary use of valuable resources in testing computer systems that have no flaws, or so few flaws that the cost of testing far exceeds the value of detecting the system defects.

Effective testing is conducted throughout the system development life cycle (SDLC). The SDLC represents the activities that must occur to build software, and the sequence in which those activities must occur.

Most of the problems associated with testing occur from one of the following causes:

Failing to define testing objectives

Testing at the wrong phase in the life cycle

Using ineffective testing techniques

The cost-effectiveness of testing is illustrated in Figure 2-4 as a testing cost curve. As the cost of testing increases, the number of undetected defects decreases. The left side of the illustration represents an under-test situation in which the cost of testing is less than the resultant loss from undetected defects. At some point, the two lines cross and an over-test condition begins. In this situation, the cost of testing to uncover defects exceeds the losses from those defects. A cost-effective perspective means testing until the optimum point is reached, which is the point where the cost of testing no longer exceeds the value received from the defects uncovered.

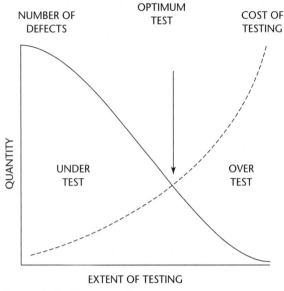

Figure 2-4 Testing cost curve.

Few organizations have established a basis to measure the effectiveness of testing. This makes it difficult for the individual systems analyst/programmer to determine the cost-effectiveness of testing. Without testing standards, the effectiveness of the process cannot be evaluated in sufficient detail to enable the process to be measured and improved.

The use of a standardized testing methodology provides the opportunity for a cause and effect relationship to be determined. In other words, the effect of a change in the methodology can be evaluated to determine whether that effect resulted in a smaller or larger number of defects. The establishment of this relationship is an essential step in improving the test process.

The objective of this book is to explain how to develop a testing methodology that enables an optimum cost-effective process to be used. The cost-effectiveness of a testing process can be determined only when the effect of that process can be measured. When the process can be measured, it can be adjusted to improve the cost-effectiveness of the test process for the organization.

Studies at IBM demonstrated that an application system built by an immature system development process will produce 60 errors (defects). These studies also showed that testing prior to coding is 50 percent effective in detecting errors, and after coding, 80 percent effective. This study and others show that it is at least 10 times as costly to correct an error after coding as before, and 100 times as costly to correct a production error.

These facts are illustrated in Figure 2-5 for a hypothetical system with 1,000 lines of source code. A normal SDLC test process is shown on the left in which testing occurs only after coding. In this example, all 60 errors remain after coding for testing, which detects 48 errors (60 times 80 percent equals 48) at an average cost ten times as great as those detected prior to coding, resulting in a cost of 480 units. To that, we must add 1,200 units of cost representing the 12 remaining errors to be detected during production at a cost of 100 units each. The net test cost is 1,680 units. Using life-cycle testing, this can be reduced to 582 units or only one-third of the normal SDLC test concept cost (illustrated on the right side of Figure 2-5).

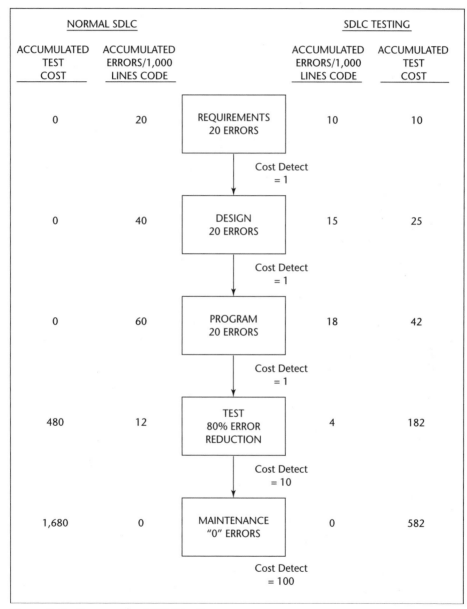

Figure 2-5 Economics of SDLC testing.

Testing—An Organizational Issue

Testing software systems is not just an IT issue, but rather is an organizational issue. The IT department can verify that the system structure functions correctly and that the executable system performs the requirements as IT understands those requirements, but the IT department cannot test to determine that the executable system satisfies the needs of the organization.

Effective testing must be done by a team comprised of information services professionals and users. Also, vendors of software may not be able, or may not want, to have users testing their systems during the developmental process. Again, in these instances, a professional test group can represent the users. The test group is known by different names, including IT testing, quality control, quality assurance, and inspectors.

The following technological developments are causing organizations to revise their approach to testing:

- **Integration.** Technology is being more closely integrated into the day-to-day business, such that the business cannot operate without computer technology. For example, the airlines can take reservations only when their computer systems are operational.

- **System chains.** More and more computer systems are interconnected into cycles of chains such that problems in one can cascade into and affect others.

- **The domino effect.** One problem condition, such as a wrong price or a program defect, can cause hundreds or even thousands of similar errors within a few minutes.

- **Reliance on electronic evidence.** With hard-copy documents being removed from processing, the validity of the transactions is dependent upon the adequacy of controls, and thus a control error may result in extensive losses.

- **Outside users.** Systems no longer belong to internal users, but rather to outside users, making it difficult to identify a single organizational unit responsible for a system.

The organizational approach to testing commences with a policy on testing computer systems. The policy should be developed under the direction of the IT department, but should represent the philosophy of the entire organization. Once the policy has been established, then the procedures and the methods of testing can be developed based upon the desires of management as expressed in the testing policy.

Management Support for Software Testing

Many IT organizations have called upon the Quality Assurance Institute (QAI) to improve their software testing process. In conducting the initial investigation, the QAI always asks the following questions:

- **How much time does the senior IT manager spend on software development, and how much time does the senior IT manager spend on software testing?** Experience has shown that in terms of developmental costs, 50 percent of the cost is spent on developing and 50 percent is spent on testing and correcting problems. Given these statistics, the senior IT manager should be spending about 50 percent of his time on development and 50 percent of his time on testing. If this ratio varies significantly (for example 80 percent on development and 20 percent on testing), the tester has a clear message that their activity is not as important as development.

- **Are the pay grades of software developers the same pay grades as given to software testers?** Since development and testing consume an equal amount of IT resources, it would seem logical that both developers and testers would have the same pay grades. If not, it again indicates to software testers that they are not as important as developers.

When testers feel this lack of management support, they lose motivation and interest. Testers also recognize that if they want to improve their career opportunities they should move to development and leave testing.

Management support for software testing is needed in the following areas:

- **Allocation of resources.** Adequate resources should be allotted to testers so that they can have effective and efficient test processes and up-to-date test tools.

- **Training.** Software testers need to be trained to improve their competency in software testing, testing processes, and the use of testing tools.

- **Motivation.** Senior IT management should undertake activities that motivate software testers. This is done by setting a "tone" at the top. For example, constantly referring to the importance of testing in staff meeting, assuring that the test schedule and budget will not be cut to compensate for developmental overruns, and periodically talking with testers about their concerns and job responsibilities.

- **Rewards.** Software testers should be rewarded for the work they do. A reward can be a "Thank you" at the end of testing, a letter of commendation to the software tester's job file, lunch or other rewards with the boss, as well as financial and promotion rewards.

- **Walking the "testing" talk.** This means that IT managers will take the time to learn testing basics, will become involved in the acquisition of testing tools, sit in on testing courses, and so forth. The goal should be to convince testers that testing is an important component of IT services.

Building a Structured Approach to Software Testing

Traditionally, the SDLC places testing immediately prior to installation and maintenance (see Figure 2-6). All too often, testing after coding is the only verification technique used to determine the adequacy of the system. When testing is constrained to a single phase and confined to the latter stages of development, severe consequences can develop. It is not unusual to hear of testing consuming 50 percent of the development budget. All errors are costly, but the later in the SDLC the error is discovered, the more costly the error. Indeed, an error discovered in the latter parts of the SDLC must be paid four different times. The first cost is developing the program erroneously, which may include writing the wrong specifications, coding the system wrong, and documenting the system improperly. Second, the system must be tested to detect the error. Third, the wrong specifications and coding must be removed and the proper specifications, coding, and documentation added. Fourth, the system must be retested to determine whether the problem(s) have been corrected.

If information services has as its goal lower cost and higher quality systems, it must not isolate verification to a single phase in the development process; rather, it must incorporate verification into each phase of development. One of the most prevalent and costly mistakes on systems development projects today is to defer the activity of detecting and correcting problems until late in the project. A major justification for an early verification activity is that many costly errors are made before coding begins.

Studies have shown that the majority of system errors occur in the design phase. Figure 2-7 represents the results of numerous studies that show that approximately two-thirds of all detected system errors can be attributed to errors made during the design phase. This means that almost two-thirds of the errors must be specified and coded into programs before they can be detected.

Table 2-1 presents the recommended testing process as a life cycle chart showing the verification activities for each phase. The success of conducting verification throughout the development cycle depends upon the existence of clearly defined and stated products at each development stage. The more formal and precise the statement of the development product, the more amenable it is to the analysis required to support verification. Many of the new system development methodologies encourage firm products even in the early development stages.

The following activities should be performed at each phase:

- Analyze the software documentation for internal testability and adequacy.

- Generate test sets based on the software documentation at this phase.

REQUIRE- MENTS	DESIGN	PROGRAM	TEST	INSTALLATION	MAINTENANCE

Figure 2-6 Traditional software development life cycle.

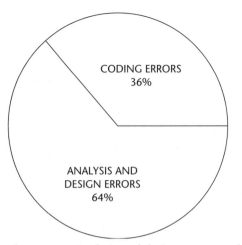

Figure 2-7 Analysis and design errors are the most numerous.

In addition, the following should be performed during the design and program phases:

- Determine that the software documentation is consistent with the software documentation produced during previous phases.
- Refine or redefine test sets generated earlier.

Table 2-1 Life Cycle Verification Activities

LIFE CYCLE PHASE	VERIFICATION ACTIVITIES
Requirements	■ Determine verification approach
	■ Determine adequacy of requirements
	■ Generate functional test data
	■ Determine consistency of design with requirements
Design	■ Determine adequacy of design
	■ Generate structural and functional test data
	■ Determine consistency with design
Program	■ Determine adequacy of implementation
	■ Generate structural and functional test data for programs
Test	■ Test application system
Installation	■ Place tested system into production
Maintenance	■ Modify and retest

The recommended test process involves testing in every phase of the life cycle. During the requirements phase, the emphasis is on validation to determine that the defined requirements meet the needs of the organization. During the design and program phases, the emphasis is on verification to ensure that the design and programs accomplish the defined requirements. During the test and installation phases, the emphasis is on inspection to determine that the implemented system meets the system specification. During the maintenance phase, the system should be retested to determine whether the changes work as planned and to ensure that the unchanged portion continues to work correctly.

Throughout the entire life cycle, neither development nor verification is a straight-line activity. Modifications or corrections to the software at one phase will require modifications or re-verification of software produced during previous phases.

Requirements

The verification activities performed during the requirements phase of software development are extremely significant. The adequacy of the requirements must be thoroughly analyzed and initial test cases generated with the expected (correct) responses. Developing scenarios of expected system use may help to determine the test data and anticipated results. These tests will form the core of the final test set. Vague or untestable requirements will leave the validity of the delivered product in doubt. Requirements defined to later phases of development can be very costly. A determination of the importance of software quality attributes should be made at this stage. Both product requirements and validation requirements should be established.

Design

Organization of the verification effort and test management activities should be closely integrated with preliminary design. During the design phase, the general testing strategy is formulated and a test plan is produced. If needed, an independent test team is organized. A test schedule with observable milestones should be determined. At this same time, the framework for test documentation should be established.

During the design phase, validation support tools should be acquired or developed and the test procedures themselves should be produced. Test data to exercise the functions introduced during the design process, as well as test cases based upon the structure of the system, should be generated. Thus, as the software development proceeds, a more effective set of test cases is built.

In addition to test organization and the generation of test cases, the design itself should be analyzed and examined for errors. Simulation can be used to verify properties of the system structures and subsystem interaction, design walkthroughs should be used by the developers to verify the flow and logical structure of the system, while design inspection should be performed by the test team. Areas of concern include missing cases, faulty logic, module interface mismatches, data structure inconsistencies, erroneous I/O assumptions, and user interface inadequacies. The detailed design must prove to be internally coherent, complete, and consistent with the preliminary design and requirements.

Program

Actual testing occurs during the program stage of development. Many testing tools and techniques exist for this stage of system development. Code walkthrough and code inspection are effective manual techniques. Static analysis techniques detect errors by analyzing program characteristics such as data flow and language construct usage. For programs of significant size, automated tools are required to perform this analysis. Dynamic analysis, performed as the code actually executes, is used to determine test coverage through various instrumentation techniques. Formal verification or proof techniques are used to provide further quality assurance.

Test

During the test process, careful control and management of test information is critical. Test sets, test results, and test reports should be catalogued and stored in a database. For all but very small systems, automated tools are required to do an adequate job—the bookkeeping chores alone become too large to be handled manually. A test driver, test data generation aids, test coverage tools, test results management aids, and report generators are usually required.

Installation

The process of placing tested programs into production is an important phase normally executed within a narrow time span. Testing during this phase must ensure that the correct versions of the program are placed into production, that data if changed or added is correct, and that all involved parties know their new duties and can perform them correctly.

Maintenance

More than 50 percent of a software system's life cycle costs are spent on maintenance. As the system is used, it is modified either to correct errors or to augment the original system. After each modification, the system must be retested. Such retesting activity is termed *regression testing*. The goal of regression testing is to minimize the cost of system revalidation. Usually only those portions of the system impacted by the modifications are retested. However, changes at any level may necessitate retesting, re-verifying, and updating documentation at all levels below it. For example, a design change requires design re-verification, unit retesting, and subsystem retesting. Test cases generated during system development are reused or used after appropriate modifications. The quality of the test documentation generated during system development and modified during maintenance will affect the cost of regression testing. If test data cases have been catalogued and preserved, duplication of effort is minimized.

Developing a Test Strategy

If IT management selects a structured approach to testing software, they need a strategy to implement it. This strategy explains "what to do." Testing tactics explain "how to" implement the strategy.

The objective of testing is to reduce the risks inherent in computer systems. The strategy must address the risks and present a process that can reduce those risks. The system concerns or risks then establish the objectives for the test process. The two components of the testing strategy are the test factors and the test phase, defined as follows:

- **Test factor.** The risk or issue that needs to be addressed as part of the test strategy. The strategy will select those factors that need to be addressed in the testing of a specific application system.

- **Test phase.** The phase of the SDLC in which testing will occur.

Not all test factors will be applicable to all software systems. The development team will need to select and rank the test factors for the specific software system being developed. Once selected and ranked, the strategy for testing will be partially defined.

The test phase will vary based on the testing methodology used. For example, the test phases in a traditional SDLC methodology will be much different from the phases in a rapid application development methodology.

Figure 2-8 illustrates a generic strategy, the one presented in this book. However, this strategy should be customized for any specific software system. The applicable test factors would be listed and ranked, and the phases of development would be listed as the phases in which testing must occur.

You must perform the following four steps to develop a customized test strategy. The test strategy can be represented as the test factor/test phase matrix, as illustrated in Figure 2-8.

1. **Select and rank test factors.** The customers/key users of the system in conjunction with the test team should select and rank the test factors. In most instances, only three to seven factors will be needed. Statistically, if the key factors are selected and ranked, the other factors will normally be addressed in a manner consistent with supporting the key factors. These should be listed in the matrix in sequence from the most significant test factor to the least significant. Rank your factors in sequence from the most to the least significant on Work Paper 2-1. Specific test risks can be substituted for factors, or you can expand the factors to describe risks in more detail.

2. **Identify the system development phases.** The project development team should identify the phases of their development process. This is normally obtained from the system development methodology. These phases should be recorded in the test phase component of the matrix. Record these phases in the test phase component of Work Paper 2-2, and then copy the appropriate test factor from Work Paper 2-1 to Work Paper 2-2.

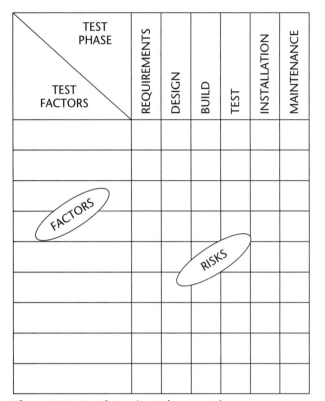

Figure 2-8 Test factor/test phase matrix.

3. **Identify the business risks associated with the system under development.**
   The developers, key users, customers, and test personnel should brainstorm
   the risks associated with the software system. Most organizations have a brainstorming technique, and it is appropriate for individuals to use the technique in
   which they have had training and prior use. Using this technique, the risks
   should be identified and agreed upon by the group. The risks should then be
   ranked into high, medium, and low. This is a relational severity indicator,
   meaning that one-third of all risks should be indicated as high; one-third,
   medium; and one-third, low.

4. **Place risks in the matrix.** The risk team should determine the test phase in
   which the risk needs to be addressed by the test team, and the test factor to
   which the risk is associated. Take the example of a payroll system: If there were
   a concern about compliance to federal and state payroll laws, the risk would be
   the penalties associated with noncompliance. Assuming compliance was
   picked as one of the significant test factors, the risk would be most prevalent
   during the requirements phase. Thus, in the matrix, at the intersection between
   the compliance test factor and the requirements phase, the risk of "penalties

associated with noncompliance to federal and state payroll laws" should be inserted. Note that this may be done by a reference number, cross-referencing the risk. The risk would then have associated with it an H, M, or L, for high, medium, or low risk, respectively.

Use Work Paper 2-1

Work Paper 2-1 enables you to make the most important factors your test specifications. The Work Paper should be completed jointly by the project and test teams. Rank the 15 factors from 1 to 15, with 1 as the most important factor and 15 as the least. You can also rank them as high, medium, or low. To use this tool correctly, five factors should be high, five medium, and five low. Table 2-2 describes the fields in Work Paper 2-1.

Use Work Paper 2-2

Copy the test factors from Work Paper 2-1 to Work Paper 2-2 and list the most important factor at the top and the least important factor at the bottom in the Test Factors column. Do not list any inconsequential test factors. Next, list the matching concerns in the appropriate test phase column. In the Figure 2-9 example, if accuracy was your highest test factor, the concern you'd list would be incomplete identification of all software requiring Year 2000 date corrections. A detailed example of how to complete and use this Work Paper follows. Table 2-3 describes the fields in Work Paper 2-2.

Table 2-2   Field Requirements

FIELD	DESCRIPTION
Number	A sequential number identifying the 15 test factors described in this chapter.
Test Factor	The 15 test factors described in this chapter.
Factor Rank	Rank the most important test factors, ideally 1 through 15; but in practice, this has proven difficult. As an alternative, pick the top five without ranking them; for example, just indicate a check in the Factor Ranked column. Or rank five of them high, five medium, and five low in importance.
Ranking Rationale	Explain why a particular test factor was ranked as indicated. For example, if correctness was ranked as the number 1 factor, the ranking rationale might explain that outputs would be sent to governmental agencies which have viewed incorrect reports negatively.

Table 2-3   Field Requirements

FIIELD	DESCRIPTION
Test Factors	Contains the factors ranked in importance. If the testers ranked the factors 1–15, then the number 1 test factor would be first in this column and the number 15 test factor would be last. However, if five test factors were ranked as important, then just those five test factors would be listed in this column.
Test Phase	The six most common test phases, as described in the text.
Test Concerns	In the horizontal column under each of the six test phases, list the test concern together with the strategy used to address that test concern. Figure 2-9 further describes documenting the test concerns and test strategy.

Test Factors (Ranked High to Low)	Year 2000 Phase			
	Assessment	Plan	Implement	Dynamic Test
Compliance (Can tax information be transmitted after 1/2/2000?)	**Concern** Has tax transmission risk for our company and government been identified? **Test Strategy** Examine the assessment document to determine that a risk regarding transmission of tax data has been identified.	**Concern** Is there a tax transmission Y2K plan? **Test Strategy** Review the Y2K plan to determine how, and which, systems will be modified to ensure that tax data can be transmitted to the appropriate governmental agencies.	**Concern** Was the plan implemented? **Test Strategy** Inspect the programs that govern transmission of tax information to determine whether they were appropriately modified.	**Concern** Was the implementation tested? **Test Strategy** Create a test, which will transmit to appropriate government agencies with a year 2000 date.

Figure 2-9   Example of a complete test strategy matrix for a Year 2000 test strategy.

Summary

Establishing the right environment for software testing is an essential component of an effective and efficient software testing process. Senior IT management has the primary responsibility for establishing an environment that is conducive to software testing. The key component of the environment is the "tone" at the top established by management regarding software testing. This tone includes management's personal involvement in software testing, how they motivate the software testing staff to perform the testing activities, the effort they are willing to expend to ensure the testing staff has the necessary competencies, and providing the resources needed to develop/acquire the software testing process including tools. This chapter has emphasized management's role and responsibility in creating an environment for effective software testing.

Once management has established a "tone" at the top regarding software testing, the remaining pieces of the environment need to be developed. Although there are many components of the environment, the three major ones are:

- Software testing work processes
- Software testing tools
- A competent software testing staff

The following three chapters will address those three key components of the software testing environment.

WORK PAPER 2-1   Test Factor/Risk Ranking

Field Requirements

FIELD	INSTRUCTIONS FOR ENTERING DATA
Number	A sequential number identifying the 15 test factors described in this chapter.
Test Factor	The 15 test factors described in this chapter.
Factor Rank	Rank the most important test factors, ideally 1 through 15; but in practice, this has proven difficult. As an alternative, pick the top five without ranking them; for example, just indicate a check in the Factor Rank column. Or rank five of them high, five medium, and five low.
Ranking Rationale	Explain why a particular test factor was ranked as indicated. For example, if accuracy was ranked as the number 1 factor, the ranking rationale might explain that outputs would be sent to governmental agencies that have viewed incorrect reports negatively.

NUMBER	TEST FACTOR	FACTOR RANK	RANKING RATIONALE
1	Accuracy		
2	File Integrity		
3	Authorization		
4	Audit Trail		
5	Processing Continuity		
6	Service Levels		
7	Access Control		
8	Compliance		
9	Reliability		
10	Ease of Use		
11	Ease of Maintenance		
12	Portability		
13	Coupling		
14	Performance		
15	Ease of Operation		

WORK PAPER 2-2   Test Factors/Test Phase/Test Concerns

TEST PHASE / TEST FACTORS (RANKED HIGH TO LOW)	REQUIREMENTS	DESIGN	PROGRAM	TEST	INSTALLATION	MAINTAINENANCE
Factors or Risks						
			Test Concerns			

Building the Software Testing Process

The testing process is the means by which the test strategy is achieved. The team that develops the testing process uses the test strategy as the requirements for the process. Their task is to determine the tests and methods of performance needed to address the risks that the test strategy identifies.

Following a test process has two significant advantages. First, the tester does not have to determine the process to be used for software testing because that process already exists. Second, when all testers follow the same process, they will develop better means for testing. These means will be incorporated into the process by continually improving the software testing process.

This chapter describes the construction of a workbench for building software. The workbench illustrates both the "do" and the "check" procedures. The "do" procedures are the test procedures, and the "check" procedures determine whether the "do" procedures were performed correctly. The chapter then identifies the considerations for customizing a process for testing, as well as explains the need for a test process. Part Three of this book details the seven steps proposed as a generic test process.

Software Testing Guidelines

Experience has shown there are six general software testing guidelines that, if followed, can significantly improve software testing. These guidelines are the primary reason for building the software testing process:

1. **Software testing should reduce software development risk.** Risk is present in all software development projects, and testing is a control that reduces those risks.

2. **Testing should be performed effectively.** Testing should be performed in a manner in which the maximum benefits are achieved from the software testing efforts.

3. **Testing should uncover defects.** Ideally, at the conclusion of testing there should be no defects in the software.

4. **Testing should be performed using business logic.** Money should not be spent on testing unless it can be spent economically to reduce business risk. In other words, it does not make business sense to spend more money on testing than the losses that might occur from the business risk.

5. **Testing should occur throughout the development life cycle.** Testing is not a phase, but rather a process. It begins when development begins and ends when the software is no longer being used.

6. **Testing should test both structure and function.** Testing should test the functional requirements to ensure they are correct, and test the adequacy of the software structure to process those functional requirements in an effective and efficient manner.

NOTE To learn how to customize the test process for a specific software system, see the section "Customizing the Software-Testing Process" later in this chapter.

Guideline #1: Testing Should Reduce Software Development Risk

Senior IT executives need to develop their IT strategy. Strategic plans are converted into business initiatives. The planning cycle comprising the plan-do components of the plan-do-check-act (PDCA) cycle is easy to understand. From a senior IT executive's perspective, the check component must address business risk.

Risk is the probability that undesirable events will occur. These undesirable events will prevent the organization from successfully implementing its business initiatives. For example, there is the risk that the information used in making business decisions will be incorrect or late. If the risk turns into reality and the information is late or incorrect, an erroneous business decision may result in a failed initiative.

Controls are the means an organization uses to minimize risk. Software testing is a control that contributes to eliminating or minimizing risks; thus, senior executives rely on controls such as software testing to assist them in fulfilling their business objectives.

The purpose of controls such as software testing is to provide information to management so that they can better react to risky situations. For example, testing may indicate that the system will be late or that there is a low probability that the information produced will be correct. Knowing this information, management can then make decisions to minimize that risk: Knowing that the project may be late, they could assign additional personnel to speed up the software development effort.

Testers must understand that their role in a business is to evaluate risk and report the results to management. Viewed from this perspective, testers must first ensure they understand the business risk, and then develop test strategies focused on those risks. The highest business risk should receive the most test resources, whereas the lowest business risk should receive the fewest resources. This way, the testers are assured that they are focusing on what is important to their management.

Guideline #2: Testing Should Be Performed Effectively

Effectiveness means getting the maximum benefit from minimum resources. The process is well-defined. There should be little variance in the cost of performing the task from tester to tester. If no well-defined process is in place, the cost variance for performing a task between testers can vary significantly.

The object of the test process from an effective viewpoint is two-fold. First, processes reduce variance by having the process performed in a consistent manner by each tester. The second processes reduce variance through continuous process improvement. Once variance is minimized, testers can perform those tests they say they will perform in the timeframe and cost they say they can be performed in.

Guideline #3: Testing Should Uncover Defects

All testing focuses on discovering and eliminating defects or variances from what is expected. There are two types of defects:

- **Variance from specifications.** A defect from the perspective of the builder of the product.

- **Variance from what is desired.** A defect from a user's (or customer's) perspective. Testers need to identify both types of defects. Defects generally fall into one of the following three categories:

  - **Wrong.** The specifications have been implemented incorrectly. This defect is a variance from what the customer/user specified.

  - **Missing.** A specified or wanted requirement is not in the built product. This can be a variance from specification, an indication that the specification was not implemented, or a requirement of the customer identified during or after the product was built.

  - **Extra.** A requirement incorporated into the product was not specified. This is always a variance from specifications, but may be an attribute desired by the user of the product. However, it is considered a defect.

Defects Versus Failures

A defect found in the system being tested can be classified as wrong, missing, or extra. The defect may be within the software or in the supporting documentation. While the defect is a flaw in the system, it has no negative impact until it affects the operational system.

A defect that causes an error in operation or negatively impacts a user/customer is called a failure. The main concern with defects is that they will turn into failures. It is the failure that damages the organization. Some defects never turn into failures. On the other hand, a single defect can cause millions of failures.

Why Are Defects Hard to Find?

Some defects are easy to spot, whereas others are more subtle. There are at least two reasons defects go undetected:

- **Not looking.** Tests often are not performed because a particular test condition is unknown. Also, some parts of a system go untested because developers assume software changes don't affect them.

- **Looking but not seeing.** This is like losing your car keys only to discover they were in plain sight the entire time. Sometimes developers become so familiar with their system that they overlook details, which is why independent verification and validation should be used to provide a fresh viewpoint.

Defects typically found in software systems are the results of the following circumstances:

- **IT improperly interprets requirements.** Information technology (IT) staff misinterpret what the user wants, but correctly implement what the IT people believe is wanted.

- **The users specify the wrong requirements.** The specifications given to IT staff are erroneous.

- **The requirements are incorrectly recorded.** Information technology staff fails to record the specifications properly.

- **The design specifications are incorrect.** The application system design does not achieve the system requirements, but the design as specified is implemented correctly.

- **The program specifications are incorrect.** The design specifications are incorrectly interpreted, making the program specifications inaccurate; however, it is possible to properly code the program to achieve the specifications.

- **There are errors in program coding.** The program is not coded according to the program specifications.

- **There are data entry errors.** Data entry staff incorrectly enter information into the computers.

- **There are testing errors.** Tests either falsely detect an error or fail to detect one.

- **There are mistakes in error correction.** The implementation team makes errors in implementing your solutions.

- **The corrected condition causes another defect.** In the process of correcting a defect, the correction process itself institutes additional defects into the application system.

Usually, you can identify the test tactics for any test process easily; it's estimating the costs of the tests that is difficult. Testing costs depend heavily on when in the project life cycle testing occurs. As noted in Chapter 2, the later in the life cycle testing occurs, the higher the cost. The cost of a defect is twofold: You pay to identify a defect and to correct it.

Guideline #4: Testing Should Be Performed Using Business Logic

The cost of identifying and correcting defects increases exponentially as the project progresses. Figure 3-1 illustrates the accepted industry standard for estimating costs and shows how costs dramatically increase the later you find a defect. A defect encountered during the execution of a SDLC phase is the cheapest to fix if corrected in the same SDLC phase where the defect occurred. Let's assume a defect found and corrected during the SDLC design phase costs x to fix. If that same defect is corrected during the system test phase, it will cost $10x$ to fix. The same defect corrected after the system goes into production will cost $100x$. Clearly, identifying and correcting defects early is the most cost-effective way to develop an error-free system.

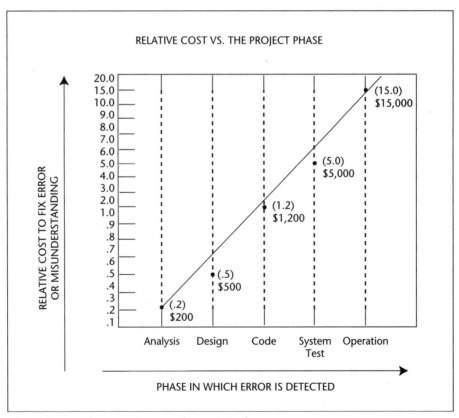

Figure 3-1   Relative cost versus the project phase.

Testing should begin during the first phase of the life cycle and continue throughout the life cycle. Although this book is centered on V-concept testing (detailed in Chapter 6), it's important to recognize that life-cycle testing is essential to reducing the cost of testing.

Guideline #5: Testing Should Occur Throughout the Development Life Cycle

Life-cycle testing involves continuous testing of the solution even after software plans are complete and the tested system is implemented. At several points during the development process, the test team should test the system to identify defects at the earliest possible point.

Life-cycle testing cannot occur until you formally develop your test process. IT must provide and agree to a strict schedule for completing various phases of the test process for proper life-cycle testing to occur. If IT does not determine the order in which they deliver completed pieces of software, appropriate tests are impossible to schedule and conduct.

Testing is best accomplished by forming a test team. The test team must use structured methodologies; they should not use the same methodology for testing that they used to develop the system. The effectiveness of the test team depends on developing the system under one methodology and testing it under another. As illustrated in Figure 3-2, when the project starts, both the development process and system test process also begin. Thus, the testing and implementation teams begin their work at the same time and with the same information. The development team defines and documents the requirements for implementation purposes, and the test team uses those requirements for the purpose of testing the system. At appropriate points during the development process, the test team runs the compliance process to uncover defects. The test team should use the structured testing techniques outlined in this book as a basis of evaluating the corrections.

As you're testing the implementation, prepare a series of tests that your IT department can run periodically after your revised system goes live. Testing does not stop once you've completely implemented your system; it must continue until you replace or update it again.

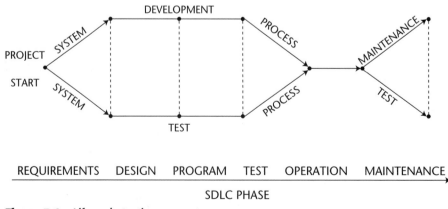

Figure 3-2 Life-cycle testing concepts.

Guideline #6: Testing Should Test Both Function and Structure

When testers test your project team's solution, they'll perform functional or structural tests. Functional testing is sometimes called *black box testing* because no knowledge of the system's internal logic is used to develop test cases. For example, if a certain function key should produce a specific result when pressed, a functional test would be to validate this expectation by pressing the function key and observing the result. When conducting functional tests, you'll be using validation techniques almost exclusively.

Conversely, structural testing is sometimes called *white box testing* because knowledge of the system's internal logic is used to develop hypothetical test cases. Structural tests predominantly use verification techniques. If a software development team creates a block of code that will allow a system to process information in a certain way, a test team would verify this structurally by reading the code, and given the system's structure, see if the code could work reasonably. If they felt it could, they would plug the code into the system and run an application to structurally validate the code. Each method has its pros and cons, as follows:

- Functional testing advantages:
  - Simulates actual system usage
  - Makes no system structure assumptions
- Functional testing disadvantages:
  - Includes the potential to miss logical errors in software
  - Offers the possibility of redundant testing
- Structural testing advantages:
  - Enables you to test the software's logic
  - Enables you to test structural attributes, such as efficiency of code
- Structural testing disadvantages:
  - Does not ensure that you've met user requirements
  - May not mimic real-world situations

Why Use Both Testing Methods?

Both methods together validate the entire system. For example, a functional test case might be taken from the documentation description of how to perform a certain function, such as accepting bar code input. A structural test case might be taken from a technical documentation manual. To effectively test systems, you need to use both methods.

Structural and Functional Tests Using Verification and Validation Techniques

Testers use verification techniques to confirm the reasonableness of a system by reviewing its structure and logic. Validation techniques, on the other hand, strictly apply to physical testing, to determine whether expected results occur. You'll conduct structural tests primarily using verification techniques, and functional tests using validation techniques. Using verification to conduct structural tests would include

- **Feasibility reviews.** Tests for this structural element would verify the logic flow of a unit of software.
- **Requirements reviews.** These reviews verify software attributes; for example, in any particular system, the structural limits of how much load (transactions or number of concurrent users) a system can handle.

Functional tests are virtually all validation tests, and inspect how the system performs. Examples of this include

- **Unit testing.** These tests verify that the system functions properly—for example, pressing a function key to complete an action.
- **Integrated testing.** The system runs tasks that involve more than one application or database to verify that it performed the tasks accurately.
- **System testing.** These tests simulate operation of the entire system, and verify that it ran correctly.
- **User acceptance.** This real-world test means the most to your business. Unfortunately, there's no way to conduct it in isolation. Once your organization staff, customers, or vendors begin to interact with your system, they'll verify that it functions properly for you.

Verification and validation are not mutually exclusive, so you will conduct functional tests with verification and structural tests with validation during your project. Table 3-3 shows the relationships just explained, listing each of the six test activities, who performs them, and whether the activity is an example of verification or validation. For example, when conducting a feasibility review, developers and users verify that the software could conceivably perform after the solution is implemented the way the developers expect.

NOTE You can learn more about verification and validation techniques in Chapters 9 and 10, respectively.

Table 3-3 Functional Testing

TEST PHASE	PERFORMED BY	VERIFICATION	VALIDATION
Feasibility Review	Developers, users	X	
Requirements Review	Developers, users	X	
Unit Testing	Developers		X
Integration Testing	Developers		X
System Testing	Developers with user assistance		X
User Acceptance	Users		X

Now that you've seen how you must verify and validate your system structurally and functionally, the last tool to introduce is a process template for employing these tactics, called the *tester's workbench*.

Workbench Concept

To understand testing methodology, you must understand the workbench concept. In IT organizations, workbenches are more frequently referred to as phases, steps, or tasks. The workbench is a way of illustrating and documenting how a specific activity is to be performed. Defining workbenches is normally the responsibility of a process management committee, which in the past has been more frequently referred to as a standards committee. There are four components to each workbench:

1. **Input.** The entrance criteria or deliverables needed to complete a task.

2. **Procedures to do.** The work tasks or processes that will transform the input into the output.

3. **Procedures to check.** The processes that determine that the output meet the standards.

4. **Output.** The exit criteria or deliverables produced from the workbench.

NOTE Testing tools are not considered part of the workbench because they are incorporated into either the procedures to do or procedures to check. The workbench is illustrated in Figure 3-3, and the software development life cycle, which is comprised of many workbenches, is illustrated in Figure 3-4.

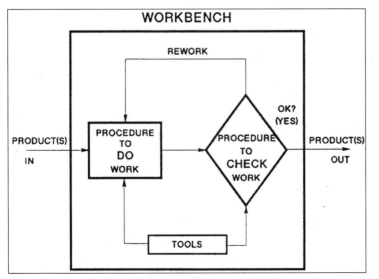

Figure 3-3　The workbench for testing software.

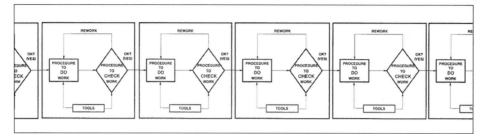

Figure 3-4   The test process contains multiple workbenches.

The workbench concept can be used to illustrate one of the steps involved in building systems. The programmer's workbench consists of the following steps:

1. Input products (program specs) are given to the producer (programmer).

2. Work is performed (e.g., coding/debugging); a procedure is followed; a product or interim deliverable (e.g., a program/module/unit) is produced.

3. Work is checked to ensure product meets specs and standards, and that the do procedure was performed correctly.

4. If the check process finds problems, the product is sent back for rework.

5. If the check process finds no problems, the product is released to the next workbench

Chapters 6 through 13, which walk you through testing your software development project, describe each step in workbench format. Each chapter begins with a workbench description for that step.

Testing That Parallels the Software Development Process

When the processes for developing software and testing software are shown in a single diagram, they are frequently presented as what is known as a "V diagram." On one side of the V are the steps for developing software, and on the other side are the steps for testing software. Figure 3-5 illustrates the V diagram for the seven-step software-testing process presented in this book.

The process for *developing* software contains the following generic steps:

1. Define the requirements for the software system.

2. Design the software system based on the requirements.

3. Build the software based on the design.

4. Test the software (which involves unit testing and frequently integration testing).

5. Install the software in an operational environment.

6. Maintain the software as changes are needed (Note: unless changes are significant, the developers will test the changes and then install the new version.)

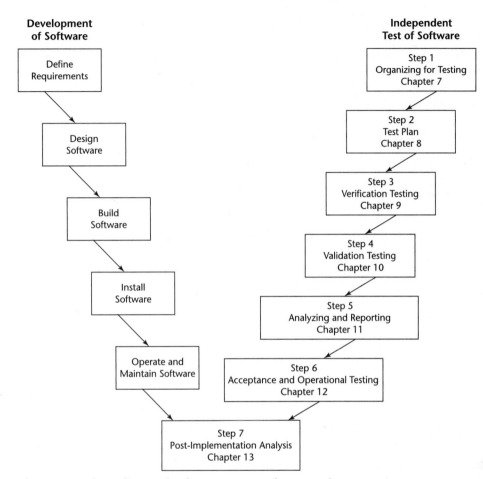

Figure 3-5 The V diagram for the seven-step software-testing process.

The process for *testing* software involves the following steps:

1. Prepare for testing a software system.

2. Plan the tests that will be conducted on the software system.

3. Execute the steps as defined in the test plan.

4. Conduct acceptance testing by the software system users. (Note: This testing may be assisted by the IT independent test group.)

5. Analyze test results and report them to the appropriate software system stakeholders.

6. Test the installation of the software into the operational environment, and test changes made to the software after it is placed into the operational environment.

7. Conduct a post-implementation analysis to evaluate the effectiveness and efficiency of the test process.

Each of the seven steps in the software-testing process can be represented by the software testing workbench. In the seven-step process, these testing workbenches comprise multiple steps. Therefore, there would be multiple workbenches within the overall workbench for each step.

An IT organization should customize the seven-step testing process for its particular situation. The seven-step process presented in this book is one that testers might use for a large, complex software system. The following sections discuss eight considerations that your organization should use when customizing the seven-step software-testing process.

Customizing the Software-Testing Process

The following are eight considerations you need to address when customizing the seven-step software-testing process:

1. Determine the test strategy objectives.
2. Determine the type of development project.
3. Determine the type of software system.
4. Determine the project scope.
5. Identify the software risks.
6. Determine when testing should occur.
7. Define the system test plan standard.
8. Define the unit test plan standard.

NOTE You can use the CD included with this book to customize the templates in the seven-step software-testing process for your organization.

Determining the Test Strategy Objectives

Test strategy is normally developed by a team very familiar with the business risks associated with the software; tactics are developed by the test team. Thus, the test team needs to acquire and study the test strategy. In this study, the test team should ask the following questions:

- What is the ranking of the test factors?
- Which of the high-level risks are the most significant?
- What damage can be done to the business if the software fails to perform correctly?

- What damage can be done to the business if the software is not completed on time?
- Which individuals are most capable of understanding the impact of the identified business risks?

Determining the Type of Development Project

The *type of development project* refers to the environment/methodology in which the software will be developed. As the environment changes, so does the testing risk. For example, the risks associated with the traditional development effort differ from the risks associated with off-the-shelf purchased software. Different testing approaches must be used for different types of projects, just as different development approaches are used (see Figure 3-6).

TYPE	CHARACTERISTICS	TEST TACTICS
Traditional system development (and most perfective maintenance)	- Uses a system development methodology	- Test at end of each task/step/phase
	- User knows requirements	- Verify that specs match need
	- Development determines structure	- Test function and structure
Iterative development/ prototyping	- Requirements unknown	- Verify that tools are used properly
	- Structure predefined	- Test functionality
System maintenance	- Modify structure	- Test structure
		- Works best with release methods
		- Requires regression testing
Purchased/contracted software	- Structure unknown	- Verify that functionality matches need
	- May contain defects	
	- Functionality defined in user documentation	- Test functionality
	- Documentation may vary from software	- Test fit into environment

Figure 3-6 Test tactics for different project types.

Determining the Type of Software System

The *type of software system* refers to the processing that will be performed by that system. This step contains 16 different software system types. However, a single software system may incorporate more than one of these types. Identifying the specific software type will help build an effective test plan.

- **Batch (general).** Can be run as a normal batch job and makes no unusual hardware or input-output actions (for example, a payroll program or a wind tunnel data analysis program).

- **Event control.** Performs real-time data processing as a result of external events (for example, a program that processes telemetry data).

- **Process control.** Receives data from an external source and issues commands to that source to control its actions based on the received data.

- **Procedure control.** Controls other software (for example, an operating system that controls the execution of time-shared and batch computer programs).

- **Advanced mathematical models.** Resembles simulation and business strategy software, but has the additional complexity of heavy use of mathematics.

- **Message processing.** Handles input and output messages, processing the text or information contained therein.

- **Diagnostic software.** Detects and isolates hardware errors in the computer where it resides or in other hardware that can communicate with that computer.

- **Sensor and signal processing.** Similar to that of message processing, but requires greater processing to analyze and transform the input into a usable data processing format.

- **Simulation.** Simulates an environment, mission situation, other hardware; inputs from these to enable a more realistic evaluation of a computer program or hardware component.

- **Database management.** Manages the storage and access of (typically large) groups of data. Such software can also prepare reports in user-defined formats based on the contents of the database.

- **Data acquisition.** Receives information in real time and stores it in some form suitable for later processing (for example, software that receives data from a space probe and files it for later analysis).

- **Data presentation.** Formats and transforms data, as necessary, for convenient and understandable displays for humans. Typically, such displays would be for some screen presentation.

- **Decision and planning aids.** Uses artificial intelligence techniques to provide an expert system to evaluate data and provide additional information and consideration for decision and policy makers.

- **Pattern and image processing.** Generates and processes computer images. Such software may analyze terrain data and generate images based on stored data.

- **Computer system software.** Provides services to operational computer programs.
- **Software development tools.** Provides services to aid in the development of software (for example, compilers, assemblers, and static and dynamic analyzers).

Determining the Project Scope

The *project scope* refers to the totality of activities to be incorporated into the software system being tested—the range of system requirements/specifications to be understood. The scope of new system development is different from the scope of changes to an existing system. This step describes some of the necessary characteristics, but this list must be expanded to encompass the requirements of the specific software system being tested. The scope of the project usually delimits the scope of the testing effort. Consider the following issues:

- **New systems development:**
    - What business processes are included in the software?
    - Which business processes will be affected?
    - Which business areas will be affected?
    - What existing systems will interface with this system?
    - Which existing systems will be affected?
- **Changes to existing systems:**
    - Are the changes corrective or is new functionality being added?
    - Is the change caused by new standards?
    - What other systems are affected?
    - Is regression testing needed?

Identifying the Software Risks

Strategic risks are the high-level business risks faced by the software system; software system risks are subsets. The purpose of decomposing the strategic risks into tactical risks is to assist in creating the test scenarios that will address those risks. It is difficult to create test scenarios for high-level risks.

Tactical risks can be categorized as follows:

Structural risks

Technical risks

Size risks

Work Papers 3-1, 3-2, and 3-3 provide the method for assessing the structural, technical, and size risks, respectively. These Work Papers are to be completed by the test team interacting with the development team and selected end users/customers. Each of the three Work Papers identifies a risk, a rating for the risk, and a weight associated with the risk. The identification of the risk and its associated weight are supplied as part of the tactical risk assessment process. Weight is an indication of the relative importance of each risk in relationship to the other risks.

To complete Work Papers 3-1, 3-2, and 3-3, perform the following steps:

1. **Understand the risk and the ratings provided for that risk.** The higher the predefined rating, the greater the risk. In most instances, ratings will be between 1 and 4.

2. **Determine the applicable rating for the software system being tested.** Select one of the listed ratings for each risk and place it in the Ratings column. For example, on the Structural Risk Assessment Work Paper (3-1), if you determined that the amount of time since the last major change to the existing area of business was more than two years, you would note that a low rating was indicated, and put a 1 in the Ratings column.

3. **Calculate and accumulate the risk score.** The ratings you provided in the Ratings column should be multiplied by the weight to get a score. The score for each work paper should then be accumulated and the total score posted to Work Paper 3-4. When the three work papers have been completed, you will have posted three scores to the Risk Score Analysis Work Paper.

To complete Work Paper 3-4, perform the following steps:

1. **Calculate average risk score by risk area.** To do this, total the number of risks on Work Papers 3-1, 3-2, and 3-3 and divide that into the total score on Work Paper 3-4 to obtain an average score for the three risk areas. Do the same for the total risk score for the software.

2. **Post comparative ratings.** After you have used these Work Papers a number of times, you will develop average scores for your application systems. Take the score totals for your application systems and rank them from high to low for each of the three risk areas. Then determine an average for the high third of the scores, the middle third of the scores, and the low third of the scores. This average is the cumulative rating for your company's applications and can be permanently recorded on Work Paper 3-4. This will enable you to compare the score of the system you are testing against comparative ratings so you can determine whether the system you are working on is high, medium, or low risk in each of the three risk areas and overall.

3. **List at the bottom of Work Paper 3-4 all the risk attributes from the three worksheets that received a high-risk rating.** Identify the area (for example, structure) and list the specific risk that was given a high rating. Then, for each of those risks, determine the specific test concern and list it on Work Paper 3-4.

When you have completed this assessment process, the tactical risks will be well defined, enabling the insight gained from this step to be embedded into the test plan. Obviously, areas of high risk may need special attention; for example, if size puts the project in a high-risk rating, extra test effort may be needed, focused on ensuring that the system can handle the volume or size of transactions specified for the software. Test concerns can be addressed by specific tests designed to evaluate the magnitude of the risk and the adequacy of controls in the system to address that risk.

Determining When Testing Should Occur

The previous steps have identified the type of development project, the type of software system, the project scope, and the technical risks. Using that information, the point in the development process when testing should occur must be determined. The previous steps have identified what type of testing needs to occur, and this step will tell when it should occur.

Testing can and should occur throughout the phases of a project (refer to Figure 3-2). Examples of test activities to be performed during these phases are:

A. Requirements phase activities
  - Determine test strategy
  - Determine adequacy of requirements
  - Generate functional test conditions

B. Design phase activities
  - Determine consistency of design with requirements
  - Determine adequacy of design
  - Generate structural and functional test conditions

C. Program phase activities
  - Determine consistency with design
  - Determine adequacy of implementation
  - Generate structural and functional test conditions for programs/units

D. Test phase activities
  - Determine adequacy of the test plan
  - Test application system

E. Operations phase activities
  - Place tested system into production

F. Maintenance phase activities
  - Modify and retest

Defining the System Test Plan Standard

A tactical test plan must be developed to describe when and how testing will occur. This test plan will provide background information on the software being tested, on the test objectives and risks, as well as on the business functions to be tested and the specific tests to be performed.

Information on the test environment part of the test plan is described in Part Two of this book. Reference other parts of the book for development methodologies other than the SDLC methodology; for example, Chapter 15 addresses client/server systems.

The test plan is the road map you should follow when conducting testing. The plan is then decomposed into specific tests and lower-level plans. After execution, the results are rolled up to produce a test report. The test reports included in Chapter 11 are designed around standardized test plans. A recommended test plan standard is illustrated in Figure 3-7; it is consistent with most of the widely accepted published test plan standards.

---

1. GENERAL INFORMATION

   1.1   Summary. Summarize the functions of the software and the tests to be performed.

   1.2   Environment and Pretest Background. Summarize the history of the project. Identify the user organization and computer center where the testing will be performed. Describe any prior testing and note results that may affect this testing.

   1.3   Test Objectives. State the objectives to be accomplished by testing.

   1.4   Expected Defect Rates. State the estimated number of defects for software of this type.

   1.5   References. List applicable references, such as:

      a) Project request authorization.
      b) Previously published documents on the project.
      c) Documentation concerning related projects.

2. PLAN

   2.1   Software Description. Provide a chart and briefly describe the inputs, outputs, and functions of the software being tested as a frame of reference for the test descriptions.

   2.2   Test Team. State who is on the test team and their test assignment(s).

   2.3   Milestones. List the locations, milestone events, and dates for the testing.

   2.4   Budgets. List the funds allocated to test by task and checkpoint.

   2.5   Testing (systems checkpoint). Identify the participating organizations and the system checkpoint where the software will be tested.

      2.5.1   Schedule (and budget). Show the detailed schedule of dates and events for the testing at this location. Such events may include familiarization, training, data, as well as the volume and frequency of the input. Resources allocated for test should be shown.

Figure 3-7 System test plan standard.

2.5.2   Requirements. State the resource requirement, including:

    a)   Equipment. Show the expected period of use, types, and quantities of the equipment needed.

    b)   Software. List other software that will be needed to support the testing that is not part of the software to be tested.

    c)   Personnel. List the numbers and skill types of personnel that are expected to be available during the test from both the user and development groups. Include any special requirements such as multishift operation or key personnel.

2.   PLAN

2.5.3   Testing Materials. List the materials needed for the test, such as:

    a)   System documentation
    b)   Software to be tested and its medium
    c)   Test inputs
    d)   Test documentation
    e)   Test tools

2.5.4   Test Training. Describe or reference the plan for providing training in the use of the software being tested. Specify the types of training, personnel to be trained, and the training staff.

2.5.5   Test to be Conducted. Reference specific tests to be conducted at this checkpoint.

2.6   Testing (system checkpoint). Describe the plan for the second and subsequent system checkpoint where the software will be tested in a manner similar to paragraph 2.5.

3.   SPECIFICATIONS AND EVALUATION

3.1   Specifications

3.1.1   Business Functions. List the business functional requirement established by earlier documentation, or Task 1 of Step 2.

3.1.2   Structural Functions. List the detailed structural functions to be exercised during the overall test.

3.1.3   Test/Function Relationships. List the tests to be performed on the software and relate them to the functions in paragraph 3.1.2.

3.1.4   Test Progression. Describe the manner in which progression is made from one test to another so that the entire test cycle is completed.

Figure 3.7   *(continued)*

3.2   Methods and Constraints.

    3.2.1   Methodology. Describe the general method or strategy of the testing.

    3.2.2   Test Tools. Specify the type of test tools to be used.

    3.2.3   Extent. Indicate the extent of the testing, such as total or partial. Include any rationale for partial testing.

    3.2.4   Data Recording. Discuss the method to be used for recording the test results and other information about the testing.

    3.2.5   Constraints. Indicate anticipated limitations on the test due to test conditions, such as interfaces, equipment, personnel, data- bases.

3.   SPECIFICATIONS AND EVALUATION

3.3   Evaluation.

    3.3.1   Criteria. Describe the rules to be used to evaluate test results, such as range of data values used, combinations of input types used, maximum number of allowable interrupts or halts.

    3.3.2   Data Reduction. Describe the techniques to be used for manipulating the test data into a form suitable for evaluation, such as manual or automated methods, to allow comparison of the results that should be produced to those that are produced.

4.   TEST DESCRIPTIONS

4.1   Test (Identify). Describe the test to be performed (format will vary for on-line test script).

    4.1.1   Control. Describe the test control, such as manual, semiautomatic or automatic insertion of inputs, sequencing of operations, and recording of results.

    4.1.2   Inputs. Describe the input data and input commands used during the test.

    4.1.3   Outputs. Describe the output data expected as a result of the test and any intermediate messages that may be produced.

    4.1.4   Procedures. Specify the step-by-step procedures to accomplish the test. Include test setup, initialization, steps and termination.

4.2   Test (Identify). Describe the second and subsequent tests in a manner similar to that used in paragraph 4.1.

Figure 3.7   *(continued)*

Defining the Unit Test Plan Standard

During internal design, the system is divided into the components or units that perform the detailed processing. Each of these units should have its own test plan. The plans can be as simple or as complex as the organization requires based on its quality expectations.

The importance of a unit test plan is to determine when unit testing is complete. It is a bad idea economically to submit units that contain defects to higher levels of testing. Thus, extra effort spent in developing unit test plans, testing units, and ensuring that units are defect free prior to integration testing can have a significant payback in reducing overall test costs.

Figure 3-8 presents a suggested unit test plan. This unit test plan is consistent with the most widely accepted unit test plan standards. Note that the test reporting in Chapter 11 for units assumes that a standardized unit test plan is utilized.

Converting Testing Strategy to Testing Tactics

Developing tactics is not a component of establishing a testing environment. However, understanding the tactics that will be used to implement the strategy is important in creating work processes, selecting tools, and ensuring that the appropriate staff is acquired and trained. The objective of this section is to introduce you to the testing tactics that will be incorporated into the approach to software testing presented in this book.

The testing methodology proposed in this book incorporates both testing strategy and testing tactics. The tactics address the test plans, test criteria, testing techniques, and testing tools used in validating and verifying the software system under development.

The testing methodology cube represents a detailed work program for testing software systems (see Figure 3-9). A detailed testing work program is important to ensure that the test factors have been adequately addressed at each phase of the systems development life cycle. This book provides a detailed description of the work program represented by the testing methodology cube.

The cube is a three-dimensional work program. The first and most important dimensions are the test factors that are selected for a specific application system test strategy. If the testing process can show that the selected test factors have been adequately handled by the application system, the test process can be considered satisfactorily completed. In designing the test work program, there are concerns in each phase of the life cycle that the test factors will not be achieved. While the factors are common to the entire life cycle, the concerns vary according to the phase of the life cycle. These concerns represent the second dimension of the cube. The third dimension of the cube is the test tactics. There are criteria that, if satisfied, would assure the tester that the application system has adequately addressed the risks. Once the test tactics have ensured that the risks are addressed, the factors can also be considered satisfied and the test tactics are complete.

1. **PLAN**

   1.1   Unit Description. Provide a brief description and flowchart of the unit which describes the input, outputs, and functions of the unit being tested as a frame of reference for the specific tests.

   1.2   Milestones. List the milestone events and dates for testing.

   1.3   Budget. List the funds allocated to test this unit.

   1.4   Test Approach. The general method or strategy used to test this unit.

   1.5   Functions not Tested. List those functions which will not be validated as a result of this test.

   1.6   Test Constraints. Indicate anticipated limitations on the test due to test conditions, such as interfaces, equipment, personnel, and data bases.

2. **BUSINESS AND STRUCTURAL FUNCTION TESTING**

   2.1   Business Functions. List the business functional requirements included in this unit.

   2.2   Structural Functions. List the structural functions included in the unit.

   2.3   Test Descriptions. Describe the tests to be performed in evaluating business and structural functions.

   2.4   Expected Test Results. List the desired result from each test. That which will validate the correctness of the unit functions.

   2.5   Conditions to Stop Test. The criteria which if occurs will result in the tests being stopped.

   2.6   Test Number Cross-Reference. A cross-reference between the system test identifiers and the unit test identifiers.

3. **INTERFACE TEST DESCRIPTIONS**

   3.1   Interface. List the interfaces that are included in this unit.

   3.2   Test Description. Describe the tests to be performed to evaluate the interfaces.

   3.3   Expected Test Results. List the desired result from each test. That which will validate the correctness of the unit functions.

   3.4   Test Number Cross-Reference. A cross-reference between the system test identifiers and the unit test identifiers.

4. **TEST PROGRESSION**

   List the progression in which the tests must be performed. Note that this is obtained from the system test plan. This section may be unnecessary if the system test plan progression worksheet can be carried forward.

Figure 3-8   Unit test plan standard.

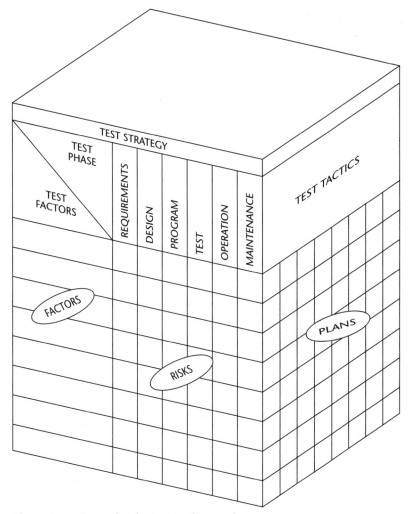

Figure 3-9   Example of a test-tactics matrix.

The three dimensions of the cube will be explained in detail in later chapters, together with the tools and techniques needed for the testing of the application system. The test factors have been previously explained. The test tactics outline the steps to be followed in conducting the tests, together with the tools and techniques needed for each aspect of testing. The test phases are representative of the more commonly accepted system development life cycles. Later chapters are devoted to testing in each phase of the life cycle, and in those chapters, the phase and test tactics for that phase are explained in detail.

Process Preparation Checklist

Work Paper 3-5 is a checklist that you can use to assess the items to be addressed by the test planning process. Use this checklist as you build your test process; it will help ensure that the test process will address the components of effective testing.

A Yes response to any checklist items means that you've chosen an effective process component for your test process. If you don't want to include a particular item in your test process, insert No for that item. Use the Comments column to clarify your response and to provide guidance for building the test process. A blank worksheet has been provided for your use at the end of this chapter.

Summary

Effective and efficient testing will occur only when a well-defined process exists. This chapter presented six guidelines to improve the effectiveness and efficiency of software-testing process. The chapter explained the workbench concept to be used in building your software-testing process. A seven-step software-testing process was presented that can be viewed as seven major testing workbenches; each of these steps incorporate several minor or sub-workbenches within the step workbench. Normally, that generic seven-step process requires customization to fit into your culture and IT mission. Customization considerations were provided to help you with the customization process.

The seven-step process designed in this book is recommended as a generic software-testing process you should use in your organization. The next chapter will provide guidance on selecting and incorporating tools into the software testing process.

WORK PAPER 3-1   Structural Risk Assessment

TEST DOCUMENT
Structural Risk Assessment

RISK	RATINGS	RATING × WEIGHT= SCORE
Ratings: L - Low M - Medium H - High NA - Not Applicable		
1. Amount of time since last major change to existing area of business		3
• More than 2 years	L=1	
• 1 to 2 years; unknown	M=2	
• Less than 1 year	H=3	
• No automated system	H=3	
2. Estimated frequency of change to proposed/existing systems		3
• No existing automated system; or development effort insufficient for estimate	NA=0	
• Fewer than 2 per year	L=1	
• 2 to 10 per year	M=2	
• More than 20 per year	H=3	
3. Estimated extent of total changes in business area methods in last year in percentage of methods affected		3
• No changes NA=0		
• Less than 10%	L=1	
• 10 to 25% M=2		
• More than 25%	H=3	
4. Magnitude of changes in business area associated with this project		3
• Minor change(s)	L=1	
• Significant but manageable change	M=2	
• Major changes to system functionality and/or resource needs	H=4	
5. Project performance site		2
• Company facility	L=1	
• Local noncompany facility	M=2	
• Not in local area	H=5	
6. Critical staffing of project		2
• In-house	L=1	
• Contractor, sole-source	M=2	
• Contractor, competitive-bid	H=6	
7. Type of project organization		2
• Line and staff: project has total management control of personnel	L=1	
• Mixture of line and staff with matrix-managed elements	M=2	
• Matrix: no management control transferred to project	H=3	

(continues)

WORK PAPER 3-1   *(continued)*

TEST DOCUMENT
Structural Risk Assessment

Ratings: L - Low M - Medium H - High NA - Not Applicable		RATING × WEIGHT=
RISK	RATINGS	SCORE

RISK	RATINGS	SCORE
8. Potential problems with subcontractor relationship		5
• Not applicable to this project	NA=0	
• Subcontractor not assigned to isolated or critical task: prime contractor has previously managed subcontractor successfully	L=1	
• Subcontractor assigned to all development tasks in subordinate role to prime contractor: company has favorable experience with subcontractor on other effort(s)	M=2	
• Subcontractor has sole responsibility for critical task; subcontractor new to company	H=3	
9. Status of the ongoing project training		2
• No training plan required	NA=0	
• Complete training plan in place	L=1	
• Some training in place	M=2	
• No training available	H=3	
10. Level of skilled personnel available to train project team		3
• No training required	NA=0	
• Knowledgeable on all systems	L=1	
• Knowledgeable on major components	M=2	
• Few components understood	H=3	
11. Accessibility of supporting reference and or compliance documents and other information on proposed/existing system		3
• Readily available	L=1	
• Details available with some difficulty and delay	M=2	
• Great difficulty in obtaining details, much delay	H=3	
12. Status of documentation in the user areas		3
• Complete and current	L=1	
• More than 75% complete and current	M=2	
• Nonexistent or outdated	H=6	
13. Nature of relationship with users in respect to updating project documentation to reflect changes that may occur during project development		3
• Close coordination	L=1	
• Manageable coordination	M=2	
• Poor coordination	H=5	
14. Estimated degree to which project documentation reflects actual business need		3
• Excellent documentation	L=1	
• Good documentation but some problems with reliability	M=2	
• Poor or inadequate documentation	H=3	

WORK PAPER 3-1   *(continued)*

TEST DOCUMENT
Structural Risk Assessment

Ratings: L - Low M - Medium H - High NA - Not Applicable		RATING × WEIGHT=
RISK	**RATINGS**	**SCORE**
15. Quality of documentation for the proposed system		3
• Excellent standards: adherence and execution are integral part of system and program development	L=1	
• Adequate standards: adherence is not consistent	M=2	
• Poor or no standards: adherence is minimal	H=3	
16. Quality of development and production library control		3
• Excellent standards: superior adherence and execution	L=1	
• Adequate standards: adherence is not consistent	M=2	
• Poor or no standards: adherence is minimal	H=3	
17. Availability of special test facilities for subsystem testing		2
• Complete or not required	L=1	
• Limited	M=2	
• None available	H=3	
18. Status of project maintenance planning		2
• Current and complete	L=1	
• Under development	M=2	
• Nonexistent	H=3	
19. Contingency plans in place to support operational mission should application fail		2
• None required	NA=0	
• Complete plan	L=1	
• Major subsystems addressed	M=2	
• Nonexistent	H=3	
20. User approval of project specifications		4
• Formal, written approval based on structured, detailed review processes	L=1	
• Formal, written approval based on informal unstructured, detailed review processes	M=2	
• No formal approval; cursory review	H=3	
21. Effect of external systems on the system		5
• No external systems involved	NA=0	
• Critical intersystem communications controlled through interface control documents; standard protocols utilized: stable interfaces	L=1	
• Critical intersystem communications controlled through interface control documents: some nonstandard protocols: interfaces change infrequently	M=2	
• Not all critical intersystem communications controlled through interface control documents: some nonstandard protocols: some interfaces change frequently	H=3	

(continues)

WORK PAPER 3-1   (*continued*)

TEST DOCUMENT
Structural Risk Assessment

RISK	RATINGS	RATING × WEIGHT= SCORE
Ratings: L - Low M - Medium H - High NA - Not Applicable		
22. Type and adequacy of configuration management planning		2
• Complete and functioning	L=1	
• Undergoing revisions for inadequacies	M=2	
• None available	H=3	
23. Type of standards and guidelines to be followed by project		4
• Standards use structured programming concepts, reflect current methodology, and permit tailoring to nature and scope of development project	L=1	
• Standards require a top-down approach and offer some flexibility in application	M=2	
• Standards are out of date and inflexible	H=3	
24. Degree to which system is based on well-specified requirements		5
• Detailed transaction and parametric data in requirements documentation	L=1	
• Detailed transaction data in requirements documentation	M=2	
• Vague requirements documentation	H=5	
25. Relationships with those who are involved with system (e.g., users, customers, sponsors, interfaces) or who must be dealt with during project effort		3
• No significant conflicting needs: system primarily serves one organizational unit	L=1	
• System meets limited conflicting needs of cooperative organization units	M=2	
• System must meet important conflicting needs of several cooperative organization units	H=3	
• System must meet important conflicting needs of several uncooperative organizational units	H=4	
26. Changes in user area necessary to meet system operating requirements		3
• Not applicable	NA=0	
• Minimal	L=1	
• Somewhat	M=2	
• Major	H=3	
27. General user attitude		5
• Good: values data processing solution	L=1	
• Fair: some reluctance	M=2	
• Poor: does not appreciate data processing solution	H=3	

WORK PAPER 3-1 *(continued)*

TEST DOCUMENT
Structural Risk Assessment

Ratings: L - Low M - Medium H - High NA - Not Applicable		RATING × WEIGHT=
RISK	RATINGS	SCORE
28. Status of people, procedures, knowledge, discipline, and division of details of offices that will be using system		4
• Situation good to excellent	L=1	
• Situation satisfactory but could be improved	M=2	
• Situation less than satisfactory	H=3	
29. Commitment of senior user management to system		3
• Extremely enthusiastic	L=1	
• Adequate	M=3	
• Some reluctance or level of commitment unknown	H=3	
30. Dependence of project on contributions of technical effort from other areas (e.g., database administration)		2
• None	L=1	
• From within IT	M=2	
• From outside IT	H=3	
31. User's IT knowledge and experience		2
• Highly capable	L=1	
• Previous exposure but limited knowledge	M=2	
• First exposure	H=3	
32. Knowledge and experience of user in application area		2
• Previous experience	L=1	
• Conceptual understanding	M=2	
• Limited knowledge	H=4	
33. Knowledge and experience of project team in application area		3
• Previous experience	L=1	
• Conceptual understanding	M=2	
• Limited knowledge	H=4	
34. Degree of control by project management		2
• Formal authority commensurate with assigned responsibility	L=1	
• Informal authority commensurate with assigned responsibility	M=2	
• Responsibility but no authority	H=3	
35. Effectiveness of project communications		2
• Easy access to project manager(s); change information promptly transmitted upward and downward	L=1	
• Limited access to project manager(s); downward communication limited	M=2	
• Aloof project management; planning information closely held	H=3	

(continues)

WORK PAPER 3-1 *(continued)*

TEST DOCUMENT
Structural Risk Assessment

Ratings: L - Low M - Medium H - High NA - Not Applicable	RATING × WEIGHT=	
RISK	RATINGS	SCORE
36. Test team's opinion about conformance of system specifications to business needs based on early tests and/or reviews		3
• Operational tests indicate that procedures and operations produce desired results	L=1	
• Limited tests indicate that procedures and operations differ from specifications in minor aspects only	M=2	
• Procedures and operations differ from specifications in important aspects: specifications insufficient to use for testing	H=3	
37. Sensitivity of information		1
• None L=0		
• High H=3		

		Total	107.00
PREPARED BY:	DATE:	Total Score / Total Weight = Risk Average	

WORK PAPER 3-2   Technical Risk Assessment

TEST DOCUMENT
Technical Risk Assessment

			RATING × WEIGHT=
Ratings: L - Low M - Medium H - High NA - Not Applicable			
RISK		**RATINGS**	**SCORE**

RISK	RATINGS	SCORE
1. Ability to fulfill mission during hardware or software failure		2
• Can be accomplished without system	L=1	
• Can be accomplished without fully operational system, but some minimum capability required	M=2	
• Cannot be accomplished without fully automated system	H=6	
2. Required system availability		2
• Periodic use (weekly or less frequently)	L=1	
• Daily use (but not 24 hours per day)	M=2	
• Constant use (24 hours per day)	H=5	
3. Degree to which system's ability to function relies on exchange of data with external systems		2
• Functions independently: sends no data required for the operation of other systems	L=0	
• Must send and/or receive data to or from another system	M=2	
• Must send and/or receive data to or from multiple systems	H=3	
4. Nature of system-to-system communications		1
• System has no external interfaces	L=0	
• Automated communications link using standard protocols	M=2	
• Automated communications link using nonstandard protocals	H=3	
5. Estimated system's program size limitations		2
• Substantial unused capacity	L=1	
• Within capacity	M=2	
• Near limits of capacity	H=3	
6. Degree of specified input data control procedures		3
• Detailed error checking	L=1	
• General error checking	M=2	
• No error checking	H=3	
7. Type of system hardware to be installed		3
• No hardware needed	NA=0	
• Standard batch or on-line systems	L=1	
• Nonstandard peripherals	M=2	
• Nonstandard peripherals and mainframes	H=3	
8. Basis for selection of programming and system software		3
• Architectural analysis of functional and performance requirements	L=1	
• Similar system development experience	M=2	
• Current inventory of system software and existing programming language skills	H=3	

(continues)

WORK PAPER 3-2   *(continued)*

TEST DOCUMENT
Technical Risk Assessment

Ratings: L - Low M - Medium H - High NA - Not Applicable	RATING × WEIGHT=	
RISK	**RATINGS**	**SCORE**
9. Complexity of projected system		2
• Single function (e.g., word processing only)	L=1	
• Multiple but related function (e.g., message generation, editing, and dissemination)	M=2	
• Multiple but not closely related functions (e.g., database query, statistical manipulation, graphics plotting, text editing)	H=3	
10. Projected level of programming language		2
• High level, widely used	L=1	
• Low-level or machine language, widely used	M=2	
• Special-purpose language, extremely limited use	H=3	
11. Suitability of programming language to application(s)		2
• All modules can be coded in straightforward manner in chosen language	L=1	
• All modules can be coded in a straightforward manner with few exit routines, sophisticated techniques, and so forth	H=3	
• Significant number of exit routines, sophisticated techniques, and so forth are required to compensate for deficiencies in language selected	H=3	
12. Familiarity of hardware architecture		2
• Mainframe and peripherals widely used	L=1	
• Peripherals unfamiliar	M=2	
• Mainframe unfamiliar	H=4	
13. Degree of pioneering (extent to which new, difficult, and unproven techniques are applied)		5
• Conservative: no untried system components; no pioneering system objectives or techniques	L=1	
• Moderate: few important system components and functions are untried; few pioneering system objectives and techniques	H=3	
• Aggressively pioneering: more than a few unproven hardware or software components or system objectives	H=3	
14. Suitability of hardware to application environment		2
• Standard hardware	NA=0	
• Architecture highly comparable with required functions	L=1	
• Architecture sufficiently powerful but not particularly efficient	M=2	
• Architecture dictates complex software routines	H=3	

WORK PAPER 3-2　*(continued)*

TEST DOCUMENT
Technical Risk Assessment

		RATING × WEIGHT=
Ratings: L - Low　M - Medium　H - High　NA - Not Applicable		
RISK	RATINGS	SCORE

RISK	RATINGS	SCORE
15. Margin of error (need for perfect functioning, split-second timing, and significant cooperation and coordination)		5
• Comfortable margin	L=1	
• Realistically demanding	M=2	
• Very demanding; unrealistic	H=3	
16. Familiarity of project team with operating software		2
• Considerable experience	L=1	
• Some experience or experience unknown	M=2	
• Little or no experience	H=3	
17. Familiarity of project team with system environment supporting the application		2
• Considerable experience	L=1	
• Some experience or experience unknown	M=2	
• Little or no experience with:		
Operating System	H=3	
DBMS	H=3	
Data Communications	H=3	
18. Knowledgeability of project team in the application area		2
• Previous experience	L=1	
• Conceptual understanding	M=2	
• Limited knowledge	H=3	
19. Type of test tools used		5
• Comprehensive test/debut software, including path analyzers	L=1	
• Formal, documented procedural tools only	M=2	
• None	H=3	
20. Realism of test environment		4
• Tests performed on operational system: total database and communications environment	L=1	
• Tests performed on separate development system: total database, limited communications	M=2	
• Tests performed on dissimilar development system: limited database and limited communications	H=3	
21. Communications interface change testing		4
• No interfaces required	NA=0	
• Live testing on actual line at operational transaction rates	L=1	
• Loop testing on actual line, simulated transactions	M=2	
• Line simulations within development system	H=3	

(continues)

WORK PAPER 3-2   *(continued)*

TEST DOCUMENT
Technical Risk Assessment

Ratings: L - Low M - Medium H - High NA - Not Applicable		RATING × WEIGHT=
RISK	RATINGS	SCORE
22. Importance of user training to the success of the system		1
• Little training needed to use or operate system: documentation is sufficient for training	L=1	
• Users and or operators need no formal training, but experience is required in addition to documentation	M=2	
• Users essentially unable to operate system without formal, hands-on training in addition to documentation	H=3	
23. Estimated degree of system adaptability to change		3
• High: structured programming techniques used: relatively unpatched, well documented	L=1	
• Moderate	M=2	
• Low: monolithic program design, high degree of inner/ intrasystem dependency, unstructured development, minimal documentation	H=4	

			Total	61.00
PREPARED BY:	DATE:		Total Score / Total Weight = Risk Average	

WORK PAPER 3-3   Size Risk Assessment

TEST DOCUMENT
Size Risk Assessment

RISK	Ratings: L - Low M - Medium H - High NA - Not Applicable	RATINGS	RATING × WEIGHT= SCORE
1.	Ranking of this project's total worker-hours within the limits established by the organization's smallest and largest system development projects (in number of worker-hours)		3
	• Lower third of systems development projects	L=1	
	• Middle third of systems development projects	M=2	
	• Upper third of systems development projects	H=3	
2.	Project implementation time		3
	• 12 months or less	L=1	
	• 13 months to 24 months	M=2	
	• More than 24 months, with phased implementation	H=3	
	• More than 24 months; no phasing	H=4	
3.	Estimated project adherence to schedule		1
	• Ahead of schedule	L=1	
	• On schedule	M=2	
	• Behind schedule (by three months or less)	H=3	
	• Behind schedule (by more than three months)	H=4	
4.	Number of systems interconnecting with the application		3
	• 1 to 2	L=1	
	• 3 to 5	M=2	
	• More than 5	H=3	
5.	Percentage of project resources allocated to system testing		2
	• More than 40%	L=1	
	• 20 to 40%	M=2	
	• Less than 20%	H=3	
6.	Number of interrelated logical data groupings (estimate if unknown)		1
	• Fewer than 4	L=1	
	• 4 to 6	M=2	
	• More than 6	H=3	
7.	Number of transaction types		1
	• Fewer than 6	L=1	
	• 6 to 25	M=2	
	• More than 25	H=3	
8.	Number of output reports		1
	• Fewer than 10	L=1	
	• 10 to 20	M=2	
	• More than 20	H=3	

(continues)

WORK PAPER 3-3   *(continued)*

TEST DOCUMENT
Size Risk Assessment

Ratings: L - Low M - Medium H - High NA - Not Applicable		RATING × WEIGHT=
RISK	**RATINGS**	**SCORE**
9. Ranking of this project's number of lines of program code to be maintained within the limits established by the organization's smallest and largest systems development projects (in number of lines of code)		3
• Lower third of systems development projects	L=1	
• Middle third of systems development projects	M=2	
• Upper third of systems development projects	H=3	

		Total	18.00
PREPARED BY:	DATE:	Total Score / Total Weight = Risk Average	

WORK PAPER 3-4   Risk Score Analysis

TEST DOCUMENT
Risk Score Analysis

APPLICATION SYSTEM _____

RISK AREA	SCORE		COMPARATIVE RATING WITH COMPANY APPLICATIONS			COMMENTS
	TOTAL	AVERAGE	HIGH	MEDIUM	LOW	
STRUCTURE						
TECHNOLOGY						
SIZE						
TOTAL RISK SCORE						

HIGH RISK ATTRIBUTES

RISK AREA	RISK ATTRIBUTES	TEST CONCERN

PREPARED BY: DATE:

WORK PAPER 3-5   Testing Tactics Checklist

		YES	NO	COMMENTS
1.	Did you use your test strategy as a guide for developing the test tactics?			
2.	Did you decompose your strategy into test tactics? (May not fully occur until the test planning step.)			
3.	Did you consider trade-offs between test factors when developing test tactics (e.g., choosing between continuity of processing and accuracy)?			
4.	Did you compare your test tactics to the test strategy to ensure they support the strategy?			
5.	Have you identified the individuals who can perform the tests?			
6.	Did you compose a strategy for recruiting those individuals?			
7.	Did management agree to let the team members accept the proposed responsibilities on your project team?			
8.	Has a test plan for testing been established? If so does the test team have the following responsibilities:			
	Set test objectives.			
	Develop a test strategy.			
	Develop the test tactics.			
	Define the test resources.			
	Execute tests needed to achieve the test plan.			
9.	Modify the test plan and test execution as changes occur.			
	Manage use of test resources.			
	Issue test reports.			
	Ensure the quality of the test process.			
	Maintain test statistics.			
10.	Does the test team adequately represent the following:			
	User personnel			
	Operation's staff			
	Data administration			
	Internal auditors			
	Quality assurance staff			
	Information technology			
	Management			
	Security administrator			
	Professional testers			

WORK PAPER 3-5   *(continued)*

		YES	NO	COMMENTS
11.	Did you develop test team assignments for each test member?			
	Does the test team accept responsibility for finding users/customer type defects?			
12.	Does the test team accept responsibility for finding defects?			
13.	Does the team recognize the benefit of removing defects earlier in the correction life cycle process?			
14.	Will testing begin when the development process begins?			
15.	Does one person have primary responsibility for testing?			
16.	Will the test team perform validation tests?			
17.	Will the test team perform verification tests?			
18.	Will verification tests include requirement reviews?			
19.	Will verification tests include design reviews?			
20.	Will verification tests include code walkthroughs?			
21.	Will verification tests include code inspections?			
22.	Will validation tests include unit testing?			
23.	Will validation tests include integration testing?			
24.	Will validation tests include system testing?			
25.	Will validation tests include user acceptance testing?			
26.	Will testers develop a testers' workbench?			
27.	Will the workbench identify the deliverables/products to be tested?			
28.	Will the workbench include test procedures?			
29.	Will the workbench check accuracy of test implementation?			
30.	Will you identify test deliverables?			
31.	Does your workbench identify the tools you'll use?			
32.	Have the testers identified a source of these generic test tools?			

CHAPTER 4

Selecting and Installing Software Testing Tools

A tool can be defined as "anything that serves as a means to get something done." It is important to recognize that you first must determine what that something is before acquiring a tool. Chapter 3 discussed the concept of a work process (the means for accomplishing a testing objective). Within the work process would be one or more tools to accomplish the objective. For example, in developing scripts, one might wish to use a capture/playback tool.

This chapter describes the relationship between tools and work processes. The chapter then explains the steps involved in selecting and installing a tool, as well as creating a toolbox for testers. Finally, the chapter proposes how to train testing staff in the use of tools, as well as designate a tool manager to provide testers the support they need in using those tools.

Integrating Tools into the Tester's Work Processes

It is important to recognize the relationship between a tool and a technique. A *technique* is a procedure for performing an operation; a *tool* is anything that serves as a means to get something done. Let's look at a non-testing example. If you want to attach two pieces of wood together, you might choose a nail as the means for accomplishing that bonding process. Joining the two pieces of wood together is a technique for building an object; a nail is a tool used to join two pieces of wood together. A technique for inserting the nail into the two pieces of wood might be a swinging motion hitting the nail on the head; a hammer is a tool that would help that technique.

Stress testing is a technique that a software tester might use to validate that software can process large volumes of data. Tools that would be helpful in stress testing software might include a test data generator or a capture/ playback tool for using and re-using large amounts of test data.

Although software testing techniques are limited, software tools are almost unlimited. Testers can select a variety of software tools to accomplish any specific software testing technique, just as a carpenter could use tools such as nails, screws, or glue to fasten two pieces of wood together.

NOTE This chapter will not discuss specific vendor tools. There are too many operating platforms and too many vendor tools to effectively identify and describe the availability of tools in this book. Search the Web for "software testing tools" and you find a variety of sources to identify what is currently available in the marketplace.

It is important that tools be integrated into the software tester's work processes. The use of tools should always be mandatory. This does not mean that an individual tester may not select among several tools to accomplish a specific task, but rather that the process should identify specific tools or provide the tester a choice of tools to accomplish a specific work task. However, for that work task, the tester must use one of the tools specified in the work process.

Tools Available for Testing Software

This section is designed to cause you to think "outside of the box" regarding tools available for software testing. When the concept of the software testing tool is discussed, many testers think of automated tools provided by vendors of testing software. However, there are many manual tools available that can aid significantly in testing software (for example, code inspections).

The objective of this discussion is to categorize the tools used by testers into generic categories. A test script, for example, is a means for accomplishing some aspect of software testing. There are both manual tools to help you create scripts, such as building use cases, as well as automated tools that can both generate and execute a test script.

Testing tools are the aids used by individuals with testing responsibility to fulfill that responsibility. The tools cover a wide range of activities and are applicable for use in all phases of the systems development life cycle. Some of the techniques are manual, some automated; some perform static tests, others dynamic; some evaluate the system structure, and others, the system function.

The skill required to use the tools and the cost of executing the tools vary significantly. Some of the skills are highly technical and involve in-depth knowledge of computer programming and the system being tested. Other tools are general in nature and are useful to almost anyone with testing responsibilities. Some techniques involve only a short expenditure of man-hours, whereas others must be conducted by a team and make heavy use of computer resources in the test process.

The following is a list of the more common testing tools:

- **Boundary value analysis.** A method of dividing application systems into segments so that testing can occur within the boundaries of those segments. The concept complements top-down system design.

- **Capture/playback.** A technique that enables you to capture the data and results of testing, and then play it back for future tests.

- **Cause-effect graphing.** Attempts to show the effect of each test event processed. The purpose is to categorize tests by the effect that will occur as a result of testing. This should reduce the number of test conditions by eliminating the need for multiple test events that all produce the same effects.

- **Checklist.** A series of probing questions designed to review a predetermined area or function.

- **Code comparison.** Identifies differences between two versions of the same program. You can use this tool with either object or source code.

- **Compiler-based analysis.** Utilizes the diagnostics produced by a compiler or diagnostic routines added to a compiler to identify program defects during the compilation of the program.

- **Confirmation/examination.** Verifies the correctness of many aspects of the system by contacting third parties, such as users, or examining a document to verify that it exists.

- **Control flow analysis.** Requires the development of a graphic representation of a program to analyze the branch logic within the program to identify logic problems.

- **Correctness proof.** Involves developing a set of statements or hypotheses that define the correctness of processing. These hypotheses are then tested to determine whether the application system performs processing in accordance with these statements.

- **Data dictionary.** The documentation tool for recording data elements and the attributes of the data elements that, under some implementations, can produce test data to validate the system's data edits.

- **Data flow analysis.** A method of ensuring that the data used by the program has been properly defined, and that the defined data is properly used.

- **Database.** A repository of data collected for testing or about testing that can be summarized, re-sequenced, and analyzed for test purposes.

- **Design-based functional testing.** Recognizes that functions within an application system are necessary to support the requirements. This process identifies those design-based functions for test purposes.

- **Design reviews.** Reviews conducted during the systems development process, normally in accordance with systems development methodology. The primary objective of design reviews is to ensure compliance to the design methodology.

- **Desk checking.** Reviews by the originator of the requirements, design, or program as a check on the work performed by that individual.

- **Disaster test.** A procedure that predetermines a disaster as a basis for testing the recovery process. The test group then causes or simulates the disaster as a basis for testing the procedures and training for the recovery process.

- **Error guessing.** Uses the experience or judgment of people to predict what the most probable errors will be and then test to ensure that the system can handle those test conditions.

- **Executable specs.** Requires a computer system for writing system specifications so that those specifications can be compiled into a testable program. The compiled specs have less detail and precision than will the final implemented programs, but they are sufficient to evaluate the completeness and proper functioning of the specifications.

- **Fact finding.** Information needed to conduct a test or to ensure the correctness of a document's information, achieved through an investigative process requiring obtaining information or searching for the facts about a predetermined condition.

- **Flowchart.** Graphically represents the system and/or program flow in order to evaluate the completeness of the requirements, design, or program specifications.

- **Inspections.** A highly structured step-by-step review of the deliverables produced by each phase of the systems development life cycle in order to identify potential defects.

- **Instrumentation.** The use of monitors and/or counters to determine the frequency with which predetermined events occur.

- **Integrated test facility.** A concept that permits the introduction of test data into a production environment so that applications can be tested at the same time they are running in production. The concept permits testing the accumulation of data over many iterations of the process, and facilitates intersystem testing.

- **Mapping.** A process that analyzes which parts of a computer program are exercised during the test and how frequently each statement or routine in a program is executed. This can be used to detect system flaws, determine how much of a program is executed during testing, and identify areas where more efficient code may reduce execution time.

- **Modeling.** A method of simulating the functioning of the application system and/or its environment to determine if the design specifications will achieve the system objectives.

- **Parallel operation.** Runs both the old and new version within the same time frame in order to identify differences between the two processes. The tool is most effective when there is minimal change between the old and new processing versions of the system.

- **Parallel simulation.** Develops a less precise version of a segment of a computer system in order to determine whether the results produced by the test are reasonable. This tool is effective when used with large volumes of data to automatically determine the correctness of the results of processing. Normally, this tool approximates only actual processing

- **Peer review.** A review process that uses peers to review that aspect of the systems development life cycle with which they are most familiar. Typically, the peer review offers compliance to standards, procedures, guidelines, and the use of good practices, as opposed to efficiency, effectiveness, and economy of the design and implementation.

- **Ratios/relationships.** Quantitative analysis that enables testers to draw conclusions about some aspect of the software to validate the reasonableness of the software. For example, in test planning, they may want to compare the proposed test budget to the number of function points being tested.

- **Risk matrix.** Tests the adequacy of controls through the identification of risks and the controls implemented in each part of the application system to reduce those risks to a level acceptable to the user.

- **Scoring.** A method to determine which aspects of the application system should be tested by determining the applicability of problem criteria to the application being tested. The process can be used to determine the degree of testing (for example, high-risk systems would be subject to more tests than low-risk systems) or to identify areas within the application system to determine the amount of testing needed.

- **Snapshot.** A method of printing the status of computer memory at predetermined points during processing. Computer memory can be printed when specific instructions are executed or when data with specific attributes are processed.

- **Symbolic execution.** Permits the testing of programs without test data. The symbolic execution of a program results in an expression that can be used to evaluate the completeness of the programming logic.

- **System logs.** Uses information collected during the operation of a computer system to analyze how well the system performed. System logs are produced by operating software such as database management systems, operating systems, and job accounting systems.

- **Test data.** System transactions that are created for the purpose of testing the application system.

- **Test data generator.** Software systems that can be used to automatically generate test data for test purposes. Frequently, these generators require only parameters of the data element values in order to generate large amounts of test transactions.

- **Test scripts.** A sequential series of actions that a user of an automated system would enter to validate the correctness of software processing.

- **Tracing.** A representation of the paths followed by computer programs as they process data or the paths followed in a database to locate one or more pieces of data used to produce a logical record for processing.

- **Use cases.** Test transactions that focus on how users will use the software in an operational environment.

- **Utility programs.** A general-purpose software package that can be used to test an application system. The most valuable utilities are those that analyze or list data files.

- **Walkthroughs.** A process that asks the programmer or analyst to explain the application system to a test team, typically by using a simulation of the execution of the application system. The objective of the walkthrough is to provide a basis for questioning by the test team to identify defects.

Selecting and Using Test Tools

This chapter presents an extensive array of tools for systems testing. Many of these tools have not been widely used. The principal reasons for this include: 1) specialized use (simulation); 2) the high cost of their use (symbolic execution); and 3) their unproven applicability (correctness proof). Many of these tools represent the state of the art and are in areas where research is continuing. However, this should not prevent organizations from experimenting with some of the newer test concepts. The tools attracting the most interest and activity at present include automated test support systems (capture/playback) and automated analysis (compiler-based analysis).

As better tools are developed for testing during the requirements and design phases of software testing, an increase in automatic analysis is possible. In addition, more sophisticated analysis tools are being applied to the code during construction. More complete control and automation of the actual execution of tests, both in assistance in generating the test cases and in the management of the testing process and result, are also taking place.

It is important that testing occur throughout the software development life cycle. One reason for the great success of disciplined manual techniques is the uniform applicability at the requirements, design, and coding phases. These tools can be used without massive capital expenditure. However, to be most effective they require a serious commitment and a disciplined application. Careful planning, clearly stated testing objectives, precisely defined tools, good management, organized record keeping, and a strong commitment are critical to successful testing. A disciplined approach must be followed during both planning and execution of the testing activities.

An integral part of this process is the selection of the appropriate testing tool. The following four steps are involved in selecting the appropriate testing tool:

1. Match the tool to its use.

2. Select a tool appropriate to its life cycle phase.

3. Match the tool to the tester's skill level.

4. Select an affordable tool.

Matching the Tool to Its Use

The better a tool is suited to accomplish its task, the more efficient the test process will be. The wrong tool not only decreases the efficiency of testing, it may not permit testers to achieve their objectives. The test objective can be a specific task in executing tests, such as using an Excel spreadsheet to track defects, or to accomplish the testing technique, such as stress testing, using a tool such as capture/playback.

The objective for using a tool should be integrated into the process in which the tool is to be incorporated. Again, the tool is the means to accomplish a test objective. When test processes are developed, a decision is made as to whether a specific task should be performed manually or whether it can be more effectively and efficiently performed using a test tool. The test process comes first, the test tool second.

In some instances, an IT testing organization will become aware of a testing tool that offers an opportunity to do more effective testing than is currently being performed. It may be necessary to modify the test process to incorporate the capabilities of the new tool. In this instance, the tool will help determine the process. What is important is that the tool is integrated into the process and not used externally to the process at the discretion of the tester.

As test processes are continually improved, new tools will be integrated into the process. The search for and analysis of available tools is a continuous process. The objective is to improve the testing process by incorporating more effective and efficient tools.

You can use Work Paper 4-1 to identify the tools that will be considered for selection. Note that this Work Paper does not contain all the tools that might be considered.

Chapter 8 describes a variety of testing techniques. Many of the tools used in testing will be utilized to effectively perform those techniques. Again, stress testing is a technique for which tools are necessary to support a large volume of test data.

Selecting a Tool Appropriate to Its Life Cycle Phase

The type of testing varies by the life cycle in which it occurs. Just as the methods change, so do the tools. Thus, it becomes necessary to select a tool appropriate for the life cycle in which it will be used.

As the life cycle progresses, the tools tend to shift from manual to automatic. However, this should not imply that the manual tools are less effective than the automatic, because some of the most productive testing can occur during the early phases of the life cycle using manual tools.

Table 4-1 lists the life cycle phases in which the identified test tools are most effective. This matrix shows the 41 test tools and for which of the 6 systems development life cycle phases each tool is most appropriate. You can use this matrix for the second step of the selection process, in which the population of tools identified in the first step can be reduced to those tools that are effective in the life cycle phase where the test will be occurring.

Table 4-1   SDLS Phase/Test Tool Matrix

TOOL	SDLC PHASE					
	Require-ments	Design	Program	Test	Oper-ation	Mainte-nance
Boundary value analysis			X	X		
Capture/playback				X		X
Cause-effect graphing		X	X			
Checklist	X	X	X	X	X	X
Code comparison						X
Compiler-based analysis			X			
Confirmation/examination	X	X	X	X	X	X
Control flow analysis				X		X
Correctness proof		X		X		
Data dictionary				X		
Data flow analysis			X			
Database				X		X
Design-based functional testing		X		X		
Design reviews		X				
Desk checking	X	X	X			X
Disaster test				X		X
Error guessing	X	X	X	X	X	X
Executable specs		X				
Fact finding	X	X	X	X	X	X
Flowchart	X	X	X			
Inspections	X	X	X	X	X	X
Instrumentation				X	X	X
Integrated test facility						X
Mapping			X			
Modeling	X	X				
Parallel operation					X	
Parallel simulation				X		

Table 4-1 *(continued)*

TOOL	SDLC PHASE					
	Require-ments	Design	Program	Test	Oper-ation	Mainte-nance
Peer review	X	X	X	X	X	X
Ratios/relationships				X		x
Risk matrix	X	X				
Scoring	X	X				
Snapshot				X		
Symbolic execution			x			
System logs				X	X	X
Test data		X	X	X		X
Test data generator				X		X
Test scripts				X		X
Tracing			x			X
Use cases				X		X
Utility programs				X	X	X
Walkthroughs	X	X	X			

Matching the Tool to the Tester's Skill Level

The individual performing the test must select a tool that conforms to his or her skill level. For example, it would be inappropriate for a user to select a tool that requires programming skills when the user does not possess those skills. This does not mean that an individual will not have to be trained before the tool can be used but rather that he or she possesses the basic skills necessary to undertake training to use the tool. Table 4-2 presents the tools divided according to the skill required. This table divides skills into user skill, programming skill, system skill, and technical skill.

- **User skill.** Requires the individual to have an in-depth knowledge of the application and the business purpose for which that application is used. Skills needed include general business specializing in the area computerized, general management skills used to achieve the mission of the user area, and a knowledge of identifying and dealing with user problems.

- **Programming skill.** Requires understanding of computer concepts, flowcharting, programming in the languages used by the organization, debugging, and documenting computer programs.

- **System skill.** Requires the ability to translate user requirements into computer system design specifications. Specific skills include flowcharting, problem analysis, design methodologies, computer operations, some general business skills, error identification and analysis in automated applications, and project management. The individual normally possesses a programming skill.

- **Technical skill.** Requires an understanding of a highly technical specialty and the ability to exhibit reasonable performance at that specialty.

Table 4-2 indicates which skills are required to execute which tools. In some instances, different skills are needed to develop the tool, and if this is the case, that has been indicated in the Comments column. The comments also indicate any skill qualification or specific technical skill needed.

Table 4-2 Skill Levels for Using Testing Tools

SKILL	TOOL	COMMENTS
User skill	Checklist	
	Integrated test facility	
	Peer review	
	Risk matrix	
	Scoring	
	Use case	
	Walkthroughs	
Programmer skill	Boundary value analysis	
	Capture playback	
	Checklist	
	Code comparison	
	Control flow analysis	
	Correctness proof	
	Coverage-based metric testing	
	Data dictionary	
	Data flow analysis	
	Database	
	Design-based functional testing	
	Desk checking	
	Error guessing	

Table 4-2   *(continued)*

SKILL	TOOL	COMMENTS
	Flowchart	
	Instrumentation	
	Mapping	
	Modeling	
	Parallel simulation	
	Peer review	
	Snapshot	
	Symbolic execution	
	System logs	
	Test data	
	Test data generator	
	Test scripts	
	Tracing	
	Volume testing	
	Walkthroughs	
System skill	Cause/effect graphing	
	Checklist	
	Confirmation/examination	
	Correctness proof	
	Design-based functional testing	
	Design reviews	
	Desk checking	
	Disaster test	
	Error guessing	
	Executable specs	Few such languages in existence
	Fact finding	
	Flowchart	
	Inspections	Helpful to have application knowledge

(continues)

Table 4-2   *(continued)*

SKILL	TOOL	COMMENTS
	Integrated test facility	Skills needed to develop but not using ITF
	Mapping	
	Modeling	
	Parallel simulation	
	Peer review	
	System logs	
	Test data	
	Test scripts	
	Tracing	
	Volume testing	
	Walkthroughs	
Technical skill	Checklist	
	Coverage-based metric testing	Requires statistical skill to develop
	Instrumentation	System programmer skill
	Parallel operation	Requires operations skill
	Peer review	Must be taught how to conduct review
	Ratio/relationships	Requires statistical skills to identify, calculate, and interpret the results of a statistical analysis

Selecting an Affordable Tool

Typically, testing must be accomplished within a budget or time span. An extremely time-consuming and hence costly tool, while desirable, may not be affordable under the test budget and schedule. Therefore, the last selection criterion is to pick those tools that are affordable from the population of tools remaining after the preceding step. Work Paper 4-2 can be used to document selected tools.

Some test tools are extremely costly to execute, whereas others involve only nominal costs. It is difficult to put a specific price tag on many of the tools because they require the acquisition of hardware or software, the cost of which may vary significantly from vendor to vendor.

Table 4-3 lists three categories of cost: high, medium, and low. Where costs are extremely high or low, the Comments column is used to further clarify the cost category.

It is possible that you will have gone through the selection process and ended up with no tools to select from. In this instance, you have two options. First, you can repeat the process and be more generous in your selection criteria. In other words, be more inclined to include tools as you move from step to step. Second, you can ignore the formal selection process and use judgment and experience to select the tool that appears most appropriate to accomplish the test objective.

Table 4-3 Cost To Use Testing Tools

COST	TOOL	COMMENTS
High	Correctness proof	
	Coverage-based metric testing	Cost to develop metrics is high—not usage
	Executable specs	
	Inspections	
	Modeling	
	Parallel operation	
	Parallel simulation	
	Symbolic execution	
	Test data	Cost varies by volume of test transactions
Medium	Capture/playback	
	Cause-effect graphing	
	Code comparison	Major cost is acquisition of utility program
	Control flow analysis	
	Database	
	Design-based functional testing	
	Design reviews	Cost varies with size of review team
	Disaster test	Cost varies with size of test
	Instrumentation	
	Integrated test facility	Major cost is building ITF
	Mapping	Software is major cost

(continues)

Table 4-3 *(continued)*

COST	TOOL	COMMENTS
	Peer review	
	Risk matrix	
	Snapshot	Major cost is building snapshot routines into programs
	Systems logs	Assumes logs already in operation
	Test data generator	Major cost is acquiring software
	Test scripts	
	Utility programs	Assumes utility already available
	Volume testing	
	Walkthroughs	Cost varies with size of walkthrough team
Low	Boundary value analysis	Requires establishing boundaries during development
	Checklist	
	Compiler-based analysis	
	Confirmation/examination	
	Data dictionary	Assumes cost of DD is not a test cost
	Desk checking	
	Error guessing	
	Fact finding	
	Flowchart	Assumes software is available
	Ratio/relationship	
	Scoring	

Training Testers in Tool Usage

Training testers in the use of test tools is a "no-brainer." Not training testers in how to use tools before they begin to use them in practice is like letting someone drive an automobile without any training: It's dangerous. The danger is that cost can escalate unnecessarily and by misusing the test tools, testers may not perform effective testing.

It is recommended that test tools be used only by testers who have demonstrated proficiency in their use. If it is necessary for the testers to use a tool in which they are not proficient, a mentor or supervisor should assist the tester in the use of that tool to ensure its effective and efficient use.

Appointing Tool Managers

The objective of appointing a tool manager is twofold:

- **More effective tool usage.** Having a tool manager is, in fact, like establishing a help desk for testers. Because the tool manager is knowledgeable in what the tool does and how it works, that individual can speed the learning of other users and assist with problems associated with the tool's usage.

- **Managerial training.** The individual appointed to be a tool's manager should have total responsibility for that tool. This includes contacting the vendor, budgeting for maintenance and support, overseeing training, and providing supervisory support. Being appointed a tool manager is an effective way to provide managerial training for individuals; it is also effective in evaluating future managerial candidates.

Managing a tool should involve budgeting, planning, training, and related managerial responsibilities.

The workbench for managing testing tools using a tool manager is illustrated in Figure 4-1. The three steps involve appointing a tool manager; assigning the duties the tool manager will perform; and limiting the tool manager's tenure. This concept not only facilitates the use of tools but builds future managers at the same time.

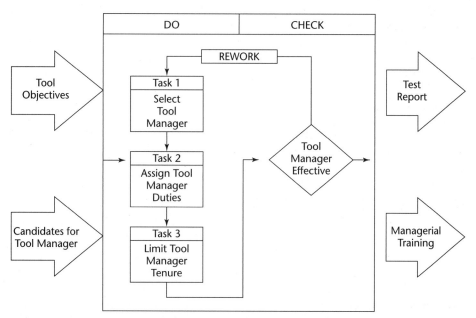

Figure 4-1   Tool manager's workbench for managing testing tools.

Prerequisites to Creating a Tool Manager Position

Before appointing a tool manager, IT management should answer the following questions:

1. Has management established objectives for the tool to be managed?
2. Has the use of the tool been specified in IT work procedures?
3. Has a training program been established for using the tool?
4. Have the potential candidates for tool manager been trained in the use of the tool they would manage?
5. Have potential candidates for tool manager effectively used the tool in a production environment?
6. Do the candidates for tool manager have managerial potential?
7. Does the individual selected for tool manager want to be manager of the tool?
8. Do the candidates for tool manager believe that this tool is effective in accomplishing the organization's mission?
9. Does the candidate for manager have sufficient time to perform the tool manager duties?
10. Have reasonable duties been assigned to the tool manager?
11. Does the tool manager understand and agree that these are reasonable duties to perform?
12. Has a tenure been established on the length of service for tool managers?

Once management has determined that a specific tool is needed (and selected that tool), a tool manager can be appointed. There are two inputs needed for this workbench: a clear definition of the objective for acquiring and using the tool, and a list of potential tool manager candidates.

Tool usage should be mandatory. In other words, work processes should indicate when to use a specific tool. The work process should indicate whether a tool user can select among two or more recommended tools. The tool manager should not be in the mode of marketing a tool but rather assisting and making tool usage more effective.

This section describes a three-step process for using a tool manager.

Selecting a Tool Manager

Ideally, the tool manager should be selected during the process of selecting the tool, and have ownership in the selection decision. The tool manager should possess the following:

- Training skills
- Tool skills
- Managerial skills
  - Planning
  - Organizing

- Directing
- Controlling

If the tool manager candidate lacks the preceding skills, they can be developed during the tool manager tenure. If the tool manager position is used to train future managers, technical proficiency and competency in tool usage is the only real requirement. The other skills can be developed during the tenure as tool manager. A mentor must be assigned to a tool manager to develop the missing skills.

In addition to the tool manager, an assistant tool manager should also be named for each tool. This individual will not have any direct managerial responsibilities but will serve as backup for the tool manager. The primary responsibility of the assistant tool manager will be to gain competency in the use of the tool. Normally, the assistant tool manager is a more junior employee than the tool manager. The assistant is the most logical person to become the next manager for the tool.

Assigning the Tool Manager Duties

A tool manager can be assigned any or all of the following duties:

- **Assist colleagues in the use of the tool.** The tool manager should be available to assist other staff members in the use of the tool. This is normally done using a "hotline." Individuals having problems using the tool or experiencing operational problems with the tool can call the tool manager for assistance. Note: The hours of "hotline" activities may be restricted; for example, 8 to 9 A.M. and 2 to 5 P.M. This restriction will be dependent upon the other responsibilities of the tool manager and the expected frequency of the calls.

- **Train testers how to use the tool.** The initial tool training normally comes from the vendor. However, additional tool training is the responsibility of the tool manager. Note that the tool manager may subcontract this training to the training department, the tool vendor, or other competent people. The tool manager has the responsibility to ensure the training occurs and may or may not do it personally.

- **Act as the tool vendor's contact.** The tool manager would be the official contact for the tool vendor. Questions from staff regarding the use of the tool that can only be answered by the vendor should be funneled through the tool manager to the vendor. Likewise, information from the vendor to the company should be directed through the tool manager.

- **Develop annual tool plans.** The tool manager should develop an annual tool plan complete with planned tool usage, schedule, and resources needed to effectively utilize the tool. Tool managers may want to define penetration goals (the percent of the department that will use the tool by the end of the planning period) and should budget for upgrades, training, and other expenditures involved in tool usage. The tool manager's time should be budgeted and accounted for.

- **Install tool upgrades.** As vendors issue new versions of the tool, the tool manager is responsible for ensuring that those upgrades are properly incorporated and that the involved parties are made aware and trained, if necessary. Note that the tool manager may not have to do a lot of this personally but is responsible to make sure it happens.

- **Prepare annual reports.** At the end of each year, or planning period, the tool manager should prepare for IT management an overview of the use of the tool during the year. This will require the tool manager to maintain statistics on tool usage, problems, costs, upgrades, and so forth. (Note that tool usage for mainframe tools can normally be obtained from job accounting software systems. Non-mainframe usage may have to be estimated.)

- **Determine timing of tool replacements.** The tool manager, being responsible for a specific software tool, should also be responsible for determining when the tool is no longer effective or when better tools can be acquired to replace it. When these situations occur, the tool manager should prepare proposals to senior IT management regarding tool replacement.

The role of a tool manager can be enhanced in the following ways:

- **Allow individuals adequate time to perform the tool manager's role.** The assignment of a tool manager should be scheduled and budgeted so that the individual knows the amount of time and resources that can be allocated to it.

- **Incorporate tool manager performance into individual performance appraisals.** The performance of the tool manager's duties should be considered an important part of an individual's work.

Limiting the Tool Manager's Tenure

It is recommended that an individual serve two years as a manager for a specific tool. The rationale for the two years is that individuals tend to lose interest over a period of time. Also, after a period of time, the manager tends to lose perspective of new uses for the tool or deficiencies in the tool. Bringing in a new tool manager every two years tends to revitalize the use of that tool in the organization. Note that the tool managers can be transferred to manage another tool.

In instances where tools are highly specialized, very complex, or have minimal usage, it may be desirable to keep an individual manager for longer than a two-year period.

Summary

Efficient testing necessitates the use of testing tools. Each testing organization should have a portfolio of tools used in testing. This chapter described the more common software-testing tools. It also proposed the establishment of a test manager function for each tool.

The selection of the appropriate tool in testing is an important aspect of the test process. Techniques are few in number and broad in scope, whereas tools are large in number and narrow in scope. Each provides different capabilities; each tool is designed to accomplish a specific testing objective.

WORK PAPER 4-1   Selecting Tools

Tool	Use	Include in Tester's Toolbox?	
		Yes	**No**
Boundary value analysis	Divides system top down into logical segments and then limits testing within the boundaries of each segment.		
Capture/ playback	Testing used to capture transactions from the testing process for re-use in future tests.		
Cause-effect graphing	Limits the number of test transactions by determining which of the number of variable conditions pose minimal risk based on system actions.		
Checklist	Provides a series of questions designed to probe potential system problem areas.		
Code comparison	Compares two versions of the same program in order to identify differences between the two versions.		
Compiler-based analysis	Detects errors during the program-compilation process.		
Confirmation/ examination	Verifies that a condition has or has not occurred.		
Control flow analysis	Identifies processing inconsistencies, such as routines with no entry point, potentially unending loops, branches into the middle of a routine, and so on.		
Correctness proof	Requires a proof hypothesis to be defined and then used to evaluate the correctness of the system.		
Data dictionary	Generates test data to verify data validation programs based on the data contained in the dictionary.		
Data flow analysis	Identifies defined data not used and used data that is not defined.		
Database	Repository for collecting information for or about testing for later use analysis		
Design-based functional testing	Evaluates functions attributable to the design process as opposed to design requirements; for example, capability may be a design process.		
Design reviews	Requires reviews at predetermined points throughout systems development in order to examine progress and ensure the development process is followed.		

(continues)

WORK PAPER 4-1   *(continued)*

Tool	Use	Include in Tester's Toolbox?	
		Yes	**No**
Desk checking	Provides an evaluation by programmer or analyst of the propriety of program logic after the program is coded or the system is designed.		
Disaster test	Simulates an operational or systems failure to determine if the system can be correctly recovered after the failure.		
Error guessing	Relies on the experience of testers and the organization's history of problems to create test transactions that have a high probability of detecting an error.		
Executable specs	Provides a high-level interpretation of the system specs in order to create the response to test data. Interpretation of expected software packages requires system specs to be written in a high-level language.		
Fact finding	Performs those steps necessary to obtain facts to support the test process.		
Flowchart	Pictorially represents computer systems logic and data flow.		
Inspections	Requires a step-by-step explanation of the product with each step checked against a predetermined list of criteria.		
Instrumentation	Measures the functioning of a system structure by using counters and other monitoring instruments.		
Integrated test facility	Permits the integration of test data in a production environment to enable testing to run during production processing.		
Mapping	Identifies which part of a program is exercised during a test and at what frequency.		
Modeling	Simulates the functioning of the environment or system structure in order to determine how efficiently the proposed system solution will function.		
Parallel operation	Verifies that the old and new version of the application system produce equal or reconcilable results.		
Parallel simulation	Approximates the expected results of processing by simulating the process to determine if test results are reasonable.		

WORK PAPER 4-1   *(continued)*

Tool	Use	Include in Tester's Toolbox?	
		Yes	**No**
Peer review	Provides an assessment by peers of the efficiency, style, adherence to standards, and so on of the product that is designed to improve the quality of the product.		
Ratio/ Relationships	To provide a high-level proof quantitatively that some aspect of the software or testing is reasonable.		
Risk matrix	Produces a matrix showing the relationship between system risk, the segment of the system where the risk occurs, and the presence or absence of controls to reduce that risk.		
Scoring	Identifies areas in the application that require testing, through the rating of criteria that have been shown to correlate to problems.		
Snapshot	Shows the content of computer storage at predetermined points during processing.		
Symbolic execution	Identifies processing paths by testing the programs with symbolic rather than actual test data.		
System logs	Provides an audit trail of monitored events occurring in the environment area controlled by system software.		
Test data	Creates transactions for use in determining the functioning of a computer system.		
Test data generator	Provides test transactions based on the parameters that need to be tested.		
Test scripts	Creating test transactions in the sequence in which those transactions will be processed for an online software system.		
Tracing	Follows and lists the flow of processing and database searches.		
Use case	Preparing test conditions that represent real world uses of the software.		
Volume testing	Identifies system restriction (e.g., internal table size) and then creates a large volume of transactions that exceed those limits.		
Walkthroughs	Leads a test team through a manual simulation of the product using test transactions.		

WORK PAPER 4-2   Documenting Tools

Tool Name: _____

Tool Vendor: _____

Tool Capabilities: _____

_____

_____

Tool Purpose: _____

_____

_____

Process That Will Use Tool: _____

_____

_____

Tool Training Availability: _____

_____

_____

Tool Limitations: _____

_____

_____

Building Software
Tester Competency

Effective software testing will not occur unless the testers are confident. They must be confident in both testing basics and the use of their organization's testing process and tools. It is as important to build the competency of the individual testers as it is to build test processes and acquire test tools.

Many colleges and universities that offer curriculums in computer science do not include courses on software testing. In many IT organizations, it is assumed that if you can build software, you can test it. This concept is changing, albeit slowly.

The emphasis in this chapter will be on building the competency of the software tester. The chapter will use the Common Body of Knowledge (CBOK) for the Certified Software Tester (CSTE) designation offered by Software Certifications (`www.software certifications.org`) and administered by the Quality Assurance Institute (`www .qaiusa.com`).

What Is a Common Body of Knowledge?

Many professions have the following characteristics in common:

- A common body of knowledge
- A code of ethics
- An examination to demonstrate competency
- Continuing professional education

Normally, senior members of the profession establish the board to oversee certification. This board comprises individuals well respected within their profession, who then define the CBOK, administer the certification examination, develop the code of ethics, and oversee the profession's continuing education policies and the conduct of the certified professionals.

Software Certifications, an organization that offers IT certifications, recently approved the 2006 Common Body of Knowledge for Software Testers. The new CBOK contains ten knowledge categories, each of which will be discussed in this chapter.

The CBOK is what the certification board believes individuals need to know to practice software testing effectively. If, based on results of the CSTE examination, it is determined that an individual is competent in software testing, that individual will receive a certification in software testing.

Who Is Responsible for the Software Tester's Competency?

IT management is responsible for the competency of software testers. They, or their designated subordinates, develop job descriptions for software testers, select the individuals who will become software testers, and approve the necessary resources for training.

This, of course, does not preclude the individual's responsibility for competency. Would-be software testers need to demonstrate to management that they have the necessary competency to practice software testing. This competency can be obtained by self-study or by formal study paid for by the tester and conducted on his or her time. Competency can also be obtained on the employer's cost and time.

How Is Personal Competency Used in Job Performance?

To understand the role of personal competency in effective job performance, you need to understand the continuum of work processes (see Figure 5-1). A work process comprises both personal competency and the maturity or effectiveness of the work process. Maturity of the work process defines the amount of variance expected when the work procedures are followed precisely. Implicit in process maturity is the worker's ability to understand and follow the process.

Personal competency is the experience that the worker brings to the job. This experience is assumed in the process, but not integrated into the process. For example, the process to write a computer program in a particular language assumes that the programmer knows how to code in that language and thus the focus is on how the language is used, not how to use the language. Consider a non-IT example: When performing an operation on an individual, it is assumed that the doctor has been trained in surgery prior to following the surgical process in a specific hospital.

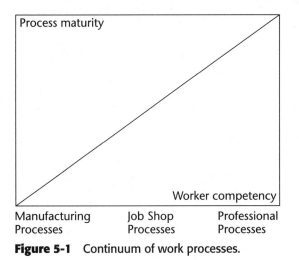

Figure 5-1   Continuum of work processes.

As shown in Figure 5-1, the processes in a manufacturing environment are very mature and require workers to be only minimally competent. One would expect a worker whose responsibility is simply to follow a routine series of steps to recognize any obvious deviations. For example, if an auto worker is confronted with three black tires and one yellow tire, he should speak up.

In a "job shop" environment, on the other hand, no two like products are created (although the products are similar), so greater personal competency is required than in a manufacturing environment.

Professional work processes require extensive personal competency and less mature work processes. For most IT organizations, software testing is a professional work process. In many IT organizations, the testing processes serve more as guidelines than step-by-step procedures for conducting tests. For example, the testing process may state that all branches in a computer program should be tested. If a tester saw a large number of very similar decision instructions, it may be more prudent to perform other tests rather than testing each processing decision both ways.

Using the 2006 CSTE CBOK

The CSTE CBOK can be used for any of the following purposes:

- Developing the job description for software testers
- Assessing an individual's competency in software testing
- Developing an examination to evaluate an individual's competency
- Formulating a curriculum to improve an individual's software testing competency

Work Paper 5-1 presents the discussion draft of the 2006 CSTE CBOK in a format that will enable you to identify skills in which you are competent and those you need to improve. Each Knowledge Category in the CBOK lists multiple skills. For example,

Knowledge Category 1, "Software Testing Principles and Concepts," requires testers to be proficient in the vocabulary of testing.

For each skill, you should make one of the following three assessments:

- **Not Competent.** It is a skill you do not have or a skill you do not believe you could use in the process of testing software. For example, for the vocabulary skill, you do not have a sufficient vocabulary to adequately discuss the job of software testing. Terms such as "regression testing," "black box testing," and "boundary value analysis" are not within your vocabulary.

- **Competent.** You have learned the skill but have not practiced it sufficiently to believe you have fully mastered the skill. For example, you understand regression testing and know what to do, but you have not practiced it enough to feel you could perform it effectively.

- **Fully Competent.** You understand the skill, know what to do, and feel very confident that you can perform the skill effectively. For example, you can develop and execute a regression test with high confidence that you can identify changes that occurred in the unchanged portion of the software.

At this point, read each skill in Work Paper 5-1 and assess your competency in one of the three assessment categories.

To develop a competency score, total the number of skills you have checked in each of the three columns. Then, at the bottom of Work Paper 5-2, multiply the number of skills checked in the Fully Competent column by 3; multiply the number of skills in the Competent column by 2; and multiply the number of skills in the Not Competent column by 1. Total those three amounts and divide by 120 (the number of skills assessed).

The number produced will be between one and three. A score of three indicates that you are a world-class software tester, whereas a score of one means that you are not competent in software testing. If your score is between one and two, you do not have the basic skills necessary to perform software testing; if your score is between 2 and 3, you should consider yourself a software tester. The closer your score comes to a three, the more competent you are.

Developing a Training Curriculum

Every software testing organization should develop a curriculum for training software testers. When an individual is hired or transferred to become a software tester, that individual's skill competency should be assessed. The competency assessment on Work Papers 5-1 and 5-2 can be used for that purpose. Based on that assessment, the individual can be placed into the curriculum at the appropriate point.

The following is a proposed curriculum to move individuals from "not competent" to "fully competent."

- **Course 1: The Basics of Software Testing.** Individuals need a basic understanding of the vocabulary, principles, and concepts for testing. Consider a job in the math profession: The basics include the ability to add, subtract, multiply, and divide. Without these basic abilities, it would be difficult to perform any significant mathematical computation. Likewise, without mastering the basics of software testing, one could not test effectively.

- **Course 2: The Process for Testing the Software System.** Testers need to know the right way to test a software project. Without an understanding of how to prepare for testing or how to develop and execute a test plan, testers might just prepare and run test conditions. The equivalent to this course is the seven-step testing process presented in this book.

- **Course 3: Software Testing Tools.** If the tester's organization uses tools to test software, the tester should become proficient in the use of those tools. It is recommended that testers not be allowed to use a specific tool until they have been sufficiently trained.

- **Course 4: Test Case Design.** Preparing the appropriate test cases is an important part of testing software. Testers need to know sources of test data, the various types of test data that can be prepared (for example, use cases), and how to prepare, use, and maintain those test cases.

- **Course 5: Variance Analysis and Defect Tracking.** Testers need to know how to identify a variance from expected processes. Once they have identified the variance, testers need to know how to document that variance and how to track it until appropriate action has been taken.

- **Course 6: Preparing Test Reports.** Testers need to know the type of reports that should be prepared, how to prepare them, who should get them, and how to present them in an acceptable manner.

- **Course 7: Test Process Improvement.** Testers need to know how to use the results of testing many different projects to identify opportunities for improving the testing process.

NOTE QAI offers public, in-house, and e-learning courses to assist you in improving your competency in software testing. For more information, visit www.qaiworldwide.org.

Table 5-1 cross-references the seven courses described in this chapter to the corresponding chapters in the book. If testers do not go to a formal course, a mentor should be assigned to help them master the material for each of the courses.

Using the CBOK to Build an Effective Testing Team

You can use Work Paper 5-3 to create a team that has mastery of all the competencies in the CSTE CBOK. Simply transfer the rating number you developed in Work Paper 5-2 to the corresponding columns for each team member. For example, if team member A was deemed "Competent" in Knowledge Category 1, then enter 2 in the corresponding column of Work Paper 5-3.

Table 5-1 Chapters Supporting the Software Tester's Curriculum

COURSE NAME	SEE CHAPTER(S)
Course 1: The Basics of Software Testing	1–13
Course 2: The Process for Testing the Software System	6–13
Course 3: Software Testing Tools	4
Course 4: Test Case Design	9–10
Course 5: Variance Analysis and Defect Tracking	11
Course 6: Preparing Test Reports	11
Course 7: Test Process Improvement	4, 23

After all the team members' ratings are recorded, you can determine whether there is adequate competency in each of the knowledge categories deemed necessary for this specific software project. For example, if knowledge of testing security was not necessary for a specific project, team members would not have to be competent in that particular knowledge category.

Generally, you would look for at least one member to be fully competent in each of the knowledge categories needed. However, if no one is fully competent in a specific skill category, having two or more individuals who are partially competent in that category would probably be adequate to make the team effective.

If the proposed software testing team does not have the necessary competency, you should take one of the following actions:

- Replace one member with another tester who possesses the needed competency.
- Add another tester to the team with the needed competency.
- Assign a mentor to work with one or more team members to help them in testing tasks in which that knowledge competency is needed.

The following are additional guidelines that can help to build an effective team:

- You can match team personalities by using techniques such as the Myers-Briggs Type Indicator (MBTI).
- It is better to have a smaller test team than to add a tester who has a very negative attitude about testing or the assignment, which demoralizes the team and requires extra supervisory effort.
- The number one skill for success in software testing is the ability to communicate. Any member of the test team who will interact with developers and/or users should be an effective communicator.
- Test teams are most effective when there is only one leader. If two members want to set direction for the test team, conflict usually occurs.

Summary

Effective testing cannot occur unless the testers are competent. The best measure of a tester's competency is to assess him or her using the CSTE CBOK, which represents the most current thinking in software tester competency. You can use the results of this assessment for two purposes. The first is to determine the strengths and weaknesses of an individual software tester so that the plan can be developed to improve his or her competency. Second, you can use the assessment to help build a software testing team, which, as a group, has the necessary competency to test a specific software project.

WORK PAPER 5-1   2006 Common Body of Knowledge

Knowledge Category 1: Software Testing Principles and Concepts   The "basics" of software testing are represented by the vocabulary of testing, testing approaches, methods, and techniques, as well as the materials used by testers in performing their test activities.

		FULLY COMPETENT	PARTIALLY COMPETENT	NOT COMPETENT
1	**Testing Techniques** Understanding the various approaches used in testing, including static (e.g., desk checking), white-box (logic-driven), black-box (requirements-driven), load testing, coverage testing, and regression testing. Also included are the methods for designing and conducting tests.			
2	**Levels of Testing** Identifying testing levels such as unit, performance, string, integration, systems recovery, acceptance, parallel, performance, and interface testing.			
3	**Testing Different Types of Software** The changes in the approach to testing when testing different development approaches such as batch processing, client/server, Web-based, object-oriented, and wireless systems.			
4	**Independent Testing** Testing by individuals other than those involved in product/system development.			
5	**Vocabulary** The technical terms used to describe various testing techniques, tools, principles, concepts, and activities.			
6	**The Multiple Roles of Software Testers** The objectives that can be incorporated into the mission of software testers. This would include the testing to determine whether requirements are met, testing effectiveness and efficiency, testing user needs versus software specifications, and testing software attributes such as maintainability, ease of use, and reliability.			

WORK PAPER 5-1   *(continued)*

		FULLY COMPETENT	PARTIALLY COMPETENT	NOT COMPETENT
7	**Testers Workbench** An overview of the process that testers use to perform a specific test activity, such as developing a test plan or preparing test data.			
8	**The V Concept of Testing** The V concept relates the build components of the development phases to the test components that occur during the test phases.			

Knowledge Category 2: Building the Test Environment   The test environment comprises all the conditions, circumstances, and influences surrounding and affecting software testing. The environment includes the organization's policies, procedures, culture, attitudes, rewards, test processes, test tools, methods for developing and improving test processes, management's support of software testing, as well as any test labs developed for the purpose of testing software and multiple operating environments. This category also includes ensuring the test environment fairly represents the production environment.

		FULLY COMPETENT	PARTIALLY COMPETENT	NOT COMPETENT
1	**Knowledge of Test Process Selection and Analysis**			
	Concepts of Test Processes—The concepts of policies, standards, and procedures, and their integration into the test process.			
	Test Process Selection—Selecting processes that lead to efficient and effective testing activities and products.			
	Acquisition or Development of a Test Bed/ Test Lab/Test Processes—Designing, developing, and acquiring a test environment that simulates the "real" world, including the capability to create and maintain test data.			
	Quality Control—Testing quality control to ensure that the test process has been performed correctly.			

(continues)

WORK PAPER 5-1 *(continued)*

	FULLY COMPETENT	PARTIALLY COMPETENT	NOT COMPETENT
Test Process Analysis—Analyzing the test process to ensure a. Its effectiveness and efficiency b. Test objectives are applicable, reasonable, adequate, feasible, and affordable c. The test program meets the test objectives d. The correct test program is being applied to the project e. The test methodology, including the processes, infrastructure, tools, methods, and planned work products and reviews, is adequate to ensure that the test program is conducted correctly f. Test progress, performance, and process adherence are assessed to determine the adequacy of the test program g. Adequate, not excessive, testing is performed			
Continuous Improvement—Identifying and making improvements to the test process using formal process improvement processes.			
Adapting the Test Environment to Different Software Development Methodologies—Establishing the environment to properly test the methodologies used to build software systems, such as waterfall, Web-based, object-oriented, agile, and so forth.			
Competency of the Software Testers—Providing the training necessary to ensure that software testers are competent in the processes and tools included in the test environment.			

WORK PAPER 5-1   *(continued)*

		FULLY COMPETENT	PARTIALLY COMPETENT	NOT COMPETENT
2	**Test Tools**			
	Tool Development and/or Acquisition—Understanding the processes for developing and acquiring test tools.			
	Tool Usage—Understanding how tools are used for automated regression testing, defect management, performance/load testing; understanding manual tools such as checklists, test scripts, and decision tables; using traceability tools, code coverage, and test case management.			
3	**Management Support for Effective Software Testing**			
	Creating a tone that encourages testers to work in an efficient and effective manner.			
	Aligning test processes with organizational goals, business objectives, release cycles, and different developmental methodologies.			

Knowledge Category 3: Managing the Test Project   Software testing is a project with almost all the same attributes as a software development project. Software testing involves project planning, project staffing, scheduling and budgeting, communicating, assigning and monitoring work, and ensuring that changes to the project plan are incorporated into the test plan.

		FULLY COMPETENT	PARTIALLY COMPETENT	NOT COMPETENT
1	**Test Planning, Scheduling, and Budgeting**			
	Alignment—Ensuring the test processes are aligned with organizational goals, user business objectives, release cycles, and different development methodologies.			
	Test Performance—Monitoring test performance for adherence to the plan, schedule and budget, reallocating resources as required, and averting undesirable trends.			

(continues)

WORK PAPER 5-1 *(continued)*

	FULLY COMPETENT	PARTIALLY COMPETENT	NOT COMPETENT
Staffing—Acquiring, training, and retaining a competent test staff.			
Management of Staff—Keeping staff appropriately informed, and effectively utilizing the test staff.			
Differences Between Traditional Management—Using a hierarchical structure versus quality management using a flattened organization structure.			
2 Personal and Organizational Effectiveness			
Communication Skills a. *Written Communication*—Providing written confirmation and explanation of a variance from expectations. Being able to describe on paper a sequence of events to reproduce the defect. b. *Oral Communication*—Demonstrating the ability to articulate a sequence of events in an organized and understandable manner. c. *Listening Skills*—Actively listening to what is said, asking for clarification when needed, and providing feedback. d. *Interviewing Skills*—Developing and asking questions for the purpose of collecting data for analysis or evaluation. e. *Analyzing Skills*—Determining how to use the information received.			

WORK PAPER 5-1 *(continued)*

	FULLY COMPETENT	PARTIALLY COMPETENT	NOT COMPETENT
Personal Effectiveness Skills a. *Negotiation*—Working effectively with one or more parties to develop options that will satisfy all parties. b. *Conflict Resolution*—Bringing a situation into focus and satisfactorily concluding a disagreement or difference of opinion between parties. c. *Influence and Motivation*—Influencing others to participate in a goal-oriented activity. d. *Judgment*—Applying beliefs, standards, guidelines, policies, procedures, and values to a decision. e. *Facilitation*—Helping a group to achieve its goals by providing objective guidance.			
Project Relationships—Developing an effective working relationship with project management, software customers, and users.			
Recognition—Showing appreciation to individuals and teams for work accomplished.			
Motivation—Encouraging individuals to do the right thing and do it effectively and efficiently.			
Mentoring—Working with testers to ensure they master the needed skills.			
Management and Quality Principles—Understanding the principles needed to build a world-class testing organization.			

(continues)

WORK PAPER 5-1   *(continued)*

		FULLY COMPETENT	PARTIALLY COMPETENT	NOT COMPETENT
3	**Leadership**			
	Meeting Chairing—Organizing and conducting meetings to provide maximum productivity over the shortest time period.			
	Facilitation—Helping the progress of an event or activity. Formal facilitation includes well-defined roles, an objective facilitator, a structured meeting, decision-making by consensus, and defined goals to be achieved.			
	Team Building—Aiding a group in defining a common goal and working together to improve team effectiveness.			

Knowledge Category 4: Test Planning   Testers need the skills to plan tests. Test planning assesses the business and technical risks of the software application and then develops a plan to determine if the software minimizing those risks. Test planners must understand the development methods and environment to effectively plan for testing.

		FULLY COMPETENT	PARTIALLY COMPETENT	NOT COMPETENT
1	**Prerequisites to Test Planning**			
	Identifying Software Risks—Demonstrating knowledge of the most common risks associated with software development.			
	Identifying Testing Risks—Demonstrating knowledge of the most common risks associated with software testing.			
	Identifying Premature Release Risk—Understanding how to determine the risk associated with releasing unsatisfactory, untested software products.			
	Risk Contributors—Identifying the contributors to risk.			
	Identifying Business Risks—Demonstrating knowledge of the most common risks associated with the business using the software.			

WORK PAPER 5-1 *(continued)*

		FULLY COMPETENT	PARTIALLY COMPETENT	NOT COMPETENT
	Risk Methods—Understanding of the strategies and approaches for identifying risks or problems associated with implementing and operating information technology, products, and processes; assessing their likelihood, and initiating strategies to test for those risks.			
	Risk Magnitude—Demonstrating the ability to calculate and rank the severity of a risk quantitatively.			
	Risk Reduction Methods—Understanding the strategies and approaches that can be used to minimize the magnitude of a risk.			
	Contingency Planning—Planning to reduce the magnitude of a known risk.			
2	**Test Planning Entrance Criteria**			
	Success Criteria/Acceptance Criteria—Understanding the criteria that must be validated to provide user management with the information needed to make an acceptance decision.			
	Test Objectives—Understanding the objectives to be accomplished through testing.			
	Assumptions—Establishing the conditions that must exist for testing to be comprehensive and on schedule.			
	Issues—Identifying specific situations/products/processes that, unless mitigated, will impact forward progress.			
	Constraints—Limiting factors to success.			
	Entrance Criteria/Exit Criteria—Understanding the criteria that must be met prior to moving software to the next level of testing or into production.			

(continues)

WORK PAPER 5-1 *(continued)*

	FULLY COMPETENT	PARTIALLY COMPETENT	NOT COMPETENT
Test Scope—Understanding what is to be tested.			
Test Plan—Understanding the activities and deliverables to meet a test's objectives.			
Requirements/Traceability—Defining the tests needed and relating them to the requirements to be validated.			
Estimating—Determining the resources and timeframes required to accomplish the planned activities.			
Scheduling—Establishing milestones for completing the testing effort and their dependencies on meeting the rest of the schedule.			
Staffing—Selecting the size and competency of the staff needed to achieve the test plan objectives.			
Test Check Procedures—Incorporating test cases to ensure that tests are performed correctly.			
Software Configuration Management—Organizing the components of a software system, including documentation, so that they fit together in working order.			
Change Management—Modifying and controlling the test plan in relationship to actual progress and scope of system development.			
Version Control—Understanding the methods to control, monitor, and achieve change.			

WORK PAPER 5-1   *(continued)*

Knowledge Category 5: Executing the Test Plan   This category addresses the skills required to execute tests, design test cases, use test tools, and monitor testing.

		FULLY COMPETENT	PARTIALLY COMPETENT	NOT COMPETENT
1	**Test Design and Test Data/Scripts Preparation**			
	Specifications—Ensuring test data scripts meet the objectives included in the test plan.			
	Cases—Developing test cases, including techniques and approaches for validation of the product. Determination of the expected result for each test case.			
	Test Design—Understanding test design strategies and attributes.			
	Scripts—Developing the online steps to be performed in testing; focusing on the purpose and preparation of procedures; emphasizing entrance and exit criteria.			
	Data—Developing test inputs; using data generation tools; determining the data set or sub-sets to ensure a comprehensive test of the system; determining data that suits boundary value analysis and stress testing requirements.			
	Test Coverage—Achieving the coverage objectives in the test plan to specific system components.			
	Platforms—Identifying the minimum configuration and platforms on which the test must function.			
	Test Cycle Strategy—Determining the number of test cycles to be conducted during the test execution phase of testing; determining what type of testing will occur during each test cycle.			

(continues)

WORK PAPER 5-1   *(continued)*

		FULLY COMPETENT	PARTIALLY COMPETENT	NOT COMPETENT
2	**Performing Tests**			
	Execute Tests—Performing the activities necessary to execute tests in accordance with the test plan and test design—including setting up tests, preparing test data base(s), obtaining technical support, and scheduling resources.			
	Compare Actual Versus Expected Results—Determining whether the actual results meet expectations.			
	Documenting Test Results—Recording test results in the appropriate format.			
	Use of Test Results—Understanding how test results should be used and who has access to them.			
3	**Defect Tracking**			
	Defect Recording—Recording defects to describe and quantify deviations from requirements/expectations.			
	Defect Reporting—Reporting the status of defects, including severity and location.			
	Defect Tracking—Monitoring defects from the time of recording until satisfactory resolution has been determined and implemented.			
4	**Testing Software Changes**			
	Static Testing—Evaluating changed code and associated documentation at the end of the change process to ensure correct implementation.			
	Regression Testing—Testing the whole product to ensure that unchanged functionality performs as it did prior to implementing a change.			

WORK PAPER 5-1 *(continued)*

	FULLY COMPETENT	PARTIALLY COMPETENT	NOT COMPETENT
Verification—Reviewing requirements, design, and associated documentation to ensure they are updated correctly as a result of the change.			

Knowledge Category 6: Test Status, Analysis, and Reporting   Testers need to demonstrate the ability to develop status reports. These reports should show the status of the testing based on the test plan. Reporting should document what tests have been performed and the status of those tests. To properly report status, testers should review and conduct statistical analysis on the test results and discovered defects. The lessons learned from the test effort should be used to improve the next iteration of the test process.

		FULLY COMPETENT	PARTIALLY COMPETENT	NOT COMPETENT
1	**Metrics of Testing**			
	Using quantitative measures and metrics to manage the planning, execution, and reporting of software testing.			
2	**Test Status Reports**			
	Code Coverage—Monitoring the execution of software and reporting on the degree of coverage at the statement, branch, or path level.			
	Requirement Coverage—Monitoring and reporting the number of requirements tested, and whether they are correctly implemented.			
	Test Status Metrics—Understanding the following metrics: a. *Metrics Used to Test*—Includes metrics such as defect removal efficiency, defect density, and mean time to last failure. b. *Complexity Measurements*—Quantitative values, accumulated by a predetermined method, that measure the complexity of a software product.			

(continues)

WORK PAPER 5-1 *(continued)*

		FULLY COMPETENT	PARTIALLY COMPETENT	NOT COMPETENT
	c. *Project Metrics*—The status of a project, including milestones, budget and schedule variance, and scope changes.			
	d. *Size Measurements*—Methods primarily developed for measuring the software size of information systems, such as lines of code and function points.			
	e. *Defect Metrics*—Values associated with the number or types of defects, usually related to system size, such as "defects/1000 lines of code" or "defects/100 function points."			
	f. *Product Measures*—Measures of a product's attributes, such as performance, reliability, and usability.			
3	**Final Test Reports**			
	Reporting Tools—Using word processing, database, defect tracking, and graphic tools to prepare test reports.			
	Test Report Standards—Defining the components that should be included in a test report.			
	Statistical Analysis—Demonstrating the ability to draw statistically valid conclusions from quantitative test results.			

Knowledge Category 7: User Acceptance Testing The objective of software development is to meet the true needs of the user, not just the system specifications. Testers should work with the users early in a project to clearly define the criteria that would make the software acceptable in meeting the user needs. As much as possible, once the acceptance criteria have been established, they should integrate it into all aspects of development.

		FULLY COMPETENT	PARTIALLY COMPETENT	NOT COMPETENT
1	**Concepts of Acceptance Testing**			
	Understanding the difference between system test and acceptance test.			

WORK PAPER 5-1 *(continued)*

		FULLY COMPETENT	PARTIALLY COMPETENT	NOT COMPETENT
2	**Acceptance Test Planning Process**			
	Defining the acceptance criteria.			
	Developing an acceptance test plan for execution by user personnel.			
	Testing data using use cases.			
3	**Acceptance Test Execution**			
	Executing the acceptance test plan.			
	Developing an acceptance decision based on the results of acceptance testing.			
	Signing off on successful completion of the acceptance test plan.			

Knowledge Category 8: Testing Software Developed by Outside Organizations   Many organizations do not have the resources to develop the type and/or volume of software needed to effectively manage their business. The solution is to obtain or contract for software developed by another organization. Software can be acquired by purchasing commerical off-the-shelf software (COTS) or contracting for all or parts of the software development to be done by outside organizations.

		FULLY COMPETENT	PARTIALLY COMPETENT	NOT COMPETENT
1	Understanding the difference between testing software developed in-house and software developed by outside organizations.			
2	Understanding the election process for selecting COTS software.			
3	Verifying that testers are able to			
	a. Ensure that requirements are testable.			
	b. Review the adequacy of the test plan to be performed by the outsourcing organization.			
	c. Oversee acceptance testing.			

(continues)

WORK PAPER 5-1 *(continued)*

	FULLY COMPETENT	PARTIALLY COMPETENT	NOT COMPETENT
d. Issue a report on the adequacy of the software to meet the contractual specifications.			
e. Ensure compatibility of software standards, communications, change control, and so on between the two organizations.			
4 Using the same approach as used for in-house software, but may need to be modified based on documentation available from the developer.			
5 Understanding the following objectives: a. Testing the changed portion of the software b. Performing regression testing c. Comparing the documentation to the actual execution of the software d. Issuing a report regarding the status of the new version of the software			

Knowledge Category 9: Testing Software Controls and the Adequacy of Security Procedures The software system of internal control includes the totality of the means developed to ensure the integrity of the software system and the products created by the software. Controls are employed to control the processing components of software, ensure that software processing is in accordance with the organization's policies and procedures, and according to applicable laws and regulations.

	FULLY COMPETENT	PARTIALLY COMPETENT	NOT COMPETENT
1 **Principles and Concepts of a Software System of Internal Control and Security**			
Vocabulary of Internal Control and Security—Understanding the vocabulary of internal control and security, including terms such as risk, threat, control, exposure, vulnerability, and penetration.			

WORK PAPER 5-1   *(continued)*

	FULLY COMPETENT	PARTIALLY COMPETENT	NOT COMPETENT
Internal Control and Security Models— Understanding internal control and security models (specifically, the COSO [Committee of Sponsoring Organizations] model).			
2 Testing the System of Internal Controls			
*Perform Risk Analysis—*Determining the risk faced by the transactions/events processed by the software.			
Determining the controls for each of the processing segments for transactions processing, including a. Transaction origination b. Transaction entry c. Transaction processing d. Database control e. Transaction results			
Determining whether the identified controls are adequate to reduce the risks to an acceptable level.			
3 Testing the Adequacy of Security for a Software System			
Evaluating the adequacy of management's security environment.			
Determining the types of risks that require security controls.			
Identifing the most probable points where the software could be penetrated.			
Determining the controls at those points of penetration.			
Assessing whether those controls are adequate to reduce the security risks to an acceptable level.			

(continues)

WORK PAPER 5-1   *(continued)*

Knowledge Category 10: Testing New Techniques   Testers require skills in their organization's current technology, as well as a general understanding of the new information technology that might be acquired by their organization.

		FULLY COMPETENT	PARTIALLY COMPETENT	NOT COMPETENT
1	**Understanding the Challenges of New Technologies**			
	New application architecture			
	New application business models			
	New communication methods			
	New testing tools			
2	**Evaluating New Technologies to Fit into the Organization's Policies and Procedures**			
	Assessing the adequacy of the controls within the technology and the changes to existing policies and procedures that will be needed before the new technology can be implemented effectively. This would include:			
	Testing new technology to evaluate actual performance versus supplier's stated performance.			
	Determining whether current policies and procedures are adequate to control the operation of the new technology and modify to bring in currency.			
	Assessing the need to acquire new staff skills to effectively implement the new technology			

WORK PAPER 5-2   Evaluating Individual Competency

	KNOWLEDGE CATEGORY	NUMBER OF SKILLS	FULLY COMPETENT	PARTIALLY COMPETENT	NOT COMPETENT
1	Software Testing Principles and Concepts	8			
2	Building the Test Environment	12			
3	Managing the Test Project	16			
4	Test Planning	27			
5	Executing the Test Plan	19			
6	Test Status, Analysis and Reporting	8			
7	User Acceptance Testing	5			
8	Testing Software Developed by Outside Organizations	6			
9	Testing Software Controls and the Adequacy of Security Procedures	11			
10	Testing New Technologies	8			
	Total	**120**			
	Multiply Total By		3	2	1
	Multiplied Total				
	Total the Sum in Each of the Three Columns				
	Divide by 120				
	Software Testing Competency Score				

WORK PAPER 5-3   Building Test Team Competency

	CATEGORY	A	B	C	D	E
		SOFTWARE TEST TEAM MEMBER				
1	Software Testing Principles and Concepts					
2	Building the Test Environment					
3	Managing the Test Project					
4	Test Planning					
5	Executing the Test Plan					
6	Test Status, Analysis and Reporting					
7	User Acceptance Testing					
8	Testing Software Developed by Outside Organizations					
9	Testing Software Controls and the Adequacy of Security Procedures					
10	Testing New Technologies					

PART

Three

The Seven-Step
Testing Process

CHAPTER 6

Overview of the Software Testing Process

Chapters 2 through 5 explained how to establish a test environment. Now you're ready to:

- Understand the advantages of following a process
- Understand the costs associated with testing
- Introduce the seven-step process that will take you through organizing, planning, testing, and completing your testing project
- Customize the seven-step process to the needs of your organization
- Establish a process to manage the seven-step testing process

The process for software testing described in this chapter is based on the experience of more than 1,000 organizations affiliated with the Quality Assurance Institute.

Advantages of Following a Process

There is no best process for testing software. However, the seven-step process described in this chapter incorporates the best aspects of many different processes. Understanding and using a process for testing software provides the following advantages:

- **Testing is consistent.** With a process, testing can be performed in a consistent manner from test to test. The use of the process will reduce variability of testing and improve confidence in the test process.

- **Testing can be taught.** When testing is performed by a process, the process is teachable. When testing is performed as an art or craft, one must study under a master tester to learn how to test. The test process breaks testing into steps and tasks that are easy to teach.

- **Test processes can be improved.** By using processes, one learns advantages and disadvantages of the process. Disadvantages can be identified and the process changed to continually improve testing.

- **Test processes are manageable.** With processes, the test manager can manage the process. Without the test process, the test manager must manage people. From a control perspective, it's much easier to manage or control a process than an individual.

The Cost of Computer Testing

There are two general categories of testing: pre-implementation and post-implementation testing. The first encompasses those activities that occur prior to placing the application system in an operational status. The objective of pre-implementation testing is to determine that the system functions as specified and that defects in the system are removed prior to placing the system into production. The second type of testing occurs after the system goes into operation and is normally considered part of systems maintenance.

The cost of removing system defects prior to the system going into production includes:

- Building the defect into the system
- Identifying the defect's existence
- Correcting the defect
- Testing to determine that the defect has been removed

Defects uncovered after the system goes into operation generate the following costs:

- Specifying and coding the defect into the system
- Detecting the problem within the application system
- Reporting the problem to the project manager and/or user
- Correcting the problems caused by the defect
- Operating the system until the defect is corrected
- Correcting the defect
- Testing to determine that the defect no longer exists
- Integrating the corrected program(s) into production

Testing should include the cost to test *plus* the cost of undetected defects. Few organizations consolidate all the named costs as testing costs; therefore, an organization rarely knows the true cost of testing. Testing is normally considered to be that process used to find defects and ensure that the system functions properly. However, as illustrated, the cost of building and correcting defects may far exceed the cost of detecting those defects.

The National Institute of Standards and Technology has estimated that testing, including the correction of defects prior to the application going into production, accounts for at least half of the total system development effort.

The high cost of system defects poses the following two challenges to organizations: how to quantify the true cost of removing defects, and how to reduce the cost of testing.

Quantifying the Cost of Removing Defects

Quality Assurance Institute surveys indicate that there are in the range of 20 to 60 defects in many application systems per 1,000 source statements. These surveys indicate that approximately two-thirds of the defects per 1,000 lines of source code occur in the requirements and design phases of application systems. Thus, while the defects are normally caught in the test phase of the system development life cycle, they occur early in the development process. (Note that as development processes mature, the number of defects produced is reduced.)

The causes of the defects built into application systems include:

- **Improperly interpreted requirements.** IT personnel misinterpret what the user wants, but correctly implement what the IT people believe is wanted.

- **Users specify wrong requirements.** The specifications given to IT personnel are erroneous.

- **Requirements are incorrectly recorded.** IT personnel fail to record the specifications properly.

- **Design specifications incorrect.** The application system design does not achieve the system requirements, but the design as specified may be correctly implemented.

- **Program specifications incorrect.** The design specifications are incorrectly interpreted, making the program specifications inaccurate, but the program can be properly coded to achieve the correct program specifications.

- **Program coding error.** The program is not coded according to the program specifications.

- **Program structural or instruction error.** The programming capabilities are improperly utilized, resulting in defects attributable to misuse of a program instruction or the method in which the instruction is used.

- **Data entry error.** The system and/or program information is incorrectly entered into the computer.

- **Testing error.** The test either detects an error where there is no error or fails to detect an existing error in the application system.

- **Error correction mistake.** In the process of correcting an error, the corrected condition contains a defect.

- **Corrected condition causes another defect.** In the process of correcting a defect, a defect occurs in the unchanged portion of the software.

The areas associated with the test process can usually be readily identified. It is the estimation of the costs associated with these areas that is difficult to obtain. However, until the total cost of testing is known, the cost of uncovering and correcting defects will be unknown.

There are two methods for developing a more realistic estimate of testing. The first is to ask IT personnel to identify all the preceding conditions and allocate their time and effort accordingly. Although this concept works in theory, in practice it is difficult to record the time and effort associated with incurring defects until that defect is actually known. Because the point of uncovering defects may be many weeks or months after the actual day they were built into the system, it may be difficult to go back and recover these costs.

The second, and more practical, approach is to record the number of defects encountered as a result of testing. As each defect is uncovered, it should be noted, as well as the point in the system development life cycle process where it was uncovered.

The actual cost to redesign and correct the system should then be recorded. These are the costs required for correcting the programs by some recompilation and change of documentation. The costs are then multiplied by a factor that represents the totality of the error and problems associated with the defect as follows:

- **Defects corrected during design requirements phase.** The cost to correct will be the total cost associated with the correction of the defect.

- **Defects corrected during building the software.** The cost to correct requirement defects should be multiplied by a factor of 10 because the additional costs are associated with removing the defective components of the software.

- **Defects corrected after the system goes into production.** The cost to correct will be approximately 100 times the cost to correct the same defect prior to placing the software into production.

Reducing the Cost of Testing

The economics of computer testing clearly demonstrate that the method to reduce the cost of defects is to locate those defects as early in the system development life cycle as possible. This involves beginning testing during the requirements phase of the life cycle and continuing testing throughout the life cycle. The objective of testing would then become to detect the error as early in the life cycle as possible.

The Seven-Step Software Testing Process

The seven-step software testing process follows the "V" concept of testing (see Figure 6-1). The V represents both the software development process and the seven-step software testing process. Both processes commence at the same time and proceed concurrently through the end of the project. Note that step 7, post-implementation analysis, will occur for both the development process and the test process. The purpose of this analysis is to determine whether development and/or testing can be performed more effectively in the future.

Figure 6-1 The seven-step software testing process.

A brief overview of the seven-step software testing process follows:

1. **Organizing for testing**

   a. **Define test scope.** Determine which type of testing is to be performed.

   b. **Organize the test team.** Determine, based on the type of testing to be performed, who should be assigned to the test team.

   c. **Assess development plan and status.** This is a prerequisite to building the test plan that will be used to evaluate the software implementation plan. During this step, testers will challenge the completeness and correctness of the development plan. Based on the extensiveness and completeness of the project plan, the testers will be in a position to estimate the amount of resources they will need to test the implemented software solution.

2. **Developing the test plan**

   a. **Perform risk analysis.** Identify the test risks.

b. **Write the test plan.** Forming the plan for testing will follow the same pattern as any software planning process. The structure of all plans should be the same, but the content will vary based on the degree of risk the testers perceive as associated with the software being developed.

3. **Verification testing**

   a. **Test software requirements.** Incomplete, inaccurate, or inconsistent requirements lead to most software failures. The inability to get the right requirements during the requirements phase will increase the cost of implementation significantly. Testers, through verification, must determine that the requirements are accurate and complete and that they do not conflict with one another.

   b. **Test software design.** This step tests both external and internal design through the verification techniques. The testers are concerned that the design will in fact achieve the objectives of the project as well as being effective and efficient on the designated hardware.

   c. **Test software construction.** The method chosen to build the software from the internal design document will determine the type and extensiveness of tests needed. As the construction becomes more automated, less testing will be required during this phase. However, if software is constructed by a manual coding process, it is subject to error and should be verified. Experience has shown that it is significantly cheaper to identify defects during the construction phase than through dynamic testing during the validation testing step.

4. **Validation testing**

   a. **Perform validation testing.** This involves the testing of code in a dynamic state. The approach, methods, and tools specified in the test plan will be used to validate that the executable codes meets the stated software requirements and the structural specifications of the design.

   b. **Record test results.** Document the results achieved through testing.

5. **Analyzing and reporting test results**

   a. **Analyze the test results.** Examine the results of testing to determine where action is required because of variance between "what is" and "what should be."

   b. **Develop test reports.** Test reporting is a continuous process. It may be both oral and written. It is important that defects and concerns be reported to the appropriate parties as early as possible so that the can be corrected at the lowest possible cost.

6. **Acceptance and operational testing**

   a. **Perform acceptance testing.** Acceptance testing enables users of the software to evaluate the applicability and usability of the software in performing their day-to-day job functions. This tests what the user believes the software should perform, as opposed to what the documented requirements state the software should perform.

b. **Test software installation.** Once the test team has confirmed that the software is ready for production, the ability to execute that software in a production environment should be tested. This tests the interface to operating software, related software, and operating procedures.

c. **Test software changes.** While this is shown as step 6 in the context of performing maintenance after the software is implemented, the concept is also applicable to changes throughout the implementation process. Whenever requirements change, the test plan must change, and the impact of that change on software systems must be tested and evaluated.

7. **Post-implementation analysis.** Test improvements can best be achieved by evaluating the effectiveness of testing at the end of each software test assignment. Although this assessment is primarily performed by the testers, it should involve the developers, users of the software, and quality assurance professionals if the function exists in the IT organization.

Objectives of the Seven-Step Process

The following are the objectives of the seven-step testing process:

1. **Organizing for testing.** This step has two objectives. The first objective is to define what is to be tested. This is the *scope* of testing. It is not the objectives for a specific application, but the scope of the testing that will be performed to determine whether the application objectives have been met. Scope includes such things as the test to determine whether or not user needs have been met. Do you perform both static and dynamic testing? Do you test security? Do you test internal control? Second, you need to determine who will perform the test. This involves establishing the test team and determining what the individuals on that team will test.

2. **Developing the test plan.** The plan will determine how testing will be performed. During planning, the specific objectives for testing will be determined. For example, in the payroll system, a test objective might be to test the calculation of the payroll taxes. Both the specific project objectives and the scope objectives will be used to develop the detailed test plan.

3. **Verification testing.** The objective of verification testing is primarily to ensure that you are building the right system. You will also perform tracing to ensure that no requirements are lost as you move between developmental phases, but the main objective is verifying that you have built the right system. During verification testing, you will challenge the requirements and design of the system. The objective is to remove defects as close to the point they occur as possible.

4. **Validation testing.** The objective of validation testing is to determine whether you built the system right. In other words, does the system perform as expected? During validation testing, you will create test data and scripts and run those in a dynamic mode against the software to validate that, in fact, the output is the expected output.

5. **Analyzing and reporting test results.** The objective of this step is to determine what you have learned from testing and then inform the appropriate individuals. This would include what works, what doesn't work, as well as any suggestions that the testers might make. It would also include analyzing whether such things as internal controls and security are adequate.

6. **Acceptance and operational testing.** The objective of this type of testing is to determine if you can use the system now, and that as the system is changed over time, it is still effective and efficient. Acceptance testing might be performed immediately prior to the software going into production, or it may be performed whenever changes are made to the system. The step also addresses controlling changes to the software application.

7. **Post-implementation analysis.** The objective of this step is future-oriented. It attempts to determine whether testing was performed effectively, and if not, what changes could be made to the testing process so that future testing will be more effective and efficient. Note that this can be done individually on a single system or on multiple systems simultaneously. This step can be performed by testers or by another group, such as quality assurance personnel.

Customizing the Seven-Step Process

The seven-step process defined in this chapter is a generic process. It is designed to test the most complex software testing system. It is designed to be used by both developers and an independent test team. If the seven-step process is to be effective, it must be customized for the organization using that process.

In order to get buy-in from those responsible for testing, they should be involved in the customization process. It is recommended that a small team of well-respected testers be organized for the purpose of customizing the process.

To customize the process, the following steps must be undertaken:

1. **Understand the seven-step process.** This involves reading Part Three of this book and perhaps discussing the process among the group.

2. **Customize for "who" tests.** Testing can be performed by both developers and testers. In some organizations, those who develop the software also test the software. In other organizations, those who test may be independent of the development team. As the test process is reviewed, it will become obvious that some of the steps are designed for independent testers and will not be needed for developers if they perform their own testing. For example, independent testers may want to know that the project has allocated adequate time for testing. Since it is the estimate of the developers, if the developers tested they would not have to do that step.

3. **Customize for the size and type of system to be tested.** The seven-step process is designed to enable you to test any software system and many different types of systems. For some systems, those which may pose no risk to the organization, it is not necessary to perform risk analysis as a prerequisite to testing. For small systems, the scope of the test plan might be reduced, for example, eliminating sections such as when to stop testing.

4. **Customize for "what" to test.** The seven step process is a generic testing process. It does not address such things as the platform to be tested, the type of developmental process, or specific testing needs, such as testing internal controls. Part Four of this book includes many different types of testing that may need to be incorporated into the seven-step testing process. The customization team should become familiar with the materials in Part Four of this book plus any specific testing needs they may have for their organization. These needs should be incorporated into the testing process if appropriate.

5. **Customize for in-house developed and/or contracted software.** The generic seven-step testing process is designed to be used with both in-house developed and contracted or purchased software. However, depending on whether the software is developed in-house or contracted, the steps in the process may need to be modified. For example, in contracted software, the testers may not have access to source code. Thus, they will be limited to black box testing and precluded from white box testing.

6. **Customize for vocabulary.** It is important that the testing process use the vocabulary of the organization. For example, if your organization does not use the terms verification and validation, you will want to change those phrases to vocabulary suitable to your organization. For example, your organization may refer to verification testing as static testing and validation testing as dynamic testing.

7. **Integrate testing into the development process.** Development and testing should not be completely independent processes. It is important that development and testing be integrated into a process that will produce quality software. If static testing is to be performed, for example, conducting a requirement review, that should be incorporated into the overall process of building software. If not, the developers may not allot adequate time for their participation in that aspect of testing.

Customization is a very important component of getting the software testing process implemented, accepted, and used by testers. It is important that they be involved in customizing this process for their organization. Even if you decide to use the seven-step process as is, your decision should involve the users of the process.

Managing the Seven-Step Process

The test manager uses the seven-step process to manage the entire testing process. The test manager should also manage by process, by facts, and by results.

- **Manage by process.** The test manager uses the test process to manage day-to-day testing activities. In preparing for testing, the test manager selects the test team and defines the specific test objectives for the software system being tested. The test process will then enable testers to accomplish those objectives.

  The test plan provides the detailed budget, schedule, and tasks to be accomplished during testing. The test plan, combined with the test objectives, is in fact a contract with the stakeholders of the tested system. It is what the testers agreed to do in performing testing. The test manager needs to manage that plan as though it were a contract and ensure that all aspects of the plan are accomplished.

- **Manage by facts.** The test manager needs to develop metrics in order to monitor quantitatively some key aspects of testing. This is considered the *dashboard* for test management. The test manager should select between three and eight key metrics to help manage testing. These metrics might include:

  - Budget

  - Schedule

  - Requirements tested/not tested

  - Status of testing, including such things as requirements tested that were implemented incorrectly

  - Requirements tested and not corrected as of a certain time period (for example, 10 days)

  - Status of defects

- **Manage by results.** The process of testing is performed in order to accomplish specific objectives. For many organizations, the objectives will be the criteria for software acceptance—for example, the following customer needs:

  - Transactions can be processed by someone with X skills.

  - Ninety-six percent of all input transactions are acceptable for processing.

  - Changes to a product's price can be made within 24 hours.

The test manager should create a quantitative dashboard of key indicators that will enable him or her to accomplish the test objectives. The types of key indicators the test manager may want on the dashboard include

- Leaving customers satisfied with the testing process (customers may be developers, users, and/or management)

- Meeting testing objectives

- Completing the test plan's contractual components

- Accomplishing special test needs, such as validating the adequacy of system security

Using the Tester's Workbench with the Seven-Step Process

Chapter 3 introduced the tester's workbench, which forms the template describing the procedures your test team will perform within the seven testing steps. Chapters 7 through 13 use the following workbench:

- **Overview.** A brief description of the step. This will expand on the overview given earlier in this chapter for each step.

- **Objective.** A detailed description of the purpose of the step that you can use to measure your progress at each step.

- **Concerns.** Specific challenges that testers will have to overcome to complete the step effectively.

- **Workbench.** A description of the process that the testers should follow to complete the step.

- **Input.** The documents, information, and skills needed to complete the step.

- **Do procedures.** Detailed, task-by-task procedures that testers must follow to perform the step.

- **Check procedures.** A checklist that testers use to verify that they have performed a step correctly. These procedures will be related to the test's objective.

- **Output.** The deliverables that the testers must produce at the conclusion of each step.

- **Guidelines.** Suggestions for performing each step more effectively and for avoiding problems.

Workbench Skills

Manufacturing positions frequently are designed so that workers require minimal skills to perform their tasks effectively. Job descriptions for these positions are accompanied by detailed documentation so that any worker could perform that function correctly. Professional positions, however, require more advanced skills and are usually accompanied by far inferior documentation. (It's assumed that the person coming into the position will bring in a certain level of knowledge.)

A surgeon, for example, has to undergo 12 years of training before becoming licensed. Although there are detailed do and check procedures for performing a given operation, much of the execution depends on the doctor's skills. The same is true when the systems analyst defines end-user requirements. The systems analyst is guided by work papers, but much of the innovative work needed to properly define requirements depends on his or her years of experience and skill level.

Figure 6-2 illustrates the relationship between the tester's competency and the tester's workbench. The workbench assumes an average skill level on the part of the reader, incorporating these assumptions into its descriptions of procedures and tools. The skills that a professional tester should possess are defined in the common body of knowledge (CBOK) for a software testing professional. Developed by the Software Certification Organization Certification Board, the CBOK is the basis used for evaluating the competency of testers.

If the people involved in the tester's workbenches do not possess the basic testing skills in the CBOK, one or more of the following recommendations should be pursued to improve testing skills:

- Attend a basic course on software testing

- Take the necessary courses from the Quality Assurance Institute to prepare for the Certified Software Tester Examination

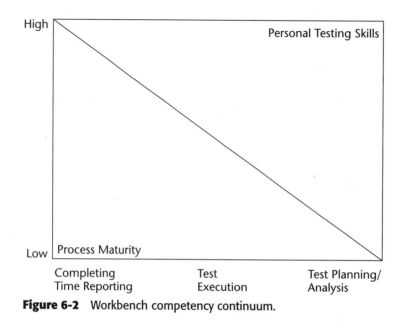

Figure 6-2   Workbench competency continuum.

Summary

This chapter presented the proposed seven-step testing process. The chapter also introduced issues surrounding the costs associated with testing. This will be helpful for justifying testing and attempting to test in a cost-effective manner. The chapter presented six areas for customizing the seven-step process to make it more effective in your organization. The chapter also addressed how test managers should manage the seven-step process.

Chapters 7 through 13 describe each of the seven steps, respectively. Each chapter includes all the necessary templates and checklists to perform those steps. It is important when reading a chapter to recognize the objective is to provide the templates, checklists, and tasks needed to perform those steps. This differs from many testing books, which focus on *what* to do; these seven steps focus on *how* to perform software testing.

CHAPTER 7

Step 1: Organizing for Testing

Software development involves two concurrent processes: building the software and testing it. It does not matter whether testing is performed by developers or by an independent test team; what is important is that someone has responsibility for testing. This chapter defines the tasks to prepare for testing and to organize the test team.

If the developers do the testing, it is probably not necessary for the testers to ensure the project estimate is adequate and to develop a process to track the project's status. However, when independent testers perform the testing, unless they can control their own test budget and the project team has an effective project status reporting process, the testers should perform the last task.

Objective

Testing can fall short of expectations for two reasons. First, the necessary preparation may not be accomplished. This chapter and the next discuss the needed preparatory work prior to executing tests. Second, many testing tasks are never completed because inadequate resources are allocated.

The objective of this chapter is to enable you to define the scope of testing and ensure that adequate time and resources are available for testing. If testing is included within the developer's budget, the test manager needs to ensure that the estimate is adequate for testing. The test manager must also ensure that overruns in project development will not restrict the amount of testing as defined in the test plan.

Workbench

Figure 7-1 shows the workbench for organizing for testing. The workbench input is the current documentation for the software system being tested. Five tasks are listed, but some of the tasks may have been completed prior to starting the first task. The output from this step is an organized test team, ready to begin testing.

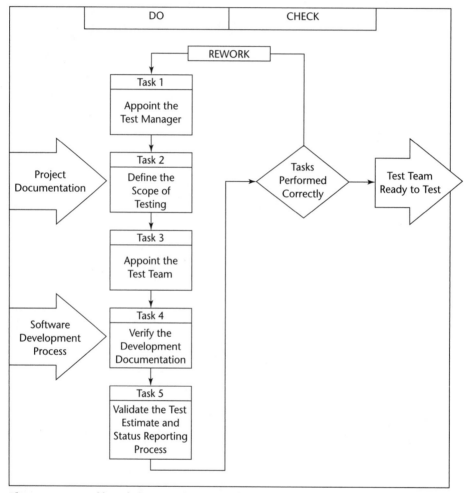

Figure 7-1   Workbench for organizing testing.

Input

The following two inputs are required to complete this step:

- **Project documentation.** This includes the project plan, objectives, scope, and defined outputs.
- **Software development process.** This includes the procedures and standards to be followed during the project's implementation.

Do Procedures

The following five tasks are recommended for organizing the testing process:

1. **Appoint the test manager.** If testing is part of the in-house development effort, the project leader should determine who is responsible for testing. If testing is performed by independent testers, IT management should appoint the test manager.
2. **Define the scope of testing.** The test manager defines the scope of testing, although all or part of the scope may be defined by testing standards.
3. **Appoint the test team.** The test manager, project manager, or IT management should appoint the test team.
4. **Verify the development documentation.** The test manager should verify that adequate development documentation is available to perform effective testing.
5. **Validate the test estimate and project status process.** The test estimate can be developed by either the test manager or the project manager.

Task 1: Appoint the Test Manager

Regardless of whether testing is performed by in-house developers or independent testers, someone needs to be responsible for testing. The test manager has the following responsibilities:

Define the scope of testing

Appoint the test team

Define the testing process and the deliverables produced

Write/oversee the test plan

Analyze test results and write the test report(s)

If the test manager cannot fulfill these responsibilities alone, other individuals should be assigned to the test team to assist him or her. Responsibilities may change based on the size of the project.

The skills required to be a test manager vary by the size of the project. For small projects (1–2 testers), the more experienced tester can fulfill the manager role; for medium-sized projects (3–5 testers), the test manager must be both a tester and a manager; and for larger projects (6 or more testers), managerial skills are more important than test skills.

Task 2: Define the Scope of Testing

Chapters 1–3 discussed the options available for testing scope. Traditionally, software testing validated that the specifications were implemented as specified. Previous discussions on testing scope expand that definition to include determining whether user needs are met, identifying whether the project was implemented in the most effective and efficient manner, ensuring the software system has met the desired quality factors, and testing for specialized software attributes, such as the adequacy of the system of internal control, and so forth.

The scope of testing may be defined in the test mission. In other words, if the testers are to ensure that the system meets the user's needs, the test manager would not have to define that in the test scope. Likewise, if testers are to assist users in developing and implementing an acceptance test plan, it would not have to be defined in the scope of testing for a specific project.

If the test mission is not specific about testing scope and/or there are specific objectives to be accomplished from testing, the test manager should define that scope. It is important to understand the scope of testing prior to developing the test plan.

Task 3: Appoint the Test Team

The test team is an integral part of the testing process. Without the formalization of the test team, it is difficult to introduce a formalized testing concept into the development process. Extensive "desk checking" by the individual who developed the work is not a cost-effective testing method. The disadvantages of a person checking his or her own work include the following:

- Misunderstandings will not be detected, because the checker will assume what he or she was told is correct.

- Improper use of the development process may not be detected, because the individual may not understand the process.

- The individual may be "blinded" into accepting erroneous test results because he or she falls into the same trap during testing that led to the introduction of the defect in the first place.

- The IT staff is optimistic in their ability to do defect-free work and thus sometimes underestimate the need for extensive testing.

- Without a formal division between software development and software testing, an individual may be tempted to improve the system structure and documentation rather than allocate that time and effort to the testing process.

This section describes the four approaches to appointing a test team (see Figure 7-2).

TEST TEAM APPROACH	COMPOSITION OF TEST TEAM MEMBERS	ADVANTAGES	DISADVANTAGES
Internal	Project team	• Minimize cost • Training • Knowledge of project	• Time allocation • Lack of independence • Lack of objectivity
External	Quality assurance Professional testers	• Independent view • IT professionals • Multiple project testing experience	• Cost • Overreliance • Competition
Non-IT	Users Auditors Consultants	• Independent view • Independence in assessment • Ability to act	• Cost • Lack of IT knowledge • Lack of project knowledge
Combination	Any or all of the above	• Multiple skills • Education • Clout	• Cost • Scheduling reviews • Diverse backgrounds

Figure 7-2   Test team composition.

Internal Team Approach

In the internal test team approach, the members of the project team become the members of the test team. In most instances, the systems development project leader is the test team project leader. It is not necessary to have all the development team members participate on the test team, although there is no reason why they cannot. What is important is that one member of the test team will be primarily responsible for testing other members' work. The objective of the team is to establish a test process that is independent of the people who developed the particular part of the project being tested.

The advantage of the internal IT test team approach is that it minimizes the cost of the test team. The project team is already responsible for testing, so using project members on the test team is merely an alternate method for conducting the tests. Testing using the test team approach not only trains the project people in good testing methods, it cross-trains them in other aspects of the project. The internal IT test team approach uses those people in testing who are most knowledgeable about the project.

A potential disadvantage of the internal test team approach is that the team will not allocate appropriate time for testing. In addition, the project team members may lack independence and objectivity in conducting the test. The tendency is for the project team members to believe that the project solution is correct and thus find it difficult to challenge the project assumptions.

External Team Approach

Testing by an external team does not relieve the project personnel of responsibility for the correctness of the application system. The external team approach provides extra assurance of the correctness of processing. Typically, external testing occurs after the project team has performed the testing it deems necessary. The development team verifies that the system structure is correct, and the independent test team verifies that the system satisfies user requirements.

External testing is normally performed by either quality assurance personnel or a professional testing group in the IT department. While the project team is involved in all aspects of the development, the quality assurance test teams specialize in the testing process (although most individuals in these testing groups have experience in systems design and programming).

The advantage of external testers is the independent perspective they bring to the testing process. The group comprises IT professionals who have specialized in the area of testing. In addition, these groups have testing experience in multiple projects and, thus, are better able to construct and execute tests than those individuals who test only periodically.

The disadvantage of external IT testing is the additional cost required to establish and administer the testing function. Also, the development team may place too much reliance on the test team and thus fail to perform adequate testing themselves. In addition, the competition between the test team and the project team may result in a breakdown of cooperation, making it difficult for the test team to function properly.

Non-IT Team Approach

Testing also can be performed by groups external to the IT department. The three most common groups are users, auditors, and consultants. These groups represent the organizational needs and test on behalf of the organization. The advantage of a non-IT test team is that they provide an independent assessment. The non-IT group is not restricted by loyalty to report unfavorable results only to the IT department. The non-IT group has a greater capacity to cause action to occur once problems are detected than a group within an IT department.

The disadvantage of non-IT testing is its cost. Generally, these groups are not familiar with the application and must first learn the application, and then learn how to test within the organization.

Combination Team Approach

In the combination test team approach, any or all the preceding groups can participate on a test team. The combination team can be assembled to meet specific testing needs. For example, if the project has significant financial implications, an auditor could be added to the test team; if the project has communication concerns, a communications consultant could be added.

The advantage of drawing on multiple skills for the test team is to enable a multi-disciplined approach to testing. In other words, the skills and backgrounds of individuals from different disciplines can be drawn into the test process. For some of the test participants, particularly users, it can be helpful to make them aware of both the system and the potential pitfalls in an automated system. In addition, a combination test team has greater clout in approving, disapproving, or modifying the application system.

The disadvantage of the combination test team is the cost associated with assembling and administering the test team. It also may pose some scheduling problems determining when the tests will occur. Finally, the diverse backgrounds of the test team may make the determination of a mutually acceptable test approach difficult.

Task 4: Verify the Development Documentation

Testers rely on the development documentation to prepare tests and to determine the desired results. If the development documentation is vague, testers cannot determine the expected results. For example, an expectation that the system should be "easy to use" is not specific enough to test. It is not good practice for the tester to define the expected result or to indicate results are "adequate."

It is important prior to test planning to determine the completeness and correctness of development documentation. In organizations where good development documentation standards exist, and IT management enforces compliance to those standards, this task is not necessary. However in that case it is necessary for the testers to have a thorough understanding of the development documentation standards.

Testers should be concerned that the documentation process will fail to

- Assist in planning and managing resources
- Help to plan and implement testing procedures
- Help to transfer knowledge of software development throughout the life cycle
- Promote common understanding and expectations about the system within the organization and—if the software is purchased—between the buyer and seller
- Define what is expected and verify that is what is delivered
- Provide managers with technical documents to review at the significant development milestones, to determine that requirements have been met and that resources should continue to be expended

Development Phases

Programs and systems are developed in phases, from the initial idea for a system to a properly working system. The terminology used to identify 170these inputs, phases, and the stages within these phases is defined in the following list:

- **Initiation.** The objectives and general definition of the software requirements are established during the initiation phase. Feasibility studies, cost/benefit analyses, and the documentation prepared in this phase are determined by the organization's procedures and practices.

- **Development.** During the development phase, the requirements for the software are determined and then the software is defined, specified, programmed, and tested. The following documentation is prepared during the four stages of this phase:

  - **Definition.** During the definition stage, the requirements for the software and documentation are determined. The functional requirements document and the data requirements document should be prepared.

  - **Design.** During this stage, the design alternatives, specific requirements, and functions to be performed are analyzed and a design is specified. Documents that may be prepared include the system/subsystem specification, program specification, database specification, and test plan.

  - **Programming.** During the programming stage, the software is coded and debugged. Documents that should be prepared during this stage include the user manual, operations manual, program maintenance manual, and test plan.

  - **Testing.** During the test stage, the software and related documentation are evaluated and the test analysis report is prepared.

- **Operation.** During the operation phase, the software is maintained, evaluated, and changed as additional requirements are identified.

The 14 documents needed for system development, maintenance, and operations are listed in Figure 7-3 and described in the following list:

- **Project request.** The purpose of the project request document is to provide a means for users to request the development, purchase, or modification of software or other IT-related services. It serves as the initiating document in the software life cycle and provides a basis for communication with the requesting organization to further analyze system requirements and assess the possible effects of the system.

- **Feasibility study.** Feasibility studies help analyze system objectives, requirements, and concepts; evaluate alternative approaches for achieving objectives; and identify proposed approaches. The feasibility study document, in conjunction with a cost/benefit analysis, should help management make decisions to initiate or continue an IT project or service. The study can be supplemented with an appendix containing details of a cost/benefit analysis or considered with a separate cost/benefit analysis document.

- **Cost/benefit analysis.** Such analyses can help managers, users, designers, and auditors evaluate alternative approaches. The analysis document, in conjunction with the feasibility study document, should help management decide to initiate or continue an IT project or service.

- **Software summary.** This document is used for very small projects to substitute for other development-phase documentation when only a minimal level of documentation is needed.

INITIATION PHASE	DEVELOPMENT PHASE				OPERATION PHASE
	Definition Stage	**Design Stage**	**Programming Stage**	**Test Stage**	
SOFTWARE SUMMARY					
Project Request Document	Functional Requirements Document	System/ Subsystem Specification	User Manual		(Uses and updates many of the initiation and development phase documents.)
Feasibility Study Document		Program Specification	Operations Manual		
Cost/Benefit Analysis Document	Data Requirements Document	Database Specification	Program Maintenance Manual		
TEST PLAN					
				Test Analysis Report	

Figure 7-3 Documentation within the software life cycle.

- **Functional requirements.** The purpose of the functional requirements document is to provide a basis for users and designers to mutually develop an initial definition of the software, including the requirements, operating environment, and development plan.

- **Data requirements.** During the definition stage, the data requirements document provides data descriptions and technical information about data collection requirements.

- **System/subsystem specifications.** Designed for analysts and programmers, this document specifies requirements, operating environment, design characteristics, and program specifications.

- **Program specification.** The purpose of the program specification is to specify program requirements, operating environment, and design characteristics.

- **Database specifications.** This document specifies the logical and physical characteristics of a particular database.

- **User manual.** Written in non-technical terminology, this manual describes system functions so that user organizations can determine their applicability and when and how to use them. It should serve as a reference document for preparation of input data and parameters and for interpretation of results.

- **Operations manual.** The purpose of this manual is to provide computer operation personnel with a description of the software and its required operational environment.

- **Program maintenance manual.** This manual provides the information necessary to understand the programs, their operating environment, and their maintenance procedures.

- **Test plan.** This document provides detailed specifications, descriptions, and procedures for all tests and test data reduction and evaluation criteria.

- **Test analysis report.** The purpose of the test analysis report is to document test results, present the proven capabilities and deficiencies for review, and provide a basis for preparing a statement of software readiness for implementation.

The standards for preparing documentation, as developed by your IT organization, are the second input to this test process.

Measuring Project Documentation Needs

The formality, extent, and level of detail of the documentation to be prepared depend on the organization's IT management practices and the project's size, complexity, and risk. What is adequate for one project may be inadequate for another.

Too much documentation can also be wasteful. An important part of testing documentation is to determine first that the right documentation is prepared; there is little value in confirming that unneeded documentation is adequately prepared.

The testing methodology uses 12 criteria to establish the need for documentation:

- **Originality required.** The uniqueness of the application within the organization.

- **Degree of generality.** The amount of rigidity associated with the application and the need to handle a variety of situations during processing.

- **Span of operation.** The percentage of total corporate activities affected by the system.

- **Change in scope and objective.** The frequency of expected change in requirements during the life of the system.

- **Equipment complexity.** The sophistication of the hardware and communications lines needed to support the application.

- **Personnel assigned.** The number of people involved in developing and maintaining the application system.

- **Developmental cost.** The total dollars required to develop the application.

- **Criticality.** The importance of the application system to the organization.

- **Average response time to program change.** The average amount of time available to install a change to the application system.

- **Average response time to data input.** The average amount of time available to process an application transaction.

- **Programming language.** The language used to develop the application.

- **Concurrent software development.** Other applications and support systems that need to be developed concurrently to fulfill the total mission.

A five-point weighting system is used for each of the 12 criteria, as shown in Figure 7-4. For example, if two people have been assigned to the project, a weight of 1 is allocated for criterion 6, but if seven people were assigned, a weight of 3 would be used.

Work Paper 7-1 should be used in developing the total weighted documentation score, as follows:

1. **Determine the weight for each of the 12 criteria.** This is done by determining which weights for each criterion are appropriate for the application being tested. The descriptive information in the five weight columns should be the basis of this determination.

2. **Enter the weight number on Work Paper 7-1 for each of the 12 criteria.** For example, if under the originality criterion weight 5 is most applicable, enter 5 in the Weight column.

3. **Total the weights for the 12 criteria.** The minimum score is 12; the maximum is 60.

The weighted score is used in determining what specific documents should be prepared for the software system being tested.

Determining What Documents Must Be Produced

Figure 7-5 relates the total weighted criteria score in Work Paper 7-1 to the previously described software documents and recommends which document testers should prepare. The need for several of the documents depends on the situation. (For example, database specifications and data requirement documents are usually required for systems using database technology.) A project request document is needed in organizations that require formal approvals before conducting a feasibility study. Cost/benefit analysis documents are needed in organizations requiring that such analyses be performed before a project is put into development.

With the total weighted criteria score developed, Figure 7-5 can be used as follows:

- The appropriate row for selecting documents is determined by cross-referencing the score developed in Work Paper 7-1 to the score in the Total Weighted Criteria column. Some of the scores in this column overlap to accommodate highly critical projects, regardless of their scores.

- For the row selected, the columns indicate which documents are needed.

If the project did not generate these documents, the test team should question the documentation. If unneeded documents were prepared, the test team should challenge the need for maintaining them.

CRITERIA		WEIGHTS			
	1	**2**	**3**	**4**	**5**
1. Originality required	None—reprogram on different equipment	Minimum—more stringent requirements	Limited—new interfaces	Considerable—apply existing state of the art to environment	Extensive—requires advance in state of the art
2. Degree of generality	Highly restricted— single purpose	Restricted— parameterized for a range of capacities	Limited flexibility— allows some change in format	Multipurpose— flexible format, range of subjects	Very flexible—able to handle a broad range of subject matter on different equipment
3. Span of operation	Local or utility	Small group	Department	Division	Entire corporation
4. Change in scope and objective	None	Infrequent	Occasional	Frequent	Continuous
5. Equipment complexity	Single machine— routine processing	Single machine— routine processing, extended peripheral system	Multicomputer— standard peripheral system	Multicomputer— advanced programming, complex peripheral system	Master control system— multicomputer, auto input/output, and display equipment
6. Personnel assigned	1 to 2	3 to 5	6 to 10	11 to 18	More than 18
7. Developmental cost ($)	1K to 10K	10K to 50K	50K to 200K	200K to 500K	More than 500K
8. Criticality	Limited to data processing	Routine corporate operations	Important corporate operations	Area/product survival	Corporate survival
9. Average response time to program change	2 or more weeks	1 to 2 weeks	3 to 7 days	1 to 3 days	1 to 24 hours
10. Average response time to data input	2 or more weeks	1 to 2 weeks	1 to 7 days	1 to 24 hours	0 to 60 minutes
11. Programming languages	High-level language	High-level and limited assembly language	High-level and extensive assembly language	Assembly language	Machine language
12. Concurrent software development	None	Limited	Moderate	Extensive	Exhaustive

Figure 7-4 Example of weighting criteria.

TOTAL WEIGHTED CRITERIA	SOFTWARE SUMMARY	USER MANUAL	OPERATIONS MANUAL	PROGRAM MAINTENANCE MANUAL	TEST PLAN	FEASIBILITY STUDY DOCUMENT	FUNCTIONAL REQUIREMENTS DOCUMENT	SYSTEM/SUBSYSTEM SPECIFICATION	TEST ANALYSIS REPORT	PROGRAM SPECIFICATION	DATA REQUIREMENTS DOCUMENT	DATABASE SPECIFICATION	PROJECT REQUEST DOCUMENT	COST/BENEFIT ANALYSIS DOCUMENT
0 to 12*	X													
12 to 15*	X	X												
16 to 26	X	X	X	X	X	X			**		***	***	***	***
24 to 38	X	X	X	X	X	X	X		**		***	***	***	***
36 to 50	X	X	X	X	X	X	X	X	X		***	***	***	***
48 to 60	X	X	X	X	X	X	X	X	X	X	***	***	***	***

Notes:

*Additional document types may be required at lower-weighted criteria totals to satisfy local requirements.

**The test analysis report logically should be prepared, but may be informal.

***Preparation of the project request document, cost/benefit analysis document, data requirements document, and database specification is situationally dependent.

Figure 7-5   Total weighted documentation criteria versus required document types.

Figure 7-6 illustrates a simpler method to determine the level of documentation needed. The four levels of documentation are:

1. **Minimal.** Level 1 documentation applies to single-use programs of minimal complexity. This documentation should include the type of work being produced and a description of what the program really does. Therefore, the documentation that results from the development of the programs (i.e., program abstract, compile listing, test cases) should be retained as well. The criteria for categorizing a program as level 1 can be its expected use or its cost to develop (in hours or dollars) and may be modified for the particular requirements of the installation. Suggested cost criteria are programs requiring less than one worker-month of effort or less than $1,000 (these are not assumed to be equal).

2. **Internal.** Level 2 documentation applies to special-purpose programs that, after careful consideration, appear to have no sharing potential and to be designed for use only by the requesting department. Large programs with a short life expectancy also fall into this category. The documentation required (other than

level 1) includes input/output formats, setup instructions, and sufficient comments in the source code to provide clarification in the compile listing. The effort spent toward formal documentation for level 2 programs should be minimal.

3. **Working document.** Level 3 documentation applies to programs that are expected to be used by several people in the same organization or that may be transmitted on request to other organizations, contractors, or grantees. This level should include all documentation types. The documentation should be typed but need not be in a finished format suitable for publication. Usually, it is not formally reviewed or edited; however, certain programs that are important to the using organization but not considered appropriate for publication should undergo a more stringent documentation review.

4. **Formal publication.** Level 4 documentation applies to programs that are of sufficient general interest and value to be announced outside the originating installation. This level of documentation is also desirable if the program is to be referenced by a technical publication or paper. You should include programs that are critical to installation activities. These programs also should be formally documented, reviewed in depth, and subjected to configuration control procedures. You should include recurring applications (payroll, for example) in this level so that you maintain an accurate history of how the system has conformed to changing laws, rules, and regulations.

LEVEL	USE	DOCUMENTATION ELEMENTS	EXTENT OF EFFORT
1	Minimal	Software summary plus any incidentally produced documentation.	No special effort, general good practice.
2	Internal	Level 1 plus user manual and operations manual.	Minimal documentation effort spent on informal documentation. No formal documentation effort.
3	Working Document	Level 2 plus functional requirements document, program specification, program maintenance manual, test plan, test analysis report, system/subsystem specification, and feasibility study document.*	All basic elements of documentation should be typewritten, but need not be prepared in finished format for publication or require external edit or review.
4	Formal Publication	Level 3 produced in a form suitable for publication.*	At a minimum, all basic elements prepared for formal publication, including external review and edit.

*In addition, the following documents should be prepared, depending on the situation: data requirements, database specification, project report, and cost/benefit analysis.

Figure 7-6 Alternate method for determining documentation.

Figure 7-6 summarizes the criteria for determining these levels of documentation. Additional criteria specific to an installation regarding program-sharing potential, life expectancy, and use frequency should also be considered when determining documentation levels.

You can determine which of the four documentation levels is appropriate:

- As an alternate to the total weighted criteria score method.

- As a means of validating the correctness of the total weighted score to the application system. If the same types of documentation are indicated by both methods, you have greater assurance that the documentation indicated is the correct one.

Determining the Completeness of Individual Documents

Testers should use Work Paper 7-2 to document the results of the completeness test. If the documentation does not meet a criterion, the Comments column should be used to explain the deficiency. This column becomes the test report on the completeness of the documentation.

The 12 criteria used to evaluate the completeness of a document are as follows:

- **Content.** The suggested content for all the documents (except the software summary) is included in a later section. A table of contents for each document is followed by a brief description of each element within the document. These document content guidelines should be used to determine whether the document contains all the needed information.

- **Audience.** Each document type is written for a particular audience. The information should be presented with the terminology and level of detail appropriate to the audience.

- **Redundancy.** The 14 document types in this section have some redundancy. In addition, most document types are specific (e.g., descriptions of input, output, or equipment). Information that should be included in each of the document types differs in context and sometimes in terminology and level of detail because it is intended to be read by different audiences at different points in the software life cycle.

- **Flexibility.** Flexibility in the use of the document results from the organization of its contents.

- **Size.** Each document-type outline can be used to prepare documents that range in size from a few to several hundred pages. Length depends on the size and complexity of the project and the project manager's judgment as to the level of detail necessary for the environment in which the software will be developed or run.

- **Combining and expanding document types.** It is occasionally necessary to combine several document types under one cover or to produce several volumes of the same document type. Document types that can be combined are manuals for users, operations, and program maintenance. The contents of each document type should then be presented with the outline (e.g., Part I—Users, Part II—Operations, and Part III—Program Maintenance).

For large systems, you can prepare a document for each module. Sometimes, the size of a document may require it to be issued in multiple volumes to allow ease of use. In such cases, the document should be separated at a section division (e.g., the contents of the test plan may be divided into sections of plan, specifications and evaluation, and specific test descriptions).

- **Format.** The content guidelines have been prepared in a generally consistent format. This particular format has been tested, and its use is encouraged.

- **Content sequence.** In general, the order of the sections and paragraphs in a particular document type should be the same as shown in the content guidelines. The order may be changed if it significantly enhances the presentation.

- **Documenting multiple programs or multiple files.** Many of the document content outlines anticipate and are adaptable to documenting a system and its subsystems, multiple programs, or multiple files. All these outlines can, of course, be used for a single system, subsystem, program, database, or file.

- **Section titles.** These titles are generally the same as those shown in the content guidelines. They may be modified to reflect terminology unique to the software being documented if the change significantly enhances the presentation. Sections or paragraphs may be added or deleted as local requirements dictate.

- **Flowcharts and decision tables.** The graphic representations of some problem solutions in the form of flowcharts or decision tables may be included in or appended to the documents produced.

- **Forms.** The use of specific forms depends on organizational practices. Some of the information specified in a paragraph in the content guidelines may be recorded on such forms.

Determining Documentation Timeliness

Documentation that is not current is worthless. Most IT professionals believe that if one part of the documentation is incorrect, other parts are probably incorrect, and they are reluctant to use it.

The documentation test team can use any or all the following four tests to validate the timeliness of documentation. These tests can be done on complete documents or parts of documents. Testers familiar with statistics can perform sampling and validate the timeliness of that sample. Testers should strive for a 95 percent confidence level that the documentation is current.

- **Use the documentation to change the application.** Timeliness can be validated with the same test process described in the preceding section. The timeliness test enables the tester to search for and confirm consistency between the various documents and to determine whether the documentation supports the operational system.

- **Compare the code with the documentation.** This test uses the current version of the programs as the correct basis for documentation. This test is usually done on a sampling basis; the tester randomly selects several parts of the program and traces them to the appropriate levels of documentation. The objective is to determine whether the code is properly represented in the documentation. Because this test is done statistically, a few variations might imply extensive segments of obsolete documentation.

- **Confirm documentation timeliness with documentation preparers.** The individuals who prepare the documentation should be asked whether it is current. Specific questions include:

  - Is this documentation 100 percent representative of the application in operation?

  - Is the documentation changed every time that a system change is made?

  - Do the individuals who change the system rely on the documentation as correct?

- **Confirm the timeliness of documentation with end users.** End users should be asked whether the documentation for the system is current. Because end users might not be familiar with all the contents of the documentation, they may need to be selected on a sampling basis and asked about specific pieces of documentation. Again, because sampling is used, a few variances may mean extensive amounts of obsolete documentation.

Task 5: Validate the Test Estimate and Project Status Reporting Process

Troubled projects have two common characteristics: The project estimate is inadequate and the status report of the development effort is misleading.

The objective of validating the project estimate is to determine what resources will be available to produce and test software. Resources include staff, computer time, and elapsed time. Because a good estimate shows when and how costs will be incurred, it can be used not only to justify software development and testing but also as a management control tool.

Testers need to know the progress of the system under development. The purpose of project management systems and accounting systems is to monitor this progress. However, many of these systems are more budget- and schedule-oriented than project completion–oriented.

The tester's main concern during the development is that inadequate resources and time will be allocated to testing. Because much of the testing will be performed after development is complete, the time period between completing development and the due date for production may be inadequate for testing.

There are three general concerns regarding available time and resources for testing:

- **Inaccurate estimate.** The estimate for resources in time will not be sufficient to complete the project as specified.

- **Inadequate development process.** The tools and procedures will not enable developers to complete the project within the time constraints.

- **Incorrect status reporting.** The project leaders will not know the correct status of the project during early developmental stages and thus cannot take the necessary corrective action in time to meet the scheduled completion dates.

Validating the Test Estimate

Many software projects are essentially innovative, and both history and logic suggest that cost overruns may be to the result of an ineffective estimating system. Software cost estimating is a complicated process because project development is influenced by a large number of variables, many of which are subjective, non-quantifiable, and inter-related in complex ways.

Some reasons for not obtaining a good estimate include:

- A lack of understanding of the process of software development and maintenance

- A lack of understanding of the effects of various technical and management constraints

- A view that each project is unique, which inhibits project-to-project comparisons

- A lack of historic data against which the model can be checked

- A lack of historic data for calibration

- An inadequate definition of the estimate's objective (whether it is intended as a project management tool or purely to aid in making a go-ahead decision) and at what stage the estimate is required so that inputs and outputs can be chosen appropriately

- Inadequate specifications of the scope of the estimate (what is included and what is excluded)

- An inadequate understanding of the premises on which the estimate is based

Strategies for Software Cost Estimating

There are five commonly used methods for estimating the cost of developing and maintaining a software system:

- **Seat-of-the-pants method.** This method, which is often based on personal experience, is still very popular because no better method has been proven. One of its problems is that each estimate is based on different experience, and therefore different estimates of the cost of a single project may vary widely. A second problem is that the estimator must have experience with a similar project, of a similar size. Experience does not work on systems larger than those used for comparison nor on systems with a totally different content.

- **Constraint method.** The constraint method is equivalent to taking an educated guess. Based on schedule, cost, or staffing constraints, a manager agrees to develop the software within the constraints. The constraints are not related to the complexity of the project. In general, this method will result in delivery of the software within the specified constraints, but with the specification adjusted to fit the constraints.

- **Percentage-of-hardware method.** This method is based on the following two assumptions:

    - Software costs are a fixed percentage of hardware costs.

    - Hardware cost estimates are usually reasonably accurate.

    A study on estimating has indicated that the first of these assumptions is not justified.

- **Simulation method.** Simulation is widely used in estimating life cycle support costs for hardware systems, but it is not appropriate for software cost estimating because it is based on a statistical analysis of hardware failure rates and ignores logistics for which there is no software equivalent.

- **Parametric modeling method.** Parametric models comprise the most commonly used estimating method and are described in the following section.

Parametric Models

Parametric models can be divided into three classes: regression, heuristic, and phenomenological.

- **Regression models.** The quantity to be estimated is mathematically related to a set of input parameters. The parameters of the hypothesized relationship are arrived at by statistical analysis and curve fitting on an appropriate historical database. There may be more than one relationship to deal with different databases, different types of applications, and different developer characteristics.

- **Heuristic models.** In a heuristic model, observation and interpretation of historical data are combined with supposition and experience. Relationships between variables are stated without justification. The advantage of heuristic models is that they need not wait for formal relationships to be established that describe how the cost-driving variables are related. Over a period of time, a given model can become very effective in a stable predicting environment. If the model fails, it is adjusted to deal with the situation. It therefore becomes a repository for the collected experiences and insights of the designers.

- **Phenomenological models.** The phenomenological model is based on a hypothesis that the software development process can be explained in terms of some more widely applicable process or idea. For example, the Putnam model is based on the belief that the distribution of effort during the software life cycle has the same characteristics as the distribution of effort required to solve a given number of problems given a constant learning rate.

Most of the estimating models follow a similar pattern, based on the following six steps. Not all steps occur in all models. For example, some models do not initially perform a total project labor or cost estimate, but start by estimating the different phases separately, so Step 4 aggregates the separate estimates instead of dividing up the total estimate. Similarly the adjustments for special project characteristics may occur between Steps 1 and 2 as well as or instead of between Steps 2 and 3.

1. **Estimate the software size.** Most models start from an estimate of project size, although some models include algorithms for computing size from various other system characteristics, such as units of work.

2. **Convert the size estimate (function points or lines of code) to an estimate of the person-hours needed to complete the test task.** Some models convert from size to labor, whereas others go directly from size to money estimates.

3. **Adjust the estimate for special project characteristics.** In some models, an effective size is calculated from the basic size estimate obtained in Step 1; in others, a person-hours or cost estimate is calculated from the estimates obtained in Step 2. The estimate is an adjustment of the basic estimate intended to take account of any special project characteristics that make it dissimilar to the pattern absorbed in the underlying historical database. Such variations, which include the effect of volatility of the requirements, different software tools, difficulty above the level of projects in the database, or a different method of dealing with support costs, are frequently based on intuitively derived relationships, unsupported by statistical verification.

   The adjustment may precede amalgamation of the costs of the different phases, or a single adjustment may be applied to the total.

4. **Divide the total estimate into the different project phases.** Each model dealing with a project's schedule makes assumptions about the allocation of effort in the different project phases. The simplest assumption defines a percentage of the effort for each phase, for example, the much-quoted 40 percent design, 20 percent code, and 40 percent test rule. It should be noted that this is not a universally agreed-on rule. Some estimating research shows that other percentages may be more appropriate, and the percentage in each phase may depend on other software characteristics. Some models assume that staffing allocation with respect to time follows a rectangular distribution; others assume that it follows a beta distribution, or a Rayleigh distribution. In general, the assumptions on staffing allocation with respect to time are based on historical data. The effect of deviating from historical patterns has not been considered.

5. **Estimate the computer time and non-technical labor costs.** Where these costs are explicitly included, they are often calculated as a percentage of the technical labor costs. Sometimes such costs are included implicitly because they were included in the database from which the model was derived.

6. **Sum the costs.** The non-technical labor costs and the cost of computer time, where these are included in the estimates, are added to the technical costs of the different phases of the software life cycle to obtain an aggregated cost estimate.

Testing the Validity of the Software Cost Estimate

An improper cost estimate can do more damage to the quality of a software project than almost any other single factor. People tend to do that which they are measured on. If they are measured on meeting a software cost estimate, they will normally meet that estimate. If the estimate is incorrect, the project team will make whatever compromises are necessary to meet that estimate. This process of compromise can significantly undermine the quality of the delivered project. The net result is increased maintenance costs, dissatisfied customers, increased effort in the customer area to compensate for software system weaknesses, and discouraged, demoralized project personnel.

Estimating software costs is just that—estimating. No one can guarantee that the software estimate will be correct for the work to be performed. However, testing can increase the validity of the estimate, and thus is a worthwhile endeavor. Testing of a software estimate is a three-part process, as follows:

1. Validate the reasonableness of the estimating model.
2. Validate that the model includes all the needed factors.
3. Verify the correctness of the cost-estimating model estimate.

Validate the Reasonableness of the Estimating Model

Work Paper 7-3 lists the 14 characteristics of a desirable estimating model. The worksheet provides a place to indicate whether the attributes are present or absent, and any comments you care to make about the inclusion or exclusion of those characteristics. The closer the number comes to 14, the more reliance you can place on your software-estimating model.

Validate That the Model Includes All the Needed Factors

The factors that influence the cost of a software project can be divided into those contributed by the development and maintenance organization, many of which are subjective, and those inherent in the software project itself. Current models differ with respect to the factors that are required as specific inputs. Many different factors may be subsumed in a single parameter in some models, particularly the more subjective parameters.

Depending on the information fed to the model, the estimate produced can vary significantly. It is important that all the factors that influence software costs are properly entered into the model. Models can produce incorrect results in two ways. First, the factor can be excluded from the model, resulting in an incorrect estimate. Second, the factor can be incomplete or incorrectly entered into the model, again causing incorrect software cost estimates to be produced.

Work Paper 7-4 lists the factors that can influence software costs. Testers must determine whether a missing factor will significantly affect the actual costs of building the software. Factors that influence the software system include:

- **Size of the software.** A favorite measure for software system size is lines of operational code, or deliverable code (operational code plus supporting code, for example, for hardware diagnostics) measured either in object code statements or in source code statements. It is rarely specified whether source code statements include non-executable code, such as comments and data declarations.

- **Percentage of the design and/or code that is new.** This is relevant when moving existing software systems to new hardware, when planning an extension to or modification of an existing software system, or when using software prototypes.

- **Complexity of the software.** Different software projects have different degrees of complexity, usually measured by the amount of interaction between the different parts of the software system, and between the software and the external world. The complexity affects programmer productivity and is an input parameter for several models.

- **Difficulty of implementing the software requirements.** Different application areas are considered to have different levels of difficulty in design and coding, affecting programmer productivity. For example, operating system software is usually regarded as more difficult than standalone commercial applications. Software projects might be given a difficulty or an application mix rating, according to the degree to which they fall into one (or more) of the following areas:

  - Operating systems

  - Self-contained real-time projects

  - Standalone, non–real-time applications

  - Modifications to an existing software system

  There are, of course, other categories. Each model deals with the difficulty in its own way, some requiring estimates of the percentage of each type of software system, others asking for a number on a predefined scale. Others merge the factor with the complexity rating.

- **Quality.** Quality, documentation, maintainability, and reliability standards required are all included in a single factor. This factor is sometimes called the *platform type*, reflecting the fact that the documentation and reliability requirements for software in a manned spacecraft are higher than in a standalone statistical package. The documentation and reliability requirements may be given a defined numeric scale—for example, from 1 to 10. Some estimating models include a parameter for the number of different locations at which the software will be run.

- **Languages to be used.** The choice of programming language affects the cost, size, timescale, and documentation effort.

- **Security classification.** The higher the security classification of the project, the more it will cost because of the additional precautions required. The security classification is not an input factor in most models.

- **Volatility of the requirement.** The firmness of the requirement specification and the interface between developer and customer affect the amount of rework that will be needed before the software is delivered. This highly subjective but nonetheless important factor is an input factor to several models. The following are included in this factor:

- Amount of change expected in the requirement
- Amount of detail omitted from the requirement specification
- Concurrent development of associated hardware, causing changes in the software specification
- Unspecified target hardware

Organization-dependent factors include the following:

- **Project schedule.** Attempts to save time by adding more people to a project prove counterproductive because more time and effort are expended in communication between project team members than can be gained by adding extra people. There must therefore be either a minimum time below which the project cannot be completed or at least a time below which the costs of saving a small amount of time become prohibitive. Conversely, if more time is allocated to a project than is required, it has been argued that the cost decreases. However, other models show costs increasing if more than some optimum time is allocated because more personnel are consumed. One effect of the compression of timescales is that work that should be done in series is undertaken in parallel, with the increased risk that some of the work will have to be scrapped (e.g., if coding is started before design is complete).

  Not all models deal with project schedules. Of those that do, some assume the 40-20-40 rule (40 percent design, 20 percent coding, and 40 percent testing), and others use more elaborate scheduling assumptions. Some research throws doubt on the validity of the 40-20-40 rule and indicates that phases are strongly interrelated, so effort skimped in one phase will probably result in a considerable increase in the effort needed in a later phase.

- **Personnel.** The personnel assigned to a project contribute to the cost. Most projects are resource limited, in that the number of people with a given skill who are available to the project is limited. The number of personnel available at any stage in a project will affect the timescales, and hence the cost. An industrial engineering model called the "Raleigh Curve" shows the relationship between the number of assigned staff and project effectiveness.

  - **Technical competence.** Effective projects are staffed with personnel with the competence needed to complete the project successfully. A less competent staff will increase the cost and schedule of the defined testing tasks.

  - **Non-technical staff.** Estimates of the non-technical personnel levels required by a project are frequently made as a percentage of the technical personnel levels.

- **Development environment.** The adequacy of the development environment, both in hardware and software, depends largely on the management of the development organization. This factor is not usually requested as an explicit input to a model, but may be implicit in the calibration of the model, or in some general management parameter. The following are three aspects of the development environment that are sometimes required as inputs:

- **Development machine.** The adequacy of the development machine as a host for developing software for the selected target, and the availability of the development machine to the software development personnel, will affect both the schedule and the cost of a software development. The study showed that time sharing, where the development machine is constantly available, is 20 percent more productive than batch systems for software development.

- **Availability of associated software and hardware.** Projected late delivery of some item of associated hardware or software can affect schedules and costs.

- **Software tools and techniques used during system design and development.** Newer tools and techniques, properly applied, can reduce development effort.

- **Resources not directly attributable to technical aspects of the project.** The development organization's management style affects the amount of effort team members expend communicating with each other, the level of non-technical effort involved, as well as software/hardware costs, subcontracting costs, and profit. These factors are usually ignored, are implicit in the database from which the model is derived, or are taken care of by a general management factor. The geographical distribution of the development organization may affect costs because of travel and the cost of transmitting data between sites, and is therefore input to some models.

- **Labor rates.** If the model estimates costs in terms of money rather than staff-hours, the relationship of labor costs to staff-hours within the development organization may be required by the model. The model may be capable of reflecting increased rates for staff required to work irregular hours because of decreases in the development timescale or lack of availability of development tools.

- **Inflation.** Costs estimated in terms of money rather than staff hours should include inflation rates if the project will last more than 12 months.

Verify the Correctness of the Cost-Estimating Model Estimate

The amount of testing of the produced estimate will depend on the reasonableness of the estimating model and the completeness of the influencing factors included in the model. The less the tester can rely on the model, the more testing that needs to be performed on the validity of the estimate produced by the model.

The following four steps are suggested when testing the validity of the estimate produced by the software cost-estimating model:

- **Recalculate the estimate.** The tester can validate the processing of the estimate by rerunning the estimating model. The purpose of this is to:

- Validate the input was entered correctly
- Validate the input was reasonable
- Validate the mathematical computation was performed correctly

This test can be done in totality or in part. For example, the tester can completely recalculate the estimate, check that the input going into the estimating model was correct, test the reasonableness of some of the input test by recalculating all or parts of the estimate, and so forth.

- **Compare produced estimate to similar projects.** The tester can determine how long it took to develop projects of similar size and complexity. These actual project costs should be available from the organization's accounting system. The estimate produced by the estimating system is then compared to the actual costs for like projects completed in the past. If there is any significant difference, the tester can challenge the validity of the estimate. This challenge may result in a recalculation or change of the estimate based on previous experience.

- **The prudent person test.** This test is similar to the preceding test in that past experience is utilized. The tester documents the factors influencing the cost estimate, documents the estimate produced by the estimating system, and then validates the reasonableness of that estimate by asking experienced project leaders for their opinions regarding the validity of the estimate. It is recommended that three experienced project leaders be asked to validate the estimate. If one or more does not feel that the estimate is reasonable, the validity of the estimate should be challenged.

- **Redundancy in software cost estimating.** This test has the tester recalculate the estimate using another cost-estimating model. For example, assume that your organization has developed a cost-estimating model. The project people have used that model to develop the cost estimate. The tester uses another method, for example, a software-estimating package. If the two estimating systems produce approximately the same estimate, the reliance on that estimate is increased. On the other hand, if there is a significant variance between the estimates using the two methods, then the tester needs to pursue additional investigation.

Sources of software estimating models include:

- Organization-developed estimating models
- Estimating models included in system development methodologies
- Software packages for developing software estimates
- Function points in estimating software costs

Calculating the Project Status Using a Point System

The suggested project status test is based on a simple point-accumulation system. The points can then be compared to the project management or accounting system progress report. If the results of the two progress measurement systems differ, testers can challenge the validity of the results produced by the project management and/or accounting system.

The point system provides an objective, accurate, efficient means of collecting and reporting performance data in an engineering field that often lacks visibility. The method uses data based on deliverable software items and collected as a normal part of the development process. The results are easily interpreted and can be presented in a number of formats and sub-divisions. The scheme is flexible and can be modified to meet the needs of projects, both large and small.

Overview of the Point Accumulation Tracking System

The increasing complexity of software systems, combined with the requirements for structured and modular designs, has increased significantly the number of software elements developed and delivered on recent simulator programs. The increased number of elements and the traditionally "soft" milestones used to measure progress have made monitoring software development and predicting future progress time-consuming, subjective, and often unreliable.

A tracking system that uses an earned point scheme has been successfully used to monitor software development on several large tests. Points are assigned for each step in the software development cycle on a per-element basis. The steps are "hard" milestones in which a generated product is accepted by program management. As the products are accepted, the associated points are earned. The ratio of earned points to total possible points is compiled on an element, functional area, or total software system basis to determine progress achieved. A program that generates reports, usually resident on the simulator computational system, tabulates the data in a variety of management reports.

The system as implemented is flexible, highly automated, and closely coupled to configuration management systems and software quality assurance procedures to ensure the validity of data. Simple calculations or comparisons of the accumulated point values provide an accurate measure of progress, deviation from schedule, and prediction of future progress.

Typical Methods of Measuring Performance

Performance in software development is measured typically either by estimating the percentage of a task completed or by counting the number of predetermined milestones that have been reached. In the estimate of percent completed method, the person performing the work estimates the percent of the work that has been accomplished in reaching a milestone or completing a task. The percent completed method has several faults. The major fault is that the measurement is subjective. The manager is asking a person with a vested interest in completing the task as early as possible to make an educated guess as to how nearly complete it is. Most people tend to be optimistic in their ability to complete a task—particularly if their manager subtly encourages optimism. The old bromide of a task being 95 percent complete for months is all too true.

A potential shortcoming of this method when used with tasks rather than milestones is that the definition of completion is not always stated. Therefore, the person making the estimate may have one perception of what the task includes, whereas the manager may have another. Hence, when the programmer states the task is 100 percent complete—written, tested, and documented—the manager may have an unpleasant surprise when he or she asks to see the installation guide. Therefore, because the end of the task may not be clearly defined, the estimates of completion may be quite inaccurate.

Because the estimates are subjective, the interpretation of the results may also be subjective. In trying to ascertain the degree of completeness of a job, a manager may ask who made the estimate and then apply a "correction factor" to the estimate for that person to get a number he feels comfortable with.

The second method, the milestone method, attempts to alleviate these problems by defining specific milestones that must be met and measuring performance by summing the number of milestones that have been met. This method is much more objective, tends to describe the overall task more fully, and, as a result, is easier to interpret. The shortcomings of this method are more in the area of resolution of the measurement versus the efficiency of collecting, collating, and presenting the results in a meaningful way.

To get the resolution of measurement fine enough to show incremental progress on a periodic basis, numerous milestones need to be defined. However, the large number of milestones makes it more difficult to collect and present the data in a timely and meaningful way. A common method is to present the data on bar graphs, but on a large project with thousands of milestones, the upkeep of bar graphs can be a slow, expensive effort.

Another potential problem is that the milestone may not accurately reflect the real task. If care is not taken to define the milestone, the milestone may not be based on deliverable items, but on something that appears to show progress, such as lines of code generated. Also, if the milestones are not carefully chosen, it may be difficult to determine if the milestone has been reached.

These performance measurement tools and techniques emphasize functions performed early in the life of a project. Less information is available on the ongoing management function of control. Control can be thought of as a three-step process: An attribute or characteristic of interest is measured, the measured value is compared with an expected or baseline value, and an appropriate action is taken if an unacceptable deviation exists. Any number of items of interest during software development may be controlled in this manner. Development time, development costs, computer memory usage, and computer time are some of the more common items.

A performance measurement scheme should meet several criteria. First and most important, the scheme should be objective. The person claiming performance should not be required to estimate degree of completion. Likewise, the person monitoring performance should know exactly what a performance measurement represents. Ideally, the state of development should be sufficiently visible and the measurement means sufficiently clear to enable any project member to make the actual measurement.

Second, the scheme should measure performance in accomplishing the real task (i.e., the development of deliverable software). Further, the resolution of the measuring scheme should be sufficiently fine to measure incremental progress on a weekly or monthly basis, and the measurement should be timely in that it measures the current state of development. Providing accurate, current performance information on a periodic basis can be a positive motivating factor for a programming staff.

Finally, the scheme must be efficient. It should require minimal resources to collect, collate, and report performance data and should require minimum time to interpret the results. Systems that require constant inputs from the programming staff, updates by clerical personnel, or integration of large amounts of data by management should not be used.

Using the Point System

The point system is really an extension to the milestone system that lends itself to automation. In its simplest form, it is assumed that each software module goes through a similar development process and that the process comprises clearly identifiable milestones. For example, assume ten modules will be developed and four milestones will define the development process. The milestones may represent a reviewed and accepted design, a completed code walkthrough, verified test results, and a released module.

In the simple case, each milestone for each software item is worth 1 point. In the case of the system with ten modules, 40 points can be earned. As part of each design review, code walkthrough, test verification, or release audit, the milestone is achieved and the corresponding point earned. By including the milestones achieved (points earned) and creating a few simple generators, you can get an objective, accurate, and timely measure of performance. Figure 7-7 shows what a simple status report might look like.

This simplified scheme works well for a homogeneous set of modules, where all modules are of the same complexity and each of the milestones represents an approximately equal amount of work. Through an introduction of weighting factors, you can easily handle modules of varying complexity or milestones representing unequal effort to complete.

Before this and other extensions are discussed, however, a brief description of implementation is in order. The heart of the system is a computer data file and a few simple report generators. The data file is simply a collection of records, one for each item that is to be tracked, that contains fields to indicate whether a particular milestone has been met. Usually, it is advantageous to include the following fields: item description, analyst responsible, work package identification, as well as various file identification fields. Often such a file will serve multiple uses, particularly if a few additional fields are added. Typical uses include family tree definition, specification cross-references, configuration control lists, and documentation cross-references.

Maintaining or updating the file can be as straightforward as modifying records with a line editor or as complex as building a special-purpose interactive update program. Some means of limited access should be used to restrict unauthorized modification of the file, particularly if some of the other uses of the file are sensitive to change.

Once the file is updated to include an entry of the module under development, the milestone status fields are updated as the milestones are met. In some cases this may be a manual process; once an event has occurred and the milestone achieved, a program librarian or other authorized person updates the status file. In other instances, in a more sophisticated system, a computer program could determine that a milestone event has occurred and automatically update the milestone status.

SOFTWARE STATUS REPORT					
	DESIGN	CODE	TEST	RELEASE	POINTS EARNED
Module A	1	1			2
Module B	1				1
Module C	1				1
Module D	1	1	1		3
Module E	1	1			2
Module F	1				1
Module G	1	1			2
Module H	1	1	1	1	4
Module I	1				1
Module J	1	1			2
TOTALS	10	6	2	1	19
PERCENT COMPLETE = 19/40 = 48%					

Figure 7-7   Simple status report.

After the file has been built, programs to generate reports are written to print the status. For smaller projects, a program that simply prints each record, sums the earned and defined points, and calculates the percent points earned may be sufficient. Larger projects may need several reports for different subsystems or summary reports that emphasize change.

Extensions

A number of extensions can be added to the scheme as described so far. The first is to add a method of weighting modules and/or milestones. While weighting all modules equally on a large program where many (over 1,000) modules exist appears to give good results, smaller programs with few modules may need to weight the modules to give a sufficiently accurate performance measurement. Also, depending on the level of visibility of the measuring system and the attitude of the personnel involved, there may be a tendency to do all the "easy" modules first to show early performance.

A similar argument can be made for weighting milestones. Depending on the acceptance criteria, some milestones may involve more work than others. Therefore, achieving those milestones represents accomplishing a greater amount of work than in meeting other milestones. Further, there may be instances where a combination of module weight and milestone weight may interact. An example is a module that was previously written on another project in a different language. The amount of design work for that module may be considerably less than a module designed from scratch, but the amount of effort to code the routine might be more because an unfamiliar language may be involved.

The weighting scheme is easily implemented by assigning points to each milestone for all modules. Then, as a milestone is earned, the assigned points are added to the total earned and divided by the total defined points to compute percent completion. The number of points assigned to each milestone is in proportion to the difficulty in achieving the milestone, and, in fact, relates directly to the estimated number of hours needed to complete the milestone. When assigning points, it is recommended that points first be assigned to each of the modules and then reapportioned to the milestones.

A second extension is to add selecting and sorting options to the programs that generate the reports. Selecting options allows the user to select all entries in the file by some field, such as work package number, file name, software family tree component, or responsible analyst. Once the entries of interest are selected, the sort option allows the user to order the entries by some key. The points earned and points defined are summed from the selected entries and the percent complete calculated. Therefore, reports can be printed listing all modules and percent complete for a certain analyst, work package, or other selected criteria. It has been found valuable to allow Boolean operations on selection fields (analyst A and subsystem B) and to provide for major and minor sort fields (for example, to list modules in alphabetical order by analyst).

A third extension is to add target dates and actual completion dates to each module record. In this extension the individual milestone status fields are replaced by two dates. The first date field is a target date indicating when the milestone should be met. The target dates do not have to be used for all modules or milestones but are useful where interdependency exists between a particular module milestone and some other element in the system. These interdependencies may exist in the design stage to some extent, but they become very important during the integration phase of a project.

The actual completion date field becomes a flag identifying when the milestone is achieved. By adding up the points assigned to a milestone that have an actual date entered in the file, the percent complete can be computed.

Using the two date fields has two advantages: You can monitor schedule interdependence and a historical record exists for future analysis. By making the date fields selectable and sortable, additional reports can be generated. Assuming that an integration milestone has been identified, a list of all modules of interest can be selected by work package number, family tree identification, or individual module name. Target dates for the milestone of interest can then be entered. As the date of the integration milestone comes closer, lists of all modules of interest that have a particular due date and have not been completed can be provided to the responsible analyst or work package manager. Judicious use of these lists on a periodic basis can be used to monitor and motivate the programming staff to ensure that the milestone is met. Usually, several of these lists in various stages are active at once as key milestones are coming up. It has been found that choosing approximately one major milestone a month and starting the list several months in advance of the target date is very effective. More milestones than this tend to set up multiple or conflicting goals for the individual analysts. Also, the lists need to be started well enough in advance to allow suitable time for the work to be completed and to enable you to institute workarounds if problems arise.

It should be noted that the meeting of these interdependency dates is really separate from performance measurement. It is possible that in a given subsystem the performance may be fully adequate, say 75 percent complete, but a key integration event may have been missed. The manager must be aware of both elements. If performance is where it should be but an integration event has been missed, it may mean the manager's people are not concentrating on the right item and need to be redirected.

Rolling Baseline

A potential problem with the point system described thus far has to do with an effect known as a *rolling baseline*. The rolling baseline occurs over the life of a program as new items are continually defined and added to the status file. This has the effect of changing the baseline, which causes percent complete to vary independently of milestones earned. During periods when few new items are added to the file, the percent complete accurately reflects real performance. At other times, as new items are added as quickly as previously defined milestones are met, reported progress tends to flatten out. In some instances where more new items were added than old items completed, negative progress is reported.

This problem is overcome by freeing the baseline for a unit of work or work package and reporting progress on the unit. That is, once a package of work is defined, no new points are allocated to the package. If, for some reason, it is decided certain modules have to be split up for the sake of modularity or computing efficiency, the points are likewise split up. In the instance where the scope of work changes because of an oversight or contract change, the effort is reprogrammed and either new work packages are created or existing work packages are expanded with a corresponding increase of points.

This has the effect of measuring performance on active or open work packages only, not on the system as a whole. However, because performance is being compared to an established schedule, which is also made up of units of work, the comparison is valid and useful.

Reports

Several informative detail and summary reports can be generated from the data file. The most encompassing detail report, of course, is a listing of all elements. Such a list may be useful in creating inventory lists of software items to be delivered and might be used during physical configuration audits. Other lists may be sorted and/or selected by work package or family tree identification number. Such lists show status of specific modules within subsets of the work breakdown structure or functional items of the system. Other sorts or selections by a responsible analyst show status of a particular individual's effort. Figures 7-8 through 7-11 show sample summary reports. Collecting data from several summary runs allows rates of completion to be calculated, upon which trends or predictions of future performance can be made.

FILENAME	ID	RA	CLASS	DESCRIPTION	DESIGN	CODE	TEST	RELEASE
F.UDHEAD	DF-U150	MKM	U	PRINT HEADING FOR DELTA LISTING (CONFIG)	--/--/-- 01/27/00	--/--/-- 02/08/00	--/--/-- 03/15/00	04/15/00 04/21/00
F.UDLIST	DF-U151	MKM	U	PRINT DELTA LISTING (CONFIG)	--/--/-- 01/31/00	--/--/-- 02/10/00	--/--/-- 03/15/00	04/15/00 04/21/00
F.UDLTST	DF-U152	MKM	U	START UDELTA SUBTASKING (CONFIG)	--/--/-- 01/31/00	--/--/-- 02/15/00	--/--/--	04/15/00
F.UDMAT	DF-U153	MKM	U	CHECK BUFFERS FOR MATCH (CONFIG)	--/--/-- 01/14/00	--/--/--	--/--/--	04/15/00
F.UDMOVE	DF-U154	MKM	U	MOVE DATA INTO MEMORY (CONFIG)	--/--/-- 02/02/00	--/--/-- 03/01/00	--/--/-- 04/04/00	04/15/00 04/11/00
F.UDOPT	DF-U155	MKM	U	SET OPTIONS IN DELTA (CONFIG)	--/--/-- 02/01/00	--/--/-- 02/28/00	--/--/-- 04/14/00	04/15/00 04/11/00

Detail Interdependency Listing

Figure 7-8 Detail interdependency listing.

WORK PACKAGE	FILENAME	WEIGHT	------MILESTONES------				------MODULE STATUS------		
			DESIGN	CODE	TEST	RELE-ASE	STATUS CODE	SCORE	% COMPLETE
173F	F.LEDCPY	8	2	2	2	2	3	4	50
173F	F.LEDEL	8	2	2	2	2	3	4	50
173F	F.LEDFIL	44	11	11	11	11	1	11	25
173F	F.LEDINF	20	5	5	5	5	1	5	25
173F	F.LEDPRT	12	3	3	3	3	7	12	75
173F	F.LIBEDT	16	4	4	4	4	3	8	75
173F	F.LIBGEN	28	7	7	7	7	15	28	100
173F	F.LTACGN	16	4	4	4	4	3	8	50
173F	F.LTACID	8	2	2	2	2	15	8	100
173F	F.LTASTA	32	16	0	0	16	7	16	50
173F	F.LTCMPR	16	8	0	0	8	15	16	100
173F	F.LTCMST	56	28	14	14	0	0	0	0
173F	F.LTCVRT	12	3	0	0	3	0	0	0
173F	F.LTGNUM	12	3	3	3	3	0	0	0
173F	F.LTINIT	12	3	3	3	3	0	0	0
173F	F.LTMDID	16	4	4	4	4	0	0	0
173F	F.LTREC	32	8	8	8	8	0	0	0
173F	F.LTSSTM	48	24	6	12	6	1	24	50
173F	F.LTUCHK	8	4	1	2	1	3	5	63
173F	F.LTUCVT	12	6	2	3	1	7	11	92
173F	F.LTVALU	8	4	1	2	1	15	8	100
TOTALS:	21	424	106	106	106	106		168	40

Figure 7-9 Detail status listing.

WORK PACKAGE: 1234

	DESIGN		CODE		TEST		RELEASE		TOTAL	
TOTAL ITEMS	24		24		24		24		96	
TARGET COMPLETE	10	42%	7	29%	3	13%	0	0%	20	21%
ACTUAL COMPLETE	9	38%	5	21%	1	4%	0	0%	15	16%
LATE	1	4%	2	8%	2	8%	0	0%	5	5%
LESS THAN 1 WEEK LATE	0		1		0		0			
1-2 WEEKS LATE	1		0		2		0			
2-4 WEEKS LATE	0		1		0		0			
4-8 WEEKS LATE	0		0		0		0			
MORE THAN 8 WEEKS LATE	0		0		0		0			

Figure 7-10 Summary report.

| WORK PACKAGE | DESCRIPTION | MGR | WEIGHT | ----------MILESTONES---------- | | | | ------WP STATUS------ | |
				DESIGN	CODE	TEST	RELEASE	SCORE	% COMPLETE
173G	SCAN LIBRARY SOFTWARE	NFB	480	120	120	120	120	150	31
173H	PPG LIBRARY SOFTWARE	NFB	296	74	74	74	74	74	25
173K	EMITTER SCRIPTING: EMTR 1-50	NFB	2500	2250	250	0	0	1055	42
17A1	TD REPORTING CPPS	TJR	310	155	155	0	310	310	100
17A3	TD REPORTING SW DEVELOPMENT	TJR	1230	375	375	240	240	575	47
17A4	SCAN PROCESSOR DOCUMENTATION	TJR	1078	863	215	0	0	0	0
17A5	TIMS, DEBUG, SVL DOCUMENTATION	TJR	7420	6550	870	0	0	3465	47
17A7	SOFTWARE DEV TOOLS DOCUMENT	TJR	4818	3563	1255	0	0	3563	73
TOTALS:			18132	13950	3314	434	434	9192	51

Figure 7-11 Summary status report.

Check Procedures

Work Paper 7-5 is a quality control checklist for this step. It is designed so that Yes responses indicate good test practices and No responses warrant additional investigation. A Comments column is provided to explain No responses and to record investigation results. The N/A column should be used when the checklist item is not applicable to the test situation.

Output

The output from this step includes a test manager, a definition of the scope of testing, an organized test team, and verification that development documentation is complete. Another output from this step is a report to the project personnel on the adequacy of the test estimate and the reasonableness of the project status. Note that this step may need to be repeated periodically as the project plan changes. Testers may also want to evaluate the reasonableness of the status report multiple times during the development process.

Summary

Time spent organizing for a test project will reduce the overall test effort. The five organizing tasks described in this chapter are an important prerequisite to test planning. It is less important as to who does the tasks, and when the tasks are performed, than the fact that the tasks are performed.

WORK PAPER 7-1   Calculation of Total Weighted Documentation Criteria Score

	CRITERION	WEIGHT	EXPLANATION
1.	Originality required		
2.	Degree of generality		
3.	Span of operation		
4.	Change in scope and objective		
5.	Equipment complexity		
6.	Personnel assigned		
7.	Developmental cost		
8.	Criticality		
9.	Average response time to program change		
10.	Average response time to data input		
11.	Programming languages		
12.	Concurrent software development		

Total Weighted Criteria Score:

WORK PAPER 7-2   Testing Documentation Completeness

	COMPLETENESS CRITERION	ADEQUATE	INADEQUATE	COMMENTS
1.	Content			
2.	Audience			
3.	Redundancy			
4.	Flexibility			
5.	Size			
6.	Combining and expanding of document types			
7.	Format			
8.	Content sequence			
9.	Documenting of multiple programs or multiple files			
10.	Section titles			
11.	Flowcharts and decision tables			
12.	Forms			

WORK PAPER 7-3   Characteristics Included/Excluded from Your Organization's Software Estimating Model

Name of Model: _____

CHARACTERISTIC	INCLUDED	EXCLUDED	COMMENTS
1. The model should have well-defined scope. (It should be clear which activities associated with the software life cycle are taken into account in the model and which are excluded. It should also be clear which resources—manpower, computer time, and elapsed time—are being estimated, and whether costs of support software are included.)			
2. The model should be widely applicable. (It should be possible to tailor a model to fit individual organizations, and types of software development.)			
3. The model should be easy to use. (Input requirements should be kept to a minimum, and output should be provided in an immediately useful format.)			
4. The model should be able to use actual project data as it becomes available. (Initial project cost estimates are likely to be based on inadequate information. As a project proceeds, more accurate data becomes available for cost estimating. It is essential that any estimating model be capable of using actual data gathered at any stage in the project life to update the model and provide refined estimates, probably with a lower likely range of values than achieved initially. Estimating is based on a probabilistic model. This means that an estimate is a number in the likely range of the quantity being estimated, and confidence in the estimate depends on the likely range of the quantity being estimated. The better the information we have on which to base an estimate, the smaller the likely range and the greater the confidence.)			
5. The model should allow for the use of historic data in the calibration for a particular organization and type of software.			
6. The model should have been checked against a reasonable number of historic projects.			

(continues)

WORK PAPER 7-3 *(continued)*

Name of Model: _____

CHARACTERISTIC	INCLUDED	EXCLUDED	COMMENTS
7. The model should only require inputs based on properties of the project which are well defined and can be established with a reasonable degree of certainty at the time the estimate is required.			
8. The model should favor inputs based on objective rather than subjective criteria.			
9. The model should not be oversensitive to subjective input criteria.			
10. The model should be sensitive to all the parameters of a project which have been established as having a market effect on the cost, and should not require input of parameters which do not have a marked effect on cost.			
11. The model should include estimates of how and when the resource will be needed. (This is particularly important if the estimates are to be used for resource allocation, but also important if the results are given in financial terms since inflation needs to be taken into account.)			
12. The model should produce a range of likely values for the quantity being estimated. (It is important to realize that an estimate cannot provide a precise prediction of the future. It must, of course, predict sufficiently closely to be useful, and to do this it should ideally be able to place bounds on either side of the estimate within a stated probability that the actual figures will lie within the stated bounds.)			
13. The model should include possibilities for sensitivity analysis, so that the response of the estimates to variation of selected input parameters can be seen.			
14. The model should include some estimate of the risk of failure to complete within the estimated time or cost.			
TOTAL CHARACTERISTICS INCLUDED			

WORK PAPER 7-4   Factors that Influence Software Cost Estimate

FACTOR	INCLUDED	EXCLUDED	COMMENTS
Project-Specific Factors			
1. Size of the software			
2. Percentage of the design and/or code that is new			
3. Complexity of the software system			
4. Difficulty of design and coding			
5. Quality			
6. Programming language			
7. Security classification level			
8. Target machine			
9. Utilization of the target hardware			
10. Requirement volatility			
Organization-Dependent Factors			
1. Project schedule			
2. Personnel			
• Technical competence			
• Nontechnical manpower			
3. Development environment			
• Development machine			
• Availability of associated software and hardware			
• Software tools and techniques to be used during design and development			
4. Resources not directly attributable to technical aspects of the project			
5. Computing resources			
6. Labor rates			
7. Inflation			

WORK PAPER 7-5 Organizing for Testing Quality Control Checklist

	YES	NO	N/A	COMMENTS
1. Has the test team manager been appointed?				
2. Has the test team manager's role been defined?				
3. Is the scope of testing consistent with the competency of the test manager?				
4. Is the test team competent?				
5. Are there standards for system documentation?				
6. Are the members of the test team in total knowledgeable of the intent and content of those standards?				
7. Are the standards customizable for systems of various sizes, so that small projects may not need as extensive documentation as large projects?				
8. Are the testers provided a complete copy of system documentation current to the point where the tests occur?				
9. Have the testers measured the documentation needs for the project based on the twelve criteria included in this chapter?				
10. Have the testers determined what documents must be produced?				
11. Do the project personnel agree with the testers' assessment as to what documents are needed?				
12. Have the testers determined the completeness of individual documents using the 13 criteria outlined in Task 3?				
13. Have the testers used the inspection process to determine the completeness of system documentation?				
14. Have the testers determined the currentness of the project documentation at the point of test?				
15. Have the testers prepared a report that outlines documentation deficiency?				
16. Do the testers ensure that the documentations deficiency outlined in their report is acted upon?				
17. Does project management support the concept of having the test team assess the development estimate and status?				

WORK PAPER 7-5 *(continued)*

		YES	NO	N/A	COMMENTS
18.	If so, is the test team knowledgeable in the estimation process?				
19.	If so, is the test team knowledgeable in the method that will be used to report project status?				
20.	Does the test team understand how the software estimate was calculated?				
21.	Has the test team performed a reasonable test to determine the validity of the estimate?				
22.	If the test team disagrees with the validity of the estimate, will a reasonable process be followed to resolve that difference?				
23.	Does the project team have a reasonable status reporting system?				
24.	Have the testers determined that the project status system will be utilized on a regular basis?				
25.	Is there a process to follow if the status reporting system indicates that the project is ahead or behind estimates?				
26.	Have the test team taken into account the influencing factors in evaluating the estimate (e.g., size of the software and so forth)?				
27.	Will the team receive copies of the status reports?				
28.	Is there a process in the test plan to act upon the status reports when received?				
29.	Does the test team have a knowledge of how projects are planned and how the content of a project is planned?				
30.	Does the test team have an understanding of the project estimating process used to estimate this project?				
31.	Does the project team have an understanding of the developmental process that will be used to build the software specified in this project?				
32.	Is the project plan complete?				
33.	Is the project estimate fully documented?				
34.	Is the developmental process documented?				
35.	Is the estimating method used for this project reasonable for the project characteristics?				

(continues)

WORK PAPER 7-5 *(continued)*

	YES	NO	N/A	COMMENTS
36. Is the estimate reasonable to complete the project as specified in the plan?				
37. Has the project been completed using the development process?				
38. Does the project team have a method for determining and reporting project status?				
39. Is that project status method used?				
40. Do the testers agree that the project status as reported is representative of the actual status?				

CHAPTER 8

Step 2: Developing the Test Plan

The scope of the effort to determine whether software is ready to be placed into production should be defined in a test plan. To expend the resources for testing without a plan will almost certainly lead to waste and the inability to evaluate the status of corrections prior to installation. The test planning effort should follow the normal test planning process, although the content will vary because it will involve not only in-house developed software but also vendor-developed software and software embedded into computer chips.

Overview

The test plan describes how testing will be accomplished. Its creation is essential to effective testing and should take about one-third of the total testing effort. If you develop the plan carefully, test execution, analysis, and reporting will flow smoothly.

Consider the test plan as an evolving document. As the developmental effort changes in scope, the test plan must change accordingly. It is important to keep the test plan current and to follow it, for it is the execution of the test plan that management must rely on to ensure that testing is effective; and it is from this plan that testers will ascertain the status of the test effort and base opinions on its results.

This chapter contains a standard that defines what to include in the test plan. The procedures described here are amplified with work papers and checklists detailing how to develop the planning material. The organizing test described in Chapter 7 will assist in developing the test plan. Chapters 9 through 13 discuss executing the test plan and summarizing and reporting the results.

Objective

The objective of a test plan is to describe all testing that is to be accomplished, together with the resources and schedule necessary for completion. The test plan should provide background information on the software being tested, test objectives and risks, and specific tests to be performed. Properly constructed, the test plan is a contract between the testers and the project team/users. Thus, status reports and final reports will be based on that contract.

Concerns

The concerns testers face in ensuring that the test plan will be complete include the following:

- **Not enough training.** The majority of IT personnel have not been formally trained in testing, and only about half of full-time independent testing personnel have been trained in testing techniques. This causes a great deal of misunderstanding and misapplication of testing techniques.

- **Us-versus-them mentality.** This common problem arises when developers and testers are on opposite sides of the testing issue. Often, the political infighting takes up energy, sidetracks the project, and negatively impacts relationships.

- **Lack of testing tools.** IT management may consider testing tools to be a luxury. Manual testing can be an overwhelming task. Although more than just tools are needed, trying to test effectively without tools is like trying to dig a trench with a spoon.

- **Lack of management understanding/support of testing.** If support for testing does not come from the top, staff will not take the job seriously and testers' morale will suffer. Management support goes beyond financial provisions; management must also make the tough calls to deliver the software on time with defects or take a little longer and do the job right.

- **Lack of customer and user involvement.** Users and customers may be shut out of the testing process, or perhaps they don't want to be involved. Users and customers play one of the most critical roles in testing: making sure the software works from a business perspective.

- **Not enough time for testing.** This is common complaint. The challenge is to prioritize the plan to test the right things in the given time.

- **Over-reliance on independent testers.** Sometimes called the "throw it over the wall" syndrome. Developers know that independent testers will check their work, so they focus on coding and let the testers do the testing. Unfortunately, this results in higher defect levels and longer testing times.

- **Rapid change.** In some technologies, especially rapid application development (RAD), the software is created and/or modified faster than the testers can test it. This highlights the need for automation, but also for version and release management.

- **Testers are in a lose-lose situation.** On the one hand, if the testers report too many defects, they are blamed for delaying the project. Conversely, if the testers do not find the critical defects, they are blamed for poor quality.

- **Having to say no.** The single toughest dilemma for testers is to have to say, "No, the software is not ready for production." Nobody on the project likes to hear that, and frequently, testers succumb to the pressures of schedule and cost.

Workbench

The workbench in Figure 8-1 shows the six tasks required to complete the test plan.

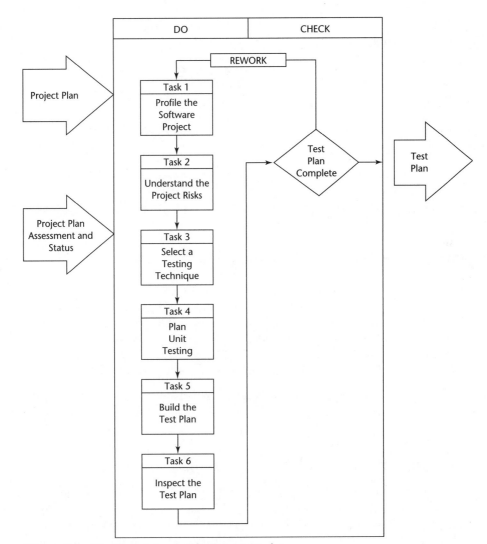

Figure 8-1 Workbench for developing a test plan.

Input

Accurate and complete inputs are critical for developing an effective test plan. The following two inputs are used in developing the test plan:

- **Project plan.** This plan should address the totality of activities required to implement the project and control that implementation. The plan should also include testing.

- **Project plan assessment and status report.** This report (developed from Step 1 of the seven-step process) evaluates the completeness and reasonableness of the project plan. It also indicates the status of the plan as well as the method for reporting status throughout the development effort.

Do Procedures

The following six tasks should be completed during the execution of this step:

1. Profile the software project.
2. Understand the software project's risks.
3. Select a testing technique.
4. Plan unit testing and analysis.
5. Build the test plan.
6. Inspect the test plan.

Task 1: Profile the Software Project

Effective test planning can occur only when those involved understand the attributes of the software project being tested. Testers need more information than is normally contained in a software development plan. Also, because testers should begin the testing process early in the developmental process, the project plan may not be complete when planning begins.

This task can be divided into the following two subtasks:

1. Conduct a walkthrough of the customer/user areas.
2. Develop a profile of the software project.

Conducting a Walkthrough of the Customer/User Area

Many, including this author, believe that testers work for the customers/users of the project, particularly if the scope of testing is greater than simply testing against specifications. And because testers represent the customer/users, they should have access to the users of the system.

A walkthrough of the customer/user area is designed for two purposes: to give an overview of the totality of activities users perform, and to gain an appreciation of the how the software will be used. For example, if your organization is building a software system to calculate employee tax deductions, testers should understand the totality of payroll responsibility so that they can put the tax deductions in the proper perspective of the overall payroll responsibilities.

Testers can gain an understanding of user responsibilities in two ways. The first is an orientation to the user area. This orientation should focus on user responsibilities before data is entered into the software project and the types of processing or uses of software deliverables during and at the conclusion of the software development process. Second, they need to follow the major business transactions as they move through the user area. If possible, it is helpful for testers to sit and observe for several hours activity in the user areas. By doing so, testers can gain an insight into busy and slack times in the user area, problems that users have in processing business transactions, and the frequency of transaction processing events.

Developing a Profile of the Software Project

The primary objective of understanding the business responsibilities of the user(s) is to develop a profile for the software project. Some of the needed profile information can be collected by the developmental project team, some can be collected by testers conducting a walkthrough of the user area, and other profile information can be gathered directly from the user or other stakeholders in the software project.

The following is the profile information that is helpful in preparing for test planning:

- **Project objectives.** The test team should understand the high-level project objectives. Without this information, team members may make problematic test decisions. For example, if the user wants a particular screen to be easy to use but testers are not aware of that objective, they could conduct tests on the screen but never look at the "easy-to-use" attribute.

- **Development process.** The type of development process for implementing software can have a significant impact on the test plan. For example, the process could be developed in-house or outsourced, and it can be waterfall, spiral, or agile.

    An important component of the development process is the maturity of that process. Testers can expect much higher defect rates at lower levels of process maturity than at higher levels.

- **Customer/users.** Testers need to identify the software's customers and users. For example, in an insurance company, the customer might be the organizational function responsible for writing property damage, whereas the users are the independent agents who write that type of insurance. If testers know the needs and competencies of users/customers, they can develop tests to assess whether the software performs appropriately.

- **Project deliverables.** Just as it is important to know the deliverables to be produced by the test team, the testers need to know the deliverables produced by the project, including both interim and final deliverables. For example, in a payroll system, an interim deliverable may be the calculation of withholding tax, whereas a final deliverable would be a paycheck. Just as objectives help focus the tester on the real needs of the software system, the deliverables focus the tester on what the system is attempting to accomplish.

■ **Cost/schedule.** Resources for testing should be included in a project's budget and schedule. In the preceding walkthrough step, there were tasks for the tester to validate the project costs and schedule through status reports. For the profile, both the costs and the schedule must be defined in much more detail. The testers need to know checkpoints, and they need to know how resources will be allocated.

■ **Project constraints.** Every software project should have a list of constraints, or conditions that will limit the type of software system produced. For example, a constraint in the payroll system may be the implementation of a new tax withholding table. Other constraints include expected turnaround time, volumes of transactions to be processed in a specific time period, skill sets of individuals entering data, relationships with other organizations, and the number of staff assigned to the project. These constraints can affect the extensiveness of testing, as well as conditions that need to be evaluated such as the probability of implementing a new tax withholding table on January 1 with existing developmental staff.

■ **Developmental staff competency.** The testers need to know the competency of the developmental staff. For example, with a relatively new and inexperienced staff, the testers might expect a much higher defect rate than with a very experienced staff.

■ **Legal/industry issues.** Software projects need to comply with governmental laws and industry standards and guidelines. For example, when building patient systems in hospitals, developers should be aware of laws such as HIPPA (the Health Insurance Portability and Accountability Act of 1996), as well as guidelines issued by leading hospital associations.

■ **Implementation technology.** Systems developed using proven technologies tend to have fewer defect rates than systems built using cutting-edge technology. For example, systems built around wireless technology may have to pioneer the use and control of that technology. On the other hand, building batch systems has been perfected over years and testers should have confidence that batch systems developed today will have minimal problems in development.

■ **Databases built/used.** Testers need to know the types of databases that will be used by the software system. These databases can be built specifically for that system or they can be existing databases. In establishing a software-testing environment, the testers will have to use controlled versions of databases or create equivalent databases for test purposes.

■ **Interfaces to other systems.** The more systems interfaced by the system being tested, the greater the test effort. Testers must ensure that proper coordination exists among all the systems affected by the software being developed. Testers should develop an inventory of systems directly interfaced as well as systems that will use the data but may not be directly interfaced. For example, if the system being tested creates a database that is used by many individuals on their own PCs, there may be issues with accounting cut-offs, which, if not controlled, would enable users to produce accounting information different than that produced by the software system that created the database.

- **Project statistics.** Testers should attempt to gather as many statistics about the software system being developed as practical. For example, knowing the number of transactions, the periods in which those transactions exist, the number of users on the system, as well as any historical data on the application (such as problems encountered, downtime occurring, customer complaints, and so forth) will help testers develop appropriate test data.

Task 2: Understand the Project Risks

The test factors describe the broad objectives of testing. These are the risks/concerns that testers need to evaluate to ensure the objectives identified by that factor have been achieved. The following discussion (and Figure 8-2) delineates the type of system characteristics that testers should evaluate to determine whether test factors have been met. (Note: Testers should customize these factors for their specific system.)

- **Reliability**
  - The level of accuracy and completeness expected in the operational environment is established.
  - Data integrity controls are implemented in accordance with the design.
  - Manual, regression, and functional tests are performed to ensure the data integrity controls work.
  - The completeness of the system installation is verified.
  - The accuracy requirements are maintained as the applications are updated.
- **Authorization**
  - The rules governing the authorization of transactions are defined.
  - The application is designed to identify and enforce the authorization rules.
  - The application implements the authorization rules.
  - Unauthorized data changes are prohibited during the installation process.
  - The method and rules for authorization are preserved during maintenance.
- **File integrity**
  - Requirements for file integrity are defined.
  - The design provides for the controls to ensure the integrity of the file.
  - The specified file integrity controls are implemented.
  - The file integrity functions are tested to ensure they perform properly.
  - The integrity of the files is preserved during the maintenance phase.

- **Audit trail**
  - The requirements to reconstruct processing are defined.
  - The audit trail requirements are incorporated into the system.
  - The audit trail functions are tested to ensure the appropriate data is saved.
  - The audit trail of installation events is recorded.
  - The audit trail requirements are updated during systems maintenance.
- **Continuity-of-processing**
  - The impact of each system failure is defined.
  - The contingency plan and procedures have been written.
  - Recovery testing verifies that the contingency plan functions properly.
  - The integrity of the previous systems is ensured until the integrity of the new system is verified.
  - The contingency plan is updated and tested as system requirements change.
- **Service level**
  - The desired service level for all aspects of the system is defined.
  - The method to achieve the predefined service levels is incorporated into the system design.
  - The programs and manual systems are designed to achieve the specified service level.
  - Stress testing is conducted to ensure that the system can achieve the desired service level when both normal and above normal volumes of data are processed.
  - A fail-safe plan is used during installation to ensure service is not disrupted.
  - The predefined service level is preserved as the system is maintained.
- **Access control**
  - Access to the system is defined.
  - The procedures to enforce the access rules are designed.
  - The defined security procedures are implemented.
  - Compliance tests are utilized to ensure that the security procedures function in a production environment.
  - Access to the computer resources is controlled during installation.
  - The procedures controlling access are preserved as the system is updated.
- **Methodology**
  - The system requirements are defined and documented in compliance with the development methodology.
  - The system design is executed in accordance with the design methodology.

- The programs are constructed and documented in compliance with the programming methodology.
- Testing is performed in compliance with the test methodology.
- The integration of the application system in a production environment complies with the installation methodology.
- System maintenance is performed in compliance with the maintenance methodology.

- **Correctness**
  - The user has fully defined the functional specifications.
  - The developed design conforms to the user requirements.
  - The developed program conforms to the system design specifications.
  - Functional testing ensures that the requirements are properly implemented.
  - The proper programs and data are placed into production.
  - The user-defined requirement changes are properly implemented in the operational system.

- **Ease-of-use**
  - The usability specifications for the application system are defined.
  - The system design attempts to optimize the usability of the implemented requirements.
  - The program optimizes ease of use by conforming to the design.
  - The relationship between the manual and automated system is tested to ensure the application is easy to use.
  - The usability instructions are properly prepared and disseminated to the appropriate individuals.
  - As the system is maintained, its ease of use is preserved.

- **Maintainable**
  - The desired level of maintainability is specified.
  - The design is developed to achieve the desired level of maintainability.
  - The program is coded and designed to achieve the desired level of maintainability.
  - The system is inspected to ensure that it is maintainable.
  - The system documentation is complete.
  - Maintainability is preserved as the system is updated.

- **Portable**
  - The portability in moving the system among hardware or software components is determined.

- The design is prepared to achieve the desired level of portability.
- The program is designed and implemented to conform to the portability design.
- The system is subjected to a disaster test to ensure that it is portable.
- The documentation is complete to facilitate portability.
- Portability is preserved as the system is maintained.

- **Coupling**
  - The interface between the system being developed and related systems is defined.
  - The design takes into account the interface requirements.
  - The program conforms to the interface design specifications.
  - Functional and regression testing are performed to ensure that the interface between systems functions properly.
  - The interface between systems is coordinated prior to the new system being placed into production.
  - The interface between systems is preserved during the systems maintenance process.

- **Performance**
  - The performance criteria are established.
  - The design specifications ensure that the desired level of performance is achieved.
  - The program is designed and implemented to achieve the performance criteria.
  - The system is compliance tested to ensure that the desired performance levels are achieved.
  - System performance is monitored during the installation phase.
  - The desired level of performance is preserved during system maintenance.

- **Ease-of-operation**
  - The operational needs are incorporated into the system design.
  - The operational procedures are tested to ensure they achieve the desired level of operational usability.
  - The operating procedures are implemented during the installation phase.
  - Changes to the operational system are updated in the operating procedures.

The test team should investigate the system characteristics to evaluate the potential magnitude of the risk, as follows:

1. **Define what meeting project objectives means.** These are the objectives to be accomplished by the project team.

TEST FACTOR	REQUIREMENTS	DESIGN	PROGRAM	TEST	OPERATION	MAINTENANCE
Reliability	Tolerances established	Data integrity controls designed	Data integrity controls implemented	Manual, regression, and functional testing	Accuracy and completeness of installation verified	Update accuracy requirements
Authorization	Authorization rules defined	Authorization rules designed	Authorization rules implemented	Compliance testing	Data changes during installation prohibited	Preserve authorization rules
File Integrity	File integrity requirements defined	File integrity controls designed	File integrity controls implemented	Functional testing	Integrity of production files verified	Preserve file integrity
Audit Trail	Reconstruction requirements defined	Audit trail designed	Implement audit trail	Functional testing	Installation audit trail recorded	Update audit trail
Continuity of Processing	Impact of failure defined	Contingency plan designed	Write contingency plan and procedures	Recovery testing	Integrity of previous testing ensured	Update contingency plan
Service Level	Desired service level defined	Method to achieve service level designed	Design system to achieve service level	Stress testing	Fail-safe installation plan implemented	Preserve service level
Access Control	Access defined	Access procedure designed	Implement security procedures	Compliance testing	Access during integration controlled	Preserve security
Methodology	Requirements comply with methodology	Design complies with methodology	Programs comply with methodology	Compliance testing	Integration complies with methodology	Maintenance complies with methodology

(continues)

Figure 8.2 Testing concerns matrix.

TEST FACTOR	REQUIREMENTS	DESIGN	PROGRAM	TEST	OPERATION	MAINTENANCE
Correctness	Functional specifications designed	Design conforms to requirements	Programs conform to design	Functional testing	Proper programs and data placed into production	Update requirements
Ease of use	Usability specifications determined	Design facilitates use	Programs conform to design	Manual support testing	Usability instructions disseminated	Preserve ease of use
Maintainable	Maintenance specifications determined	Design is maintainable	Programs are maintainable	Inspection	Documentation completed	Preserve maintainability
Portable	Portability needs determined	Design is portable	Programs conform to design	Disaster testing	Documentation completed	Preserve portability
Coupling	Systems interface defined	Interface design complete	Programs conform to design	Functional and regression testing	Interface coordinated	Ensure proper interface
Performance	Performance criteria established	Design achieves criteria	Programs achieve criteria	Compliance testing	Integration performance monitored	Preserve level of performance
Ease of operation	Operational needs defined	Communicate needs to operations	Develop operating procedures	Operations testing	Operating procedures implemented	Update operating procedures

Figure 8.2 (continued)

2. **Understand the core business areas and processes.** All information systems are not created equal. Systems that support mission-critical business processes are clearly more important than systems that support mission-support functions (usually administrative), although these, too, are necessary functions. A focus on core business areas and processes is essential to the task of assessing the impact of the problem on the enterprise and for establishing priorities.

3. **Assess the severity of potential failures.** This step must be performed for each core business area and its associated processes.

4. **Identify the system components:**
   - Links to core business areas or processes
   - Platforms, languages, and database management systems
   - Operating system software and utilities
   - Telecommunications
   - Internal and external interfaces
   - Owners
   - Availability and adequacy of source code and associated documentation

5. **Identify, prioritize, and estimate the test resources required.** Achieving test objectives requires significant investment in two vital resources: money and people. Accordingly, the organization has to make informed choices about priorities by assessing the costs, benefits, and risks of competing projects. In some instances, it may be necessary to defer or cancel new system development efforts and reprogram the freed resources to achieve and test a project.

6. **Develop validation strategies and testing plans for all converted or replaced systems and their components.** The testing and validation of converted or replaced systems require a phased approach. Consider the specific objectives for the following phases:
   - **Phase 1, unit testing.** This phase focuses on functional and compliance testing of a single application or software module.
   - **Phase 2, integration testing.** This phase tests the integration of related software modules and applications.
   - **Phase 3, system testing.** This phase tests all the integrated components of a system.
   - **Phase 4, acceptance testing.** This phase tests that the system will function with live, operational data.

7. **Identify and acquire automated test tools and write test scripts.** Regardless of the strategy selected, the scope of the testing and validation effort requires careful planning and use of automated tools, including test case analyzers and test data libraries.

8. **Define requirements for the test facility.** Organizations should operate in an adequate testing environment to avoid potential contamination or interference with the operation of production systems.

9. **Address implementation schedule issues.** This step includes:
   - Selecting conversion facilities
   - Determining the time needed to put converted systems into production
   - Converting backup and archival data

10. **Address interface and data exchange issues.** The test team should consider the following issues when conducting this step:
    - Development of a model showing the internal and external dependency links among enterprise core business areas, processes, and information systems
    - Notification of all outside data exchange entities
    - Data bridges and filters
    - Contingency plans if no data is received from an external source
    - The validation process for incoming external data
    - Contingency plans for invalid data

11. **Evaluate contingency plans.** These should be realistic contingency plans, including the development and activation of manual or contract procedures to ensure the continuity of core business processes.

12. **Identify vulnerable parts of the system and processes operating outside the information resource management area.** This includes telephone and network switching equipment and building infrastructure systems. Testers should develop a separate plan for their testing.

Task 3: Select a Testing Technique

Testing techniques should be selected based on their ability to accomplish test objectives. The technique selection process begins with selecting the test factor. Once the factor has been selected, testers know in which life cycle phase the technique will be utilized.

Both structural and functional testing can be accomplished using a predetermined set of techniques. Once the technique has been selected, the test method for implementing that technique needs to be determined. The test method can be either dynamic or static. Dynamic techniques attempt to determine whether the system functions properly while the programs are being operated, and static testing looks at the system in a non-operating environment.

The following describes the generic techniques testers can use for structural and functional testing.

Structural System Testing Techniques

The objective of structural testing is to ensure that the system is structurally sound. It attempts to determine that the technology has been used properly and that when all the component parts are assembled they function as a cohesive unit. The techniques are not designed to ensure that the application system is functionally correct but rather that it is structurally sound. The following techniques are briefly described in Figure 8-3 and then individually explained:

- Stress testing
- Execution testing
- Recovery testing
- Operations testing
- Compliance testing
- Security testing

TECHNIQUE	DESCRIPTION	EXAMPLE
Stress	System performs with expected volumes	• Sufficient disk space allocated • Communication lines adequate
Execution	System achieves desired level of proficiency	• Transaction turnaround time adequate • Software/hardware use optimized
Recovery	System can be returned to an operational status after a failure	• Induce failure • Evaluate adequacy of backup data
Operations	System can be executed in a normal operational status	• Determine systems can run using documentation • JCL adequate
Compliance	System is developed in accordance with standards and procedures	• Standards followed • Documentation complete
Security	System is protected in accordance with importance to organization	• Access denied • Procedures in place

Figure 8-3   Structural testing techniques.

Stress Testing

Stress testing is designed to determine whether the system can function when subjected to larger volumes than normally would be expected. Areas stressed include input transactions, internal tables, disk space, output, communications, and computer capacity. If the application functions adequately under stress testing, testers can assume that it will function properly with normal volumes of work.

Objectives

Specific objectives of stress testing include

- Normal or above-normal volumes of transactions can be processed within the expected time frame.

- System capacity, including communication lines, has sufficient resources to meet expected turnaround times.

- Users can perform their assigned tasks and maintain the desired turnaround time.

How to Use Stress Testing

Stress testing should simulate the production environment as closely as possible. Online systems should be stress tested by having people enter transactions at a normal or above-normal pace. Batch systems can be stress tested with large input batches. Error conditions should be included in tested transactions. Transactions for use in stress testing can be obtained from one of the following three sources:

Test data generators

Test transactions created by the test group

Transactions previously processed in the production environment

In stress testing, the system should be run as it would in the production environment. Operators should use standard documentation, and the people entering transactions or working with the system should be the clerical personnel that will work with the system after it goes into production. Online systems should be tested for an extended period of time, and batch systems tested using more than one batch of transactions.

When to Use Stress Testing

Stress testing should be used when there is uncertainty regarding the volume of work the application system can handle without failing. Stress testing is most common with online applications because it is difficult to simulate heavy-volume transactions using the other testing techniques. The disadvantage of stress testing is the amount of time it takes to prepare for the test, as well as the number of resources consumed during the execution of the test. Testers should weigh these costs against the risk of not identifying volume-related failures until the application is placed into an operational mode.

Execution Testing

Execution testing is designed to determine whether the system achieves the desired level of proficiency in a production status. Execution testing can verify response and turnaround times, as well as design performance. The execution of a system can be tested in whole or in part, using the actual system or a simulated model.

Objectives

Specific objectives of execution testing include:

- Determining the performance of the system structure
- Verifying the optimum use of hardware and software
- Determining response time to online requests
- Determining transaction processing turnaround time

How to Use Execution Testing

Testers can conduct execution testing in any phase of the system development life cycle. The testing can evaluate a single aspect of the system—for example, a critical routine in the system—or the ability of the proposed structure to satisfy performance criteria. Execution testing can be performed in any of the following manners:

- Using hardware and software monitors
- Using a simulation model
- Creating a quick and dirty program(s) to evaluate the approximate performance of a completed system

The earlier the technique is used, the greater the likelihood that the completed application will meet the performance criteria.

When to Use Execution Testing

Execution testing should be used early in the development process. Although there is value in knowing that the completed application does not meet performance criteria, if that assessment is not known until the system is operational, it may be too late or too costly to make the necessary modifications. Therefore, execution testing should be used at that point in time when the results can be used to affect or change the system structure.

Recovery Testing

Recovery is the ability to restart operations after the integrity of the application has been lost. The process normally involves reverting to a point where the integrity of the system is known, and then reprocessing transactions up until the point of failure. The time required to recover operations is affected by the number of restart points, the volume of applications run on the computer center, the training and skill of the people conducting the recovery operation, and the tools available. The importance of recovery will vary from application to application.

Objectives

Recovery testing is used to ensure that operations can be continued after a disaster. Recovery testing not only verifies the recovery process, but also the effectiveness of the component parts of that process. Specific objectives of recovery testing include the following:

- Adequate backup data is preserved.
- Backup data is stored in a secure location.
- Recovery procedures are documented.
- Recovery personnel have been assigned and trained.
- Recovery tools have been developed.

How to Use Recovery Testing

Testers should conduct recovery testing in two modes. First, they should assess the procedures, methods, tools, and techniques. Then, after the system has been developed, they should introduce a failure into the system and test the ability to recover.

Evaluating the procedures and documentation is a process that primarily calls for judgment and checklists. The actual recovery test may involve off-site facilities and alternate processing locations. Normally, procedural testing is conducted by skilled systems analysts, professional testers, or management personnel. Testing the actual recovery procedures should be performed by computer operators and other clerical personnel who would, in fact, be involved had it been an actual disaster instead of a test disaster.

A simulated disaster is usually performed on one aspect of the application system. For example, the test may be designed to determine whether people using the system can continue processing and recover computer operations after computer operations cease. While several aspects of recovery need to be tested, it is better to test one segment at a time rather than induce multiple failures at a single time. When multiple failures are induced, it may be more difficult to pinpoint the cause of the problem than when only a single failure is induced.

It is preferable not to advise system participants when a disaster test will be conducted. When people are prepared, they may perform the recovery test in a manner different from the performance when it occurs at an unexpected time. Even if the participants know that recovery may be part of the test, I recommend that you don't let them know specifically when the test will occur or what type of recovery will be necessary.

When to Use Recovery Testing

Recovery testing should be performed whenever the user of the application states that the continuity of operation is essential to the proper functioning of the user area. The user should estimate the potential loss associated with inability to recover operations over various time spans—for example, the inability to recover within five minutes, one hour, eight hours, and one week. The potential loss should determine both the amount of resources to be devoted to disaster planning as well as recovery testing.

Operations Testing

After an application has been tested, it is integrated into the operating environment. At this point, the application will be executed using the normal operations staff, procedures, and documentation. Operations testing is designed to verify prior to production that the operating procedures and staff can properly execute the application.

Objectives

Specific objectives of operations testing include

- Determining the completeness of computer operator documentation
- Ensuring that the necessary support mechanisms, such as job control language, have been prepared and function properly
- Evaluating the completeness of operator training

How to Use Operations Testing

Operations testing evaluates both the process and the execution of the process. During the requirements phase, operational requirements can be evaluated to determine their reasonableness and completeness. During the design phase, the operating procedures should be designed and evaluated.

The execution of operations testing can normally be performed in conjunction with other tests. However, if operations testing is included, the operators should not be prompted or helped by outside parties. The test needs to be executed as though it were part of normal computer operations so that it adequately evaluates the system's effectiveness in an operational environment.

When to Use Operations Testing

Operations testing should occur prior to placing any application into a production status. If the application is to be tested in a production-type setting, operations testing can piggyback that process at a very minimal cost.

Compliance Testing

Compliance testing verifies that the application was developed in accordance with IT standards, procedures, and guidelines. The methodologies are used to increase the probability of success, to enable the transfer of people in and out of the project with minimal cost, and to increase the maintainability of the application system.

Objectives

Specific objectives of compliance testing include the following:

- Determining that systems development and maintenance methodologies are followed
- Ensuring compliance to departmental standards, procedures, and guidelines
- Evaluating the completeness and reasonableness of system documentation

How to Use Compliance Testing

Compliance testing requires that the prepared document/program be compared to organizational standards. The most effective method for compliance testing is the inspection process.

When to Use Compliance Testing

The type of testing conducted varies based on the phase of the development life cycle. However, it may be more important to test adherence to the process during the requirements phase than at later stages because it is difficult to correct applications when requirements are not adequately documented.

Security Testing

The level of security required depends on the risks associated with compromise or loss of information. Security testing is designed to evaluate the adequacy of protective procedures and countermeasures.

Objectives

Specific objectives of security testing include the following:

- Determining that adequate attention has been devoted to identifying security risks
- Determining that a realistic definition and enforcement of access to the system has been implemented
- Determining that sufficient expertise exists to perform adequate security testing
- Conducting reasonable tests to ensure that the implemented security measures function properly

How to Use Security Testing

Security testing is a highly specialized part of the test process. Most organizations can evaluate the reasonableness of security procedures to prevent the average perpetrator from penetrating the application. However, the highly skilled perpetrator using sophisticated techniques may use methods undetectable by novices designing security measures and/or testing those measures.

The first step is to identify the security risks and the potential loss associated with those risks. If either the loss is low or the penetration method routine, IT personnel can conduct the necessary tests. On the other hand, if either the risks are very high or the technology that might be used is sophisticated, specialized help should be acquired in conducting the security tests.

When to Use Security Testing

Security testing should be used when the information and/or assets protected by the application system are of significant value to the organization. The testing should be performed both before and after the system goes into an operational status. The extent of testing depends on the security risks, and the individual assigned to conduct the test should be selected based on the estimated sophistication that might be used to penetrate security.

Functional System Testing Techniques

Functional system testing is designed to ensure that the system requirements and specifications are achieved. The process normally involves creating test conditions to evaluate the correctness of the application. The following techniques are briefly described in Figure 8-4 and then individually explained:

Requirements testing

Regression testing

Error-handling testing

Manual-support testing

Intersystems testing

Control testing

Parallel testing

TECHNIQUE	DESCRIPTION	EXAMPLE
Requirements	System performs as specified	• Prove system requirements • Compliance to policies, regulations regulations
Regression	Verifies that anything unchanged still performs correctly	• Unchanged system segments function • Unchanged manual procedures correct
Error Handling	Errors can be prevented or detected, and then corrected	• Error introduced into test • Errors reentered
Manual support	The people-computer interaction works	• Manual procedures developed • People trained
Intersystems	Data is correctly passed from system to system	• Intersystem parameters changed • Intersystem documentation updated
Control	Controls reduce system risk to an acceptable level	• File reconciliation procedures work • Manual controls in place
Parallel	Old system and new system are run and the results compared to detect unplanned differences	• Old and new system can reconcile • Operational status of old system maintained

Figure 8-4 Functional testing techniques.

Requirements Testing

Requirements testing must verify that the system can perform correctly over a continuous period of time. The system can be tested throughout the life cycle, but it is difficult to test the reliability before the program becomes operational.

Objectives

Specific objectives of requirements testing include the following:

- User requirements are implemented.
- Correctness is maintained over extended processing periods.
- Application processing complies with the organization's policies and procedures.
- Secondary user needs have been included, such as:
  - Security officer
  - Database administrator
  - Internal auditors
  - Comptroller
- The system processes accounting information in accordance with procedures.
- Systems process information in accordance with governmental regulations.

How to Use Requirements Testing

Requirements testing is primarily performed through the creation of test conditions and functional checklists. Test conditions are generalized during the requirements phase, and become more specific as the life cycle progresses.

Functional testing is more effective when the test conditions are created directly from user requirements. When test conditions are created from the system documentation, defects in that documentation will not be detected through testing. When the test conditions are created from other than the system documentation, defects introduced into the documentation will be detected.

When to Use Requirements Testing

The process should begin in the requirements phase and continue through every phase of the life cycle. It is not a question as to whether requirements must be tested but, rather, the extent and methods used.

Regression Testing

One of the attributes that has plagued IT professionals for years is the cascading effect of making changes to an application system. One segment of the system is developed and thoroughly tested, and then a change is made to another part of the system, which has a disastrous effect on the tested portion. Regression testing retests previously tested segments to ensure that they still function properly after a change has been made to another part of the application.

Objectives

Specific objectives of regression testing include the following:

- Determining that system documentation remains current
- Determining that system test data and conditions remain current
- Determining that previously tested system functions perform properly after changes are introduced

How to Use Regression Testing

Regression testing is retesting unchanged segments of the application system. It normally involves rerunning tests that have been previously executed to ensure that the same results can be achieved. While the process is simple in that the test transactions have been prepared and the results known, unless the process is automated it can be a very time-consuming and tedious operation. It is also one in which the cost/benefit needs to be carefully evaluated or large amounts of effort can be expended with minimal payback.

When to Use Regression Testing

Regression testing should be used when there is a high risk that new changes may affect unchanged areas of the application system. In the developmental process, regression testing should occur after a predetermined number of changes are incorporated into the application system. In the maintenance phase, regression testing should be conducted if the potential loss that could occur due to affecting an unchanged portion is very high. The determination as to whether to conduct regression testing should be based on the significance of the loss that could occur as a result of improperly tested applications.

Error-Handling Testing

One of the characteristics that differentiate automated from manual systems is the predetermined error-handling feature. Manual systems can deal with problems as they occur, but automated systems must preprogram error handling. In many instances, the completeness of error handling affects the usability of the application. Error-handling testing determines the ability of the application system to properly process incorrect transactions.

Objectives

Specific objectives of error-handling testing include:

- Determining that all reasonably expected error conditions are recognizable by the application system
- Determining that the accountability for processing errors has been assigned and that the procedures provide a high probability that the error will be corrected
- Determining that reasonable control is maintained during the correction process

How to Use Error-Handling Testing

Error-handling testing requires a group of knowledgeable people to anticipate what can go wrong with the application system. Most other forms of testing involve verifying that the application system conforms to requirements. Error-handling testing uses exactly the opposite concept.

A successful method for developing error conditions is to have IT staff, users, and auditors brainstorm what might go wrong with the application. The totality of their thinking must then be organized by application function so that a logical set of test transactions can be created. Without this type of synergistic interaction, it is difficult to develop a realistic body of problems prior to production.

Error-handling testing should test the introduction of the error, the processing of the error, the control condition, and the reentry of the condition properly corrected.

When to Use Error-Handling Testing

Error testing should occur throughout the system development life cycle. At all points in the developmental process the impact from errors should be identified and appropriate action taken to reduce those errors to an acceptable level. Error-handling testing assists in the error management process of systems development and maintenance. Some organizations use auditors, quality assurance, or professional testing personnel to evaluate error processing.

Manual-Support Testing

The manual part of the system requires the same attention to testing as does the automated segment. Although the timing and testing methods may differ, the objectives of manual testing remain the same as testing the automated segment of the system.

Objectives

Specific objectives of manual-support testing include the following:

- Verifying that the manual-support procedures are documented and complete
- Determining that manual-support responsibility has been assigned
- Determining that the manual-support personnel are adequately trained
- Determining that the manual support and the automated segment are properly interfaced

How to Use Manual-Support Testing

Manual testing involves first the evaluation of the adequacy of the process, and second, the execution of the process. The process itself can be evaluated in all phases of the development life cycle. Rather than preparing and entering test transactions themselves, testers can have the actual clerical and supervisory people prepare, enter, and use the results of processing from the application system.

Manual-support testing normally involves several iterations of the process. Testing people processing requires testing the interface between people and the application system. This means entering transactions, getting the results back from that processing, and taking additional action based on the information received, until all aspects of the manual computer interface have been adequately tested.

Manual-support testing should occur without the assistance of the systems personnel. The manual-support group should operate using the training and procedures provided them by the systems personnel. However, the results should be evaluated by the systems personnel to determine if they have been adequately performed.

When to Use Manual-Support Testing

Although manual-support testing should be conducted throughout the development life cycle, extensive manual-support testing is best done during the installation phase so that clerical personnel do not become involved with the new system until immediately prior to its entry into operation. This avoids the confusion of knowing two systems and not being certain which rules to follow. During the maintenance and operation phases, manual-support testing may involve only providing people with instructions on the changes and then verifying that they understand the new procedures.

Intersystem Testing

Application systems are frequently interconnected to other application systems. The interconnection may be data coming into the system from another application, leaving for another application, or both. Frequently, multiple applications—sometimes called cycles or functions—are involved. For example, there could be a revenue cycle that interconnects all the income-producing applications, such as order entry, billing, receivables, shipping, and returned goods. Intersystem testing is designed to ensure that the interconnection between applications functions correctly.

Objectives

Specific objectives of intersystem testing include the following:

- Determining that the proper parameters and data are correctly passed between applications
- Ensuring that proper coordination and timing of functions exists between the application systems
- Determining that the documentation for the involved systems is accurate and complete

How to Use Intersystem Testing

One of the best testing tools for intersystem testing is the integrated test facility. This permits testing to occur in a production environment and thus the coupling of systems can be tested at minimal cost.

When to Use Intersystem Testing

Intersystem testing should be conducted whenever there is a change in parameters between application systems. The extent and type of testing will depend on the risk associated with those parameters being erroneous. If the integrated test facility concept is used, the intersystem parameters can be verified after the changed or new application is placed into production.

Control Testing

Approximately one-half of the total system development effort is directly attributable to controls. Controls include data validation, file integrity, audit trails, backup and recovery, documentation, and the other aspects of systems related to integrity. Control testing is designed to ensure that the mechanisms that oversee the proper functioning of an application system work.

Objectives

Specific objectives of control testing include the following:

- Accurate and complete data
- Authorized transactions
- Maintenance of an adequate audit trail of information
- Efficient, effective, and economical process
- Process meeting the needs of the user

How to Use Control Testing

The term "system of internal controls" is frequently used in accounting literature to describe the totality of the mechanisms that ensure the integrity of processing. Controls are designed to reduce risks; therefore, to test controls, the risks must be identified.

One method for testing controls is to develop a risk matrix. The matrix identifies the risks, the controls, and the segment within the application system in which the controls reside.

When to Use Control Testing

Control testing should be an integral part of system testing. Controls must be viewed as a system within a system, and tested in parallel with other systems tests. Because approximately 50 percent of the total development effort goes into controls, a proportionate part of testing should be allocated to evaluating the adequacy of controls.

Parallel Testing

In the early days of computer systems, parallel testing was one of the more popular testing techniques. However, as systems become more integrated and complex, the difficulty in conducting parallel tests increased and thus the popularity of the technique diminished. Parallel testing is used to determine that the results of the new application are consistent with the processing of the previous application or version of the application.

Objectives

Specific objectives of parallel testing include the following:

- Conducting redundant processing to ensure that the new application performs correctly
- Demonstrating consistency and inconsistency between two versions of the same application system

How to Use Parallel Testing

Parallel testing requires that the same input data be run through two versions of the same application. Parallel testing can be done with the entire application or with a segment of the application. Sometimes a particular segment, such as the day-to-day interest calculation on a savings account, is so complex and important that an effective method of testing is to run the new logic in parallel with the old logic.

If the new application changes data formats, the input data will have to be modified before it can be run through the new application. The more difficulty encountered in verifying results or preparing common input, the less attractive the parallel testing technique becomes.

When to Use Parallel Testing

Parallel testing should be used when there is uncertainty regarding the correctness of processing of the new application, and the old and new versions of the application are similar. For example, in payroll, banking, and other financial applications where the results of processing are similar, even though the methods may change significantly— for example, going from batch to online banking—parallel testing is one of the more effective methods of ensuring the integrity of the new application.

Task 4: Plan Unit Testing and Analysis

This section examines the techniques, assessment, and management of unit testing and analysis. The strategies are categorized as functional, structural, or error-oriented. Mastery of the material in this section assists the software engineer to define, conduct, and evaluate unit tests and analyses and to assess new unit testing techniques.

Unit testing and analysis are the most practiced means of verifying that a program possesses the features required by its specification. *Testing* is a dynamic approach to verification in which code is executed with test data to assess the presence (or absence) of required features. *Analysis* is a static approach to verification in which required features are detected by analyzing, but not executing, the code. Many analysis techniques, such as proof of correctness, safety analysis, and the more open-ended analysis procedures represented by code inspections and reviews, have become established technologies with their own substantial literature. These techniques are not discussed in this section.

This section focuses on unit-level verification. What constitutes a "unit" has been left imprecise; it may be as little as a single statement or as much as a set of coupled subroutines. The essential characteristic of a unit is that it can meaningfully be treated as a whole. Some of the techniques presented here require associated documentation that states the desired features of the unit. This documentation may be a comment in the source program, a specification written in a formal language, or a general statement of requirements. Unless otherwise indicated, this documentation should not be assumed to be the particular document in the software life cycle called a "software specification," "software requirements definition," or the like. Any document containing information about the unit may provide useful information for testing or analysis.

Functional Testing and Analysis

Functional testing and analysis ensure that major characteristics of the code are covered.

Functional Analysis

Functional analysis seeks to verify, without execution, that the code faithfully implements the specification. Various approaches are possible. In the proof-of-correctness approach, a formal proof is constructed to verify that a program correctly implements its intended function. In the safety-analysis approach, potentially dangerous behavior is identified and steps are taken to ensure such behavior is never manifested. Functional analysis is mentioned here for completeness, but a discussion of it is outside the scope of this section.

Functional Testing

Unit testing is functional when test data is developed from documents that specify a module's intended behavior. These documents include, but are not limited to, the actual specification and the high- and low-level design of the code to be tested. The goal is to test for each software feature of the specified behavior, including the input domains, the output domains, categories of inputs that should receive equivalent processing, and the processing functions themselves.

Testing Independent of the Specification Technique

Specifications detail the assumptions that may be made about a given software unit. They must describe the interface through which access to the unit is given, as well as the behavior once such access is given. The interface of a unit includes the features of its inputs, its outputs, and their related value spaces (called domains). The behavior of a module always includes the function(s) to be computed (its semantics), and sometimes the runtime characteristics, such as its space and time complexity.

Functional testing can be based either on the interface of a module or on the function to be completed.

- **Testing based on the interface.** Testing based on the interface of a module selects test data based on the features of the input and output domains of the module and their interrelationships.

  - **Input domain testing.** In external testing, test data is chosen to cover the extremes of the input domain. Similarly, midrange testing selects data from the interiors of domains. The motivation is inductive—it is hoped that conclusions about the entire input domain can be drawn from the behavior elicited by some of its representative members. For structured input domains, combinations of extreme points for each component are chosen. This procedure can generate a large quantity of data, although considerations of the inherent relationships among components can ameliorate this problem somewhat.

  - **Equivalence partitioning.** Specifications frequently partition the set of all possible inputs into classes that receive equivalent treatment. Such partitioning is called *equivalence partitioning*. A result of equivalence partitioning is the identification of a finite set of functions and their associated input and output domains. Input constraints and error conditions can also result from this partitioning. Once these partitions have been developed, both external and midrange testing are applicable to the resulting input domains.

- **Syntax checking.** Every robust program must parse its input and handle incorrectly formatted data. Verifying this feature is called *syntax checking*. One means of accomplishing this is to execute the program using a broad spectrum of test data. By describing the data with documentation language, instances of the input language can be generated using algorithms from automata theory.

- **Testing based on the function to be computed.** Equivalence partitioning results in the identification of a finite set of functions and their associated input and output domains. Test data can be developed based on the known characteristics of these functions. Consider, for example, a function to be computed that has fixed points (that is, certain of its input values are mapped into themselves by the function). Testing the computation at these fixed points is possible, even in the absence of a complete specification. Knowledge of the function is essential in order to ensure adequate coverage of the output domains.

  - **Special-value testing.** Selecting test data on the basis of features of the function to be computed is called *special-value testing*. This procedure is particularly applicable to mathematical computations. Properties of the function to be computed can aid in selecting points that will indicate the accuracy of the computed solution.

  - **Output domain coverage.** For each function determined by equivalence partitioning there is an associated output domain. Output domain coverage is performed by selecting points that will cause the extremes of each of the output domains to be achieved. This ensures that modules have been checked for maximum and minimum output conditions and that all categories of error messages have, if possible, been produced. In general, constructing such test data requires knowledge of the function to be computed and, hence, expertise in the application area.

Testing Dependent on the Specification Technique

The specification technique employed can aid in testing. An executable specification can be used as an oracle and, in some cases, as a test generator. Structural properties of a specification can guide the testing process. If the specification falls within certain limited classes, properties of those classes can guide the selection of test data. Much work remains to be done in this area of testing.

- **Algebraic.** In algebraic specification, properties of a data abstraction are expressed by means of axioms or rewrite rules. In one testing system, the consistency of an algebraic specification with an implementation is checked by testing. Each axiom is compiled into a procedure, which is then associated with a set of test points. A driver program supplies each of these points to the procedure of its respected axiom. The procedure, in turn, indicates whether the axiom is satisfied. Structural coverage of both the implementation and the specification is computed.

- **Axiomatic.** Despite the potential for widespread use of predicate calculus as a specification language, little has been published about deriving test data from such specifications. A relationship between predicate calculus specifications and path testing has been explored.

- **State machines.** Many programs can be specified as state machines, thus providing an additional means of selecting test data. Because the equivalence problem of two finite automata is decidable, testing can be used to decide whether a program that simulates a finite automation with a bounded number of nodes is equivalent to the one specified. This result can be used to test those features of programs that can be specified by finite automata—for example, the control flow of a transaction-processing system.

- **Decision tables.** Decision tables are a concise method of representing an equivalence partitioning. The rows of a decision table specify all the conditions that the input may satisfy. The columns specify different sets of actions that may occur. Entries in the table indicate whether the actions should be performed if a condition is satisfied. Typical entries are "Yes," "No," or "Don't care." Each row of the table suggests significant test data. Cause-effect graphs provide a systematic means of translating English specifications into decision tables, from which test data can be generated.

Structural Testing and Analysis

In structural program testing and analysis, test data is developed or evaluated from the source code. The goal is to ensure that various characteristics of the program are adequately covered.

Structural Analysis

In structural analysis, programs are analyzed without being executed. The techniques resemble those used in compiler construction. The goal here is to identify fault-prone code, to discover anomalous circumstances, and to generate test data to cover specific characteristics of the program's structure.

- **Complexity measures.** As resources available for testing are always limited, it is necessary to allocate these resources efficiently. It is intuitively appealing to suggest that the more complex the code, the more thoroughly it should be tested. Evidence from large projects seems to indicate that a small percentage of the code typically contains the largest number of errors. Various complexity measures have been proposed, investigated, and analyzed in the literature.

- **Data flow analysis.** A program can be represented as a flow graph annotated with information about variable definitions, references, and indefiniteness.

From this representation, information about data flow can be deduced for use in code optimization, anomaly detection, and test data generation. Data flow anomalies are flow conditions that deserve further investigation, as they may indicate problems. Examples include: defining a variable twice with no intervening reference, referencing a variable that is undefined, and undefining a variable that has not been referenced since its last definition. Data flow analysis can also be used in test data generation, exploiting the relationship between points where variables are defined and points where they are used.

- **Symbolic execution.** A symbolic execution system accepts three inputs: a program to be interpreted, symbolic input for the program, and the path to follow. It produces two outputs: the symbolic output that describes the computation of the selected path, and the path condition for that path. The specification of the path can be either interactive or preselected. The symbolic output can be used to prove the program correct with respect to its specification, and the path condition can be used for generating test data to exercise the desired path. Structured data types cause difficulties, however, because it is sometimes impossible to deduce what component is being modified in the presence of symbolic values.

Structural Testing

Structural testing is a dynamic technique in which test data selection and evaluation are driven by the goal of covering various characteristics of the code during testing. Assessing such coverage involves the instrumentation of the code to keep track of which characteristics of the program text are actually exercised during testing. The low cost of such instrumentation has been a prime motivation for adopting this technique. More important, structural testing addresses the fact that only the program text reveals the detailed decisions of the programmer. For example, for the sake of efficiency, a programmer might choose to implement a special case that appears nowhere in the specification. The corresponding code will be tested only by chance using functional testing, whereas use of a structural coverage measure such as statement coverage should indicate the need for test data for this case. Structural coverage measures form a rough hierarchy, with higher levels being more costly to perform and analyze, but being more beneficial, as described in the list that follows:

- **Statement testing.** Statement testing requires that every statement in the program be executed. While it is obvious that achieving 100 percent statement coverage does not ensure a correct program, it is equally obvious that anything less means that there is code in the program that has never been executed!

- **Branch testing.** Achieving 100 percent statement coverage does not ensure that each branch in the program flow graph has been executed. For example, executing an if...then statement (no else) when the tested condition is true, tests only one of two branches in the flow graph. Branch testing seeks to ensure that every branch has been executed. Branch coverage can be checked by probes inserted at points in the program that represent arcs from branch points in the flow graph. This instrumentation suffices for statement coverage as well.

- **Conditional testing.** In conditional testing, each clause in every condition is forced to take on each of its possible values in combination with those of other clauses. Conditional testing thus subsumes branch testing and, therefore, inherits the same problems as branch testing. Instrumentation for conditional testing can be accomplished by breaking compound conditional statements into simple conditions and nesting the resulting if statements.

- **Expression testing.** Expression testing requires that every expression assume a variety of values during a test in such a way that no expression can be replaced by a simpler expression and still pass the test. If one assumes that every statement contains an expression and that conditional expressions form a proper subset of all the program expressions, then this form of testing properly subsumes all the previously mentioned techniques. Expression testing does require significant runtime support for the instrumentation.

- **Path testing.** In path testing, data is selected to ensure that all paths of the program have been executed. In practice, of course, such coverage is impossible to achieve, for a variety of reasons. First, any program with an indefinite loop contains an infinite number of paths, one for each iteration of the loop. Thus, no finite set of data will execute all paths. The second difficulty is the infeasible path problem: It is undecided whether an arbitrary path in an arbitrary program is executable. Attempting to generate data for such infeasible paths is futile, but it cannot be avoided. Third, it is undecided whether an arbitrary program will halt for an arbitrary input. It is therefore impossible to decide whether a path is finite for a given input.

  In response to these difficulties, several simplifying approaches have been proposed. Infinitely many paths can be partitioned into a finite set of equivalence classes based on characteristics of the loops. Boundary and interior testing require executing loops zero times, one time, and, if possible, the maximum number of times. Linear sequence code and jump criteria specify a hierarchy of successively more complex path coverage.

  Path coverage does not imply condition coverage or expression coverage because an expression may appear on multiple paths but some subexpressions may never assume more than one value. For example, in

  ```
  if a / b then S₁ else S₂
  ```

  b may be false and yet each path may still be executed.

Error-Oriented Testing and Analysis

Testing is necessitated by the potential presence of errors in the programming process. Techniques that focus on assessing the presence or absence of errors in the programming process are called error oriented. There are three broad categories of such techniques: statistical assessment, error-based testing, and fault-based testing. These are stated in order of increasing specificity of what is wrong with the program. Statistical methods attempt to estimate the failure rate of the program without reference to the number of remaining faults.

Error-based testing attempts to show the absence of certain errors in the programming process. Fault-based testing attempts to show the absence of certain faults in the code. Since errors in the programming process are reflected as faults in the code, both techniques demonstrate the absence of faults. They differ, however, in their starting point: Error-based testing begins with the programming process, identifies potential errors in that process, and then asks how those errors are reflected as faults. It then seeks to demonstrate the absence of those reflected faults. Fault-based testing begins with the code and asks what are the potential faults in it, regardless of what error in the programming process caused them.

Statistical Methods

Statistical testing employs statistical techniques to determine the operational reliability of the program. Its primary concern is how faults in the program affect its failure rate in its actual operating environment. A program is subjected to test data that statistically models the operating environment, and failure data is collected. From the data, a reliability estimate of the program's failure rate is computed. This method can be used in an incremental development environment. A statistical method for testing paths that compute algebraic functions has also been developed. A prevailing sentiment is that statistical testing is a futile activity because it is not directed toward finding errors. However, studies suggest it is a viable alternative to structural testing. Combining statistical testing with an oracle appears to represent an effective tradeoff of computer resources for human time.

Error-Based Testing

Error-based testing seeks to demonstrate that certain errors have not been committed in the programming process. Error-based testing can be driven by histories of programmer errors, measures of software complexity, knowledge of error-prone syntactic constructs, or even error guessing. Some of the more methodical techniques are described in the list that follows:

- **Fault estimation.** Fault seeding is a statistical method used to assess the number and characteristics of the faults remaining in a program. Harlan Mills originally proposed this technique, and called it error seeding. First, faults are seeded into a program. Then the program is tested and the number of faults discovered is used to estimate the number of faults yet undiscovered. A difficulty with this technique is that the faults seeded must be representative of the yet-undiscovered faults in the program. Techniques for predicting the quantity of remaining faults can also be based on a reliability model.

- **Domain testing.** The input domain of a program can be partitioned according to which inputs cause each path to be executed. These partitions are called *path domains*. Faults that cause an input to be associated with the wrong path domain are called *domain faults*. Other faults are called *computation faults*. (The terms used before attempts were made to rationalize nomenclature were "domain errors" and "computation errors.") The goal of domain testing is to discover domain faults by ensuring that the test data limits the range of undetected faults.

- **Perturbation testing.** Perturbation testing attempts to decide what constitutes a sufficient set of paths to test. Faults are modeled as a vector space, and characterization theorems describe when sufficient paths have been tested to discover both computation and domain errors. Additional paths need not be tested if they cannot reduce the dimensionality of the error space.

Fault-Based Testing

Fault-based testing aims at demonstrating that certain prescribed faults are not in the code. It functions well in the role of test data evaluation: Test data that does not succeed in discovering the prescribed faults is not considered adequate. Fault-based testing methods differ in both extent and breadth. One with local extent demonstrates that a fault has a local effect on computation; it is possible that this local effect will not produce a program failure. A method with global extent demonstrates that a fault will cause a program failure. Breadth is determined by whether the technique handles a finite or an infinite class of faults. Extent and breadth are orthogonal, as evidenced by the techniques described below.

- **Local extent, finite breadth.** Input-output pairs of data are encoded as a comment in a procedure, as a partial specification of the function to be computed by that procedure. The procedure is then executed for each of the input values and checked for the output values. The test is considered adequate only if each computational or logical expression in the procedure is determined by the test; that is, no expression can be replaced by a simpler expression and still pass the test. Simpler is defined in a way that allows only a finite number of substitutions. Thus, as the procedure is executed, each possible substitution is evaluated on the data state presented to the expression. Those that do not evaluate the same as the original expression are rejected. The system allows methods of specifying the extent to be analyzed.

- **Global extent, finite breadth.** In mutation testing, test data adequacy is judged by demonstrating that interjected faults are caught. A program with interjected faults is called a mutant, and is produced by applying a mutation operator. Such an operator changes a single expression in the program to another expression, selected from a finite class of expressions. For example, a constant might be incremented by one, decremented by one, or replaced by zero, yielding one of three mutants. Applying the mutation operators at each point in a program where they are applicable forms a finite, albeit large, set of mutants. The test data is judged adequate only if each mutant in this set is either functionally equivalent to the original program or computes different output than the original program. Inadequacy of the test data implies that certain faults can be introduced into the code and go undetected by the test data.

  Mutation testing is based on two hypotheses. The *competent-programmer hypothesis* says that a competent programmer will write code that is close to being correct; the correct program, if not the current one, can be produced by some straightforward syntactic changes to the code. The *coupling-effect hypothesis* says that test data that reveals simple faults will uncover complex faults as well.

Thus, only single mutants need be eliminated, and combinatory effects of multiple mutants need not be considered. Studies formally characterize the competent-programmer hypothesis as a function of the probability of the test set's being reliable, and show that under this characterization, the hypothesis does not hold. Empirical justification of the coupling effect has been attempted, but theoretical analysis has shown that it does not hold, even for simple programs.

- **Local extent, infinite breadth.** Rules for recognizing error-sensitive data are described for each primitive language construct. Satisfaction of a rule for a given construct during testing means that all alternate forms of that construct have been distinguished. This has an obvious advantage over mutation testing—elimination of all mutants without generating a single one! Some rules even allow for infinitely many mutants. Of course, since this method is of local extent, some of the mutants eliminated may indeed be the correct program.

- **Global extent, infinite breadth.** We can define a fault-based method based on symbolic execution that permits elimination of infinitely many faults through evidence of global failures. Symbolic faults are inserted into the code, which is then executed on real or symbolic data. Program output is then an expression in terms of the symbolic faults. It thus reflects how a fault at a given location will affect the program's output. This expression can be used to determine actual faults that could not have been substituted for the symbolic fault and remain undetected by the test.

Managerial Aspects of Unit Testing and Analysis

Administration of unit testing and analysis proceeds in two stages. First, techniques appropriate to the project must be selected, and then these techniques must be systematically applied.

Selecting Techniques

Selecting the appropriate techniques from the array of possibilities is a complex task that requires assessment of many issues, including the goal of testing, the nature of the software product, and the nature of the test environment. It is important to remember the complementary benefits of the various techniques and to select as broad a range of techniques as possible, within imposed limits. No single testing or analysis technique is sufficient. Functional testing suffers from inadequate code coverage, structural testing suffers from inadequate specification coverage, and neither technique achieves the benefits of error coverage.

- **Goals.** Different design goals impose different demands on the selection of testing techniques. Achieving correctness requires use of a great variety of techniques. A goal of reliability implies the need for statistical testing using test data representative of the anticipated user environment. It should be noted, however, that proponents of this technique still recommend judicious use of "selective" tests to avoid embarrassing or disastrous situations. Testing may also be directed toward assessing the utility of proposed software. This kind of testing requires a solid foundation in human factors. Performance of the software may also be of special concern. In this case, external testing is essential. Timing instrumentation can prove useful.

Often, several of these goals must be achieved simultaneously. One approach to testing under these circumstances is to order testing by decreasing benefit. For example, if reliability, correctness, and performance are all desired features, it is reasonable to tackle performance first, reliability second, and correctness third, since these goals require increasingly difficult-to-design tests. This approach can have the beneficial effect of identifying faulty code with less effort.

- **Nature of the product.** The nature of the software product plays an important role in the selection of appropriate techniques.

- **Nature of the testing environment.** Available resources, personnel, and project constraints must be considered in selecting testing and analysis strategies.

Control

To ensure quality in unit testing and analysis, it is necessary to control both documentation and the conduct of the test:

- **Configuration control.** Several items from unit testing and analysis should be placed under configuration management, including the test plan, test procedures, test data, and test results. The test plan specifies the goals, environment, and constraints imposed on testing. The test procedures detail the step-by-step activities to be performed during the test. Regression testing occurs when previously saved test data is used to test modified code. Its principal advantage is that it ensures previously attained functionality has not been lost during a modification. Test results are recorded and analyzed for evidence of program failures. Failure rates underlie many reliability models; high failure rates may indicate the need for redesign.

- **Conducting tests.** A test bed is an integrated system for testing software. Minimally, such systems provide the ability to define a test case, construct a test driver, execute the test case, and capture the output. Additional facilities provided by such systems typically include data flow analysis, structural coverage assessment, regression testing, test specification, and report generation.

Task 5: Build the Test Plan

The development of an effective test plan involves the following four steps:

1. Set the test objectives.
2. Develop a test matrix.
3. Define test administration.
4. Write the test plan.

Setting Test Objectives

The objectives of testing should restate the project objectives from the project plan. In fact, the test plan objectives should determine whether the project plan objectives have been achieved. If the project plan does not have clearly stated objectives, testers must develop their own. In that case, testers must have them confirmed as the project objectives by the project team. Testers can:

- Set objectives to minimize the project risks
- Brainstorm to identify project objectives
- Relate objectives to the testing policy, if established

Normally, there should be ten or fewer test objectives. Having too many objectives scatters the test team's focus.

Work Paper 8-1 is designed for documenting test objectives. To complete the Work Paper:

- Itemize the objectives so that they can be referred to by number.
- Write the objectives in a measurable statement to focus testers' attention.
- Assign a priority to the objectives, as follows:
    - *High.* The most important objectives to be accomplished during testing
    - *Average.* Objectives to be accomplished only after the high-priority test objectives have been met
    - *Low.* The least important of the test objectives
- Define the completion criteria for each objective. This should state quantitatively how the testers will determine whether the objective has been accomplished. The more specific the criteria, the easier it will be for the testers to follow through.

NOTE Establish priorities so that approximately one-third are high, one-third are average, and one-third are low.

Developing a Test Matrix

The test matrix is the key component of the test plan. On one side it lists what is to be tested; on the other, it indicates which test is to be performed, or "how" software will be tested. Between the two dimensions of the matrix are the tests applicable to the software; for example, one test may test more than one software module. The test matrix is also a test "proof." It proves that each testable function has at least one test, and that each test is designed to test a specific function.

An example of a test matrix is illustrated in Table 8-1. This shows four functions in a payroll system, with three tests to validate the functions. Because payroll is a batch system, batched test data is used with various dates, the parallel test is run when posting to the general ledger, and all changes are verified through a code inspection. The test matrix can be prepared using the work papers described in the following sections. (Note: The modules that contain the function(s) to be tested will be identified.)

Table 8-1   Test Matrix Example

SOFTWARE FUNCTION	TEST DECK TRANSACTION	PARALLEL TEST	CODE INSPECTION
FICA Calculation	X		X
Gross Pay	X		X
Tax Deduction	X		X
General Ledger Charges		X	X

The recommended test process is first to determine the test factors to be evaluated in the test process, and then to select the techniques that will be used in performing the test. Figure 8-5 is a test factor/test technique matrix that shows which techniques are most valuable for the various test factors. For example, if testers want to evaluate the system structure for reliability, the execution and recovery testing techniques are recommended. On the other hand, if testers want to evaluate the functional aspects of reliability, the requirements, error handling, manual support, and control testing techniques are recommended.

Individual Software Modules

Testers should list the software modules to be tested on Work Paper 8-2, including the name of the module, a brief description, and the evaluation criteria. When document-ing software modules, testers should include the following three categories:

Modules written by the IT development group

Modules written by non-IT personnel

Software capabilities embedded in hardware chips

Structural Attributes

Testers can use Work Paper 8-3 to identify the structural attributes of software that may be affected and thus require testing. The structural attributes can be those described earlier (maintainability, reliability, efficiency, usability, and so on) or specific processing concerns regarding how changes can affect the operating performance of the software.

Structural attributes also include the impact the processing of one software system has on another software system. This is classified as a structural attribute because the structure of one system may be incompatible with the structure of another.

TEST FACTOR	STRUCTURAL TESTING						FUNCTIONAL TESTING							UNIT TESTING
	Stress	Execution	Recovery	Operations	Compliance	Security	Requirements	Regression	Error Handling	Manual Support	Inter-systems	Control	Parallel	
Reliability		x	x				x		x					x
Authorization						x	x							x
File Integrity			x				x		x					x
Audit Trail			x				x							x
Continuity of Processing	x		x	x										x
Service Level	x	x		x										
Access Control						x								
Methodology					x									
Correctness							x	x	x	x	x	x	x	x
Ease of Use					x		x			x				x
Maintainable					x									x
Portable				x	x									
Coupling				x							x	x		
Performance	x	x		x	x									x
Ease of Operation					x									

Figure 8-5 Test factor/technique matrix.

Batch Tests

Batch tests are high-level tests. They must be composed during the execution phase in specific test transactions. For example, a test identified at the test plan level might validate that all dating in a software module is correct. During execution, each date-related instruction in a software module would require a test transaction. (It is not necessary for test descriptions at the test planning level to be that detailed.)

Work Paper 8-4 describes each batch test to perform during testing. If you use our previous example of the testing-related processing date, that task can be described in the test plan and related to all the software modules in which that test will occur. However, during execution, the test data for each module that executes that test will be a different transaction. To complete Work Paper 8-4, you must identify the software project, unless it is applicable to all software projects, in which case the word "all" should be used to describe the software project.

Each test should be named and numbered. In our example, it might be called Date Compliance test and given a unique number. Numbering is important both to control tests and to roll test results back to the high-level test described in the test plan.

Figure 8-6 shows a completed test document for a hypothetical test of data validation routines. Although all the detail is not yet known because the data validation routines have not been specified at this point, there is enough information to enable a group to prepare the data validation routines.

Conceptual Test Script for Online System Test

Work Paper 8-5 serves approximately the same purpose for online systems as Work Paper 8-4 does for batch systems. Work Paper 8-4 is a high-level description of the test script, not the specific transaction that will be entered during online testing. For the test planning perspective, it is unimportant whether the individual items will be manually prepared or generated and controlled using a software tool.

The example given for entering a batch test to validate date-related processing is also appropriate for test scripts. The primary differences are the sequence in which the events must occur and the source or location of the origin of the online event.

Figure 8-7 shows an example of developing test scripts for the data validation function of an order-entry software project. It lists two scripting events, the evaluation criteria, and comments that would be helpful in developing these tests.

Verification Tests

Testers can use Work Paper 8-6 to document verification testing. Verification is a static test performed on a document developed by the team responsible for creating software. Generally, for large documents, the verification process is a review; for smaller documents, the verification process comprises inspections. Other verification methods include the following:

- Static analyzers incorporated into the compilers
- Independent static analyzers
- Walkthroughs
- Third-party confirmation of the document's accuracy

Software Project: <u>Payroll Application</u>

Name of Test: Validate Input   **Test No. 1**

Test Objective

Exercise data validation routines.

Test Input

Prepare the following types of input data for each input field:

- valid data
- invalid data
- range of codes
- validation of legitimate values and tables

Test Procedures

Create input transactions that contain the conditions described in test input. Run the entire test deck until all conditions are correctly processed.

Test Output

Reject all invalid conditions and accept all valid conditions.

Test Controls

Run the entire test each time the test is conducted. Rerun the test until all specified output criteria have been achieved.

Software or Structure Attribute Tested

The data validation function.

Figure 8-6 Conducting batch tests.

Verification tests normally relate to a specific software project, but because of the extensiveness of testing, a single verification test may be applicable to many software projects. For example, it may be determined that each source code listing that is changed will be inspected prior to unit testing. In this case, the software project should be indicated as "all."

Software/Test Matrix

The objective of Work Paper 8-7 is to illustrate that the tests validate and verify all the software modules, including their structural attributes. The matrix also illustrates which tests exercise which software modules.

			EVALUATION	
SEQUENCE	SOURCE	SCRIPT EVENT	CRITERIA	COMMENTS
1	Data entry clerk	The data entry clerk enters an invalid customer order.	The customer number should be rejected as invalid.	A help routine would help to locate the proper customer number.
2	Data entry clerk	The data entry clerk enters a correct order into the system for one or more invalid company products.	The system should, first, confirm that the information entered is valid and for legitimate values, and, second, ask the data entry clerk to verify that all the information has been entered correctly.	This tests the entry of a valid order through the data validation routines.

Software Project: *Order Entry*

Software Module: _____ **Test No.: 2**

Figure 8-7   Example of a test script for a data validation function.

The information to complete this matrix has already been recorded in Work Papers 8-2 through 8-6. The vertical axis of the matrix lists the software modules and structural attributes from Work Papers 8-2 and 8-3. The horizontal axis lists the tests indicated on Work Papers 8-4, 8-5, and 8-6. The intersection of the vertical and horizontal axes indicates whether the test exercises the software module/structural attributes listed. This can be indicated by a check mark or via a reference to a more detailed description that relates to the specific test and software module.

Defining Test Administration

The administrative component of the test plan identifies the schedule, milestones, and resources needed to execute the test plan as illustrated in the test matrix. This cannot be undertaken until the test matrix has been completed.

Prior to developing the test plan, the test team has to be organized. This initial test team is responsible for developing the test plan and then defining the administrative resources needed to complete the plan. Thus, part of the plan will be executed as the plan is being developed; that part is the creation of the test plan, which itself consumes resources.

The test plan, like the implementation plan, is a dynamic document—that is, it changes as the implementation plan changes and the test plan is being executed. The test plan must be viewed as a "contract" in which any modifications must be incorporated.

Work Papers 8-8 through 8-10, described in the following sections, are provided to help testers develop and document the administrative component of the test plan.

Test Plan General Information

Work Paper 8-8 is designed to provide background and reference data on testing. In many organizations this background information will be necessary to acquaint testers with the project. It is recommended that, along with this background data, testers be required to read all or parts of Chapters 1 through 4.

Define Test Milestones

Work Paper 8-9 is designed to indicate the start and completion date of each test. These tests are derived from the matrix in Work Papers 8-4, 8-5, and 8-6. The start/completion milestones are listed as numbers. If you prefer, these may be days or dates. For example, milestone 1 could just be week 1, day 1, or November 18. The tests from the test matrix are then listed in this work paper in the Test column; a start and completion milestone are checked for each test.

NOTE Organizations that have scheduling software should use that in lieu of this work paper. Both the work paper and the scheduling software should include the person responsible for performing that test as the assignment becomes known.

Define Checkpoint Administration

Test administration contains all the attributes associated with any other project. Test administration is, in fact, project management; the project is testing. Administration involves identifying what is to be tested, who will test it, when it will be tested, when it is to be completed, the budget and resources needed for testing, any training the testers need, and the materials and other support for conducting testing.

Work Paper 8-10, which is completed for each milestone, can be used to schedule work as well as to monitor its status. Work Paper 8-10 also covers the administrative aspects associated with each testing milestone. If the test plan calls for a different test at six milestones, testers should prepare six different work papers. Because budgeting information should be summarized, a total budget figure for testing is not identified in the administrative part of the plan.

Writing the Test Plan

The test plan can be as formal or informal a document as the organization's culture dictates. When the test team has completed Work Papers 8-1 through 8-10, they have completed the test plan. The test plan can either be the ten work papers or the information on those work papers transcribed to a more formal test plan. Generally, if the test team is small, the work papers are more than adequate. As the test team grows, it is better to formalize the test plan.

Figure 8-8 illustrates a four-part test plan standard. It is a restatement and slight clarification of the information contained on the work papers in this chapter.

1. **GENERAL INFORMATION**

   1.1 Summary. Summarize the functions of the software and the tests to be performed.

   1.2 Environment and Pretest Background. Summarize the history of the project. Identify the user organization and computer center where the testing will be performed. Describe any prior testing and note results that may affect this testing.

   1.3 Test Objectives. State the objectives to be accomplished by testing.

   1.4 Expected Defect Rates. State the estimated number of defects for software of this type.

   1.5 References. List applicable references, such as:

      a) Project request authorization.
      b) Previously published documents on the project.
      c) Documentation concerning related projects.

2. **PLAN**

   2.1 Software Description. Provide a chart and briefly describe the inputs, outputs, and functions of the software being tested as a frame of reference for the test descriptions.

   2.2 Test Team. State who is on the test team and their test assignment(s).

   2.3 Milestones. List the locations, milestone events, and dates for the testing.

   2.4 Budgets. List the funds allocated to test by task and checkpoint.

   2.5 Testing (systems checkpoint). Identify the participating organizations and the system checkpoint where the software will be tested.

      2.5.1 Schedule (and budget). Show the detailed schedule of dates and events for the testing at this location. Such events may include familiarization, training, data, as well as the volume and frequency of the input. Resources allocated for test should be shown.

      2.5.2 Requirements. State the resource requirement, including:

         a) Equipment. Show the expected period of use, types, and quantities of the equipment needed.
         b) Software. List other software that will be needed to support the testing that is not part of the software to be tested.
         c) Personnel. List the numbers and skill types of personnel that are expected to be available during the test from both the user and development groups. Include any special requirements such as multishift operation or key personnel.

Figure 8-8 System test plan standard.

2.5.3   Testing Materials. List the materials needed for the test, such as:

a)   System documentation
b)   Software to be tested and its medium
c)   Test inputs
d)   Test documentation
e)   Test tools

2.5.4   Test Training. Describe or reference the plan for providing training in the use of the software being tested. Specify the types of training, personnel to be trained, and the training staff.

2.5.5   Test to be Conducted. Reference specific tests to be conducted at this checkpoint.

2.6   Testing (system checkpoint). Describe the plan for the second and subsequent system checkpoint where the software will be tested in a manner similar to paragraph 2.5.

3.   SPECIFICATIONS AND EVALUATION

3.1   Specifications

3.1.1   Business Functions. List the business functional requirement established by earlier documentation.

3.1.2   Structural Functions. List the detailed structural functions to be exercised during the overall test.

3.1.3   Test/Function Relationships. List the tests to be performed on the software and relate them to the functions in paragraph 3.1.2.

3.1.4   Test Progression. Describe the manner in which progression is made from one test to another so that the entire test cycle is completed.

3.2   Methods and Constraints.

3.2.1   Methodology. Describe the general method or strategy of the testing.

3.2.2   Test Tools. Specify the type of test tools to be used.

3.2.3   Extent. Indicate the extent of the testing, such as total or partial. Include any rationale for partial testing.

3.2.4   Data Recording. Discuss the method to be used for recording the test results and other information about the testing.

3.2.5   Constraints. Indicate anticipated limitations on the test due to test conditions, such as interfaces, equipment, personnel, data-bases.

Figure 8-8   *(continued)*

3.   **SPECIFICATIONS AND EVALUATION**   *(continued)*

   3.3   Evaluation.

      3.3.1   Criteria. Describe the rules to be used to evaluate test results, such as range of data values used, combinations of input types used, maximum number of allowable interrupts or halts.

      3.3.2   Data Reduction. Describe the techniques to be used for manipulating the test data into a form suitable for evaluation, such as manual or automated methods, to allow comparison of the results that should be produced to those that are produced.

4.   **TEST DESCRIPTIONS**

   4.1   Test (Identify). Describe the test to be performed (format will vary for on-line test script).

      4.1.1   Control. Describe the test control, such as manual, semiautomatic or automatic insertion of inputs, sequencing of operations, and recording of results.

      4.1.2   Inputs. Describe the input data and input commands used during the test.

      4.1.3   Outputs. Describe the output data expected as a result of the test and any intermediate messages that may be produced.

      4.1.4   Procedures. Specify the step-by-step procedures to accomplish the test. Include test setup, initialization, steps and termination.

   4.2   Test (Identify). Describe the second and subsequent tests in a manner similar to that used in paragraph 4.1.

Figure 8-8   *(continued)*

Task 6: Inspect the Test Plan

This task describes how to inspect the corrected software prior to its execution. This process is used, first, because it is more effective in identifying defects than validation methods; and second, it is much more economical to remove the defects at the inspection stage than to wait until unit or system testing. This task describes the inspection process, including the role and training of the inspectors, and the step-by-step procedures to complete the process.

The implementation/rework step of the project team involves modifying software and supporting documentation to make it compliant. Thereafter, the software needs to be tested. However, as already noted, identifying defects in dynamic testing is more costly and time-consuming than performing a static inspection of the changed products or deliverables.

Inspection, then, is a process by which completed but untested products are evaluated as to whether the specified changes were installed correctly. To accomplish this, inspectors examine the unchanged product, the change specifications, and the changed product to determine the outcome. They look for three types of defects: errors, meaning the change has not been made correctly; missing, meaning something should have been changed but was not changed; and extra, meaning something not intended was changed or added.

The inspection team reviews the product after each inspector has reviewed it individually. The team then reaches a consensus on the errors and missing/extra defects. The author (the person implementing the project change) is given those defect descriptions so that the product can be changed prior to dynamic testing. After the changes are made, they are re-inspected to verify correctness; then dynamic testing can commence. The purpose of inspections is twofold: to conduct an examination by peers, which normally improves the quality of work because the synergy of a team is applied to the solution, and to remove defects.

Inspection Concerns

The concerns regarding the project inspection process are basically the same associated with any inspection process. They are as follows:

- **Inspections may be perceived to delay the start of testing.** Because inspection is a process that occurs after a product is complete but before testing, it does in fact impose a delay to dynamic testing. Therefore, many people have trouble acknowledging that the inspection process will ultimately reduce implementation time. In practice, however, the time required for dynamic testing is reduced when the inspection process is used; thus, the total time is reduced.

- **There is resistance to accepting the inspection role.** There are two drawbacks to becoming an inspector. The first is time; an inspector loses time on his or her own work assignments. The second is that inspectors are often perceived as criticizing their peers. Management must provide adequate time to perform inspections and encourage a synergistic team environment in which inspectors are members offering suggestions, as opposed to being critics.

- **Space may be difficult to obtain for conducting inspections.** Each deliverable is inspected individually by a team; therefore, meeting space is needed in which to conduct inspections. Most organizations have limited meeting space, so this need may be difficult to fulfill. Some organizations use cafeteria space during off hours; or if the group is small enough, they can meet in someone's work area. However, it is important to hold meetings in an environment that does not affect others' work.

- **Change implementers may resent having their work inspected prior to testing.** Traditional software implementation methods have encouraged sloppy developments, which rely on testing to identify and correct problems. Thus, people instituting changes may resist having their products inspected prior to having the opportunity to identify and correct the problems themselves. The solution is to encourage team synergism with the goal of developing optimal solutions, not criticizing the work of individuals.

- **Inspection results may affect individual performance appraisal.** In a sense, the results of an inspection are also a documented list of a person's defects, which can result in a negative performance appraisal. Management must emphasize that performance appraisals will be based on the final product, not an interim defect list.

Products/Deliverables to Inspect

Each software project team determines the products to be inspected, unless specific inspections are mandated by the project plan. Consider inspecting the following products:

- Project requirements specifications
- Software rework/maintenance documents
- Updated technical documentation
- Changed source code
- Test plans
- User documentation (including online help)

Formal Inspection Roles

The selection of the inspectors is critical to the effectiveness of the process. It is important to include appropriate personnel from all impacted functional areas and to carefully assign the predominant roles and responsibilities (project, operations, external testing, etc.). There should never be fewer than three inspection participants but not more than five.

Each role must be filled on the inspection team, although one person may take on more than one role. The following subsections outline the participants and identify their roles and responsibilities in the inspection process.

Moderator

The moderator coordinates the inspection process and oversees any necessary follow-up tasks. It is recommended that the moderator *not* be a member of the project team. Specifically, the moderator does the following:

- Organizes the inspection by selecting the participants; verifies the distribution of the inspection materials; and schedules the overview, inspection, and required follow-up sessions.
- Leads the inspection process; ensures that all participants are prepared; encourages participation; maintains focus on finding defects; controls flow and direction; and maintains objectivity.

- Controls the inspection by enforcing adherence to the entry and exit criteria; seeks consensus on defects; makes the final decision on disagreements; directs the recording and categorizing of defects; summarizes inspection results; and limits inspections to one to two hours.
- Ensures the author completes the follow-up tasks.
- Completes activities listed in moderator checklist (reference Work Paper 8-11):
  - Determine if the product is ready for inspection, based on entry criteria for the type of inspections to be conducted.
  - Select inspectors and assign the roles of reader and recorder.
  - Estimate inspection preparation time (e.g., 20 pages of written documentation per two hours of inspections).
  - Schedule the inspection meeting and send inspection meeting notices to participants.
  - Determine if overview is required (e.g., if the product is lengthy or complex) with author and project leader.
  - Oversee the distribution of the inspection material, including the meeting notice.

Reader

The reader is responsible for setting the pace of the inspection. Specifically, the reader:

- Is not also the moderator or author
- Has a thorough familiarity with the material to be inspected
- Presents the product objectively
- Paraphrases or reads the product material line by line or paragraph by paragraph, pacing for clarity and comprehension

Recorder

The recorder is responsible for listing defects and summarizing the inspection results. He or she must have ample time to note each defect because this is the only information that the author will have to find and correct the defect. The recorder should avoid using abbreviations or shorthand that may not be understood by other team members. Specifically, the recorder:

- May also be the moderator but cannot be the reader or the author
- Records every defect
- Presents the defect list for consensus by all participants in the inspection
- Classifies the defects as directed by the inspectors by type, class, and severity, based on predetermined criteria

Author

The author is the originator of the product being inspected. Specifically, the author:

- Initiates the inspection process by informing the moderator that the product is ready for inspection

- May also act as an inspector during the inspection meeting

- Assists the moderator in selecting the inspection team

- Meets all entry criteria outlined in the appropriate inspection package cover sheet

- Provides an overview of the material prior to the inspection for clarification, if requested

- Clarifies inspection material during the process, if requested

- Corrects the defects and presents finished rework to the moderator for sign-off

- Forwards all materials required for the inspection to the moderator as indicated in the entry criteria

Inspectors

The inspectors should be trained staff who can effectively contribute to meeting objectives of the inspection. The moderator, reader, and recorder may also be inspectors. Specifically, the inspectors:

- Must prepare for the inspection by carefully reviewing and understanding the material

- Maintain objectivity toward the product

- Record all preparation time

- Present potential defects and problems encountered before and during the inspection meeting

Formal Inspection Defect Classification

The classification of defects provides meaningful data for their analysis and gives the opportunity for identifying and removing their cause. This results in overall cost savings and improved product quality.

Each defect should be classified as follows:

- **By origin.** Indicates the development phase in which the defect was generated (requirements, design, program, etc.).

- **By type.** Indicates the cause of the defect. For example, code defects could be errors in procedural logic, or code that does not satisfy requirements or deviates from standards.

- **By class.** Defects should be classified as missing, wrong, or extra, as described previously.

- **By severity.** There are two severity levels: major (those that either interrupt system operation or cause an incorrect result) and minor (all those that are not major).

Inspection Procedures

The formal inspection process is segmented into the following five subtasks, each of which is distinctive and essential to the successful outcome of the overall process:

1. Planning and organizing
2. Overview session (optional)
3. Individual preparation
4. Inspection meeting
5. Rework and follow-up

Planning and Organizing

The planning step defines the participants' roles and defines how defects will be classified. It also initiates, organizes, and schedules the inspection.

Overview Session

This task is optional but recommended. Its purpose is to acquaint all inspectors with the product to be inspected and to minimize individual preparation time. This task is especially important if the product is lengthy, complex, or new; if the inspection process is new; or if the participants are new to the inspection process.

Individual Preparation

The purpose of this task is to allot time for each inspection participant to acquire a thorough understanding of the product and to identify any defects (per exit criteria).

The inspector's responsibilities are to:

- Become familiar with the inspection material
- Record all defects found and time spent on the inspection preparation report (see Work Paper 8-12) and inspection defect list (see Work Paper 8-13)

Each inspector performs a "desk review" of the material, with the following recommended guidelines:

- It should be performed in one continuous time span.
- The inspector must disregard the style of the work product (for example, the way a programmer chooses to build a report).
- The emphasis should be on meeting standards and ensuring that output meets the product specification.
- Every defect must be identified.

The activities involved in performing an individual inspection are as follows:

- Review the input product (product specification).

- Review the output product (author's work).

- Identify each input specification by a unique identifier on the input product document.

- Trace specifications one by one to the output product, essentially repeating the author's process.

- Cross-reference the output to the input specification (block out output that relates to the input specification).

- Continue this process until all specifications have been traced and all output has been referenced.

During the individual inspection, each inspector records defects, questions, and concerns to be addressed during the inspection meeting. Recommended guidelines for recording these items are that:

- Every defect should be recorded, no matter how small.

- Areas of concern regarding correctness of input specifications should be noted as issues to discuss.

- Significant inefficiencies in the output product should be noted as issues to discuss.

- Any output that does not have an input specification should be marked as a defect (that is, "extra").

Inspection Meeting

The purpose of the inspection meeting is to find defects in the product, not to correct defects or suggest alternatives. A notice is sent to all participants notifying them of the meeting (see Work Paper 8-14). The following are the responsibilities of the meeting participants, in the sequence they occur:

- **Moderator responsibilities (at the beginning of the inspection)**
  - Introduce participants and identify roles.
  - Restate the objective of the inspection.
  - Verify inspectors' readiness by checking time spent in preparation and whether all material was reviewed prior to the meeting (as indicated on each inspector's inspection preparation report). If any of the participants are not prepared, the moderator must decide whether to continue with the inspection or reschedule it to allow for further preparation.
- **Reader responsibilities**
  - Read or paraphrase the material.

- **Inspector responsibilities**
  - Discuss potential defects and reach a consensus about whether the defects actually exist.
- **Recorder responsibilities**
  - Record defects found, by origin, type, class, and severity, on the inspection defect list.
  - Classify each defect found, with concurrence from all inspectors.
  - Prepare the inspection defect summary (see Work Paper 8-15).
- **Author responsibilities**
  - Clarify the product, as necessary.
- **Moderator responsibilities (at the end of the inspection)**
  - Call the inspection to an end if a number of defects are found early, indicating that the product is not ready for inspection. The author then is responsible for reinitiating an inspection, through the moderator, once the product is ready.
  - Determine the disposition of the inspection and any necessary follow-up work.
  - Approve the inspection defect list and the inspection summary, and then forward copies to the author and quality assurance personnel.
  - Sign off on the inspection certification report if no defects were found (see Work Paper 8-16).

Rework and Follow-Up

The purpose of this task is to complete required rework, obtain a sign-off or initiate a reinspection, and capture inspection results. Listed next are the responsibilities of the participants, in order of occurrence:

- **Author responsibilities**
  - Complete all rework to correct defects found during the inspection.
  - Reinitiate the inspection process if the inspection ended with major rework required.
  - Contact the moderator to approve the rework if the inspection ended with minor rework required.
- **Moderator responsibilities**
  - Review all rework completed and sign off on the inspection report after all the defects have been corrected.
- **Recorder responsibilities**
  - Summarize defect data and ensure its entry into an inspection defect database.

Check Procedures

Work Paper 8-17 contains the items to evaluate to determine the accuracy and completeness of the test plan. The questions are designed so that a Yes response is desirable, and a No response requires that testers evaluate whether that item should be addressed. If the item is not applicable, a check mark should be placed in the N/A column. For No responses, a comment should be entered; if action is required, the results of the action should also be recorded in the Comments column.

Output

The single deliverable from this step is the test plan. It should be reviewed with appropriate members of management to determine its adequacy. Once approved, the tester's primary responsibility is to execute the test in accordance with that plan, and then report the results. Once the test plan is approved, testers should not be held responsible for potential omissions.

Guidelines

Planning can be one of the most challenging aspects of the software testing process. The following guidelines can make the job a little easier:

1. **Start early.** Even though you might not have all the details at hand, you can complete a great deal of the planning by starting on the general and working toward the specific. By starting early, you can also identify resource needs and plan for them before they are subsumed by other areas of the project.

2. **Keep the test plan flexible.** Make it easy to add test cases, test data, and so on. The test plan itself should be changeable, but subject to change control.

3. **Review the test plan frequently.** Other people's observations and input greatly facilitate achieving a comprehensive test plan. The test plan should be subject to quality control just like any other project deliverable.

4. **Keep the test plan concise and readable**. The test plan does not need to be large and complicated. In fact, the more concise and readable it is, the more useful it will be. Remember, the test plan is intended to be a communication document. The details should be kept in a separate reference document.

5. **Calculate the planning effort.** You can count on roughly one-third of the testing effort being spent on planning, execution, and evaluation, respectively.

6. **Spend the time to develop a complete test plan.** The better the test plan, the easier it will be to execute the tests.

Summary

The test plan drives the remainder of the testing effort. Well-planned test projects tend to cost less and get completed earlier than projects with incomplete test plans. It is not unusual to spend approximately one-third of the total test effort on planning, but that time reaps rewards during test execution and reporting.

This chapter covers test planning from a risk-oriented approach. Test objectives are designed to address the significant risks. The objectives are decomposed into test transactions. The test plan is completed when the administrative data, such as schedule and budget, are added to the written test plan.

WORK PAPER 8-1 Test Objective

Number	Objective	Priority	Completion Criteria

WORK PAPER 8-2   Software Module

Software Project: _____

Number	Software Module Name	Description	Evaluation Criteria

WORK PAPER 8-3   Structural Attribute

Software Project: _____

Software Model Number	Structural Attribute	Description	Evaluation Criteria

WORK PAPER 8-4   Batch Tests

Software Project: _____

Name of Test: **Test No.** _____

Test Objective
_____

Test Input
_____

Test Procedures
_____

Test Output
_____

Test Controls
_____

Software or Structure Attribute Tested
_____

_____

WORK PAPER 8-5   Conceptual Test Script for Online System Test

Software Project: _____

Software Module: _____   Test No. _____

Sequence	Source	Script Event	Evaluation Criteria	Comments

WORK PAPER 8-6   Verification Tests

Software Project: _____

Number	Verification Test	System Product	Purpose	Responsibility	Test Point/ Schedule

WORK PAPER 8-7   Software/Test Matrix

Software Project: _____

Tests

Software Module	1	2	3	4	5	6	7	8	9	10

WORK PAPER 8-8   Test Plan General Information

Field Requirements

FIELD	INSTRUCTIONS FOR ENTERING DATA
Software Project	The name or number that uniquely identifies the project or system that will be tested for compliance.
Summary	A one- or two-paragraph overview of what is to be tested and how the testing will be performed.
Pretest Background	Summary of any previous test experiences that might prove helpful with testing. The assumption is, if there were problems in the past, they will probably continue; however, if there were few problems with test tools, the test team can expect to use those tools effectively.
Test Environment	The computer center or facilities used to test the application. In a single computer center installation, this subsection is minimal. If the software is used in multiple installations, the test environments may need to be described extensively.
Test Constraints	Certain types of testing may not be practical or possible during testing. For example, in banking systems in which the software ties into the Fed Wire system, it is not possible to test software with that facility. In other cases, the software cannot yet interface directly with production databases, and therefore the test cannot provide assurance that some of those interfaces work. List all known constraints.
References	Any documents, policies, procedures, or regulations applicable to the software being tested or the test procedures. It is also advisable to provide a brief description of why the reference is being given and how it might be used during the testing process.
When to stop testing	What type of test results or events should cause testing to be stopped and the software returned to the implementation team for more work.

Software Project: _____

_____

Summary

_____

Pretest Background

_____

Test Environment

_____

Test Constraints

_____

References

_____

When to Stop Testing

_____

WORK PAPER 8-9   Test Milestones

Field Requirements

FIELD	INSTRUCTIONS FOR ENTERING DATA
Tests	Tests to be conducted during execution (the tests described on Work Papers 8-4, 8-5, and 8-6 and shown in matrix format in Work Paper 8-7). The vertical column can contain either or both the test number and/or name.
Start/Completion Milestone	The names to identify when tests start and stop. The milestones shown in Work Paper 8-9 are numbers 1–30, but these could be week numbers, day numbers, or specific dates such as November 18, 1999, included in the heading of the vertical columns.
Intersection between Tests and Start/ Completion Milestones	Insert a check mark in the milestone where the test starts, and a check mark in the column where the tests are to be completed.

Tests   **Start/Completion Milestones**

	1	2	3	4	5	6	7	8	9	10	11	12	13	14	15	16	17	18	19	20	21	22	23	24	25	26	27	28	29	30

WORK PAPER 8-10   Administrative Checkpoint

Field Requirements

FIELD	INSTRUCTIONS FOR ENTERING DATA
Software Project	The name or number that uniquely identifies the project or system that will be tested for compliance.
Project	The name of the project being tested.
Checkpoint for Test	The name of the systems development checkpoint at which testing occurs. Unless the test team knows which development documents have been completed, testing is extremely difficult to perform.
Schedule	The dates on which the following items need to be started and completed: • plan • train test group • obtain data • test execution • test report(s)
Budget	The test resources allocated at this milestone, including both test execution and test analysis and reporting.
Resources	The resources needed for this checkpoint, including: • equipment (computers and other hardware needed for testing) • software and test personnel (staff to be involved in this milestone test, designated by name or job function)
Testing Materials	Materials needed by the test team to perform the test at this checkpoint, including: • system documentation (specific products and documents needed to perform the test at this point) • software to be tested (names of the programs and subsystems to be tested at this point) • test input (files or data used for test purposes) • test documentation (any test documents needed to conduct a test at this point) • test tools (software or other test tools needed to conduct the test at this point) *Note:* Not all these materials are needed for every test.
Test Training	It is essential that the test team be taught how to perform testing. They may need specific training in the use of test tools and test materials, the performance of specific tests, and the analysis of test results.

(continues)

WORK PAPER 8-10   *(continued)*

Software Project: _____

Test Milestone Number: _____	**Start**	**Finish**
Schedule: Test Plan: _____		
Tester Training: _____		
Obtaining Data: _____		
Execution: _____		
Report: _____		

Budget:

_____

Resources

Equipment:

Support Personnel:

Test Personnel:

_____

Testing Materials

Project Documentation:

Software to Be Tested:

Test Input:

Test Documentation:

Test Tools:

_____

Test Training

_____

WORK PAPER 8-11   Moderator Checklist

_____   Check that entry criteria (inspection package cover sheet) have been met.

_____   Meet with author and team leader to select qualified inspection participants and assign roles.

_____   Determine need for an overview session.

_____   Schedule inspection meeting; complete inspection meeting notice.

_____   Gather materials from author, and distribute to inspection participants.

_____   Talk with inspectors to ensure preparation time.

_____   Complete self-preparation of material for inspection.

_____   Conduct inspection meeting.

_____   Ensure completion and distribution of inspection defect list and inspection summary.

_____   Verify conditional completion (moderator review or reinspection).

_____   Complete inspector certification report.

WORK PAPER 8-12   Inspection Preparation Report

Software Project: _____   Date: _____

Name of Item Being Inspected: _____

Item Version Identification: _____

Material Size (lines/pages): _____   Expected Preparation Time: _____

Preparation Log:

Date   Time Spent

_____   _____

_____   _____

Total Preparation Time: _____

Defect List:

Location	Defect Description	Exit Criteria Violated
_____	_____	_____
_____	_____	_____
_____	_____	_____
_____	_____	_____
_____	_____	_____
_____	_____	_____
_____	_____	_____

WORK PAPER 8-13   Inspection Defect List

Field Requirements

FIELD	INSTRUCTIONS FOR ENTERING DATA
Project Name	The name of the project in which an interim deliverable is being inspected.
Date	The date on which this workpaper is completed.
Name of Item Being Inspected	The number or name by which the item being Inspected is known.
Item Version Identification	The version number if more than one version of the item is being inspected.
Material Size	The size of the item being inspected. Code is frequently described as number of lines of executable code. Written documentation is frequently described as number of pages.
Expected Preparation Time	Total expected preparation time of all the inspectors.
Moderator	The name of the person leading the inspection.
Phone	The phone number of the moderator.
Inspection Type	Indicates whether an initial inspection or a reinspection of the item to verify defect correction.
Release #	A further division of version number indicating the sequence in which variations of a version are released into test.
Product Type	The type of product being inspected, such as source code.
Location	The location of a defect determined to be a defect by the formal inspection meeting.
Origin/Defect Description	The name by which the defect is known in the organization; inspectors' opinion as to where that defect originated.
Defect Phase	The phase in the development process at which the defects were uncovered.
Defect Type	A formal name assigned to the defect. This Work Paper suggests 17 different defect types. Your organization may wish to modify or expand this list.
Severity Class	Indicate whether the defect is an extra, missing, or wrong class. (See Chapter 8 for explanation of defect class.)
Severity MAJ/MIN	Indicate whether the defect is of major or minor severity. (See Chapter 8 for a discussion of the meaning of major and minor.
	Note: This form is completed by the inspector filling the reporter role during the formal inspection process.

(continues)

WORK PAPER 8-13   *(continued)*

Project Name: _____ Date: _____

Name of Item Being Inspected: _____

Item Version Identification: _____

Material Size (lines/pages): _____ Expected Preparation Time: _____

Moderator: _____ Phone: _____

Inspection Type: _____ Inspection   Release #: _____

_____ Reinspection   Product Type: _____

Location	Origin Defect Description	Defect Phase	Defect Type	Severity	
				Class	**Maj/Min**
_____	_____	_____	_____	_____	_____
_____	_____	_____	_____	_____	_____
_____	_____	_____	_____	_____	_____
_____	_____	_____	_____	_____	_____
_____	_____	_____	_____	_____	_____
_____	_____	_____	_____	_____	_____
_____	_____	_____	_____	_____	_____
_____	_____	_____	_____	_____	_____
_____	_____	_____	_____	_____	_____
_____	_____	_____	_____	_____	_____
_____	_____	_____	_____	_____	_____
_____	_____	_____	_____	_____	_____
_____	_____	_____	_____	_____	_____
_____	_____	_____	_____	_____	_____

Defect Types:

CM	Comments	LO	Logic	PF	Performance
DA	Data	LR	Linkage Requirements	RQ	Requirements
DC	Documentation	MN	Maintainability	SC	Spec Clarification
EN	English Readability	MS	Messages/Return Codes	ST	Standards
IF	Interface	OT	Other	TP	Test Plan
LD	Logical Design	PD	Physical Design		

Defect Class: E   Extra   M   Missing   W   Wrong

WORK PAPER 8-14   Inspection Meeting Notice

Project Name: _____ Date: _____

Name of Item Being Inspected: _____

Item Version Identification: _____

Material Size (lines/pages): _____ Expected Preparation Time: _____

Moderator: _____ Phone: _____

Inspection Type: _____ Inspection

_____ Reinspection

Schedule:

Date: _____

Time: _____

Location: _____

Duration: _____

Participants:

Name	Phone	Role
_____	_____	_____
_____	_____	_____
_____	_____	_____
_____	_____	_____
_____	_____	_____

(continues)

WORK PAPER 8-14   *(continued)*

Comments:

_____

_____

_____

_____

_____

_____

_____

WORK PAPER 8-15   Inspection Defect Summary

Project Name: _____ Date: _____

Name of Item Being Inspected: _____

Item Version Identification: _____

Material Size (lines/pages): _____

Moderator: _____ Phone: _____

Inspection Type: _____ Inspection

_____ Reinspection

Defect Types	Minor Defect Class				Major Defect Class			
	E	M	W	Total	E	M	W	Total
CM (Comments)								
DA (Data)								
DC (Documentation)								
EN (English Readability)								
IF (Interfaces)								
LD (Logical Design)								
LO (Logic)								
LR (Linkage Requirements)								
MN (Maintainability)								
MS (Messages/Return Codes)								
OT (Other)								
PD (Physical Design)								
PF (Performance)								
RQ (Requirements)								
SC (Spec Clarification)								
ST (Standards)								
TP (Test Plan)								
Totals:								

WORK PAPER 8-16   Inspection Certification Report

Project Name: _____   Date: _____

Name of Item Being Inspected: _____

Item Version Identification: _____

The following people have inspected the named item and have agreed that all technical, contractual, quality, and other requirements and inspection criteria have been satisfied:

Moderator: _____

Recorder: _____

Reader: _____

Author: _____

Software Quality Representative: _____

Inspectors: _____

_____

_____

_____

_____

_____

_____

_____
Moderator Signature/Date

WORK PAPER 8-17   Quality Control Checklist

	YES	NO	NA	COMMENTS
Software Function/Software Attribute Work Papers				
1. Have all the business software functions been identified?				
2. Does the sponsor/user agree that these are the appropriate software functions?				
3. Is the software function identified by a commonly used name?				
4. Are all the software functions described?				
5. Have the criteria for evaluating the software functions been identified?				
6. Are the evaluation criteria measurable?				
7. Has the structure addressed: Reliability? Efficiency? Integrity? Usability? Maintainability? Testability? Flexibility? Portability? Reusability? Interoperability?				

(continues)

WORK PAPER 8-17 *(continued)*

	YES	NO	NA	COMMENTS
8. Have the criteria for each structural attribute been stated?				
9. Are the evaluation criteria measurable?				
10. Has the description for each structural attribute been given?				
Work Papers on Tests to Be Conducted				
1. Has the test been named?				
2. Has the test been given a unique identifying number?				
3. Has the test objective been stated clearly and distinctly?				
4. Are the tests appropriate to evaluate the functions defined?				
5. Is the level of detail on the document adequate for creating actual test conditions once the system is implemented?				
6. Are the verification tests directed at project products?				
7. Is the verification test named?				

WORK PAPER 8-17 *(continued)*

	YES	NO	NA	COMMENTS
8. Is the name of the verification test adequate for test personnel to understand the intent of the test?				
9. Have the products to be tested been identified?				
10. Has the purpose of the verification test been stated?				
11. Has the sequence in which each online test will be performed been identified?				
12. Has the name for each test been included (optional)?				
13. Have the criteria that would cause testing to be stopped been indicated?				
14. Are the stop criteria measurable (i.e., there is no question that the criteria have been met)?				
15. Are the stop criteria reasonable?				
Software Function/Test Matrix				
1. Does the matrix contain all the software functions defined on Work Paper 8-2?				
2. Does the matrix contain all the structural attributes defined on Work Paper 8-3?				
3. Does the matrix contain all the tests described in test Work Papers 8-4, 8-5, and 8-6?				

(continues)

WORK PAPER 8-17 *(continued)*

	YES	NO	NA	COMMENTS
4. Are the tests related to the functions?				
5. Are there tests for evaluating each software function?				
6. Are there tests for evaluating each structural attribute?				
Administrative Work Papers				
1. Has a work paper been prepared for each test milestone?				
2. Has the date for starting the testing been identified?				
3. Has the date for starting test team training been identified?				
4. Has the date for collecting the testing material been identified?				
5. Has the concluding date of the test been identified?				
6. Has the test budget been calculated?				
7. Is the budget consistent with the test workload?				
8. Is the schedule reasonably based on the test workload?				
9. Have the equipment requirements for the test been identified?				

WORK PAPER 8-17 *(continued)*

	YES	NO	NA	COMMENTS
10. Have the software and documents needed for conducting the test been identified?				
11. Have the personnel for the test been identified?				
12. Have the system documentation materials for testing been identified?				
13. Has the software to be tested been identified?				
14. Has the test input been defined?				
15. Have the needed test tools been identified?				
16. Has the type of training that needs to be conducted been defined?				
17. Have the personnel who require training been identified?				
18. Will the test team be notified of the expected defect rate at each checkpoint?				
19. Has a test summary been described?				
20. Does this summary indicate which software is to be included in the test?				
21. Does the summary indicate the general approach to testing?				

(continues)

WORK PAPER 8-17   *(continued)*

	YES	NO	NA	COMMENTS
22. Has the pretest background been defined?				
23. Does the pretest background describe previous experience in testing?				
24. Does the pretest background describe the sponsor's/user's attitude to testing?				
25. Has the test environment been defined?				
26. Does the test environment indicate which computer center will be used for testing?				
27. Does the test environment indicate permissions needed before beginning testing (if appropriate)?				
28. Does the test environment state all the operational requirements that will be placed on testing?				
29. Have all appropriate references been stated?				
30. Has the purpose for listing references been stated?				
31. Are the number of references complete?				
32. Are the test tools consistent with the departmental standards?				
33. Are the test tools complete?				

WORK PAPER 8-17 *(continued)*

		YES	NO	NA	COMMENTS
34.	Has the extent of testing been defined?				
35.	Have the constraints of testing been defined?				
36.	Are the constraints consistent with the resources available for testing?				
37.	Are the constraints reasonable based on the test objectives?				
38.	Has the general method for recording test results been defined?				
39.	Is the data reduction method consistent with the test plan?				
40.	Is the information needed for data reduction easily identifiable in the test documentation?				
Test Milestones Work Paper					
1.	Has the start date of testing been defined?				
2.	Are all the test tasks defined?				
3.	Are the start and stop dates for each test indicated?				
4.	Is the amount of time allotted for each task sufficient to perform the task?				
5.	Will all prerequisite tasks be completed before the task depending on them is started?				

Step 3:
Verification Testing

Verification testing is the most effective way to remove defects from software. If most of the defects are removed prior to validation testing (i.e., unit, integration, system, and acceptance testing), validation testing can focus on testing to determine whether the software meets the true operational needs of the user and can be effectively integrated into the computer operations activity.

Because the experience of many testers is limited to unit, integration, systems, and acceptance testing, these testers are not experienced in verification techniques. The verification techniques are not complex, and once understood, can be easily implemented into the test process.

Typically, verification testing—testing in a static mode—is a manual process. Verification testing provides two important benefits: defects can be identified close to the point where they originate, and the cost to correct defects is significantly less than when detected in dynamic testing.

Verification testing normally occurs during the requirements, design, and program phases of software development, but it can also occur with outsourced software. There are many different techniques for verification testing, most of which focus on the documentation associated with building software. This chapter discusses the many different ways to perform verification testing during the requirements, design, and programming phases of software development.

Overview

Most but not all verification techniques are manual. However, even in manual techniques, automated tools can prove helpful. For example, when conducting a software review, reviewers might want to use templates to record responses to questions.

Because most testing focuses on validation/dynamic testing, verification technique names are not consist. Consider, for example, a review, which is an independent investigation of some developmental aspect. Some call these reviews System Development Reviews, others call them End-of-Phase Reviews, still others refer to them as Peer Reviews, and some use Requirements Review. Because some of the verification techniques are similar, they may also be referred to as a walkthrough or inspection.

For the purposes of this chapter, specific names are assigned to the review techniques, as follows:

- **Reviews.** A review is a formal process in which peers and/or stakeholders challenge the correctness of the work being reviewed. For example, in a requirements review, the correctness and completeness of requirements is challenged. It is a formal process usually based on the experience of the organization or outside experts, and uses a predetermined set of questions to accomplish the objectives of the review.

- **Walkthroughs.** A walkthrough is an informal process by which peers and other stakeholders interact with project personnel to help ensure the best possible project is implemented. Frequently, the walkthrough is requested by the project team, to resolve issues that they are not sure they have resolved in the most effective and efficient manner. For example, they may be uncertain that they have the best design for a specific requirement and want an independent process to "brainstorm" better methods.

- **Inspections.** Inspections are a very formal process in which peers and project personnel assume very specific roles. The objective of an inspection is to ensure that the entrance criteria for a specific workbench were correctly implemented into the exit criteria. The inspection process literally traces the entrance criteria to the exit criteria to ensure that nothing is missing, nothing is wrong, and nothing has been added that was not in the entrance criteria.

- **Desk debugging.** This can be a formal or informal process used by a worker to check the accuracy and completeness of his/her work. It is most beneficial when the process is formalized so that the worker has a predefined series of steps to perform. The objective is basically the same as an inspection, tracing the entrance criteria to the exit criteria; unlike the inspection, however, it is performed by the worker who completed the task.

- **Requirements tracing.** Requirements tracing, sometimes called quality function deployment (QFD), ensures that requirements are not lost during implementation. Once defined, the requirements are uniquely identified. They are then traced from work step to work step to ensure that all the requirements have been processed correctly through the completion of that process.

- **Testable requirements.** A testable requirement has a built-in validation technique. Incorporation of testable requirements is sometimes referred to as developing a "base case," meaning that the method of testing all the requirements has been defined. If you use this method, the requirements phase of software development or contracting cannot be considered complete until the testable component of each requirement has been defined. Some organizations use testers to help define and/or agree to a test that will validate the requirements.

- **Test factor analysis.** This verification technique is unique to the test process incorporated in this book. It is based on the test factors described in an earlier chapter. Under this analysis, a series of questions helps determine whether those factors have been appropriately integrated into the software development process. Note that these test factors are attributes of requirements such as ease of use.

- **Success factors.** Success factors are the factors that normally the customer/user will define as the basis for evaluating whether the software system meets their needs. Success factors correlate closely to project objectives but are in measurable terms so that it can be determined whether the success factor has been met. Acceptance criteria are frequently used as the success factors.

- **Risk matrix.** The objective of a risk matrix is to evaluate the effectiveness of controls to reduce those risks. (Controls are the means organizations use to minimize or eliminate risk.) The risk matrix requires the identification of risk, and then the matching of controls to those risks so an assessment can be made as to whether the risk has been minimized to an acceptable level.

- **Static analysis.** Most static analysis is performed through software. For example, most source code compilers have a static analyzer that provides information as to whether the source code has been correctly prepared. Other static analyzers examine code for such things as "non-entrant modules" meaning that for a particular section of code there is no way to enter that code.

These techniques are incorporated into either the verification process of requirements, design, or programming the software. However, just because a specific technique is included in one phase of development does not mean it cannot be used in other phases. Also, some of the techniques can be used in conjunction with one another. For example, a review can be coupled with requirements tracing.

Objective

Research has shown that the longer it takes to find and correct a defect, the more costly the correction process becomes. The objectives of verification testing during the requirements, design, and programming phases are twofold. The first is to identify defects as close to the point were they originated as possible. This will speed up development and at the same time reduce the cost of development. The second objective is to identify improvement opportunities. Experienced testers can advise the development group of better ways to implement user requirements, to improve the software design, and/or to make the code more effective and efficient.

Concerns

Testers should have the following concerns when selecting and executing verification testing:

- **Assurance that the best verification techniques will be used.** The verification technique can be determined during the development of the test plan or as detailed verification planning occurs prior to or during an early part of the developmental phase. Based on the objectives to be accomplished, testers will select one or more of the verification techniques to be used for a specific developmental phase.

- **Assurance that the verification technique will be integrated into a developmental process.** Development should be a single process, not two parallel processes of developing and testing during implementation. Although two processes are performed by potentially different groups, they should be carefully integrated so that development looks like a single process. This is important so that both developers and testers know when and who is responsible for accomplishing a specific task. Without this, developers may not notify testers that a particular phase has begun or ended, or budget the developer's time, so that testers are unable to perform the verification technique. If verification has been integrated into the developmental process, verification will be performed.

- **Assurance that the right staff and appropriate resources will be available when the technique is scheduled for execution.** Scheduling the staff and funding the execution of the verification technique should occur in parallel with the previous action of integrating the technique into the process. It is merely the administrative component of integration, which includes determining who will execute the technique, when the technique will be executed, and the amount of resources allocated to the execution of the technique.

- **Assurance that those responsible for the verification technique are adequately trained.** If testers who perform the verification technique have not been previously trained, their training should occur prior to executing the verification technique.

- **Assurance that the technique will be executed properly.** The technique should be executed in accordance with the defined process and schedule.

Workbench

Figure 9-1 illustrates the workbench for performing verification testing. The input to the workbench is the documentation prepared by the development team for the phase being tested. Near the end of the requirements, design, and programming phases, the appropriate verification technique will be performed. The quality control procedures are designed to ensure the verification techniques were performed correctly. At the end of each development phase test, testers should list the defects they've uncovered, plus any recommendations for improving the effectiveness and efficiency of the software.

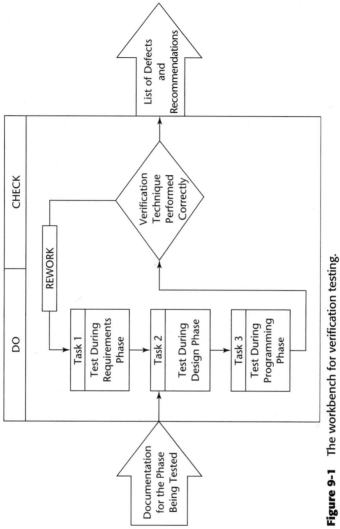

Figure 9-1 The workbench for verification testing.

Input

This section describes the inputs required to complete the verification testing during each phase of development: requirements, design, and programming.

The Requirements Phase

The requirements phase is undertaken to solve a business problem. The problem and its solution drive the system's development process. Therefore, it is essential that the business problem be well defined. For example, the business problem might be to improve accounts receivable collections, reduce the amount of on-hand inventory through better inventory management, or improve customer service.

The analogy of building a home illustrates the phases in a system's development life cycle. The homeowner's needs might include increased living space, and the results of the requirements phase offer a solution for that need. The requirements phase in building a home would specify the number of rooms, the location of the lot on which the house will be built, the approximate cost to construct the house, the type of architecture, and so on. At the completion of the requirements phase, the potential homeowner's needs would be specified. The deliverables produced from the homeowner's requirements phase would be a functional description of the home and a plot map of the lot on which the home is to be constructed. These are the inputs that go to the architect to design the home.

The requirements phase should be initiated by management request and should conclude with a proposal to management on the recommended solution for the business need. The requirements team should study the business problem, the previous methods of handling the problem, and the consequences of that method, together with any other input pertinent to the problem. Based on this study, the team develops a series of solutions. The requirements team should then select a preferred solution from among these alternatives and propose that solution to management.

The most common deliverables from the requirements phase needed by the testers for this step include the following:

- Proposal to management describing the problem, the alternatives, and proposing a solution

- Cost/benefit study describing the economics of the proposed solution

- Detailed description of the recommended solution, highlighting the recommended method for satisfying those needs. (Note: This becomes the input to the systems design phase.)

- List of system assumptions, such as the life of the project, the value of the system, the average skill of the user, and so on

The Design Phase

The design phase verification process has two inputs: test team understanding of how design, both internal and external, occurs; and the deliverables produced during the design phase that will be subject to a static test.

The design process could result in an almost infinite number of solutions. The system design is selected based on an evaluation of multiple criteria, including available time, desired efficiency, skill of project team, hardware and software available, as well as the requirements of the system itself. The design will also be affected by the methodology and tools available to assist the project team.

In home building, the design phase equivalent is the development of blueprints and the bill of materials for supplies needed. It is much easier to make changes in the early phases of design than in later phases.

From a project perspective, the most successful testing is that conducted early in the design phase. The sooner the project team becomes aware of potential defects, the cheaper it is to correct those defects. If the project waited until the end of the design phase to begin testing, it would fall into the same trap as many projects that wait until the end of programming to conduct their first tests: When defects are found, the corrective process can be so time-consuming and painful that it may appear cheaper to live with the defects than to correct them.

Testing normally occurs using the deliverables produced during the design phase. The more common design phase deliverables include the following:

Input specifications

Processing specifications

File specifications

Output specifications

Control specifications

System flowcharts

Hardware and software requirements

Manual operating procedure specifications

Data retention policies

The Programming Phase

The more common programming phase deliverables that are input for testing are as follows:

Program specifications

Program documentation

Computer program listings

Executable programs

Program flowcharts

Operator instructions

In addition, testers need to understand the process used to build the program under test.

Do Procedures

Testers should perform the following steps during requirements phase testing:

1. Prepare a risk matrix.
2. Perform a test factor analysis.
3. Conduct a requirements walkthrough.
4. Perform requirements testing.
5. Ensure requirements are testable.

Testers should perform the following steps during design phase testing:

1. Score success factors.
2. Analyze test factors.
3. Conduct design review.
4. Inspect design deliverables.

Testers should perform the following steps during programming phase testing:

1. Desk debug the program.
2. Perform programming phase test factor analysis.
3. Conduct a peer review.

Task 1: Test During the Requirements Phase

System development testing should begin during the requirements phase, when most of the critical system decisions are made. The requirements are the basis for the systems design, which is then used for programming to produce the final implemented application. If the requirements contain errors, the entire application will be erroneous.

Testing the system requirements increases the probability that the requirements will be correct. Testing at this point is designed to ensure the requirements are properly recorded, have been correctly interpreted by the software project team, are reasonable when measured against good practices, and are recorded in accordance with the IT department's guidelines, standards, and procedures.

The requirements phase should be a user-dominated phase. In other words, the user should specify the needs and the information services personnel should record the needs and provide counseling about the alternative solutions, just as the builder and architect would counsel the homeowner on building options. This means that the user, being the dominant party, should take responsibility for requirements phase testing.

Having responsibility for testing does not necessarily mean responsibility for performing the test. Performance of the test is different from the party having responsibility for the test—responsibility means the acceptance or rejection of the product based on the test results.

If there are multiple users, responsibility may be assigned to a committee, which may be the same committee that develops the requirements. One of the primary objectives of testing during requirements is to ensure that the requirements have been properly stated and recorded. Normally, only the user can look at recorded requirements and make that determination. Therefore, it is important for the user to accept testing responsibility during the requirements phase and to be an active participant in the test process.

People undertaking the test process must understand the requirements phase objectives and then evaluate those objectives through testing. Should the requirements phase be found inadequate as a result of testing, the phase should be continued until requirements are complete. Without testing, inadequacies in the requirements phase may not be detected.

Customarily, a management review occurs after the requirements phase is complete. Frequently, this is done by senior management, who are not as concerned with the details as with the economics and the general business solution. Unfortunately, inadequate details can significantly affect the cost and timing of implementing the proposed solution.

The recommended test process outlined in this book is based on the 15 requirements phase test factors and the test concerns for each factor (see the section "Requirements Phase Test Factors"). The test team determines which of those factors apply to the application being tested, and then conducts those tests necessary to determine whether the test factor has been adequately addressed during the requirements phase. This chapter defines the test factors and recommends tests to enable you to address the requirements phase testing concerns.

Requirements Phase Test Factors

The following list provides a brief description of the 15 requirement phase test factors (concerns):

- **Requirements comply with methodology (methodology test factor).** The process used by the information services function to define and document requirements should be adhered to during the requirements phase. The more formal these procedures, the easier the test process. The requirements process is one of fact gathering, analysis, decision making, and recording the requirements in a predefined manner for use in design.

- **Functional specifications defined (correctness test factor).** User satisfaction can only be ensured when system objectives are achieved. The achievement of these objectives can only be measured when the objectives are measurable. Qualitative objectives—such as improving service to users—are not measurable objectives, whereas processing a user order in four hours is measurable.

- **Usability specifications determined (ease-of-use test factor).** The amount of effort required to use the system and the skill level necessary should be defined during requirements. Experience shows that difficult-to-use applications or features are not often used, whereas easy-to-use functional systems are highly used. Unless included in the specifications, the ease-of-use specifications will be created by default by the systems analyst or programmer.

- **Maintenance specifications determined (maintainable test factor).** The degree of expected maintenance should be defined, as well as the areas where change is most probable. Specifications should then determine the methods of maintenance—such as user-introduced change of parameters—and the time span in which certain types of maintenance changes need to be installed; for example, a price change must be operational within 24 hours after notification to information services.

- **Portability needs determined (portable test factor).** The ability to operate the system on different types of hardware, to move it at a later time to another type of hardware, or to move from version to version of software should be stated as part of the requirements. The need to have the application developed as a portable one can significantly affect the implementation of the requirements.

- **System interface defined (coupling test factor).** The information expected as input from other computer systems, and the output to be delivered to other computer systems, should be defined. This definition not only includes the types of information passed, but the timing of the interface and the expected processing to occur as a result of that interface. Other interface factors that may need to be addressed include privacy, security, and retention of information.

- **Performance criteria established (performance test factor).** The expected efficiency, economy, and effectiveness of the application system should be established. These system goals are an integral part of the design process and, unless established, default to the systems analyst/programmer. When this happens, user dissatisfaction is almost guaranteed to occur with the operational system. An end product of the requirements phase should be a calculation of the cost/benefit to be derived from the application. The financial data should be developed based on procedures designed to provide consistent cost and benefit information for all applications.

- **Operational needs defined (ease-of-operations test factor).** The operational considerations must be defined during the requirements phase. This becomes especially important in user-driven application systems. The processes that must be followed at terminals to operate the system—in other words, the procedures needed to get the terminal into a state ready to process transactions—should be as simple as possible. Central site operating procedures also need to be considered.

- **Tolerances established (reliability test factor).** The expected reliability from the system controls should be defined. For example, the requirements phase should determine the control requirements for the accuracy of invoicing, the percent of orders that need to be processed within 24 hours, and other such concerns. An invoicing tolerance might state that invoices are to be processed with a tolerance of plus or minus 1 percent from the stated current product prices. If you don't establish these tolerances, there is no basis to design and measure the reliability of processing over an extended period of time. If you don't define an expected level of defects, zero defects are normally expected. Controls to achieve zero defects are normally not economical. It is usually more economical and to the advantage of the user to have some defects occur in processing, but to control and measure the number of defects.

- **Authorization rules defined (authorization test factor).** Authorization requirements specify the authorization methods to ensure that transactions are, in fact, processed in accordance with the intent of management.

- **File integrity requirements defined (file integrity test factor).** The methods of ensuring the integrity of computer files need to be specified. This normally includes the control totals that are to be maintained both within the file and independently of the automated application. The controls must ensure that the detail records are in balance with the control totals for each file.

- **Reconstruction requirements defined (audit trail test factor).** Reconstruction involves both substantiating the accuracy of processing and recovery after an identified problem. Both of these needs involve he retention of information to backup processing. The need to substantiate processing evolves both from the organization and regulatory agencies, such as tax authorities requiring that sufficient evidential matter be retained to support tax returns.

    Application management needs to state if and when the system recovery process should be executed. If recovery is deemed necessary, management needs to state the time span in which the recovery process must be executed. This time span may change based upon the time of the day and the day of the week. These recovery requirements affect the type and availability of data retained.

- **Impact of failure defined (continuity-of-processing test factor).** The necessity to ensure continuity of processing is dependent upon the impact of failure. If system failure causes only minimal problems, ensuring continuous processing may be unnecessary. On the other hand, where continuity of operations is essential, it may be necessary to obtain duplicate data centers so that one can continue processing should the other experience a failure.

- **Desired service level defined (service level test factor).** Service level implies response time based on the requirements. The service level required will vary based on the requirements. Each level of desired service needs to be stated; for example, there is a service level to process a specific transaction, a service level to correct a programming error, a service level to install a change, and a service level to respond to a request.

- **Access defined (security test factor).** Security requirements should be developed showing the relationship between system resources and people. Requirements should state all of the available system resources subject to control, and then indicate who can have access to those resources and for what purposes. For example, access may be authorized to read, but not change, data.

At the conclusion of the testing, the test team can judge the adequacy of each of the criteria, and thus of all the test concerns included in the test process for the requirements phase. The test team should make one of the following four judgments about each criterion:

1. **Very adequate.** The project team has done more than normally would be expected for the criterion.

2. **Adequate evaluation.** The project team has done sufficient work to ensure the reasonableness of control over the criterion.

3. **Inadequate assessment.** The project team has not done sufficient work, and should do more work in this criterion area.

4. **Not applicable (N/A).** Because of the type of application or the system design philosophy by the organization, the implementation of this criterion is not applicable to the application being reviewed.

Each test process contains a test that can be performed for each evaluation criterion. The objective of the test is to assist the team in evaluating each criterion. The test should be conducted prior to assessing the adequacy of the project being tested. It should be noted that because of time limitations, review experience, and tests previously performed, the test team may choose not to assess each criterion.

The 15 test processes are recommended in Work Paper 9-1 as a basis for testing the requirements phase. One test program is constructed to evaluate each of the requirements phase concerns. Work Paper 9-2 is a quality control checklist for this task.

Preparing a Risk Matrix

A risk matrix is a tool designed to assess the adequacy of controls in computer systems. The term *controls* is used in its broadest context, meaning all the mechanisms, methods, and procedures used in the application to ensure that it functions in accordance with the intent of management. It is estimated that in automated systems, controls account for at least one-half of the total developmental effort. Therefore, effort expended to ensure the adequacy of controls is essential to the success and credibility of the application system.

One of the major benefits of the risk matrix is the identification of risks and what the system must do for each of those risks. The risk matrix is primarily a design tool, but it can be used as a test tool because it is infrequently used in the design process.

The risk matrix can be used in both the requirements phase and the design phase. The following discussion explains how to use the risk matrix. Ideally, the risk matrix starts in the requirements phase and is expanded and completed in the design phase. The execution of the risk matrix requires five actions. The actions should be performed in the following sequence.

Establishing the Risk Team

The key to a successful risk matrix is the establishment of the correct risk team, whose responsibility will be to complete the matrix. The objective of completing the matrix is to determine the adequacy of the control requirements and design to reduce the risks to an acceptable level.

The risk team may be part of the requirements team or part of the test team, or it may be a team specifically selected for the purpose of completing the risk matrix. The team should consist of three to six members and at a minimum possess the following skills:

Knowledge of the user application

Understanding of risk concepts

Ability to identify controls

Familiarity with both application and information services risks

Understanding of information services concepts and systems design

Understanding of computer operations procedures

The candidates for the risk team should, at a minimum, include someone from the user area and any or all of the following:

Internal auditor

Risk consultant

Data processor

Security officer

Computer operations manager

Identifying Risks

The objective of the risk team is first to identify the application-oriented, not environmental, risks associated with the application system. For example, the risks that relate to all applications equally (for example, environmental risks) need not be identified unless they have some special relevance to the applicants. The risk team can use one of the following two methods for risk identification:

1. **Risk analysis scenario.** In this method, the risk team "brainstorms" the potential application risks using their experience, judgment, and knowledge of the application area. It is important to have the synergistic effect of a group so that group members can challenge one another to develop a complete list of risks that are realistic for the application.

2. **Risk checklist.** The risk team is provided with a list of the more common risks that occur in automated applications. From this list, the team selects those risks applicable to the application. In this method, the team needs fewer skills because the risk list provides the stimuli for the process, and the objective of the team is to determine which of the risks on the list are applicable to the application. Figure 9-2 provides a list of risks for the purpose of identification.

Establishing Control Objectives (Requirements Phase Only)

During the requirements phase, the control objectives for each risk should be established. These objectives define the acceptable level of loss for each of the identified risks. Another way of stating the acceptable level of loss is the measurable objective for control. When control can be stated in measurable terms, the controls to achieve that objective have a requirement to use for control-decision purposes.

The adequacy of control cannot be tested until the acceptable level of loss from each risk has been defined. Therefore, although the definition of the control objectives is a user and project responsibility, it may take the formation of a risk team to get them defined. After the control objectives have been defined, the requirements can be tested to determine whether those objectives are achievable.

CATEGORY: Uncontrolled System Access

1. Date or programs may be stolen from the computer room or other storage areas.

2. Information services facilities may be destroyed or damaged by either intruders or employees.

3. Individuals may not be adequately identified before they are allowed to enter the information services area.

4. Remote terminals may not be adequately protected from use by unauthorized persons.

5. An unauthorized user may gain access to the system and an authorized user's password.

6. Passwords may be inadvertently revealed to unauthorized individuals. A user may write his or her password in some convenient place, or the password may be obtained from card decks, discarded printouts, or by observing the user as he or she types it.

7. A user may leave a logged-in terminal unattended, allowing an unauthorized person to use it.

8. A terminated employee may retain access to an information services system because his or her name and password are not immediately deleted from authorization tables and control lists.

9. An unauthorized individual may gain access to the system for his or her own purposes (e.g., theft of computer services or data or programs, modification of data, alteration of programs, sabotage, denial of services).

10. Repeated attempts by the same user or terminal to gain unauthorized access to the system or to a file may go undetected.

CATEGORY: Ineffective Security Practices for the Application

1. Poorly defined criteria for authorized access may result in employees not knowing what information they, or others, are permitted to access.

2. The person responsible for security may fail to restrict user access to only those processes and data which are needed to accomplish assigned tasks.

3. Large disbursements, unusual price changes, and unanticipated inventory usage may not be reviewed for correctness.

4. Repeated payments to the same party may go unnoticed because there is no review.

5. Sensitive data may be carelessly handled by the application staff, by the mail service, or by other personnel within the organization.

6. Post-processing reports analyzing system operations may not be reviewed to detect security violations.

Figure 9-2   List of generalized application risks.

CATEGORY: Ineffective Security Practices for the Application *(continued)*

7. Inadvertent modification or destruction of files may occur when trainees are allowed to work on live data.

8. Appropriate action may not be pursued when a security variance is reported to the system security officer or to the perpetrating individual's supervisor; in fact, procedures covering such occurrences may not exist.

CATEGORY: Procedural Errors at the Information Services Facility

Procedures and Controls

1. Files may be destroyed during database reorganization or during release of disk space.

2. Operators may ignore operational procedures (for example, by allowing programmers to operate computer equipment).

3. Job control language parameters may be erroneous.

4. An installation manager may circumvent operational controls to obtain information.

5. Careless or incorrect restarting after shutdown may cause the state of a transaction update to be unknown.

6. An operator may enter erroneous information at CPU console (e.g., control switch in wrong position, terminal user allowed full system access, operator cancels wrong job from queue).

7. Hardware maintenance may be performed while production data is online and the equipment undergoing maintenance is not isolated.

8. An operator may perform unauthorized acts for personal gain (e.g., make extra copies of competitive bidding reports, print copies of unemployment checks, delete a record from a journal file).

9. Operations staff may sabotage the computer (e.g., drop pieces of metal into a terminal).

10. The wrong version of a program may be executed.

11. A program may be executed twice using the same transactions.

12. An operator may bypass required safety controls.

13. Supervision of operations personnel may not be adequate during nonworking hour shifts.

14. Due to incorrectly learned procedures, an operator may alter or erase the master files.

15. A console operator may override a label check without recording the action in the security log.

Figure 9-2 *(continued)*

CATEGORY: Procedural Errors at the Information Services Facility

Storage Media Handling

1. Critical tape files may be mounted without being write-protected.

2. Inadvertently or intentionally mislabeled storage media are erased. In a case where they contain backup files, the erasure may not be noticed until the backup is needed.

3. Internal labels on storage media may not be checked for correctness.

4. Files with missing or mislabeled expiration dates may be erased.

5. Incorrect processing of data or erroneous updating of files may occur when card decks have been dropped, partial input decks are used, write rings are mistakenly placed in tapes, paper tape is incorrectly mounted, or wrong tape is mounted.

6. Scratch tapes used for jobs processing sensitive data may not be adequately erased after use.

7. Temporary files written during a job step for use in subsequent steps may be erroneously released or modified through inadequate protection of the files or because of an abnormal termination.

8. Storage media containing sensitive information may not get adequate protection because operations staff is not advised of the nature of the information content.

9. Tape management procedures may not adequately account for the current status of all tapes.

10. Magnetic storage media that have contained very sensitive information may not be degaussed before being released.

11. Output may be sent to the wrong individual or terminal.

12. Improperly operating output or post-processing units may result in loss of output.

13. Surplus output material may not be disposed of properly.

14. Tapes and programs that label output for distribution may be erroneous or not protected from tampering.

CATEGORY: Program Errors

1. Records may be deleted from sensitive files without a guarantee that the deleted records can be reconstructed.

2. Programmers may insert special provisions in programs that manipulate data concerning themselves (e.g., payroll programmer may alter his or her own payroll records).

Figure 9-2   *(continued)*

CATEGORY: Program Errors   *(continued)*

3. Data may not be stored separately from code with the result that program modifications are more difficult and must be made more frequently.

4. Program changes may not be tested adequately before being used in a production run.

5. Changes to a program may result in new errors because of unanticipated interactions between program modules.

6. Program acceptance tests may fail to detect errors that only occur for unusual combinations of input (e.g., a program that is supposed to reject all except a specified range of values actually accepts an additional value).

7. Programs, the contents of which should be safeguarded, may not be identified and protected.

8. Code, test data with its associated output, and documentation for certified programs may not be filed and retained for reference.

9. Documentation for vital programs may not be safeguarded.

10. Programmers may fail to keep a change log, to maintain backup copies, or to formalize recordkeeping activities.

11. An employee may steal programs he or she is maintaining and use them for personal gain.

12. Poor program design may result in a critical data value being initialized twice. An error may occur when the program is modified to change the data value— but only changes it in one place.

13. Production data may be disclosed or destroyed when it is used during testing.

14. Errors may result when the programmer misunderstands requests for changes to the program.

15. Errors may be introduced by a programmer who makes changes directly to machine code.

16. Programs may contain routines not compatible with their intended purpose, which can disable or bypass security protection mechanisms. For example, a programmer who anticipates being fired inserts code into a program that will cause vital system files to be deleted as soon as his/her name no longer appears in the payroll file.

17. Inadequate documentation or labeling may result in the wrong version of program being modified.

Figure 9-2   *(continued)*

CATEGORY: Operating System Flaws

1. User jobs may be permitted to read or write outside assigned storage area.

2. Inconsistencies may be introduced into data because of simultaneous processing of the same file by two jobs.

3. An operating system design or implementation error may allow a user to disable audit controls or to access all system information.

4. An operating system may not protect a copy of information as thoroughly as it protects the original.

5. Unauthorized modification to the operating system may allow a data entry clerk to enter programs and thus subvert the system.

6. An operating system crash may expose valuable information such as password lists or authorization tables.

7. Maintenance personnel may bypass security controls.

8. An operating system may fail to record that multiple copies of output have been made from spooled storage devices.

9. An operating system may fail to maintain an unbroken audit trail.

10. When restarting after a system crash, the operating system may fail to ascertain that all terminal locations that were previously occupied are still occupied by the same individuals.

11. A user may be able to get into monitor or supervisory mode.

12. The operating system may fail to erase all scratch space assigned to a job after the normal or abnormal termination of the job.

13. Files may be allowed to be read or written without having been opened.

CATEGORY: Communication System Failure

Accidental Failures

1. Undetected communications errors may result in incorrect or modified data.

2. Information may be accidentally misdirected to the wrong terminal.

3. Communication nodes may leave unprotected fragments of messages in memory during unanticipated interruptions in processing.

4. Communication protocols may fail to positively identify the transmitter or receiver of a message.

Figure 9-2   *(continued)*

CATEGORY: Communication System Failure *(continued)*

Intentional Acts

1. Communication lines may be monitored by unauthorized individuals.

2. Data or programs may be stolen via telephone circuits from a remote job entry terminal.

3. Programs in the network switching computers may be modified to compromise security.

4. Data may be deliberately changed by individuals tapping the line.

5. An unauthorized user may "take over" a computer communication port as an authorized user disconnects from it. Many systems cannot detect the change. This is particularly true in much of the currently available communication protocols.

6. If encryption is used, keys may be stolen.

7. A terminal user may be "spoofed" into providing sensitive data.

8. False messages may be inserted into the system.

9. True messages may be deleted from the system.

10. Messages may be recorded and replayed into the system.

Figure 9-2 *(continued)*

Table 9-1 shows an example risk matrix at the end of the requirements phase for a typical billing and distribution system. This matrix lists four risks for the billing and distribution system and lists control objectives for each of those risks. For example, one of the risks is that the product will be shipped but not billed. In this instance, the control objective is to ensure that all shipments are billed. In other words, the acceptable level of loss for this risk is zero, and the project team must install a system that ensures that for each shipment leaving the distribution area an invoice will be prepared. However, note that the next risk is that the product will be billed at the wrong price or quantity and that the controls have a greater than zero level of loss established, as do the other two risks.

Table 9-1 Requirements Phase Risk Matrix Example

RISK	CONTROL OBJECTIVE
Shipped but not billed	Ensure all shipments are billed.
Billed for wrong quantity price	Bill at current price on 99 percent of line items and or have error pricing less than plus or minus 10 percent.
Billed to wrong customer	Reduce incorrect billings to less than 0.1 percent of invoices.
Shipped wrong product quantity	Ship correct product and quantity on 99 percent of or line items.

Identifying Controls in Each System Segment

The following are the common system segments:

- **Origination.** The creation of the source document plus the authorization associated with that transaction origination.
- **Data entry.** The transfer of information to machine-readable media.
- **Communication.** The movement of data from one point in the system to another. Movement may be manual or electronic.
- **Processing.** Application of the system logic to the data.
- **Storage.** The retention of data, for both temporary and extended periods of time.
- **Output.** The translation of data from computer media to media understandable and usable by people.
- **Use.** Satisfaction of the business need through the results of system processing.

The risk team determines which controls are applicable to which risk and records them in the correct segment of the system. At the conclusion of the development of the risk matrix, the risk team assesses whether the controls are adequate to reduce the risk to the acceptable level identified in the control objective. This will test the adequacy of the controls at the conclusion of the design process. An example of a risk matrix for billing and distribution systems at the end of the design phase is illustrated in Table 9-2.

The same four risks that were identified during the requirements phase (refer to Table 9-1) are listed on this matrix also, as are the controls associated with each risk. In this example, the shipped-but-not-billed risk shows that three controls (1, 2, and 3) will help reduce that risk. (Note that for an actual matrix these controls must be described.) The matrix shows in which segment of the application system those controls reside. After the controls have been identified and recorded, the risk team must determine whether those three controls and the segments in which they exist are adequate to reduce the shipped-but-not-billed risk to the point where all shipments will be billed.

Determining the Adequacy of Controls

The test concludes when the risk team assesses whether controls are adequate to reduce each identified risk to an acceptable level.

Performing a Test Factor Analysis

Work Paper 9-1 provides a process to assess the concerns associated with the requirements phase of the system's development life cycle. A test program is included for each concern. There are 15 concerns, covering each phase of the development process. For each concern, there is a test program comprising eight criteria. The test program lists those criteria that, if proved to be adequately addressed through testing, should ensure the test team that the concern is minimal.

Table 9-2 Design Phase Risk Matrix Example

SYSTEM SEGMENT RISK	ORIGINATION	DATA ENTRY	COMMUNICATION	PROCESSING	STORAGE	OUTPUT	USE
Shipped but not billed	1			2			6
Billed for wrong quantity or price		6		7 8 9	10	11	
Billed to wrong customer				12 3	14	15	16
Shipped wrong product or quantity	17	18		19 20		21	22

The test team must perform sufficient testing to evaluate the adequacy with which the project team has handled each of the test criteria. For example, in the requirements phase, one test criterion is "Have the significant financial fields been identified?" To determine that the project team has adequately addressed this criterion, the test team conducts such tests as necessary to assure themselves that the significant financial fields have been identified. The testing may require fact finding in the accounting department to verify that the fields indicated as financial fields are complete.

Conducting a Requirements Walkthrough

The requirements phase involves creativity, experience, and judgment, as well as a methodology to follow. During this phase, the methodology helps, but it is really creativity and problem solving that is needed. Of the review processes, the walkthrough is the least structured and the most amenable to creativity. Therefore, the walkthrough becomes a review process that complements the objectives of the requirements phase. The objective of the walkthrough is to create a situation in which a team of skilled individuals can help the project team in the development of the project solutions. The walkthrough attempts to use the experience and judgment of the review team as an adjunct or aid in the developmental process. The walkthrough in the requirements phase is oriented toward assistance in problem solving as opposed to compliance to methodology.

The walkthrough involves five actions to be completed in the sequence listed below. The amount of time allocated to each step will depend on the size of the application being reviewed and the degree of assistance desired from the walkthrough team.

Establishing Ground Rules

The walkthrough concept requires that the project participants make a presentation explaining the functioning of the system as developed at the time of the presentation. The presentation, or reading of the requirements, is the vehicle for initiating discussion between the project team and the walkthrough team. The prime objective is to elicit questions, comments, and recommendations.

The walkthrough is most productive when ground rules are established before the actual walkthrough. The ground rules should be understood by both the project team and the walkthrough team and should normally include the following:

- Size and makeup of the walkthrough team (Three to six skilled participants is a good size. Three members are needed to get sufficient perspective and discussion, but more than six members makes the process too large and unwieldy.)

- Responsibility of the walkthrough team, which is usually limited to recommendations, comments, and questions.

- Obligation of the project team to answer all questions and respond to recommendations.

- Approximate length, time, and location of the walkthrough.

- Confidentiality of information discussed at the walkthrough.

- Non-negotiable aspects of the system.

- Who will receive the results of the walkthrough and how are those results to be used? (For example, if a report is to be prepared, who will receive it, what is the purpose of the report, and what is the most likely action based on that report?)

Selecting the Team

The ground rules establish the size and makeup of the team. The ground rules are normally generic in nature, and must be converted into action. For example, if the ground rules say that the team should consist of two members of user management and two project leaders, the most appropriate individuals must then be selected.

The walkthrough team should be selected based on the objectives to be accomplished. Any of the involved parties (i.e., users, information services, and senior management) may want to recommend walkthrough team participants. These tend to be selected based on project concerns. For example, if operations is a major concern, operations people should be selected for the walkthrough team.

The most common participants on a walkthrough team include the following:

- Information services project manager/systems analyst.
- Senior management with responsibility over the computerized area.
- Operations management.
- User management.
- Consultants possessing needed expertise. (The consultants may be from inside or outside the corporation. For example, the consultants may be internal auditors, database administrators, or independent computer consultants.)

A good review team has at least one member of user management, one senior member of information services, and one member of senior management. Additional participants can be added as necessary.

The team participants should be notified as soon as possible that they have been selected for the walkthrough and advised of the responsibility and time commitments and the date for the walkthrough. Generally, if people do not want to participate in the walkthrough, they should be relieved of that responsibility and another person selected. If a team participant has a scheduling conflict and cannot complete the review in time, it may be more advisable to change the time of the review than to lose the participant.

Presenting Project Requirements

The project personnel should present the project requirements to the walkthrough team. A good walkthrough includes a presentation of the following:

- Statement of the goals and objectives of the project.
- Background information, including appropriate statistics on the current and proposed application area. (Note that these statistics should be business statistics and not computer system statistics.)
- List of any exceptions made by the project team.
- Discussion of the alternatives considered and the alternative selected.

■ A walkthrough of the requirements using representative transactions as a baseline. (Rather than describing the system, it is better to select the more common transaction types and explain how those transactions will be processed based on the defined requirements.)

Responding to Questions/Recommendations

The project presentation should be interrupted with questions, comments, and recommendations as they occur to the walkthrough team. The objective of the walkthrough is to evoke discussion and not to instruct the walkthrough team on the application requirements. The project team should be prepared to deviate from any presentation plan to handle questions and recommendations as they occur.

It is generally good to appoint one person as recorder for the walkthrough. This is normally a member of the project team. The recorder's duty is to capture questions for which appropriate answers are not supplied during the walkthrough, and to indicate recommendations for which acceptance and implementation are possible.

Issuing the Final Report (Optional)

The ground rules determine whether a report will be issued, and if so, to whom. However, if it is determined that a walkthrough report should be issued, responsibility should be given to a single person to write the report. State in advance to whom the report is to be issued. The entire walkthrough team should agree on the contents of the report; if they do not, the report should state minority opinions. The information captured by the recorder may prove valuable in developing the report. To be most valuable to the project team, the report should be issued within five days of the walkthrough.

Performing Requirements Tracing

Requirements tracing is a simple but difficult-to-execute concept. The objective is to uniquely identify each requirement to be implemented, and then determine at each checkpoint whether that requirement has been accurately and completely processed.

Requirements tracing requires the following three actions:

1. **Uniquely identify each requirement.** The identification process can be as simple as 1 through x, or requirements can be named or any other method chosen that can uniquely identify the requirement. The end process of this step is a detailed listing of all the requirements (see the requirements tracing matrix in Figure 9-2).

2. **Identify the development checkpoints at which requirements will be traced.** In most developmental processes, requirements will be traced at predefined checkpoints. For small projects, the checkpoints may be at the end of a phase, whereas in larger projects, sub-phases might require checkpoints. The checkpoints will be incorporated into the requirements tracing matrix. Note that in this matrix five checkpoints have been listed (a, b, c, d, e) as well as four requirements (1, 2, 3, 4).

3. **Check that the requirements have been accurately and completely implemented at the end of a checkpoint.** Use the requirements tracing matrix to investigate whether the identified requirements have been accurately and correctly implemented at the end of a specific checkpoint. In Figure 9-3, for example, at developmental checkpoint A, a decision would be made as to whether requirements 1, 2, 3, and 4 have been accurately and correctly implemented. If they have not been, the developmental team must make the necessary corrections.

Ensuring Requirements Are Testable

Many believe this is one of the most valuable verification techniques. If requirements are testable, there is a high probability that they will, in fact, meet the user needs as well as simplify implementation. Ideally, users of the requirement would develop the means for validating whether the requirement has been correctly implemented. For example, if there was a requirement that customers could not exceed their credit limit on purchases, the users might define three tests that test below the credit limit, at the credit limit, and above the credit limit.

Ensuring that requirements are testable requires only that some stakeholder develop the means for testing the requirement. As previously discussed, ideally this is the user. However, some users do not have the background necessary to develop the test conditions without the assistance of someone experienced in creating test data. Note that developing testable requirements is very similar to a concept called "use cases." A use case is a case that tests how the outputs from the software will be used by the operating personnel.

Use cases are helpful in three ways:

■ Testing that requirements are accurately and completely implemented

■ Assisting developers in implementing requirements because the implementers will know how the outputs will be used

■ Developing cases for the acceptance testing of the software by the users

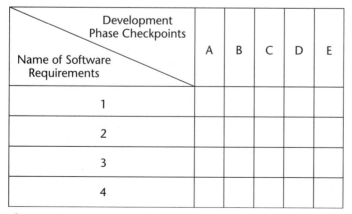

Name of Software Requirements \ Development Phase Checkpoints	A	B	C	D	E
1					
2					
3					
4					

Figure 9-3 Requirement tracing matrix.

Task 2: Test During the Design Phase

During the design phase, the user and the system designer must work together closely. Neither party should be dominant during this period, the phase during which the user-defined requirements are converted into a process that can be accomplished by a computer. It is important that both the user and system designer work as partners to develop not only an efficient application system, but also one that is acceptable to the user.

Testing during the design phase should be jointly shared by the user and the information services project team. If the team consists of both users and IT personnel, the project team can accept test responsibility.

The system design is an IT responsibility. It is therefore logical to assume that IT should accept responsibility for the adequacy of that design, and thus have test responsibility. Unfortunately, this logic shifts responsibility from the user to information services. The danger is that the system may become information services' system, as opposed to the user's system. When the user is involved in establishing test criteria, the ultimate responsibility for the application is more clearly established.

The design phase provides the opportunity to test the structure (both internal and external) of the software application. The greater the assurance of the project team that the structure is sound and efficient, the higher the probability that the project will succeed.

Current test tools permit the structure to be tested in both a static and a dynamic mode. It is possible through modeling and simulation to model the structure on the computer to analyze the performance characteristics of the structure. However, the testing concepts must be developed hand in hand with the design process to gain maximum test advantages. State testing of the adequacy of the design has proved to be effective.

The design phase can be viewed as a funnel that takes the broad system requirements at the wide end of the funnel and narrows them down through a design process to very detailed specifications. This is a creative phase of the life cycle. Along with this creativity is a concern that some important design aspects will be overlooked.

Understanding design phase concerns produces more effective testing. Testing can then be directed at specific concerns instead of attempting broad-based testing.

Scoring Success Factors

Scoring is a predictive tool that utilizes previous systems experience. Existing systems are analyzed to determine the attributes of those systems and their correlation to the success or failure of that particular application. When attributes that correlate to success or failure can be identified, they can be used to predict the behavior of systems under development.

Attributes of an effective scoring tool are as follows:

- **Sampling.** The criteria that represent a sample of all the criteria involved in the implementation of an automated application system. The sampling criteria are not meant to be complete.

- **High positive correlation.** The criteria picked will have shown a high positive correlation in the past with either success or failure of an automated application. These criteria should not be judgmental or intuitive, but rather, those criteria for which it can be demonstrated that the absence or presence of that attribute has shown a high correlation to the outcome of the project.

- **Ease of use.** To be effective, the process of scoring must be simple. People will use an easy predictive concept, but will be hesitant to invest significant amounts of time and effort.

- **Develop risk score.** The score for each attribute should be determined in a measurable format so that a total risk score can be developed for each application. This will indicate the degree of risk, the area of risk, and a comparison of risk among application systems.

The scoring test tool is prepared for use in evaluating all applications. The tool should be general in nature so that it will apply to diverse applications, because the degree of risk must be compared against a departmental norm.

The scoring tool can be used in one of the following two ways under the direction of the test team:

1. **Project leader assessment.** The application project leader can be given the scoring mechanism and asked to rate the degree of risk for each of the attributes for his or her project. The project leader need not know the importance of any of the attributes in a risk score, but only needs to measure the degree of project risk based on his or her in-depth knowledge of the project.

2. **Test team assessment.** A member of the test team can be assigned the responsibility to develop the risk score. If the test team has worked on the project from the beginning, that person may be knowledgeable enough to complete the scoring instrument. However, if the test team member lacks knowledge, investigation may be needed to gather sufficient evidence to score the project.

At the conclusion of the scoring process, the result can be used in any of the following ways:

- **Estimate extent of testing.** The higher the risk, the more testing that management may desire. Knowing that an application is high risk alerts management to the need to take those steps necessary to reduce that risk to an acceptable level.

- **Identify areas of test.** Depending on the sophistication of the scoring instrument, specific areas may be identified for testing. For example, if computer logic is shown to be high risk, testing should thoroughly evaluate the correctness of that processing.

- **Identify composition of test team.** The types of risks associated with the application system help determine the composition of the test team. For example, if the risks deal more with technology than with logic, the test team should include individuals thoroughly knowledgeable in that technology.

A scoring instrument for application systems is presented in Work Paper 9-3 at the end of the chapter. This scoring instrument develops a computer application system profile on many different system characteristics/attributes. The user is then asked to determine whether the system being reviewed is high, medium, or low risk for the identified characteristic. For example, the first characteristic deals with the importance of the function being computerized. If that function is important to several organizational units, it is a high-risk application. If the requirements are only of limited significance to cooperating units, the risk drops to medium; if there are no significant conflicting needs and the application is primarily for one organizational unit, the risk is low. The person doing the assessment circles the appropriate indicator. At the conclusion, a score can be developed indicating the number of high-risk, medium-risk, and low-risk indicators.

A risk score is achieved by totaling the number of characteristics rated high, medium, and low, respectively, and then multiplying each of these totals by the risk factor (high = 3, medium = 2, low = 1) to arrive at a risk score. The three resulting risk score numbers are then added together to arrive at a total risk score, which you can use to compare application systems against a norm. Another way to use the information is to divide the total score by the total number of risk characteristics to obtain a score between one and three. The closer the score is to three, the higher the risk, and conversely, the lower the score, the lower the risk.

Analyzing Test Factors

Work Paper 9-4 contains a test process for each of the design phase test factors. The person conducting the test can select the concerns of interest and use the appropriate test programs, keeping in mind the following general objectives for the design phase:

- Develop a solution to the business problem.
- Determine the role of the computer in solving the business problem.
- Develop specifications for the manual and automated segments of the system.
- Comply with policies, procedures, standards, and regulations.
- Define controls that will reduce application risks to an acceptable level.
- Complete the project within budgetary, staffing, and scheduling constraints.

The concerns to be analyzed during the design phase are as follows:

- **Data integrity controls designed.** Data integrity commences with risk identification, followed by management decisions on the acceptability of that risk, stated in terms of the amount of loss acceptable. The data integrity controls are then designed to these risk-tolerance specifications.

- **Authorization rules designed.** Authorization in automated systems may be manual and/or automated. The procedures for manual authorization should be specified during the design phase. Automated authorization methods must be specified in more detail than manual procedures because they cannot rely on people to react to unexpected situations.

- **File integrity controls designed.** File integrity is ensured by file identification methods, automated file controls, and independently maintained file integrity controls. The specifications for this three-part integrity process must be determined during the design phase.

- **Audit trail designed.** The audit trail provides the capability to trace transactions from their origination to control totals, and to identify all the transactions substantiating a control total. In addition, the audit trail is used to substantiate individual transaction processing, and to recover the integrity of computer operations after it has been lost. Frequently, governmental agencies specify the types of information that need to be retained for audit trail purposes—this information must be defined during the design phase. The audit trail should be designed to achieve those purposes.

- **Contingency plan designed.** The contingency plan outlines the actions to be performed in the event of problems. This plan includes the manual methods to be followed while the automated applications are not in operation, the backup and recovery procedures, as well as physical site considerations. Contingency plan specifications should be outlined during the design phase.

- **Method to achieve service level designed.** The requirements phase defined the service levels to be achieved during the operation of the application. This concern deals primarily with the performance of the system and its ability to satisfy user needs on a timely basis.

- **Access procedures defined.** Security in an automated system is achieved by predefining who can have access and for what purpose and then enforcing those access rules. A security profile indicates who can have access to what resources.

- **Design complies with methodology.** The system design process should be performed and documented in accordance with IT methodology. Standardized design procedures ensure ease of understanding by all parties trained in that methodology, and at the same time help ensure the completeness of the design process. The purpose of the methodology is to develop better systems at a lower cost.

- **Design conforms to requirements.** The system design is a translation of the user requirements into detailed system specifications. During any translation, misunderstandings or misinterpretations can occur. Steps need to be taken to ensure that the completed design achieves the objectives and intent of the defined requirements.

- **Design facilitates use.** The final product must be used by people. The easier the system is to use, the more likely that the features will be utilized and the transactions processed correctly. The design must take into consideration the skill levels and job motivation of the people using the application system.

- **Design is maintainable.** The cost of maintaining a computer application normally far exceeds the cost to develop. Identifying those system aspects that are most likely to be changed and building those parts of the system for ease of maintenance is an important aspect of the design process. The system design needed for maintainability may change significantly depending on the expected frequency of change.

- **Design is portable.** If the requirements indicate that the application system should be transferable from one piece of hardware to another or from one version of software to another, the design should incorporate those portability features. When future hardware and software is uncertain, the design should be generalized, and not attempt to take advantage of features or facilities of existing hardware and software.

- **Interface design is complete.** The interface to other applications needs to be identified and the specifications for that interface designed. Interface specifications should also consider secondary uses of application information. Understanding these secondary uses may result in additional capabilities included within the design process.

- **Design fulfills criteria.** The cost/benefit study performed during the requirements phase may not supply a high-precision evaluation. During the design phase, the performance estimates can be more accurately stated so that a better prediction can be made as to whether the performance criteria can be achieved. A guideline used by one corporation is that the accuracy of estimating the achievement of the performance criteria at the end of the design phase should be within plus or minus 10 percent.

- **Needs communicated to operations.** Operations needs to identify future processing requirements to prepare to handle those requirements when the system becomes operational. The larger the processing requirements, the greater the need to involve operations in the design alternative considerations.

A detailed work program is provided for each of the 15 design phase test concerns. These work programs follow and outline the criteria to be assessed for each concern, together with the recommended test, test technique, and test tool to be used in evaluating each criterion. Note that the person conducting the test should use judgment regarding the extent of testing relative to the importance of the criteria to the application.

Conducting a Design Review

The design review is structured using the same basic information that formed the basis for scoring. However, in the case of the design review, the criteria is more specific. The objective is to pre-identify those attributes of design that correlate to system problems. The design review then investigates those attributes to determine that they have been appropriately addressed by the project team.

The design review is conducted by a team knowledgeable in the design process. They are responsible for reviewing the application system for completeness and reasonableness. It is not necessary that the team be knowledgeable about the specific application, but they must be knowledgeable about the design methodology.

In conducting a design review, the team follows a predetermined review process. The design review is normally formal and highly structured in nature, in that the review team has predetermined investigations to make and has known start and stop points. The design review normally follows the design methodology. Team members attempt to determine that all the tasks have been properly performed. At the conclusion of the design review, the team normally issues a formal report indicating their findings and recommendations about the project.

The design review team may consist of the following members:

- **Project personnel.** The project personnel can conduct their own design review. Typically, the individual on the project who is assigned review responsibility is not the same person that actually designed the system; however, the reviewer may have had partial design responsibility. This requires team members to accept different roles and responsibilities during the review process than they have held during the design process. Because of the possible ties to the actual design of the system, having the design review checklist as a self-assessment tool normally fulfills a valuable function for the reviewer(s).

- **Independent review team.** The members of this review team are not members of the project being reviewed. They can be from other projects or quality-assurance groups, or they can be professional testers. This mode of operation provides a greater degree of independence in conducting the review in that there is no conflict of interest between the design and review roles. On the other hand, it is frequently difficult for peers to be critical of each other, especially in situations where a reviewer might eventually work for the person being reviewed.

These general guidelines should be followed when conducting a review:

1. **Select the review team.** The members of the review team should be selected in advance of the review process.

2. **Train the review team members.** The individuals who will be conducting the review should be trained in how to conduct the review. At a minimum, this means reviewing the checklist and explaining the objective and intent of each question. It is also advisable to train the people in the interpersonal relationships involved in conducting a review so that the review can be held in a non-threatening environment.

3. **Notify the project team.** The project team should be notified several days in advance of the review as to when the review will occur and the responsibility of the project team during the review. Obviously, if the project team conducts the review, this task is less important, but it is still necessary to formally schedule the review so that all members will be present.

4. **Allot adequate time.** The review should be conducted in a formal, businesslike manner, as efficiently as possible, but should not be rushed. Sufficient time should be allocated to probe and investigate areas of concern. Even when the same people conduct the review that designed the system, the interpersonal relationships and synergistic effect of a review can produce many positive effects if sufficient time is allocated to enable appropriate interaction.

5. **Document the review facts.** All the factual findings of the review should be recorded. Normally, this can be done on the review checklist unless the comments are lengthy or supporting evidence is required. In any case, facts should be referenced to the specific checklist questions that uncovered them.

6. **Review the facts with the project team.** The correctness of the facts should be substantiated with all individuals involved, and the review should not proceed until this is done. It is better to do this at the end of the review for important findings than intermittently during the review process.

7. **Develop review recommendations.** Based on the facts, the review team should offer their recommendations to correct any problem situation. These recommendations are an important part of the review process.

8. **Review recommendations with the project team.** The project team should be the first to receive the recommendations and have an opportunity to accept, modify, or reject the recommendations.

9. **Prepare a formal report.** A report documenting the findings, the recommendations, and the action taken or to be taken on the recommendations should be prepared. This report may or may not be sent to higher levels of management, depending on the review ground rules established by the organization. However, it is important to have a formal record of the review process, what it found, and the actions taken on recommendations.

One or more reviews may occur during the design phase. The number of reviews will depend on the importance of the project and the time span of the design phase. A program for a two-point design phase review is shown in Work Papers 9-5 and 9-6. This provides for the first review at the end of the business system design (Work Paper 9-5) that part of the design where it is determined how the business problem will be solved. The second review point would occur after the computer system design (Work Paper 9-6) is complete. Note that the questions in the two review checklists are taken from an actual organization's review process, and therefore may not be applicable to all organizations. Normally, the review process needs to be customized based on the design methodology, information services policies and procedures, and the criteria found to be causing problems in the organization.

Inspecting Design Deliverables

Inspection is a process by which completed but untested design products are evaluated as to whether the specified changes were installed correctly. To accomplish this, inspectors examine the unchanged product, the change specifications, and the changed product to determine the outcome. They look for three types of defects: errors, meaning the change has not been made correctly; missing, meaning something that should have been changed, but was not changed; and extra, meaning something not intended was changed or added.

The inspection team reviews the product after each inspector has reviewed it individually. The team then reaches a consensus on the errors, missing, and extra defects. The author (the person implementing the project change) is given those defect descriptions so that the product can be changed prior to dynamic testing. After the changes are made, they are re-inspected to verify correctness; then dynamic testing can commence. The purpose of inspections is twofold: to conduct an examination by peers, which normally improves the quality of work because the synergy of a team is applied to the solution; and to remove defects.

The following items can enhance the benefits of formal inspections:

- **Training.** Use inspections to train new staff members in the department's standards and procedures.

- **Product quality.** Do not inspect obviously poor products; that is, the inspectors should not do the developers' work. Developers should not submit a product for inspection if they are not satisfied with the quality of the product.

Work Paper 9-7 is a quality control checklist for this task.

Task 3: Test During the Programming Phase

Building an information system (i.e., programming) is purely an IT-related function, with little need for user involvement, except where questions arise about design specifications and/or requirements.

Wherever possible, changes requested by users should be discouraged through more complete design reviews, or postponed until the system is placed into operation. If changes cannot be postponed, they should be implemented through the regular development process and (preferably) tested before changing the original program specifications.

The complexity of performing the programming phase depends on the thoroughness of the design phase and the tool used to generate code. Well-defined and measurable design specifications greatly simplify the programming task. On the other hand, the failure to make decisions during the early phases necessitates those decisions being made during the programming phase. Unfortunately, if not made earlier, these decisions may be made by the wrong individual—the programmer.

Testing during the programming phase may be static or dynamic. During most of the phase, programs are being specified, designed, and coded. In this phase, the resultant code may not be executable, and therefore may require different test tools. The efficiency gained from early testing is just as appropriate to the programming phase as it is to other phases. For example, problems detected during program design can be corrected more economically than if they are detected while testing the executable program.

NOTE The importance of testing programs will vary based on the means of code generation. The more automated code generation becomes, the less emphasis needs to be placed on programming phase testing. Because many organizations use a variety of methods for code generation, this verification task is designed to incorporate all the programming phase components needed. The user of this test process must adjust this task according to the method used to generate code.

The programming phase consists of three segments: The program specifications are written from the design specifications; a programmer con- verts the program specifications into machine-executable instructions; and then the programmer verifies that these instructions meet the program specifications.

The programming equivalent in home construction is the building of the house by masons, carpenters, plumbers, and electricians. These are the craftsmen who take the design specifications and materials and convert them into the desired product. However, just as aids are available to the programmer, aids are also available to the construction worker. For example, preconstructed roof trusses and other parts of the house can be purchased. The more pieces that can be produced automatically, the greater the probability of a successfully built home.

The programming phase in the construction of a system produces a large volume of deliverables. During this phase, the number of items to be tested increases significantly. Therefore, it becomes important to understand the deliverables, their risk, and which segments of the deliverables need to be tested.

The IT project leader should be responsible for testing during the programming phase. The primary objective for this testing is to ensure that the design specifications have been correctly implemented. Program testing is not concerned with achieving the user's needs, but rather that the developed structure satisfies the design specifications and works. Much of the testing will be conducted by the programmer. Testing at this point is highly technical, and it normally requires someone with programming experience. These tests should be complete prior to interconnecting the entire application and testing the application system.

This verification task describes a test process to use during programming. Desk debugging and peer reviews are recommended as effective test methods during the programming phase. This relatively low-cost test approach has proven to be effective in detecting problems and can be used at any point during the programming activity. The task includes a complete test program addressing all of the programming phase concerns, as follows:

1. **Program testing will consist exclusively of dynamic testing as opposed to including static testing.** Static testing using techniques such as desk debugging and peer reviews is much more effective in uncovering defects than is dynamic testing. The concern is that the proper testing technique will not be used for the needed test objective.

2. **Program testing will be too costly.** Programmers have a tendency to identify defects, assume there are no more, and then correct those defects and retest. This has proven to be a time-consuming and costly approach to testing. Using static methods to remove defects and dynamic testing to verify functionality is a much more efficient method of program testing.

3. **Programs will be released for string, system, and acceptance testing before they are fully debugged.** The shortest and most economical testing is to remove all the defects at one level of testing before moving to the next level. For example, it is much more economical to continue program testing to remove program defects than to identify those defects in string testing.

Desk Debugging the Program

Desk debugging enables the programmer to evaluate the completeness and correctness of the program prior to conducting more expensive testing. In addition, desk debugging can occur at any point in the programming process, including both program design and coding. Desk debugging can be as extensive or as minimal as desired. The amount of desk debugging performed will depend on the following:

Wait time until the next program deliverable is received

Implementation schedule

Testing resources

Efficiency of test tools

Departmental policy

Desk debugging can be syntactical, structural, or functional.

Syntactical Desk Debugging

Program specifications and program statements must be developed in accordance with departmental methodology and compiler requirements. The programmer can check the appropriate syntax of the documentation and statements to ensure they are written in compliance with the rules. Syntactical checking asks questions such as these:

- Is the job identification correct?
- Are program statements appropriately identified?
- Are program statements constructed using the appropriate structure?
- Are data elements properly identified?
- Do the program statements use the proper data structure; for example, do mathematical instructions work on mathematical fields?
- Are the data structures adequate to accommodate the data values that will be used in those structures?

Structural Desk Debugging

Structural problems account for a significant number of defects in most application systems. These defects also mask functional defects so that their detection becomes more difficult. The types of questions to be asked during structural desk debugging include these:

- Are all instructions entered?
- Are all data definitions used in the instructions defined?
- Are all defined data elements used?
- Do all branches go to the correct routine entrance point?
- Are all internal tables and other limits structured so that when the limit is exceeded processing can continue?

Functional Desk Debugging

The functions are the requirements that the program is to perform. The questions to be asked about the function when desk debugging include the following:

- Will the program perform the specified function in the manner indicated?
- Are any of the functions mutually exclusive?
- Will the system detect inaccurate or unreasonable data?
- Will functional data be accumulated properly from run to run?

Performing Programming Phase Test Factor Analysis

The depth of testing in the programming phase depends on the adequacy of the system at the end of the design phase. The more confidence the test team has in the adequacy of the application at the end of the design phase, the less concern they will have during the programming phase. During requirements and design testing, the concerns over the test factors may change based on test results. In the programming phase, the test team should identify the concerns of most interest, and then develop the test process to address those concerns. In identifying these concerns, the test team must take into account changes that have occurred in the system specifications since the last test was conducted. The objectives that the test team members should continually consider when testing during the programming phase include the following:

- Are the systems maintainable?
- Have the system specifications been implemented properly?
- Do the programs comply with information services standards and procedures as well as good practice?
- Is there a sufficient test plan to evaluate the executable programs?
- Are the programs adequately documented?

The test concerns to be considered during this subtask are as follows:

- **Data integrity controls implemented.** Specific controls need to be implemented in a manner that will achieve the desired processing precision. Improperly implemented controls may not achieve the established level of control tolerance, and because of the widespread misunderstanding of the purpose of controls (i.e., reduced risk), simplistic solutions might be implemented where complex controls are needed to achieve the control objectives.

- **Authorization rules implemented.** Authorization rules need to be implemented in a manner that makes it difficult to circumvent them. For example, when authorization limits are set, people should not be able to circumvent these limits by entering numerous items under the prescribed limit. Therefore, authorization rules must not only consider the enforcement of the rules, but also take into account the more common methods to circumvent those rules.

- **File integrity controls implemented.** File integrity controls should be implemented in a manner that minimizes the probability of loss of file integrity, and they should both prevent the loss of integrity and detect that loss, should it occur, on a timely basis.

- **Audit trail implemented.** The audit trail needs to be implemented in a manner that facilitates retrieval of audit trail information. If the audit trail contains needed information, but it is too costly or time-consuming to use, its value diminishes significantly. The implementation considerations include the amount of information retained, sequencing for ease of retrieval of that information, cross-referencing of information for retrieval purposes, as well as the length of time that the audit trail information needs to be retained.

- **Contingency plan written.** The contingency plan is a set of detailed procedures in step-by-step format outlining those tasks to be executed in the event of problems. The plan should describe the preparatory tasks so that the necessary data and other resources are available when the contingency plan needs to be activated. The design contingency approach is of little value until it is documented and in the hands of the people who need to use it.

- **System to achieve service level designed.** The desired service level can only become a reality when the procedures and methods are established. One procedure that should be set up is the monitoring of the level of service to ensure that it meets specifications. The inclusion of monitoring routines provides assurance over an extended period of time that service levels will be achieved, or if not, that fact will be detected early so corrective action can be taken.

- **Security procedures implemented.** Security is the combination of employee awareness and training, plus the necessary security tools and techniques. The procedures ensuring that these two parts are available and working together must be developed during the programming phase.

- **Program complies with methodology.** Procedures should be implemented that ensure compliance with developmental standards, policies, procedures, and methods. If noncompliance is detected, appropriate measures must be taken to either obtain a variance from the methodology or modify the system or design so that compliance is achieved. Although methodology does not necessarily satisfy user objectives, it is necessary to satisfy information services design objectives.

- **Program conforms to design.**

  - **Correctness.** Changing conditions cause many information services project personnel to ignore project objectives during the program phase. The argument is that there are sufficient changes so that monitoring compliance to system objectives is meaningless. The test team should discourage this thinking and continually monitor the implementation of objectives. If objectives have not been met, either they should be changed or the system changed to bring it into compliance with the functional specifications of the application.

  - **Ease of use.** The implementation of system specs may negate some of the ease-of-use design aspects unless those aspects are specifically defined. Programming is a translation of design specifications and it may fail to achieve the ease-of-use intent. Programming must achieve this ease-of-use design spec as it does other functional specifications.

- **Portability.** The portability of programs depends on the language selected and how that language is used. The specifications should indicate the do's and don'ts of programming for portability, and the coding should conform to those design specifications. If portability is a major concern and the program specifications fail to define portability coding adequately, the programmer should make every effort to write in as straightforward a method as possible.

- **Coupling.** The design specifications should indicate parameters passing to and from other application systems. It is normally good practice for the programmer to verify that the system's specifications are up-to-date prior to coding intersystem functions. This ensures not only that the programs conform to the design, but that the specifications of interconnected applications have not changed since the design was documented.

- **Performance.** The creation of the program provides the first operational opportunity for users to assess whether the system can achieve the desired performance level. At this point, the instructions to perform the requirements have been defined and can be evaluated. An early assessment of potential performance provides an opportunity to make performance adjustments if necessary.

- **Program is maintainable.** The method of program design and coding may have a greater significance for maintainability than the design specifications themselves. The rules of maintainable code should be partially defined by departmental standards, and partially defined by system specifications. In addition, the programmer should use judgment and experience in developing highly maintainable code.

- **Operating procedures developed.** Procedures should be developed during programming to operate the application system. During the next phase, the executable programs will be operated, and the necessary instructions should be developed prior to that phase of the SDLC. The operating procedures should be consistent with the application system operational requirements.

A detailed test process is illustrated in Work Paper 9-8 for each of the 15 identified programming phase test concerns. The test process includes test criteria, recommended test processes, techniques, and tools. The team conducting the test is urged to use judgment in determining the extent of tests and the applicability of the recommended techniques and tools to the application being tested. Work Paper 9-9 is a quality control checklist for this task.

Conducting a Peer Review

The peer review provides a vehicle for knowledgeable people (peers) to contribute to the construction of the computer program by informally but effectively reviewing the functioning of the program in a non-threatening environment. The peer review provides a static analysis that evaluates both the structure and the functioning of the program. The peer review can detect syntactical errors, but more through personal observation than as a direct result of the walkthrough.

Peer reviews can also be formal. Whether the formal or informal version is used, management should approve the peer review concept. Formal peer reviews are an integral task in the programming process, whereas informal peer reviews are called for at the discretion of the lead programmer.

The peer review team should consist of between three and six members. It is important to have at least three members on the peer review team to obtain sufficiently varied opinion and to keep discussion going. Individuals who should be considered for the peer review team include the following:

Computer programmers (at least two)

Job control specialists

Computer operator

Control clerk

Programming supervisor

Program peer reviews are performed by executing the following tasks.

Establishing Peer Review Ground Rules

This need not be done for every peer review, but it is important to have good ground rules. Among the ground rules that need to be decided are the following:

- Areas included and excluded from the peer review; for example, whether efficiency of programs will be included
- Whether reports will be issued
- Method for selecting peer review team leader
- Location of conducting the peer review
- Method for selecting a peer review

Selecting the Peer Review Team

The members of the peer review team should be selected sufficiently in advance so that they can arrange their schedules to allocate sufficient time and acquire training for the peer review exercise.

Training Team Members

If an individual on the team has not participated in the program peer review previously, that individual should be trained in the process. Training includes an understanding of the peer review ground rules, preferably some training in interpersonal relationships such as how to interview and work with people in a peer review process, and training in the intent of the standards and program methodologies.

Selecting a Review Method

The team leader should select the review method. The review itself consists of two parts. The first part is a general explanation of the objectives and functioning of the program. The second part is the review of the program(s) using the selected method. Four methods can be used to conduct the peer review:

1. **Flowchart.** The program is explained from a flowchart of the program logic. This is most effective when the flowchart is produced directly from the source code.

2. **Source code.** The review examines each line of source code in order to understand the program.

3. **Sample transactions.** The lead programmer explains the programs by explaining the processing that occurs on a representative sample of transactions.

4. **Program specifications.** The program specifications are reviewed as a means of understanding the program.

Conducting the Peer Review

The project lead programmer normally oversees the peer review. The peer review commences by having the lead programmer briefly review the ground rules, explain the program's objectives, and then lead the team through the program processing. The review team is free to question and comment on any aspect of the project programmer's explanations and to make recommendations and suggestions about the program. Generally, the peer review is conducted in a democratic manner. The role of the team leader is to ensure that the team's questions and comments are in order, ensure the team members' rights to ask questions, to make recommendations, or to stop interrogation on a specific point if, in the opinion of the inspection team leader, there is no benefit from continuing discussion.

Drawing Conclusions

At the end of the formal peer review, the lead programmer indicates that he or she has no more comments to make and turns the meeting over to the peer review team leader. The peer review team leader now takes control of the meeting and summarizes the factual information drawn from the review and presents the review team's recommendations. Ideally, this is done as a group activity, but some peer review teams, especially when the process is formalized, may want some time alone to discuss among themselves what they have heard and what they are going to recommend. The findings and recommendations are then presented to the project team for their consideration.

Preparing Reports

In the formal peer review process, reports may be prepared documenting the results. However, this is optional and not an essential part of the peer review process.

Check Procedures

Three quality control checklists are provided for this chapter. Testers should complete Work Paper 9-2 at the end of the requirements phase, Work Paper 9-7 at the end of the design phase, and Work Paper 9-9 at the end of the programming phase. The checklists are designed so that "Yes" responses indicate that the verification technique was performed correctly and "No" responses warrant further investigation.

Output

The only output from Task 1 is a report indicating requirements deficiencies. These will indicate where requirements are not accurate and/or complete. It is important that this report be prepared prior to completing the requirements checkpoint.

In Task 2, both the design review and the design deliverables inspection process will produce a defects list. Because the review is more general in nature, it may include some recommendations and areas of concern. Because inspections are more specific and tied to standards, these defects are usually variances from standards and are not debatable.

One of three categories of results can be produced from each design deliverables inspection:

No defects found

Minor work required

Major rework required

After all the steps in Task 2 have been performed, there should be only one deliverable: the moderator's certification of the product, releasing the product to the next phase of the process to make the organization software compliant.

Two outputs should occur from Task 3. The first is a fully debugged program, after you have used static testing to uncover and remove defects. The second is a list of the defects uncovered during testing. Note that if the organization has a quality assurance activity, that list of defects should be forwarded to them, so that they may address weaknesses in processes to eliminate reoccurrence of the same defects in other programs. In the formal peer review process in Task 3, reports may be prepared documenting the results. However, this is optional and not an essential part of the peer review process.

Guidelines

The walkthrough test tool and risk matrix are two of the more effective test tools for the requirements phase. The use of these tools will help determine whether the requirements phase test factors have been adequately addressed. These recommendations are not meant to exclude from use the other test tools applicable to the requirements phase, but rather to suggest and explain in detail two of the more effective tools for this phase.

Many of the available test tools for systems design are relatively new and unproven. Some of the more promising techniques require design specifications to be recorded in predetermined formats. Although the long-run potential for design phase testing is very promising, few proven design phase test tools currently exist.

Two design phase test tools that are receiving widespread acceptance are scoring and design reviews. Scoring is a tool designed to identify the risk associated with an automated application. The design review concept involves a formal assessment of the completeness of the process followed during the design phase. These two recommended test tools complement each other. Scoring is a process of identifying the system attributes that correlate to risk and then determining the extent to which those attributes are present or absent in the system being scored. The result of scoring is a determination of the degree of risk in the application system, and thus establishes the extent to which testing is needed. The design review then becomes the vehicle for testing the design specifications. The higher the risk, the more detailed the design review should be; for minimal-risk systems, the design review could be limited or even nonexistent.

Two test tools have proven themselves over the years in programming phase testing: desk debugging and peer review. These two tools are closely related and complement each other. Desk debugging is performed by the individual programmer prior to peer reviews, which are normally performed by other members of the information services department. A combination of the two tools is effective in detecting both structural and functional defects.

Summary

This chapter covers three tasks for performing verification during three phases of system development. Task 1 provides a process for assessing the accuracy and completeness of requirements. The cost of uncovering and correcting requirement deficiencies at this phase of development is significantly less than during acceptance testing. Estimates indicate that it would cost at least ten times as much to correct a requirement deficiency in acceptance testing than during this phase. If testers can increase the accuracy and completeness of requirements at this point of development, the test effort during the design phase can emphasize structural concerns and implementation concerns as opposed to identifying improper requirements at later test phases.

Task 2 describes a process for testers to evaluate the accuracy and completeness of the design process. Once verified as accurate and complete, the design can be moved to the build phase to create the code that will produce the needed results from the user-provided input.

Task 3 describes static testing during the build/programming phase. The method of generating computer code varies significantly from organization to organization, and from project to project.

The programming phase testing approach outlined in this task is designed to cover all methods of code generation. However, all of the techniques should be used when code is generated through statement languages. When code generators are used from design specifications, the program testing will be minimal. Some of these programming testing techniques may be incorporated in design phase testing. After the static verification testing is done, the testing emphasis shifts to dynamic testing.

WORK PAPER 9-1 Requirements Test Phase Process

TEST FACTOR: Requirements Comply with Methodology

| TEST CRITERIA | ASSESSMENT | | | | RECOMMENDED TEST | TEST TECHNIQUE | TEST TOOL |
	Very Ade-quate	Ade-quate	Inade-quate	N/A			
1. Have the applicable organization's policies and procedures been identified?					Confirm with those individuals responsible for developing the policies and procedures that all the applicable policies have been identified.	Compliance	Confirmation/examination
2. Do the requirements comply with these policies and procedures?					Review requirement to ensure compliance.	Compliance	Fact finding
3. Have the requirements been documented in accordance with the requirements methodology?					Examine requirements to ensure all needed documentation is complete.	Compliance	Checklist
4. Is the cost/benefit analysis prepared in accordance with the appropriate procedures?					Examine cost/benefit analysis to ensure it was prepared in accordance with procedures.	Compliance	Checklist
5. Has the requirements phase met the intent of the requirements methodology?					Review the deliverables from requirements and assess if they meet the intent of the methodology.	Compliance	Checklist
6. Is the requirements phase staffed according to procedures?					Verify that the project is appropriately staffed.	Compliance	Peer review
7. Will all of the applicable policies, procedures, and requirements be in effect at the time the system goes in operation?					Confirm with the appropriate parties the effective dates of existing policies, procedures, and regulations.	Compliance	Fact finding
8. Will there be new standards, policies, and procedures in effect at the time the system goes operational?					Confirm with the appropriate parties the effective dates of new standards, policies, and procedures.	Compliance	Fact finding

(continues)

WORK PAPER 9-1 *(continued)*

TEST FACTOR: Functional Specifications Defined

TEST CRITERIA	ASSESSMENT				RECOMMENDED TEST	TEST TECHNIQUE	TEST TOOL
	Very Adequate	Adequate	Inadequate	N/A			
1. Can the data required by the application be collected with the desired degree of reliability?					Confirm with the people who would generate the data that it can be generated with the desired degree of reliability.	Requirements	Fact finding
2. Can the data be collected within the time period specified?					Confirm with the people generating the data that it can be collected within the required time frame.	Requirements	Fact finding
3. Have the user requirements been defined in writing?					Confirm with the user that the requirements in writing are complete.	Requirements	Checklist
4. Are the requirements stated in measurable terms?					Examine the reasonableness of the criteria for measuring successful completion of the requirements.	Requirements	Walkthroughs
5. Has the project solution addressed the user requirements?					Examine the system specifications to confirm they satisfy the user's stated objectives.	Requirements	Walkthroughs
6. Could test data be developed to test the achievement of the objectives?					Verify that the requirements are stated in enough detail that they could generate test data to verify compliance.	Requirements	Test data
7. Have procedures been specified to evaluate the implemented system to ensure the requirements are achieved?					Examine the specifications that indicate a post-installation review will occur.	Requirements	Confirmation/ examination
8. Do the measurable objectives apply to both the manual and automated segments of the application system?					Examine to verify that the system objectives cover both the manual and automated segments of the application.	Requirements	Confirmation/ examination

WORK PAPER 9-1 *(continued)*

TEST FACTOR: Usability Specifications Defined

TEST CRITERIA	ASSESSMENT				RECOMMENDED TEST	TEST TECHNIQUE	TEST TOOL
	Very Adequate	Adequate	Inadequate	N/A			
1. Have the user functions been identified?					Confirm with the user that all user functions are defined in requirements.	Manual support	Confirmation/ examination
2. Have the skill levels of the users been identified?					Examine requirements documentation describing user skill level.	Manual support	Confirmation/ examination
3. Have the expected levels of supervision been identified?					Examine requirements documentation describing expected level of supervision.	Manual support	Confirmation/ examination
4. Has the time span for user functions been defined?					Confirm with the user that the stated time span for processing is reasonable.	Manual support	Confirmation/ examination
5. Will the counsel of an industrial psychologist be used in designing user functions?					Confirm that the industrial psychologist's services will be used.	Manual support	Confirmation/ examination
6. Have clerical personnel been interviewed during the requirements phase to identify their concerns?					Confirm with clerical personnel that their input has been obtained.	Manual support	Confirmation/ examination
7. Have tradeoffs between computer and people processing been identified?					Examine reasonableness of identified tradeoffs.	Manual support	Design reviews
8. Have the defined user responsibilities been presented to the user personnel for comment?					Confirm that users have examined their responsibilities.	Manual support	Confirmation/ examination

(continues)

WORK PAPER 9-1 *(continued)*

TEST FACTOR: Maintenance Specifications Defined

TEST CRITERIA	ASSESSMENT				RECOMMENDED TEST	TEST TECHNIQUE	TEST TOOL
	Very Adequate	Adequate	Inadequate	N/A			
1. Has the expected life of the project been defined?					Confirm with the user that the stated project life is reasonable.	Compliance	Confirmation/ examination
2. Has the expected frequency of change been defined?					Confirm with the user that the expected frequency of change is reasonable.	Compliance	Confirmation/ examination
3. Has the importance of keeping the system up to date functionally been defined?					Confirm with the user that the stated importance of functional updates is correct.	Compliance	Confirmation/ examination
4. Has the importance of keeping the system up to date technologically been defined?					Confirm with IT management that the importance of technological updates is correct.	Compliance	Confirmation/ examination
5. Has it been decided who will perform maintenance on the project?					Confirm with IT management who will perform maintenance.	Compliance	Confirmation/ examination
6. Are the areas of greatest expected change identified?					Examine documentation for areas of expected change.	Compliance	Peer review
7. Has the method of introducing change during development been identified?					Examine project change procedures.	Compliance	Checklist
8. Have provisions been included to properly document the application for maintenance purposes?					Examine the completeness of project maintenance documentation.	Compliance	Peer review

WORK PAPER 9-1   *(continued)*

TEST FACTOR: Portability Needs Determined

TEST CRITERIA	ASSESSMENT				RECOMMENDED TEST	TEST TECHNIQUE	TEST TOOL
	Very Ade-quate	Ade-quate	Inade-quate	N/A			
1. Are significant hardware changes expected during the life of the project?					Confirm with computer operations expected hardware changes.	Operations	Confirmation/ examination
2. Are significant software changes expected during the life of the project?					Confirm with computer operations expected software changes.	Operations	Confirmation/ examination
3. Will the application system be run in multiple locations?					Confirm with the user the locations where the application will be operated.	Compliance	Confirmation/ examination
4. If an online application, will different types of terminals be used?					Examine terminal hardware requirements.	Compliance	Confirmation/ examination
5. Is the proposed solution dependent on specific hardware?					Review requirements to identify hardware restrictions.	Compliance	Inspections
6. Is the proposed solution dependent on specific software?					Review requirements to identify software restrictions.	Compliance	Inspections
7. Will the application be run in other countries?					Confirm with the user the countries in which the application will be run.	Compliance	Confirmation/ examination
8. Have the portability requirements been documented?					Examine the requirements documentation for portability requirements.	Compliance	Inspections

(continues)

WORK PAPER 9-1 *(continued)*

TEST FACTOR: Systems Interface Defined

TEST CRITERIA	ASSESSMENT				RECOMMENDED TEST	TEST TECHNIQUE	TEST TOOL
	Very Adequate	Adequate	Inadequate	N/A			
1. Have data to be received from other applications been identified?					Confirm with the project team that interfaced applications have been identified.	Intersystems	Confirmation/ examination
2. Have data going to other applications been identified?					Confirm with the project team that interfaced applications have been identified.	Intersystems	Confirmation/ examination
3. Has the reliability of interfaced data been defined?					Confirm with other applications the reasonableness of reliability requirements.	Control	Fact finding
4. Has the timing of transmitting data been defined?					Confirm with other applications the reasonableness of timing requirements.	Control	Fact finding
5. Has the timing of data being received been defined?					Confirm with other applications the reasonableness of timing requirements.	Control	Fact finding
6. Has the method of interfacing been defined?					Examine documentation to ensure the completeness of interface methods.	Intersystems	Walkthroughs
7. Have the interface requirements been documented?					Verify completeness of the interface requirements documentation.	Intersystems	Walkthroughs
8. Have future needs of interfaced systems been taken into consideration?					Confirm with interfaced projects the need to consider future requirements.	Intersystems	Fact finding

WORK PAPER 9-1 *(continued)*

TEST FACTOR: Performance Criteria Established

	ASSESSMENT						
TEST CRITERIA	Very Ade-quate	Ade-quate	Inade-quate	N/A	RECOMMENDED TEST	TEST TECHNIQUE	TEST TOOL
1. Will hardware and software be obtained through competitive bidding?					Examine the reasonableness of the competitive bidding procedures.	Compliance	Acceptance test criteria
2. Have cost-effectiveness criteria been defined?					Examine the cost-effectiveness criteria.	Compliance	Confirmation/ examination
3. Has the cost-effectiveness for this application system been calculated in accordance with the procedures?					Examine the calculation and confirm that it has been prepared in accordance with the procedures.	Compliance	Checklist
4. Are the cost-effectiveness procedures applicable to this application?					Confirm with the user that the procedures are applicable to this application.	Compliance	Confirmation/ examination
5. Could application characteristics cause the actual cost to vary significantly from the projections?					Confirm with the user that there are no unusual characteristics that could cause the cost to vary significantly.	Compliance	Confirmation/ examination
6. Are there application characteristics that could cause the benefits to vary significantly from the projected benefits?					Confirm with the user that there are no characteristics that would cause the actual benefits to vary significantly from the projected benefits.	Compliance	Confirmation/ examination
7. Is the expected life of the project reasonable?					Confirm with the user the reasonable life for the project.	Compliance	Confirmation/ examination
8. Does a design phase schedule exist that identifies tasks, people, budgets, and costs?					Examine the completeness of the design phase work program.	Compliance	Design review

(continues)

WORK PAPER 9-1 *(continued)*

TEST FACTOR: Operational Needs Defined

TEST CRITERIA	ASSESSMENT				RECOMMENDED TEST	TEST TECHNIQUE	TEST TOOL
	Very Ade-quate	Ade-quate	Inade-quate	N/A			
1. Have the volume of transactions been identified?					Confirm with user that the volume of transactions is correct.	Compliance	Confirmation/examination
2. Has the timing of processing been determined?					Confirm with user that the timing is reasonable.	Compliance examination	Confirmation/examination
3. Has the frequency of processing been determined?					Confirm with user that the frequency is reasonable.	Compliance	Confirmation/examination
4. Has the number of documents that need to be stored online been determined?					Confirm with user that the storage requirements are correct.	Compliance	Confirmation/examination
5. Will communication capabilities be required for processing?					Confirm with user that the communication needs are correct.	Compliance	Confirmation/examination
6. Will special processing capabilities such as optical scanners be required?					Review documentation to identify special processing needs.	Operations	Peer review
7. Will computer operations be expected to perform special tasks, such as data entry?					Review documentation to identify special operating requirements.	Operations	Peer review
8. Has it been confirmed with computer operations that they havebeen advised of project requirements?					Confirm with computer operations that they have been advised of project requirements.	Operations	Confirmation/examination

WORK PAPER 9-1 *(continued)*

TEST FACTOR: Tolerances Established

TEST CRITERIA	ASSESSMENT				RECOMMENDED TEST	TEST TECHNIQUE	TEST TOOL
	Very Adequate	Adequate	Inadequate	N/A			
1. Have the significant financial fields been identified?					Confirm with the accounting department that the indicated financial fields are the key financial fields for the application system.	Control	Confirmation/ examination
2. Has responsibility for the accuracy and completeness of each financial field been assigned?					Examine system documentation indicating individual responsible for each key financial field.	Control	Inspections
3. Have the accuracy and completeness risks been identified?					Assess the completeness of the identified risks.	Requirements	Walkthroughs
4. Has the individual responsible for each field stated the required precision for financial accuracy?					Review the system documentation to determine that the stated accuracy precision is recorded.	Control	Confirmation/ examination
5. Has the accounting cutoff method been determined?					Confirm with the user that the projected cutoff procedure is realistic.	Control	Confirmation/ examination
6. Have procedures been established to ensure that all of the transactions will be entered on a timely basis?					Examine the reasonableness of the procedures to ensure the timely recording of transactions.	Control	Walkthroughs
7. Has a procedure been specified to monitor the accuracy of financial information?					Review the reasonableness of the procedures to monitor financial accuracy.	Control	Walkthroughs
8. Are rules established on handling inaccurate and incomplete data?					Review the reasonableness of the procedures to handle inaccurate and incomplete data.	Error handling	Inspections

(continues)

TEST FACTOR: Authorization Rules Defined

TEST CRITERIA	ASSESSMENT				RECOMMENDED TEST	TEST TECHNIQUE	TEST TOOL
	Very Adequate	Adequate	Inadequate	N/A			
1. Have all of the key transactions been identified?					Confirm with the user that all of the key transactions are identified.	Security	Confirmation/ examination
2. Have the rules for authorizing each of the key transactions been determined?					Verify that the authorization rules comply with organizational policies and procedures.	Control	Confirmation/ examination & Peer review
3. Are the authorization rules consistent with the value of the resources controlled by the transaction?					Review the reasonableness of the authorization rules in relationship to the resources controlled.	Requirements	Walkthroughs and Peer review
4. Have the individuals who can authorize each transaction been identified?					Verify that the individuals have been granted that specific authorization by management.	Control	Confirmation/ examination & Peer review
5. Have specifications been determined requiring the name of the individual authorizing the transaction to be carried with the transaction?					Review the documentation to verify the specifications require the system to maintain records on who authorized each transaction.	Requirements	Inspection
6. Have the transactions that will be automatically generated by the system been identified?					Confirm with the user that all of the transactions that will be computer generated have been identified.	Security	Confirmation/ examination
7. Have the rules for authorizing computer-generated transactions been identified?					Verify that these authorization rules are consistent with the organization's policies and procedures.	Control	Confirmation/ examination
8. Have procedures to monitor the reasonableness of computer-generated transactions been specified?					Review the reasonableness of the procedures that will monitor computer-generated transactions.	Requirements	Walkthroughs

WORK PAPER 9-1 *(continued)*

TEST FACTOR: File Integrity Requirements

TEST CRITERIA	ASSESSMENT				RECOMMENDED TEST	TEST TECHNIQUE	TEST TOOL
	Very Ade-quate	Ade-quate	Inade-quate	N/A			
1. Have key computer files been identified?					Confirm with the user that the identified files are the key files.	Requirements	Confirmation/ examination
2. Has the composition of the data on each of the key files been identified?					Confirm with the user that the major data fields have been identified.	Requirements	Confirmation/ examination
3. Have the key control fields been identified?					Confirm with the user that the identified key fields are the key control fields.	Requirements	Confirmation/ examination
4. Has the method of internal file integrity for each of the key fields been determined?					Verify the reasonableness of the method to ensure the integrity of the key fields within the automated system.	Control	Walkthroughs
5. In a multiuser system, has one user been assigned data integrity responsibility?					Determine the reasonableness of assigning responsibility to the named individual.	Control	Fact finding
6. Has a decision been made as to whether the integrity of the field warrants an external, independently maintained control total?					Confirm with the organization's comptroller the importance of the key fields with which independent external control totals are not maintained.	Control	Confirmation/ examination
7. Has the method of maintaining independent control totals on the key fields been determined?					Examine the reasonableness of the method for maintaining independent control totals on key fields.	Control	Fact finding
8. Have tolerances been established on the degree of reliability expected from file integrity controls?					Confirm the reasonableness of the integrity tolerances with the organization's comptroller.	Control	Confirmation/ examination

(continues)

WORK PAPER 9-1 *(continued)*

TEST FACTOR: Reconstruction Requirements Defined

TEST CRITERIA	ASSESSMENT				RECOMMENDED TEST	TEST TECHNIQUE	TEST TOOL
	Very Ade-quate	Ade-quate	Inade-quate	N/A			
1. Does the organization's record retention policy include automated applications?					Review the applicability of the record retention policy to automated applications.	Control	Walkthroughs
2. Have the criteria for reconstructing transaction processing been determined?					Review the reasonableness of the reconstruction criteria with the application user.	Requirements	Fact finding
3. Have the criteria for reconstructing computer files been determined?					Verify the reasonableness of reconstruction procedures with the manager of computer operations.	Requirements	Fact finding
4. Is requirements documentation adequate and in compliance with standards?					Verify the completeness and adequacy of requirements documentation.	Requirements	Inspections
5. Have the criteria for reconstructing processing from a point of known integrity been determined?					Confirm the reasonableness of the processing reconstruction requirements with the manager of computer operations.	Requirements	Confirmation/ examination
6. Has the project stated a requirement to trace transactions to application control totals?					Verify that the system specifications include this requirement.	Control	Confirmation/ examination
7. Has the project stated a requirement specifying that control totals must be supportable by identifying all the transactions comprising that control total?					Verify that the system specifications include this requirement.	Control	Confirmation/ examination
8. Has the retention period for all of the reconstruction information been specified?					Confirm that the retention periods are in accordance with the organization's record retention policy.	Requirements	Inspections

WORK PAPER 9-1 (continued)

TEST FACTOR: Impact of Failure Defined

TEST CRITERIA	ASSESSMENT				RECOMMENDED TEST	TEST TECHNIQUE	TEST TOOL
	Very Ade-quate	Ade-quate	Inade-quate	N/A			
1. Has the dollar loss of an application system failure been defined?					Examine the reasonableness of the dollar loss.	Recovery	Fact finding
2. Has the dollar loss calculation for a failure been extended to show the loss at different time intervals, such as one hour, eight hours, one day, one week, etc.?					Examine the reasonableness of the loss amounts at various time intervals.	Recovery	Fact finding
3. Is the proposed system technology reliable and proven in practice?					Confirm with independent sources the reliability and track record of the recommended hardware and software.	Recovery	Confirmation/ examination
4. Has a decision been made as to whether it is necessary to recover this application in the event of a system failure?					Confirm the correctness of the decision with the system user.	Recovery	Confirmation/ examination
5. Are alternate processing procedures needed in the event that the system becomes unoperational?					Confirm with the user the need for alternate processing procedures.	Recovery	Confirmation/ examination
6. If alternate processing procedures are needed, have they been specified?					Confirm with the user the reasonableness of those alternate processing procedures.	Recovery	Confirmation/ examination
7. Has a procedure been identified for notifying users in the event of a system failure?					Confirm with the user the reasonableness of the notification procedure.	Recovery	Confirmation/ examination
8. Has the desired percent of up-time for the system been specified?					Confirm with the user the reasonableness of the up-time.	Recovery	Confirmation/ examination

(continues)

WORK PAPER 9-1 (continued)

TEST FACTOR: Desired Service Level Defined

TEST CRITERIA	ASSESSMENT				RECOMMENDED TEST	TEST TECHNIQUE	TEST TOOL
	Very Ade-quate	Ade-quate	Inade-quate	N/A			
1. Has the response time for each transaction been identified?					Confirm with the user that the response times are reasonable.	Operations	Confirmation/examination
2. Has a schedule been established indicating which part of the system is run on which day?					Confirm with computer operations that there is sufficient capacity to meet these service levels.	Operations	Confirmation/examination
3. Do all vendor contracts indicate maintenance support for key hardware and software?					Review contractual specifications to ensure they include maintenance.	Operations	Confirmation/examination
4. Have processing tolerances been established for each part of the system?					Confirm with the user that these service level tolerances are correct.	Operations	Confirmation/examination
5. Can computer operations process the requirements within the expected tolerances?					Confirm with the manager of computer operations the reasonableness of the tolerances.	Operations	Confirmation/examination
6. Has the priority of each part of system processing been decided to determine which segment runs first in the event computer time is limited?					Confirm with the user the reasonableness of the priorities.	Operations	Confirmation/examination
7. Has the priority of each application been established in relationship to other applications to determine priority of processing after a failure and in the event of limited computer time?					Confirm with a member of executive management the reasonableness of the application system priority.	Operations	Confirmation/examination
8. Has the volume of processing requirements been projected for a reasonable period of time in the future?					Confirm with the manager of operations there will be sufficient capacity to meet these increased volumes.	Operations	Confirmation/examination

TEST FACTOR: Access Defined

TEST CRITERIA	ASSESSMENT				RECOMMENDED TEST	TEST TECHNIQUE	TEST TOOL
	Very Adequate	Adequate	Inadequate	N/A			
1. Have the application resources been identified?					Confirm with the user that the identified resources are complete.	Security	Risk matrix & Confirmation/ examination
2. Have the users of those resources been identified?					Confirm with the individual responsible for those resources that the users are authorized.	Security	Risk matrix & Confirmation/ examination
3. Have the individuals responsible for those resources been identified?					Confirm with user management that these are the individuals responsible for those resources.	Security	Risk matrix & Confirmation/ examination
4. Has a profile been established matching resources with the users authorized to access those resources?					Examine the completeness of the user profile.	Security	Risk matrix & Peer review
5. Have procedures been identified to enforce the user profile?					Confirm with the manager of computer operations that the procedures are workable.	Security	Confirmation/ examination
6. Has the importance of each resource been identified?					Confirm with the individual responsible that the security classifications are correct.	Security	Confirmation/ examination
7. Has a procedure been established for monitoring access violations?					Evaluate the reasonableness of the monitoring procedures.	Control	Fact finding
8. Has a process been established to punish access violators?					Confirm with management that they intend to enforce violation procedures.	Control	Confirmation/ examination

WORK PAPER 9-2 Quality Control Checklist

	YES	NO	N/A	COMMENTS
1. Are the defined requirements testable?				
2. Does the user agree the defined requirements are correct?				
3. Do the developers understand the requirements?				
4. Do the stated requirements meet the stated business objectives for the project?				
5. Have the project risks been identified?				
6. Was a reasonable process followed in defining the requirements?				
7. Are project control requirements adequate to minimize project risks?				
8. Was a project requirements walkthrough conducted?				

WORK PAPER 9-3 Computer Applications Risk Scoring Form[1]

SIGNIFICANT CHARACTERISTICS	INDICATIVE OF HIGH RISK	INDICATIVE OF MEDIUM RISK	INDICATIVE OF LOW RISK	COMMENTS
System Scope and Complexity				
Organizational breadth				
a) Important functions	Must meet important conflicting needs of several organizational units.	Meets limited conflicting requirements of cooperative organizational units.	No significant conflicting needs, serves primarily one organizational unit.	
b) Unrelated organizational units deeply involved	Dependent upon data flowing from many organizational units not under unified direction.	Dependent upon data from a few organizational units with a common interest; if not unified control.	Virtually all input data comes from a small group of sections under unified control.	
Information services breadth				
a) Number of transaction types	More than 25	6 to 25	Fewer than 6	
b) Number of related record segments	More than 6	4 to 6	Fewer than 4	
c) Output reports	More than 20	10 to 20	Fewer than 10	
Margin of error				
a) Necessity for everything to work perfectly, for "split-second timing" for great cooperation (perhaps including external parties), etc.	Very demanding	Realistically demanding	Comfortable margin	
Technical complexity				
a) Number of programs including sort/merge	More than 35	20 to 35	Fewer than 20	

[1]Risk scoring method developed by the General Accounting Office.

(continues)

WORK PAPER 9-3 *(continued)*

SIGNIFICANT CHARACTERISTICS	INDICATIVE OF HIGH RISK	INDICATIVE OF MEDIUM RISK	INDICATIVE OF LOW RISK	COMMENTS
b) Programming approach (number of module/functions interacting within an update/file maintenance program)	More than 20	10 to 20	Fewer than 10	
c) Size of largest program	More than 60K	25K to 60K	Fewer than 25K	
d) Adaptability of program to change	Low, due to monolithic program design.	Can support problems with adequate talent and effort.	Relatively high; program straightforward, modular, roomy, relatively unpatched, well-documented, etc.	
e) Relationship to equipment in use	Pushes equipment capacity near limits.	Within capacities.	Substantial unused capacity.	
f) Reliance on online data entry, automatic document reading, or other advanced techniques	Heavy, including direct entry of transactions and other changes into the master files.	Remote-batch processing under remote operations control.	None or limited to file inquiry.	
Pioneering aspects Extent to which the system applies new, difficult, and unproven techniques on a broad scale or in a new situation, thus placing great demands on the non-IS departments, systems and programming groups, IS operations personnel, customers, or vendors, etc.	More than a few relatively untried equipment or system software components or system techniques or objectives, at least one of which is crucial.	Few untried systems components and their functions are moderately important; few, if any, pioneering system objectives and techniques.	No untried system components; no pioneering system objectives or techniques.	

WORK PAPER 9-3 *(continued)*

SIGNIFICANT CHARACTERISTICS	INDICATIVE OF HIGH RISK	INDICATIVE OF MEDIUM RISK	INDICATIVE OF LOW RISK	COMMENTS
System stability				
a) Age of system (since inception or last big change)	Less than 1 year	1 to 2 years	Over 2 years	
b) Frequency of significant change	More than 4 per year	2 to 4 per year	Fewer than 2 per year	
c) Extent of total change in last year	Affecting more than 25% of programs.	Affecting 10 to 25% of programs.	Affecting less than 10% of programs.	
d) User approval of specifications	Cursory, essentially uninformed.	Reasonably informed as to general but not detailed specifications; approval apt to be informal.	Formal, written approval, based on informed judgment and written, reasonably precise specifications.	
Satisfaction of user requirements				
a) Completeness	Incomplete, significant number of items not processed in proper period.	Occasional problems but normally no great difficulties.	No significant data omitted or processed in wrong period.	
b) Accuracy	Considerable error problem, with items in suspense or improperly handled.	Occasional problems but normally not great difficulties.	Errors not numerous or of consequence.	
c) Promptness in terms of needs	Reports and documents delayed so as to be almost useless; forced to rely on informal records.	Reports and documents not always available when desired; present timetable inconvenient but tolerable.	Reports and documents produced soon enough to meet operational needs.	

(continues)

WORK PAPER 9-3 (continued)

SIGNIFICANT CHARACTERISTICS	INDICATIVE OF HIGH RISK	INDICATIVE OF MEDIUM RISK	INDICATIVE OF LOW RISK	COMMENTS
d) Accessibility of details (to answer inquiries, review for reasonableness, make corrections, etc.)	Great difficulty in obtaining details of transactions or balances except with much delay.	Complete details available monthly; in interim, details available with some difficulty and delay.	Details readily available.	
e) Reference to source documents (audit trail)	Great difficulty in locating documents promptly.	Audit trail excellent; some problems with filing and storage.	Audit trail excellent; filing and storage good.	
f) Conformity with established system specifications	Actual procedures and operations differ in important respects.	Limited tests indicate that actual procedures and operations differ in only minor respects and operations produce desired results.	Limited tests indicate actual procedures and operations produce desired results.	
Source data origin and approval				
a) People, procedures, knowledge, discipline, division of duties, etc. in departments that originate and/or approve data	Situation leaves much to be desired.	Situation satisfactory, but could stand some improvement.	Situation satisfactory.	
b) Data control procedures outside the information services organization	None or relatively ineffective; e.g., use of noncritical fields, loose liaison with IT department, little concern with rejected items.	Control procedures based on noncritical fields; reasonably effective liaison with IT department.	Control procedures include critical fields; good tie-in with IT department; especially good on rejected items.	
c) Error rate	Over 7% of transactions rejected after leaving source data department.	4–7% of transactions rejected after leaving source data department.	Less than 4% of transactions rejected after leaving source data department.	

WORK PAPER 9-3 *(continued)*

SIGNIFICANT CHARACTERISTICS	INDICATIVE OF HIGH RISK	INDICATIVE OF MEDIUM RISK	INDICATIVE OF LOW RISK	COMMENTS
d) Error backing	Many 30-day-old items.	Mostly 10–15-day-old items.	Items primarily less than 7 days old.	
Input data control (within IT department)				
a) Relationship with external controls	Loose liaison with external control units; little concern with rejected items; batch totals not part of input procedures; only use controls like item counts; no control totals of any kind.	Reasonably effective liaison with external data control units; good control over new items, but less satisfactory control over rejected items; batch totals received, but generated by computer.	Good tie-in with external control units for both valid and rejected items; batch totals received as part of input process.	
b) Selection of critical control fields	Control based on noncritical fields.	Control based on a mixture of critical and noncritical fields, with effective supplementary checks.	Control established on critical fields.	
c) Controls over key transcription	Control based on batch totals.	Control based on transmittal sheets; batch totals and key verification of critical fields not batch controlled.	Control based on transmittal sheets; batch totals maintained on data logs; key verification of all critical fields; written "sign-off" procedures.	
Data validation				
a) Edit tests	Alphanumeric tests.	Range and alphanumeric tests.	Range, alphanumeric, and check-digit tests.	
b) Sophistication	Simple, based on edit of one field at a time.	Simple editing, plus some editing based on the interrelationship of two fields.	Simple editing, plus extensive edit tests based on the interrelationship of two or more fields.	

(continues)

WORK PAPER 9-3 *(continued)*

SIGNIFICANT CHARACTERISTICS	INDICATIVE OF HIGH RISK	INDICATIVE OF MEDIUM RISK	INDICATIVE OF LOW RISK	COMMENTS
c) Application to critical data	A considerable amount of critical data is not edited.	A few critical fields are edited only indirectly.	Editing performed on critical fields.	
d) Error balancing, retrieval, and correction procedures	Error rejected by system and eliminated from controls; treated as new items when reintroduced.	Number and value of rejected items carried in suspense account without electronically maintained details.	Error carried in suspense account in total and in detail until removed by correction.	
Computer processing control procedure				
a) Controls within machine room	Informal operating instructions.	Written operating procedures.	Operations are based on a schedule and use up-to-date instructions.	
b) Manual and electronic safeguards against incorrect processing of files	Tape library controls by serial number; no programmed checks.	Tape library controls by serial number; programmed checks applied to file identification.	Programmed label check applied to serial number, expiration date, and the identification.	
c) Recording of run-to-run debit, credit, and balance totals for both transaction processing and master field records	Run-to-run totals not used.	Run-to-run totals printed and compared manually.	Run-to-run totals printed and compared by program.	
d) Documentation status	Poor or no standards; uneven adherence; not part of system and program development.	Adequate practices not uniformly adhered to; documentation done "after the fact."	Excellent standards closely adhered to and carried out as part of system and program development.	
e) System test practices	Some transaction paths not tested.	Each transaction path tested individually.	Each transaction path tested in combination with all other transactions.	

WORK PAPER 9-3 *(continued)*

SIGNIFICANT CHARACTERISTICS	INDICATIVE OF HIGH RISK	INDICATIVE OF MEDIUM RISK	INDICATIVE OF LOW RISK	COMMENTS
Output control				
a) Quantitative controls	Virtually nonexistent.	Hard to tie back meaningfully to input controls.	Tied back to input controls.	
b) Qualitative controls	Documents and reports accepted virtually without review.	Documents and reports receive limited review.	Documents and reports tested in detail, in addition to receiving a "common sense" review of reasonable data limits.	
c) Distribution controls	No routine report distribution procedures.	Routine procedures for distribution limited to list of users and frequency of report delivery.	Written procedures requiring that control log indicate receipt by user, time of accounting for each copy, etc.	
Online processing controls				
a) Data transmission controls, including error detection, error recovery, and data security	The front-end control program does not validate operator identification codes or message sequence number, and does not send acknowledgment to origin.	The front-end control program checks terminal and operator identification codes and message sequence number, sends acknowledgment to origin, and provides a transaction log.	The front-end control program validates terminal/operator identification codes plus transaction authorization codes and message sequence number and count, corrects errors, sends acknowledgment to origin, and provides log of transactions plus copies of updated master file records.	

(continues)

WORK PAPER 9-3 *(continued)*

SIGNIFICANT CHARACTERISTICS	INDICATIVE OF HIGH RISK	INDICATIVE OF MEDIUM RISK	INDICATIVE OF LOW RISK	COMMENTS
b) Data validation controls, including error detection and correction	Neither the front-end control nor the application processing program checks for authorization approval codes; no check digits are used with identification keys; little use of extensive data relationship tests; erroneous transactions are rejected without analysis or suspense entry.	The application program checks approval codes for key transaction types only, but check digits are not used with identification keys; extensive data relationship tests are used; erroneous transactions are sent back to terminal with a note, butno suspense entry is made.	The application program validates approval codes for all transactions, and check digits are used with identification keys; data relationship tests are used extensively; erroneous transactions are noted in error suspense file when sent back to terminal with note.	
c) Information services controls, including error detection, transaction processing, master file processing, and file recovery provisions	Application program produces a total number of transactions processed; no master file processing controls; file recovery provisions limited to periodic copy of master file.	Application program produces a summary record of all debit and credit transactions processed; no master file processing controls; file recovery provisions limited to transaction log and periodic copy of master file.	Stored validation range values are used to validate transaction fields; application program summarizes all transactions processed by type, with credit and debit values for each terminal, and uses a master file control trailer record that is balanced by program routine; end-of-processing file recovery provisions include transaction log of active master file records.	

WORK PAPER 9-4 Design Phase Test Process

TEST FACTOR: Data Integrity Controls Designed

TEST CRITERIA	ASSESSMENT				RECOMMENDED TEST	TEST TECHNIQUE	TEST TOOL
	Very Adequate	Adequate	Inadequate	N/A			
1. Are controls established over accuracy and completeness during the transaction origination process?					Review the adequacy of the transaction origination accuracy and completeness control.	Control	Risk matrix & Checklist
2. Are input transactions controlled, such as through a sequential input number, to ensure that all transactions are entered?					Review the adequacy of the input controls to ensure that all input is entered.	Control	Risk matrix & Checklist
3. Are communication controls established to ensure the accurate and complete transmission of data?					Review the adequacy of transmission accuracy and completeness controls.	Control	Risk matrix & Checklist
4. For key entry transactions, such as cash receipts, are batch control totals prepared?					Verify the adequacy of the batch control total procedures.	Requirements	Control flow analysis
5. For key entry input transactions, such as purchase orders, are batch numbers prepared to ensure that batches of input are not lost?					Verify the adequacy of the batch numbering procedures.	Requirements	Control flow analysis
6. Are check digits or equivalent controls used on key control fields, such as product number, to ensure the accurate entry of product number?					Verify that key fields use procedures that ensure the accurate entry of that information.	Requirements	Error guessing & Design-based functional testing

(continues)

WORK PAPER 9-4 (continued)

TEST FACTOR: Data Integrity Controls Designed (continued)

TEST CRITERIA	ASSESSMENT				RECOMMENDED TEST	TEST TECHNIQUE	TEST TOOL
	Very Adequate	Adequate	Inadequate	N/A			
7. Is each field subject to extensive data validation checks?					Examine the type and scope of data validation checks for each key field to determine that they are adequate.	Error handling	Acceptance test criteria, Error guessing. Checklist, & Data dictionary
8. Are input numbers, batch numbers, and batch totals verified by the data validation programs to ensure the accurate and complete input of transactions?					Verify that the controls established at the time of manual input preparation are verified by the computer program.	Control	Inspections

WORK PAPER 9-4 *(continued)*

TEST FACTOR: Authorization Rules Designed

TEST CRITERIA	ASSESSMENT				RECOMMENDED TEST	TEST TECHNIQUE	TEST TOOL
	Very Ade-quate	Ade-quate	Inade-quate	N/A			
1. Has the method for authorizing each transaction been documented?					Review the documentation to ensure authorization rules are complete.	Security	Checklist & Inspections
2. For those documents whose authorization is dependent upon the source of origination as opposed to a signature, can that source of origination be verified by the application system?					Determine that for transactions whose entry itself indicates authorization, that those transactions can only originate from the properly authorized source.	Security	Checklist, Error guessing, & Inspections
3. In a multiuser system, has responsibility for authorization been assigned to a single individual?					Determine the adequacy of the assigned authorization responsibilities in a multiuser system.	Control	Inspections & Fact finding
4. Is the authorization method consistent with the value of the resources being authorized?					Review the reasonableness of the authorization method in relationship to the resources being controlled.	Requirements	Cause effect graphing, Walkthroughs, & Scoring
5. If passwords are used for authorization, are procedures adequate to protect passwords?					Review the adequacy of the password protection procedures.	Control	Error guessing
6. If passwords are used, will they be changed at reasonable frequencies?					Determine the reasonableness of the frequency for changing passwords.	Control	Error guessing

(continues)

WORK PAPER 9-4 *(continued)*

TEST FACTOR: Authorization Rules Designed *(continued)*

TEST CRITERIA	ASSESSMENT				RECOMMENDED TEST	TEST TECHNIQUE	TEST TOOL
	Very Ade-quate	Ade-quate	Inade-quate	N/A			
7. Are the authorization rules verified by the automated segment of the application?					Examine the documentation for verifying authorization rules.	Security	Checklist, Risk matrix, & Inspections
8. Are procedures established to report authorization violations to management?					Examine the reasonableness of the procedure to report authorization violations to management.	Control	Error guessing & Inspections

WORK PAPER 9-4 *(continued)*

TEST FACTOR: File Integrity Controls Designed

TEST CRITERIA	ASSESSMENT				RECOMMENDED TEST	TEST TECHNIQUE	TEST TOOL
	Very Ade-quate	Ade-quate	Inade-quate	N/A			
1. Have the fields been identified that will be used to verify file integrity?					Confirm with users that there are sufficient file integrity checks based upon the importance of data.	Control	Error guessing Confirmation/ examination
2. Are procedures established to verify the integrity of key files?					Examine the documentation indicating the file integrity verification procedures to determine they are adequate.	Requirements	Inspections
3. Are procedures established to verify the integrity of files on a regular basis?					Confirm with the user that the file integrity verification frequency is adequate to protect the integrity of the file.	Requirements	Confirmation/ examination
4. Are procedures established to report file integrity variances to management?					Examine the specifications and procedures for reporting file integrity variances to management.	Control	Inspections
5. For key files, such as cash receipts, have procedures been establishment to maintain independent control totals?					Verify for key files that independent control total procedures are adequate.	Control	Checkpoint & Inspections
6. Have procedures been established to reconcile independent control totals to the totals produced by the automated segment?					Verify the adequacy of the reconciliation procedures.	Control	Cause-effect graphing, Checklist, & Desk checking
7. Will the independent control totals be reconciled regularly to the automated control totals?					Confirm with the user that the frequency of independent reconciliation is adequate.	Requirements	Confirmation/ examination

(continues)

WORK PAPER 9-4 *(continued)*

TEST FACTOR: File Integrity Controls Designed *(continued)*

TEST CRITERIA	ASSESSMENT				RECOMMENDED TEST	TEST TECHNIQUE	TEST TOOL
	Very Ade-quate	Ade-quate	Inade-quate	N/A			
8. Are simple accounting proofs performed regularly to ensure that the updating procedures are properly performed?					Review the adequacy of the methods to ensure that updating is performed correctly.	Error handling	Boundary value analysis & Desk checking

WORK PAPER 9-4 *(continued)*

TEST FACTOR: Audit Trail Designed

TEST CRITERIA	ASSESSMENT				RECOMMENDED TEST	TEST TECHNIQUE	TEST TOOL
	Very Ade-quate	Ade-quate	Inade-quate	N/A			
1. Have the detailed specifications been documented for each audit trail objective?					Review the completeness of the documentation in relationship to the audit trail objectives.	Requirements	Walkthroughs
2. Have the data fields and records for each audit trail been defined?					Review the reasonableness of the included data fields to satisfy the audit trail objective.	Requirements	Walkthroughs
3. Has the length of time to save each audit trail been defined?					Verify that the length of time is consistent with the organization's record retention policy.	Control	Confirmation/ examination & Fact finding
4. Have the instructions been defined for utilizing the audit trail?					Review the completeness of the specifications to instruct people in using the audit trail.	Requirements	Checklist & Data flow analysis
5. Does the audit trail include both the manual and automated segments of the system?					Review the audit trail specifications to verify that both the manual and automated segments are included.	Requirements	Flowchart & Tracing
6. Is the audit trail stored in a sequence and format making the retrieval and use easy?					Confirm with audit trail users that the form and sequence are consistent with the use they would make of the audit trail.	Requirements	Confirmation/ examination & Fact finding
7. Will sufficient generations of the audit trail be stored away from the primary site so that if the primary site is destroyed processing can be reconstructed?					Examine the adequacy of the off-site facility.	Requirements	Inspections
8. Have procedures been established to delete audit trails in the prescribed manner at the completion of their usefulness?					Assess the adequacy of the audit trail destruction procedures.	Requirements	Checklist & Error guessing

(continues)

WORK PAPER 9-4 *(continued)*

TEST FACTOR: Contingency Plan Designed

TEST CRITERIA	ASSESSMENT				RECOMMENDED TEST	TEST TECHNIQUE	TEST TOOL
	Very Adequate	Adequate	Inadequate	N/A			
1. Has responsibility for the preparation of a contingency plan been assigned?					Verify that the assigned individual has the sufficient skills and time to prepare a contingency plan.	Operations	Fact finding
2. Does the contingency plan define all of the causes of failure?					Confirm with the computer operations manager that the list of potential failures is complete.	Operations	Error guessing & Confirmation/ examination
3. Does the contingency plan define responsibilities during the contingency period?					Review the completeness of the assigned responsibilities.	Operations	Checklist
4. Does the contingency plan identify contingency resources?					Confirm with the computer operations manager that the assigned resources will be available in the event of a failure.	Operations	Confirmation/ examination
5. Does the contingency plan predetermine the operating priorities after a problem?					Confirm with a member of executive management that the recovery priorities are reasonable.	Recovery	Confirmation/ examination
6. Are all the parties involved in a failure included in the development of the contingency plan?					Review the list of contingency plan participants for completeness.	Recovery	Checklist
7. Are procedures established to test the contingency plan?					Review the adequacy of the contingency plan test procedures.	Recovery	Checklist & Disaster test
8. Will the contingency plan be developed at the time the application goes operational?					Review the schedule for developing the contingency plan to ensure it will be complete when the system goes operational.	Recovery	Inspections

WORK PAPER 9-4 (continued)

TEST FACTOR: Method to Achieve Service Level Designed

TEST CRITERIA	ASSESSMENT				RECOMMENDED TEST	TEST TECHNIQUE	TEST TOOL
	Very Adequate	Adequate	Inadequate	N/A			
1. Can the system design achieve the desired service level?					Either confirm the reasonableness with computer operations personnel or run a simulation of the system to verify service levels.	Execution	Confirmation/ examination & Modeling
2. Do peak period volumes impact upon the desired service level?					Develop a simulation to test service levels based upon maximum processed volumes.	Execution	Modeling
3. Can user personnel manually handle their part of peak volume periods?					Develop a model to demonstrate the amount of time required to perform the manual part of processing.	Execution	Modeling
4. Will expected errors impact upon service levels?					Determine the expected number of errors and include that in the system simulation.	Execution	Checklist, Error guessing, Inspections, & Modeling
5. Has the cost of failing to achieve service levels been determined?					Confirm with users that the cost of failure to meet service levels has been calculated.	Execution	Confirmation/ examination
6. Are desired and projected service levels recalculated as the system is changed?					Examine the requests for system changes and determine their impact on the service level.	Execution	Inspections & Modeling
7. Are procedures established to monitor the desired service level?					Review the adequacy of the monitoring procedure.	Execution	Checklist & Inspections
8. Will sufficient computer resources be installed to meet the service levels as the volumes increase?					Confirm with the computer operations manager that computer resources will be increased in proportion to increased volumes of data.	Operations	Confirmation/ examination & Fact finding

(continues)

WORK PAPER 9-4 *(continued)*

TEST FACTOR: Access Procedures Designed

TEST CRITERIA	ASSESSMENT				RECOMMENDED TEST	TEST TECHNIQUE	TEST TOOL
	Very Ade-quate	Ade-quate	Inade-quate	N/A			
1. Have advanced security techniques such as cryptography been considered?					Confirm with the individual responsible for data security that advanced security measures have been considered and implemented where necessary.	Security	Confirmation/ examination
2. Have operating software features been evaluated for security purposes and implemented where necessary?					Confirm with system programmers that a systematic process was used to evaluate systems software features needed for security.	Security	Risk matrix & Confirmation/ examination
3. Have procedures been designed to protect the issuance and maintenance of passwords?					Confirm with the data security officer the adequacy of password protection procedures.	Security	Risk matrix & Confirmation/ examination
4. Are procedures defined to monitor security violations?					Review the adequacy of the procedures to monitor security violations.	Control	Checklist & Fact finding
5. Does senior management intend to prosecute security violators?					Confirm with senior management their intent to monitor security and prosecute violators.	Control	Confirmation/ examination
6. Have the security needs of each application resource been defined?					Review the completeness and adequacy of the security for each application resource.	Control	Risk matrix & Scoring
7. Has one individual been assigned the responsibility for security of the application?					Confirm that the individual appointed has sufficient skill and time to monitor security.	Security	Checklist & Confirmation/ examination
8. Is the system designed to protect sensitive data?					Confirm with the user the completeness of the design to protect sensitive data.	Security	Cause-effect graphing, Correctness proof, Inspections, & Scoring

WORK PAPER 9-4 (continued)

TEST FACTOR: Design Complies with Methodology

TEST CRITERIA	ASSESSMENT				RECOMMENDED TEST	TEST TECHNIQUE	TEST TOOL
	Very Adequate	Adequate	Inadequate	N/A			
1. Have the appropriate methodology specifications been determined?					Confirm with the responsible party that the specifications are correct.	Compliance	Correctness proof, Error guessing, & Confirmation/ examination
2. Has the required level of compliance to the methodology been achieved?					Verify that the project complies with the methodology.	Compliance	Design reviews
3. Will the standards, policies, etc. be monitored during implementation?					Confirm with the involved parties that they will monitor compliance to the methodology.	Compliance	Confirmation/ examination & Fact finding
4. Has the cost of compliance been determined so that it can be measured against the benefit, sanction, etc.?					Review with the involved parties the cost/benefit of compliance.	Compliance	Fact finding
5. Are procedures established to substantiate compliance to the methodology?					Review the adequacy of the specified method of substantiating compliance.	Compliance	Fact finding
6. Will the methodology be in use when the system becomes operational?					Confirm with IT management the applicability of using all or part of the methodology based on the application's expected implementation date.	Compliance	Confirmation/ examination
7. Have deviations from the methodology been documented and approved?					Verify variances from the methodology are approved.	Compliance	Design reviews & Confirmation/ examination
8. Is design documentation adequate and in compliance with standards?					Verify the completeness and adequacy of design documentation.	Compliance	Design reviews

(continues)

TEST FACTOR: Design Conforms to Requirements

TEST CRITERIA	ASSESSMENT				RECOMMENDED TEST	TEST TECHNIQUE	TEST TOOL
	Very Ade-quate	Ade-quate	Inade-quate	N/A			
1. Has the systems design group made changes to the application system without gaining user approval?					Examine all of the program change requests to verify they have been approved by the user.	Requirements	Confirmation/ examination
2. Is there a formal change request procedure that must be followed to make all system changes?					Examine the adequacy and compliance to the program change procedure.	Control	Checklist & Inspections
3. Are the objectives of the system reevaluated and changed where necessary based on each approved change request?					Determine the effect of the approved system changes on the objectives, and determine if the objectives have been changed accordingly.	Requirements	Inspections & Walkthroughs
4. Does the user continually reevaluate the application system objectives in regard to changing business conditions?					Confirm with the user that the objectives are updated based on changing business conditions.	Requirements	Acceptance test criteria, Confirmation/ examination, & Fact finding
5. Are user personnel heavily involved in the design of the application system?					Confirm with the information services project personnel that the user is heavily involved in the system design.	Requirements	Confirmation/ examination & Fact finding
6. If user management changes, does the new management reconfirm the system objectives?					Verify that the design specifications achieve the intent of the application requirements.	Requirements	Acceptance test criteria, Confirmation/ examination

WORK PAPER 9-4 *(continued)*

TEST FACTOR: Design Conforms to Requirements *(continued)*

TEST CRITERIA	ASSESSMENT				RECOMMENDED TEST	TEST TECHNIQUE	TEST TOOL
	Very Ade-quate	Ade-quate	Inade-quate	N/A			
7. If the objectives are changed, is the means of measuring those objectives changed accordingly?					Verify that the criteria to measure the objectives are reasonable.	Requirements	Acceptance test criteria, Cause-effect graphing, Design-based functional testing, Executable specs, & Symbolic execution
8. Do the design specifications achieve the intent of the requirements?					Verify that the design specifications achieve the intent of the application requirements.	Requirements	Correctness proof, Data flow analysis, Design-based functional testing, Desk checking, Executable specs, & Symbolic execution

(continues)

WORK PAPER 9-4 *(continued)*

TEST FACTOR: Design Facilitates Use

TEST CRITERIA	ASSESSMENT				RECOMMENDED TEST	TEST TECHNIQUE	TEST TOOL
	Very Ade-quate	Ade-quate	Inade-quate	N/A			
1. Have the people tasks been defined?					Examine the manual processing documentation.	Manual support	Inspections
2. Are the tasks realistic based on the skill level of the people?					Review the application system processing.	Manual support	Peer review
3. Is the timing of the tasks realistic?					Calculate the adequacy of manual turnaround time.	Requirements	Modeling
4. Will the information needed to do the people tasks be available?					Confirm with users the expected availability of needed information.	Requirements	Confirmation/ examination
5. Is the workload reasonable based on the expected staffing?					Estimate the time required to complete assigned tasks.	Requirements	Modeling
6. Have the people involved been presented their tasks for comment?					Confirm with users their independence in systems design.	Manual support	Confirmation/ examination
7. Could some of the people tasks be better performed on the computer?					Review the application system processing.	Requirements	Cause-effect graphing & Error guessing
8. Will adequate instruction manuals be prepared for these tasks?					Review the design specifications for preparation of instruction manuals.	Manual support	Checklist

WORK PAPER 9-4 (continued)

TEST FACTOR: Design Is Maintainable

TEST CRITERIA	ASSESSMENT				RECOMMENDED TEST	TEST TECHNIQUE	TEST TOOL
	Very Ade-quate	Ade-quate	Inade-quate	N/A			
1. Is system design logically constructed?					Review the application design structure.	Compliance	Peer review
2. Are data attributes fully defined?					Examine the data documentation for completeness.	Compliance	Inspections
3. Is computer logic presented in an easy-to-follow manner?					Review the application system logic.	Compliance	Peer review
4. Are changes to the system incorporated into the design documentation?					Trace changes to the system specifications.	Compliance	Inspections
5. Have areas of expected high frequency of change been designed to facilitate maintenance?					Review the maintainability of logic in areas of expected high change.	Compliance	Fact finding
6. Are business functions designed using a standalone concept?					Review the application design structure.	Compliance	Inspections
7. Is design documentation complete and usable?					Examine the design documentation for usability.	Compliance	Inspections
8. Are maintenance specialists involved in the design process?					Confirm with maintenance specialists that they are involved in the design process.	Compliance	Confirmation/ examination

(continues)

WORK PAPER 9-4 *(continued)*

TEST FACTOR: Design Is Portable

TEST CRITERIA	ASSESSMENT				RECOMMENDED TEST	TEST TECHNIQUE	TEST TOOL
	Very Adequate	Adequate	Inadequate	N/A			
1. Does the design avoid specialized hardware features?					Review hardware specifications for special features.	Operations	Inspections
2. Does the design avoid specialized software features?					Review software specifications for special features.	Operations	Inspections
3. Will the system be coded in a common computer language?					Examine coding rules for the project.	Operations	Fact finding
4. Will the system be restricted to common features of the language?					Examine coding rules for the project.	Operations	Fact finding
5. Does the system avoid the use of specialized software packages?					Review software specifications for specialized software.	Operations	Inspections
6. Are data values restricted to normal data structures?					Review data documentation for type of data structure used.	Operations	Inspections
7. Does documentation avoid specialized jargon?					Review documentation for use of specialized jargon.	Operations	Inspections
8. Have the portability implementation considerations been documented?					Review the adequacy of the portability documentation.	Operations	Inspections

WORK PAPER 9-4 (continued)

TEST FACTOR: Interface Design Complete

TEST CRITERIA	ASSESSMENT				RECOMMENDED TEST	TEST TECHNIQUE	TEST TOOL
	Very Adequate	Adequate	Inadequate	N/A			
1. Have the transactions to be received from other applications been defined?					Examine interfaced input data documentation.	Intersystems	Checklist
2. Have the transactions going to other applications been defined?					Examine interfaced output data documentation.	Intersystems	Checklist
3. Has the timing of interfaced transactions been defined?					Review system specifications for definition of timing.	Intersystems	Flowchart
4. Is the timing of interfaced transactions realistic?					Confirm with interfaced application personnel that timing is reasonable.	Operations	Confirmation/ examination
5. Has the media for transferring data to interfaced applications been defined?					Review system specifications for documentation of media.	Operations	Inspections
6. Are common data definitions used on interfaced data?					Compare common data definitions of interfaced applications.	Control	Fact finding
7. Are common value attributes used on interfaced data?					Compare common value attributes of interfaced applications.	Control	Fact finding
8. Has interface documentation been exchanged with interfaced applications?					Confirm with interfaced projects that documentation has been exchanged.	Intersystems	Confirmation/ examination

(continues)

WORK PAPER 9-4 (continued)

TEST FACTOR: Design Achieves Criteria

TEST CRITERIA	ASSESSMENT				RECOMMENDED TEST	TEST TECHNIQUE	TEST TOOL
	Very Adequate	Adequate	Inadequate	N/A			
1. Have the systems development and acceptance criteria costs been recalculated based on the systems design?					Confirm with the user that the new system costs and acceptance criteria are reasonable.	Execution	Acceptance test criteria & Confirmation/ examination
2. Have the criteria for developing the manual processing segments been confirmed?					Confirm with the user that the manual effort has been defined and the cost confirmed.	Execution	Acceptance test criteria & Confirmation/ examination
3. Has the cost of operating the computer programs been confirmed based on the systems design?					Confirm with computer operations that the operational costs are reasonable.	Execution	Acceptance test criteria & Confirmation/ examination
4. Have the costs to operate the manual segments of the system been confirmed?					Confirm with the user that the cost to operate the manual segments of the application are reasonable.	Execution	Acceptance test criteria & Confirmation/ examination
5. Have the benefits of the system been confirmed based upon the systems design?					Confirm with the user the reasonableness of the benefits.	Execution	Acceptance test criteria & Confirmation/ examination
6. Has the useful life of the system been confirmed based upon the systems design?					Confirm with the user the reasonableness of the expected life of the application.	Execution	Acceptance test criteria & Confirmation/ examination

WORK PAPER 9-4 *(continued)*

TEST FACTOR: Design Achieves Criteria *(continued)*

TEST CRITERIA	ASSESSMENT				RECOMMENDED TEST	TEST TECHNIQUE	TEST TOOL
	Very Ade-quate	Ade-quate	Inade-quate	N/A			
7. Has the cost-effectiveness of the new system been recalculated if changes in the factors have occurred?					Confirm with the organization's accountants that the cost is correct.	Execution	Confirmation/ examination
8. Does the cost-effectiveness after design warrant the continuance of the system?					Confirm with senior management that the system design is still cost-effective.	Execution	Confirmation/ examination

(continues)

WORK PAPER 9-4 *(continued)*

TEST FACTOR: Needs Communicated to Operations

TEST CRITERIA	ASSESSMENT				RECOMMENDED TEST	TEST TECHNIQUE	TEST TOOL
	Very Ade-quate	Ade-quate	Inade-quate	N/A			
1. Have special hardware needs been defined?					Review specifications for special hardware needs.	Operations	Inspections
2. Have special software needs been defined?					Review specifications for special software needs.	Operations	Inspections
3. Have operations timing specifications been defined?					Review specifications for operations timing specifications.	Operations	Inspections
4. Have system volumes been projected over an extended time period?					Confirm with users the reasonableness of projections.	Compliance	Confirmation/ examination
5. Have operations capacity requirements been specified?					Review specifications to determine whether the capacity requirements are reasonable.	Operations	Checklist
6. Have computer test requirements been specified?					Examine test specifications for reasonableness.	Operations	Fact finding
7. Have supplies/forms been specified?					Review specifications to verify that all supplies/ forms have been identified.	Operations	Fact finding
8. Has computer operations been notified of the anticipated workload and other requirements?					Confirm with computer operations their awareness of operation requirements.	Operations	Confirmation/ examination

WORK PAPER 9-5   Business System Design Review Checklist[2]

	YES	NO	N/A	COMMENTS
Systems Overview				
1. Is there a brief description of interfaces with other systems?				
2. Is there an outline of the major functional requirements of the system?				
3. Are the major functions defined into discrete steps with no boundary overlapping?				
4. Have manual and automatic steps been defined?				
5. Has the definition of what data is required to perform each step been indicated along with a description of how the data is obtained?				
System Description				
6. Has a system structure chart been developed, showing the logical breakdown into subsystems and interfaces with other systems?				
7. Have the major inputs and outputs been defined as well as the functional processing required to produce the output?				
8. Is there a narrative description of the major functions of the system?				
9. Have subsystem functional flow diagrams been developed showing the inputs, processing, and outputs relevant to the subsystem?				
10. Has subsystem narrative description been developed?				
11. Do the functional outlines follow the logical structure of the system?				
12. Are they hierarchical in nature—that is, by function and by steps within function?				
Design Input and Output Data—Data Structure				
13. Has the data been grouped into logical categories (i.e., customer product, accounting, marketing sales, etc.)?				
14. Has the data been categorized as follows: a) Static b) Historical data likely to be changed c) Transaction-related				
15. Have standard data names (if possible) been used?				
16. Has the hierarchical relationship among data elements been defined and described?				

[2]Based on case study included in *Effective Methods of EDP Quality Assurance.*

(continues)

WORK PAPER 9-5 *(continued)*

	YES	NO	N/A	COMMENTS

Design Output Documents

17. Are there headings?
18. Do the headings include report titles, department, date, page number, etc.?
19. Are the output documents adaptable to current filing equipment?
20. Are processing dates, system identification, titles, and page numbers shown?
21. Has consideration been given to output devices?
22. Is each data column identified?
23. Where subtotals are produced (e.g., product within customer) are they labeled by control break?

Design Input Elements

24. Are the data elements clearly indicated?
25. Has the source of the data been defined (department and individual)?
26. Have input requirements been documented?
27. Is the purpose of the input document clear?
28. Is the sequence indicated?

Design Computer Processing

29. Has each function been described using functional terminology (e.g., if salary exceeds maximum, print message)?
30. Has validity checking been defined with reference to the data element dictionary?
31. In cases where the same data may be coming from several sources, have the sources been identified as to priorities for selection by the system?
32. Has processing been classified according to type of function (e.g., transaction, calculation, editing, etc.)?

Design Noncomputer Processing

33. Has the preparation of input been described?
34. Has the distribution of output been described?
35. Has an error correction procedure been described?

Organizational Controls

36. Have organizational controls been established?

WORK PAPER 9-5 *(continued)*

	YES	NO	N/A	COMMENTS
37. Have controls been established across department lines?				
38. Have the control fields been designed?				
39. Are there control validation procedures prior to proceeding to the next step?				
Overall System Controls				
40. Have controls been designed to reconcile data received by the computer center?				
41. Have controls for error correction and reentry been designed?				
42. Have controls been designed that can be reconciled to those of another system?				
Input Controls				
43. Have some or all of the following criteria been used for establishing input controls?				
a) Sequence numbering				
b) Prepunched cards				
c) Turnaround documents				
d) Batch numbering				
e) Input type				
f) Predetermined totals				
g) Self-checking numbers				
h) Field length checks				
i) Limit checks				
j) Reasonability checks				
k) Existence/nonexistence checks				
44. Do controls and totals exist for:				
a) Each value column				
b) Cross-foot totals				
c) Counts of input transactions, errors, accepted transactions				
d) Input transactions, old master, new master				
45. Are the results of all updates listed for each transaction showing the before and after condition?				
46. As the result of an update, are the number of adds, deletes, and changes processed shown?				
47. If relationship tests have been used, are they grouped and defined?				
48. Have control total records been utilized to verify that all records have been processed between runs?				

(continues)

WORK PAPER 9-5   *(continued)*

	YES	NO	N/A	COMMENTS
Output Controls				
49. Have output controls been established for all control fields?				
50. Is there a separate output control on errors rejected by the system?				
System Test Plan				
51. Have acceptance criteria been identified?				
52. Has a tentative user acceptance strategy been developed?				
53. Have test data requirements been defined?				
54. Have data element dictionary forms been completed?				
55. Have organizational changes been defined?				
56. Have new organizational charts or new positions been required?				
57. If required, have areas for special user procedures been identified?				
58. Has a timetable for operating the system been developed?				
59. Were separate timetables developed for different cycles (weekly, monthly)?				
60. Has the documentation been gathered and organized?				
61. Has a financial analysis been performed?				
Plan User Procedures—Conversion Design				
62. Have the scope, objectives, and constraints been developed?				
63. Has a plan for user procedures and conversion phases been completed?				
64. Has the plan been broken down into approximate work units (days) to serve as a basis for a schedule for the other phases?				
65. Have the resources and responsibilities been arranged?				
66. Have schedules been prepared for the next phases?				
67. Have appropriate budgets for the next phases been prepared?				
68. Has a project authorization been properly prepared for remaining phases?				

WORK PAPER 9-6 Computer Systems Design Review Checklist[3]

	YES	NO	N/A	COMMENTS
Develop Outline Design				
1. Has a detailed review of the business system design resulted in requiring additional information or changes?				
2. Have these revisions been reviewed by the user?				
3. Have existing sources of data been identified?				
4. Has a data management alternative been considered because of the nature of the system?				
5. Have the data elements been grouped by category?				
6. Have the record layout forms been used for listing the data elements?				
7. Has the file description form been used to show the characteristics of each file?				
8. Have the access methods been determined?				
9. Has use been made of blocking factors to reduce accesses for a sequential file?				
10. If a database has been used, has the relationship between segments (views of the database) been included?				
11. If new data elements have been required, have they been included as part of the data dictionary?				
12. Has the description of processing been translated into system flowcharts showing programs and their relationships, as well as reports?				
13. Has the processing been isolated by frequency as well as function?				
14. Does each file requiring updating have an associated, unique transaction file?				
15. Does each main file have a separate validation and update function?				
16. Have the following been addressed in order to reduce excessive passing of files: a) Sort verbs (statements) b) Input procedure c) Output procedure d) Random updating				
17. Has a matrix been prepared showing which programs create, access, and update each file?				

---

[3]ibid.

(continues)

WORK PAPER 9-6   *(continued)*

		YES	NO	N/A	COMMENTS
18.	Has a separate section been set up for each program in the system showing:				
	a) Cover page showing the program name, systems and/or subsystem name, run number, and a brief description of the program				
	b) Input/output diagram				
	c) Processing description				
19.	Does the processing description contain a brief outline of the processing that the program is going to perform?				
20.	Has the content and format of each output been defined?				
21.	Has the content and format of each input been defined?				
22.	Have data items been verified against to the rules specified in the data dictionary?				
23.	Have transactions that update master files been assigned record types?				

Hardware/Software Configuration

		YES	NO	N/A	COMMENTS
24.	Does the hardware configuration show the following:				
	a) CPU				
	b) Minimum core storage				
	c) Number and type of peripherals				
	d) Special hardware				
	e) Numbers of tapes and/or disk packs				
	f) Terminals, minicomputers, microfilm, microfiche, optical scanning, etc.				
25.	Has the following software been defined:				
	a) Operating system				
	b) Telecommunications				
	c) Database management				
26.	If telecommunications equipment is involved, has a communications analyst been consulted regarding type, number, speed, etc.?				

File Conversion

		YES	NO	N/A	COMMENTS
27.	Have the file conversion requirements been specified?				
28.	Have program specifications for the file conversion programs been completed?				
29.	Can the main program(s) be utilized to perform the file conversion?				
30.	Has a schedule been established?				

WORK PAPER 9-6 *(continued)*

	YES	NO	N/A	COMMENTS
Design System Tests				
31. Has the user's role for testing been defined?				
32. Have responsibilities and schedules for preparing test data been agreed to by the user?				
33. Has the input medium been agreed to?				
34. Is special hardware/software required, and if so, will programmers and/or users require additional training?				
35. Have turnaround requirements been defined?				
36. Have testing priorities been established?				
37. If an online system, has an investigation of required space as opposed to available space been made?				
38. Has an analysis of the impact upon interfacing systems been made and have arrangements been made for acquiring required information and data?				
39. Have testing control procedures been established?				
40. Has the possibility of utilizing existing code been investigated?				
41. Has a system test plan been prepared?				
42. Has the user prepared the system test data as defined by the conditions to be tested in the system test plan?				
43. Has computer operations been consulted regarding keypunching and/or verification?				
Revise and Complete Design				
44. Have all required forms from previous phases as well as previous task activities in this phase been completed?				
45. Has the processing description for program specifications been categorized by function?				
46. For validation routines, have the editing rules been specified for:				
a) Field format and content (data element description)				
b) Interfield relationships				
c) Intrafield relationships				
d) Interrecord relationships				
e) Sequence				
f) Duplicates				
g) Control reconciliation				

(continues)

WORK PAPER 9-6 *(continued)*

	YES	NO	N/A	COMMENTS
47. Have the rejection criteria been indicated for each type of error situation, as follows: a) Warning message but transaction is accepted b) Use of the default value c) Outright rejection of record within a transaction set d) Rejection of an entire transaction e) Rejection of a batch of transactions f) Program abort				
48. Have the following validation techniques been included in the specifications: a) Validation of entire transaction before any processing b) Validation to continue regardless of the number of errors on the transaction unless a run abort occurs c) Provide information regarding an error so the user can identify the source and determine the cause				
49. Has a procedure been developed for correction of rejected input either by deletion, reversal, or reentry?				
50. Do the specifications for each report (output) define: a) The origin of each item, including the rules for the selection of optional items b) The rules governing calculations c) The rules for printing and/or print suppression				
51. Have the following been defined for each intermediate (work) file: a) Origins or alternative origins for each element b) Calculations c) Rules governing record types, sequence, optional records, as well as inter- and intrarecord relationships				
52. Have the following audit controls been built in where applicable: a) Record counts (in and out) b) Editing of all source input c) Hash totals on selected fields d) Sequence checking of input files e) Data checking f) Listing of errors and review g) Control records				

WORK PAPER 9-6 *(continued)*

	YES	NO	N/A	COMMENTS
Determine Tentative Operational Requirements				
53. Has the impact of the system upon existing computer resources been evaluated?				
54. Have the computer processing requirements been discussed with computer operations?				
55. Have backup procedures been developed?				
Online Systems				
56. Have testing plans been discussed with computer operations to ensure that required resources (core, disk space) for "sessions" will be available?				
57. Have terminal types been discussed with appropriate technical support personnel?				
58. Have IMS considerations (if applicable) been coordinated with computer operations, technical support, and DBA representatives?				
59. Has a user training program been developed?				
60. Have run schedules been prepared to provide computer operations with the basic information necessary to schedule computer usage?				
61. Have run flowcharts including narrative (where required) been prepared?				
62. Have "first cut" estimates of region sizes, run times, etc. been provided on the flowcharts or some other documentations?				
63. Have restart procedures been described for each step of the job?				
64. Have restart procedures been appended to the security and backup section of the documentation?				
Plan Program Design				
65. Has all relevant documentation for each program been gathered?				
66. Has the sequence in which programs are to be developed been defined in accordance to the system test plan?				
67. Has the number of user and project personnel (including outside vendors) required been ascertained?				
68. Has computer time required for program testing (compiles, test runs) been estimated?				
69. Have data preparation requirements been discussed with computer operations regarding data entry?				

(continues)

WORK PAPER 9-6 *(continued)*

	YES	NO	N/A	COMMENTS
70. Has a development cost worksheet been prepared for the next phase or phases?				
71. Have personnel been assigned and project work schedules been prepared?				
72. Has the project schedule and budget been reviewed and updated?				
Prepare Project Authorization				
73. Has a project authorization form been completed?				

WORK PAPER 9-7   Quality Control Checklist

	YES	NO	N/A	COMMENTS
1. Is the test team knowledgeable in the design process?				
2. Are the testers experienced in using design tools?				
3. Have the testers received all of the design phase deliverables needed to perform this test?				
4. Do the users agree that the design is realistic?				
5. Does the project team believe that the design is realistic?				
6. Have the testers identified the success factors, both positive and negative, that can affect the success of the design?				
7. Have the testers used those factors in scoring the probability of success?				
8. Do the testers understand the 15 design-related test factors?				
9. Have the testers analyzed those design test factors to evaluate their potential impact on the success of the design?				
10. Do the testers understand the design review process?				
11. Has a review team been established that represents all parties with a vested interest in the success of the design?				
12. Does management support using the design review process?				
13. Is the design review process conducted at an appropriate time?				
14. Were the items identified in the design review process reasonable?				
15. Does the project team agree that the identified items need to be addressed?				
16. Does management support performing inspections on project rework?				
17. Has appropriate time been allotted in the project scheduling for performing inspections?				
18. Have the individuals responsible for project rework been educated in the importance of participating in the inspection process?				

(continues)

WORK PAPER 9-7 *(continued)*

	YES	NO	N/A	COMMENTS
19. Does management view inspections as an integral part of the process rather than as an audit to identify participants' performance?				
20. Has the inspection process been planned?				
21. Have the inspectors been identified and assigned their specific roles?				
22. Have the inspectors been trained to perform their role?				
23. Have the inspectors been given the necessary materials to perform the review?				
24. Have the inspectors been given adequate time to complete both the preparation and the review meeting inspection process?				
25. Did the individual inspectors adequately prepare for the inspection?				
26. Did the individual inspectors prepare a defect list?				
27. Was the inspection scheduled at a time convenient for all inspectors?				
28. Did all inspectors come to the inspection meeting?				
29. Did all inspectors agree on the final list of defects?				
30. Have the inspectors agreed upon one of the three acceptable inspection dispositions (i.e., certification, reexamination, or reinspection)?				
31. Were the defects identified during the review meeting recorded and given to the author?				
32. Has the author agreed to make the necessary corrections?				
33. Has a reasonable process been developed to determine that those defects have been corrected satisfactorily?				
34. Has a final moderator certification been issued for the product/deliverable inspected?				

WORK PAPER 9-8 Initial Supplier Capability Assessment

TEST FACTOR: Data Integrity Controls Implemented

TEST CRITERIA	ASSESSMENT				RECOMMENDED TEST	TEST TECHNIQUE	TEST TOOL
	Very Adequate	Adequate	Inadequate	N/A			
1. Have procedures been written indicating how to record transactions for entry into the automated system?					Examine the usefulness of data error messages.	Manual support	Correctness proof, Exhaustive testing, & Flowchart
2. Have data validation checks been implemented to ensure that input complies with system specifications?					Review the completeness of the data validation checks.	Requirements	Compiler-based analysis, Data dictionary, & Inspections
3. Have anticipation controls been installed, where appropriate, to ensure that valid, but unreasonable, data is noted for manual investigation?					Examine the extensiveness of anticipation controls to identify potential problems.	Error handling	Correctness proof, Error guessing, & Inspections
4. Are errors properly identified and explained so that follow-up action can be readily conducted?					Examine the completeness of the data entry procedures.	Error handling	Exhaustive testing
5. Have procedures been established to take corrective action on data errors?					Examine the reasonableness of the procedures to take corrective action on identified errors.	Error handling	Cause-effect graphing
6. Are procedures established to ensure that errors are corrected on a timely basis?					Verify that the procedures will ensure that errors are corrected on a timely basis.	Error handling	Correctness proof & Flowchart

(continues)

WORK PAPER 9-8 *(continued)*

TEST FACTOR: Data Integrity Controls Implemented

TEST CRITERIA	ASSESSMENT				RECOMMENDED TEST	TEST TECHNIQUE	TEST TOOL
	Very Adequate	Adequate	Inadequate	N/A			
7. Are run-to-run controls installed to ensure the completeness and accuracy of transactions as they move from point to point in the system?					Examine the reasonableness of the procedures that ensure accuracy and completeness of transactions as they flow through the system.	Requirements	Control flow analysis & Data flow analysis
8. Have procedures been implemented to ensure that complete and accurate input is recorded?					Verify the adequacy of the procedures to ensure that controls established during data origination are verified during processing.	Control	Correctness proof & Exhaustive testing

WORK PAPER 9-8   *(continued)*

TEST FACTOR: Authorization Rules Implemented

TEST CRITERIA	ASSESSMENT				RECOMMENDED TEST	TEST TECHNIQUE	TEST TOOL
	Very Ade-quate	Ade-quate	Inade-quate	N/A			
1. Have the authorization methods been divided between manual and automated?					Evaluate the reasonableness of the authorization method selected.	Security	Fact finding
2. Have procedures been prepared to specify the manual authorization process for each transaction?					Review the adequacy of the manual authorization procedures.	Security	Inspections
3. Have the methods been implemented for authorizing transactions in the automated segment of the system?					Examine the program specifications to determine that authorization method has been properly implemented.	Requirements	Inspections
4. Have procedures been established to indicate violations of manual authorization procedures?					Examine the reasonableness of the violation procedures for manual authorization.	Control	Checklist & Fact finding
5. Have procedures been established to identify and act upon violations of automated authorization procedures?					Examine the adequacy of the automated authorization violation procedures.	Requirements	Walkthroughs
6. Do the implemented authoriza-tion methods conform to the authorization rules defined in the requirements phase?					Verify compliance of implemented authorization methods to the defined authorization rules.	Requirements	Inspections

(continues)

WORK PAPER 9-8   (continued)

TEST FACTOR: Authorization Rules Implemented

TEST CRITERIA	ASSESSMENT				RECOMMENDED TEST	TEST TECHNIQUE	TEST TOOL
	Very Adequate	Adequate	Inadequate	N/A			
7. Have procedures been implemented to verify the source of transactions where the source becomes the basis for authorizing the transaction?					Verify that the system authenticates the source of transaction where that source itself authorizes the transaction.	Security	Inspections
8. Does the system maintain a record of who authorized each transaction?					Verify that procedures are implemented to identify the authorizer of each transaction.	Requirements	Inspections

WORK PAPER 9-8 *(continued)*

TEST FACTOR: File Integrity Controls Implemented

TEST CRITERIA	ASSESSMENT				RECOMMENDED TEST	TEST TECHNIQUE	TEST TOOL
	Very Adequate	Adequate	Inadequate	N/A			
1. Has someone been appointed accountable for the integrity of each file?					Verify that the assigned individual has the necessary skills and time available.	Control	Fact finding
2. Have the file integrity controls been implemented in accordance with the file integrity requirements?					Compare the implemented controls to the integrity requirements established during the requirements phase.	Requirements	Inspections
3. Have procedures been established to notify the appropriate individual of file integrity problems?					Examine the adequacy of the procedures to report file integrity problems.	Error handling	Walkthroughs
4. Are procedures established to verify the integrity of files on a regular basis?					Review the reasonableness of the file integrity verification frequency.	Requirements	Walkthroughs
5. Are there subsets of the file that should have integrity controls?					Confirm with the user that all file subsets are appropriately safeguarded through integrity controls.	Control	Error guessing & Confirmation/ examination
6. Are procedures written for the regular reconciliation between automated file controls and manually maintained control totals?					Verify the reasonableness and timeliness of procedures to reconcile automated controls to manually maintained controls.	Control	Walkthroughs
7. Are interfile integrity controls maintained where applicable?					Confirm with the user that all applicable file relationships are reconciled as a means of verifying file integrity.	Control	Confirmation/ examination
8. Are sensitive transactions subject to special authorization controls?					Verify with legal counsel that sensitive transaction authorization controls are adequate.	Control	Confirmation/ examination

(continues)

WORK PAPER 9-8 (continued)

TEST FACTOR: Implement Audit Trail

TEST CRITERIA	ASSESSMENT				RECOMMENDED TEST	TEST TECHNIQUE	TEST TOOL
	Very Ade-quate	Ade-quate	Inade-quate	N/A			
1. Has the audit trail relationship from source record to control total been documented?					Examine the completeness of the audit trail from source document to control total.	Requirements	Walkthroughs
2. Has the audit trail from the control total to the supporting source transaction been documented?					Examine the completeness of the audit trail from the control total to the source document.	Requirements	Walkthroughs
3. Have all the defined fields been included in the audit trail?					Verify that the audit trail records include all of the defined audit trail fields.	Requirements	Walkthroughs
4. Does the implemented audit trail satisfy the defined reconstruction requirements?					Verify that the implemented audit trail is in compliance with the reconstruction requirements phase.	Requirements	Inspections
5. Have procedures been defined to test the audit trail?					Verify that an audit trail test plan has been devised.	Requirements	Fact finding
6. Are procedures defined to store part of the audit trail off-site?					Examine the reasonableness of the procedures that require application audit trail records to be stored off-site.	Recovery	Cause-effect graphing & Peer review
7. Does the implemented audit trail permit reconstruction of transaction processing?					Review the completeness of the transaction reconstruction process.	Requirements	Exhaustive testing & Inspections
8. Does the audit trail contain the needed information to restore a failure?					Confirm with the computer operations manager that the audit trail information is complete.	Requirements	Confirmation/ examination

TEST FACTOR: Write Contingency Plan

TEST CRITERIA	ASSESSMENT				RECOMMENDED TEST	TEST TECHNIQUE	TEST TOOL
	Very Adequate	Adequate	Inadequate	N/A			
1. Does the contingency plan identify the people involved in recovering processing after a failure?					Confirm with the operations manager that all the appropriate people are identified in the contingency plan.	Recovery	Confirmation/ examination
2. Has the contingency plan been approved by the operations manager?					Examine the evidence indicating the operations manager approves of the plan.	Recovery	Confirmation/ examination
3. Does the plan identify all the resources needed for recovery?					Confirm with the operations manager that all the needed resources are identified.	Recovery	Confirmation/ examination
4. Does the contingency plan include the priority for restarting operations after a failure?					Review the reasonableness of the priority with senior management.	Recovery	Error guessing & Fact finding
5. Does the recovery plan specify an alternate processing site?					Confirm that an alternate site is available for backup processing.	Recovery	Confirmation/ examination
6. Does the contingency plan provide for security during a recovery period?					Review the reasonableness of the security plan with the security officer.	Recovery	Inspections
7. Has a plan been developed to test the contingency plan?					Examine the completeness of the test plan.	Operations	Inspections
8. Has the role of outside parties, such as the hardware vendor, been included in the test plan and confirmed with those outside parties?					Confirm with outside parties that they can supply the support indicated in the contingency plan.	Operations	Confirmation/ examination

(continues)

WORK PAPER 9-8 *(continued)*

TEST FACTOR: Design System to Achieve Service Level

TEST CRITERIA	ASSESSMENT				RECOMMENDED TEST	TEST TECHNIQUE	TEST TOOL
	Very Ade-quate	Ade-quate	Inade-quate	N/A			
1. Do the implemented programs perform in accordance with the desired service level?					Verify the performance criteria of the programs during testing.	Stress	Instrumentation
2. Does the system performance achieve the desired level of service?					Verify the performance of the system during testing.	Stress	Instrumentation
3. Have the training programs been prepared for the people who will use the application system?					Examine the completeness of the training programs.	Execution	Checklist & Inspections
4. Is the support software available and does it meet service-level requirements?					Confirm with computer operations personnel that the support software is available and does meet performance criteria.	Operations	Confirmation/ examination
5. Is the support hardware available and does it provide sufficient capacity?					Confirm with computer operations personnel that the support hardware is available and does meet the capacity requirements.	Operations	Confirmation/ examination
6. Is sufficient hardware and software on order to meet anticipated future volumes?					Confirm with computer operations that sufficient hardware and software is on order to meet anticipated future volumes.	Operations	Confirmation/ examination
7. Has a test plan been defined to verify that service-level performance criteria can be met?					Examine the completeness of the test plan.	Execution	Checklist & Inspections
8. Can the required input be delivered to processing in time to meet production schedules?					Confirm with the individuals preparing input that they can prepare input in time to meet production schedules.	Execution	Confirmation/ examination

TEST FACTOR: Implement Security Procedures

TEST CRITERIA	ASSESSMENT				RECOMMENDED TEST	TEST TECHNIQUE	TEST TOOL
	Very Adequate	Adequate	Inadequate	N/A			
1. Is the required security hardware available?					Confirm with the security officer that the needed security hardware is available.	Security	Confirmation/ examination
2. Is the required security software available?					Confirm with the security officer that the needed security software is available.	Security	Confirmation/ examination
3. Has a procedure been established to disseminate and maintain passwords?					Examine the completeness and adequacy of the password dissemination and maintenance plan.	Security	Exhaustive testing
4. Have the involved personnel been trained in security procedures?					Examine the adequacy and completeness of the security training procedures.	Security	Exhaustive testing
5. Has a procedure been established to monitor violations?					Examine the completeness and adequacy of the test violation procedure.	Control	Exhaustive testing
6. Has management been instructed on the procedure for punishing security violators?					Confirm with management that they have been adequately instructed on how to implement security prosecution procedures.	Control	Confirmation/ examination
7. Have procedures been established to protect the programs, program listings, data documentation, and other systems documentation defining how the system works?					Verify with the security officer the adequacy of the procedures to protect the system documentation and program.	Security	Risk matrix & Confirmation/ examination
8. Has one individual been appointed accountable for security of the application when it becomes operational?					Verify that the accountable individual has the necessary skills and the time available.	Security	Fact finding

(continues)

WORK PAPER 9-8 *(continued)*

TEST FACTOR: Programs Comply with Methodology

TEST CRITERIA	ASSESSMENT				RECOMMENDED TEST	TEST TECHNIQUE	TEST TOOL
	Very Ade-quate	Ade-quate	Inade-quate	N/A			
1. Have the organization's policies and procedures been incorporated into the application programs?					Examine the programs to ensure that they comply with the necessary organization policies and procedures.	Compliance	Inspections
2. Have the organization's information services policies and procedures been incorporated into the application programs?					Examine the programs to ensure that they comply with the necessary information services policies and procedures.	Compliance	Inspections
3. Have the organization's accounting policies and procedures been incorporated into the application programs?					Examine the programs to ensure that they comply with the necessary accounting policies and procedures.	Compliance	Inspections
4. Have the governmental regulations been incorporated into the application program?					Examine the programs to ensure that they comply with the necessary government regulations.	Compliance	Inspections
5. Have the industry standards been incorporated into the application programs?					Examine the programs to ensure that they comply with the necessary industry standards.	Compliance	Inspections
6. Have the organization's user department policies and procedures been incorporated into the application programs?					Examine the programs to ensure that they comply with the user department's policies and procedures.	Compliance	Inspections

WORK PAPER 9-8 (continued)

TEST FACTOR: Programs Comply with Methodology

TEST CRITERIA	ASSESSMENT				RECOMMENDED TEST	TEST TECHNIQUE	TEST TOOL
	Very Ade-quate	Ade-quate	Inade-quate	N/A			
7. Are the policies, procedures, and regulations used as a basis for system specifications up-to-date?					Confirm with the appropriate party that the regulations used for specifications are current.	Compliance	Confirmation/examination
8. Are there anticipated changes to the policies, standards, or regulations between this phase and the time the system will become operational?					Confirm with the involved parties the probability of changes to the policies, standards, or regulations prior to the system becoming operational.	Compliance	Confirmation/examination

(continues)

TEST FACTOR: Programs Conform to Design (Correctness)

TEST CRITERIA	ASSESSMENT				RECOMMENDED TEST	TEST TECHNIQUE	TEST TOOL
	Very Adequate	Adequate	Inadequate	N/A			
1. Have changes in user management affected their support of system objectives?					Confirm with user management that the stated objectives are still desired.	Requirements	Confirmation/examination
2. Does the program implementation comply with stated objectives?					Compare program results to stated objectives.	Requirements	Design reviews
3. Will the implemented systems produce correct results?					Verify that the implemented systems will produce correct results.	Requirements	Correctness proof
4. Have the desired reports been produced?					Confirm that the reports produced by the application program comply with user-defined specifications.	Requirements	Design reviews
5. Does the system input achieve the desired data consistency and reliability objectives?					Confirm with the user that the input to the system achieves the desired consistency and reliability objectives.	Requirements	Design reviews
6. Are the manuals explaining how to use the computer outputs adequate?					Confirm with the user the adequacy of the output use manuals.	Requirements	Checklist & Confirmation/examination
7. Are the input manuals and procedures adequate to ensure the preparation of valid input?					Confirm with the input preparers that the manuals appear adequate to produce valid input.	Requirements	Checklist & Confirmation/examination
8. Has the user involvement in the developmental process continued through the programming phase?					Confirm with the project personnel that the user participation has been adequate.	Requirements	Checklist & Confirmation/examination

TEST FACTOR: Programs Conform to Design (Ease of Use)

TEST CRITERIA	ASSESSMENT				RECOMMENDED TEST	TEST TECHNIQUE	TEST TOOL
	Very Adequate	Adequate	Inadequate	N/A			
1. Do the application documents conform to design specifications?					Verify that the implemented ease of use segment of the application conforms to design.	Compliance	Design reviews
2. Have easy-to-use instructions been prepared for interfacing with the automated application?					Examine the usability of the people interface instructions.	Manual support	Checklist
3. Have provisions been made to provide assistance to input clerks?					Verify that provisions are implemented to assist input clerks in the proper entry of data.	Manual support	Checklist & Walkthroughs
4. Are the training sessions planned to train personnel on how to interact with the computer system?					Examine the course content to verify the appropriateness of the material.	Manual support	Walkthroughs
5. Are the output documents implemented for ease of use?					Verify the ease of use of the output documents.	Requirements	Checklist & Walkthroughs
6. Is the information in output documents prioritized?					Verify that the information in output documents is prioritized.	Requirements	Inspections
7. Are the input documents implemented for ease of use?					Verify the ease of use of the input documents.	Requirements	Checklist & Walkthroughs
8. Do clerical personnel accept the application system as usable?					Confirm with clerical personnel their acceptance of the usability of the application.	Manual support	Confirmation/ examination

(continues)

WORK PAPER 9-8 *(continued)*

TEST FACTOR: Programs Are Maintainable

TEST CRITERIA	ASSESSMENT				RECOMMENDED TEST	TEST TECHNIQUE	TEST TOOL
	Very Ade-quate	Ade-quate	Inade-quate	N/A			
1. Do the programs conform to the maintenance specifications?					Verify that the programs conform to the maintenance specifications.	Compliance	Inspections
2. Is the program documentation complete and usable?					Review the documentation for completeness and usability.	Compliance	Compiler-based analysis & Inspections
3. Do the programs contain a reasonable number of explanatory statements?					Review the programs to determine they contain a reasonable number of explanatory statements.	Compliance	Inspections
4. Is each processing segment of the program clearly identified?					Verify that each processing segment of the program is adequately identified.	Compliance	Inspections
5. Do the programs avoid complex program logic wherever possible?					Review programs for complex programming logic.	Compliance	Checklist & Inspections
6. Are the expected high-frequency change areas coded to facilitate maintenance?					Determine ease of maintenance of high-change areas.	Compliance	Peer review
7. Have the programs been reviewed from an ease-of-maintenance perspective?					Review programs to determine their maintainability.	Compliance	Peer review
8. Are changes introduced during programming incorporated into the design documentation?					Review changes and verify that they have been incorporated into the design documentation.	Compliance	Design reviews & Confirmation/ examination

WORK PAPER 9-8 *(continued)*

TEST FACTOR: Programs Conform to Design (Portable)

TEST CRITERIA	ASSESSMENT				RECOMMENDED TEST	TEST TECHNIQUE	TEST TOOL
	Very Adequate	Adequate	Inadequate	N/A			
1. Does the system avoid the use of any vendor-specific hardware features?					Review application for vendor-specific hardware restrictions.	Operations	Inspections
2. Does the system avoid the use of any vendor-specific software features?					Review application for vendor-specific software restrictions.	Operations	Inspections
3. Are the programs written using the common program language statements?					Review programs for use of uncommon programming statements.	Compliance	Inspections
4. Are all portability restrictions documented?					Determine the completeness of the portability documentation.	Compliance	Inspections
5. Are all operating characteristics documented?					Determine the completeness of operating characteristics documentation.	Compliance	Inspections
6. Does program documentation avoid technical jargon?					Review documentation for use of technical jargon.	Compliance	Inspections
7. Are the data values used in the program machine independent?					Review data values to determine they are machine independent.	Compliance	Checklist, Confirmation/ examination & Fact finding
8. Are the data files machine independent?					Review data files to determine they are machine independent.	Compliance	Checklist, Confirmation/ examination & Fact finding

(continues)

WORK PAPER 9-8 *(continued)*

TEST FACTOR: Programs Conform to Design (Coupling)

TEST CRITERIA	ASSESSMENT				RECOMMENDED TEST	TEST TECHNIQUE	TEST TOOL
	Very Adequate	Adequate	Inadequate	N/A			
1. Are common record layouts used for interfaced programs?					Verify that common record layouts are used by interfaced applications.	Intersystems	Inspections
2. Are the values in the data fields common to interfaced programs?					Verify that common data values are used by interfaced applications.	Intersystems	Inspections
3. Do the interfaced systems use the same file structure?					Verify that common file structures are used by interfaced applications.	Intersystems	Inspections
4. Have the interfaced segments been implemented as designed?					Verify that the interface segments of the application are implemented as designed.	Intersystems	Correctness proof, Desk checking, & Inspections
5. Have changes to the interfaced system been coordinated with any affected application?					Confirm that changes affecting interfaced applications are coordinated with those applications.	Intersystems	Exhaustive testing & Confirmation/ examination
6. Is the program/interface properly documented?					Verify that the interface document is complete.	Intersystems	Error guessing & Inspections
7. Is the data transfer media common to interfaced applications?					Verify that common media is used for interfaced application files.	Operations	Confirmation/ examination & Fact finding
8. Can the required timing for the transfer of data be achieved?					Verify that the data transfer timing between interfaced applications is reasonable.	Intersystems	Error guessing & Fact finding

WORK PAPER 9-8   *(continued)*

TEST FACTOR: Develop Operating Procedures

TEST CRITERIA	ASSESSMENT				RECOMMENDED TEST	TEST TECHNIQUE	TEST TOOL
	Very Ade-quate	Ade-quate	Inade-quate	N/A			
1. Has the size of the largest program been identified?					Review programs to determine their maximum size.	Operations	Inspections
2. Have changes made during programming affected operations?					Review changes to ascertain if they affect operations.	Operations	Inspections
3. Have any deviations from designed operations been communicated to computer operations?					Review application for operation design variations and confirm operations have been notified of these changes.	Operations	Error guessing
4. Have operations documentation been prepared?					Review the completeness of operations documentation.	Compliance	Design reviews
5. Have special forms and other needed media been ordered?					Determine if needed media has been ordered.	Operations	Confirmation/examination & Fact finding
6. Have data media retention procedures been prepared?					Review the adequacy of data retention procedures.	Compliance	Inspections
7. Has needed computer time for tests been scheduled?					Examine the computer schedule to ascertain if needed test time has been scheduled.	Operations	Fact finding
8. Have off-site storage needs been defined?					Determine the reasonableness of off-site storage requirements.	Operations	Fact finding

(continues)

WORK PAPER 9-8 *(continued)*

TEST FACTOR: Programs Achieve Criteria (Performance)

TEST CRITERIA	ASSESSMENT				RECOMMENDED TEST	TEST TECHNIQUE	TEST TOOL
	Very Ade-quate	Ade-quate	Inade-quate	N/A			
1. Has the cost to design and test the system approximated the cost estimate?					Examine the projected budget to verify that actual costs approximate budget costs.	Execution	Fact finding
2. Does the operational cost as represented by information services approximate the projected operational costs?					Use the data from the job accounting system to substantiate that the actual test operational costs approximate the projected operational costs.	Execution	Fact finding
3. Are the costs monitored during the developmental process?					Confirm with the information services manager that project costs are monitored.	Compliance	Confirmation/ examination
4. Will changes made during the programming phase affect anticipated system costs?					Confirm with the project manager that changes during the program phase will not affect operational costs.	Execution	Confirmation/ examination & Fact finding
5. Are the projected benefits still reasonable?					Confirm with user management that projected benefits are still reasonable.	Execution	Confirmation/ examination & Fact finding
6. Is the projected life of the project still reasonable?					Confirm with user management that the expected life of the project is still reasonable.	Execution	Confirmation/ examination
7. Is the project on schedule?					Compare the current status versus projected status in the schedule.	Execution	Fact finding
8. Are there any expected changes in the test or conversion phases that would impact the projected return on investment?					Confirm with the project leader whether there would be any changes during the test or conversion phase that could affect the projected return on investment.	Execution	Error guessing & Confirmation/ examination

WORK PAPER 9-9   Quality Control Checklist

	YES	NO	N/A	COMMENTS
1. Is verifying and validating programs considered to be a responsibility of the programmer?				
2. Does the programmer understand the difference between static and dynamic testing?				
3. Will the program be subject to static testing as the primary means to remove defects?				
4. Does the programmer understand the process that will generate the program code?				
5. Does the programmer understand and use desk debugging?				
6. Does the programmer understand the 15 programming concerns, and will they be incorporated into testing?				
7. Is the program tested using either the peer review technique or code inspections?				
8. Will the program be subject to full testing prior to moving to a higher-level testing (e.g., string testing)?				
9. Are all of the uncovered defects recorded in detail?				
10. Are all of the uncovered defects corrected prior to moving to the next level of testing?				

Step 4: Validation Testing

This step provides the opportunity to evaluate a system in an executable mode. Although the previous verification steps ensure that the system will function as specified, it is not until the software is executed as a system that there is complete assurance it will function properly.

Testing tradeoffs can be made between the various phases of the life cycle. The more verification testing is performed during the requirements, design, and program phases, the less validation testing that needs to be performed. On the other hand, when only minimal verification testing is performed during the early phases, extensive validation testing may be needed during the test phase.

Overview

Although testers primarily use system documentation to conduct verification testing, they use test data and test scripts to conduct validation testing. Validation testing attempts to simulate the system's operational environment. Validation testing is effective only when the test environment is equivalent to the production environment.

There are two types of validation testing. The first is the test that the developers implemented to software as specified. At a minimum, this is unit testing and integration testing of the units. The second type of testing tests that the developed software system can operate in a production environment. That is, it tests that the system's various components can be integrated effectively. Although this second type of testing may be conducted by software developers, the preferred method is to use independent testers. This second type of dynamic testing is covered in Chapter 12.

Objective

The objective of this step is to determine whether a software system performs correctly in an executable mode. The software is executed in a test environment in approximately the same mode as it would be in an operational environment. The test should be executed in as many different ways as necessary to address the 15 concerns described in this test process, with any deviation from the expected results recorded. Depending on the severity of the problems, uncovered changes may need to be made to the software before it is placed in a production status. If the problems are extensive, it may be necessary to stop testing completely and return the software to the developers.

Concerns

Validation testing presents testers with the following concerns:

- **Software not in a testable mode.** The previous testing steps will not have been performed adequately to remove most of the defects and/or the necessary functions will not have been installed, or correctly installed in the software. Thus, testing will become bogged down in identifying problems that should have been identified earlier.

- **Inadequate time/resources.** Because of delays in development or failure to adequately budget sufficient time and resources for testing, the testers will not have the time or resources necessary to effectively test the software. In many IT organizations management relies on testing to ensure that the software is ready for production prior to being placed in production. When adequate time or resources are unavailable, management may still rely on the testers when they are unable to perform their test as expected.

- **Significant problems will not be uncovered during testing.** Unless testing is planned and executed adequately, problems that can cause serious operational difficulties may not be uncovered. This can happen because testers at this step spend too much time uncovering defects rather than evaluating the software's operational performance.

Workbench

Figure 10-1 illustrates the workbench for executing tests and recording results. This shows that the testers use a test environment at this point in the testing life cycle. The more closely this environment resembles the actual operational environment, the more effective the testing becomes. If test data was not created earlier in the testing process, it needs to be created as part of this step. Tests are then executed and the results recorded. The test report should indicate what works and what does not work. The test report should also give the tester's opinion regarding whether he or she believes the software is ready for operation at the conclusion of this test step.

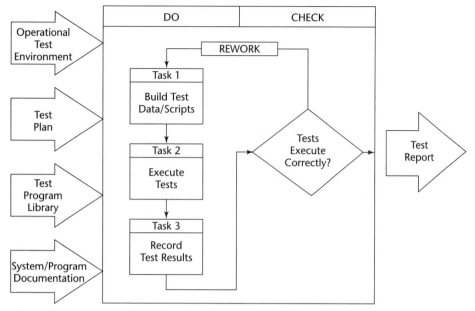

Figure 10-1   Workbench to execute dynamic tests and record results.

Input

Validation testing an application system has few new inputs. Many aspects of the developmental process are unavailable for evaluation during the test phase. Therefore, the testing during this phase must rely on the adequacy of the work performed during the earlier phases. The deliverables that are available during the validation testing include:

System test plan (may include a unit test plan)

Test data and/or test scripts

Results of previous verification tests

Inputs from third-party sources, such as computer operators

Part II of this book discussed the test environment. Ensuring that the test environment is representative of the operational environment is of critical importance to system testing and the integration testing of software systems to other systems on the operational environment. The test environment is less important for developer-conducted unit testing and testing of the integration of units. For that type of testing, what is important is that the test data include real-world test criteria.

The test environment should include the tools to perform testing effectively. For example, it is difficult to conduct regression testing unless the test environment includes the capture/playback tool. Likewise, it is difficult to create large amounts of test data without a tool that can help generate test conditions. Whereas verification testing is primarily a manual function, validation testing normally requires one or more software test tools.

Do Procedures

This step involves the following three tasks:

1. Build the test data.
2. Execute tests.
3. Record test results.

Task 1: Build the Test Data

The concept of test data is a simple one: to enable testers to create representative processing conditions. The complex part of creating test data is determining which transactions to include. Experience shows that it is uneconomical to test every condition in an application system. Experience further shows that most testing exercises fewer than one-half of the computer instructions. Therefore, optimizing testing through selecting the most important test transactions is the key aspect of the test data test tool.

Several of the test tools are structured methods for designing test data. For example, correctness proof, data flow analysis, and control flow analysis are all designed to develop extensive sets of test data. Unfortunately, although extremely effective, these tools require significant time and effort to implement, and few organizations allocate sufficient budgets. Thus, IT personnel are often not trained sufficiently to use these tools.

Sources of Test Data/Test Scripts

Effective validation testing requires you to gather all the test data/scripts that represent the type of processing that will occur in an operational environment. You can determine some of these transactions by studying the software development documentation; other test transactions may not be obvious from the documentation and require experienced testers to ensure that the data is accurate and complete.

Test data/scripts can come from any of the following sources:

- **System documentation.** Testers can use test data and scripts to test a system's documented specifications. For example, if the documentation indicates that a customer cannot exceed a preset credit limit, the testers could create test data that would validate that a customer cannot purchase items if they exceed their credit limit.

- **Use cases.** The testers should obtain from the users of the application the type of transactions they will be using. These are frequently referred to as use cases. In other words, there are test transactions that test that the software will work to process transactions by the users as they use the software.

- **Test generators.** Test generators, as the name implies, can create test conditions for use by testers. However, the type of test data that can be generated depends on the capability of the test data generator. The concern over test generators is that most do not have the capability to generate data that tests interrelationships such as pay grade and pay dollars.

- **Production data.** Testers can use production files themselves, or they can extract specific data from them.

- **Databases.** Testers need databases for testing many software applications. They can use copies of databases or live databases that have features that will block data from being updated as a result of processing test data.

- **Operational profiles.** Testers, in conjunction with the stakeholders of the software system, can analyze the type of processing that occurs in an operational environment. This is particularly useful when testing error conditions or when stress- or load-testing the system.

- **Individually created test data/scripts.** Testers can create their own data/scripts based on their knowledge of where errors are most likely to occur.

Testing File Design

To design an adequate file of test data, testers must be familiar with the IT department's standards and other relevant policies, include their provisions in the simulated transactions and procedures, and supply input and output formats for all types of transactions to be processed. To gain this knowledge, testers should review and analyze system flowcharts, operating instructions, and other documentation. This knowledge can alert the test team to possible system weaknesses for which unique test transactions should be designed.

To be effective, a test file should include transactions with a wide range of valid and invalid data—valid data for testing normal processing operations and invalid data for testing programmed controls.

Only one test transaction should be processed against each master record. This permits an isolated evaluation of specific program controls by ensuring that test results will not be influenced by other test transactions processed against the same master record. General types of conditions to test include the following:

- **Tests of normally occurring transactions.** To test a computer system's ability to accurately process valid data, a test file should include transactions that normally occur. For example, in a payroll system, transactions would include the calculations of regular pay, overtime pay, and some other type of premium pay (such as shift pay), as well as setting up master records for newly hired employees and updating existing master records for other employees.

- **Tests using invalid data.** Testing for the existence or effectiveness of programmed controls requires the use of invalid data. Examples of tests for causing invalid data to be rejected or "flagged" include the following:

  - Entering alphabetic characters when numeric characters are expected, and vice versa.

  - Using invalid account or identification numbers.

  - Using incomplete or extraneous data in a specific data field or omitting it entirely.

- Entering negative amounts when only positive amounts are valid, and vice versa.

- Entering illogical conditions in data fields that should be related logically.

- Entering a transaction code or amount that does not match the code or amount established by operating procedures or controlling tables.

- Entering transactions or conditions that will violate limits established by law or by standard operating procedures.

- **Tests to violate established edit checks.** Based on the system's documentation, an auditor should be able to determine which edit routines are included in the computer programs to be tested. He or she should then create test transactions to violate these edits to see whether they, in fact, exist.

Defining Design Goals

Before processing test data, the test team must determine the expected results. Any difference between actual and predetermined results indicates a weakness in the system. The test team should determine the effect of the weakness on the accuracy of master file data and on the reliability of reports and other computer products.

One of the test tools described earlier in this book was a function/test matrix. This matrix lists the software functions along one side and the test objectives on the other. Completing this matrix would help create a file of test conditions that would accomplish the test objectives for each of the software functions. Another objective of the test file is to ensure that the desired test coverage occurred. Coverage might include requirements coverage as well as branch coverage.

Entering Test Data

After the types of test transactions have been determined, the test data should be entered into the system using the same method as users. To test both input and computer processing, testers should ensure that all the data required for transaction processing is entered. For example, if users enter data by completing a data entry template, the tester should use that template as well.

Applying Test Files Against Programs That Update Master Records

There are two basic approaches to test programs for updating databases and/or production files. In the first approach, copies of actual master records and/or simulated master records are used to set up a separate master file. In the second approach, special routines used during testing will stop testers from updating production records.

To use the first approach, the test team must have a part of the organization's master file copied to create a test master file. From a printout of this file, the team selects records suitable for the test. The tester then updates the test file with both valid and invalid data by using the organization's transaction-processing programs. Testers can simulate master records by preparing source documents and processing them with the program the organization uses to add new records to its master file. Procedures for using simulated records as test data are the same as those for copied records. An advantage of using simulated records is that they can be tailored for particular conditions and they eliminate the need to locate and copy suitable organization records. This advantage is usually offset when many records are needed because their creation can be complex and time-consuming when compared to the relatively simple procedure of copying a part of the organization's master file.

Often, the most practical approach is to use a test master file that is a combination of copied and simulated master records. In this approach, copied records are used whenever possible and simulated records are used only when necessary to test conditions not found in the copied records.

By using copied and simulated master records in a separate test file, testers avoid the complications and dangers of running test data in a regular processing run against the current master file. A disadvantage of copied and simulated records is that computer programs must be loaded and equipment set up and operated for audit purposes only, thus involving additional cost.

Creating and Using Test Data

The following is the recommended process for creating and using test data:

1. **Identify test resources.** Testing using test data can be as extensive or limited a process as desired. Unfortunately, many programmers approach the creation of test data from a "we'll do the best job possible" perspective and then begin developing test transactions. When time expires, testing is complete. The recommended approach suggests that the amount of resources allocated for creating test data should be determined and then a process developed that creates the most important test data in the allotted time for creating test data.

2. **Identify test conditions.** Testers should use a function/test matrix to identify the conditions to test.

3. **Rank test conditions.** If resources are limited, the maximum use of those resources will be obtained by testing the most important test conditions. The objective of ranking is to identify high-priority test conditions that should be tested first.

    Ranking does not mean that low-ranked test conditions will not be tested. Ranking can be used for two purposes: first, to determine which conditions should be tested first; and second, and equally important, to determine the amount of resources allocated to each of the test conditions. For example, if testing the FICA deduction was a relatively low-ranked condition, only one test transaction might be created to test that condition, while for the higher-ranked test conditions several test transactions may be created.

4. **Select conditions for testing.** Based on the ranking, the conditions to be tested should be selected. At this point, the conditions should be very specific. For example, "testing FICA" is a reasonable condition to identify and rank, but for

creating specific test conditions it is too general. Three test situations might be identified—such as employees whose year-to-date earnings exceed the maximum FICA deduction; an employee whose current-period earnings will exceed the difference between the year-to-date earnings and the maximum deduction; and an employee whose year-to-date earnings are more than one pay period amount below the maximum FICA deductions. Each test situation should be documented in a testing matrix. This is a detailed version of the testing matrix that was started during the requirements phase.

5. **Determine correct results of processing.** The correct processing results for each test situation should be determined. Each test situation should be identified by a unique number, and then a log made of the correct results for each test condition. If a system is available to automatically check each test situation, special forms may be needed as this information may need to be converted to machine-readable media.

    The correct time to determine the correct processing results is before the test transactions have been created. This step helps determine the reasonableness and usefulness of test transactions. The process can also show if there are ways to extend the effectiveness of test transactions, and whether the same condition has been tested by another transaction.

6. **Create test transactions.** The method of creating the machine-readable transaction varies based on the application and the testing rules. The most common methods of creating test transactions include the following:

    ■ Key entry

    ■ Test-data generators

    ■ User-prepared input forms

    ■ Production data

7. **Document test conditions.** Both the test situations and the results of testing should be documented.

8. **Conduct test.** Testers should run the executable system using the test conditions or a simulated production environment.

9. **Verify and correct test results.** The results of testing should be verified and any necessary corrections to the programs performed. Problems detected as a result of testing can be attributable not only to system defects, but to test data defects. Testers should be aware of both situations.

Payroll Application Example

In making two reviews of automated civilian payroll systems, the U.S. General Accounting Office used test files to test the agencies' computer programs for processing pay and leave data. This case shows their test file development approach.

First, all available documentation was reviewed for the manual and automated parts of each system. To understand the manual operations, they interviewed payroll supervisors and clerks, reviewed laws and regulations relating to pay and leave, and familiarized themselves with standard payroll operating procedures. For the automated part of each system they interviewed system designers and programmers and reviewed system and program documentation and operating procedures.

After acquiring a working knowledge of each system, they decided to test computer programs used to update payroll master records and those used to calculate biweekly pay and leave entitlements. Although they were concerned primarily with these particular programs, they decided that other programs used in the normal biweekly payroll processing cycle (such as programs for producing pay and leave history reports, leave records, and savings bond reports) should also be tested to see how they would handle test data.

They then designed a test file of simulated pay and leave transactions to test the effectiveness of internal controls, compliance with applicable laws and regulations, and the adequacy of standard payroll operating procedures. The test file included transactions made up of both valid and invalid data. These transactions were based on specified procedures and regulations and were designed to check the effectiveness of internal controls in each installation's payroll processing. They used one transaction for each master record chosen.

The best method of obtaining suitable payroll master records for the test, they decided, would be to use copies of actual master records, supplemented with simulated records tailored for test conditions not found in the copied records.

Accordingly, they obtained a duplicate of each agency's payroll master file and had a section of it printed in readable copy. From this printout, they selected a specific master record to go with each test transaction. When none of the copied records appearing on the printout fit the specifics of a particular transaction, they made up a simulated master record by preparing source documents and processing them with the program used by each installation to add records for new employees to its master file. They then added the simulated records to the copied records to create the test master file.

They next prepared working papers on which were entered, for each test transaction, the control number assigned to the transaction, the type of input document to be used, and the nature and purpose of the test. They predetermined the correct end results for all test transactions and recorded these results in the working papers for comparison with actual results.

With some help from payroll office personnel, they next coded the test transactions onto source documents. The data was then key entered and key verified. They then processed the test data against actual agency payroll programs and compared the test results with the predetermined results to see whether there were any differences.

They found both systems accepted and processed several invalid test transactions that should have been rejected or flagged by programmed computer controls. Alternative manual controls were either nonexistent or less than fully effective because they could be bypassed or compromised through fraud, neglect, or inadvertent error. They recommended that the systems' automated controls be strengthened to ensure accurate payrolls and protect the government from improper payments.

A copy of their work papers outlining the test conditions is illustrated in Figure 10-2.

No.	TEST TRANSACTION	PURPOSE	Reject	Print error message	Reject in certain circumstances	Cut back to allowable maximum	Process without cutback	Automatically compute correct amount	Automatically adjust leave records
1.	Leave a mandatory field blank on a new employee's master record.	To determine whether the system will accept a master record with essential data missing. If missing data will cause an incorrect payment, the master record should be rejected with appropriate warning; if missing data is for administrative purposes only, the condition should be flagged by an error message.		X	X				
2.	Enter erroneous codes, such as charity, life insurance, union dues, marital status, etc. (Note: One erroneous code per master record.)	To determine whether the system will accept invalid data into employees' master records. The program should print error messages to identify invalid data and reject further processing of such transactions.		X	X				
3.	Enter an invalid annual leave category.	To determine whether the system will accept an invalid annual leave category. Federal regulations have established annual leave categories as 4, 6, or 8, depending on the amount of creditable service.	X	X					

Figure 10-2 Typical payroll transactions to include in a test file.

TEST TRANSACTION	PURPOSE	HOW A SYSTEM WITH EFFECTIVE CONTROLS WILL HANDLE THE TRANSACTION						
		Reject	Print error message	Reject in certain circumstances	Cut back to allow-able maximum	Process without cutback	Automatically compute correct amount	Automatically adjust leave records
4. Change a field in an inactive master record.	To determine whether it is possible to change fields in inactive master records and whether adequate controls exist over such changes. Processing of inactive records should be separated from the normal processing of active records to eliminate the possibility of unearned salary payments or the manipulation of records for persons who are not in a pay status.	X	X					
5. Change an employee's annual leave category before it is due to be changed.	To determine whether the system will reject invalid updates. The annual leave category is based on the amount of creditable service an employee has, computed from the employee's service computation date. Employees with less than 3 years of service are in category 4; employees with 3 to 15 years of service are in category 6; employees with more than 15 years of service are in category 8. The program should reject any attempt to change a leave category before it is due to be changed.							

Figure 10-2 (continued)

TEST TRANSACTION	PURPOSE	Reject	Print error message	Reject in certain circumstances	Cut back to allowable maximum	Process without cutback	Automatically compute correct amount	Automatically adjust leave records
6. Promote a general schedule (GS) employee above grade 5 before one year in grade has passed.	To determine whether the system rejects an invalid transaction. Federal regulations state that GS employees above grade 5 must be in grade at least one year before they can be promoted.	x	x					
7. Give a GS employee a within-grade salary increase before one year in grade has passed.	To determine how the system handles this transaction. Federal regulations state that a GS employee must be in grade at least one year before being eligible for a within-grade salary increase. The system should "flag" the transaction as being a quality step increase (which has the same effect as within-grade increase but can occur without the employee's having been in grade for one year).		x					
8. Change an employee's grade or annual salary so that the grade/step and annual salary rate are incompatible.	To determine whether the system accepts incompatible data. The program should have salary and grade controls that will reject transactions of this type from further processing.		x	x				

Figure 10-2 *(continued)*

		HOW A SYSTEM WITH EFFECTIVE CONTROLS WILL HANDLE THE TRANSACTION						
	TEST TRANSACTION	PURPOSE	Reject	Print error message	Reject in certain circumstances	Cut back to allowable maximum	Process without cutback	Automatically compute correct amount	Automatically adjust leave records
9.	Change an employee's service computation date to indicate that the leave category is due to change.	To determine whether the annual leave category is correctly changed, with a message printed to indicate the change. If the leave category is not automatically changed, a message should be printed.		x					
10.	Pay an inactive employee.	To determine whether the system will compute pay for an inactive employee (an employee who has been separated but whose record is maintained in the same master file used for active employees).	x	x					
11.	Pay a nonexistent employee.	To determine whether the system will compute pay for an employee with no record in the master file.	x	x					
12.	Input two time and attendance cards for the same employee.	To determine whether the system will compute pay twice for the same employee.	x	x					
13.	Pay a GS employee for 80 hours of work on a second-shift entitlement for a wage board (WB) employee.	To determine whether the system rejects WB entitlements for GS employees.	x	x					

Figure 10-2 *(continued)*

HOW A SYSTEM WITH EFFECTIVE CONTROLS WILL HANDLE THE TRANSACTION

	TEST TRANSACTION	PURPOSE	Reject	Print error message	Reject in certain circumstances	Cut back to allow-able maximum	Process without cutback	Automatically compute correct amount	Automatically adjust leave records
14.	Pay a GS employee for 80 hours work on a third-shift entitlement for a WB employee.	Same as above.	x	x					
15.	Pay a WB employee for 80 hours work on a night-shift differential entitlement for a GS employee.	To determine whether the system rejects GS entitlements for WB employees.	x	x					
16.	Pay a WB employee for 20 hours of overtime.	To verify the accuracy of premium (overtime) pay computation. Overtime pay is 1 and 1/2 times regular pay.						x	
17.	Pay a GS employee for 20 hours of night-differential pay.	Same as above. Premium = 10 percent.						x	
18.	Pay a WB employee for 80 hours on second shift.	Same as above. Premium = 7 1/2 percent.						x	
19.	Pay a WB employee for 80 hours on third shift.	Same as above. Premium = 10 percent.						x	

Figure 10-2 (continued)

HOW A SYSTEM WITH EFFECTIVE CONTROLS WILL HANDLE THE TRANSACTION

	TEST TRANSACTION	PURPOSE	Reject	Print error message	Reject in certain circumstances	Cut back to allow-able maximum	Process without cutback	Automatically compute correct amount	Automatically adjust leave records
20.	Pay a GS employee for 8 hours of holiday pay.	Same as above. Holiday pay is double regular pay.						X	
21.	Pay a WB employee for 8 hours of holiday pay.	Same as above.						X	
22.	Pay a GS employee for 8 hours of Sunday pay (for Sunday work that is not overtime work).	Same as above. Sunday premium is 25 percent of regular pay if Sunday is a regularly scheduled workday.						X	
23.	Pay a WB employee for 8 hours of Sunday pay.	Same as above.						X	
24.	Pay GS employees for 10 hours of environmental pay at the following premiums: a) 4 percent b) 8 percent c) 25 percent d) 50 percent	Same as above.						X	

Figure 10-2 *(continued)*

	TEST TRANSACTION	PURPOSE	Reject	Print error message	Reject in certain circumstances	Cut back to allow-able maximum	Process without cutback	Automatically compute correct amount	Automatically adjust leave records
			HOW A SYSTEM WITH EFFECTIVE CONTROLS WILL HANDLE THE TRANSACTION						
25.	Pay WB employees for 10 hours of envi-ronmental pay at the following premiums: a) 4 percent b) 8 percent c) 25 percent d) 50 percent	Same as above.						x	
26.	Pay a GS-1, 2, 3, 4, 5, 6, or 7 employee for 10 hours of over-time.	To verify accuracy of premium pay computation. For GS employees whose basic pay rate does not exceed the salary of a GS-10/1, the overtime rate is 1 and 1/2 times the basic pay rate.						x	
27.	Pay a GS-10, 11, 12, or 13 employee for 10 hours of over-time.	Same as above. For a GS employee whose basic pay rate is equal to or exceeds the rate of a GS-10/1, the over-time rate is one and 1/2 times the hourly rate for a GS-10/1.						x	

Figure 10-2 (continued)

HOW A SYSTEM WITH EFFECTIVE CONTROLS WILL HANDLE THE TRANSACTION

TEST TRANSACTION	PURPOSE	Reject	Print error message	Reject in certain circumstances	Cut back to allowable maximum	Process without cutback	Automatically compute correct amount	Automatically adjust leave records
28. Pay a GS-14 employee enough overtime pay to exceed the maximum salary limitation.	To test maximum salary limitation. Additional pay, such as overtime, night differential, holiday and Sunday pay, may be paid to the extent that it does not cause the aggregate pay for a biweekly period to exceed the rate of a GS-15/10. The program should cut back pay to this maximum.		X		X			
29. Pay a GS-14 employee enough environmental pay to exceed the maximum salary limitation.	Same as above. Program should not cut back environmental pay because it is not subject to the maximum salary limitation.					X		
30. Pay a WB employee enough premium pay to exceed the maximum salary limitation.	Same as above. Program should not cut back pay because WB employees have no maximum salary limitation.					X		
31. Pay a GS employee for one hour of holiday pay.	To determine whether the system will pay less than the two-hour minimum of holiday pay.		X				X	

Figure 10-2 (continued)

HOW A SYSTEM WITH EFFECTIVE CONTROLS WILL HANDLE THE TRANSACTION

	TEST TRANSACTION	PURPOSE	Reject	Print error message	Reject in certain circumstances	Cut back to allow-able maximum	Process without cutback	Automatically compute correct amount	Automatically adjust leave records
32.	Pay a WB employee for one hour of holiday pay.	Same as above.		x				x	
33.	Pay a GS employee for 40 hours of Sunday pay.	To determine whether the system limits Sunday pay to 32 hours maximum allowed.		x		x			
34.	Pay a WB employee for 80 hours on second shift and 10 hours for overtime into the third shift.	To verify the accuracy of premium pay. Federal regulations state that overtime pay for an employee regularly working the second or third shift will be computed at 1 and 1/2 times the second or third shift rate, respectively.						x	
35.	Pay a WB employee for 80 hours on third shift and 10 hours for overtime into the first shift.	Same as above.						x	
36.	Charge a full-time employee for 80 hours of leave without pay (LWOP).	To determine whether sick and annual leave will accrue when a full-time employee charges 80 hours of LWOP. The sick leave credit should be reduced by 4 hours, and the annual leave credit should be reduced by 4, 6, or 8 hours, depending on the annual leave category.							x

Figure 10-2 (continued)

TEST TRANSACTION	PURPOSE	HOW A SYSTEM WITH EFFECTIVE CONTROLS WILL HANDLE THE TRANSACTION						
		Reject	Print error message	Reject in certain circumstances	Cut back to allow-able maximum	Process without cutback	Automatically compute correct amount	Automatically adjust leave records
37. Charge a full-time employee for more annual leave than the employee has.	To determine whether excess annual leave is charged to LWOP. (The system should automatically reduce employee's pay for LWOP.)		X				X	X
38. Charge a full-time employee for more sick leave than the employee has.	To determine whether excess sick leave is charged to annual leave or LWOP. (The system should automatically adjust leave records and reduce pay for LWOP, if required.)		X				X	X
39. Charge a full-time employee for 99 hours of annual leave (19 hours more than a regular biweekly period).	To determine whether the system will cut back to the maximum of 80 hours for regular pay in a pay period.		X		X			
40. Charge a full-time employee for 99 hours of sick leave.	Same as above.		X		X			

Figure 10-2 (continued)

HOW A SYSTEM WITH EFFECTIVE CONTROLS WILL HANDLE THE TRANSACTION

	TEST TRANSACTION	PURPOSE	Reject	Print error message	Reject in certain circumstances	Cut back to allowable maximum	Process without cutback	Automatically compute correct amount	Automatically adjust leave records
41.	Charge a full-time employee for 80 hours of regular pay and 80 hours of annual leave in the same pay period.	Same as above. Total hours of work and leave cannot exceed 80 in a pay period.	X	X					
42.	Charge a full-time employee for enough hours of military leave to exceed 120 hours total.	To determine whether the system flags military leave in excess of 120 hours. Federal regulations state that an employee cannot charge more than 120 hours to military leave in a pay year. Because there are certain exceptions, the system should alert payroll clerks to the excess and should not reject or cut back the transaction.		X					
43.	Make a lump-sum annual leave payment to a separated employee in excess of annual leave balance.	To determine whether the system appropriately excludes excess annual leave in a lump-sum leave payment.		X		X			

Figure 10-2 (continued)

TEST TRANSACTION	PURPOSE	Reject	Print error message	Reject in certain circumstances	Cut back to allowable maximum	Process without cutback	Automatically compute correct amount	Automatically adjust leave records
	HOW A SYSTEM WITH EFFECTIVE CONTROLS WILL HANDLE THE TRANSACTION							
44. Pay a GS part-time employee for 32 hours of regular pay.	To determine whether the system correctly accrues annual and sick leave for part-time employees. For each 20 hours worked, a part-time employee receives one hour of sick leave. If in leave category 4, an employee needs 20 hours of work to earn one hour of annual leave; if in leave category 6, the employee needs 15 hours worked to earn one hour of annual leave; and if in leave category 8, the employee needs 10 hours worked to earn one hour of annual leave.							x
45. Make a lump-sum annual leave payment to an active employee.	To determine whether the system will make a lump-sum annual leave payment to an active employee. These payments should be made only to separated employees.	x	x					

Figure 10-2 (continued)

Creating Test Data for Stress/Load Testing

The objective of stress/load testing is to verify that the system can perform properly when internal program or system limitations have been exceeded. This may require that large volumes of transactions be entered during testing.

The following are the recommended steps for determining the test data needed for stress/load testing:

1. **Identify input data used by the program.** A preferred method to identify limitations is to evaluate the data. Each data element should be reviewed to determine if it poses a system limitation. This is an easier method than attempting to evaluate the programs. The method is also helpful in differentiating between system and program limitations. Another advantage is that data may need to be evaluated only once, rather than evaluating numerous individual programs.

2. **Identify data created by the program.** These would be data elements that are not input into the system but are included in internal or output data records. If testers know the input and output data, they can easily identify newly created data elements.

3. **Challenge each data element for potential limitations.** Testers should ask the following questions about each data element. A Yes answer to any of the questions means a limitation has been identified.

   - Can the data value in a field exceed the size of this data element?

   - Is the value in a data field accumulated?

   - Is data temporarily stored in the computer?

   - Is the information in a data element stored in the program until a following transaction is entered?

   - If a data element represents an accounting entity, does the number used to identify the accounting entity in itself provide a future limitation, such as using a one-character field to identify sales districts?

4. **Document limitations.** Documentation forms the basis for volume testing. Each limitation must now be evaluated to determine the extent of testing required.

5. **Perform volume testing.** The testing follows the nine steps outlined in the earlier section, "Creating and Using Test Data."

Creating Test Scripts

Several characteristics of scripting are different from batch test data development. These differences include the following:

- **Data entry procedures required.** The test procedures take on greater significance in scripting. The person using the script needs to know the details of how to enter the transaction via the terminal. This may be more complex than simply creating a test condition.

- **Use of software packages.** Scripting is a very difficult and complex task to do manually, particularly when the script has to be repeated multiple times. Therefore, most testers use a capture/playback type of software package, which enables the capture of transactions as they are entered via terminal, and then repeats them as the scripts are reused. There are many of these on the market, although they are aimed primarily at the IBM mainframe.

- **Sequencing of events.** Scripts require the sequencing of transactions. In batch systems, sequencing is frequently handled by sorting during systems execution; however, with scripts, the sequence must be predefined.

- **Stop procedures.** Batch testing continues until the batch is complete or processing abnormally terminates. Scripting may be able to continue, but the results would be meaningless; therefore, the script has to indicate when to stop, or if specific conditions occur, where to go in the script to resume testing.

To develop, use, and maintain test scripts, testers should perform the following five steps:

1. Determine testing levels.

2. Develop test scripts.

3. Execute test scripts.

4. Analyze the results.

5. Maintain test scripts.

Determining Testing Levels

There are five levels of testing for scripts, as follows:

- **Unit scripting.** Develops a script to test a specific unit/module.

- **Pseudo-concurrency scripting.** Develops scripts to test when two or more users are accessing the same file at the same time.

- **Integration scripting.** Determines that various modules can be properly linked.

- **Regression scripting.** Determines that the unchanged portions of systems remain unchanged when the system is changed. (Note: This is usually performed with the information captured on capture/playback software systems.)

- **Stress/performance scripting.** Determines whether the system will perform correctly when it is stressed to its capacity.

Developing Test Scripts

Typically, the capture/playback tool is used to develop test scripts. The development of a script involves a number of considerations, as follows:

Programs to be tested

Operating environment

Script components

Script organization

Terminal entry of scripts

Automated entry of script transactions

Manual entry of script transactions

Transaction edits

Transactions navigation

Transaction sources

Files involved

Terminal input and output

Online operating environment

Date setup

File initialization

Screen initialization

Secured initialization

File restores

Password options

Update options

Processing inquiries

Program libraries

File states/contents

Security considerations

Start and stop considerations

Logon procedures

Logoff procedures

Setup options

Menu navigation

Exit procedures

Re-prompting options

API communications

Single versus multiple terminals

Date and time dependencies

Inquiries versus updates

Unit test organization

Pseudo-concurrent test organization

Integration test organization

Regression test organization

Testers can use Work Paper 10-1 as an aid to developing test scripts. Table 10-1 summarizes the development strategies.

Table 10-1 Script Development Strategies

TEST LEVEL	SINGLE TRANSACTION	MULTIPLE TRANSACTIONS	SINGLE TERMINAL	MULTIPLE TERMINALS
Unit	X		X	
Concurrent	X			X
Integration		X	X	
Regression		X		X
Stress		X		X

Executing Test Scripts

Testers can execute test scripts either manually or by using the capture/playback tools. Considerations to incorporate when using capture/playback tools include the following:

Environmental setup

Program libraries

File states/contents

Date and time

Multiple terminal arrival modes

Serial (cross-terminal) dependencies

Processing options

Stall detection

Synchronization of different types of input data

Volume of inputs

Arrival rate of input

NOTE Be reluctant to use scripting extensively unless a software tool drives the script.

Analyzing the Results

After executing test scripts, testers must compare the actual results with the expected results. Much of this should have been done during the execution of the script, using the operator instructions provided. Note that if a capture/playback software tool is used, analysis will be more extensive after execution. The analysis should include the following:

- System components
- Terminal outputs (screens)
- File contents
- Environment variables, such as
    - Status of logs
    - Performance data (stress results)
- Onscreen outputs
- Order of outputs processing
- Compliance of screens to specifications
- Ability to process actions
- Ability to browse through data

Maintaining Test Scripts

Once developed, test scripts need to be maintained so that they can be used throughout development. The following areas should be incorporated into the script maintenance procedure:

Identifiers for each script

Purpose of scripts

Program/units tested by this script

Version of development data that was used to prepare script

Test cases included in script

Task 2: Execute Tests

Effective validation testing should be based on the test plan created much earlier in the life cycle. The test phase testing is a culmination of the previous work preparing for this phase. Without this preparation, tests may be uneconomical and ineffective.

The following describes some of the methods of testing an application system. Testers can use Work Paper 10-2 to track their progress.

- **Manual, regression, and functional testing (reliability).** Manual testing ensures that the people interacting with the automated system can perform their functions correctly. Regression testing verifies that what is being installed does not affect any portion of the application already installed or other applications interfaced by the new application. Functional testing verifies that the system requirements can be performed correctly when subjected to a variety of circumstances and repeated transactions.

- **Functional and regression testing (coupling).** The test phase should verify that the application being tested can correctly communicate with interrelated application systems. Both functional and regression testing are recommended. Functional testing verifies that any new function properly interconnects, while regression testing verifies that unchanged segments of the application system that interconnect with other applications still function properly.

- **Compliance testing**

  - **Authorization.** Testing should verify that the authorization rules have been properly implemented and complied with. Test conditions should include unauthorized transactions or processes to ensure that they are rejected, as well as ensuring authorized transactions are accepted.

  - **Performance.** Performance criteria are established during the requirements phase. These criteria should be updated if the requirements change during later phases of the life cycle. Many of the criteria can be evaluated during the test phase, and those that can be tested should be tested. However, it may be necessary to wait until the system is placed into production to verify that all of the criteria have been achieved.

- **Security.** Testers should evaluate the adequacy of the security procedures by attempting to violate them. For example, an unauthorized individual should attempt to access or modify data.

- **Functional testing**
  - **File integrity.** Testers should verify the controls over the file integrity. For example, if integrity depends on the proper functioning of an independent control total, that function should be tested along with the automated segment of the application system. In addition, sufficient updates of the file should be performed so that the integrity controls can be tested during several iterations of executing the application system.
  - **Audit trail.** Testers should test the audit trail function to ensure that a source transaction can be traced to a control total, that the transaction supporting a control total can be identified, and that the processing of a single transaction or the entire system can be reconstructed using audit trail information. It is normally advisable to list part of the audit trail file to ensure that it is complete based on the test transactions entered.
  - **Correctness.** Functional correctness testing verifies that the application functions in accordance with user-specified requirements. Because IT personnel normally concentrate their testing on verifying that the mainline requirements function properly, you may wish to emphasize the other test concerns during validation testing, or emphasize improperly entered transactions to test the data validation and error detection functions.

- **Recovery testing (continuity of testing).** If processing must continue during periods when the automated system is not operational, alternate processing procedures should be tested. In addition, the users of application systems should be involved in a complete recovery test so that not only the automated system is tested, but the procedures for performing the manual aspects of recovery are tested. This may involve intentionally causing the system to fail so that the recovery procedures can be tested.

- **Stress testing (service level).** The application under stress to verify that the system can handle high-volume processing. Stress testing should attempt to find those levels of processing at which the system can no longer function effectively. In online systems, this may be determined by the volume of transactions, whereas in batch systems the size of the batch or large volumes of certain types of transactions can test internal tables or sort capabilities.

- **Testing complies with methodology.** Testing should be performed in accordance with the organization's testing policies and procedures. The methodology should specify the type of test plan required, the recommended test techniques and tools, as well as the type of documentation required. The methodology should also specify the method of determining whether the test is successful.

- **Manual support testing (ease of use).** The ultimate success of the system is determined by whether people can use it. Because this is difficult to evaluate prior to validation testing, it is important that the system is evaluated in as realistic a test environment as possible.

- **Inspections (maintainability).** Modifications made during the system's development life cycle provide one method of testing the maintainability of the application system. Fortunately, these changes are made by the developers who are intimately familiar with the application system. The completed system should be inspected by an independent group, preferably systems maintenance specialists. System development standards should be devised with maintainability in mind.

- **Disaster testing (portability).** Disaster testing simulates problems in the original environment so that an alternative processing environment can be tested. Although it is not possible to simulate all environments into which an application system may be moved, knowing that it can transfer between two different environments provides a high probability that other moves will not cause major complications.

- **Operations testing (ease of operations).** Testing in this phase should be conducted by the normal operations staff. Project development personnel should not be permitted to coach or assist during the test process. It is only through having normal operation personnel conduct the test that the completeness of instructions and the ease with which the system can be operated can be properly evaluated.

Task 3: Record Test Results

Testers must document the results of testing so that they know what was and was not achieved. The following attributes should be developed for each test case:

- **Condition.** Tells what is.
- **Criteria.** Tells what should be.

  These two attributes are the basis for a finding. If a comparison between the two gives little or no practical consequence, no finding exists.

- **Effect.** Tells why the difference between what is and what should be is significant.
- **Cause.** Tells the reasons for the deviation.

A well-developed problem statement includes each of these attributes. When one or more of these attributes is missing, questions almost always arise, such as:

- **Condition.** What is the problem?
- **Criteria.** Why is the current state inadequate?
- **Effect.** How significant is it?
- **Cause.** What could have caused the problem?

Documenting a statement of a user problem involves three tasks, which are explained in the following sections.

Documenting the Deviation

Problem statements derive from a process of comparison. Essentially, the user compares "what is" with "what should be." When a deviation is identified between what actually exists and what the user thinks is correct or proper, the first essential step toward development of a problem statement has occurred. It is difficult to visualize any type of problem that is not in some way characterized by this deviation. The "what is" can be called the statement of condition. The "what should be" can be called the criteria. These concepts are the first two, and most basic, attributes of a problem statement.

Documenting deviation means to describe conditions as they currently exist and criteria that represent what the user wants. The actual deviation is the difference, or gap, between "what is" and "what is desired."

The statement of condition uncovers and documents facts as they exist. What is a fact? If somebody tells you something happened, is that "something" a fact? Or is it only a fact if someone told you it's a fact? The description of the statement of condition does, of course, depend largely on the nature and extent of the evidence or support that is examined and noted. For those facts making up the statement of condition, the IT professional will obviously take pains to ensure that the information is accurate, well-supported, and worded as clearly and precisely as possible.

The statement of condition should document as many of the following attributes as appropriate for the problem:

Activities involved

Procedures used to perform work

Outputs/deliverables

Inputs

Users/customers served

Deficiencies noted

The criterion is the user's statement of what is desired. It can be stated in either negative or positive terms. For example, it could indicate the need to reduce the complaints or delays as well as desired processing turnaround time.

Often, "should be" relates primarily to commonsense or general reasonableness, and the statement of condition virtually speaks for itself. These situations must be carefully distinguished from personal whims or subjective, fanciful notions. There is no room for such subjectivity in defining what is desired.

As much as possible, the criteria should directly relate to the statement of condition. For example, if volumes are expected to increase, the number of users served has changed, or the user processes have changed, they should be expressed in the same terms as used in documenting the statement of condition.

Work Paper 10-3 provides space to describe the problem and document the statement of condition and the statement of criteria. Note that an additional section could be added to Work Paper 10-3 to describe the deviation. However, if the statement of condition and statement of criteria are properly worded, the deviation should be readily determinable.

Documenting the Effect

Whereas the legitimacy of a problem statement may stand or fall on criteria, the attention that the problem statement receives after it is reported depends largely on its significance. Significance is judged by effect.

Efficiency and economy are useful measures of effect and frequently can be stated in quantitative terms such as dollars, time, units of production, number of procedures and processes, or transactions. Whereas past effects cannot be ascertained, potential future effects may be determined. Sometimes effects are intangible but are nevertheless of major significance.

Effect is frequently considered almost simultaneously with the first two attributes (condition and criteria) of the problem. Reviewers may suspect a bad effect even before they have clearly formulated these other attributes in their minds. After the statement of condition is identified, reviewers may search for a firm criterion against which to measure the suspected effect. They may hypothesize several alternative criteria, which are believed to be suitable based on experiences in similar situations. They may conclude that the effects under each hypothesis are so divergent or unreasonable that what is really needed is a firmer criterion—say, a formal policy in an area where no policy presently exists. The presentation of the problem statement may revolve around this missing criterion, although suspicions as to effect may have been the initial path.

The reviewer should attempt to quantify the effect of a problem wherever practical. Although the effect can be stated in narrative or qualitative terms, that frequently does not convey the appropriate message to management; for example, statements such as "Service will be delayed," or "Extra computer time will be required" do not really tell what is happening to the organization.

Documenting the Cause

In some cases, the cause may be obvious from the facts presented. In other instances, investigation is required to identify the origin of the problem.

Most findings involve one or more of the following causes:

- Nonconformity with standards, procedures, or guidelines
- Nonconformity with published instructions, directives, policies, or procedures from a higher authority
- Nonconformity with business practices generally accepted as sound
- Employment of inefficient or uneconomical practices

The determination of the cause of a condition usually requires the scientific approach, which encompasses the following steps:

1. Define the problem (the condition that results in the finding).
2. Identify the flow of work and/or information leading to the condition.
3. Identify the procedures used in producing the condition.

4. Identify the people involved.

5. Re-create the circumstances to identify the cause of a condition.

Document the cause for the problem on Work Paper 10-3.

Check Procedures

Work Paper 10-4 is a quality-control checklist for this step. Yes responses indicate good test practices, and No responses warrant additional investigation. A Comments column is provided to explain No responses and to record the results of investigation.

Output

Validation testing has the following three outputs:

The test transactions to validate the software system

The results from executing those transactions

Variances from the expected results

Guidelines

Validation testing is the last line of defense against defects entering the operational environment. If no testing has occurred prior to the test phase, it is unreasonable to expect testing at this point to remove all the defects. Experience has shown that it is difficult for the test phase to be more than 80 percent effective in reducing defects. Obviously, the fewer the number of defects that enter the test phase, the fewer the number of defects that get into the production environment.

At the end of the test phase, the application system is placed into production. The test phase provides the last opportunity for the user to ensure that the system functions properly. For this reason, the user should be heavily involved in testing the application system.

The IT department has an opportunity to evaluate the application system during the program phase. During this phase, they determine whether the system functions according to the requirements. The test step is best performed by a group other than the project team. This is not to say that the project team should not be involved or help, but rather that the team should not be the dominant party in the test phase. If the same individual were responsible for both the program phase testing and the test phase testing, there would be no need to have two different phases. If information services assume test responsibility during the program phase, and the user accepts it during the test phase, the two phases complement one another.

An independent test group should be given the responsibility to test the system to determine whether the system performs according to its needs. Because of communication problems, differences may exist between the specifications to which the system was built and the requirements that the user expected. Ideally, the test team will have been developing test conditions from the requirements phase, and during the test phase should uncover any remaining defects in the application system.

Summary

This chapter described how to dynamically test application software. Validation testing should not focus on removing defects, but rather on whether the system can perform as specified in operational mode. Because full testing is impractical, validation testing must concentrate on those operational aspects most important to the user. The next step is to analyze the results of testing and report the results.

WORK PAPER 10-1   Developing Test Scripts

Test Item	Entered By	Sequence	Action	Expected Result	Operator Instructions

WORK PAPER 10-2 Test Phase Test Process

TEST FACTOR: Manual, Regressional, and Functional Testing (Reliability)

TEST CRITERIA	ASSESSMENT				RECOMMENDED TEST
	Very Ade-quate	Ade-quate	Inade-quate	N/A	
1. Has data that does not conform to individual data element specifications been tested?					Verify that data validation programs reject data not conforming to data element specifications.
2. Have tests been performed to reject data relationships not conforming to system specifications?					Verify that the system rejects data relationships that do not conform to system specifications.
3. Have invalid identifiers been tested?					Verify that program rejects invalid identifiers.
4. Have tests been conducted to verify that missing sequence numbers will be detected?					Confirm that the system detects missing sequence numbers.
5. Have tests been conducted to verify that inaccurate batch totals will be detected?					Verify that the system will detect inaccurate batch totals.
6. Have tests been conducted to determine that data missing from a batch or missing scheduled data will be detected?					Verify that the programs will defect data missing from batches and scheduled data that does not arrive on time.
7. Have tests been conducted to verify that the unchanged parts of the system are not affected by invalid data?					Conduct regression test to ensure that unchanged portions of the program are not affected by invalid data.
8. Are the results obtained from the recovery process correct?					Verify the correctness of the results obtained from the recovery process.

WORK PAPER 10-2 *(continued)*

TEST FACTOR: Compliance Testing (Authorization)

TEST CRITERIA	ASSESSMENT				RECOMMENDED TEST
	Very Ade-quate	Ade-quate	Inade-quate	N/A	
1. Do manual procedures ensure that the proper authorization is received?					Test manual procedures to verify that authorization procedures are followed.
2. Have automated authorization rules been tested?					Verify that programs enforce automated authorization rules.
3. Have the current authorization names and identifiers been included as part of the test?					Confirm that the actual identifiers for authorization are included in the programs.
4. Have unauthorized transactions been entered into the system to determine if they will be rejected?					Verify that the authorization programs reject Security unauthorized transactions.
5. If multiple authorization is required, do the procedures function properly?					Verify that multiple authorization procedures perform properly.
6. If authorizers are limited in the size of transactions they can testing authorize, have multiple transactions below that limit been entered to determine if the system checks against limit violations?					Verify that the system can identify potential violations of authorization limits caused by entering multiple transactions below the limit.
7. Have the procedures to change the name or identifier of individuals authorized to change a transaction been tested?					Verify that the procedure to change the authorization rules of a program performs properly.
8. Have the procedures to report authorization violations to management been tested?					Verify that the authorization reports are properly prepared and delivered.

(continues)

WORK PAPER 10-2 *(continued)*

TEST FACTOR: Functional Testing (File Integrity)

TEST CRITERIA	ASSESSMENT				RECOMMENDED TEST
	Very Ade-quate	Ade-quate	Inade-quate	N/A	
1. Have the file balancing controls been tested?					Verify that the procedures to balance the files function properly.
2. Have the independently maintained control totals been tested?					Verify that the independently maintained control totals can confirm the automated file control totals.
3. Have integrity procedures been tested to ensure that updates are properly recorded?					Verify that the new control totals properly reflect the updated transactions.
4. Have tests been performed to ensure that integrity can be retained after a program failure?					Cause a program to fail to determine if it affects the file integrity.
5. Has erroneous data been entered to determine if it can destroy the file integrity?					Enter erroneous data to determine that it cannot affect the integrity of the file totals.
6. Have the manual procedures to develop independent control totals been tested?					Verify that the manual procedures can be properly performed to produce correct independent control totals.
7. If multiple files contain the same data, will all like elements of data be changed concurrently to ensure the integrity of all computer files?					Change a data element in one file that is redundant in several files to verify that the other files will be changed accordingly.
8. Have nil and one record file conditions been tested?					Run system with one and no records on each file.

WORK PAPER 10-2 *(continued)*

TEST FACTOR: Functional Testing (Audit Trail)

TEST CRITERIA	ASSESSMENT				RECOMMENDED TEST
	Very Ade-quate	Ade-quate	Inade-quate	N/A	
1. Has a test been conducted to verify that source documents can be traced to control totals?					Verify that a given source transaction can be traced to the appropriate control total.
2. Has a test been conducted to verify that all of the supporting data for a control total can be identified?					Determine for a control total that all the supporting transactions can be identified.
3. Can the processing of a single transaction be reconstructed?					Verify that the processing of a single transaction can be reconstructed.
4. Has a test been conducted to verify that the audit trail contains the appropriate information?					Examine the audit trail to verify that it contains the appropriate information.
5. Will the audit trail be saved for the appropriate time period?					Verify that a audit trail is marked to be saved for the appropriate time period.
6. Have tests been conducted to determine that people can reconstruct processing from the audit trail procedures?					Verify that by using the audit trail procedures people can reconstruct processing.
7. Have tests been conducted to verify that the audit trail is economical to use?					Determine the cost of using the audit trail.
8. Does the audit trail satisfy review requirements?					Verify with the auditors that the audit trail is satisfactory for their purpose.

(continues)

WORK PAPER 10-2 *(continued)*

TEST FACTOR: Recovery Testing (Continuity of Processing)

TEST CRITERIA	ASSESSMENT				RECOMMENDED TEST
	Very Adequate	Adequate	Inadequate	N/A	
1. Has a simulated disaster been created to test recovery procedures?					Simulate a disaster to verify that recovery can occur after a disaster.
2. Can people perform the recovery operation from the recovery procedures?					Verify that a recovery can be performed directly from the recovery procedures.
3. Has a test been designed to determine recovery can occur within the desired frame?					Conduct a recovery test to determine that it can be performed within the required time frame.
4. Have operation personnel been trained in recovery procedures?					Confirm with operation personnel that they have received appropriate recovery training.
5. Has each type of system failure been tested?					Verify that the system can recover from each of the various types of system failures.
6. Have the manual backup procedures been tested using full volume for system failures?					Simulate a system disaster to verify that the manual procedures are adequate.
7. Have the manual procedures been tested for entering data received during downtime into the system after the integrity of the system has been restored?					Verify that the system users can properly enter data that has been accumulated during system failures.
8. Can alternate processing procedures be performed using the manual procedures?					Require the manual alternate processing procedures to be performed exclusively from the procedures.

WORK PAPER 10-2 _(continued)_

TEST FACTOR: Stress Testing (Service Level)

TEST CRITERIA	ASSESSMENT				RECOMMENDED TEST
	Very Ade-quate	Ade-quate	Inade-quate	N/A	
1. Have the limits of all internal tables and other restrictions been documented?					Confirm with the project leader that all the project limits are documented.
2. Have each of the documented units been tested?					Verify that the application limits have been tested.
3. Have programmed procedures been included so that transactions that cannot be processed within current capacity are retained for later processing?					Confirm that when more transactions are entered than the system can handle they are stored for later processing.
4. Has the input portion of the system been subject to stress testing?					Verify that excessive input will not result in system problems.
5. Has the manual segment of the system been subject to stress testing?					Verify that when people get more transactions than they can process, no transactions will be lost.
6. Have communication systems been stress tested?					Verify that when communication systems are required to process more transactions than their capability, transactions are not lost.
7. Have procedures been written outlining the process to be followed when the system volume exceeds capacity?					Evaluate the reasonableness of the excess capacity procedures.
8. Have tests using backup personnel been performed to verify that the system can process normal volumes without the regular staff present?					Test the functioning of the system when operated by backup personnel.

(continues)

WORK PAPER 10-2 *(continued)*

TEST FACTOR: Compliance Test (Performance)

TEST CRITERIA	ASSESSMENT				RECOMMENDED TEST
	Very Ade-quate	Ade-quate	Inade-quate	N/A	
1. Can systems be operated at expected volumes with the anticipated manual support?					Verify that the systems can be operated with anticipated manual support.
2. Can transactions be processed at expected volumes for the expected cost?					Verify that the transaction processing costs are within expected tolerances.
3. Has the test phase been conducted within the test budget?					Verify from the accounting reports that the test phase has been performed within budget.
4. Have problems been encountered in testing that will affect the cost-effectiveness of the system?					Confirm with the project leader that uncovered problems will not significantly affect the cost effectiveness of the system.
5. Does the test phase indicate that the expected benefits will be received?					Confirm with user management that the expected benefit should be received.
6. Will projected changes to hardware and software significantly reduce operational or maintenance costs?					Confirm with computer operations whether projected changes to hardware and software will significantly reduce operations and maintenance costs.
7. Does a test phase schedule exist that identifies tasks, people, budgets, and costs?					Examine the completeness of the test phase work program.
8. Is the technology used for implementation sound?					Confirm with an independent source the soundness of the implementation technology.

WORK PAPER 10-2 *(continued)*

TEST FACTOR: Compliance Testing (Security)

TEST CRITERIA	ASSESSMENT				RECOMMENDED TEST
	Very Ade-quate	Ade-quate	Inade-quate	N/A	
1. Do the identified security risks have adequate protection?					Examine the completeness of the protection against the identified security risks.
2. Have tests been conducted to violate physical security?					Attempt to violate physical security.
3. Have tests been conducted to violate access security?					Attempt to violate access security.
4. Have tests been conducted to determine if computer resources can be used without authorization?					Attempt to violate access security.
5. Have tests been conducted to determine if security procedures are adequate during off hours?					Conduct security violations during nonworking hours.
6. Are repetitive tests conducted to attempt to violate security by continual attempts?					Conduct repetitive security violations.
7. Are tests conducted to obtain access to program and system documentation?					Attempt to gain access to program and system documentation.
8. Are employees adequately trained in security procedures?					Verify that employees know and follow security procedures.

(continues)

WORK PAPER 10-2 *(continued)*

TEST FACTOR: Test Complies with Methodology

TEST CRITERIA	ASSESSMENT				RECOMMENDED TEST
	Very Ade-quate	Ade-quate	Inade-quate	N/A	
1. Does testing verify that the system processing is in compliance with the organization's policies and procedures?					Verify that the operational system results comply with the organization's policies and procedures.
2. Does testing verify that the system processing is in compliance with the information services processing policies and procedures?					Verify that the operational system results comply with the information services policies and procedures.
3. Does testing verify that the system processing is in compliance with the accounting policies and procedures?					Verify that the operational system results comply with the accounting policies and procedures.
4. Does testing verify that the system processing is in compliance with governmental regulations?					Verify that the operational system results comply with the governmental regulations.
5. Does testing verify that the system processing is in compliance with industry standards?					Verify that the operational system results comply with the industry standards.
6. Does testing verify that the system processing is in compliance with the user procedures?					Verify that the operational system results comply with the user department policies and procedures.
7. Did testing procedures conform to the test plan?					Verify that the test plan was fully implemented.
8. Has the testing verified that sensitive data is adequately protected?					Confirm with the user the completeness of the test to verify sensitive data is protected.

WORK PAPER 10-2 *(continued)*

TEST FACTOR: Functional Testing (Correctness)

TEST CRITERIA	ASSESSMENT				RECOMMENDED TEST
	Very Ade-quate	Ade-quate	Inade-quate	N/A	
1. Do the normal transaction origination procedures function in accordance with specifications?					Verify that the transaction origination procedures perform in accordance with systems requirements.
2. Do the input procedures function in accordance with specifications?					Verify that the input procedures perform in accordance with systems requirements.
3. Do the processing procedures function in accordance with specifications?					Verify that the processing procedures perform in accordance with systems requirements.
4. Do the storage retention procedures function in accordance with specifications?					Verify that the storage retention procedures perform in accordance with systems requirements.
5. Do the output procedures function in accordance with specifications?					Verify that the output procedures perform in accordance with systems requirements.
6. Do the error-handling procedures function in accordance with specifications?					Verify that the error-handling procedures perform in accordance with systems requirements.
7. Do the manual procedures function in accordance with specifications?					Verify that the manual procedures perform in accordance with systems requirements.
8. Do the data retention procedures function in accordance with specifications?					Verify that the data retention procedures perform in accordance with systems requirements.

(continues)

WORK PAPER 10-2 *(continued)*

TEST FACTOR: Manual Support Testing (Ease of Use)

TEST CRITERIA	ASSESSMENT				RECOMMENDED TEST
	Very Ade-quate	Ade-quate	Inade-quate	N/A	
1. Do the clerical personnel understand the procedures?					Confirm with clerical personnel that they understand the procedures.
2. Are the reference documents easy to use?					Examine results of using reference documents.
3. Can input documents be completed correctly?					Examine processing for correctness.
4. Are output documents used properly?					Examine correctness of use of output documents.
5. Is manual processing completed within the expected time frame?					Identify time span for manual processing.
6. Do the outputs indicate which actions should be taken first?					Examine outputs for priority of use indications.
7. Are documents clearly identified regarding recipients and use?					Examine documents for clarity of identification.
8. Are the clerical personnel satisfied with the ease of use of the system?					Confirm with clerical personnel the ease of use of the system.

WORK PAPER 10-2 *(continued)*

TEST FACTOR: Inspections (Maintainability)

TEST CRITERIA	ASSESSMENT				RECOMMENDED TEST
	Very Ade-quate	Ade-quate	Inade-quate	N/A	
1. Do the programs contain nonentrant code?					Determine all program statements are entrant.
2. Are the programs executable?					Examine the reasonableness of program processing results.
3. Can program errors be quickly located?					Introduce an error into the program.
4. Does the program conform to the documentation?					Verify the executable version of the program conforms to the program documentation.
5. Is a history of program changes available?					Examine the completeness of the history of program changes.
6. Are test criteria prepared so that they can be used for maintenance?					Examine the usability of test data for maintenance.
7. Are self-checking test results prepared for use during maintenance?					Examine the usability of expected test results for maintenance.
8. Are all errors detected during testing corrected?					Verify that errors detected during testing have been corrected.

(continues)

WORK PAPER 10-2   *(continued)*

TEST FACTOR: Disaster Testing (Portability)

	ASSESSMENT				
TEST CRITERIA	Very Ade-quate	Ade-quate	Inade-quate	N/A	RECOMMENDED TEST
1. Have alternate processing sites and/or requirements been identified?					Confirm that alternate site requirements have been identified.
2. Are data files readable at the new facilities?					Execute data files at the new facilities.
3. Are programs executable at the new facilities?					Execute programs at the new facilities.
4. Are operating instructions usable at the new facilities?					Request that normal operators execute system at the new facilities.
5. Are outputs usable at the new facilities?					Examine usability of outputs produced using the new facilities.
6. Is execution time acceptable at the new facilities?					Monitor execution time at the new facility.
7. Are programs recompilable at the new facilities?					Recompile programs at the new facility.
8. Are the user procedures usable at the new facilities?					Request users to operate system at the new facilities.

WORK PAPER 10-2 *(continued)*

TEST FACTOR: Functional and Regression Testing (Coupling)

TEST CRITERIA	ASSESSMENT				RECOMMENDED TEST
	Very Ade-quate	Ade-quate	Inade-quate	N/A	
1. Are inputs from other appliance systems correct?					Verify correctness of computerized data.
2. Are outputs going to other applications correct?					Verify correctness of computerized data.
3. Does input from other applications conform to specifications documents?					Verify actual input conforms to specifications.
4. Does output going to other applications conform to specifications documents?					Verify actual output conforms to specifications.
5. Does input from other applications impact nonrelated functions?					Perform appropriate regression testing.
6. Can the intersystem requirements be processed within time frame specifications?					Monitor time span of processing for adherence to specifications.
7. Are intersystem operation instructions correct?					Verify intersystem operation instructions are correct.
8. Are the retention dates on intersystem files correct?					Confirm that intersystem file retention dates are correct.

(continues)

WORK PAPER 10-2 *(continued)*

TEST FACTOR: Operations Test (Ease of Operations)

TEST CRITERIA	ASSESSMENT				RECOMMENDED TEST
	Very Ade-quate	Ade-quate	Inade-quate	N/A	
1. Are operating instructions in the proper format?					Verify documented instructions conform to standards.
2. Have operators been instructed in how to operate the new applications?					Confirm with operators completeness of instructions.
3. Has a trouble call-in list been prepared?					Examine call-in list.
4. Are operating instructions complete?					Determine operator instructions are complete.
5. Has appropriate operations and test time been scheduled?					Examine schedule for reasonable allocation of time.
6. Are data retention procedures prepared?					Verify completeness of retention procedures.
7. Have normal operators successfully executed the application?					Verify that operators can operate the system by only using operator instructions.
8. Have operator recommendations for improvements been reviewed?					Verify that operator recommendations have been adequately reviewed.

WORK PAPER 10-3   Test Problem Documentation

Name of Software Tested

_____

**Problem
Description**

_____

_____

Actual Results

_____

_____

Expected Results

_____

_____

Effect of Deviation

_____

_____

Cause of Problem

_____

_____

Location of Problem

_____

_____

**Recommended
Action**

_____

_____

WORK PAPER 10-4   Quality Control Checklist

	YES	NO	N/A	COMMENTS
1. Has an appropriate test environment been established to perform the dynamic test of the application software?				
2. Are the testers trained in the test tools that will be used during this step?				
3. Has adequate time been allocated for this step?				
4. Have adequate resources been assigned to this step?				
5. Have the methods for creating test data been appropriate for this system?				
6. Has sufficient test data been developed to adequately test the application software?				
7. Have all the testing techniques that were indicated in the test plan been scheduled for execution during this step?				
8. Have the expected results from testing been determined?				
9. Has a process been established to determine variance/deviation between expected results and actual results?				
10. Have both the expected and actual results been documented when there's a deviation between the two?				
11. Has the potential impact of any deviation been determined?				
12. Has a process been established to ensure that appropriate action/resolution will be taken on all identified test problems?				

Step 5: Analyzing and Reporting Test Results

Testers should write two types of reports: interim reports and final reports. Interim test reports are necessary for both testers and management; testers need to know testing defect identification and correction status, and management needs to know the status of the overall project effort and the risks the organization faces as a consequence.

This chapter builds on the material presented so far in this book. In earlier steps, the test objectives are decomposed into a test plan, which eventually is decomposed into specific tests; tests are executed, and then the results are rolled up into test reports. The test results are compared against the expected results and experience with similar software systems. Reports are then prepared to provide the information that the user of the software system needs to make effective business decisions.

Overview

The user of the software system is responsible for deciding whether the software system should be used as presented and, if so, which precautions must be taken to ensure high-quality results. It is the testers who provide the information on which those decisions will be based. Thus, the testers are responsible not only for testing, but to consolidate and present data in a format that is conducive to good business decision making.

The project team is responsible for reporting the project's status. However, experience has shown that project teams tend to be overly optimistic about their ability to complete projects on time and within budget. Testers can provide management with an independent assessment of the status of the project.

By maintaining a status report of their activities, testers can report regularly to management what works and what does not work. Not working may mean a variety of statuses, including not tested, partially working, and not working at all.

Reporting on how the system will perform in operation uses the results of acceptance testing. Management may be interested in knowing only that the software system is acceptable to the system users. Math-oriented management may want statistical reliability measurements, in addition to user acceptance. Reliability assessment would include statistical measurements such as the expected mean time between failures.

Whether to place a software system in production is a user management decision, although testers can offer factual data about the status of the system together with their opinion regarding that decision.

Concerns

Testers should have the following concerns about the development and delivery of test reports:

- Test results will not be available when needed.
- Test information is inadequate.
- Test status is not delivered to the right people.

Workbench

Figure 11-1 shows the workbench for reporting test results. To report the results of testing, testers need not only the data collected during testing, but also the plans and the expected processing results. Tasks 1 and 2, which report the project's status and interim test results, should be performed on a regular basis. In the early stages of testing, reports may be prepared only monthly, but during the later stages of testing the reports should become more frequent.

The type and number of final reports will vary based on the scope of the project and the number of software systems involved. There may be a final report for each software system or a single report if all of the software systems are placed into production concurrently.

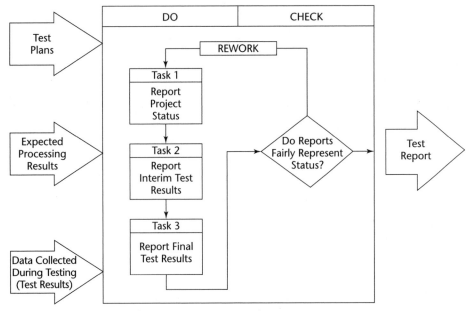

Figure 11-1   Workbench for reporting test results.

Input

This section describes the three types of input needed to answer management's questions about the status of the software system.

Test Plan and Project Plan

Testers need both the test plan and the project plan, both of which should be viewed as contracts. The project plan is the project's contract with management for work to be performed, and the test plan is a contract indicating what the testers will do to determine whether the software is complete and correct. It is against these two plans that testers will report status.

Expected Processing Results

Testers report the status of actual results against expected results. To make these reports, the testers need to know what results are expected. For software systems, the expected results are the business results.

Data Collected during Testing

This section explains the four categories of data to be collected during testing.

Test Results Data

The test results data includes but is limited to the following:

- **Test factors.** The factors incorporated in the plan, the validation of which becomes the test objective.

- **Business objectives.** The validation that specific business objectives have been met.

- **Interface objectives.** The validation that data/objects can be correctly passed among software components.

- **Functions/subfunctions.** Identifiable software components normally associated with the requirements for the software.

- **Units.** The smallest identifiable software components.

- **Platform.** The hardware and software environment in which the software system will operate.

Test Transactions, Test Suites, and Test Events

These are the test products produced by the test team to perform testing. They include but are not limited to the following:

- **Test transactions/events.** The type of tests that will be conducted during the execution of tests, which will be based on software requirements.

- **Inspections.** A verification of process deliverables against their specifications.

- **Reviews.** A verification that the process deliverables/phases are meeting the user's true needs.

Defects

This category includes a description of the individual defects uncovered during testing. Work Paper 11-1 can be used for recording and monitoring defects. This description includes but is not limited to the following:

Data the defect uncovered

The name of the defect

The location of the defect

The severity of the defect

The type of defect

How the defect was uncovered

The results of later investigations should be added to this information—for example, where the defect originated, when it was corrected, and when it was entered for retest.

Efficiency

Two types of efficiency can be evaluated during testing: software system and test. As the system is being developed, a process decomposes requirements into lower and lower levels. These levels normally include high- and low-level requirements, external and internal design, and the construction or build phase. While these phases are in progress, the testers decompose the requirements through a series of test phases, which are described in Steps 3 and 4 of the seven-step process.

Conducting testing is normally the reverse of the test development process. In other words, testing begins at the lowest level and the results are rolled up to the highest level. The final test report determines whether the requirements were met. Documenting, analyzing, and rolling up test results depend partially on the process of decomposing testing through a detailed level. The roll-up is the exact reverse of the test strategy and tactics.

Storing Data Collected During Testing

A database should be established in which to store the results collected during testing. I also suggest that the database be available online through a client/server system so that individuals with a vested interest in the status of the project have ready access.

The most common test report is a simple spreadsheet that indicates the project component for which status is requested, the test that will be performed to determine the status of that component, and the results of testing at any point in time. Interim report examples illustrated in Task 2 of this chapter show how to use such a spreadsheet.

Do Procedures

Three tasks are involved in reporting test results. They are described here as individual steps because each is a standalone effort. For example, reporting the status of the project is an activity independent of other test reports. Testers could issue interim and final test reports without reporting or knowing the status of the project. However, Tasks 2 and 3 are more closely linked. Interim test results will normally be used in developing the final test report. On the other hand, some testers prepare only interim reports and others only final reports.

The three tasks and their associated reports detailed in this chapter are representative of what testers could report. Testers should not limit themselves to these reports but rather use their creativity to develop others appropriate to the project and the organization.

What is important about test reports is that they supply management with the information it needs to make decisions. Reporting extraneous information is a waste of the tester's time, and not reporting information needed by management is an ineffective use of testing. Testers are encouraged early in the project to consult with management to learn the types of reports they should prepare during and at the conclusion of testing.

Task 1: Report Software Status

This task offers an approach for reporting project status information. These reports enable senior IT management to easily determine the status of the project, and can be issued as needed.

The two levels of project status reports are as follows:

- **Summary status report.** This report provides a general view of all project components. It is used to determine which projects need immediate attention and which are on schedule with no apparent problems.

- **Project status report.** This report shows detailed information about a specific project component, allowing the reader to see up-to-date information about schedules, budgets, and project resources. Each report should be limited to one page so that only vital statistics are included.

Both reports are designed to present information clearly and quickly. Colorful graphics can be used to highlight status information. Senior management does not have time to read and interpret lengthy status reports from all project teams in the organization. Therefore, this step describes a process that enables management to quickly and easily assess the status of all projects.

NOTE An individual software system that needs rework is referred to as a *project.*

The best way to produce "user-friendly" reports is to incorporate simple graphics and color-coding. For example, projects represented in green would be those with no apparent problems, projects in yellow would indicate potentially problematic situations, and projects in red would indicate those needing management's immediate attention.

This step describes reporting on three status conditions for each project: implementation, schedule, and budgets. The number of status conditions should be kept to as few as possible; four is still manageable. Some organizations list quality as the fourth, beginning with system testing in later development phases.

In addition to serving as the input to project status reports, the data collected can be used for internal benchmarking, in which case the collective data from all projects is used to determine the mean level of performance for all enterprise projects. This benchmark is used for comparison purposes, to make judgments on the performance of individual projects.

Prior to effectively implementing a project reporting process, two inputs must be in place.

- **Measurement units.** IT must have established reliable measurement units that can be validated. Management must be willing to use this quantitative data as an integral part of the decision-making process. All those involved in IT projects must be trained in collecting and using this data.

- **Process requirements.** Process requirements for a project reporting system must include functional, quality, and constraint attributes. Functional attributes describe the results the process is to produce; quality attributes define the particular attributes that should be included in the software requirement; and constraint attributes include tester skill levels, budget, and schedule.

The following sections describe the six subtasks for this task.

Establishing a Measurement Team

The measurement team should include individuals who:

- Have a working knowledge of quality and productivity measurements
- Are knowledgeable in the implementation of statistical process control tools
- Have a working understanding of benchmarking techniques
- Know of the organization's goals and objectives
- Are respected by their peers and management

Representatives should come from management and personnel responsible for software development and maintenance. For an IT organization of fewer than 50 people, the measurement team should be between three and five members.

Creating an Inventory of Existing Project Measurements

An inventory of existing measurements should be performed in accordance with a plan. If problems arise during the inventory, the plan and the inventory process should be modified accordingly. The formal inventory is a systematic and independent review of all existing measurements and metrics. All identified data must be validated to determine if they are valid and reliable.

The inventory process should start with an introductory meeting of the participants. The objective of this meeting is to review the inventory plan with management and representatives of the projects. A sample agenda for the introductory meeting would be to:

1. Introduce all members.
2. Review the scope and objectives of the inventory process.
3. Summarize the inventory processes to be used, including work papers and data repositories.
4. Establish communications channels.
5. Confirm the inventory schedule with major target dates.

Creating an inventory involves the following activities:

1. Review all measurements.
2. Document all findings.
3. Conduct interviews to determine what and how measurement data is captured and processed.

Developing a Consistent Set of Project Metrics

To enable senior management to quickly access the status of each project, it is critical to develop a list of consistent measurements spanning all project lines. Initially, this can be challenging, but with cooperation and some negotiating, you can establish a reasonable list of measurements. Organizations with development and maintenance standards will have an easier time completing this step.

Defining Process Requirements

The objective of this step is to use the management criteria and measurement data developed in Steps 2 and 3 to define the process requirements for the management project reporting system. Major criteria of this specification include the following:

- A description of desired output reports
- A description of common measurements
- The source of common measurements and associated software tools to capture the data
- A determination of how the data will be stored (centralized and/or segregated)

Developing and Implementing the Process

The objective of this step is to document the work process used to output the reports of the project data. The implementation will involve the following activities:

1. Document the workflow of the data capture and reporting process.
2. Procure software tools to capture, analyze, and report the data.
3. Develop and test system and user documentation.
4. Beta-test the process using a small- to medium-sized project.
5. Resolve all management and project problems.
6. Conduct training sessions for management and project personnel on how to use the process and interrelate the reports.
7. Roll out the process across all project lines.

Monitoring the Process

Monitoring the reporting process is very important because software tools are constantly being upgraded and manual supporting activities sometimes break down. The more successful the system, the better the chance that management will want to use it and perhaps expand the reporting criteria.

The two primary reports from this step are Summary Status and Project Status.

Summary Status Report

The Summary Status report (see Figure 11-2) provides general information about all projects and is divided into the following four sections:

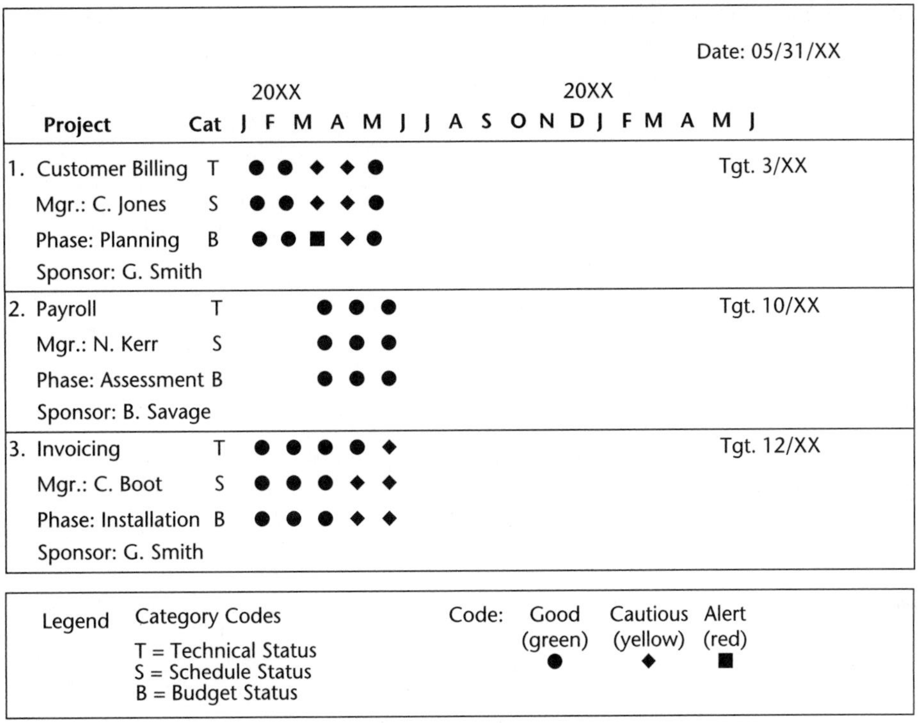

Figure 11-2   A Summary Status report.

- **Report date information.** The information in the report is listed as current as of the date in the top-left corner. The date the report was produced appears in the top-right corner.

- **Project information.** Project information appears in a column on the left side of the report. Each cell contains the project's name, manager, phase, and sponsor.

- **Timeline information.** Timeline information appears in a chart that displays a project's status over an 18-month period. It shows project status by measuring technical, budgeting, and scheduling considerations. The year and month (abbreviated with initials) appear along the top of the chart to indicate the month-by-month status of each project.

  Technical (T), scheduling (S), and budget (B) information also appears in the chart, and is specific to each project. These three considerations measure the status of each project:

  - *Technical status* (T) shows the degree to which the project is expected to function within the defined technical and/or business requirements.

  - *Scheduling status* (S) shows the degree to which the project is adhering to the current approved schedule.

  - *Budgeting status* (B) shows the degree to which the project is adhering to the current approved budget. Expenditures for the budget include funds, human resources, and other resources.

- **Legend information.** The report legend, which is located along the bottom of the page, defines the colors and symbols used in the report, including category and color codes. The following colors could be used to help to quickly identify project status:

  - A green circle could mean there are no major problems and that the project is expected to remain on schedule.

  - A yellow circle could indicate potentially serious deviation from project progression.

  - A red circle could mean a serious problem has occurred and will have a negative effect on project progression.

Project Status Report

The Project Status report (see Figure 11-3) provides information related to a specific project component. The design of the report and use of color in your report enables the reader to quickly and easily access project information. It is divided into the following six sections:

- **Vital project information.** Vital project information appears along the top of the report. This information includes:

  - Date the report is issued

  - Name of the executive sponsoring the project

  - Name of project manager

  - Official name of project

  - Quick-status box containing a color-coded circle indicating the overall status of the project

- **General Information.** This section of the report appears inside a rectangular box that contains general information about the project. The work request number and a brief description of the project appear in the top half of the box. The lower half of the box shows the phase of the project (e.g., planning, requirements, development, and implementation), as well as important project dates and figures, which include:

  - Project start date, determined by official approval, sponsorship, and project management

  - Original target date for project completion

  - Current target date for project completion

  - Phase start date of the current phase

  - Original target date for completion of the current phase

  - Current target date for completion of the current phase

  - Original budget allotted for the project

  - Current budget allotted for the project

  - Expenses to date for the project

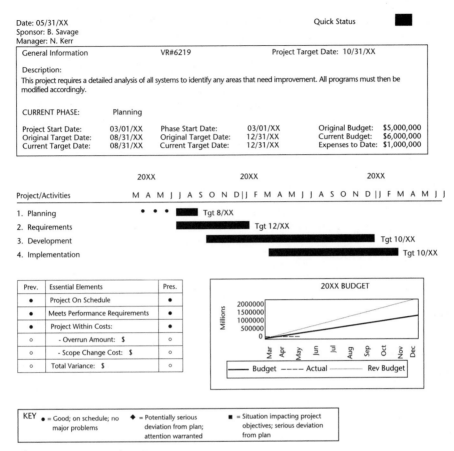

Figure 11-3   A Project Status report.

- **Project/Activities.** The Project/Activities chart measures the status according to the phase of the project.

  Future activities for the project are indicated by a bar, which extends to the expected date of project completion, or the current target date, identified by the abbreviation Tgt.

- **Essential Elements.** The Essential Elements section indicates the current status of the project by comparing it to the previous status of the project. The chart could use the color-coded circles and list considerations that allow the reader to quickly gather project statistics. These considerations ask:

  - Is the project on schedule?

  - Do the current project results meet the performance requirements?

  - Are the project costs within the projected budget?

  - Are the project costs over budget?

  - What is the dollar amount of the project budget overrun?

These questions can be answered by comparing the previous report results (on the left side of the chart) to the current report results (on the right side of the chart).

This section of the report also includes a graph that compares projected costs to actual costs. The projected cost line appears in one color; the actual cost line appears in another. The dollar amounts appear on the left side of the graph, and the time line appears along the bottom of the graph. This graph shows you whether the project is adhering to the current approved budget.

- **Legend information.** The report legend, which is located along the bottom of the page, defines the colors and symbols used in the report, including category and color codes.

- **Project highlights information.** The project highlights appear in a rectangular box located at the bottom of the report. This section may also contain comments explaining specific project developments.

Task 2: Report Interim Test Results

The test process should produce a continuous series of reports that describe the status of testing. The frequency of the test reports should be at the discretion of the team and based on the extensiveness of the test process.

This section describes ten interim reports. Testers can use all ten or select specific ones to meet their individual needs. However, I recommend that if available test data permits at the end of the testing phase, all ten test reports be prepared and incorporated into the final test report.

Function/Test Matrix

The function/test matrix shows which tests must be performed to validate the software functions, and in what sequence to perform the tests. It will also be used to determine the status of testing.

Many organizations use a spreadsheet package to maintain test results. The intersection of the test and the function can be color-coded or coded with a number or symbol to indicate the following:

- 1 = Test is needed but not performed.
- 2 = Test is currently being performed.
- 3 = Minor defect noted.
- 4 = Major defect noted.
- 5 = Test is complete and function is defect-free for the criteria included in this test.

Testers should complete Work Paper 11-1 each time they uncover a defect. This information should be maintained electronically so that test managers and/or software users can review it. The information collected about each defect can be as simple or as complex as desired. For simplification purposes, it is suggested that the following guidelines be used:

- **Defect naming.** Name defects according to the phase in which the defect most likely occurred, such as a requirements defect, design defect, documentation defect, and so forth.

- **Defect severity.** Use three categories of severity, as follows:

    Critical. The defect(s) would stop the software system from operating.

    Major. The defect(s) would cause incorrect output to be produced.

    Minor. The defect(s) would be a problem but would not cause improper output to be produced, such as a system documentation error.

- **Defect type.** Use the following three categories:

    Missing. A specification was not included in the software.

    Wrong. A specification was improperly implemented in the software.

    Extra. An element in the software was not requested by a specification.

The information from Work Paper 11-1 should be used to produce the function/test matrix, as shown in Table 11-1.

The report is designed to show the results of performing a specific test on a function. Therefore, no interpretation can be made about the results of the entire software system, only about the results of individual tests. However, if all the tests for a specific function are successful, testers can assume that function works. Nevertheless, "working" means that it has met the criteria in the test plan.

Functional Testing Status Report

The purpose of this report is to show the percentage of functions, including the functions that have been fully tested, the functions that have been tested but contain errors, and the functions that have not been tested.

A sample of this test report is illustrated in Figure 11-4. It shows that approximately 45 percent of the functions tested have uncorrected errors, 35 percent were fully tested, and 10 percent were not tested.

Table 11-1 Function/Test Matrix

TEST	1	2	3	4	5	6	7	8	9	10
Function										
A		X		X				X	X	
B			X		X				X	
C			X				X	X		
D			X						X	
E		X		X				X		X

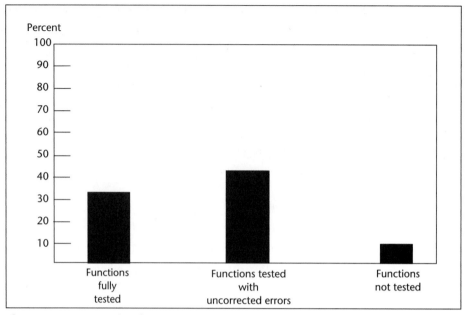

Figure 11-4 A Functional Testing Status report.

The report is designed to show the status of the software system to the test manager and/or customers. How the status is interpreted will depend heavily on the point in the test process at which the report was prepared. As the implementation date approaches, a high number of functions tested with uncorrected errors and functions not tested should raise concerns about meeting the implementation date.

Functions Working Timeline Report

The purpose of this report is to show the status of testing and the probability that the software will be ready on the projected date.

Figure 11-5 shows an example of a Functions Working Timeline report. This report assumes a September implementation date and shows from January through September the percent of functions that should be working correctly at any point in time. The "Actual" line shows that the project is doing better than anticipated.

If the actual performance is better than planned, the probability of meeting the implementation date is high. On the other hand, if the actual percent of functions working is less than planned, both the test manager and development team should be concerned and may want to extend the implementation date or add resources to testing and/or development.

Expected Versus Actual Defects Uncovered Timeline Report

The purpose of this report is to show whether the number of defects is higher or lower than expected. This assumes that the organization has sufficient historical data to project defect rates. It also assumes that the development process is sufficiently stable so that the defect rates are relatively consistent.

The example chart for the Expected versus Actual Defects Uncovered Timeline report in Figure 11-6 shows a project beginning in January with a September implementation date. For this project, almost 500 defects are expected; the expected line shows the cumulative anticipated rate for uncovering those defects. The "Actual" line shows that a higher number of defects than expected have been uncovered early in the project.

Generally, an actual defect rate varies from the expected rate because of special circumstances, and investigation is warranted. The cause may be the result of an inexperienced project team. Even when the actual defects are significantly less than expected, testers should be concerned because it may mean that the tests have not been effective and a large number of undetected defects remain in the software.

Defects Uncovered Versus Corrected Gap Timeline Report

The purpose of this report is to list the backlog of detected but uncorrected defects. It requires recording defects as they are detected, and then again when they have been successfully corrected.

The example in Figure 11-7 shows a project beginning in January with a projected September implementation date. One line on the chart shows the cumulative number of defects uncovered during testing, and the second line shows the cumulative number of defects corrected by the development team, which have been retested to demonstrate that correctness. The gap represents the number of uncovered but uncorrected defects at any point in time.

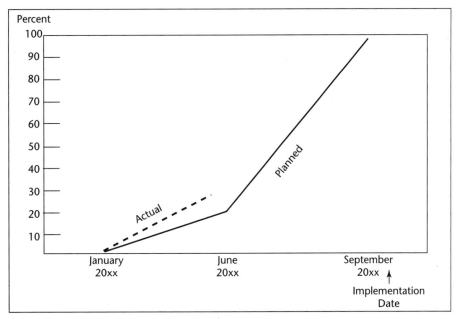

Figure 11-5   A Functions Working Timeline report.

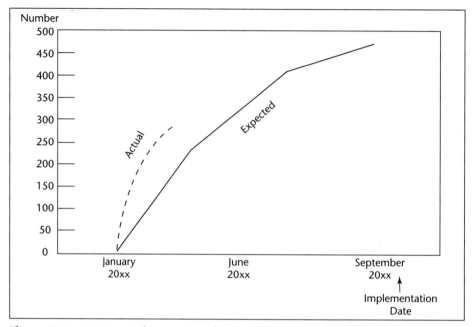

Figure 11-6 An Expected versus Actual Defects Uncovered Timeline report.

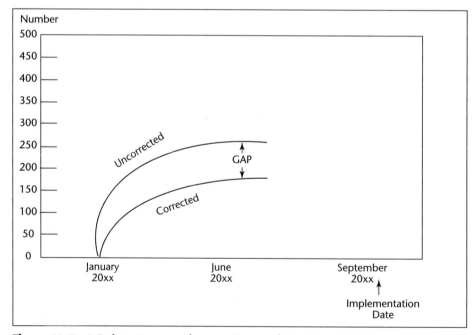

Figure 11-7 A Defects Uncovered versus Corrected Gap Time Line report.

The ideal project would have a very small gap between these two timelines. If the gap becomes wide, it indicates that the backlog of uncorrected defects is growing, and that the probability the development team will be able to correct them prior to implementation date is decreasing. The development team must manage this gap to ensure that it remains narrow.

Average Age of Uncorrected Defects by Type Report

The purpose of this report is to show the breakdown of the gap presented in Figure 11-7 by defect type—that is, the actual number of defects by the three severity categories.

The Average Age of Uncorrected Defects by Type report example shows the three severity categories aged according to the average number of days since the defect was detected. For example, it shows that the average critical defect is about 3 days old, the average major defect is about 10 days old, and the average minor defect is about 20 days old. The calculation is to accumulate the total number of days each defect has been waiting to be corrected, divided by the number of defects. Average days should be working days.

Figure 11-8 shows a desirable result, demonstrating that critical defects are being corrected faster than major defects, which are being corrected faster than minor defects. Organizations should have guidelines for how long defects at each level should be maintained before being corrected. Action should be taken accordingly based on actual age.

Defect Distribution Report

The purpose of this report is to explain how defects are distributed among the modules/units being tested. It lists the total cumulative defects for each module being tested at any point in time.

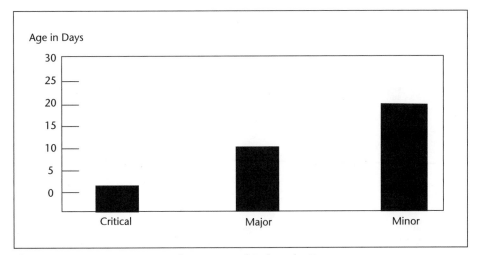

Figure 11-8   An Average Age of Uncorrected Defects by Type report.

The sample Defect Distribution report, shown in Figure 11-9, shows eight units along with the number of defects for each. The report could be enhanced to show the extent of testing that has occurred on the modules (for example, by color-coding the number of tests or by incorporating the number of tests into the bar as a number).

This report can help identify modules that have an excessive defect rate. A variation of the report could list the cumulative defects by test—for example, defects uncovered in test 1, the cumulative defects uncovered by the end of test 2, the cumulative defects uncovered by test 3, and so forth. Frequently, modules that have abnormally high defect rates are those that have ineffective architecture and, thus, are candidates to be rewritten rather than for additional testing.

Normalized Defect Distribution Report

The purpose of this report is to normalize the defect distribution presented in Figure 11-9. The normalization can be by function points or lines of code. This will enable testers to compare the defect density among the modules/units.

The Normalized Defect Distribution report example in Figure 11-10 shows the same eight modules presented in Figure 11-9. However, in this example, the defect rates have been normalized to defects per 100 function points or defects per 1,000 lines of code, to enable the reader of the report to compare defect rates among the modules. This was not possible in Figure 11-9, because there was no size consideration. Again, a variation that shows the number of tests can be helpful in drawing conclusions.

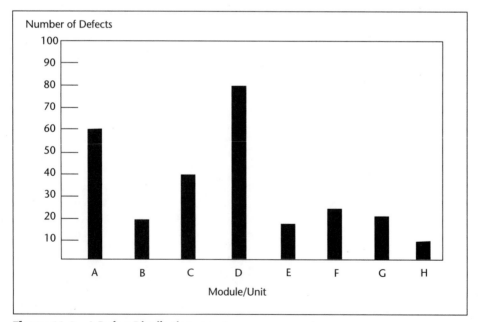

Figure 11-9 A Defect Distribution report.

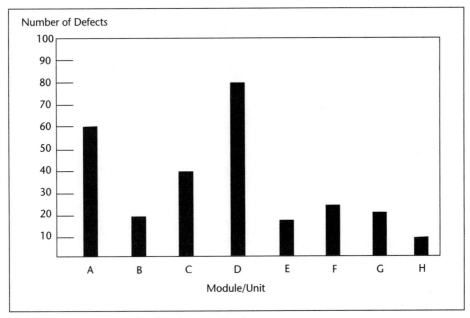

Figure 11-10   A Normalized Defect Distribution report.

This report can help identify modules that have excessive defect rates. A variation of the report could show the cumulative defects by test: for example, the defects uncovered in test 1, the cumulative defects uncovered by the end of test 2, the cumulative defects uncovered by test 3, and so forth. Frequently, modules that have abnormally high defect rates are those that have ineffective architecture and, thus, are candidates for rewrite rather than additional testing.

Testing Action Report

This is a summary action report prepared by the test team. The information contained in the report should be listed as necessary to the test manager and/or the development manager so that they can properly direct the team toward a successful implementation date.

The Testing Action report example (see Figure 11-11) lists four pieces of information helpful to most test managers: total number of tests behind schedule, uncorrected critical defects, major uncorrected defects more than five days old, and the number of uncovered defects not corrected.

These items are examples of what could be included in the Testing Action report. Most are included in the other reports, but this report is a summation, or a substitute, for the other reports.

The test manager should carefully monitor the status of testing and take action when testing falls behind schedule.

<u>Tests Behind Schedule:</u>
<u>Uncorrected Critical Defects:</u>
<u>Major Uncorrected Defects More Than 5 Days Old:</u>
<u>Number of Uncovered Defects Not Corrected:</u>

Figure 11-11   A Testing Action report.

Interim Test Report

As testers complete an individual project they should issue an Interim Test report. The report should discuss the scope of the test, the results, what works and does not work, and recommendations (see Figure 11-12).

Any report about testing should indicate the test's scope; otherwise, the reader will assume that exhaustive testing has occurred, which is never the case. Testing is a risk-oriented activity in which resources should be expended to minimize the major risks. Exhaustive testing is not possible, practical, or economical. Thus, testing is never designed to ensure that there are no defects remaining in the software, and the scope will explain what the testers accomplished.

The recommendations section is a critical part of the report, because the reader is usually removed from the project being tested and the technical recommendations provided by the testers can help with the reader's business decision. For example, testers may indicate that there is a 50/50 probability that the system will terminate abnormally in production because of dating problems. A business decision might then be made to put the software into operation, but develop effective backup recovery procedures in case the termination occurs.

Task 3: Report Final Test Results

A final report should be prepared at the conclusion of each test activity. The report should summarize the information from the following reports:

---

1. Scope of Test

This section indicates which functions were and were not tested.

---

2. Test Results

This section indicates the results of testing, including any variance between what is and what should be.

---

3. What Works/What Does Not Work

This section defines the functions that work and do not work and the interfaces that work and do not work.

---

4. Recommendations

This section recommends actions that should be taken to:

a. Fix functions/interfaces that do not work.

b. Make additional improvements.

Figure 11-12   An Interim Test report.

- Individual Project report
- Integration Test report
- System Test report
- Acceptance Test report

A final test report is designed to document the results of testing as defined in the test plan. Without a well-developed test plan, it is difficult to develop a meaningful test report. It is designed to accomplish three objectives: to define the scope of testing (normally a brief recap of the test plan), to present the results of testing, and to draw conclusions and make recommendations. The test report may be a combination of electronic and hard copy data. For example, if the function/test matrix is maintained electronically, there is no reason to print it because the paper report will summarize that data, draw the appropriate conclusions, and present recommendations.

The test report has one immediate and two long-term purposes. The immediate purpose is to enable customers to determine whether the system is ready for production (and if not, to assess the potential consequences and initiate appropriate actions to minimize those consequences). The first of the two long-term uses is for the project development team to trace problems in the event the application malfunctions in production. By knowing which functions have been correctly tested and which functions still contain defects, testers can take corrective action. The second long-term purpose is to enable testers to analyze the rework process and make changes to prevent defects from occurring in the future.

Individual Project Test Report

This report focuses on individual projects. When different testers test individual projects, they should prepare a report on their results. Refer to Figure 11-12 for a sample report format.

Integration Test Report

Integration testing tests the interfaces between individual projects. A good test plan will identify the interfaces and institute test conditions that will validate interfaces between software systems. Given this, the integration report follows the same format as the Individual Project Test report, except that the conditions tested are the interfaces between software systems.

System Test Report

Chapter 8 presented a system test plan standard that identified the objectives of testing, what was to be tested, how it was to be tested, and when tests should occur. The System Test report should present the results of executing that test plan (see Figure 11-13). If test data is maintained electronically, it need only be referenced, not included in the report.

---

1. General Information

    1.1 *Summary.* Summarize both the general functions of the software tested and the test analysis performed.

    1.2 *Environment.* Identify the software sponsor, developer, user organization, and the computer center where the software is to be installed. Assess the manner in which the test environment may be different from the operation environment, and the effects of this difference on the tests.

    1.3 *References.* List applicable references, such as:
    a. Project request (authorization).
    b. Previously published documents on the project.
    c. Documentation concerning related projects.

2. Test Results and Findings

    Identify and present the results and findings of each test separately in paragraphs 2.1 through 2.*n*.

Figure 11-13   A System Test report.

2.1   *Test (identify)*

    2.1.1   *Validation tests.* Compare the data input and output results, including the output of internally generated data, of this test with the data input and output requirements. State the findings.

    2.1.2   *Verification tests.* Compare what is shown on the document to what should be shown.

2.*n*   *Test (identify).* Present the results and findings of the second and succeeding tests in a manner similar to that of paragraph 2.1.

3.   Software Function Findings

Identify and describe the findings on each function separately in paragraphs 3.1 through 3.*n*.

3.1   *Function (identify)*

    3.1.1   *Performance.* Describe briefly the function. Describe the software capabilities designed to satisfy this function. State the findings as to the demonstrated capabilities from one or more tests.

    3.1.2   *Limits.* Describe the range of data values tested. Identify the deficiencies, limitations, and constraints detected in the software during the testing with respect to this function.

3.*n*   *Function (identify).* Present the findings on the second and succeeding functions in a manner similar to that of paragraph 3.1.

4.   Analysis Summary

4.1   *Capabilities.* Describe the capabilities of the software as demonstrated by the tests. Where tests were to demonstrate fulfillment of one or more specific performance requirements, compare the results with these requirements. Compare the effects any differences in the test environment versus the operational environment may have had on this test demonstration of capabilities.

4.2   *Deficiencies.* Describe the deficiencies of the software as demonstrated by the tests. Describe the impact of each deficiency on the performance of the software. Describe the cumulative or overall impact on performance of all detected deficiencies.

4.3   *Risks.* Describe the business risks if the software is placed in production.

4.4   *Recommendations and estimates.* For each deficiency, provide any estimates of time and effort required for its correction, and any recommendations as to:
a. The urgency of each correction.
b. Parties responsible for corrections.
c. How the corrections should be made.

4.5   *Option.* State the readiness for implementation of the software.

Figure 11-13   *(continued)*

Acceptance Test Report

Testing has two primary objectives. The first is to ensure that the system as implemented meets the software requirements. The second objective is to ensure that the software system can operate in the real-world user environment, which includes people with varying skills, attitudes, time pressures, business conditions, and so forth. This final report should address these issues. See Chapter 12 for conducting and reporting the results of acceptance testing.

Check Procedures

Work Paper 11-2 is a questionnaire that enables testers to verify that they have performed the test reporting processes correctly. The checklist is divided into three parts: Quality Control over Writing the Status Report, Quality Control for Developing Interim Test Result Reports, and Control over Writing Final Test Reports. Work Paper 11-3 is a questionnaire that will guide testers to writing effective reports.

Output

This step should produce the following three categories of reports:

- **Project status reports.** These reports are designed both for the project team and senior management. Senior management includes information services management, user/customer management, and executive management. These reports provide a check and balance against the status reports submitted by the project team, and any discrepancies between the two reports should be reconciled.

- **Interim test reports.** These reports describe the status of testing. They are designed so that the test team can track its progress in completing the test plan. They are also important for the project implementers, as the test reports will identify defects requiring corrective action. Other staff members may wish to access the reports to evaluate the project's status.

- **Final test reports.** These reports are designed for staff members who need to make decisions regarding the implementation of developed software. The reports should indicate whether the software is complete and correct, and if not, which functions are not working.

Guidelines

Testers can use the data from individual project reports to develop a baseline for the enterprise based on mean scores of the reporting criteria. Rather than comparing quality, productivity, budget, defects, or other categories of metrics to external organizations, valuable management information can be made available. From this baseline, individual projects can be compared. Information from projects consistently scoring above the enterprise baseline can be used to improve those projects that are marginal or fall below the enterprise baseline.

Testers should heed the following guidelines when preparing reports:

1. Use Work Papers 11-2 and 11-3 to ensure reports are written effectively.

2. Allow project team members to review report drafts and make comments before reports are finalized.

3. Don't include names or assign blame.

4. Stress quality.

5. Limit the report to two or three pages stressing important items and include other information in appendixes.

6. Eliminate small problems from the report and give these directly to the project people.

7. Deliver the report to the project leader by hand.

8. Offer to have the testers work with the project team to explain their findings and recommendations.

Summary

The emphasis of this chapter has been on summarizing, analyzing, and reporting test results. Once the decision to implement software has been made, the next step (as discussed in Chapter 12) is to determine whether the system meets the real needs of the users regardless of system requirements and specifications.

WORK PAPER 11-1   Defect Reporting

Field Requirements

FIELD	INSTRUCTIONS FOR ENTERING DATA
Software/System Tested	Name of software being tested.
Date	Date on which the test occurred.
Defect Found	The name and type of a single defect found in the software being tested.
Location Found	The individual unit or system module in which the defect was found.
Severity of Defect	Critical means the system cannot run without correction; major means the defect will impact the accuracy of operation; minor means it will not impact the operation.
Type of Defect	Whether the defect represents something missing, something wrong, or something extra.
Test Data/Script Locating Defect	Which test was used to uncover the defect.
Origin of Defect/ Phase of Development	The phase in which the defect occurred.
Date Corrected	The date on which the defect was corrected.
Retest Date	The date on which the testers were scheduled to validate whether the defect had been corrected.
Result of Retest	Whether the software system functions correctly and the defect no longer exists; or if additional correction and testing will be required.

WORK PAPER 11-1   *(continued)*

Software/System Tested: _____

_____

Date: _____

_____

Defect Found: _____

_____

Location Found: _____

_____

Severity of Defect: ❑ Critical
                           ❑ Major
                           ❑ Minor

Type of Defect: ❑ Missing
                           ❑ Wrong
                           ❑ Extra

Test Data/Script Locating Defect:

_____

_____

Origin of Defect/Phase of Development: _____

_____

Date Corrected: _____

_____

Retest Date: _____

_____

Result of Retest: _____

_____

WORK PAPER 11-2   Report Writing Quality Control Checklist

	YES	NO	N/A	COMMENTS
Part 1: Quality Control over Writing Status Reports				
1. Has management been involved in defining the information to be used in the decision-making process?				
2. Have the existing units of measure been validated?				
3. Are software tools in place for collecting and maintaining a database to support the project reporting process?				
4. Has the completed requirements document been signed off by management and project personnel?				
5. Have management and project personnel been trained in collecting quantitative data and using the reports?				
Part 2: Quality Control for Developing Interim Test Result Reports				
1. Do the report writers have the expected results from testing?				
2. Is there a method of reporting uncovered defects?				
3. Is there a method of reporting the status of defects?				
4. Is there a method to relate the defects to the function that is defective?				
5. Have the testers consulted with management to determine what type of reports are wanted?				
6. Have the following reports been prepared? • Function Test/Matrix • Functional Testing Status • Function Working Timeline • Expected vs. Actual Defects Uncovered Timeline • Defects Uncovered vs. Corrected Gap Timeline • Average Age of Uncorrected Defects by Type • Defect Distribution • Normalized Defect Distribution • Testing Action				

WORK PAPER 11-2   *(continued)*

		YES	NO	N/A	COMMENTS
7.	Do the reports appear reasonable to those involved in testing?				
8.	Have the reports been delivered to the person desiring the report?				
9.	Have the reports been delivered on a timely basis?				
Part 3: Control over Writing Final Test Reports					
1.	Have reports been issued for the final results of individual project testing?				
2.	Have reports been issued for the final results of integration testing?				
3.	Has a summary report been issued on the overall results of testing?				
4.	Did these reports identify the scope of testing?				
5.	Did these reports indicate what works and what doesn't?				
6.	Do these reports provide recommendations on actions to take if appropriate?				
7.	Do these reports provide an opinion to management on whether the software system should be placed into the production?				

WORK PAPER 11-3   Guidelines for Writing Test Reports

	YES	NO	N/A	COMMENTS
Reporting Complete				
1. Does it give all necessary information?				
2. Is it written with the reader in mind, and does it answer all his or her questions?				
3. Is there a plan for a beginning, middle, and end?				
4. Are specific illustrations, cases, or examples used to best advantage?				
5. Are irrelevant ideas and duplications excluded?				
6. Are the beginning and the ending of the report effective?				
Clarity				
7. Are the ideas presented in the best order?				
8. Does each paragraph contain only one main idea?				
9. Is a new sentence started for each main idea?				
10. Are the thoughts tied together so the reader can follow from one to another without getting lost?				
11. Are most sentences active? Are the verbs mostly action verbs?				
12. Is the language adapted to the readers; are the words the simplest to carry the thought?				
13. Is underlining used for emphasis, or parentheses for casual mention?				
14. Will your words impart exact meaning to the reader?				
Concise				
15. Does report contain only essential facts?				
16. Are most of the sentences kept short?				
17. Are most paragraphs kept short?				
18. Are unneeded words eliminated?				
19. Are short words used for long ones?				
20. Are roundabout and unnecessary phrases eliminated?				
21. Is the practice followed of using pronouns instead of repeating nouns?				
22. Is everything said in the fewest possible words?				

WORK PAPER 11-3   *(continued)*

	YES	NO	N/A	COMMENTS
Correct				
23. Is the information accurate?				
24. Do the statements conform to policy?				
25. Is the writing free from errors in grammar, spelling, and punctuation?				
Tone				
26. Is the tone natural? Is conversational language used?				
27. Is it personal? Are the "we" and "you" appropriately emphasized?				
28. Is it friendly, courteous, and helpful?				
29. Is it free from words that arouse antagonism?				
30. Is it free from stilted, hackneyed, or technical words and phrases?				
Effectiveness				
31. Is there variety in the arrangement of words, sentences, and pages so that it is interesting to read?				
32. Was it given the "ear" test?				
Conclusion				
33. Is the report satisfactory and ready for publication?				

Step 6: Acceptance and Operational Testing

Acceptance testing is formal testing conducted to determine whether a software system satisfies its acceptance criteria and to enable the buyer to determine whether to accept the system. Software acceptance testing at delivery is usually the final opportunity for the buyer to examine the software and to seek redress from the developer for insufficient or incorrect software. Frequently, the software acceptance test period is the only time the buyer is involved in acceptance and the only opportunity the buyer has to identify deficiencies in a critical software system. (The term *critical* implies economic or social catastrophe, such as loss of life; as used in this chapter, it implies the strategic importance to an organization's long-term economic welfare.) The buyer is thus exposed to the considerable risk that a needed system will never operate reliably (because of inadequate quality control during development). To reduce the risk of problems arising at delivery or during operation, the buyer must become involved with software acceptance early in the acquisition process.

Overview

At the conclusion of Step 5, developers and testers have tested the system and reported their conclusions. If the report follows the proposed format, it will list not only strengths and weaknesses but also recommendations. The customer/users of the software have one of three decisions to make:

1. The software system is usable as is and can be placed into a production state.

2. The software has some deficiencies; when corrected, the software can be placed into an operational state.

3. The software is severely deficient and it may or may not ever be placed into an operational state depending on the type of deficiencies, the alternatives available to the customer/users, and the cost to correct the deficiencies.

The user may or may not want to conduct acceptance testing before making one of these three decisions. If the decision is to conduct acceptance testing, acceptance testing would occur and the results of the acceptance testing plus the tester's report would be input to making one of the preceding three decisions.

The tested software system at the conclusion of Step 5 should be ready to move to an operational state. This does not mean that all the requirements are implemented, or that it does not include defects, but rather, it's at a decision point regarding placing the software into operation. This decision point occurs for both the initial version of the software system as well as changed versions of the software system. Normally, moving the initial version into an operational state is more complex than moving a changed version into an operational state.

Testers need to be heavily involved in ensuring that the software as tested can be moved effectively into an operational state. The activities performed vary based on the risks associated with placing the software into production.

Acceptance testing is designed to determine whether the software is "fit" for the user to use. The concept of fit is important in both design and testing. Design must attempt to build the application to fit into the user's business process; the test process must ensure a prescribed degree of fit. Testing that concentrates on structure and requirements may fail to assess fit, and thus fail to test the value of the automated application to the business. The four components of fit are as follows:

- **Data.** The reliability, timeliness, consistency, and usefulness of the data included in the automated application

- **People.** The skills, training, aptitude, and desire to properly use and interact with the automated application

- **Structure.** The proper development of application systems to optimize technology and satisfy requirements

- **Rules.** The procedures to follow in processing the data

The system must fit into these four components of the business environment. If any of the components fails to fit properly, the success of the application system will be diminished. Therefore, testing must ensure that all the components are adequately prepared and/or developed, and that the four components fit together to provide the best possible solution to the business problem.

Objective

The objective of acceptance testing is to determine throughout the development cycle that all aspects of the development process meet user needs. There are many ways to accomplish this. The user may require that the implementation plan be subject to an independent review, of which the user may choose to be a part or just input acceptance criteria into the process.

Acceptance testing should not only occur at the end of the development process but as an ongoing activity that tests both interim and final products, so that unnecessary time is not expended making corrections that prove unacceptable to the system user.

The overall objective of testing for software changes is to ensure that the changed application functions properly in the operating environment. This includes both the manual and automated segments of the computerized application. The specific objectives of this aspect of testing include the following:

Develop tests to detect problems prior to placing the change into production.

Correct problems prior to placing the change in production.

Test the completeness of training material.

Involve users in the testing of software changes.

Concerns

When considering acceptance testing, users must be aware of the following concerns:

- Acceptance testing must be integrated into the overall development process.
- Cost and time for acceptance testing will not be available.
- The implementers of the project plan will be unaware of the acceptance criteria.
- The users will not have the skill sets needed to perform acceptance testing.

Typically, the user/customers conduct acceptance testing only for the initial release of the software system. However, if extensive changes are made to the software system, the customer/user may repeat this task before a new version of the software is placed into an operational state.

Pre-operational testing involves ensuring that the software that operated effectively and efficiently in the test environment still operates efficiently and effectively in the production environment. Post-operational testing is involved in testing changes made to the new system that will create new operational versions of the software system.

Placing the initial version of the software into an operational state may involve all three tasks because the movement of the software into an operational state identifies defects that must be corrected. When new versions are created that incorporate changes in the software, normally just pre-operational and post-operational testing need to be performed.

The installation phase testing does not verify the functioning of the application system, but rather the process that places that application system into a production status. The process is attempting to validate the following:

- Proper programs are placed into the production status.
- Needed data is properly prepared and available.

- Operating and user instructions are prepared and used.

- An effective test of the installation phase cannot be performed until the results expected from the phase have been identified. The results should be predetermined and then tests performed to validate that what is expected has happened. For example, a control total of records updated for installation might be determined, and then an installation phase test would be performed to validate that the detailed records in the file support the control total.

IT management should be concerned about the implementation of the testing and training objectives. These concerns need to be addressed during the development and execution of the testing and training for software changes. The first step in addressing control concerns is identifying the concerns that affect these software changes:

- **Will the testing process be planned?** Inadequate testing is synonymous with unplanned testing. Unless the test is planned, there is no assurance that the results will meet change specifications.

- **Will the training process be planned?** People rarely decide on the spur of the moment to hold a training class or develop training material. What tends to happen is that training is given one on one after problems begin to occur. This is a costly method of training.

- **Will system problems be detected during testing?** Even the best training plans rarely uncover all the potential system problems. What is hoped is that the serious problems will be detected during testing.

- **Will training problems be detected during testing?** How people will react to production situations is more difficult to predict than how computerized applications will perform. Thus, the objective in training should be to prepare people for all possible situations.

- **Will already-detected testing and training problems be corrected prior to the implementation of the change?** An unforgivable error is to detect a problem and then fail to correct it before serious problems occur. Appropriate records should be maintained and controls implemented so that detected errors are immediately acted on.

Workbench

The acceptance testing workbench begins with software that has been system tested for the system specifications. The tasks performed in this step lead to an acceptance decision, which does not necessarily mean that the software works as desired by the user, or that all problems have been corrected; it means that the software user is willing to accept and use the software in its current state. The acceptance test workbench is illustrated in Figure 12-1.

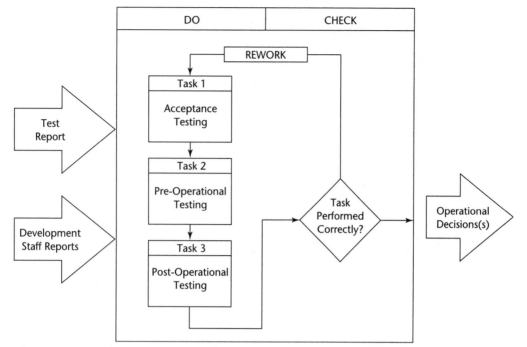

Figure 12-1   Acceptance testing workbench.

Input Procedures

The three inputs to Task 1 are as follows:

Interim work products

Tested software

Unresolved defect list

Task 2, the installation phase, is the process of getting a new system operational. The process may involve any or all of the following areas:

Changing old data to a new format

Creating new data

Installing new and/or change programs

Updating computer instructions

Installing new user instructions

The installation process may be difficult to execute within the time constraints. For example, many system installations are performed over a weekend. If the installation cannot be successfully completed within this two-day period, the organization may face serious operational problems Monday morning. For this reason, many organizations have adopted a fail-safe method. They pick a deadline by which the new system must be successfully installed; if it is not, they revert back and use the old system.

Much of the test process will be evaluating and working with installation phase deliverables. The more common deliverables produced during the installation phase include the following:

Installation plan

Installation flowchart

Installation program listings and documentations (assuming special installation programs are required)

Test results from testing special installation programs

Documents requesting movement of programs into the production library and removal of current programs from that library

New operator instructions

New user instructions and procedures

Results of installation process

Testers need four inputs to adequately perform testing on a changed version of software, as follows:

Change documentation

Current test data/test plan

Changed version of software

Prior test results

Task 1: Acceptance Testing

Software acceptance is an incremental process of approving or rejecting software systems during development or maintenance, according to how well the software satisfies predefined criteria. In this chapter, for the purpose of software acceptance, the activities of software maintenance are assumed to share the properties of software development. "Development" and "developer" include "maintenance" and "maintainer."

Acceptance decisions occur at pre-specified times when processes, support tools, interim documentation, segments of the software, and finally the total software system must meet predefined criteria for acceptance. Subsequent changes to the software may affect previously accepted elements. The final acceptance decision occurs with verification that the delivered documentation is adequate and consistent with the executable system and that the complete software system meets all buyer requirements. This decision is usually based on software acceptance testing. Formal final software acceptance testing must occur at the end of the development process. It consists of tests to determine whether the developed system meets predetermined functionality, performance, quality, and interface criteria. Criteria for security or safety may be mandated legally or by the nature of the system.

Defining the Acceptance Criteria

The user must assign the criteria the software must meet to be deemed acceptable. (Note: Ideally, this is included in the software requirements specifications.) In preparation for developing the acceptance criteria, the user should do the following:

- Acquire full knowledge of the application for which the system is intended.
- Become fully acquainted with the application as it is currently implemented by the user's organization.
- Understand the risks and benefits of the development methodology that is to be used in correcting the software system.
- Fully understand the consequences of adding new functions to enhance the system.

Acceptance requirements that a system must meet can be divided into these four categories:

- **Functionality.** Internal consistency of documents and code and between stages; traceability of functionality; adequate verification of logic; functional evaluation and testing; preservation of functionality in the operating environment.
- **Performance.** Feasibility analysis of performance requirements; correct simulation and instrumentation tools; performance analysis in the operating environment.
- **Interface quality.** Interface documentation; interface complexity; interface and integration test plans; interface ergonomics; operational environment interface testing.
- **Overall software quality.** Quantification of quality measures; criteria for acceptance of all software products; adequacy of documentation and software system development standards; quality criteria for operational testing.

Assessing the criticality of a system is important in determining quantitative acceptance criteria. By definition, all safety criteria are critical; and by law, certain security requirements are critical. Some typical factors affecting criticality include the following:

Importance of the system to organization or industry

Consequence of failure

Complexity of the project

Technology risk

Complexity of the user environment

For specific software systems, users must examine their projects' characteristics and criticality to develop expanded lists of acceptance criteria for those software systems. Some of the criteria may change according to the phase of correction for which criteria are being defined. For example, for requirements, the "testability" quality may mean that test cases can be developed automatically.

The user must also establish acceptance criteria for individual elements of a product. These criteria should be the acceptable numeric values or ranges of values. The buyer should compare the established acceptable values against the number of problems presented at acceptance time. For example, if the number of inconsistent requirements exceeds the acceptance criteria, the requirements document should be rejected. At that time, the established procedures for iteration and change control go into effect.

Work Paper 12-1 is designed to document the acceptance criteria. It should be prepared for each hardware or software project within the overall project. Acceptance criteria requirements should be listed and uniquely numbered for control purposes. After defining the acceptance criteria, a determination should be made as to whether meeting the criteria is critical to the success of the system.

Developing an Acceptance Plan

The first step to achieve software acceptance is the simultaneous development of a software acceptance plan, general project plans, and software requirements to ensure that user needs are represented correctly and completely. This simultaneous development will provide an overview of the acceptance activities, to ensure that resources for them are included in the project plans. Note that the initial plan may not be complete and may contain estimates that will need to be changed as more complete project information becomes available.

After the initial software acceptance plan has been prepared, reviewed, and approved, the acceptance manager is responsible for implementing the plan and for ensuring that the plan's objectives are met. It may have to be revised before this assurance is warranted.

Table 12-1 lists examples of information that should be included in a software acceptance plan.

Table 12-1   Acceptance Plan Contents

Project Description	Type of system; life cycle methodology; user community of delivered system; major tasks system must satisfy; major external interfaces of the system; expected normal usage; potential misuse; risks; constraints; standards and practices.
User Responsibilities	Organization and responsibilities for acceptance activities; resource and schedule requirements; facility requirements; requirements for automated support, special data, training; standards, practices, and conventions; updates and reviews of acceptance plans and related products.
Administrative Procedures	Anomaly reports; change control; recordkeeping; communication between developer and manager organizations.
Acceptance Description	Objectives for entire project; summary of acceptance criteria; major acceptance activities and reviews; information requirements; types of acceptance decisions; responsibility for acceptance decisions.

The plan must include the techniques and tools that will be utilized in acceptance testing. Normally, testers will use the organization's current testing tools, which should be oriented toward specific testing techniques.

Two categories of testing techniques can be used in acceptance testing: structural and functional. (Again, acceptance testing must be viewed in its broadest context; it should not be the minimal testing that some users perform after the information system professionals have concluded their testing.)

The functional testing techniques help ensure that the requirements/specifications are properly satisfied by the software system. Functional testing is not concerned with how processing occurs, but with the results of processes.

Structural testing ensures sufficient checking of the implementation of the function by finding test data that will force sufficient coverage of the structured presence in the implemented software. It evaluates all aspects of this structure to verify that the structure is sound.

Executing the Acceptance Plan

The objective of this step is to determine whether the acceptance criteria have been met in a delivered product. This can be accomplished through reviews, which involve looking at interim products and partially developed deliverables at various points throughout the developmental process. It can also involve testing the executable software system. The determination of which (or both) of these techniques to use will depend on the criticality of the software, the size of the software program, the resources involved, and the time period over which the software is being developed.

Software acceptance criteria should be specified in the formal project plan. The plan identifies products to be tested, the specific pass/fail criteria, the reviews, and the types of testing that will occur throughout the entire life cycle.

Acceptance decisions need a framework in which to operate; items such as contracts, acceptance criteria, and formal mechanisms are part of this framework. Software acceptance must state or refer to specific criteria that products must meet to be accepted. A principal means of reaching acceptance in the development of critical software systems is to hold a periodic review of interim software documentation and other software products.

A disciplined acceptance program for software of any type may include reviews as a formal mechanism. When the acceptance decision requires change, another review becomes necessary to ensure that the required changes have been properly configured and implemented, and that any affected segments are acceptable. For large or complicated projects, several reviews may be necessary during the development of a single product.

Some software acceptance activities may include testing pieces of the software; formal software acceptance testing occurs at the point in the development life cycle when the user accepts or rejects the software. This means a contractual requirement between the user and the project team has been met. Rejection normally means additional work must be done on the system to render it acceptable to the user. Final software acceptance testing is the last opportunity for the user to examine the software for functional, interface, performance, and quality features prior to the final acceptance review. The system at this time must include the delivered software, all user documentation, and final versions of other software deliverables.

Developing Test Cases (Use Cases) Based on How Software Will Be Used

Incomplete, incorrect, and missing test cases can cause incomplete and erroneous test results, which, at minimum, means that rework is necessary, and at worst, means that a flawed system is developed. It is necessary to ensure that all required test cases are identified so that all system functionality requirements are tested.

A *use case* is a description of how a user (or another system) uses the system being designed to perform a given task. A system is described by the sum of its use cases. Each instance or scenario of a use case will correspond to one test case. Incorporating the use case technique into the development life cycle will address the effects of incomplete, incorrect, and missing test cases. Use cases represent an easy-to-use approach applicable to both conventional and object-oriented system developments.

Use cases provide a powerful means of communication between customer, developers, testers, and other project personnel. Test cases can be developed with system users and designers as the use cases are being developed. Having the test cases this early in the project provides a baseline for the early planning of acceptance testing. Another advantage to having test cases early on is that if a packaged software solution is indicated, the customer can use them to evaluate purchased software earlier in the development cycle. Using the use case approach will ensure not only meeting requirements but also expectations.

Building a System Boundary Diagram

A system boundary diagram depicts the interfaces between the software being tested and the individuals, systems, and other interfaces. These interfaces or external agents in this work practice will be referred to as "actors." The purpose of the system boundary diagram is to establish the scope of the system and to identify the actors (i.e., the interfaces) that need to be developed.

An example of a system boundary diagram for an automatic automated teller machine for an organization called "Best Bank" is illustrated in Figure 12-2.

Work Paper 12-2 is designed to document a system boundary diagram for the software under test. For that software each system boundary needs to be defined. System boundaries can include the following:

Individuals/groups that manually interface with the software.

Other systems that interface with the software.

Libraries.

Objects within object-oriented systems.

Each system boundary should be described. For each boundary, an actor must be identified.

Two aspects of actor definition are required. The first is the actor description, and the second is the name of an individual or group who can play the role of the actor (i.e., represent that boundary interface). For example, in Figure 12-2 the security alarm system is identified as an interface. The actor is the security alarm company. The name of a person in the security alarm company or the name of someone who can represent the security alarm company must be identified. Note that in some instances the actor and the individual may be the same, such as the ATM system administrator listed in Figure 12-2.

Defining Use Cases

An individual use case consists of the following:

Preconditions that set the stage for the series of events that should occur for the use case

Post-conditions that state the expected outcomes of the preceding process

Sequential narrative of the execution of the use case

Use cases are used to do the following:

Manage (and trace) requirements

Identify classes and objects (OO)

Design and code (non-OO)

Develop application documentation

Develop training

Develop test cases

The use case definition is done by the actor. The actor represents the system boundary interface and prepares all the use cases for that system boundary interface. Note that this can be done by a single individual or a team of individuals.

Work Paper 12-3 is used for defining a use case. An example of a completed Work Paper 12-3 for an ATM system is illustrated in Figure 12-3. This example is for an ATM system. The case is a bank customer making a withdrawal from their checking account on an ATM.

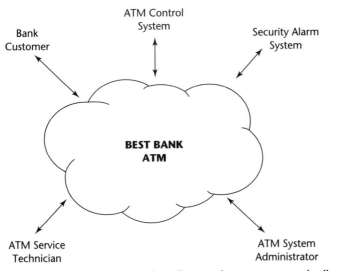

ATM Control System

Bank Customer

Security Alarm System

BEST BANK ATM

ATM Service Technician

ATM System Administrator

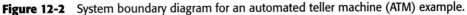

Figure 12-2   System boundary diagram for an automated teller machine (ATM) example.

Use Case Definition		
Last Updated By:	Last Updated On:	
Use Case Name: Withdraw From Checking		UC ID: ATM-01
Actor: Bank Customer		
Objective: To allow a bank customer to obtain cash and have the withdrawal taken from their checking account.		
Preconditions: Bank customer must have an ATM cash card, valid account, valid PIN and their available checking account balance must be greater than, or equal to, withdrawal amount. ATM in idle mode with greeting displayed (main menu).		
Results (Postconditions): The cash amount dispensed must be equal to the withdrawal amount. The ATM must print a receipt and eject the cash card. The checking account is debited by amount dispensed.		

Detailed Description	
Action	**Model (System) Response**
1. Customer inserts ATM cash Card.	1. ATM reads cash card and prompts customer to enter PIN.
2. Customer enters PIN.	2. ATM validates PIN and displays menu with a list of transactions that can be selected.
3. Customer selects Withdraw From Checking transacton.	
4. Customer enters withdrawal amount.	3. ATM validates account and prompts customer for withdrawal amount.
5. Customer takes cash.	4. ATM validates account balance is greater than, or equal to, withdrawal amount. ATM dispenses cash equal to withdrawal amount and prompts customer to take cash.
6. Customer indicates not to continue.	
7. Customer takes card and receipt.	5. ATM asks customer whether they want to continue.
	6. ATM prints receipt, ejects cash, prompts customer to take card, sends debit message to ATM Control System, returns to idle mode and displays main menu.

Exceptions:
If ATM cannot read cash card, then ATM ejects cash card.
   If incorrect PIN is entered, then customer is given two additional chances to enter correct PIN. If correct PIN not entered on third try, then ATM keeps cash card and informs customer that they must retrieve card from bank personnel during business hours.
   If account is not valid, ATM ejects card and informs customer that they must contact bank personnel during business hours regarding their invalid account.
If account balance is less than withdrawal amount, ATM informs customer that the withdrawal amount exceeds their account balance and to reenter a withdrawal amount that does not exceed account balance. If amount reentered still exceeds account balance, ATM ejects card, informs customer that amount requested still exceeds account balance and bank policy does not permit exceptions.

Alternative Courses:
At any time after reaching the main menu and before finishing a transaction, including before selecting a transaction, the customer may press the cancel key. If the cancel key is pressed, the specified transaction (if there is one) is canceled, the customer's cash card is returned, the ATM returns to idle mode and the main menu is displayed.

Original Author: Larry Creel	Original Date: 9-25-X

Figure 12-3   Example of completed Work Paper 12-3 (use case definition) for an ATM system.

Developing Test Cases

A test case is a set of test inputs, execution conditions, and expected results developed for a particular test objective. There should be a one-to-one relationship between use case definitions and test cases. There needs to be at least two test cases for each use case: one for successful execution of the use case and one for an unsuccessful execution of a test case. However, there may be numerous test cases for each use case.

Additional test cases are derived from the exceptions and alternative courses of the use case. Note that additional detail may need to be added to support the actual testing of all the possible scenarios of the use case.

The use case description is the input into Work Paper 12-4. The actor who prepared the use case description also prepares the test case work paper. There will be at least two test conditions for each use case description and normally many more. The actor tries to determine all of the possible scenarios that occur for each use case. Figure 12-4 is an example of a test case work paper designed to test the function "withdrawal from checking from an ATM." Note that this is Action 3 from Figure 12-3. Work Paper 12-1 becomes the input for Work Paper 12-4, as shown in Figure 12-5.

At the conclusion of acceptance testing, a decision must be made for each acceptance criterion as to whether it has been achieved.

Reaching an Acceptance Decision

Final acceptance of software based on acceptance testing usually means that the software project has been completed, with the exception of any caveats or contingencies. Final acceptance for the software occurs, and the developer has no further development obligations (except, of course, for maintenance, which is a separate issue).

Typical acceptance decisions include the following:

- Required changes are accepted before progressing to the next activity.
- Some changes must be made and accepted before further development of that section of the product; other changes may be made and accepted at the next major review.
- Progress may continue and changes may be accepted at the next review.
- No changes are required and progress may continue.

The goal is to achieve and accept "perfect" software, but usually some criteria will not be completely satisfied for each product, in which case the user may choose to accept less-than-perfect software.

Task 2: Pre-Operational Testing

If the decision is made to place the software system into an operational state, pre-operational testing should occur. This is testing performed to validate that the developed/acquired system will operate as intended in the production environment. Much of this testing involves ensuring that the configuration management system has, in effect, the right configuration items in the production environment. The testing also includes high-level integration testing which validates whether the tested software system effectively and efficiently integrates with other systems and other parts of the production environment.

Test Case Worksheet

Test Case ID: T-ATM-01	Original Author: Larry Creel	Last Updated By:
Parent Use Case ID: ATM-01	Original Date: 9-26-XX	Last Updated On:

Test Objective: To test the function *Withdraw From Checking*, the associated exceptions and alternative courses.

ITEM NO.	TEST CONDI-TION	OPERATOR ACTION	INPUT SPECIFI-CATIONS	OUTPUT SPECIFICATIONS (EXPECTED RESULTS)	PASS OR FAIL	COMMENTS
1	Successful withdrawal.	1-Insert card. 2-Enter PIN. 3-Select Withdraw From Checking transaction. 4-Enter withdrawal amount. 5-Take cash. 6-Indicate not to continue. 7-Take card and receipt.	1-ATM can read card. 2-Valid account. 3-Valid PIN. 4-Account balance greater than, or equal to, withdrawal amount.	1-ATM reads card and prompts customer to enter PIN. 2-ATM validates PIN and displays menu with a list of transactions that can be selected. 3-ATM validates account and prompts customer to enter withdrawal amount. 4-ATM validates account balance greater than, or equal to, withdrawal amount. ATM dispenses cash equal to withdrawal amount and prompts customer to take cash. 5-ATM asks customer whether they want to continue. 6-ATM prints receipt, ejects cash card, prompts customer to take card, sends debit message to ATM Control System. ATM returns to idle mode and displays Main Menu.		Re-execute test and use the Continue option Verify correct debit message received by ATM Control System.
2	Unsuccess-ful with-drawal due to unread-able card.	1-Insert card. 2-Take card.	1-ATM cannot read card. 2-Valid account. 3-Valid PIN. 4-Account bal-ance greater than or equal to, with-drawal amount.	1-ATM ejects card, prompts customer to take card and displays message "Cash Card unreadable. Please contact bank personnel during business hours." ATM returns to idle mode and displays Main Menu.		

Fiigure 12-4 Example of completed Work Paper 12-4 (test case work paper) for an ATM withdrawal.

ITEM NO.	TEST CONDITION	OPERATOR ACTION	INPUT SPECIFICATIONS	OUTPUT SPECIFICATIONS (EXPECTED RESULTS)	PASS OR FAIL	COMMENTS
3	Unsuccessful withdrawal due to incorrect PIN entered three times.	1-Insert Card. 2-Enter PIN. 3-Reenter PIN. 4-Reenter PIN.	1-ATM can read card. 2-Valid account. 3-Invalid PIN. 4-Account balance greater than, or equal to, withdrawal amount.	1-ATM reads card and prompts customer to enter PIN. 2-ATM does not validate PIN and prompts customer to reenter PIN. 3-ATM does not validate PIN and prompts customer to reenter PIN. 4-ATM does not validate PIN, keeps card, displays message "For return of your card, please contact bank personnel during business hours." ATM returns to idle mode and displays Main Menu.		
4	Unsuccessful withdrawal due to invalid account.	1-Insert card. 2-Enter PIN. 3-Select Withdrawal transaction. 4-Enter withdrawal amount. 5-Take card.	1-ATM can read card. 2-Invalid account. 3-Valid PIN. 4-Account balance greater than, or equal to, withdrawal amount.	1-ATM reads card and prompts customer to enter PIN. 2-ATM validates PIN and displays menu with a list of transactions that can be selected. 3-ATM prompts customer for withdrawal 4-ATM does not validate account, ejects card, prompts customer to take card and displays message "Your account is not valid. Please contact bank personnel during business hours." ATM returns to idle mode and displays Main Menu.		
5	Unsuccessful withdrawal due to account balance less than	1-Insert card. 2-Enter PIN. 3-Select Withdraw From Checking transaction. 4-Enter withdrawal amount that is greater	1-ATM can read card. 2-Valid account. 3-Valid PIN. 4-Account balance less	1-ATM reads card and prompts customer to enter PIN. 2-ATM validates PIN and displays menu with a list of transactions that can be selected. 3-ATM prompts customer for withdrawal amount.		

Figure 12-4 (continued)

ITEM NO.	TEST CONDITION	OPERATOR ACTION	INPUT SPECIFICATIONS	OUTPUT SPECIFICATIONS (EXPECTED RESULTS)	PASS OR FAIL	COMMENTS
	withdrawal amount.	than account balance. 5-Reenter withdrawal amount that is greater than account balance. 6-Take card.	than withdrawal amount.	4-ATM ejects card and displays message informing customer that the withdrawal amount exceeds their account balance and to reenter a withdrawal amount that does not exceed account balance. 5-ATM ejects card, prompts customer to take card and displays message "Amount requested still exceeds account balance and bank policy does not permit exceptions." ATM returns to idle mode and displays Main Menu.		
6	Unsuccessful withdrawal due to customer pressing Cancel key before entering PIN.	1-Insert card. 2-Press Cancel key. 3-Take card.	1-ATM can read card. 2-Valid account. 3-Valid PIN 4-Account balance greater than, or equal to, withdrawal amount.	1-ATM reads card and prompts customer to enter PIN. 2-ATM ejects card and prompts customer to take card. ATM returns to idle mode and displays Main Menu.		
7	Unsuccessful withdrawal due to customer pressing Cancel key after entering PIN.	1-Insert card. 2-Enter PIN. 3-Press Cancel key. 4-Take card.	1-ATM can read card. 2-Valid account. 3-Valid PIN. 4-Account balance greater than, or equal to, withdrawal amount.	1-ATM reads card and prompts customer to enter PIN. 2-ATM validates PIN and displays menu with a list of transactions that can be selected. 3-ATM ejects card and prompts customer to take card. ATM returns to idle mode and displays Main Menu.		

Figure 12-4 *(continued)*

ITEM NO.	TEST CONDITION	OPERATOR ACTION	INPUT SPECIFICATIONS	OUTPUT SPECIFICATIONS (EXPECTED RESULTS)	PASS OR FAIL	COMMENTS
8	Unsuccessful withdrawal; due to customer pressing Cancel key after entering PIN and selecting Withdrawal transaction.	1-Insert card. 2-Enter PIN. 3-Select Withdraw From Checking transaction. 4-Press Cancel key. 5-Take card.	1-ATM can read card. 2-Valid account. 3-Valid PIN. 4-Account balance greater than, or equal to, withdrawal amount.	1-ATM reads card and prompts customer to enter PIN. 2-ATM validates PIN and displays menu with a list of transactions that can be selected. 3-ATM validates account and prompts customer to enter withdrawal amount. 4-ATM ejects card and prompts customer to take card. ATM returns to idle mode and displays Main Menu.		

Figure 12-4 *(continued)*

No.	Acceptance Requirement	Critical Yes No	Test Result Accept Reject	Comments
1	The system must execute to end of job during a payroll production run after January 1, 20xx.	X		Payroll will not be run in a pro-duction status until this require-ment has been met.
2	The results of payroll must be correct even if there are date problems in the report or other processing components.	X		Payroll will not be run in a pro-duction status until this require-ment is met.

Figure 12-5 Acceptance criteria.

The installation phase is the primary responsibility of the IT department. Specifi-cally, computer operations personnel have the responsibility for getting the system into operation. However, the project team and the users may share responsibility for developing the appropriate data files and user and operator instructions for the appli-cation system.

As with other aspects of the life cycle, many parties are involved in the installation. Assigning one of those parties to be responsible for the installation pinpoints both accountability and action. The recommended party for that responsibility would be a key individual in computer operations.

However, in some online systems the user operations personnel may have primary operating responsibilities because they initiate work at terminals, and in that instance, it may be more appropriate to assign user operations personnel installation responsi-bility than to assign responsibility to a centralized operations group.

The installation team performs a standalone, one-time process. This enables them to be independent of the development team so that they can perform their installation tasks concurrently with the development process. This does not prohibit both teams from comprising the same individuals.

Most phases in the systems development life cycle are sequential in nature, and the execution of the installation phase is part of this sequential life cycle process. However, preparing for the installation can overlap with any or all of the previous phases. This installation process may encompass requirements, design, programming, and testing, all of which become the responsibility of the individual in charge of the installation process.

Placing a system under development into an operational status may require a mini-system to handle the process. The installation phase specifications need to be deter-mined and the mechanism developed to install the new system. Programming may be required to convert files from an old format to a new format. Those programs should be tested prior to executing the actual system conversion. However, because this is a one-time process the attention to detail and control exhibited in the system being developed may not exist in the development of the installation system.

Testing New Software Installation

The installation phase poses two difficulties for the test team. First, installation is a process separate from the rest of the application development. Its function relates not to satisfying user needs, but to placing a completed and tested application into production. In many instances, this test will be performed by a different group than the one that tested the other portions of the application system. Second, installation normally occurs in a very short time span. It is not uncommon for an installation to occur within an hour or several hours. Therefore, tests must be well planned and executed if they are to be meaningful and helpful to the installation process.

Test results that are not available until hours or days after the installation are worthless. It is important that the test results be available prior to the completion of the installation. The objective of testing is to determine whether the installation is successful; therefore, the results must be available as quickly as possible. In many instances, this means that the test results must be predetermined before the test starts.

Work Paper 12-5 lists the installation test process. A test program is provided for each of the installation phase concerns. Each test program describes the criteria that should be evaluated through testing and the recommended tests, including suggested test techniques and tools. This generalized installation phase test program may need to be customized for a specific installation. The individual responsible for the test should take into account unique application characteristics that may require special testing.

Testing the Changed Software Version

IT management establishes both the software maintenance changes for its department and the objectives for making the changes. The establishment of clear-cut objectives helps the software maintenance analyst and operation personnel understand some of the procedures they are asked to follow. This understanding often results in a better controlled operation.

The specific objectives of installing the change are as follows:

- **Put changed application systems into production.** Each change should be incorporated through a new version of a program. The production system should have the capability to move these versions in and out of production on prescribed dates. To do this, it is necessary first to uniquely identify each version of a program, and second to pinpoint the dates when individual program versions are to be placed into and taken out of production.

- **Assess the efficiency of changes.** If a change results in extensive time and effort to do additional checking, or to locate information not provided by the system, additional changes may be desirable.

- **Monitor the correctness of the change.** People should not assume that testing will uncover all of the problems. For example, problems may be encountered in untouched parts of the application. People should be assigned the responsibility to review output immediately following changes. If this is a normal function, then those people should be notified that a change has occurred and should be informed where the change is in the system and what potentially bad outputs might be expected.

- **Keep systems library up to date.** When programs are added to the production and source library, other versions should be deleted. This will not happen unless specific action is taken. The application system project team should ensure that unwanted versions in the source and object code libraries are deleted when they have fulfilled their purposes.

When the change is put into production, IT management can never be sure what type of problems may be encountered shortly thereafter. The concerns during the change process deal with properly and promptly installing the change. It is during the installation that the results of these change activities become known. Thus, many of the concerns culminate during the installation of the change.

IT management must identify the concerns so that they can establish the proper control mechanisms. The most common concerns during the installation of the change include the following:

Will the change be installed on time?

Is backup data compatible with the changed system?

Are recovery procedures compatible with the changed system?

Is the source/object library cluttered with obsolete program versions?

Will errors in the change be detected?

Will errors in the change be corrected?

Testing the installation of the changes is divided into three tasks, some of which are manual and others heavily automated. Each is explained in detail in the following subsections.

Testing the Adequacy of the Restart/Recovery Plan

Restart and recovery are important stages in application systems processing. Restart means computer operations begin from a point of known integrity. Recovery occurs when the integrity of the system has been compromised. In a recovery process, the systems processing must be backed up to a point of known integrity; thereafter, transactions are rerun to the point at which the problem was detected.

Many aspects of system changes affect the recovery process. Among those to evaluate for their impact on recovery are the following:

Addition of a new function

Change of job control

Additional use of utility programs

Change in retention periods

Change in computer programs

Change in operating documentations

Introduction of a new or revised form

The testers should assess each change to determine its impact on the recovery process. If a program is changed, the tester must ensure that those changes are included in backup data. Without the latest version of the program, the tester may not be able to correctly recover computer processing.

If the tester determines that recovery has been affected by the change, that impact on the recovery plan must be updated. The tester can use Work Paper 12-6 to document the restart/recovery planning process, and forward it to the person responsible for recovery.

Verifying the Correct Change Has Been Entered into Production

A positive action must be taken to move a changed program from test status to production status. This action should be taken by the owner of the software. When the user department is satisfied with the change, the new program version can be moved into production.

The production environment should be able to control programs according to production date. Each version of a program in production should be labeled according to when it is to go into and be taken out of production. If there is no known replacement, the date to take that version out of production is the latest date that can be put into that field. When a new version has been selected, that date can be changed to the actual date.

A history of changes should be available for each program, to provide a complete audit trail of everything that has happened to the program since first written. The change history, together with a notification to operations that a change is ready for production, provides the necessary controls during this step.

To verify that the correct change has been placed into production, the tester should answer the following two questions:

1. **Is a change history available?** Changes to an application program should be documented using a work paper similar to Work Paper 12-7. The objective of this history-of-change form is to show all of the changes made to a program since its inception. This serves two purposes: First, if problems occur, this audit trail indicates whether the changes have been made; and second, it discourages unauthorized changes. In most organizations, changes to programs/systems are maintained in source code libraries, test libraries, and production libraries. Work Paper 12-7 is a hardcopy format of the type of information that testers should be looking for in software libraries.

2. **Is there a formal notification of production changes?** The procedure to move a version from testing to production should be formalized. Telephone calls and other word-of-mouth procedures are not sufficient. The formal process can be enhanced to prevent the loss of notification forms by using a prenumbered form. The project leader should prepare the notification of production change form, which should then be sent to the computer operations department, which installs the new version. A sample form is illustrated in Work Paper 12-8.

The owner of the software decides when a new version of the software will be placed into production. This approval gives operations the go-ahead to initiate its procedures for notifying the appropriate staff that changes are to be installed. The tester must verify that the appropriate notification has been given, pending the owner's approval, and that the information is correct.

Verifying Unneeded Versions Have Been Deleted

It may or may not be desirable to delete old versions of programs when a new version is entered. The most obvious argument against doing so is to maintain a fallback version in case the new version proves defective. Organizations should establish standards regarding when old versions should be automatically deleted from the library. Some, while not automating this function, periodically notify the project team that older versions will be deleted unless the project team takes specific action to have them retained in the library. Other organizations charge the projects a fee for retaining old versions.

In any case, programs should not be deleted from libraries without authorization. Some type of form should be prepared to authorize computer operations personnel to delete programs from a library. This form also provides a history of additions to the libraries. A source/object library deletions notice form is illustrated in Work Paper 12-9. This form becomes a more effective control if a sequential number is added, so that its loss is more likely to be detected. The form should be filled out by the software maintenance project leader and sent to computer operations for action.

The computer operations department should have a process for deleting unneeded versions of source libraries, test libraries, and production libraries—after receiving authorization to do so, of course. It is recommended that those authorizations be in writing from the owner of the item. The type of information needed for deleting programs from a library is contained in Work Paper 12-9, which also contains instructions for deleting programs.

The objective of the entire correction process is to satisfy the new date need. This is accomplished by incorporating that need into the application system and running it in production status. If all parts of the software change process have been properly performed, the production step is mechanical. The program library automatically calls in the correct version of the program on the proper day. However, if there are special operator instructions, the operator should be alerted to that change on the appropriate day. Most information services organizations have procedures for this purpose.

Monitoring Production

Application systems are most vulnerable to problems immediately following the introduction of new versions of a program(s). For this reason, many organizations monitor the output immediately following the introduction of a new program version. In organizations that normally monitor output, extra effort or attention may be applied at the time a changed program version is first run.

The following groups may monitor the output of a new program version:

Application system control group

User personnel

Software maintenance personnel

Computer operations personnel

Regardless of who monitors the output, the software maintenance analyst and user personnel should provide clues about what to look for. User and software maintenance personnel must attempt to identify the specific areas where they believe problems might occur.

The types of clues that could be provided to monitoring personnel include the following:

- **Transactions to investigate.** Specific types of transactions, such as certain product numbers, that they should monitor

- **Customers.** Specific customers or other identifiers to help them locate problems on specific pages of reports

- **Reports.** Specific outputs that should be reviewed

- **Tape files.** Data records or files that have been changed that they may need to examine by extracting information to determine if data was properly recorded

- **Performance.** Anticipated improvements in the effectiveness, efficiency, and economy of operations that they should review

This process is normally more effective if it is formalized. This means documenting the type of clues to look for during the monitoring process. A program change monitor notification form is illustrated in Work Paper 12-10. This form should be completed by the user and/or software maintenance personnel and then given to the people monitoring the transaction. The information contained on the program change monitor notification form is outlined on the form's completion instructions sheet.

Documenting Problems

Individuals detecting problems when they monitor changes in application systems should formally document them. The formal documentation process can be made even more effective if the forms are controlled through a numbering sequence. This enables software maintenance personnel to detect lost problem forms. The individual monitoring the process should keep a duplicate copy of the form on hand, in case the copy sent to the project is lost.

The person monitoring the process should be asked both to document the problem and to assess the risk associated with that problem. Although this individual may not be the ideal candidate to make a risk assessment, a preliminary assessment is often very helpful in determining the seriousness of the problem. If the initial estimate about the risk is erroneous, it can be corrected at a later time.

The report of a system problem caused by system change, because of the program change monitor notification, enables the individual to associate the problem with a specific problem change. This additional piece of information is usually invaluable in correcting the problem.

A form to record a system problem caused by a system change is illustrated in Work Paper 12-11. This form should be completed by the individual monitoring the application system. The completed form should be given to the software maintenance analyst for correction. The information contained on the system problem caused by system change form is described on the form's completion instructions sheet.

Task 3: Post-Operational Testing

Post-operational testing is used in this book to signify testing changed versions of the software system. The process as presented is equally applicable to testing changed versions during development, as well as changed versions after the system has been placed into an operational state. If the IT organization has well-developed change management, version control, and an effective configuration management system, the extensiveness of testing new versions will be significantly reduced. In those instances, much of the testing from the versions will center on the specific change made to the software system.

Testing and training are as important to software maintenance as they are to new systems development. Frequently, even small changes require extensive testing and training. It is not unusual to spend more time testing a change and training users to operate a new facility than incorporating the change into the application system. This task explains the process that should be performed when testing system changes.

Too frequently, software maintenance has been synonymous with "quick and dirty" programming, which is rarely worth the risk. Frequently, it takes considerable time to correct problems that could have been prevented by adequate testing and training. If testing is properly conducted, it should not take longer to do the job right.

IT management has the responsibility for establishing the testing and training procedures for software changes. Many organizations establish change control procedures but do not carry them through testing and training. A checklist is provided for management to review the effectiveness of their testing.

The process outlined in this task is designed to be used two ways. First, it is written as if changes occur after the software has been placed into production. The second and perhaps equally important use will be testing changes during the development of software.

Both of these uses of the process for testing changes require some reiteration of previous steps. For example, the test plan will need to be updated, and the test data will need to be updated. Because those activities are presented in previous chapters, they are not reiterated in this task.

The following five tasks should be performed to effectively test a changed version of software.

Developing and Updating the Test Plan

The test plan for software maintenance is a shorter, more directed version of a test plan used for a new application system. Whereas new application testing can take many weeks or months, software maintenance testing often must be done within a single day or a few hours. Because of time constraints, many of the steps that might be performed individually in a new system are combined or condensed into a short time span. This increases the need for planning so that all aspects of the test can be executed within the allotted time.

The types of testing will vary based upon the implemented change. For example, if a report is modified, there is little need to test recovery and backup plans. On the other hand, if new files are created or processing procedures changed, restart and recovery should be tested.

The preparation of a test plan is a two-part process. The first part is the determination of what types of tests should be conducted, and the second part is the plan for how to conduct them. Both parts are important in software maintenance testing.

Elements to be tested (types of testing) are as follows:

Changed transactions

Changed programs

Operating procedures

Control group procedures

User procedures

Intersystem connections

Job control language

Interface to systems software

Execution of interface to software systems

Security

Backup/recovery procedures

The test plan should list the testing objective, the method of testing, and the desired result. In addition, regression testing might be used to verify that unchanged segments have not been unintentionally altered. Intersystem connections should be tested to ensure that all systems are properly modified to handle the change.

An acceptance test plan is included as Work Paper 12-12. This work paper should be completed by the software maintenance analyst and countersigned by the individual responsible for accepting the changed system.

Developing and Updating the Test Data

Data must be prepared for testing all the areas changed during a software maintenance process. For many applications, the existing test data will be sufficient to test the new change. However, in many situations new test data will need to be prepared.

In some cases, the preparation of test data can be significantly different for software maintenance than for new systems. For example, when the system is operational it may be possible to test the application in a live operational mode, thus eliminating the need for technical test data, and enabling maintenance software analysts to use the same input the users of the application prepare. Special accounts can be established to accumulate test data processed during testing in a production mode. The information in these accounts can then be eliminated after the test, which negates the effect of entering test data into a production environment.

It is important to test both what should be accomplished, as well as what can go wrong. Most tests do a good job of verifying that the specifications have been implemented properly. Where testing frequently is inadequate is in verifying the unanticipated conditions. Included in this category are the following:

Transactions with erroneous data

Unauthorized transactions

Transactions entered too early

Transactions entered too late

Transactions that do not correspond with master data contained in the application

Grossly erroneous transactions, such as transactions that do not belong to the application being tested

Transactions with larger values in the fields than anticipated

These types of transactions can be designed by doing a simple risk analysis scenario. The risk analysis scenario involves brainstorming with key people involved in the application, such as users, maintenance systems analysts, and auditors. These people attempt to ask all the questions, such as, "What if this type of error were entered? What would happen if too large a value were entered in this field?"

The three methods that can be used to develop/update test data are as follows:

- **Update existing test data.** If test files have been created for a previous version, they can be used for testing a change. However, the test data will need to be updated to reflect the changes to the software. Note that testers may wish to use both versions in conducting testing. Version 1 is to test that the unchanged portions perform now as they did in the previous versions. The new version is to test the changes. Updating the test data should follow the same processes used in creating new test data.

- **Create new test data.** The creation of new test data for maintenance follows the same methods as creating test data for a new software system.

- **Use production data for testing.** Tests are performed using some or all of the production data for test purposes (date-modified, of course), particularly when there are no function changes. Using production data for test purposes may result in the following impediments to effective testing:

    - **Missing test transactions.** The transaction types on a production data file may be limited. For example, if the tester wants to test an override of a standard price, that transaction may not occur on the production data file.

    - **Multiple tests of the same transaction.** Production data usually represents the production environment, in which 80 to 90 percent of the transactions are of approximately the same type. This means that some transaction types are not tested at all, while others are tested hundreds of times.

    - **Unknown test results.** An important part of testing is to validate that correct results are produced. When testers create test transactions, they have control over the expected results. When production data is used, however, testers must manually calculate the correct processing results, perhaps causing them to misinterpret the intent of the transaction and thereby to misinterpret the results.

    - **Lack of ownership.** Production data is owned by the production area, whereas test data created by testers is owned by the testers. Some testers are more involved and interested in test data they created themselves than in test data borrowed from another owner.

Although these potential impediments might cause production data testing to be ineffective, steps can be taken to improve its usefulness. Production data should not be completely excluded as a source of test data.

Testing the Control Change Process

Listed next are three tasks commonly used to control and record changes. If the staff performing the corrections does not have such a process, the testers can give them these subtasks and then request the work papers when complete. Testers should verify completeness using these three tasks as a guide.

Identifying and Controlling Change

An important aspect of changing a system is identifying which parts of the system will be affected by that change. The impact may be in any part of the application system, both manual and computerized, as well as in the supporting software system. Regardless of whether affected areas will require changes, at a minimum there should be an investigation into the extent of the impact.

The types of analytical action helpful in determining the parts affected include the following:

Review system documentation.

Review program documentation.

Review undocumented changes.

Interview user personnel regarding procedures.

Interview operations personnel regarding procedures.

Interview job control coordinator regarding changes.

Interview systems support personnel if the implementation may require deviations from standards and/or IT departmental procedures.

This is a very important step in the systems change process, as it controls the change through a change identification number and through change documentation. The time and effort spent executing this step is usually returned in the form of more effective implementation procedures and fewer problems during and after the implementation of the change. A change control form is presented as Work Paper 12-13.

Documenting Change Needed on Each Data Element

Whereas changes in processing normally affect only a single program or a small number of interrelated programs, changes to data may affect many applications. Thus, changes that affect data may have a more significant effect on the organization than those that affect processing.

Changes can affect data in any of the following ways:

- **Length.** The data element may be lengthened or shortened.
- **Value.** The value or codes used in data elements may be expanded, modified, or reduced.
- **Consistency.** The value contained in data elements may not be the same in various applications or databases; thus, it is necessary to improve consistency.
- **Reliability.** The accuracy of the data may be changed.

In addition, changes to a data element may require further documentation. Organizations in a database environment need to expend additional effort to ensure that data documentation is consistent, reliable, and understandable. Much of this effort will be translated into data documentation.

A form for documenting data changes is presented as Work Paper 12-14. This form should be used to provide an overview of the data change. In a database environment, a copy of the data definition form should be attached to the data change form as a control vehicle.

Documenting Changes Needed in Each Program

The implementation of most changes will require some programming alterations. Even a change of data attributes often necessitates program changes. Some of these will be minor in nature, whereas others may be extremely difficult and time-consuming to implement.

The change required for each program should be documented on a separate form. This serves several purposes: First, it provides detailed instructions at the individual program level regarding what is required to change the program; second, it helps ensure that changes will be made and not lost—it is difficult to overlook a change that is formally requested; third, and equally important, it provides a detailed audit trail of changes, in the event problems occur.

Work Paper 12-15 is a form for documenting program changes. It should be completed even though doing so may require more time than the implementation of the change itself. The merits of good change documentation have been repeatedly established.

Conducting Testing

Software change testing is normally conducted by both the user and software maintenance test team. The testing is designed to provide the user assurance that the change has been properly implemented. Another role of the software maintenance test team is to aid the user in conducting and evaluating the test.

Testing for software maintenance is normally not extensive. In an online environment, the features would be installed and the user would test them in a regular production environment. In a batch environment, special computer runs must be set up to run the acceptance testing. (Because of the cost, these runs are sometimes eliminated.)

An effective method for conducting software maintenance testing is to prepare a checklist providing both the administrative and technical data needed to conduct the test. This ensures that everything is ready at the time the test is to be conducted. A checklist for conducting a software maintenance acceptance test is illustrated in Work Paper 12-16. This form should be prepared by the software maintenance analyst as an aid in helping the user conduct the test. The information contained on the conduct acceptance test checklist is described on the form's completion instructions sheet.

Developing and Updating Training Material

Updating training material for users, and training users, is not an integral part of many software change processes. Therefore, this task description describes a process for updating training material and performing that training. Where training is not part of software maintenance, the testers can give the software maintenance analyst these materials to use in developing training materials. If training is an integral part of the software maintenance process, the testers can use the material in this task as a guide for evaluating the completion of updating training materials.

Training is an often-overlooked aspect of software maintenance. Many of the changes are small; this fosters the belief that training is not needed. Also, the fact that many changes originate in the user area leads the software maintenance analyst to the conclusion that the users already know what they want and have trained their staff accordingly. All these assumptions may be wrong.

The software maintenance analyst should evaluate each change for its impact on the procedures performed by people. If the change affects those procedures, then training material should be prepared. However, changes that increase performance and have no impact on users of the system do not require training unless they affect the operation of the system. In that case, computer operations personnel would need training. Training cannot be designed by someone who is unfamiliar with existing training material. The software maintenance change is incorporated into the application system. The training requirements are likewise incorporated into existing training material. Therefore, it behooves the application project personnel to maintain an inventory of training material.

Training Material Inventory Form

Most application systems have limited training materials. The more common types of training materials include the following:

Orientation to the project narrative

User manuals

Illustrations of completed forms and instructions for completing them

Explanation and action to take on error listings

Explanation of reports and how to use them

Explanation of input data and how to enter it

A form for inventory training material is included as Work Paper 12-17. This form should be completed and filed with the software maintenance analyst. Whenever a change is made, the form can be duplicated, and at that point the "needs updating" column can be completed to indicate whether training material must be changed as a result of incorporating the maintenance need. The columns to be completed on the form are explained on the form's completion instructions sheet.

Training Plan Work Paper

The training plan work paper is a why, who, what, where, when, and how approach to training. The individual developing the plan must answer those questions about each change to determine the scope of training programs. Points to ponder in developing training programs are as follows:

- **Why conduct training?** Do the changes incorporated into the application system necessitate training people?

- **Who should be trained?** If training is needed, then it must be determined which individuals, categories of people, or departments require that training.

- **What training is required?** The training plan must determine the content of the necessary training material.

- **Where should training be given?** The location of the training session, or dissemination of the training material, can affect how and when the material is presented.

- **When should training be given?** Confusion might ensue if people are trained too far in advance of the implementation of new procedures. For example, even training provided a few days prior to the change may cause confusion because people might be uncertain as to whether to follow the new or the old procedure. In addition, it may be necessary to conduct training both immediately before and immediately after the change to reinforce the new procedures and to answer questions immediately after the new procedures are installed.

- **How should the training material be designed?** The objective of training is to provide people with the tools and procedures necessary to do their job. The type of change will frequently determine the type of training material to be developed.

- **What are the expected training results?** The developers of the training plan should have in mind the behavior changes or skills to be obtained through the training sessions. They should also determine whether training is effective.

Work Paper 12-18 documents the training plan by providing space to indicate the preceding types of information. In addition, the responsible individual and the dates needed for training can also be documented on the form. The information contained on the training plan work paper is described on the form's completion instructions sheet.

Preparing Training Material

The tasks required to perform this step are similar to those used in making a change to an application system. In most instances, training material will exist, but will need to be modified because of the change. Changes in the program must be accompanied by changes in the training material. Individuals responsible for modifying training should consider the following tasks:

- Identifying the impact of the change on people

- Determining what type of training must be "unlearned" (people must be stopped from doing certain tasks)

- Determining whether "unlearning" is included in the training material

- Making plans to delete outmoded training material

- Determining what new learning is needed (this should come from the training plan)

- Determining where in the training material that new learning should be inserted
- Preparing the training material that will teach people the new skills (this should be specified in the training plan)
- Designing that material
- Determining the best method of training (this should be documented in the training plan)
- Developing procedures so that the new training material will be incorporated into the existing training material on the right date, and that other supportive training will occur at the proper time

An inventory should be maintained of the new/modified training modules. This is in addition to the training material inventory, which is in hardcopy. The training modules are designed to be supportive of that training material. This helps determine what modules need to be altered to achieve the behavior changes/new skills required because of the change.

Work Paper 12-19 is a training module inventory form. This should be completed by the individual responsible for training. The information contained on the form is described on the form's completion instructions, and both are found at the end of the chapter.

Conducting Training

The training task is primarily one of coordination in that it must ensure that everything needed for training has been prepared. The coordination normally involves these steps:

1. Schedule training dates.
2. Notify the people who should attend.
3. Obtain training facilities.
4. Obtain instructors.
5. Reproduce the material in sufficient quantity for all those requiring the material.
6. Train instructors.
7. Set up the classroom or meeting room.

Many times, training will be provided through manuals or special material delivered to the involved parties. The type of training should be determined when the training plan is developed and the material is prepared.

A training checklist should be prepared. A sample checklist for conducting training is illustrated in Work Paper 12-20. The individual responsible for training should prepare this checklist for use during the training period to ensure all the needed training is provided. The information included on the conduct training checklist is described on the form's completion instructions sheet. Both forms are found at the end of the chapter.

Check Procedures

Work Paper 12-21 is a quality control checklist for Task 1, Work Paper 12-22 is a quality control checklist for Task 2, and Work Paper 12-23 is a quality control checklist for Task 3.

Output

Two outputs are produced from Task 1 at various times, as follows:

1. **Interim product acceptance opinion.** An opinion as to whether an interim product is designed to meet the acceptance criteria.

2. **Final acceptance decision.** Relates to a specific hardware or software component regarding whether it is acceptable for use in production.

There are both interim and final outputs to Task 2. The interim outputs are the various reports that indicate any problems that arise during installation. Problems may relate to installation, deletion of programs from the libraries, or production. Whoever performs these testing tasks should notify the appropriate organization to make adjustments and/or corrections.

The ongoing monitoring process will also identify problems. These problems may deal with both the software and/or the users of the software. For example, problems may occur in the procedures provided to users to interact with the software, or it may be that the users are inadequately trained to use this software. All of these problems need to be reported to the appropriate organization.

The output of Task 3 will answer the questions and/or provide the information in the following subsections.

Is the Automated Application Acceptable?

The automated segment of an application is acceptable if it meets the change specification requirements. If it fails to meet those measurable objectives, the system is unacceptable and should be returned for additional modification. This requires setting measurable objectives, preparing test data, and then evaluating the results of those tests.

The responsibility for determining whether the application is acceptable belongs to the user. In applications with multiple users, one user may be appointed responsible. In other instances, all users may test their own segments or they may act as a committee to verify whether the system is acceptable. The poorest approach is to delegate this responsibility to the information technology department.

Test results can be verified through manual or automated means. The tediousness and effort required for manual verification have caused many information technology professionals to shortcut the testing process. When automated verification is used, the process is not nearly as time-consuming, and tends to be performed more accurately.

A difficult question to answer in terms of acceptability is whether 100 percent correctness is required on the change. For example, if 100 items are checked and 99 prove correct, should the application be rejected because of the one remaining problem? The answer to this question depends on the importance of that one remaining item.

Users should expect that their systems will operate as specified. However, this may mean that the user may decide to install the application and then correct the error after implementation. The user has two options when installing a change known to have an error. The first is to ignore the problem and live with the results. For example, if a heading is misplaced or misspelled, the user may decide that that type of error, although annoying, does not affect the user of the output results. The second option is to make the adjustments manually. For example, if necessary, final totals can be manually calculated and added to the reports. In either case, the situation should be temporary.

Automated Application Segment Failure Notification

Each failure noted during testing of the automated segment of the application system should be documented. If it is known that the change will not be corrected until after the application is placed into production, a problem identification form should be completed to document the problem. However, if the change is to be corrected during the testing process, then a special form should be used for that purpose.

A form for notifying the software maintenance analyst that a failure has been uncovered in the automated segment of the application is illustrated in Work Paper 12-24. This form is to be used as a correction vehicle within the test phase, and should be prepared by the individual uncovering the failure. It is then sent to the software maintenance analyst in charge of the change for correction. The information contained on the automated application segment test failure notification form is described on the form's completion instructions sheet.

Is the Manual Segment Acceptable?

Users must make the same acceptability decisions on the manual segments of the application system as they make on the automated segments. Many of the manual segments do not come under the control of the maintenance systems analyst. However, this does not mean that the correct processing of the total system is not of concern to the maintenance systems analyst.

The same procedures followed in verifying the automated segment should be followed in verifying the manual segment. The one difference is that there are rarely automated means for verifying manual processing. Verifying manual segments can take as much—if not more—time than verifying the automated segment. The more common techniques to verify the correctness of the manual segment include the following:

- **Observation.** The person responsible for verification observes people performing the tasks. That person usually develops a checklist from the procedures and then determines whether the individual performs all of the required steps.

- **Application examination.** The people performing the task need to evaluate whether they can correctly perform the task. For example, in a data entry operation, the data entry operator may be asked to enter that information in a controlled mode.

- **Verification.** The person responsible for determining that the training is correct examines the results of processing from the trained people to determine whether they comply with the expected processing.

If the training is not acceptable, the user must decide again whether to delay the change. In most instances, the user will not delay the implementation of change if there are only minor problems in training, but instead will attempt to compensate for those problems during processing. On the other hand, if it becomes apparent that the users are ill-equipped to use the application, the change should be delayed until the individuals are better trained.

The methods that users can incorporate to overcome minor training deficiencies include the following:

- **Restrict personnel.** The new types of processing are performed only by people who have successfully completed the training. Thus, those who need more skills have time to obtain them before they begin using the new procedures or data.

- **Supervisory review.** Supervisors can spend extra time reviewing the work of people to ensure that the tasks are performed correctly.

- **Information technology assistance.** The software maintenance analysts/ programmers can work with user personnel during an interim period to help them process the information correctly.

- **Overtime.** Crash training sessions can be held in the evening or on weekends to bring the people up to the necessary skill level.

Training Failure Notification Form

Training failures should be documented at the same level of detail as are failures of the computerized segment. However, procedural errors can cause as many serious problems as can incorrect computer code. Unless these failures are documented, people can easily overlook the problem and assume someone else will correct it.

Each failure uncovered in training should be documented on a training failure notification form. This form should be completed by the individual who uncovers the problem, and then presented to the individual responsible for training for necessary action. A form that can be used to document training failures is illustrated in Work Paper 12-25. The information contained on the training failure notification form is described on the form's completion instructions sheet.

Guidelines

Acceptance testing is a critical part of testing. Guidelines to make it effective include the following:

- **Incorporate acceptance criteria into the test plan.** Although this chapter suggests a separate test plan and acceptance test plan, they can in fact be incorporated, in which case the test plan will use the acceptance criteria as the test plan objectives.

- **Include information systems professionals on the acceptance test team.** The acceptance test team needs information system skills as well as business skills for the areas affected by the hardware/software being acceptance tested. Acceptance testers must be able to understand information systems and to effectively communicate with information systems professionals.

Feedback enables IT management and users to monitor each phase of the software maintenance process. The feedback information relates to the processes and controls operational during each phase. During the installation of the change, management is able to measure the overall success of the software maintenance process. This gathered data is some of the most valuable. The types of feedback information that have proved most valuable include the following:

Number of changes installed

Number of changes installed by application

Number of problems encountered with installed changes

Number of old program versions deleted

Number of new program versions installed

Number of conditions monitored

Number of changes not installed on time

The following should help in performing Task 3:

- **Making test adjustments.** Corrections to problems should be implemented in the application system and then the system should be retested. When a new change is entered to the application system (even a change made during testing), the maintenance software analyst should not assume that previously tested segments will work correctly. It is quite possible that the new change has caused problems to unchanged portions. Unfortunately, it may mean that much of the testing already completed may have to be repeated.

- **Making training adjustments.** Identified training adjustments can be made in numerous ways. The methods selected will obviously depend on the type of failure uncovered. In some instances, a single individual may have been overlooked and the training can be presented to that person individually. In other cases, new training material may have to be prepared and taught.

The procedures described in this section for developing training materials apply equally to correcting training materials. In addition, if people have been improperly instructed, steps may have to be taken to inform them of the erroneous training and then to provide them with the proper training.

Summary

The IT department, both developers and testers, have processes in place to build the specified system. Developers and/or testers might challenge those specifications as accurate and complete; however, in many organizations, developers implement the specifications, and testers test to determine whether or not those specifications have been implemented as specified.

At the conclusion of the IT development and test processes, software can be placed into an operational state. This step addresses testing after the IT developers and testers have completed their work processes. This testing may involve the team that developed and tested the software, or it may be done independently of the software developers and testers.

The acceptance and operational testing included in this step involves acceptance testing by the customer/users of the software; pre-operational testing ensures that when the software system is moved from a test environment to a production environment that it performs correctly and that when the software system is changed, it is tested to ensure both the changed and unchanged portions still perform as specified.

At the conclusion of acceptance and operational testing, a decision is made as to whether the software should be placed into a production state. At that point, testing of that software system is complete. The remaining step (Step 7) is a post analysis by the testers to evaluate the effectiveness and efficiency of testing the software system and to identify areas in which testing could be improved in future projects.

WORK PAPER 12-1   Acceptance Criteria

Field Requirements

FIELD	INSTRUCTIONS FOR ENTERING DATA
Hardware/Software Project	The name of the project being acceptance-tested. This is the name the user/customer calls the project.
Number	A sequential number identifying acceptance criteria.
Acceptance Requirement	A user requirement that will be used to determine whether the corrected hardware/software is acceptable.
Critical	Indicate whether the acceptance requirement is critical, meaning that it must be met, or noncritical, meaning that it is desirable but not essential.
Test Result	Indicates after acceptance testing whether the requirement is acceptable or not acceptable, meaning that the project is rejected because it does not meet the requirement.
Comments	Clarify the criticality of the requirement; or indicate the meaning of test result rejection. For example, the software cannot be run; or management will make a judgment after acceptance testing as to whether the project can be run.

Hardware/Software Project: _____

Number	Acceptance Requirement	Critical		Test Result		Comments
		Yes	**No**	**Accept**	**Reject**	

WORK PAPER 12-2   System Boundary Diagram

Software Under Test: _____

System Boundary	Boundary Description	Actor Description	Name of Individual/Group Representing Actor

WORK PAPER 12-3   Use Case Definition

Last Updated By: Last Updated On:

Use Case Name: UC ID:

Actor:

Objective:

Preconditions:

Results (Postconditions):

Detailed Description

Action	Model (System) Response
1.	1.
2.	2.
3.	3.
4.	4.
5.	5.

Exceptions:

Alternative Courses:

Original Author: Original Date:

WORK PAPER 12-4 Test Case Work Paper

Test Case ID:

Parent Use Case ID:

Test Objective:

Original Author:

Original Date:

Last Updated By:

Last Updated On:

Item No.	Test Condition	Operator Action	Input Specifications	Output Specifications (Expected Results)	Pass or Fail	Comments

WORK PAPER 12-5 Installation Phase Test Process

TEST CRITERIA	ASSESSMENT				RECOMMENDED TEST
	Very Adequate	Adequate	Inadequate	N/A	
1. Have the accuracy and completeness of the installation been verified?					Examine the completeness of, and the results from, the installation plan.
2. Have data changes been prohibited during installation?					Compare old and new versions of important data files.
3. Has the integrity of the production files been verified?					Confirm their integrity with the users of the production files.
4. Does an audit trail exist showing installation activity?					Verify the completeness of the audit trail.
5. Will the integrity of the previous system/version be maintained until the integrity of the new system/version can be verified?					Perform parallel processing.
6. Ensure that a fail-safe installation plan is used for installation?					Determine that the option always exists to revert to the previous system/version.
7. Ensure that adequate security will occur during installation to prevent compromise?					Review the adequacy of the security procedures.
8. Verify that the defined installation process has been followed?					Confirm compliance on a sampling basis.
9. Verify that the proper system/version is placed into production on the correct date?					Determine the adequacy of the version control procedures.
10. Verify that user personnel can understand and use the documentation provided to use the new system/version?					Confirm with users during acceptance testing that their user documentation is adequate.
11. Verify that all the needed documentation has been prepared in accordance with documentation standards?					Verify on a sampling basis that specified documentation exists and meets standards.
12. Ensure that all involved with the installation are aware of the installation dates and their installation responsibilities?					Confirm with a sample of involved parties their knowledge of installation date(s) and responsibilities.
13. Ensure that the installation performance will be monitored?					Examine the monitoring process.
14. Ensure that the needed operating procedures are complete and installed when needed?					Examine the operating procedures and process for placing those procedures into operation.

WORK PAPER 12-6   Restart/Recovery Planning Data

Field Requirements

FIELD	INSTRUCTIONS FOR ENTERING DATA
Application System	The name by which the application is known.
Ident. Number	The application numerical identifier.
Change Ident. #	The sequence number that uniquely identifies the change.
	Note: Restart/recovery planning data, necessary to modify the recovery procedures, comprises the remainder of the form.
Impact on Estimated Total Downtime	If the change affects the downtime, the entire recovery process may have to be reevaluated.
Impact on Estimated Downtime Frequency	The number of times the recovery process will probably have to be executed. An important factor in determining backup data and other procedures. If the change will affect the frequency of downtime, the entire recovery process may have to be reevaluated.
Change in Downtime Risk	The probable loss when a system goes down. May be more important than either the total downtime or downtime frequency. If the loss is potentially very high, management must establish strong controls to lessen the downtime risk. If the change will probably cause a loss, the entire recovery process may have to be reevaluated.
New Program Versions for Recovery	Each new program version must be included in the recovery plan. This action documents the needed changes.
New Files/Data for Recovery	Changes in data normally impact the recovery process. This section documents those changes.
New Recovery Instructions/Procedures	If operating procedures or instructions have to be modified, this section provides space to document those changes.
Date New Version Operational	The date the new programs, files, data, recovery instructions, and procedures must be included in the recovery process.
Comments	Any additional information that may be helpful in modifying the recovery program to better reflect the changed application system.

WORK PAPER 12-6   *(continued)*

Application
System: _____

Ident.
Number: _____

Change
Ident. # _____

Impact on Estimated Total Downtime

_____

Impact on Estimated Downtime Frequency

_____

Change in Downtime Risk

_____

New Program Versions for Recovery

_____

New Files/Data for Recovery

_____

New Recovery Instructions/Procedures

_____

Date New Version Operational

_____

Comments

_____

WORK PAPER 12-7   Program Change History

Field Requirements

FIELD	INSTRUCTIONS FOR ENTERING DATA
Application System	The name by which the application is known.
Ident. Number	The numerical application identifier.
Program Name	A brief description of the program or its name.
Ident. Number	The program identifier.
Coded by	The programmer who originally coded the program.
Maintained by	The programmer who now maintains the program.
Date Entered into Production	The date on which the program was first used in production.
Version #	The original version number. *Note:* Program change history provides an audit trail of changes to a program; and is contained in the following fields.
Change ID #	The sequence number that uniquely identifies the change.
New Version #	The program version number used to code the change.
Coded by	The name of the programmer who coded the change.
Date Entered into Production	The date on which this version went into production.
Comments	Additional information valuable in tracing the history of a change to a program.

WORK PAPER 12-7   *(continued)*

Application System: _____ Ident. Number _____

_____

Program Name: _____ Ident. Number _____

_____

Coded by: _____

_____

Maintained by: _____

_____

Date Entered into Production: _____ Version # _____

Program Change History

Change ID #	New Version #	Coded by	Date Entered into Production	Comments

WORK PAPER 12-8   Production Change Instructions

Field Requirements

FIELD	INSTRUCTIONS FOR ENTERING DATA
Sent To	The name of the person in operations who controls the application system being changed.
Application Control #	A number issued sequentially to control the changes to each application system.
Application Name	The name by which the application is known.
Number	The numerical application identifier.
Change Ident. #	The sequence number that uniquely identifies the change.
	Note: The following production change information includes instructions to computer operations to move programs, job control statements, operator manual procedures, and other items associated with the change to production status. The specific instructions provide both for adding and deleting information.
Resource	The resource that needs to be added to or deleted from the production environment. The most common resources involved in a production change include programs, job statements, and operator manual procedures.
Task	Instructs whether to add or delete the resource from the production status. The Add column indicates that it is to be moved from test status to production status; the Delete column indicates that it is to be removed from production status.
Effective Dates	The date on which the tasks are to be performed.
Comments	Additional instructions that help operations personnel perform their assignments. For example, this column might include the location or the source of new pages for the operator's manual.
Prepared By	Usually, the name of the project leader.
Date	The date on which the form was prepared.

WORK PAPER 12-8   *(continued)*

Sent To: _____   Application
Control #: _____

Application Name
_____   Number: _____   Change
Ident. #: _____

Production Change Instructions

Resource	Task		Effective Dates	Comments
	Add	Delete		
Program #				
Program #				
Program #				
Program #				
Job Statements #				
Job Statements #				
Operator Manual procedure #				
Operator Manual procedure #				
Other: _____				
Other: _____				
Other: _____				

Prepared By: _____   Date: _____

WORK PAPER 12-9   Deletion Instructions

Field Requirements

FIELD	INSTRUCTIONS FOR ENTERING DATA
Application Name	The name by which the application is known.
Ident. Number	The numerical application identifier.
Deletion Control Number	A number sequentially issued to control the form.
Sent To	Typically, the person in operations responsible for deleting a program from the application.
Date	The date on which the form was prepared.
From	Usually, the name of the project leader.
Department	The organization or department authorizing the deletion of the program.
	Note: Deletion instructions guide operations personnel to delete unwanted program versions, as follows:
Library	The name or number that identifies the library in which the program resides.
Program Version to Delete	The program number and version of that program that is to be deleted.
Deletion Date	The date on which the program version may be deleted.
Comments	Any additional information helpful to operations staff in performing the required tasks.
Prepared By	The name of the person who prepared the form.
Date	The date on which the form was prepared.

WORK PAPER 12-9   *(continued)*

Application
Name: _____

Ident.
Number: _____

Deletion
Control #: _____

Sent To: _____   Date: _____

From: _____   Department: _____

Deletion Instructions

Library	Program Version to Delete	Deletion Date	Comments

Prepared By: _____   Date: _____

WORK PAPER 12-10   Form Completion Instructions: Program Change Monitor Notification

Field Requirements

FIELD	INSTRUCTIONS FOR ENTERING DATA
Application System	The name by which the application is known.
Number	The application identifier.
Change Ident. #	The sequence number that uniquely identifies the change.
Description of Change	A description which helps the people monitoring the application gain perspective on the areas impacted.
Date of Change	The date on which the change goes into production. This is the date when the monitoring should commence.
Monitoring Guidelines	The description of the type of problems to be anticipated. The information should be descriptive enough to tell the monitors both what to look for and what action to take if they find problems. Obviously, those potential problems which are identified are those most likely to occur. However, the monitors should be alert to any type of problem that might occur immediately following introduction of a new program version. The information about the high-probability items is:

- Area potentially impacted: the report, transactions, or other area in which the individuals monitoring should be looking.

- Probable impact: this section describes the type of problems that are most likely to occur within the impacted area.

- Action to take if problem occurs: the people to call, correction to make, or any other action that the individual uncovering the problem should take.

- Comments: any additional information that might prove helpful to the monitors in attempting to identify problems associated with the program change.

Prepared By	The name of the person who prepared the form, normally the software maintenance analyst.
Date	The date on which the form was prepared.

WORK PAPER 12-10   *(continued)*

Application
System: _____   Number: _____   Change
Ident. # _____

Description of Change   Date of Change

_____

Monitoring Guidelines

Area Potentially Impacted	Probable Impact	Action to Take If Problem Occurs	Comments

Prepared By: _____   Date: _____

WORK PAPER 12-11   Form Completion Instructions: System Problem Caused by System Change

Field Requirements

FIELD	INSTRUCTIONS FOR ENTERING DATA
Application name	The name by which the application is known.
Number	The application identifier.
Change Ident. #	The sequence number that uniquely identifies the change.
Problem Date	The date on which the problem was located.
Problem Time	The time the problem was encountered.
Problem Control #	A sequential number that controls the form.
Description of Problem	A brief narrative description. Normally, examples of the problem are attached to the form.
Area of Application Affected	This segment is designed to help the software maintenance analyst identify the source of the problem. If it is one of the problems outlined on the program change monitor notification form, the individual completing the form can be very specific regarding the affected area. Otherwise, the individual should attempt to identify areas such as report writing or input validation where the problem seems to originate.
Impact of Problem	The individual identifying the problem should attempt to assess the impact of that problem on the organization. This information is very valuable in determining how fast the problem must be fixed. Ideally, this risk would be expressed in quantitative units, such as number of invoices incorrectly processed, dollar loss, number of hours lost because of the problems. It is often helpful to divide the problem into various time periods. This is because some risks are not immediately serious but become serious if they are not corrected by a certain time or date. Some suggested time spans included on the form are:

• If not fixed within one hour

• If not fixed within one day

• If not fixed within one week |
Recommendation	The suggestions from the individual uncovering the problem as to what should be done to fix it. This recommendation can either be to correct the errors that have occurred and/or to correct the problems in the application system.
Prepared By	The name of the person who uncovered the system problem caused by the system change.
Date	The date on which the form was prepared.

WORK PAPER 12-11   *(continued)*

Application
Name: _____ Number: _____ Change
Ident. # _____

Problem Date _____ Problem Time _____ Problem
Control # _____

Description of Problem

_____

Area of Application Affected

_____

Impact of Problem

If not fixed within 1 hour:

If not fixed within 1 day:

If not fixed within 1 week:

_____

Recommendation

_____

Prepared By: _____ Date: _____

WORK PAPER 12-12   Form Completion Instructions: Acceptance Test Plan

Field Requirements

FIELD	INSTRUCTIONS FOR ENTERING DATA
Application Name	The name by which the application is known.
Number	The application identifier.
Change Ident. #	The sequence number that uniquely identifies the change.
Individual Responsible for Test	The name of the individual or individuals who will be conducting the test. This normally is the user and the application systems analyst/programmer.
Test Plan	The steps that need to be followed in conducting the test. For the functional, regression, stress, and performance types of testing, these test characteristics need to be defined:
	• Change objective: the description of the objective of the change that was installed. This should be specific so that test planning can be based on the characteristics of the objective.
	• Method of testing: the type of test that will be conducted to verify that the objective is achieved.
	• Desired result: the expected result from conducting the test. If this result is achieved, the implementation can be considered successful, while failure to meet this result means an unsuccessful implementation.
Regression Test Plan	The tests and procedures to be followed to ensure that unchanged segments of the application system have not been inadvertently changed by software maintenance.
Intersystem Test Plan	The tests to be conducted to ensure that data flowing from and to other systems will be correctly handled after the change.
Comments	Additional information that might prove helpful in conducting or verifying the test results.
Individual Who Accepts Tested Application	The name of the individual who should review this test plan because of the responsibility to accept the change after successful testing.
Date	The date on which the form was completed.

WORK PAPER 12-12   *(continued)*

Application
Name: _____ Number: _____ Change
Ident. # _____

Individual Responsible for Test: _____

TEST PLAN

Change Objective	Method of Testing	Desired Results

Regresssion Test Plan

Intersystem Test Plan

Comments

Individual Who Accepts Tested Application	Date

WORK PAPER 12-13   Change Control Form

Field Requirements

FIELD	INSTRUCTIONS FOR ENTERING DATA
Application System	The name by which the application system is known.
Application Ident. #	The identification number of the application system.
Change Ident. #	The control number for the change.
Description of Change	The solution and general terms for the change, such as issue a new report, add an input data edit, or utilize a new processing routine.
Changes Required	All impacted areas with instructions for the changes to be made or investigations to be undertaken regarding the impact of the proposed solution. The type of items affected include:

- data elements
- programs
- job control language
- operations manuals
- user training
- user manuals

For each of the affected items, the following information should be provided:

- Item affected: the program, data element, job control or other
- Item identification: the program number or other method of identifying the affected item

Prepared By	The name of the person completing the form.
Date	The date on which the form was completed.

Application
System: _____

Application
Ident. #: _____

Change
Ident. # _____

Description of Change:

_____

Change Overview:

_____

Changes Required

Item	Item Identification	Comments

Prepared By: _____ Date: _____

WORK PAPER 12-14   Data Change Form

Field Requirements

FIELD	INSTRUCTIONS FOR ENTERING DATA
Application System	The name by which the application is known.
Application Ident. #	The number used to identify the application system.
Change Ident. #	The sequential number used to identify the change.
Data Element Name	The name by which the data element is known.
Data Ident. #	The number used to uniquely identify the data element. In a data dictionary system, this should be the data dictionary data element number.
Record Name	The record or records in which the data element is contained.
Record Ident. #	The number that describes the record or records in which the data element is contained.
File Name	The file or files in which the data element is contained.
File Ident. #	The numbers that uniquely describe the file or files in which the data element is contained.
Assigned To	The name of the person, function, or department responsible for making the change to the data element and the associated records and files.
Date Required	The date by which the change should be made (pending user approval).
Data Change	The type of change to be made on the data element.
Description of Change	A detailed narrative description (with examples when applicable) explaining the type of change that must be made to the data element. When a data dictionary is used, the data dictionary form should be attached to the data change form.
Comments	Information helpful in implementing the data change.
Prepared By	The name of the person who completed the form.
Date	The date on which the form was completed.

(continues)

WORK PAPER 12-14   *(continued)*

Application
System: _____

Application
Ident. #: _____

Change
Ident. #: _____

Data Element
Name: _____

Data
Ident. #: _____

Record
Name: _____

Record
Ident. #: _____

File
Name: _____

File
Ident. #: _____

Assigned To: _____

Date Required: _____

Data Change
❑ Add element.
❑ Delete element.
❑ Modify element attributes.
❑ Modify element description.

Description of Change

Comments

Prepared By: _____

Date: _____

WORK PAPER 12-15   Program Change Form

Field Requirements

FIELD	INSTRUCTIONS FOR ENTERING DATA
Application System	The name by which the application to be changed is known.
Application Ident. #	The identifier that uniquely describes the application system.
Change Ident. #	The sequential number used to identify the change.
Program Name	The name by which the program to be changed is known.
Number	The number that uniquely identifies the program.
Version Number	The version number that will be assigned to the altered program.
Date Required	The date on which the change is to be implemented, assuming the user approves the changes.
Assigned To	The name of the person who will make the change in the program.
Description of Change	A narrative description of the change to be made to this specific program. It should provide examples of programs produced before and after the change.
Source Statement Affected	A description of the source statement or statements that should be changed, together with the change to be made. The change may be described in terms of specifications rather than specific source statements.
Comments	Tips and techniques on how best to install the change in the application system.
Prepared By	The name of the person who completed the form.
Date	The date on which the form was completed.

Application
System: _____

Application
Ident. #: _____

Change
Ident. #: _____

Program Name: _____   Number: _____   Version #: _____

New Version #: _____

Date
Required: _____

Assigned
To: _____

Description of Change

_____

Source Statement Affected

_____

Comments

_____

Prepared By: _____   Date: _____

WORK PAPER 12-16   Form Completion Instructions: Acceptance Test Checklist

Field Requirements

FIELD	INSTRUCTIONS FOR ENTERING DATA
Application Name	The name by which the application is known.
Number	The application identifier.
Change Ident. #	The sequence number that uniquely identifies the change.
Administrative Data	The administrative data relates to the management of the test.
Technical Data	The resources needed to conduct the acceptance test and the location of those resources. The information that should be documented about the needed resources includes:

- Resource needed: the exact resource needed.
- Location: the physical location of that resource. In many acceptance tests, the resources are marshalled in a common area to await conducting the test.

WORK PAPER 12-16 *(continued)*

Application
Name: _____ Number: _____ Change Ident. # _____

Administrative Data

Date of test   _____

Location of test   _____

Time of test   _____

Information services person in charge of test   _____

User person in charge of test   _____

Computer time available   _____

Technical Data

	Resource Needed	Location	Available Yes	No	N/A
1.	Test transactions				
2.	Master files/data base				
3.	Operator instructions				
4.	Special media/forms				
5.	Acceptance criteria				
6.	Input support personnel				
7.	Output support personnel				
8.	Control group				
9.	External control proof				
10.	Backup/recovery plan				
11.	Security plan				
12.	Error message actions				

Prepared By: _____ Date: _____

WORK PAPER 12-17   Form Completion Instructions: Training Material Inventory

Field Requirements

FIELD	INSTRUCTIONS FOR ENTERING DATA
Application Name	The name by which the application is known.
Number	The application identifier.
Change Ident. #	The sequence number that uniquely identifies the change.
Training Material Name	The name or number by which the training material is known.
Training Material Description	A brief narrative description of what is contained in the training material.
Needs Updating	Columns to be completed whenever a change is installed. The columns provide an indication of whether the training material needs updating (Yes column) or does not need updating (No column).
Prepared By	The name of the individual responsible for maintaining the inventory.
Date	The last date on which the inventory was updated.

WORK PAPER 12-17 *(continued)*

Application
Name: _____ Number: _____

Change
Ident. # _____

Training Material Name/Number	Training Material Description	Needs Updating	
		Yes	No

Prepare By: _____ Date: _____

WORK PAPER 12-18   Form Completion Instructions: Training Plan

Field Requirements

FIELD	INSTRUCTIONS FOR ENTERING DATA
Application Name	The name by which the application is known.
Number	The application identifier.
Change Ident. #	The sequence number that uniquely identifies the change.
Individual Responsible for Training	The individual with the overall responsibility for ensuring that all the training material is prepared, taught, and evaluated prior to the implementation of the change.
Training Plan	The details of why, who, what, where, when, how, and the results to be derived from the training plan. The remainder of the form deals with this plan.
Group Needing Training	The name of the individual, type of person, or department requiring training. The groups to consider include:

- Transaction origination staff: the people who originate data into the application system.
- Data entry clerk: the person who transcribes data to computer media.
- Control group—information services: the group responsible for ensuring that all input is received and that output is reasonable.
- Control group—user: the group in the user area responsible for the accuracy, completeness, and authorization of data.
- Computer operations: the group responsible for running the application on computer hardware.
- Records retention: the group or groups responsible for saving backup data.
- Third-party customers: people with unsatisfied needs or people who are the ultimate recipients of reports.
- User management and staff: the group responsible for the application.
- Other: any other involved party requiring training.

Training Approach	The why, what, where, when, and how of the training plan.
Desired Results	The expected result, behavior change, or skills to be gained from the training material.
Training Dates	Important dates for implementing the training plan.
Comments	Any material helpful in designing, teaching, or evaluating the training material.
Individual Who Accepts Training as Sufficient	The name of the individual or department who must agree that the training is adequate. This individual should also concur with the training plan.
Date	The date the training plan was developed.

WORK PAPER 12-18   *(continued)*

Application
Name: _____ Number: _____ Change Ident. # _____

Individual Responsible for Training _____

Training Plan

Group Needing Training	Training Approach	Desired Result
1. Transaction origination staff		
2. Data entry clerk		
3. Control group—information services		
4. Control group—user		
5. Computer operations		
6. Records retention		
7. Third-party customers		
8. User management and staff		
9. Other: _____		
10. Other: _____		

Training Dates

Date training material prepared   _____

Date training can commence   _____

Date training to be completed   _____

Comments

Individual Who Accepts Testing as Sufficient   Date

_____   _____

WORK PAPER 12-19   Form Completion Instructions: New/Modified Training Modules

Field Requirements

FIELD	INSTRUCTIONS FOR ENTERING DATA
Application Name	The name by which the application is known.
Number	The application identifier.
Change Ident. #	The sequence number that uniquely identifies the change.
Training Module Inventory	The remainder of the information on the form describes the modules.
Training Module Description	A brief narrative of the training module. The location of the training material should be identified so that it can be easily obtained.
Description of Change	As the training module becomes modified, this column should contain a sequential listing of all the changes made. In effect, it is a change history for the training module.
Training Material	The course material included in the training module.
Who Should Be Trained	The individual(s) to whom the training module is directed.
Method of Training	The recommended way in which the training module should be used.
Prepared By	The name of the individual who prepared the module.
Date	The date on which it was last updated.

WORK PAPER 12-19 *(continued)*

Application
Name: _____ Number: _____ Change Ident. # _____

Training Module Inventory

Training Module Description	Description of Change	Training Material	Who Should Be Trained	Method of Training					
				Meeting	Class-room	Self-study	New Procedure	Super-visor	Other

Prepared By: _____ Date: _____

**WORK PAPER 12-20   Form Completion Instructions: Conduct Training
Checklist**

Field Requirements

FIELD	INSTRUCTIONS FOR ENTERING DATA
Application Name	The name by which the application is known.
Number	The application identifier.
Change Ident. #	The sequence number that uniquely identifies the change.
Training Checklist	The remainder of the form contains the checklist information, which is:

- Name of individual requiring training: whenever possible, actual names should be used, as opposed to groups of people, so records can be maintained as to whether or not the people actually took the training.
- Department: the department/organization with which the individual is affiliated.
- Training required: the training modules and/or material to be given the individual.
- Dates: the dates on which the course is to be given or the training material to be disseminated to the individual. The schedules dates should be listed, as well as the date the individual actually took the course or received the material.
- Location: the location of the course or the location to which the training material should be distributed.
- Instructor: the name of the responsible individual should be listed.
- Comments: any other information that would verify that training took place. In classroom situations where examinations are given, the space could be used to record that grade.

Prepared By	The name of the individual preparing the form who should be the one responsible for ensuring the training is given.
Date	The date on which the form was prepared.

WORK PAPER 12-20   *(continued)*

Application
Name: _____ Number: _____

Change
Ident. # _____

Training Checklist

| Name of Individual Requiring Training | Department | Training Required | Dates | | Location | Instructor | Com-ments |
			Sched-uled	Taken			

Prepared By: _____ Date: _____

WORK PAPER 12-21   Acceptance Testing Quality Control Checklist

		YES	NO	N/A	COMMENTS
1.	Has acceptance testing been incorporated into the test plan?				
2.	Is acceptance testing viewed as a project process, rather than as a single step at the end of testing?				
3.	Have the appropriate users of the software or hardware components been selected to develop the acceptance criteria for those components?				
4.	Does the group that defines the acceptance criteria represent all uses of the component to be tested?				
5.	Do those individuals accept the responsibility of identifying acceptance criteria?				
6.	Have the acceptance criteria been identified early enough in the project so that they can influence planning and implementation?				
7.	Has an acceptance test plan been developed?				
8.	Does that plan include the components of acceptance test plan as outlined in this chapter?				
9.	Is the acceptance test plan consistent with the acceptance criteria?				
10.	Have appropriate interim products been reviewed by the acceptance testers before being used for the next implementation task?				
11.	Have the appropriate testing techniques been selected for acceptance testing?				
12.	Do the acceptance testers have the skill sets necessary to perform acceptance testing?				
13.	Have adequate resources for performing acceptance testing been allocated?				
14.	Has adequate time to perform acceptance testing been allocated?				
15.	Have interim acceptance opinions been issued?				
16.	Has the project team reacted positively to the acceptance testers' concerns?				
17.	Has a final acceptance decision been made?				

WORK PAPER 12-21   *(continued)*

		YES	NO	N/A	COMMENTS
18.	Is that decision consistent with the acceptance criteria that have been met and not met?				
19.	Have the critical acceptance criteria been identified?				
20.	Are the requirements documented in enough detail that the software interfaces can be determined?				
21.	Does both user management and customer management support use case testing?				
22.	Has a system boundary diagram been prepared for the software being tested?				
23.	Does the system boundary diagram identify all of the interfaces?				
24.	Have the individuals responsible for each interface on the new system boundary diagram been identified?				
25.	Do the actors agree to participate in developing use cases?				
26.	Has a use case been defined for each system boundary?				
27.	Do the users of the software agree that the use case definitions are complete?				
28.	Have at least two test cases been prepared for each use case?				
29.	Have both a successful and unsuccessful test condition been identified for each use case?				
30.	Do the users of the software agree that the test case work paper identifies all of the probable scenarios?				

WORK PAPER 12-22   Pre-Operational Testing Quality Control Checklist

		YES	NO	N/A	COMMENTS
1.	Is each change reviewed for its impact upon the restart/recovery plan?				
2.	If a change impacts recovery, is the newly estimated downtime calculated?				
3.	If the change impacts recovery, is the new downtime risk estimated?				
4.	Are the changes that need to be made to the recovery process documented?				
5.	Is the notification of changes to the production version of an application documented?				
6.	Are changes to application systems controlled by an application control change number?				
7.	Are there procedures to delete unwanted program versions from the source, test, and object libraries?				
8.	Are program deletion requests documented so that production is authorized to delete programs?				
9.	Are procedures established to ensure that program versions will go into production on the correct day?				
10.	If it affects operating procedures, are operators notified of the date new versions go into production?				
11.	Are procedures established to monitor changed application systems?				
12.	Do the individuals monitoring the process receive notification that an application system has been changed?				
13.	Do the people monitoring changes receive clues regarding the areas impacted and the probable problems?				
14.	Do the people monitoring application system changes receive guidance on what actions to take if problems occur?				
15.	Are problems that are detected immediately following changes documented on a special form so they can be traced to a particular change?				
16.	Are the people documenting problems asked to document the impact of the problem on the organization?				

WORK PAPER 12-22   *(continued)*

		YES	NO	N/A	COMMENTS
17.	Is software change installation data collected and documented?				
18.	Does information services management review and use the feedback data?				
19.	Does information services management periodically review the effectiveness of installing the software change?				

WORK PAPER 12-23 Testing and Training Quality Control Checklist

		YES	NO	N/A	COMMENTS
1.	Are software maintenance analysts required to develop a test plan?				
2.	Must each change be reviewed to determine if it has an impact on training?				
3.	If a change has an impact on training, do procedures require that a training plan be established?				
4.	Is an inventory prepared of training material so that it can be updated?				
5.	Does the training plan make one individual responsible for training?				
6.	Does the training plan identify the results desired from training?				
7.	Does the training plan indicate the who, why, what, where, when, and how of training?				
8.	Does the training plan provide a training schedule, including dates?				
9.	Is an individual responsible for determining if training is acceptable?				
10.	Are all of the training modules inventoried?				
11.	Does each training module have a history of the changes made to the module?				
12.	Is one individual assigned responsibility for testing?				
13.	Does the test plan list each measurable change objective and the method of testing that objective?				
14.	Does the training plan list the desired results from testing?				
15.	Does the training plan address regression testing?				
16.	Does the training plan address intersystem testing?				
17.	Is someone responsible for judging whether testing is acceptable?				
18.	Is an acceptance testing checklist prepared to determine the necessary resources are ready for the test?				

WORK PAPER 12-23   *(continued)*

		YES	NO	N/A	COMMENTS
19.	Does the acceptance testing checklist include the administrative aspects of the test?				
20.	Is a training checklist prepared which indicates which individuals need training?				
21.	Is a record kept of whether or not individuals receive training?				
22.	Is each test failure documented?				
23.	Is each training failure documented?				
24.	Are test failures corrected before the change goes into production?				
25.	Are training failures corrected before the change goes into production?				
26.	If the change is put into production before testing/training failures have been corrected, are alternative measures taken to assure the identified errors will not cause problems?				
27.	Is feedback data identified?				
28.	Is feedback data collected?				
29.	Is feedback data regularly reviewed?				
30.	Are control concerns identified?				
31.	Does information services management periodically review training and testing software changes?				

WORK PAPER 12-24   Form Completion Instructions: Automated Application Segment Test Failure Notification

Field Requirements

FIELD	INSTRUCTIONS FOR ENTERING DATA
Application Name	The name by which the application is known.
Number	The application identifier.
Change Ident. #	The sequence number that uniquely identifies the change.
Description of Failure	A brief description of the condition that is believed to be unacceptable. In most instances, the detailed information would be presented orally, as would the documentation supporting the failure. The purpose of the form is to record the problem and control the implementation. The information contained in this section includes:

Under Description of Failure:

- Test Date: the date of the test.
- Failure #: a sequentially increasing number used to control the identification and implementation of problems. If a form is lost or mislaid, it will be noticed because a failure number will be missing.
- System Change Objective Failed: the measurable change objective that was not achieved.
- Description of Failure: a brief description of what is wrong.

FIELD	INSTRUCTIONS FOR ENTERING DATA
Recommended Correction	Corrections suggested by the individual uncovering the failure or the software maintenance analyst after an analysis of the problem. The type of information included in the recommendation is:

- Programs Affected: all the programs that contributed to the failure.
- Data Affected: all the data elements, records, or files that contributed or were involved in the failure.
- Description of Correction: a brief description of the recommended solution.

FIELD	INSTRUCTIONS FOR ENTERING DATA
Correction Assignments	This section is completed by the software maintenance analyst to assign the correction of the failure to a specific individual. At a minimum, this should include:

- Correction Assigned To: the individual making the correction.
- Date Correction Needed: the date by which the correction should be made.
- Comments: suggestions on how to implement the solution.

FIELD	INSTRUCTIONS FOR ENTERING DATA
Prepared By	The name of the individual who uncovered the failure.
Date	The date on which the form was prepared.

WORK PAPER 12-24 *(continued)*

Application
Name: _____ Number: _____ Change
Ident. # _____

Description of Failure

Test Date _____ Failure # _____

System Change Objective Failed _____

_____

Desciption of Failure _____

_____

_____

Recommended Correction

Programs Affected _____

_____

Data Affected _____

_____

Description of Correction _____

_____

_____

Correction Assignments

Correction Assigned To _____

Date Correction Needed _____

Comments _____

_____

_____

_____

Prepared By: _____ Date: _____

WORK PAPER 12-25 Form Completion Instructions: Training Failure Notification

Field Requirements

FIELD	INSTRUCTIONS FOR ENTERING DATA
Application Name	The name by which the application is known.
Number	The application identifier.
Change Ident. #	The sequence number that uniquely identifies the change.
Description of Failure	The details of the training failure need to be described. At a minimum, this would include:
	• Failure #: a sequentially increasing number used to control the failure form.
	• Test Date: the date on which the test occurred.
	• People Not Adequately Trained: the name of individuals, categories of people or departments who could not adequately perform their tasks.
	• Failure Caused By Lack of Training: a description of why the training was inadequate.
Recommended Correction	Suggestions for correcting the failure. This section can be completed either by the individual uncovering the failure and/or by the systems analyst. The type of information helpful in correcting the training failure includes:
	• Training Material Needing Revisions: the specific material that should be modified to correct the problem.
	• New Method of Training Needed: suggestions for varying the training method.
	• People Needing Training: all of the people that may need new training.
	• Description of Correction: a brief explanation of the recommended solution.
Correction Assignments	Assignments made by the individual responsible for training. At a minimum, each assignment would include:
	• Correction Assigned To: name of individual who will make the necessary adjustments to training material.
	• Training Material Needing Correction: the specific training document(s) that need changing.
	• Comments: recommendations on how to change the training material.
Prepared By	The name of the individual who uncovered the failure.
Date	The date on which the failure occurred.

WORK PAPER 12-25 *(continued)*

Application
Name: _____ Number: _____ Change Ident. # _____

Description of Failure

Test Date _____ Failure # _____

People Not Adequately Trained _____

_____

Failure Caused By Lack of Training _____

_____
_____

Recommended Correction

Training Materials Needing Revisions _____

_____

New Method of Training Needed _____

_____

People Needing Training _____

_____

Description of Correction _____

_____
_____

Correction Assignments

Correction Assigned To _____

_____

Training Material Needing Correction _____

_____

Comments _____

_____
_____
_____

Prepared By _____ Date: _____

CHAPTER 13

Step 7: Post-Implementation Analysis

A significant portion of IT resources is expended testing application systems. A reasonable question for management to ask is, "Are we getting our money's worth from this testing?" Unfortunately, many IT functions cannot objectively answer that question.

This chapter describes the more common objectives for measuring testing and then recommends criteria for performing those measurements. The chapter explains who should evaluate performance, identifies the common approaches, and then recommends testing metrics for the assessment process.

Overview

Measuring a test's effectiveness serves two purposes: It evaluates the performance of the testers and, perhaps more important, enables an IT organization to modify its testing process. Identifying the ineffective aspects of testing isolates the areas for improvement. The two evaluation testing objectives of assessing individual performance and improving the test process are closely related; indeed, the same evaluation criteria can be used for both purposes. These major evaluation objectives are achieved through the collection of data about more detailed evaluation objectives. The objective of assessment is to identify problems so that corrective action can be taken. Therefore, the evaluation will be looking for the negative aspects of testing. The absence of a negative factor represents a positive evaluation.

> **NOTE** The evaluation of the test process is normally based on accumulating many individual analyses of software systems tested.

Concerns

The major concern that testers should have is that their testing processes will not improve. Without improvement, testers will continue to make the same errors and perform testing inefficiently time after time. Experience in many organizations has shown that testers make more errors than developers. Thus, testing is an error-prone process.

To improve the test process, the results of testing must be evaluated continually. Unless the results are recorded and retained, the evaluation will not occur. Without a formal process, and management's support for the process, testers need to be concerned that their processes will remain stagnant and not subject to continuous improvement.

Workbench

Figure 13-1 illustrates the workbench for evaluating a test's effectiveness. The objectives for the assessment should be clearly established; without defined objectives, the measurement process may not be properly directed.

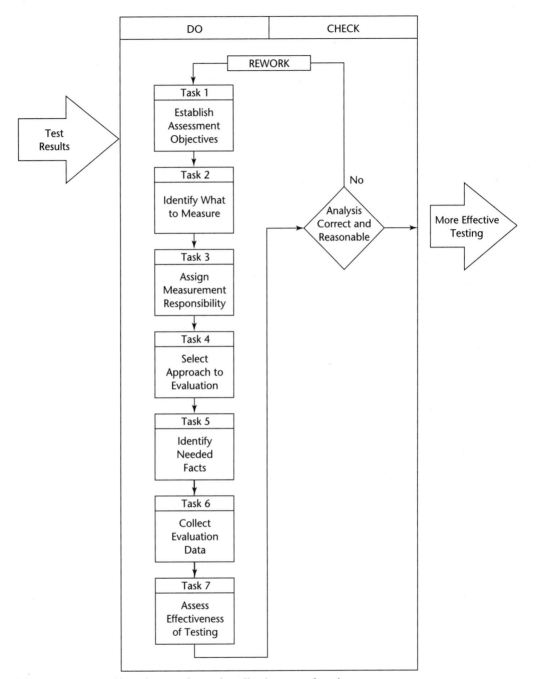

Figure 13-1   Workbench to evaluate the effectiveness of testing.

Input

The input to this step should be the results of conducting software tests. The type of information required includes but is not limited to:

Number of tests conducted

Resources expended in testing

Test tools used

Defects uncovered

Size of software tested

Days to correct defects

Defects not corrected

Defects uncovered during operation that were not uncovered during testing

Developmental phase in which defects were uncovered

Names of defects uncovered

Do Procedures

Once a decision has been made to formally assess the effectiveness of testing, an assessment process is needed. This assessment can be performed by software test, quality assurance or a team organization to do this step. This assessment process involves the following seven tasks.

Task 1: Establish Assessment Objectives

Establish the objectives for performing the assessment. If objectives are not defined, the measurement process may not be properly directed and thus may not be effective. These objectives include:

- **Identify test weaknesses.** Identify problems within the test process where the methodology is not effective in identifying system defects.
- **Identify the need for new test tools.** Determine when the existing test tools are not effective or efficient as a basis for acquiring new or improved testing tools.
- **Assess project testing.** Evaluate the effectiveness of the testing performed by a project team to reduce defects from the project at an economical cost.
- **Identify good test practices.** Determine which practices used in the test process are the most effective so that those practices can be used by all projects.
- **Identify poor test practices.** Determine which of the practices used by the project team are ineffective so that other projects can be advised not to use those practices.

- **Identify economical test practices.** Determine the characteristics that make testing most economical so that the cost-effectiveness of testing can be improved.

Task 2: Identify What to Measure

Identify the categories of information needed to accomplish the measurement objectives. The list that follows offers the five characteristics of application system testing that can be measured:

1. **Involvement.** Who is involved in testing and to what extent?

2. **Extent of testing.** What areas are covered by testing and what volume of testing will be performed on those areas?

3. **Resources.** How much information services resources, both people and computer, will be consumed in a test process?

4. **Effectiveness.** How much testing is achieved per unit of resource?

5. **Assessment.** What is the value of the results received from the test process?

Task 3: Assign Measurement Responsibility

Make one group responsible for collecting and assessing testing performance information. Without a specific accountable individual, there will be no catalyst to ensure that the data collection and assessment process occurs. The responsibility for the use of information services resources resides with IT management. However, they may desire to delegate the responsibility to assess the effectiveness of the test process to a function within the department. If the information services departments have a quality assurance function, that delegation should be made to the quality assurance group. Lacking that function, other candidates for assigning the responsibility include an information services comptroller, manager of standards, manager of software support, or the planning manager.

Task 4: Select Evaluation Approach

Evaluate several approaches that can be used in performing the assessment process. The one that best matches the managerial style should be selected. The following are the most common approaches to evaluating the effectiveness of testing.

- **Judgment.** The individual responsible for the assessment evaluates the test. This is normally an arbitrary assessment and one that is difficult to justify. However, if the individual is well respected and the judgments correlate to actual results, the process may work effectively.

- **Compliance with methodology.** Testing can be considered a success when it complies with well-established guidelines and standards, and a process defect when it does not.

- **Problems after test.** The effectiveness of the test process can be measured by the number of problems it causes. If few problems occur, testing can be considered to be good; if many problems occur, testing can be considered poor.

- **User reaction.** If the user is satisfied with the application system, it can be assumed testing is good; if the user is unhappy with the performance of the application system, testing can be judged poor.

- **Testing metrics.** Criteria are identified that show a high positive correlation to good or bad testing. This correlation or relationship between factors is called a *metric*. This process is a scientific mathematical approach to the measurement of testing.

The metrics approach is recommended because once established it is easy to use and can be proven to show a high correlation to effective and ineffective practices. A major advantage to metrics is that the assessment process can be clearly defined, will be known to those people who are being assessed, and is specific enough so that it is easy to determine which testing variables need to be adjusted to improve the effectiveness, efficiency, and/or economy of the test process.

Task 5: Identify Needed Facts

Identify the facts necessary to support the approach selected. The metrics approach clearly identifies the type of data needed for the assessment process. Using the metrics described later in this chapter, the needed information includes:

- **Change characteristics.** The frequency, size, and type of change occurring in each system.

- **Magnitude of system.** A measure used to equate testing information from system to system, the size being a factor used to relate testing in one application system to another.

- **Cost of process being tested.** The cost to develop a system or install a change, whichever is being tested.

- **Cost of test.** The resources, both people and computer, used to test the new function.

- **Defects uncovered by testing.** The number of defects uncovered as a result of the test.

- **Defects detected by phase.** A breakdown of the previous category for each phase tested to show the effectiveness of the test by system development life cycle (SDLC) phase.

- **Defects uncovered after test.** The number of defects uncovered after the new function is placed into production status.

- **Cost of testing by phase.** The amount of resources consumed for testing by each developmental phase of the SDLC in which testing occurs.

- **System complaints.** Complaints of problems by a third party after the system goes operational.

- **Quantification of defects.** The potential dollar loss associated with each defect had it not been detected.

- **Who conducted the test.** The functional unit to which the individuals conducting the test report.

- **Quantification of correctness of defect.** The cost to correct the application system defect.

Task 6: Collect Evaluation Data

Establish a system to collect and store the needed data in a form suitable for assessment. This may require a collection mechanism, a storage mechanism, and a method to select and summarize the information. Wherever possible, utility programs should be used for this purpose.

Task 7: Assess the Effectiveness of Testing

Analyze the raw information in order to draw conclusions about the effectiveness of systems testing. Using this analysis, the appropriate party can take action. The summarized results must be output into a form for presentation that provides an assessment of testing. The judgmental approach normally expresses the assessment in terms of an opinion of the assessor. The user reaction provides the same type of assessment and normally includes examples that illustrate good or poor testing performance. The problems and compliance to standards approaches normally express the assessment in terms of what has or has not happened; for example, there is a known number of problems, or X standards have been violated in a test process. Metrics assess testing by quantitatively showing the effectiveness of the test process.

Using Testing Metrics

Testing metrics are relationships that show a high positive correlation to that which is being measured. Metrics are used in almost all disciplines as a basis of performing an assessment of the effectiveness of some process. Some of the more common assessments familiar to most people in other disciplines include:

- **Blood pressure (medicine).** Identifies effectiveness of the heart and can be used to assess the probability of heart attack and stroke.

- **Student aptitude test (education).** Measures a student's achievement in high school studies.

- **Net profit (accounting).** Measures the success of the organization in profiting within its field or industry.

- **Accidents per day (safety).** Measures the effectiveness of an organization's safety program.

A metric is a mathematical number that shows a relationship between two variables. For example, the SAT score used by many colleges to determine whether to accept a student shows the student's mastery of topics as compared to the total number of topics on the examination. And gross profit is a number showing a relationship between income and the costs associated to produce that income.

The metric must then be compared to some norm or standard. For example, someone's blood pressure is compared to the norm for that person's age and sex. The metric by itself is meaningless until it can be compared to some norm. The net profit metric is expressed as a percent, such as 10 percent net profit. This does not take on its true meaning until you know that other companies in that industry are making 20 percent, 10 percent, or 5 percent. Once the norm for the industry is known, then the gross profit metric takes on more meaning.

The list that follows briefly explains 34 suggested metrics for evaluating application system testing:

1. **User participation (user participation test time divided by total test time).** Metric identifies the user involvement in testing.

2. **Instructions coverage (number of instructions exercised versus total number of instructions).** Metric shows the number of instructions in the program that were executed during the test process.

3. **Number of tests (number of tests versus size of system tested).** Metric identifies the number of tests required to evaluate a unit of information services work.

4. **Paths coverage (number of paths tested versus total number of paths).** Metric indicates the number of logical paths that were executed during the test process.

5. **Acceptance criteria tested (acceptance criteria verified versus total acceptance criteria).** Metric identifies the number of user-identified criteria that were evaluated during the test process.

6. **Test cost (test cost versus total system cost).** Metric identifies the amount of resources used in the development or maintenance process allocated to testing.

7. **Cost to locate defect (cost of testing versus the number of defects located in testing).** Metric shows the cost to locate a defect.

8. **Achieving budget (anticipated cost of testing versus the actual cost of testing).** Metric determines the effectiveness of using test dollars.

9. **Detected production errors (number of errors detected in production versus application system size).** Metric determines the effectiveness of system testing in deleting errors from the application prior to it being placed into production.

10. **Defects uncovered in testing (defects located by testing versus total system defects).** Metric shows the percent of defects that were identified as a result of testing.

11. **Effectiveness of test to business (loss due to problems versus total resources processed by the system).** Metric shows the effectiveness of testing in reducing system losses in relationship to the resources controlled by the system being tested.

12. **Asset value of test (test cost versus assets controlled by system).** Metric shows the relationship between what is spent for testing as a percent versus the assets controlled by the system being tested.

13. **Rerun analysis (rerun hours versus production hours).** Metric shows the effectiveness of testing as a relationship to rerun hours associated with undetected defects.

14. **Abnormal termination analysis (installed changes versus number of application system abnormal terminations).** Metric shows the effectiveness of testing in reducing system abnormal terminations through maintenance changes.

15. **Source code analysis (number of source code statements changed versus the number of tests).** Metrics show the efficiency of testing as a basis of the volume of work being tested.

16. **Test efficiency (number of tests required versus the number of system errors).** Metric shows the efficiency of tests in uncovering errors.

17. **Startup failure (number of program changes versus the number of failures the first time the changed program is run in production).** Metric shows the ability of the test process to eliminate major defects from the application being tested.

18. **System complaints (system complaints versus number of transactions processed).** Metric shows the effectiveness of testing and reducing third-party complaints.

19. **Test automation (cost of manual test effort versus total test cost).** Metric shows the percent of testing performed manually and that performed automatically.

20. **Requirements phase testing effectiveness (requirements test cost versus number of errors detected during requirements phase).** Metric shows the value returned for testing during the requirements phase.

21. **Design phase testing effectiveness (design test cost versus number of errors detected during design phase).** Metric shows the value returned for testing during the design phase.

22. **Program phase testing effectiveness (program test cost versus number of errors detected during program phase).** Metric shows the value returned for testing during the program phase.

23. **Test phase testing effectiveness (test cost versus number of errors detected during test phase).** Metric shows the value returned for testing during the test phase.

24. **Installation phase testing effectiveness (installation test cost versus number of errors detected during installation phase).** Metric shows the value returned for testing during the installation.

25. **Maintenance phase testing effectiveness (maintenance test cost versus number of errors detected during maintenance phase).** Metric shows the value returned for testing during the maintenance phase.

26. **Defects uncovered in test (defects uncovered versus size of systems).** Metric shows the number of defects uncovered through testing based on a unit of work.

27. **Untested change problems (number of tested changes versus problems attributable to those changes).** Metric shows the effect of testing system changes.

28. **Tested change problems (number of tested changes versus problems attributable to those changes).** Metric shows the effect of testing system changes.

29. **Loss value of test (loss due to problems versus total resources processed by system).** Metric shows the result of testing in reducing losses as related to the resources processed by the system.

30. **Scale of ten (assessment of testing rated on a scale of ten).** Metric shows people's assessment of the effectiveness of testing on a scale on which 1 is poor and 10 is outstanding.

31. **Defect removal efficiency (assessment of identifying defects in the phase in which they occurred).** Metric shows the percentage of defects uncovered by the end of a development phase versus the total number of defects made in that single phase of development.

32. **Defects made by testers (assesses the ability of testers to perform test processes in a defect-free manner).** Metric shows the number of defects made by testers as a relationship to the size of the project in which they are testing.

33. **Achieving schedule (anticipated completion date for testing versus actual completion date of testing).** Metric defines the ability of testers to meet their completion schedule or checkpoints for the test process.

34. **Requirements traceability (monitor requirements throughout the test process).** Metric shows at various points throughout the development process the percent of requirements moved to the next phase that was correctly implemented, requirements missing in the next phase, requirements implemented incorrectly in the next phase, and requirements included in the next phase that were not included in the previous phase.

Check Procedures

Work Paper 13-1 is a quality control checklist for this step. It is designed so that Yes responses indicate good test practices, and No responses warrant additional investigation. A Comments column is provided to explain No responses and to record results of investigation. The N/A column is used when the checklist item is not applicable to the test situation.

Output

The bottom line of assessment is making application system testing more effective. This is performed by a careful analysis of the results of testing, and then taking action to correct identified weaknesses. Facts precede action, and testing in many organizations has suffered from the lack of facts. Once those facts have been determined, action should be taken.

The *measurement first, action second* concept is effective when the measurement process is specific. The measurement must be able to determine the effect of action. For example, the metric approach fulfills this requirement in that it shows very specific relationships. Using this concept if a tester takes action by changing one of the metric variables, he or she can quickly measure the result of that action.

Changing the variable in one metric can normally be measured by the change in another metric. For example, if a tester detects a higher number of defects than desirable after the system goes operational, he or she should take action. The action taken might be to increase the number of instructions exercised during testing. Obviously, this increases test cost with the hopeful objective of reducing undetected defects prior to operation. If it can be shown that increasing the number of instructions exercised does, in fact, reduce the number of defects in an operation system, that action can be considered desirable and should be extended. On the other hand, if increasing the number of instructions executed does not reduce the number of defects undetected prior to production, then those resources have not been used effectively and that action should be eliminated and another action tried.

Using the measurement/action approach, the tester can manipulate the variables until the desired result is achieved. Without the measurement, management can never be sure that intuitive or judgmental actions are effective. The measurement/action approach works and should be followed to improve the test process.

Guidelines

For the process of evaluating test effectiveness to be valuable, testers must recognize that they make defects in performing the test processes. Testers need to understand the nature of test defects and be able to name them. For example, a test defect might be preparing incorrect test data.

Summary

This step concludes the recommended seven-step testing process. The results of this step will be recommendations to improve the full seven steps within the testing process. Not only must the seven testing steps be improved, but the steps taken to improve the effectiveness of testing also require improvement.

The improvement process begins by first adopting the seven-step process, and continues by customizing the process to your IT organization's specific needs. The experience gained will identify opportunities for improvement. Part Four addresses special testing needs based on the use of specific technologies and approaches.

WORK PAPER 13-1   Post-Implementation Analysis Quality Control Checklist

	YES	NO	N/A	COMMENTS
1. Does management support the concept of continuous improvement to test processes?				
2. Have resources been allocated to improving the test processes?				
3. Has a single individual been appointed responsible for overseeing the improvement of test processes?				
4. Have the results of testing been accumulated over time?				
5. Do the results of testing include the types of items identified in the input section of this chapter?				
6. Do testers have adequate tools to summarize, analyze, and report the results of previous testing?				
7. Do the results of that analysis appear reasonable?				
8. Is the analysis performed on a regular basis?				
9. Are the results of the analysis incorporated into improved test processes?				
10. Is data maintained so there can be a determination as to whether those installed improvements do in fact improve the test processes?				

Incorporating Specialized Testing Responsibilities

CHAPTER 14

Software Development Methodologies

From a tester's perspective, the software development methodology used significantly affects software testing. Suppose, for instance, that one could develop a continuum of software development methodologies from no methodology to a perfect methodology. The perfect methodology produces no defects, thus negating the need for testing. In contrast, with no methodology, one must exhaustively test to provide an opinion as to whether to place the software in operation.

The reliability of the software development process also depends significantly on whether the development team complies with the process. In many organizations, compliance with the process is not required. Those organizations use a system development methodology as a guideline, selecting those components the project staff wants to use and deleting those components they do not want to use. The benefits of using the system development methodology are significantly reduced when the methodologies are not complied with during development.

How Much Testing Is Enough?

This section covers the following six topics, each of which can affect the amount of testing required for software development:

- Methodology types
- Defining requirements
- Methodology maturity

- Project staff competency
- Project staff experience
- Configuration-management controls

This section explains why these six components affect the amount of testing required. Following this discussion, another section allows the tester to assess these six components and thus estimate the amount of testing required.

Software Development Methodologies

A software development methodology provides guidelines for how to build software. In the early days of computing, software project managers had two responsibilities: to develop a process for building software, and to follow that process to project completion. Because all project leaders need a software development methodology, standardized processes were developed. Some organizations create their own software development methodology, whereas others acquire the methodology for building software from suppliers.

This section discusses the following topics:

- The "Overview" subsection identifies the challenges a project manager faces, the guidelines for choosing a methodology, and the project manager's responsibilities when applying a specific methodology.
- The "Methodology Types" subsection concisely describes several common software development methodologies.
- The "Software Development Life Cycle" subsection covers six common phases in the software development life cycle (including responsibilities, external development services, and documentation within those phases).

Overview

Many software project managers use the development methodology as a guideline rather than a process that requires strict adherence. If these processes are not followed as written, the developers have to create the process or parts of the process to build software.

Therefore, software project managers should follow the developmental methodology for these reasons:

- To focus the entire effort on building software, not on building a developmental process
- To achieve consistency, which results because all projects use the developmental methodology
- To improve the developmental methodology itself, which is possible only if the organization gains experience (positive and negative) by following the methodology and learning from that experience

When developmental methodologies are used only as guidelines, improvements to the methodologies are unnecessary. However, when compliance is required, defect-prone components are quickly replaced by more effective developmental processes.

Thousands of different methodologies are used to build software. No single developmental methodology has proven to be best. Most work, but some may not fit the needs of the specific project. This creates a dilemma for the software project manager.

The solution is for an organization to standardize on one or a few development methodologies. For example, they may have a development methodology for a waterfall development effort, and another methodology for a prototype effort. Because of the unique characteristics of specific projects, a standardized methodology may not be effective for the whole project.

An *agile development methodology* is widely promoted. Although no definition of an agile development methodology has been generally accepted, it means flexibility in using the development methodology. In other words, the users have options when they are applying an agile development methodology.

Most organizations believe that agile development is effective only in small projects with a small number of developers. Currently, this is how most agile methodologies are used. Some, however, believe that agile techniques can be used for larger projects.

Methodology Types

Many different methodologies are available for developing software. The project manager must select the developmental methodology most appropriate to the project needs. Each methodology has advantages and disadvantages. A concise description of the six most common developmental methodologies follows.

Waterfall Methodology

The waterfall methodology is the oldest software development methodology. It follows a logical progression of defining requirements, designing the system, building the system, testing the system, and placing the system in operation. It is primarily used for the development of systems that do batch processing. The waterfall methodology assumes that at the end of the requirements phase, requirements for development are known.

Prototyping Methodology

The prototyping methodology assumes that the user does not have a rigid definition of requirements. Prototyping applies in an "I'll know it when I see it" environment. Prototyping produces an operational methodology of the user's requirements as currently defined. The user can then see the system in operation and make changes for another generation or prototype of the system. The development of prototype versions continues until the user believes it contains the requirements desired by the user. Most agree that the prototype should not be put into operation as is, because a prototype methodology lacks the necessary controls to ensure correct and high-quality processing.

Rapid Application Development Methodology

The objective of rapid application development (RAD) is a quick turnaround time with emphasis on requirements definition, which is accomplished by heavy user involvement throughout all developmental phases. RAD makes extensive use of development tools. Much of its effectiveness and reduced cycle time is due to rapid movement from one phase of development to the next.

Spiral Methodology

The spiral methodology focuses on objectives, alternatives, constraints, and risks. The spiral methodology, like RAD, heavily involves the user. At each part of the spiral development, the risks, constraints, and alternative methods are evaluated. The objective is to use the best possible system from a business perspective, although development may require a longer development cycle than RAD.

Incremental Methodology

The objective of the incremental methodology is to develop the system in parts (or increments). It is effective when single parts of the system can be used immediately without the full system being developed or when a particular part is critical to the success of the overall system, but there's some uncertainty as to whether that part can be effectively developed. The incremental method can be effective in reducing the risk of investing and building an entire system when the outcome is questionable.

The V Methodology

The V methodology is mostly associated with software testing. It develops two processes: one for building the system, and one for testing the system. The two processes are then interrelated as a V methodology. The V shows development on one side and testing on the other side. For example, during the requirements stage of development, the software acceptance testing side is developed. The V methodology assumes that approximately one-half of the total development effort will be spent on testing. The V then integrates testing so that testing is more effective and defects are uncovered earlier in the developmental process.

Software Development Life Cycle

Although no single generally accepted developmental methodology exists, all development methodologies share some attributes. The most common shared attributes are the phases or steps required, the individuals involved in development and their roles and responsibilities, and the deliverables produced.

The following example represents a large software development process. Project managers should have a general understanding of these common attributes. However, project managers should not expect that all systems can be developed in accordance with this specific software development life cycle (SDLC) methodology. This methodology is for explanatory purposes only. The following SDLC topics are discussed:

- Six common phases of the SDLC
- Roles and responsibilities

The phases described in this guide are intended to clarify the broad functions or activities that occur during the development of an automated system. The following six phases cover activities commonly performed.

Phase 1: Initiation

The initiation phase begins with the recognition of a problem and the identification of a need. During this phase, the need is validated, and alternative functional concepts to satisfy the need are explored, recommended, and approved. The decision to pursue a solution must be based on a clear understanding of the problem, a preliminary investigation of alternative solutions (including non–computer-based solutions), and a comparison of the expected benefits versus the cost (including design, construction, operation, and potential risks) of the solution. At this stage, the sensitivity of the data controlled by the SDLC under consideration should be evaluated.

Phase 2: Definition

In this phase, the functional requirements are defined, and detailed planning for the development of an operable SDLC is begun. Functional requirements and processes to be automated are documented and approved by appropriate senior management before an SDLC development effort is started. Requirements identification is iterative, as is the analysis of potential risk, and involves those who identify and solve problems. It is critical that internal control and specific security requirements be identified during this process. Requirements may be, and commonly are, modified in later phases as a better understanding of the problem is gained.

Also during the definition phase, a Project Plan is prepared that describes the unique SDLC methodology to be used during the life of the particular project. It specifies a strategy for managing SDLC development, certification, and accreditation. It defines goals and activities for all subsequent phases, and includes resource estimates during each phase, intermediate milestones, and methods for design, documentation, problem reporting, and change control. Resource planning for VV&T (verification, validation, and testing) should be included here.

Phase 3: System Design

The activities performed during this phase result in a specification of the problem solution. The solution provides a specific high-level definition, including information aggregates, information flows and logical processing steps, and all major interfaces and their inputs and outputs. The purpose is to refine, resolve deficiencies in, define additional details in, and package the solution. The design specifications describe the physical solution (algorithms and data structures) in such a way that it can be implemented in code with little or no need for additional analysis.

Organizations should define and approve security requirements prior to acquiring or starting formal development of the applications. The VV&T goals are also identified during this phase, and a plan for achieving these goals is developed. The Project Plan and Risk Analysis are reviewed and revised as required given the scope and complexity of the solution formulated.

Phase 4: Programming and Testing

This phase results in programs that are ready for testing, evaluation, certification, and installation. Programming is the process of implementing the detailed design specifications into code. Completed code then undergoes unit testing, as described in the revised VV&T Plan (also completed in this phase), and integration and system testing in Phase 5. User and Maintenance Manuals are prepared during this phase, as is a preliminary Installation Plan that specifies the approach to, and details of, the installation of the SDLC.

Phase 5: Evaluation and Acceptance

In this phase, integration and system testing of the SDLC occurs. For validation purposes, the system should be executed on test data, and the SDLC field tested in one or more representative operational sites.

Phase 6: Installation and Operation

The purpose of this final life cycle phase is to:

- Implement the approved operational plan, including extension or installation at other sites.
- Continue approved operation.
- Budget adequately.
- Control all changes and maintain or modify the SDLC during its remaining life.

Problem reporting, change requests, and other change-control mechanisms are used to facilitate the systematic correction and evolution of the SDLC. In addition, periodic performance measurement and evaluation activities are performed to ensure that the system continues to meet its requirements in a cost-effective manner in the context of a changing system environment. These reviews may be conducted by either the quality assurance (QA) staff or the audit unit or both.

Roles and Responsibilities

Software project managers must recognize that organizational structures vary significantly from organization to organization. The functions covered in this section are described as "job-title-related" functions so that organizations can look at them as specific job titles, if they have an equivalent job, or as functions that must be performed regardless of whether the specific job exists. The list is not meant to be all-inclusive, nor does it preclude smaller organizations or organizational units from combining participants or roles.

The rationale for describing the participants is to identify the role of each key participant. The project manager should verify that the respective SDLC participants have each performed his or her appropriate role. The following list describes all the participants:

- **Sponsor/user.** The sponsor/user is responsible for initially identifying the need that the SDLC must meet. The sponsor/user must identify various alternative solutions to the problem and determine the feasibility and cost/benefit of the various alternatives. The sponsor/user also conducts or oversees a Risk Analysis to assess the potential vulnerabilities of the system or application under development. The analysis must be continually updated or revised during the SDLC to ensure the inclusion of appropriate internal controls and security safeguards.

The sponsor/user is ultimately responsible for accepting (accrediting) the system as complete, meeting its requirements, and being ready for operational use. Depending on the particular system, the sponsor/user may be located at various levels in the organization.

- **Project manager.** The project manager is responsible for seeing that a system is properly designed to meet the sponsor/user's needs, and is developed on schedule. The project manager is responsible for seeing that all system documentation is prepared as the system is being developed. If the system is developed either in-house or by a contractor, the project manager is responsible for certifying that the delivered system meets all technical specifications, including security, and obtaining technical assistance from the IT manager as necessary.

- **System security specialist (SSS).** This individual is responsible, at the program or operational level, for ensuring that a system complies with the organization's computer/system security policy. The SSS approves design reviews to ensure that 1) the design meets approved security specifications and system tests, and 2) administrative, physical, and technical requirements are adequate prior to installation of the system.

- **Internal control specialist (ICS).** This individual is responsible, at the operational level, for seeing that a system complies with the organization's internal control policy. The ICS ensures that a system meets basic standards for documentation, recording of transactions, execution of transactions, separation of duties, access to resources, and all other internal control requirements.

- **Contracting officer.** The contracting officer is responsible for awarding and managing vendor contracts to provide part or all of the system development activity that is not in-house. The contract might also provide for the procurement of system software required by a new application. The contracting officer, in either case, is responsible for seeing that the vendor or contractor complies with the terms of the contract and that the deliverables are provided on time.

- **Information technology (IT) manager.** The IT manager is the technical individual responsible for the automatic data processing (ADP) installations and operations of an organization's programs (i.e., they are responsible for the operation of the data processing center and the management of the systems analysts, programmers, and so on). The IT organization may actually develop parts of the SDLC or may provide technical support to the project manager and sponsor/user during the system's life cycle.

- **Quality assurance (QA) specialist.** The operations-level QA staff is responsible for assuring the sponsor/user that an application system is developed in accordance with the system's stated objectives, contains the needed internal controls and security to produce consistently reliable results, and operates in conformance with requirements and data processing procedures. Quality assurance, as defined in the SDLC matrix, is the function that establishes the responsibilities and methods used to ensure quality in data processing products. The QA specialist may or may not be personally involved in establishing these responsibilities and methods.

The QA charter should allow for independent reviews. QA staff should actively participate in reviewing the development of new systems or applications and the significant modification of existing systems. (Coordination with security/audit and VV&T participants is essential to avoid duplication of effort.) In addition, the QA staff should ensure data integrity of systems. The presence and effective functioning of the QA staff will determine the nature and extent of audit involvement, in that they commonly perform similar functions.

Defining Requirements

Software projects require that requirements be well defined, both for the system's analysts and the users. The objective of this section is to help develop a requirements definition that meets the needs of the software project. This section explains how to identify what is a requirement, as well as what is not a requirement.

The following are working definitions of *requirements* as used in a software project:

- **Requirement.** An attribute or characteristic to be possessed by a product or service

- **Requirements definition.** A process by which customers and producers reach an understanding of requirements

- **Statement of requirements.** A specification deliverable produced as a result of a requirements definition

These definitions identify three unique aspects of requirements. The *requirements definition* is the process, a predefined series of tasks that leads to a predefined deliverable, which the IT analyst and the customer go through to identify the requirements. These requirements are then documented in the deliverable known as the *statement of requirements*.

Categories

The following four requirements categories provide a structure for discussing requirements. These categories do not represent rigid boundaries, and most people will have legitimate concerns in all four while predominantly concentrating their efforts in one.

- **Business requirements.** The customers for the business requirements are the business users. Because we're talking about what the system "must do," it's the business users who are uniquely positioned to define these requirements. The IT staff, to the extent that they have learned or are learning the business, can assist in clarifying and defining these requirements; but only active business users can own them. The list of requirements includes all of the needs and wants of the user community. Although the definition of these requirements is generally presented in a "best-case" scenario, the priority of these requirements is sorted so that needs are addressed before nice-to-haves.

- **Implementation requirements.** The customers for the implementation requirements are IT's management because they are responsible for providing future
  production services to the business community. These are the things that the system "must be," including day-to-day production service levels as well as training, enhancement, and maintenance activity; and disaster recovery and capacity
  planning. Although the business requirements present the best-case scenario,
  implementation requirements generally identify the "target-case" scenario. Business users often express direct concerns about these implementation specifics.
  The strength of this concern is usually directly proportional to the level of implementation problems associated with other application systems already in use.

- **Constraint requirements.** Constraints are generally the requirements of life
  placed on the project from the outside. The customers for these requirements
  are management—executive, line business, and information systems—who are
  allocating resources to the project effort. Typical constraint requirement examples include budgets, schedules, and operating environments. These realities
  generally force the "worst-case" scenario.

- **Enterprise-wide requirements.** Requirements applicable to all software systems, such as security.

Attributes

This subsection discusses requirement attributes from three different perspectives: a
systems analyst perspective, a tester perspective, and international industry standards.

Desired Attributes: A Systems Analyst Perspective

Attributes of a requirement do not define what something "should do." Attributes
define what something "should be." Desired attributes of a requirement define the
positive properties that a requirement should have, such as the following:

Clear

Complete

Consistent

Correct

Modifiable

Pure

Relevant

Testable

Traceable

Usable

Later, we discuss project-verification strategies that focus on ensuring that requirements reasonably embody these attributes.

Requirements Measures: A Tester's Perspective

Verifying and validating requirements is ultimately a subjective assessment based on the agreement of all stakeholders. By providing measurement scales that focus on different aspects of requirements quality, the subjective assessments can be made more objective. Each requirements measure isolates a single aspect of the requirements so that quantitative assessments can be collected and prioritized.

- **Criticality.** The requirement can be tied directly to an organizational goal or critical success factor. It's not just a nice-to-have. Failure to conform to the requirement would hurt the business.

- **Measurability.** It's possible to tell whether the requirement is being satisfied. Reasonable people would not disagree about the level of conformance.

- **Controllability.** It's possible to differentiate systemic from random variation in the processes surrounding the requirement. This means that we can identify future nonconformance and categorize them according to frequency and severity.

- **Completeness.** All items needed for the specification of the requirements of the solution to the problem have been identified.

- **Correctness.** Each item in the requirements specification is free from error.

- **Clearness.** Each item in the requirements specification is exact and not vague. There is a single interpretation of each item in the requirements specification; the meaning of each item in the requirements specification is understood; the specification is easy to read.

- **Consistency.** No item in the requirements specification conflicts with another item in the specification.

- **Relevance.** Each item in the requirements specification is pertinent to the problem and its solution.

- **Testability.** During program development and acceptance testing, it will be possible to determine whether the item in the requirements specification has been satisfied.

- **Traceability.** Each item in the requirements specification can be traced to its origin in the problem environment.

- **Pureness.** The requirements specification is a statement of the requirements that must be satisfied by the problem solution, and is not obscured by proposed solutions to the problem.

- **Usability.** Each item can be understood by its user and contains the information needed by the user.

- **Modifiability.** The requirements specification is expressed in such a way that each item can be changed without dramatically affecting other items.

International Standards

The quality of a requirement can be measured on a continuum. A standard that dictates that every requirement must be defined to a level that supports statistical process control would be unreasonable. However, we should strive to define requirements that support the most rigorous review possible.

Several internationally recognized organizations are currently developing and publishing standards for the requirements definition process. One standard described is the Institute of Electrical and Electronics Engineers (IEEE) *IEEE1233: Guide for Developing System Requirements Specification*.

The IEEE has several process standards that relate to requirements. Three standards are explained here:

- **IEEE 1233 (4.2): Properties of System Requirements Specifications (SRS)**

  - **Unique Set.** Each requirement is stated only once.

  - **Normalized.** Requirements should not overlap; that is, they shall not refer to other requirements or capabilities of other requirements.

  - **Linked Set.** Explicit relationships should be defined among individual requirements to show how the requirements are related to form a complete system.

  - **Complete.** An SRS should include all the requirements identified by the customer, as well as those needed for definition of the system.

  - **Consistent.** The SRS content should be consistent and noncontradictory in the level of detail, style of statements, and presentation of material.

  - **Bounded.** The boundaries, scope, and context for the set of requirements should be identified.

  - **Configurable.** Versions should be maintained across time and instances of the SRS.

- **IEEE 1233 (4.3.1): Organizing Requirements**

  - Identify requirements that are derived from other requirements.

  - Organize requirements of different levels of detail into their appropriate levels.

  - Verify the completeness of the set of requirements.

  - Identify inconsistencies among requirements.

  - Clearly identify the capabilities, conditions, and constraints for each requirement.

  - Develop a common understanding with the customer of the purpose and objectives of the set of requirements.

  - Identify requirements that will complete the SRS.

- **IEEE 1233 (4.4): Intended Use**

  - During systems design, requirements are allocated to subsystems, hardware, software, operations, and other major components of the system.

  - During the system build, the SRS is used to write appropriate system verification plans for all components.

  - During implementation, test procedures are defined using the SRS.

Methodology Maturity

Many organizations have developed classification schemes to evaluate the maturity of a software development methodology. One of the most successful was developed by the Software Engineering Institute (SEI) under a grant from the U.S. Department of Defense. The SEI methodology has itself matured over time and is now referred to as the CMMI (Capability Maturity Model Integrated).

The SEI methodology has four defined levels of maturity and one undefined level. For the defined levels, SEI has described the "focus" for achieving that particular level of maturity.

Note that the undefined level of maturity is level 1, referred to as *Initial*. There are no requirements for level 1; everyone who develops software begins at this level. The SEI defines what must be achieved as levels 2, 3, 4, and 5. The focus of levels 2, 3, 4, and 5 follows:

- **Level 2: Managed.** Provide more consistency and less variability in software systems by initiating good project-management processes.

- **Level 3: Defined.** At this level, the organization's attempts to minimize process variability and maximize the effectiveness and efficiency of developed software. At level 3, the processes are standardized, and a high level of compliance to process is required.

- **Level 4: Quantitatively managed.** At this level, the processes are mature enough that they can produce reliable and quantitative data. Therefore, management can rely on the quantitative data produced by the developmental processes, and therefore can take action on the quantitative data.

- **Level 5: Optimizing.** At this level, the IT organization can build software at the cost it says it can build it for, and implement it by the scheduled implementation date. Having this level of processing sophistication enables the organization to innovate new and unique ways to build software more effectively and efficiently.

Table 14-1 shows the process areas for each level that need to be developed and deployed before that level can be considered mature. For example, level 2 requires configuration management, level 3 risk management, level 4 quantitative project management, and level 5 causal analysis and resolution. Note that it is not necessary to have all process areas fully proficient to be evaluated as being at a particular maturity level.

NOTE The SEI model is continually maturing; for an updated version, visit www.sei.cmu.edu.

The methodology also is not meant to imply that the process areas only begin at the level at which they are defined. For example, validation or dynamic testing would be performed at levels 1 and 2. It is listed at level 3 to indicate that a process area such as validation itself is a mature process that can be relied on. Validation at levels 1 and 2 would not be expected to be nearly as effective as validation at level 3.

Another example is quantitative project management occurring at level 4. This does not mean that project managers do not use quantitative data until level 4. Exactly the opposite is true. At level 1, project managers use quantitative data for budgeting and scheduling. What it does mean is that the processes are not mature enough to produce reliable and valid data for use in managing projects. If project managers rely exclusively on the quantitative data produced at levels 1 and 2, they probably will make many erroneous project decisions.

Table 14-1 CMMI SS Version 1.1 Staged Representation: Process Areas by Maturity Level

LEVEL	FOCUS	PROCESS AREA
5 Optimizing	Continuous Process Improvement	Organizational Innovation and Deployment Causal Analysis and Resolution
4 Quantitatively Managed	Quantitative Management	Organizational Process Performance Quantitative Project Management
3 Defined	Process Standardization	Requirements Development Technical Solution Product Integration Verification Validation Organizational Process Focus Organizational Process Definition Organizational Training Integrated Project Management Risk Management Integrated Teaming Integrated Supplier Management Decision Analysis and Resolution Organizational Environment for Integration
2 Managed	Basic Project Management	Requirements Management Project Planning Project Monitoring and Control Supplier Agreement Management Measurement and Analysis Process and Product Quality Assurance Configuration Management
1 Initial		No Requirements; No Specific Process Areas

Competencies Required

Project management is the application of skills, tools, and techniques to meet successfully or exceed the objectives of a project in the specified time frame at a specified cost. It aims to meet the needs of the client. Another view is that software development refers to the definition, planning, control, and conclusion of a project.

To understand competencies needed to effectively develop software, examine the skills associated with successful software project managers as defined by the Software Quality Institute. The Quality Assurance Institute has also defined skills specifically needed by software developers and skills specifically needed by software testers. This section has divided all these skills into the following five categories:

- **Process-Selection Skills**

  Assessing processes

  Awareness of process standards

  Defining the product

  Evaluating alternative processes

  Managing requirements

  Managing subcontractors

  Performing the initial assessment

  Selecting methods and tools

  Tailoring processes

  Tracking product quality

  Understanding development activities

- **Project-Management Skills**

  Building a work breakdown structure

  Documenting plans

  Estimating cost

  Estimating effort

  Managing risks

  Monitoring development

  Scheduling

  Selecting metrics

  Selecting project-management tools

  Tracking processes

  Tracking project progress

- **People-Management Skills**

  Appraising performance

  Handling intellectual property

  Holding effective meetings

  Interaction and communication

  Leadership

  Managing change

  Negotiating successfully

  Planning careers

  Presenting effectively

  Recruiting

  Selecting a team

  Team building

- **Building Software Skills**

  Understanding development methodologies

  Initiating software projects

  Defining software requirements

  Designing systems

  Building systems

  Developing user documentation and training

  Installing software systems

  Changing software systems

- **Testing Software Systems**

  Developing software testing principles and concepts

  Building the test environment

  Managing the test project

  Test planning

  Executing the test plan

  Monitoring test status, analysis, and reporting

  Testing user acceptance

  Testing software developed by outside organizations

  Testing software controls and the adequacy of security procedures

  Testing new technologies

Staff Experience

The project staff is defined as the stakeholders who have a vested interest in the success of the project. Primarily this includes the software development staff and the user staff.

A good process used by an untrained individual may not work; and if it does work, it might not be nearly as efficient or effective as that process when used by someone with experience. For example, if you were trained in how to change a tire on your car, you could perform that process effectively and efficiently. However, if you've not been trained, you may have difficulty finding the jack, the tire, and other tools necessary for the tire-change process. An experienced tire changer may be able to change a tire in 10 minutes; the inexperienced tire changer may take an hour, even though the process is mature and fully defined in the owner's manual.

Experienced user staff should be knowledgeable in the software development methodology and their role and responsibilities in the building of software systems. Development project staff members need to be experienced in the business of the users and the processes and tools used to build the software.

No single method can fully assess experience. Some criteria to evaluate experience are as follows:

Number of software systems built

Training courses attended

Like work performed through many development cycles

Years of experience

Professional certifications

Configuration-Management Controls

Configuration management (CM) is one of the components of software project management that differentiates software project management from general project management. There are similarities in controlling change, but CM involves much more. It includes maintaining an inventory of the items included in the total project configuration.

Basic CM Requirements

Project managers must implement an internal CM system for the control of all configuration documentation, physical media, and physical parts representing or comprising the product. For software, the system must address the evolving developmental configuration and support environments (engineering, implementation, and test) used to generate and test the product. The product manager's CM system must consist of the following elements:

Configuration identification

Configuration control

Configuration-status accounting

Configuration audits

Configuration Identification

Configuration identification (CI) includes the following:

- Selection of CIs
- Determination of the types of configuration documentation required for each CI
- Issuance of numbers and other identifiers affixed to the CIs
- Technical documentation that comprises the CIs' configuration documentation

As a part of the configuration identification process, the project manager must determine the documentation that will be used to establish the configuration baseline(s) required by the contract.

The project manager must also identify the developmental configuration for each CI.

Configuration Control

The project manager must apply internal configuration-control measures to the configuration documentation for each CI. The project manager must apply configuration-control measures to each baselined CI, and its configuration documentation, in accordance with this standard. The configuration process must:

- Ensure effective control of all CIs and their approved configuration documentation
- Provide effective means, as applicable, for the following:
  - Proposing changes to CIs.
  - Requesting deviations or *waivers* pertaining to such items.

    A *waiver* is a written authorization to accept an item, which during manufacture, or after having been submitted for inspection or acceptance, is found to depart from specified requirements, but nevertheless is considered suitable for use "as is" or after repair by an approved method.
  - Preparing notices of revision.
  - Preparing specification-change notices.
- Ensure implementation of approved changes

Configuration-Status Accounting

The project manager must implement a configuration-status accounting (CSA) system. As a minimum, the CSA system must:

- Identify the current approved configuration documentation and identification number associated with each CI.
- Record and report the status of proposed engineering changes from initiation to final approval or contractual implementation.
- Record and report the results of configuration audits to include the status and final disposition of identified discrepancies.
- Record and report the status of all critical and major requests for deviations and waivers that affect the configuration of a CI.

- Record and report implementation status of authorized changes.
- Provide the traceability of all changes from the original base-lined configuration documentation of each CI.
- Report the affectivity and installation status of configuration changes to all CIs at all locations.

Configuration Audits

Configuration audits should be performed before establishing a product baseline for the item. A configuration audit verifies that the information in the CM system is complete and in compliance with the CM standards.

Planning

The project manager must plan a CM process in accordance with the requirements of this standard, tailored appropriately for the particular CI(s), their scope and complexity, and the contracted phase(s) of the life cycle. Planning must be consistent with the objectives of a continuous improvement process, which includes the analysis of necessary means to prevent reoccurrence. The project manager's CM planning must include the following:

- The objectives of the CM process and of each applicable CM element
- The CM organization and organizational relationships
- Responsibilities and authority of CM managers
- CM resources, such as tools, techniques, and methodologies
- Coordination with internal and external organizations.
- CM policies, processes, procedures, methods, records, reports, and forms

Data Distribution and Access

The project manager must assign distribution codes in accordance with organizational standards. Access to data must be limited in accordance with the applicable distribution codes and by data rights, security requirements, and data status level.

CM Administration

The following subsections cover the administrative activities performed to fulfill the CM responsibilities.

Project Leader's CM Plan

The project leader's CM plan must be in accordance with the IT standards and describe the processes, methods, and procedures to be used to manage the functional and physical characteristics of the assigned CI(s). The project leader must:

- Develop the project leader's CM plan
- Submit the plan and changes to the IT organization CM board
- Implement the activities required by this standard in accordance with the approved plan

Work Breakdown Structure

The project leader must ensure traceability of CIs to the Work Breakdown Structure (WBS) elements.

Technical Reviews

The project leader must ensure that the CM representatives participate in all technical reviews conducted in accordance with IT standards. The role of CM in the technical review process requires that you do the following:

- Evaluate the adequacy of the type and content of the configuration documentation.
- Ascertain that the configuration documentation is under internal configuration control.
- Determine whether problems and action items identified at the review will be addressed by the project manager.

Configuration Identification

The following tasks are those configuration-identification activities performed to fulfill the CM responsibilities.

The purpose of configuration identification is to incrementally establish and maintain a definitive basis for control and status accounting for a CI throughout its life cycle. To accomplish configuration identification, the project leader must, for both hardware and software:

- Select CIs.
- Select configuration documentation to be used to define configuration baselines for each CI.
- Establish a release system for configuration documentation.
- Define and document interfaces.
- Enter each item of configuration documentation and computer software source code into a controlled developmental configuration.
- Establish the functional, allocated, and product baselines at the appropriate points in the system or CI life cycle, upon contractual implementation of the applicable configuration documentation, and in accordance with contract requirements.

- Assign identifiers to CIs and their component parts and associated configuration documentation, including revision and version numbers where appropriate. Assign serial and lot numbers, as necessary, to establish the CI for each configuration of each item of hardware and software.

- Ensure that the marking and labeling of items and documentation with their applicable identifiers enables correlation between the item, configuration documentation, and other associated data.

- Ensure that applicable identifiers are embedded in the source and object code.

CI Selection

The project leader must select CIs. Any item requiring logistics support or designated for separate procurement is a CI. However, all CIs associated with any given development project are not necessarily designated as CIs at the same point in time. Computer hardware will be treated as CIs. Computer software will be treated as CIs throughout the life of the process regardless of how the software will be stored.

Document Library

The project leader must establish a documentation library and implement procedures for controlling the documents residing within the documentation library.

Software Development Library

The project leader shall establish a software development library and implement procedures for controlling the software residing within the software development library.

Configuration Baselines

CM establishes baselines to enable project leaders to measure change(s) from the progressive definition and documentation of the requirements, and design information describing the various CIs designation for a system.

Initial Release

Configuration documentation is first released to the involved stakeholders for their review and use. The initial release includes the incorporation of related information into the configuration-status accounting information system.

Software Marking and Labeling

The marking and labeling of software will be as follows:

- Software identifier and version (and computer program identification number where applicable) will be embedded in the source code header.

- Each software medium used must be marked and labeled. For example, for magnetic disk media containing copies of tested software entities, each medium must be marked with a label that lists cross-references to applicable software identifiers of the entities it contains.

- Media copy numbers must distinguish each copy of the software media from its identical copies. Each time a new version of the software is issued, new copy numbers, starting from 1, must be assigned.

Interface Requirements

The interface requirements for the system and its configuration items must be identified as a part of the system process. Those interface requirements must be controlled by the configuration-control board during the development of the system.

Configuration Control

Configuration control is the systematic proposal, justification, evaluation, coordination, and approval or disapproval of proposed changes. The implementation of all approved changes must be controlled. Each approved and implemented change will result in a new baseline being established.

The project leader must implement a configuration-control function that ensures the following:

- Regulation of the flow of proposed changes

- Documentation of the complete impact of the proposed changes

- Release only of approved configuration changes into configuration identifications and their related configuration documentation

Configuration control begins with the establishment of a functional baseline and continues as further configuration baselines are established. Configuration control continues throughout the life cycle of the configuration identification.

Measuring the Impact of the Software Development Process

It is important for testers to measure the impact that using the software development methodology has on the resources and time needed to test effectively. If testers *believe* that a proposed test schedule and budget is inadequate, that might not result in increased resources or time. However, when testers *know* that inadequate time or resources have been allocated to testing, they can redirect the test effort to the high-risk components of the software.

Work Paper 14-1 is an assessment worksheet for evaluating the six components of software development that affect software testing. Be aware, however, that there are more than six components that affect testing. However, statistics show that if you pick a limited number of the "right" components, they will pull other components in the same direction. What this means is that the assessment questions for staff competency do not cover all the required competencies. However, if these are the right components of staff competency, the staff should also have the other related components at the same time.

When answering the items on Work Paper 14-1, respond with either Yes or No. A Yes response means that the item is there and has shown some positive results. For example, an item in the competency of project staff asks whether the staff has competency in following and using the testing process. To answer Yes, a testing process must be in place. One or more individuals on the project staff must be competent in using that testing process, and experience in using the process has demonstrated that it is effective.

For each of the five components that affect the software development methodology, there are five questions. At this point, complete Work Paper 14-1 and answer the 30 questions on that work paper.

Upon completion of the self-assessment on Work Paper 14-1, post the results to Work Paper 14-2 ("Analysis Footprint of the Impact of the Software Development Methodology on Testing"). Total the number of Yes responses for each component. Put a dot on the line (for each of the six components) that represents the total number of Yes responses for that component. For example, if you answered Yes three times for the type of software development processes, place a dot on line number 3 for the type of process.

After you have posted all six scores to Work Paper 14-2, connect the six dots. You now have the footprint of the impact of the software development methodology on testing.

The footprint shows which of the components have the most impact on software testing. Impact is represented by the items that could not be answered Yes. In the example of posting the type of process, three Yes answers were presumed. The impact would be the two No responses.

Ideally, the footprint would be the number 5 line. Any time the footprint is not pushed out to the 5 ring, there is a negative impact from the components of the software development methodology.

Noting a negative impact, the software testing group has two options. One is to eliminate the item with the "No" response; the second is to minimize the negative impact. For example, if the project team does not have anyone competent in software testing, that can be addressed by adding someone to the team who has testing competency. The second way to address a weakness is to increase the amount of testing resources or extend the schedule.

Summary

This chapter had two major objectives: to explain to testers how attributes of the software development methodology can impact the resources and schedule needed for effective and efficient software testing and to provide an instrument to measure that impact so testers could make necessary adjustments to resources and schedules. Note that after the self-assessment is has been completed, an experienced tester must analyze the results of that self-assessment and make realistic adjustments to the budgeted testing resources and schedule.

WORK PAPER 14-1   Self-Assessment of the Components of Software Development That Impact Testing

	YES	NO

Type of Development Process

1. Has a process been developed that identifies the criteria that will be used to select the most appropriate type of software development methodology for the software project being developed?

2. Does the developmental methodology selected have quality-control processes integrated into the development methodology?

3. Does the development methodology have both entrance and exit criteria?

4. Will management require compliance to the developmental methodology selected?

5. Does the developmental methodology selected have the appropriate management checkpoints so that go/no go decisions can be made at those checkpoints?

Specifying Requirements

1. Is there a standard for requirements that definitively defines the attributes of a requirement?

2. If so, is that standard consistent with good practices and industry standards for requirement definition?

3. Are there enterprise-wide requirements, such as security, privacy, and control, that will be incorporated into all software projects?

4. Is there a process that will trace requirements from the requirements phase through implementation of the software project?

5. Is there a process in place that states that the requirements-definition phase of software development will not be complete until someone attests that the requirements are testable?

Maturity of the IT Processes

1. Does your organization have all of the processes specified for CMMI level 2?

2. Does your organization have all of the processes specified for CMMI level 3?

3. Does your organization have all of the processes specified for CMMI level 4?

4. Does your organization have all of the processes specified for CMMI level 5?

5. Does your organization have a process in place that will continuously improve the processes specified in the CMMI maturity methodology?

Competency of the Project Staff

1. Is the project staff competent in selecting the software development methodology used for building a specific software system?

2. Is the project staff competent in software testing?

3. Is the project staff competent in the procedures to be followed in developing software?

4. Is the software project staff competent in managing people?

5. Is the software project staff competent in managing projects?

(continues)

WORK PAPER 14-1   *(continued)*

	YES	NO
Experience of the Project Staff		
1. Is the project staff experienced and knowledgeable in the business of the user?		
2. Is the user associated with the project competent in the methodology used by the IT organization to develop software?		
3. Will the users be involved throughout the entire software development methodology as needed, and will they be involved when needed?		
4. Is the project staff experienced in using the selected software development methodology?		
5. Have one or more members of the project staff been recognized for their experience and competency by being awarded a professional certification?		
Configuration-Management Controls		
1. Does the configuration management consist of these four elements: Configuration identification Configuration control Configuration-status accounting Configuration audits		
2. Are there internal configuration-control measures to control each configuration item?		
3. Has a configuration-management plan been developed (or will one be) for the software project being developed?		
4. Does the configuration-management system include a version control?		
5. Does the configuration-management system restrict access to authorized individuals to protect data rights, security requirements, and data-status level?		

**WORK PAPER 14-2 Analysis Footprint of the Impact of the Software
Development Methodology on Testing**

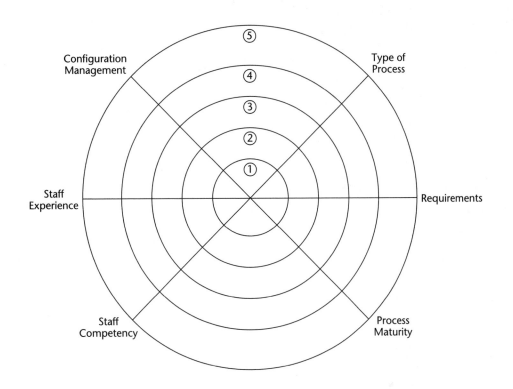

CHAPTER 15

Testing Client/Server Systems

The success of a client/server program depends heavily on both the readiness of an organization to use the technology effectively and its ability to provide clients the information and capabilities that meet their needs. If an organization is not ready to move to client/server technology, it is far better to work on changing the organization to a ready status than on installing client/server technology. Preparing the organization for client/server technology is an important component of a successful program, regardless of whether it is an organization-wide client/server technology or just a small program. If the organization is ready, the client/server approach should be evaluated prior to testing the client systems.

Overview

Figure 15-1 shows a simplified client/server architecture. There are many possible variations of the client/server architecture, but for illustration purposes, this is representative.

In this example, application software resides on the client workstations. The application server handles processing requests. The back-end processing (typically a mainframe or super-minicomputer) handles processing such as batch transactions that are accumulated and processed together at one time on a regular basis. The important distinction to note is that application software resides on the client workstation.

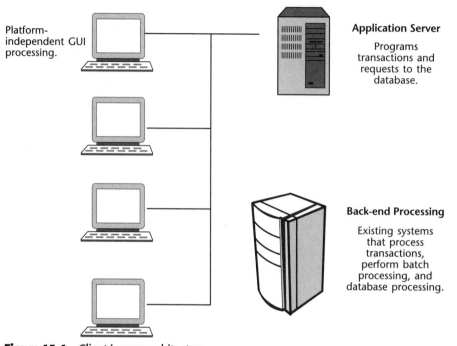

Figure 15-1   Client/server architecture.

Figure 15-1 shows the key distinction between workstations connected to the mainframe and workstations that contain the software used for client processing. This distinction represents a major change in processing control. For this reason, client/server testing must first evaluate the organization's readiness to make this control change, and then evaluate the key components of the client/server system prior to conducting tests. This chapter will provide the material on assessing readiness and key components. The actual testing of client/server systems will be achieved using the seven-step testing process.

Concerns

The concerns about client/server systems reside in the area of control. The testers need to determine that adequate controls are in place to ensure accurate, complete, timely, and secure processing of client/server software systems. The testers must address the following five concerns:

1. **Organizational readiness.** The culture is adequately prepared to process data using client/server technology. Readiness must be evaluated in the areas of management, client installation, and server support.

2. **Client installation.** The concern is that the appropriate hardware and software will be in place to enable processing that will meet client needs.

3. **Security.** There is a need for protection of both the hardware, including residence software, and the data that is processed using that hardware and software. Security must address threats from employees, outsiders, and acts of nature.

4. **Client data.** Controls must be in place to ensure that everything is not lost, incorrectly processed, or processed differently on a client workstation than in other areas of the organization.

5. **Client/server standards.** Standards must exist to ensure that all client workstations operate under the same set of rules.

Workbench

Figure 15-2 provides a workbench for testing client/server systems. This workbench can be used in steps as the client/server system is developed or concurrently after the client/server system has been developed. The workbench shows four steps, as well as the quality control procedures necessary to ensure that those four steps are performed correctly. The output will be any identified weaknesses uncovered during testing.

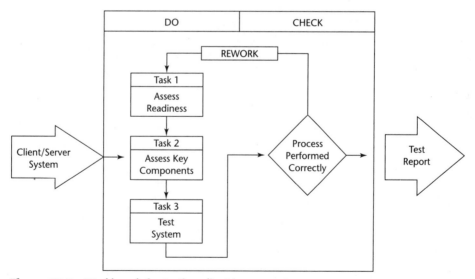

Figure 15-2   Workbench for testing client/server systems.

Input

The input to this test process will be the client/server system. This will include the server technology and capabilities, the communication network, and the client workstations that will be incorporated into the test. Because both the client and the server components will include software capabilities, the materials should provide a description of the client software, and any test results on that client software should be input to this test process.

Do Procedures

Testing client/server software involves the following three tasks:

- Assess readiness
- Assess key components
- Assess client needs

Task 1: Assess Readiness

Client/server programs should have sponsors. Ideally, these are the directors of information technology and the impacted user management. It is the responsibility of the sponsors to ensure that the organization is ready for client/server technology. However, those charged with installing the new technology should provide the sponsor with a readiness assessment. That assessment is the objective of this chapter.

The readiness assessment proposed in this chapter is a modification of the readiness approach pioneered by Dr. Howard Rubin of Rubin and Associates. There are eight dimensions to the readiness assessment, as follows:

1. **Motivation.** The level of commitment by the organization to using client/server technology to drive improvements in quality, productivity, and customer satisfaction.

2. **Investment.** The amount of monies approved/budgeted for expenditures in the client/server program.

3. **Client/server skills.** The ability of the client/server installation team to incorporate the client/server technology concepts and principles into the users' programs.

4. **User education.** Awareness by the individuals involved in any aspect of the client/server program in principles and concepts. These people need to understand how technology is used in the affected business processes.

5. **Culture.** The willingness of the organization to innovate. In other words, is the organization willing to try new concepts and new approaches, or is it more comfortable using existing approaches and technology?

6. **Client/server support staff.** The adequacy of resources to support the client/server program.

7. **Client/server aids/tools.** The availability of client/server aids and tools to perform and support the client/server program.

8. **Software development process maturity.** The ability of a software development process to produce high-quality (defect-free) software on a consistent basis.

The following section addresses how to measure process maturity. The other dimensions are more organization-dependent and require the judgment of a team of knowledgeable people in the organization.

Software Development Process Maturity Levels

Figure 15-3 illustrates the five software development process maturity levels, which have the following general characteristics:

1. **Ad hoc.** The software development process is loosely defined, and the project leader can deviate from the process whenever he or she chooses.

2. **Repeatable.** The organization has achieved a stable process with a repeatable level of quality by initiating rigorous requirements, effective project management, cost, schedules, and change control.

3. **Consistent.** The organization has defined the process as a basis for consistent implementation. Developers can depend on the quality of the deliverables.

4. **Measured.** The organization has initiated comprehensive process measurements and analysis. This is when the most significant quality improvements begin.

5. **Optimized.** The organization now has a foundation for continuing improvement and optimization of the process.

These levels have been selected because they:

- Reasonably represent the actual historical phases of evolutionary improvement of real software organizations.

- Represent a measure of improvement that is reasonable to achieve from the prior level.

- Suggest interim improvement goals and progress measurements.

- Make obvious a set of immediate improvement priorities once an organization's status in this framework is known.

Although there are many other elements to these maturity level transitions, the primary objective is to achieve a controlled and measured process as the foundation for continuing improvement.

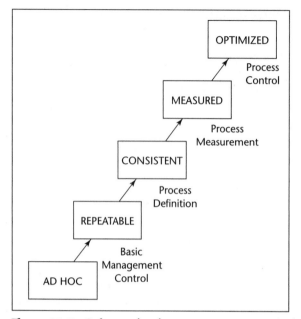

Figure 15-3 Software development process maturity levels.

This software development process maturity structure is intended for use with an assessment methodology and a management system. Assessment helps an organization identify its specific maturity status, and the management system establishes a structure for implementing the priority improvement actions. Once its position in this maturity structure is defined, the organization can concentrate on those items that will help it advance to the next level. When, for example, a software organization does not have an effective project-planning system, it may be difficult or even impossible to introduce advanced methods and technology. Poor project planning generally leads to unrealistic schedules, inadequate resources, and frequent crises. In such circumstances, new methods are usually ignored and priority is given to coding and testing.

The Ad Hoc Process (Level 1)

The ad hoc process level is unpredictable and often very chaotic. At this stage, the organization typically operates without formalized procedures, cost estimates, and project plans. Tools are neither well integrated with the process nor uniformly applied. Change control is lax, and there is little senior management exposure or understanding of the problems and issues. Because many problems are deferred or even forgotten, software installation and maintenance often present serious problems.

Although organizations at this level may have formal procedures for planning and tracking their work, there is no management mechanism to ensure that they are used. The best test is to observe how such an organization behaves in a crisis. If it abandons established procedures and essentially reverts to coding and testing, it is likely to be at the ad hoc process level. After all, if the techniques and methods are appropriate, then they should be used in a crisis; if they are not appropriate in a crisis, they should not be used at all.

One key reason why organizations behave in this fashion is that they have not experienced the benefits of a mature process and, thus, do not understand the consequences of their chaotic behavior. Because many effective software actions (such as design and code inspections or test data analysis) do not appear to directly support shipping the product, they seem expendable.

Driving an automobile is an appropriate analogy. Few drivers with any experience will continue driving for very long when the engine warning light comes on, regardless of their rush. Similarly, most drivers starting on a new journey will, regardless of their hurry, pause to consult a map. They have learned the difference between speed and progress. Without a sound plan and a thoughtful analysis of the problems, management may be unaware of ineffective software development.

Organizations at the ad hoc process level can improve their performance by instituting basic project controls. The most important are project management, management oversight, quality assurance, and change control. The fundamental role of the project management system is to ensure effective control of commitments. This requires adequate preparation, clear responsibility, a public declaration, and a dedication to performance. For software, project management starts with an understanding of the job's magnitude. In any but the simplest projects, a plan must then be developed to determine the best schedule and the anticipated resources required. In the absence of such an orderly plan, no commitment can be better than an educated guess.

A suitably disciplined software development organization must have senior management oversight. This includes review and approval of all major development plans prior to their official commitment. Also, a quarterly review should be conducted of facility-wide process compliance, installed quality performance, schedule tracking, cost trends, computing service, and quality and productivity goals by project. The lack of such reviews typically results in uneven and generally inadequate implementation of the process as well as frequent over-commitments and cost surprises.

A quality assurance group is charged with assuring management that software work is done the way it is supposed to be done. To be effective, the assurance organization must have an independent reporting line to senior management and sufficient resources to monitor performance of all key planning, implementation, and verification activities. This generally requires an organization of about 3 percent to 6 percent the size of the software organization.

Change control for software is fundamental to business and financial control as well as to technical stability. To develop quality software on a predictable schedule, requirements must be established and maintained with reasonable stability throughout the development cycle. While requirements changes are often needed, historical evidence demonstrates that many can be deferred and incorporated later. Design and code changes must be made to correct problems found in development and testing, but these must be carefully introduced. If changes are not controlled, then orderly design, implementation, and testing are impossible and no quality plan can be effective.

The Repeatable Process (Level 2)

The repeatable process has one important strength that the ad hoc process does not: It provides control over the way the organization establishes its plans and commitments. This control provides such an improvement over the ad hoc process level that the people in the organization tend to believe they have mastered the software problem. They have achieved a degree of statistical control through learning to make and meet their estimates and plans. This strength stems from using work processes that, when followed, produce consistent results. Organizations at the repeatable process level thus face major risks when they are presented with new challenges. The following are some examples of the changes that represent the highest risk at this level:

■ Unless they are introduced with great care, new tools and methods can negatively affect the testing process.

■ When the organization must develop a new kind of product, it is entering new territory. For example, a software group that has experience developing compilers will likely have design, scheduling, and estimating problems when assigned to write a real-time control program. Similarly, a group that has developed small, self-contained programs will not understand the interface and integration issues involved in large-scale projects. These changes may eliminate the lessons learned through experience.

■ Major organizational changes can also be highly disruptive. At the repeatable process level, a new manager has no orderly basis for understanding the organization's operation, and new team members must learn the ropes through word of mouth.

The key actions required to advance from the repeatable process to the next stage, the consistent process, are to establish a process group, establish a development process architecture, and introduce a family of software engineering methods and technologies.

The procedure for establishing a software development process architecture, or development life cycle, that describes the technical and management activities required for proper execution of the development process must be attuned to the specific needs of the organization. It will vary depending on the size and importance of the project as well as the technical nature of the work itself. The architecture is a structural decomposition of the development cycle into tasks, each of which has a defined set of prerequisites, functional descriptions, verification procedures, and task completion specifications. The decomposition continues until each defined task is performed by an individual or single management unit.

If they are not already in place, introduce a family of software engineering methods and technologies. These include design and code inspections, formal design methods, library control systems, and comprehensive testing methods. Prototyping should also be considered, together with the adoption of modern implementation languages.

The Consistent Process (Level 3)

With the consistent process, the organization has achieved the foundation for major and continuing progress. For example, the software teams, when faced with a crisis, will likely continue to use the process that has been defined. The foundation has now been established for examining the process and deciding how to improve it. As powerful as the process is, it is still only qualitative; there is little data to indicate how much was accomplished or how effective the process is. There is considerable debate about the value of software process measurements and the best ones to use. This uncertainty generally stems from a lack of process definition and the consequent confusion about the specific items to be measured. With a consistent process, measurements can be focused on specific tasks. The process architecture is thus an essential prerequisite to effective measurement.

The following key steps are required to advance from the consistent process level to the measured process level:

1. Establish a minimum basic set of process measurements to identify the quality and cost parameters of each process step. The objective is to quantify the relative costs and benefits of each major process activity.

2. Establish a process database and the resources to manage and maintain it. Cost and productivity data should be maintained centrally to guard against loss, to make it available for all projects, and to facilitate process quality and productivity analysis.

3. Provide sufficient process resources to gather and maintain this process data and to advise project members on its use. Assign skilled professionals to monitor the quality of the data before entry in the database and to provide guidance on analysis methods and interpretation.

4. Assess the relative quality of each product and inform management where quality targets are not being met. An independent quality assurance group should assess the quality actions of each project and track its progress against its quality plan. When this progress is compared with the historical experience on similar projects, an informed assessment can generally be made.

The Measured Process (Level 4)

In advancing from the ad hoc process through the repeatable and consistent processes to the measured process, software organizations should expect to make substantial quality improvements. The greatest potential problem with the measured process is the cost of gathering data. There are an enormous number of potentially valuable measures of the software process, but such data is expensive to gather and to maintain.

Approach data gathering with care, therefore, and precisely define each piece of data in advance. Productivity data is essentially meaningless unless explicitly defined. For example, the simple measure of lines of source code per expended development month can vary by 100 times or more, depending on the interpretation of the parameters. Lines of code need to be defined to get consistent counts. For example, if one line brings in a routine with one hundred lines of code, should that be counted as one line of code or one hundred lines of code?

When different groups gather data but do not use identical definitions, the results are not comparable, even if it makes sense to compare them. The tendency with such data is to use it to compare several groups and to criticize those with the lowest ranking. This is an unfortunate misapplication of process data. It is rare that two projects are comparable by any simple measures. The variations in task complexity caused by different product types can exceed five to one. Similarly, the cost per line of code of small modifications is often two to three times that for new programs. The degree of requirements change can make an enormous difference, as can the design status of the base program in the case of enhancements.

Process data must not be used to compare projects or individuals. Its purpose is to illuminate the product being developed and to provide an informed basis for improving the process. When such data is used by management to evaluate individuals or teams, the reliability of the data itself will deteriorate.

The two fundamental requirements for advancing from the measured process to the next level are:

1. Support automatic gathering of process data. All data is subject to error and omission, some data cannot be gathered by hand, and the accuracy of manually gathered data is often poor.

2. Use process data both to analyze and to modify the process to prevent problems and improve efficiency.

The Optimized Process (Level 5)

In varying degrees, process optimization goes on at all levels of process maturity. With the step from the measured to the optimized process, however, there is a paradigm shift. Up to this point, software development managers have largely focused on their products and will typically gather and analyze only data that directly relates to product improvement. In the optimized process, the data is available to tune the process itself. With a little experience, management will soon see that process optimization can produce major quality and productivity benefits.

For example, many types of errors can be identified and fixed far more economically by design or code inspections than by testing. Unfortunately, there is only limited published data available on the costs of finding and fixing defects. However, from experience, I have developed a useful guideline: It takes about 1 to 4 working hours to find and fix a bug through inspections, and about 15 to 20 working hours to find and fix a bug in function or system testing. To the extent that organizations find that these numbers apply to their situations, they should consider placing less reliance on testing as their primary way to find and fix bugs.

However, some kinds of errors are either uneconomical to detect or almost impossible to find except by machine. Examples are errors involving spelling and syntax, interfaces, performance, human factors, and error recovery. It would be unwise to eliminate testing completely because it provides a useful check against human frailties.

The data that is available with the optimized process provides a new perspective on testing. For most projects, a little analysis shows that two distinct activities are involved: removing defects and assessing program quality. To reduce the cost of removing defects, testing techniques such as inspections, desk debugging, and code analyzers should be emphasized. The role of functional and system testing should then be changed to one of gathering quality data on the programs. This involves studying each bug to see if it is an isolated problem or if it indicates design problems that require more comprehensive analysis.

With the optimized process, the organization has the means to identify the weakest elements of the process and to fix them. At this point in process improvement, data is available to justify the application of technology to various critical tasks, and numerical evidence is available on the effectiveness with which the process has been applied to any given product. An organization should then no longer need reams of paper to describe what is happening because simple yield curves and statistical plots can provide clear and concise indicators. It would then be possible to ensure the process and hence have confidence in the quality of the resulting products.

Conducting the Client/Server Readiness Assessment

To perform the client/server readiness assessment, you need to evaluate your organization in the eight readiness dimensions, as described in Task 1. You may want to assemble a representative group of individuals from your organization to develop the assessment and use Work Paper 15-1 to assist them in performing the assessment.

You should rate each readiness dimension in one of the following four categories:

1. **High.** The readiness assessment team is satisfied that the readiness in this dimension will not inhibit the successful implementation of client/server technology.

2. **Medium.** The readiness assessment team believes that the readiness in this dimension will not be a significant factor in causing the client/server technology to fail. While additional readiness would be desirable, it is not considered an inhibitor to installing client/server technology.

3. **Low.** While there is some readiness for client/server technology, there are serious reservations that the readiness in this dimension will have a negative impact on the implementation of client/server technology.

4. **None.** No readiness at all in this area. Without at least low readiness in all eight dimensions, the probability of client/server technology being successful is extremely low.

Work Paper 15-2 can be used to record the results of the client/server technology readiness assessment.

Preparing a Client/Server Readiness Footprint Chart

A footprint chart is a means of graphically illustrating readiness. The end result will be a footprint that indicates the degree of readiness. The chart is completed by performing the following two steps:

1. Record the point on the dimension line that corresponds to the readiness rating provided on Work Paper 15-2. For example, if the motivation dimension was scored medium, place a dot on the medium circle where it intersects with the motivation dimension line.

2. Connect all of the points and color the inside of the readiness lines connecting the eight readiness points.

The shaded area of the footprint chart is the client/server readiness footprint. It will graphically show whether your organization is ready for client/server technology. Use Work Paper 15-3 for your client/server readiness footprint chart.

Task 2: Assess Key Components

Experience shows that if the key or driving components of technology are in place and working, they will provide most of the assurance necessary for effective processing. Four key components are identified for client/server technology:

1. Client installations are done correctly.
2. Adequate security is provided for the client/server system.
3. Client data is adequately protected.
4. Client/server standards are in place and working.

These four key components need to be assessed prior to conducting the detailed testing. Experience has shown that if these key components are not in place and working, the correctness and accuracy of ongoing processing may be degraded even though the software works effectively.

A detailed checklist is provided to assist testers in evaluating these four components. The checklists are used most effectively if they are answered after an assessment of the four key areas is completed. The questions are designed to be answered by the testers and not to be asked of the people developing the key component areas.

Task 3: Assess Client Needs

Assessing client needs in a client/server system is a challenge because of the number of clients. In some organizations, clients will be homogenous, whereas in other organizations, they will be diverse and not in direct communication with one another. The tester's challenge is that a client/server system that meets the needs of some clients might not meet the needs of all clients. Thus, testers need some assurance that the client/server system incorporates the needs of the all clients.

The tester has two major challenges in evaluating the needs of the clients:

- Can the system do what the client needs?
- Can the client produce results consistent with other clients and other systems?

The tester has two options in validating whether the client/server system will meet the processing needs of the clients. The first is to test how the developers of the system documented the clients' needs. Two distinct methods might be used. The first is that the client/server system is developed for the clients. In other words, the clients were not the driving force in developing this system, but rather management determined the type of processing the clients needed to perform their job effectively and efficiently. The second method is when the client/server system is built based on the requests of the clients.

If the clients have specified their needs, it would be beneficial to conduct a review of the documented requirements for accuracy and completeness. The methods for conducting reviews were described in Chapter 9. The review process should be conducted by clients serving on the review committee.

If the system was developed for the clients, then the testers might want to validate that that system will meet the true needs of the clients. In many client/server systems, the clients are clerical in job function but most likely knowledgeable in what is needed to meet the needs of their customers/users. Through visiting a representative number of clients should prove beneficial to testers in determining whether or not the system will, in fact, meet the true needs of the clients.

Ensuring that the deliverables produced by the clients will be consistent with deliverables from other clients and other systems is a more complex task. However, it is an extremely important task. For example, in one organization, one or more clients produced accounting data that was inconsistent with the data produced by the accounting department. This was because the client did not understand the cut-offs used by the accounting department. The cut-off might mean that an order placed in November but completed in December should not be considered in November sales.

The following are some of the client/server characteristics that testers should evaluate to determine whether they meet the client needs:

- **Data formats.** The format in which the client receives data is a format that is usable by the client. This is particularly important when the client will be using other software systems to ensure that the data formats are usable by those other systems.

- **Completeness of data.** Clients may need more data to correctly perform the processing desired. For example, in our accounting cutoff discussion, it is important that the client would know in which accounting period the data belongs. In addition, there may be data needed by the user that is not provided by the client/server system.

- **Understandable documentation.** The client needs to have documentation, both written and onscreen, that is readily understandable. For example, abbreviations should be clearly defined in the accompanying written documentation.

- **Written for the competency of the client's users.** Many software developers develop software for people at higher competency levels than the typical users of their systems. This can occur if the system is complex to use, or assumes knowledge and background information not typical of the clients that will use the system.

- **Easy to use.** Surveys have shown that only a small portion of most software systems is used because of the difficulty in learning how to use all components of the system. If a processing component is not easy to use, there is a high probability that the client will not use those parts of the system correctly.

- **Sufficient help routines.** Periodically, clients will be involved in a processing situation for which they do not know how to respond. If the client/server system has "help" routines available, the probability that the client can work through those difficult situations is increased.

Check Procedures

Work Paper 15-4 is a quality control checklist for this client/server test process. It is designed so that Yes responses indicate good test practices, and No responses warrant additional investigation. A Comments column is provided to explain No responses and to record results of investigation. The N/A column is used when the checklist item is not applicable to the test situation.

Output

The only output from this system is the test report indicating what works and what does not work. The report should also contain recommendations by the test team for improvements, where appropriate.

Guidelines

The testing described in this chapter is best performed in two phases. The first phase—Tasks 1, 2, and 3—is best executed during the development of the client/server system. Task 4 can then be used after the client/server system has been developed and is ready for operational testing.

Summary

This chapter provided a process for testing client/server systems. The materials contained in this chapter are designed to supplement the seven-step process described in Part Three of this book. Readiness assessment and key component assessment (Tasks 1 and 2) supplement the seven-step process (specifically Step 2, test planning). The next chapter discusses a specialized test process for systems developed using the rapid application development method.

WORK PAPER 15-1   Client/Server Readiness Assessment

	YES	NO	N/A	COMMENTS
Installing Client System				
1. Has a personal computer installation package been developed? (If this item has a No response, the remaining items in the checklist can be skipped.)				
2. Is the installation procedure available to any personal computer user in the organization?				
3. Does the personal computer installation program provide for locating the personal computer?				
4. Does the program provide for surge protection for power supplies?				
5. Does the installation program provide for necessary physical protection?				
6. Does the installation program identify needed supplies and accessories?				
7. Does the installation program provide for acquiring needed computer media?				
8. Does the installation program address storing computer media?				
9. Does the installation program address storage area for printer supplies, books, and so on?				
10. Does the installation program address noise from printers, including providing mats and acoustical covers?				
11. Does the installation program address con- verting data from paper to computer media?				
12. Does the installation program arrange for off-site storage area?				
13. Does the installation program arrange for personal computer servicing?				
14. Does the installation program arrange for a backup processing facility?				
15. Does the installation program arrange for consulting services if needed?				
16. Are users taught how to install personal computers through classes or step-by-step procedures?				
17. Do installation procedures take into account specific organizational requirements, such as accounting for computer usage?				

(continues)

WORK PAPER 15-1   *(continued)*

	YES	NO	N/A	COMMENTS
18. Is the installation process customized depending on the phase of maturity of personal computer usage?				
19. Has a means been established to measure the success of the installation process?				
20. Have potential installation impediments been identified and counterstrategies adopted where appropriate?				
21. Has the organization determined their strategy in the event that the installation of standard personal computer is unsatisfactory to the user?				
22. Has the needed client software been supplied?				
23. Has the needed client software been tested?				

Client/Server Security

	YES	NO	N/A	COMMENTS
1. Has the organization issued a security policy for personal computers?				
2. Have standards and procedures been developed to ensure effective compliance with that policy?				
3. Are procedures established to record personal computer violations?				
4. Have the risks associated with personal computers been identified?				
5. Has the magnitude of each risk been identified?				
6. Has the personal security group identified the type of available countermeasures for the personal computer security threats?				
7. Has an awareness program been developed to encourage support of security in a personal computer environment?				
8. Have training programs been developed for personal computer users in security procedures and methods?				
9. Does the audit function conduct regular audits to evaluate personal computer security and identify potential vulnerabilities in that security?				
10. Does senior management take an active role in supporting the personal computer security program?				

WORK PAPER 15-1   *(continued)*

	YES	NO	N/A	COMMENTS
11. Have security procedures been developed for operators of personal computers?				
12. Are the security programs at the central computer site and coordinated?				
13. Has one individual at the central site been appointed responsible for overseeing security of the personal computer program?				
14. Have operating managers/personal computer users been made responsible for security over their personal computer facilities?				
15. Is the effectiveness of the total personal computer security program regularly evaluated?				
16. Has one individual been appointed responsible for the security of personal computers for the organization?				

Client Data

1. Has a policy been established on sharing data with users?				
2. Is data recognized as a corporate resource as opposed to the property of a single department or individual?				
3. Have the requirements for sharing been defined?				
4. Have profiles been established indicating what user wants which data?				
5. Have the individuals responsible for that data approved use by the proposed users of the data?				
6. Has a usage profile been developed that identifies whether data is to be uploaded and downloaded?				
7. Has the user use profile been defined to the appropriate levels to provide the needed security?				
8. Have security standards been established for protecting data at personal computer sites?				
9. Has the personal computer user been made accountable and responsible for the security of the data at the personal computer site?				

(continues)

WORK PAPER 15-1   *(continued)*

	YES	NO	N/A	COMMENTS
10. Does the user's manager share this security responsibility?				
11. Have adequate safeguards at the central site been established to prevent unauthorized access to data?				
12. Have adequate safeguards at the central site been established to prevent unauthorized modification to data?				
13. Are logs maintained that keep records of what data is transferred to and from personal computer sites?				
14. Do the communication programs provide for error handling?				
15. Are the remote users trained in accessing and protecting corporate data?				
16. Have the appropriate facilities been developed to reformat files?				
17. Are appropriate safeguards taken to protect diskettes at remote sites containing corporate data?				
18. Is the security protection required for data at the remote site known to the personal computer user?				
19. Are violations of data security/control procedures recorded?				
20. Is someone in the organization accountable for ensuring that data is made available to those users who need it? (In many organizations this individual is referred to as the data administrator.)				

Client/Server Standards

	YES	NO	N/A	COMMENTS
1. Are standards based on a hierarchy of policies, standards, procedures, and guidelines?				
2. Has the organization issued a personal computer policy?				
3. Have the standards been issued to evaluate compliance with the organization's personal computer policy?				
4. Have policies been developed for users of personal computers that are supportive of the organization's overall personal computer policy?				

WORK PAPER 15-1   *(continued)*

	YES	NO	N/A	COMMENTS
5. Have personal computer policies been developed for the following areas:				
a. Continuity of processing				
b. Reconstruction				
c. Accuracy				
d. Security				
e. Compliance				
f. File integrity				
g. Data				
6. Are all standards tied directly to personal computer policies?				
7. Has the concept of ownership been employed in the development of standards?				
8. Can the benefit of each standard be demonstrated to the users of the standards?				
9. Are the standards written in playscript?				
10. Have quality control self-assessment tools been issued to personal computer users to help them comply with the standards?				
11. Has a standards notebook been prepared?				
12. Is the standards notebook divided by area of responsibility?				
13. Are the standards explained to users in the form of a training class or users-group meeting?				
14. Does a representative group of users have an opportunity to review and comment on standards before they are issued?				
15. Are guidelines issued where appropriate?				
16. Is the standards program consistent with the objectives of the phase of maturity of the personal computer in the organization?				

WORK PAPER 15-2   Client/Server Readiness Results

#	READINESS DIMENSION		READINESS RATING			
	NAME	DESCRIPTION	HIGH	MEDIUM	LOW	NONE

WORK PAPER 15-3 Client/Server Readiness Footprint Chart

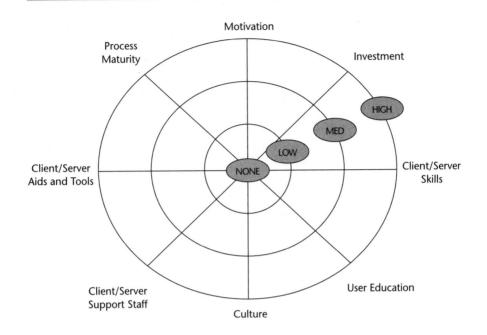

WORK PAPER 15-4   Client/Server Systems Quality Control Checklist

	YES	NO	N/A	COMMENTS
1. Does the test team in total have team members who understand client/server technology?				
2. Have the test team members acquired knowledge of client/server system to be tested?				
3. Has the readiness of the organization who installs client/server technology been evaluated?				
4. If the organization is not deemed ready to install client/server technology, have the appropriate steps been taken to achieve a readiness status prior to installing the client/server system?				
5. Has an adequate plan been developed and implemented to ensure proper installation of client technology?				
6. Are the communication lines adequate to enable efficient client/server processing?				
7. Has the server component of the system been developed adequately so that it can support client processing?				
8. Are security procedures adequate to protect client hardware and software?				
9. Are security procedures adequate to prevent processing compromise by employees, external personnel, and acts of nature?				
10. Are procedures in place to adequately protect client data?				
11. Are procedures in place to ensure that clients can only access data for which they have been authorized?				
12. Are standards in place for managing client/server systems?				
13. Does management support and enforce those standards?				

16

Rapid Application Development Testing

Rapid application development (RAD) is an effective software development paradigm that provides a systematic and automatable means of developing a software system under circumstances where initial requirements are not well known or where requirements change frequently during development. Providing high software quality assurance requires sufficient software testing. The unique nature of evolutionary, iterative development is not well suited for classical testing methodologies; therefore, the need exists for a testing methodology tailored for this developing paradigm. Part of the tailored testing methodology is ensuring RAD is the right development methodology for the system being developed.

Overview

This chapter describes a testing strategy for RAD: spiral testing. This document shows key RAD characteristics impinging on testing and the value of spiral testing to support evolutionary, iterative RAD. This testing strategy assumes the RAD system

- is iterative.
- is evolutionary.
- contains RAD language with a defined grammar.
- provides reusable components capability (library and retrieval).

- uses implementation code from reusable components written in a high-level language.

- contains a sophisticated support environment.

These characteristics will keep the RAD paradigm sufficiently general to discuss testing concerns. Because program verification and validation are the most costly activities in current development, any changes to RAD to simplify testing will accelerate the development process and increase RAD's appeal.

Objective

The RAD testing methodology described in this test process s designed to take maximum advantage of the iterative nature of RAD. It also should focus on the requirements-capturing purpose of developing. Thus, a RAD-based testing technique starts by capturing the testing information resident in the RAD process in a form suitable for thoroughly testing the RAD system. Testers must know both the assumptions and the requirements the designers are trying to meet so that a test series can be built to verify the system. Remember, the test personnel are not usually the design personnel, nor should they be; therefore, RAD-based testing must provide tools and methods to analyze system requirements and capture requirement changes.

Concerns

This section describes the four concerns testers should have about RAD-based testing.

Testing Iterations

The iterative nature of software development implies that the system must track revision histories and maintain version control of alternate RAD versions. The user's response to a demonstration may require that the RAD fall back to a previous iteration for change, or the developer might wish to demonstrate several iteration alternatives for user comment (one of which, or portions of several being selected). Requirements may be added, changed, or deleted. Test goals must easily change to fit modified requirements. Ideally, the developing environment will capture this modification explicitly, along with the accompanying purpose of the modification. Any testing tools developed must take these modifications into account to test the proper version and to appropriately consider the requirements and purpose germane to that version for test development. The tool should also exploit change as a likely source of errors. A tool that helps testers compare changes from one iteration to the next, along with system dependencies potentially affected by changes, helps test development considerably.

Testing Components

The use of reusable components raises reliability concerns. Have the components been unit tested, and if so, to what degree? Have they been used in previous implementations, and if so, which ones? What testing has been conducted on the previous implementations as well as the individual components? The testing methodology must consider how information on past component testing can be recorded and referenced to determine what unit testing might still be needed and what integration testing strategies might best check the components in their instantiated context.

Testing Performance

One necessary testing component is a set of test conditions. Requirements-based and functional testing base test conditions on some stated form of behavior or required performance standard, such as formal specifications or a requirements document. The development methodology does not provide a separate performance standard. The testing methodology must establish an objective standard of the intended behavior of the RAD under consideration. Every program must have an objective performance standard. The developing system must then, in some fashion, provide the tester and his or her tools with access to a system functionality description and system requirements to allow rapid, complete, and consistent derivation from the RAD. This access to functionality descriptions and requirements has the added benefit of helping develop scripts for demonstrations so that particular iteration changes and enhancements will be highlighted for the user's comments.

Recording Test Information

The software development environment not only should capture requirements, assumptions, and design decisions, but, ideally, should map these into the RAD in a way useful to both rapid application development and testing. This mapping automatically provides a trace, documenting the RAD's development. As the system grows, knowing why a particular design decision was made and being able to see where (and how) the RAD implements it will be difficult without automated support. The developing/testing paradigm must capture mappings from design or development decisions to the implementation. These mappings need to be rapidly revisable to quickly make the next RAD iteration.

Workbench

Figure 16-1 illustrates the workbench for testing RAD systems. Because rapid application development goes through a series of iterations, the tasks in the workbench parallel those iterations. Note that Task 3 may, in fact, perform all the iterations between the planning iteration and the final iteration multiple times.

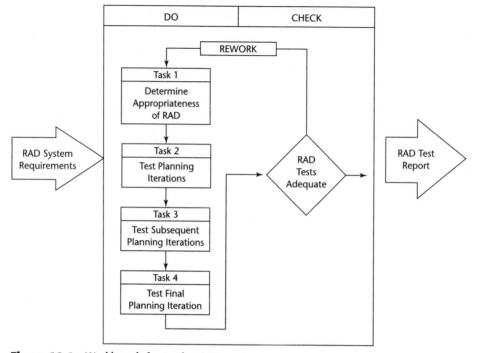

Figure 16-1   Workbench for testing RAD systems.

Input

The only input to this test process is the RAD requirements. Because of the nature of RAD, the requirements are normally incomplete when development begins. The requirements will be continually developed throughout various iterations. Thus, the input to each of the three steps in the recommended RAD test process will be different.

Do Procedures

This section begins by describing iterative RAD and spiral testing, and then integrates those topics into a three-task strategy.

Testing Within Iterative RAD

The chapter provides a framework for iterative RAD testing. The most obvious approach to testing during RAD would be to treat each development iteration as one software life cycle. An advantage is that this keeps intact the methodology of testing familiar to most testers. The lack of a conventional specification effectively removes the information basis for test planning. Under current descriptions of the developing process, a specification would need to be generated, at least in part, before conventional techniques could be applied.

The process's complexity is also compounded by the need to conduct a full cycle of testing for each iteration, even though the early iterations will almost never contain detailed or unchanging requirements. This would be inefficient and impractical testing.

An alternative test approach is to iterate test planning in parallel with the developing iterations. This will simplify testing and reduce overall testing costs when compared to the preceding approach. The initial test plan would consider only the basic system description contained in the initial RAD iteration. As RAD iterations proceed, the test plan would expand to incorporate the latest iteration modifications. One disadvantage is that this approach causes the test plan to follow the RAD process closely. The decisions in the RAD might unduly influence the test plan, causing important test conditions not to be explored. The possible disadvantage suggests that the unit and integration testing might be done iteratively, with acceptance testing occurring entirely on the final iteration of the development cycle.

By considering how the developing process closely follows the spiral process model that leads to a spiral iterative test planning process. Figure 16-2 illustrates this process.

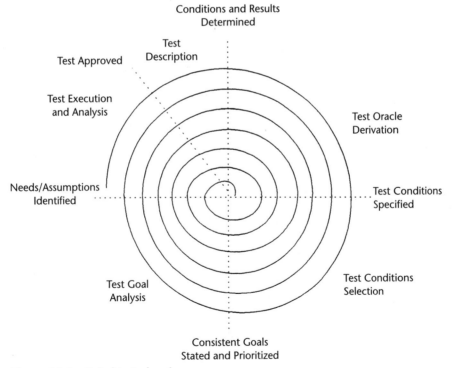

Figure 16-2 Spiral test planning process.

Spiral Testing

The proposed RAD testing strategy, termed *spiral testing*, remains iterative and parallels the RAD process. Spiral testing characterizes the varying types of RAD iterations by tailoring the testing process to account for these differences. Spiral testing distinguishes between the initial few RAD testing iterations, subsequent iterations, and the final few iterations. The major distinction between the first few testing iterations and the subsequent ones is that the first iterations, for any but the smallest of systems, probably will have only test planning and structuring activities that establish priorities and areas of test emphasis.

The framework for intermediate testing activity and final acceptance testing, to include test derivation, is laid in the initial iterations. Unit and integration testing will likely be confined to subsequent and final testing iterations. Subsequent testing iterations will have less framework-related activity and more acceptance test oracle derivation activity. The major distinction between the subsequent and final iterations is that the final iterations are where developers return to their RAD to fix identified errors and testers conduct final integration and acceptance and regression testing. Figure 16-3 shows the separation of the groups of iterations for either the development or testing spiral. The following sections cover spiral testing in detail.

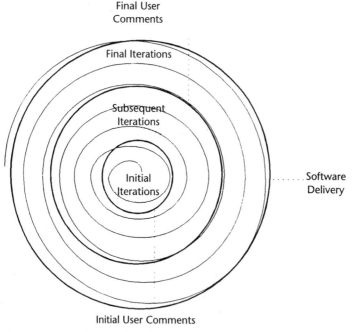

Figure 16-3   A "targeted" spiral.

Task 1: Determine Appropriateness of RAD

There are strengths and weaknesses to using the RAD concept to build software. If the advantages outweigh the disadvantages, RAD should be used. However, some applications built under the RAD concept would have been better built under other software development models.

RAD development offers the following strengths:

- System users get a quick view of the system's deliverables.

- The cost of risk associated with development is reduced because decisions can be made early regarding the usability of the first RAD prototype.

- Customer satisfaction can be improved through a series of developmental iterations rather than a focus on a single deliverable.

- If the project is developed by a project team familiar with the user's business, fewer developers are required because of their knowledge of the user business.

- Using powerful development tools can reduce the cycle time for developing the final system.

The problems associated with using the RAD model for development, on the other hand, include the following:

- Users and developers must be committed to rapid-fire activities in an abbreviated time frame; thus any lack of commitment negates most of the advantages of the RAD model.

- Diffusers are not continuously involved throughout the RAD cycles. Obtaining the necessary feedback at the appropriate times will facilitate development.

- Unless the system can be appropriately modularized and has access to reusable components, the reduced cost and schedule may not be achieved.

- Because the RAD concept does not require a fixed completion date, the risk is that the development team will continue through the RAD cycles past the point of economic return.

Understanding the strengths and weaknesses of the RAD model, testers should assess whether RAD is a desirable model for a specific software system. Using this analysis, the IT organization can be prevented from building software using the RAD model when other developmental models would be more appropriate.

Testers should use Work Paper 16-1 to determine whether the RAD model is appropriate for their software system. If the testers are uncertain whether a specific item can be answered Yes, they should give a No response. If more than 25 percent of the items have a No response, the applicability of using the RAD model for this specific software system should be re-evaluated.

Task 2: Test Planning Iterations

The first few iterations of the RAD serve varying purposes, depending on the particular software under design. When feasibility is not a consideration or when a detailed requirements document exists, the first development iterations establish the product's design framework as a base upon which to RAD the remainder of the system. When feasibility must be investigated and/or when requirements are unknown, the first several development iterations seek to construct abstract RADs to see if an acceptable system can be designed. If the RAD is feasible, developers establish the major software requirements and design a development plan upon which to build the system during successive iterations, as in the first case mentioned previously. The first few development iterations will usually be devoted to establishing an overall RAD structural framework.

To mirror this process for test planning purposes, the initial test planning iterations consider the developing results and frame the testing process for the remainder of the project. This is the logical point for testers to determine the major critical portions of the RAD, and establish test priorities. As RADs establish major requirements, the test team begins to break these down into test goals, determining derived goals as well. As development continues, the testers can define the testing emphasis in greater detail, make needed test plan adjustments, and record test justifications.

It appears prudent (although not essential) throughout the development process for the test team to review user input and generate goals independently from the RAD team, so as to identify misstated requirements and to find missing requirements. This increases the quality of the RAD versions, thereby decreasing the number of iterations needed.

The initial iterations are where the test team will forecast the most important portions of the system to test. As the implementation hierarchy of the system takes shape, the testers establish test sections for path and integration testing. The long-term testing purpose is to build the framework for constructing the final acceptance-test oracle and to fit the intermediate testing activities into the overall development plan. The process will be manual for the most part, and this would be where initial testing tools and their databases/instrumentation would be initialized. The initial iteration phase would end at the RAD iteration in which the top-level requirements specification is established.

It is recommended that the documentation for each iteration of the RAD process be subject to the inspection process, as outlined in Part Three of this book, as well as complete the checklist in Work Paper 16-2.

Task 3: Test Subsequent Planning Iterations

Once the basic RAD framework is established, subsequent iterations commence in which developers enhance the RAD's functionality and demonstrate it for user/designer review. In the typical case, additional requirements are identified and the design matures in parallel over multiple iterations. Both are validated in the review process. At some point, sufficient requirements are identified to establish the overall system design.

The subsequent testing iterations will be characterized by unit testing, integration testing, and continued requirements review to determine whether any requirements are missing. To complement the design process, the test team concurrently develops integration test plans as designers complete subsections of the system design. In addition, as reusable components are instantiated to provide required functionality, the test team or design team unit tests these modules (both approaches are acceptable in current practice) by consulting the test history of the instantiated modules and conducting additional unit testing appropriate to the developing system.

Should this additional testing be necessary, the test team updates the test history to reflect the additional testing and its results. This update could be as simple as appending a test script (although this could eventually cost a large amount of storage for a large components test library) or as complex as completely revising the test history to incorporate new test sets, assumptions tested, test case justifications, and additional test history details. The complex update may be needed to reduce a series of simple updates into a consistent and usefully compact synthesis. As performance aberrations are found during a given iteration's tests, they are readdressed to the design team for correction prior to the next iteration demonstration.

As the design team RADs system components, the test team can commence integration test planning for those components. The integration testing process is the same at any hierarchical system level for integration testing. The test team needs to keep integration testing at various levels coordinated to maximize test efficiency. If a standard structure for integration test sets could be constructed, then it might be possible to develop tools to manipulate these to conduct increasing levels of integration testing as more components and system subsections are implemented. Currently, most of this process would be manual. Final integration testing cannot commence until the RAD implementation is complete.

Throughout testing, testers consult the RAD specification and all requirements to determine the correct responses to test data. Considerable information needed for test data selection will likely be found in the RAD specification language. Automated support to extract this information would be very helpful, but will depend on the developing language in question and on possessing the capability automatically to relate the criteria to selected test data and execute the test.

Throughout the iterations, the test methodology must remain responsive to change. Existing components and specifications may change or disappear between iterations, contingent with user/developer/tester input. Additionally, each new iteration adds increased functionality or furthers the completion of existing incomplete implementations. The test development process must capture all effects of change because additional testing or retesting of previously tested code may be required. This retesting raises the issue of "phase agreement" between the RAD spiral and the test-planning spiral.

An *in-phase agreement* would have formal iteration testing proceed at the completion of a development iteration and prior to iteration demonstration to the user. The advantage here is that the test team will have tested the system and the developers are not as likely to demonstrate a system that contains undiscovered or obvious bugs. Any problems encountered in testing are corrected prior to user review. User confidence is not enhanced when bugs that are not related to design issues are discovered during the demonstration. On the other hand, many iterations will usually be demonstrating requirements not yet validated, and it is wasteful to test requirements that have not been validated.

An *out-of-phase agreement* relies on the designers to test their RAD iteration sufficiently prior to demonstration (for their reputation, not for formal testing). The test team conducts formal testing for an iteration at the conclusion of the user demonstration. They modify the formal test plan, developed during the development iteration, by removing any planned testing of eliminated, changed, or superseded requirements and by adding additional testing of corrections and modifications resulting from the user's review. Test planning proceeds in tandem with iterations development, but actual testing waits for the results of the user's review. Once the testers obtain user comments, they may assume that the stated requirements at that point represent solid requirements for the purpose of testing. This assumption continues until a requirement is explicitly or implicitly changed or eliminated. The advantages of out-of-phase testing are a savings in testing conducted (because you test only reviewed requirements) and increased test responsiveness to user review. The disadvantages are the increased likelihood of missed requirements and the possibility of bugs in the demonstrated systems. Work Paper 16-3 should be used when subsequent iterations are inspected.

Task 4: Test the Final Planning Iteration

Once developers establish all requirements (usually in the latter iterations), the final few iterations of development are devoted to implementing the remaining functionality, followed by error correction. Therefore, the testers can devote their work to completing the test for acceptance testing, and to remaining unit testing and subsection integration testing.

The final test planning iterations commence with the completion of the operational RAD and prior to final user acceptance. As any final requirements are implemented or as system components are fine-tuned, tests are developed and conducted to cover these changes. Most important, the test team completes the acceptance test plan. Once the system is completely implemented and the acceptance test design is complete, the test team conducts the acceptance test. The test team checks differences in actual results from expected results and corrects the tests as appropriate while the design team corrects system faults. The cycle continues until the system successfully completes testing. If the design team is busier than the test team, the test team can use the available time to conduct additional testing or priority-superseded testing previously skipped. The result should be a sufficiently tested software system. Work Paper 16-4 should be used when the final iteration is inspected.

Check Procedures

Work Paper 16-5 is a quality control checklist for testing RAD systems. It is designed so that Yes responses indicate good test practices and No responses warrant additional investigation. A Comments column is provided to explain No responses and to record results of investigation. The N/A column is used when the checklist item is not applicable to the test situation.

Output

This testing process will have multiple outputs of approximately the same composition. These outputs are test reports that indicate findings at the end of the testing of each iteration of the RAD development. The test reports should indicate what works and what does not work. They should also contain testers' recommendations for improvement. Note that if there are many iterations of the system being developed, the reports may be less formal so that they can be more quickly provided to the development team.

Guidelines

Spiral testing has the advantages of being flexible and maximizing the amount of testing conducted during the RAD process. It allows for the steady development of an acceptance test in the face of continual system change and facilitates lower-level testing as soon as implementation code is instantiated. The spiral testing approach particularly suits the methodology for use with evolutionary, iterative RAD that is itself spiral. Using test histories for reusable components should speed the testing process by reducing the amount of unit testing required. Testers can obtain a further benefit of the test history feature, the compounding of unit testing for reusable components, by either increasing the component confidence factor or at least delineating the bounds within which it may be successfully used.

The spiral testing approach also results in thorough documentation of the testing conducted and a formal, written test plan that can be viewed with the user for approval. The extended time for test development (considerably more than in conventional life cycle models) also should provide for a more thorough test.

The major disadvantage to the approach is that the final acceptance test remains a moving target until the completion of implementation coding. Additionally, the test team must remain vigilant against following the development process so closely that they fail to view the system objectively from the outside. The first disadvantage is inherent to the development process; therefore, the goal is to minimize its effect. Spiral testing is likely to do this. The second disadvantage may be reduced with experience but will likely require separate test teams to conduct critical acceptance tests. Note that the spiral testing strategy remains a theory at this point. Further research will be required to determine its feasibility and practicality.

Summary

This chapter provided a testing process for systems developed using the RAD methodology. Testers need to be familiar with the RAD methodology their organization uses. The materials contained in this chapter focused on the inspection process because it is more effective in uncovering defects than is dynamic testing. Dynamic testing is more effective when used in the later iterations of the RAD process. This chapter was designed to be used in conjunction with the seven-step process outlined in Part Three.

WORK PAPER 16-1   RAD Applicability Checklist

	YES	NO	COMMENTS
1. Is the system being designed a user business applications?			
2. Is the technical risk low?			
3. Is the project team familiar with the user business application?			
4. Is the project team skilled in the use of the RAD developmental tools?			
5. Is the developmental team highly motivated to develop this application using the RAD model?			
6. Can the system being developed be modularized?			
7. Are the requirements for the software system reasonably well known?			
8. Is the cost of the development not a critical concern?			
9. Is the implementation schedule not a critical concern?			
10. Is the software project small enough that it can be developed within about 60 days?			
11. Can the software functionality be delivered in increments?			
12. Is the software system relatively small in comparison to other systems developed by the IT organization?			
13. Are the users willing to become heavily involved in the development?			
14. Will the users be available during the developmental cycle?			

WORK PAPER 16-2   RAD Inspection Checklist for Task 2

	INSPECTION RESULT			DESCRIPTION/LOCATION OF NOTED DEFECT
	PASS	FAIL	N/A	
Define Purpose and Scope of System				
1. Is the defined system within the context of the organization's goals?				
2. Is the defined system within the context of the organization's information requirements?				
3. Have the objectives that are critical to the success of the organization been identified in the RAD purpose and scope?				
4. Does the system scope identify the user environment?				
5. Does the system scope identify the hardware environment?				
6. Does the system scope identify the other systems that interact with this system (e.g., regarding input and output)?				
7. Does the RAD system scope define available funding?				
8. Does the RAD system scope identify time constraints?				
9. Does the RAD system scope identify the available resources to build the system?				
10. Does the RAD system scope state the security needs for the data and software?				
11. Has the RAD team been established?				
12. Is the RAD team trained in the techniques of RAD and the use of specific fourth-generation language for implementing RAD?				
13. Is the RAD software development group enthusiastic about the RAD concept?				
14. Does the RAD team know how to control RAD?				

(continues)

WORK PAPER 16-2 *(continued)*

	INSPECTION RESULT			DESCRIPTION/LOCATION
	PASS	FAIL	N/A	OF NOTED DEFECT

Develop System Conceptual Model

		PASS	FAIL	N/A	
1.	Does the RAD team use a graphic method (e.g., a data flow diagram) to construct a model of the system to be developed?				
2.	Are the data definitions used for the RAD included in the data dictionary?				
3.	Are the critical system objectives defined in the project scope related to specific components of the conceptual model?				
4.	Has the major business input been defined?				
5.	Has the major business output been defined?				
6.	Has the cost to implement the system using traditional systems development processes been estimated?				
7.	Has the cost of the RAD been estimated? (The RAD should cost no more than 6% to 10% of the full-scale development effort.)				
8.	Have the benefits of the RAD system been developed?				
9.	Have the risks associated with developing this system when it goes into production been identified?				
10.	Have the files needed to support the RAD system when it goes into production been identified?				
11.	Has a database administrator been consulted to determine whether the needed data will be available?				
12.	Has the computer operations department been consulted to determine whether it could run the system if it were implemented?				
13.	Are there sufficient communications lines to support the system?				

WORK PAPER 16-2   *(continued)*

| | INSPECTION RESULT | | | DESCRIPTION/LOCATION |
	PASS	FAIL	N/A	OF NOTED DEFECT
Develop Logical Data Model				
1. Has a model of the local information flow for individual subsystems been designed?				
2. Has a model for the global information flow for collections of subsystems been designed?				
3. Have the conceptual schemas for the RAD system been defined?				
4. Does the conceptual schema define the attributes of each entity in the subschema?				
5. Has a model been developed for each physical external schema?				
6. Has the physical database been designed to provide optimum access for the prototype transactions?				
7. Does the physical database design provide efficiency in operation?				
8. Is the RAD design restricted to accessing the database at the logical level?				
9. Have the functions to be performed by the RAD system been defined?				
10. Has the sequence of performing the functions been defined?				
11. Has the potential source of input transactions and data been defined?				
12. Has a determination been made that the needed data can be prepared in time to meet RAD processing schedules?				

WORK PAPER 16-3   RAD Inspection Checklist for Task 3

	INSPECTION RESULT			DESCRIPTION/LOCATION
	PASS	FAIL	N/A	OF NOTED DEFECT
Develop and Demonstrate RAD System				
1. Have the basic database structures derived from the logical data modeling been defined?				
2. Have the report formats been defined?				
3. Have the interactive data entry screens been defined?				
4. Have the external file routines to process data been defined?				
5. Have the algorithms and procedures to be implemented by the RAD been defined?				
6. Have the procedure selection menus been defined?				
7. Have the test cases to ascertain that data entry validation is correct been defined?				
8. Have report and screen formatting options been defined?				
9. Has a RAD system been developed using a fourth-generation language?				
10. Has the RAD been demonstrated to management?				
11. Has management made strategic decisions about the application based on RAD appearance and objectives?				
12. Has the RAD been demonstrated to the users?				
13. Have the users been given the opportunity to identify problems and point out unacceptable procedures?				
14. Has the prototype been demonstrated before a representative group of users?				
15. If the RAD is unacceptable to management or users, have requests for changes or corrections been documented?				
16. Has a decision been made concerning whether to develop another RAD iteration?				

WORK PAPER 16-4   RAD Inspection Checklist for Task 4

	INSPECTION RESULT			DESCRIPTION/LOCATION
	PASS	FAIL	N/A	OF NOTED DEFECT

Revise and Finalize Specifications

		PASS	FAIL	N/A	
1.	Is someone on the RAD team responsible for reviewing each component for inconsistencies, ambiguities, and omissions?				
2.	Has the statement of goals and objectives been reviewed to ensure that all elements are present, that all components have been defined, and that there are no conflicts?				
3.	Has the definition of system scope been reviewed to ensure that all elements are present, that all components have been defined, and that there are no conflicts?				
4.	Have the system diagrams been reviewed to ensure that all elements are present, that all components have been defined, and that there are no conflicts?				
5.	Has the data dictionary report been reviewed to ensure that all elements are present, that all components have been defined, and that there are no conflicts?				
6.	Has the risk analysis been reviewed to ensure that all elements are present, that all components have been defined, and that there are no conflicts?				
7.	Has the logical data model been reviewed to ensure that all elements are present, that all components have been defined, and that there are no conflicts?				
8.	Have the data entry screens been reviewed to ensure that all elements are present, that all components have been defined, and that there are no conflicts?				

(continues)

WORK PAPER 16-4 *(continued)*

| | INSPECTION RESULT | | | DESCRIPTION/LOCATION |
	PASS	FAIL	N/A	OF NOTED DEFECT
9. Have the report layouts been reviewed to ensure that all elements are present, that all components have been defined, and that there are no conflicts?				
10. Have the selection menus and operational flow been reviewed to ensure that all elements are present, that all components have been defined, and that there are no conflicts?				
11. Has the physical database structure been reviewed to ensure that all elements are present, that all components have been defined, and that there are no conflicts?				
12. Has the draft user manual been reviewed to ensure that all elements are present, that all components have been defined, and that there are no conflicts?				
13. Have all of the RAD elements been indexed?				
14. Have all of the RAD elements been cross- referenced by subject and component?				
15. Does the RAD documentation contain sample reports?				
16. Does the RAD documentation contain sample data entry screens?				
17. Does the RAD documentation contain a listing of the fourth-generation commands for each programmed function?				

WORK PAPER 16-4   *(continued)*

	INSPECTION RESULT			DESCRIPTION/LOCATION
	PASS	FAIL	N/A	OF NOTED DEFECT

Develop Production System

		PASS	FAIL	N/A	
1.	Has a decision been made by the end user regarding putting the system in production?				
2.	If so, have all the significant system problems been resolved?				
3.	If the RAD is very inefficient, is it discarded in place of a production system built using traditional methods?				
4.	If the RAD does not have adequate controls, is it thrown away and a new system developed using traditional methods?				
5.	If the RAD is placed into production, does it have adequate data validation?				
6.	If the RAD is placed into production, does it have adequate system controls?				
7.	If the RAD is placed into production, does it have adequate documentation for maintenance purposes?				
8.	If the system is rebuilt using traditional methods, does the developmental project team believe that the RAD documentation is adequate for developing a production system?				

(continues)

WORK PAPER 16-4   *(continued)*

	INSPECTION RESULT			DESCRIPTION/LOCATION OF NOTED DEFECT
	PASS	FAIL	N/A	
Release Test System				
1. Has the system been approved by the test team before being released for test?				
2. Has the system design been documented in detail?				
3. Have the user manuals been revised?				
4. Has a training plan been developed?				
5. Are the users involved in the testing?				
6. Is the system put under full production conditions during testing?				
7. Does the existing system remain in place until the new system has passed testing?				
8. Have all end users been trained in the operation of the system?				
9. If the output is crucial to the organization, has a parallel operation test been performed?				
10. Are errors noted during testing documented?				
11. Are needed changes noted during testing documented?				
12. Has a formal decision procedure been developed to determine when to move the system out of testing?				
Release Production System				
1. Have the users accepted the system before it is placed into production?				
2. Have the final user manuals been prepared?				
3. Have the final user manuals been distributed to the end users?				
4. Have the end users been trained in any changes occurring between testing and placement of the system into production?				

WORK PAPER 16-5   RAD Systems Quality Control Checklist

	YES	NO	N/A	COMMENTS
1. Does the test team contain a collective knowledge and insight into how RAD systems are developed?				
2. Does the test team collectively understand the tool that is used in RAD?				
3. Do the testers understand that the RAD's requirements will be continually changing as development progresses?				
4. Does the test team collectively understand how to use the inspection tools?				
5. Is the inspection process used at the end of each iteration of RAD?				
6. Are new requirements documented prior to developing each RAD iteration?				
7. Did the testers test each RAD iteration?				
8. Is the tester's input incorporated into the process of updating requirements for the next iteration of a RAD?				

Testing Internal Controls

Internal control has always been important. However, passage of the Sarbanes-Oxley Act of 2002 by the U.S. Congress increased management's awareness of this importance. Under this law, both the CEO and CFO must personally certify the adequacy of their organization's system of internal control. An improper certification may result in criminal or civil charges against the certifier.

This chapter focuses on the internal controls within software systems. It is important for the tester to know that there are two general categories of controls: environmental (or general) controls, and controls within a specific business application (internal controls). This chapter covers three types of controls in the latter category (specific business application controls): preventive, detective, and corrective. The chapter then explains how to evaluate controls within an information system.

Overview

There are two systems in every business application: the system that processes transactions and the system that controls the processing of such (see Figure 17-1). From the perspective of the system designer, these two are designed and implemented as one system. For example, edits that determine the validity of input are included in the part of the system in which transactions are entered. However, those edits are part of the system that controls the processing of business transactions.

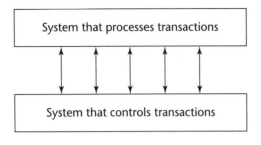

Business application processing

Figure 17-1   The two systems in every business application.

Because these two systems are designed as a single system, most software testers do not conceptualize the two systems. Furthermore, the system documentation is not divided into the system that processes transactions and the system that controls the processing of transactions.

When you visualize a single system, you may have difficulty visualizing the total system of internal control. If you look at edits of input data by themselves, it is difficult to see how the totality of control over the processing of a transaction is accomplished. Thus, you are at risk of processing invalid transactions. This risk occurs throughout the system, not just during data editing. A system of internal controls must address all the risk of invalid processing from the point that a transaction is entered into the system to the point that the output is used for business purposes.

The following three terms are associated with an undesirable occurrence during processing:

- **Risk.** The probability that an undesirable event will occur
- **Exposure.** The amount of loss that might occur if an undesirable event occurs
- **Threat.** A specific event that might cause an undesirable event to occur

Controls are required to mitigate risks, exposure, and the specific threats that might cause loss. Therefore, to evaluate the adequacy of internal controls, testers must know the risks, exposures, and threats associated with the business application being tested. The objective of a system of internal controls in a business application is to minimize business risks.

As mentioned previously, one category of control is environmental controls. Such a system refers to the management-established and -maintained environment. Environmental (or general) controls are the means by which management manages the organization, including organizational policies and structures, hiring practices, training programs, supervisory/evaluation functions, and the day-to-day employee work processes, such as a system development methodology for building software systems.

Without strong environmental controls, transaction-processing (internal) controls may not be effective. For example, if passwords to access computer systems are not adequately protected, the password system will not work. Individuals will either protect or not protect their password based on environmental controls such as the attention management pays to password protection, the monitoring of the use of passwords, and management's actions regarding failure to protect passwords.

Internal Controls

Internal application controls are designed to meet the specific control requirements of each processing application. They contrast with and are complemented by environmental controls applicable where the processing occurs. Application controls are designed to ensure that the recording, classifying, and summarizing of authorized transactions and the updating of master files will produce accurate and complete information on a timely basis.

Normally, the processing cycle includes all the procedures in the source and user departments and in the IT departments to record and prepare source data and ultimately produce useful information during a specific time period. When you discuss application controls, it is useful to classify them according to whether they are preventive, detective, or corrective.

NOTE Some input errors may be acceptable if they do not cause an interruption in the processing run—for example, a misspelling. When deciding tolerance limits, an organization must compare the cost of correcting an error to the consequences of accepting it. Such tradeoffs must be determined for each application. Unfortunately, however, no universal guidelines are available.

Control Objectives

Controls typically are classified according to the location of their implementation: input, process, and output. However, the location of controls is not important to their evaluation. The auditor's prime concern should be the objective of a control.

The objectives of internal application controls are to prevent, detect, or correct the various causes (assumed to always exist) of risk exposure, as follows:

- To ensure that all authorized transactions are completely processed once and only once

- To ensure that transaction data are complete and accurate

- To ensure that transaction processing is correct and appropriate to the circumstances

- To ensure that processing results are utilized for the intended benefits

- To ensure that the application can continue to function

In most instances, controls can be related to multiple exposures. A single control can also fulfill multiple objectives. For these reasons, internal application controls are classified according to whether they prevent, detect, or correct causes of exposure. The following subsections describe these types of controls, using key controls as examples (instead of trying to present an exhaustive list).

Preventive Controls

Preventive controls are the most desirable (cost-effective, and from a PR perspective) controls because they stop problems from occurring. Therefore, application designers should focus on preventive controls. Preventive controls include standards, training, segregation of duties, authorization, forms design, prenumbered forms, documentation, passwords, consistency of operations, etc.

You might ask, "At what point in the processing flow is it most desirable to exercise computer data edits?" Computer data edits are one example of preventive control, and the answer to this question is this: "As soon as possible, to uncover problems early and avoid unnecessary computer processing." Some input controls depend on access to master files and so must be timed to coincide with file availability. However, many input-validation tests may be performed independently of the master files. Preferably, these tests should be performed in a separate edit run at the beginning of the processing. Normally, the input-validation tests are included in programs to perform data-conversion operations such as scanning data into the computer. If these tests are included in programs performing such operations, the controls may be used without significantly increasing the computer run time.

Preventive controls are located throughout the entire IT system. Many of these controls are executed prior to the data entering the computer programs. This section discusses the following preventive controls:

Source-data authorization

Data input

Source-data preparation

Turnaround documents

Prenumbered forms

Input validation

File auto-updating

Processing controls

Source-Data Authorization

After data have been recorded properly, there should be control techniques to ensure that the source data have been authorized. Typically, authorization should be given for source data such as credit terms, prices, discounts, commission rates, overtime hours, and so forth.

The input documents, where possible, should have evidence of authorization and should be reviewed by the internal control group in data processing. To the extent practical, the computer should be utilized as much as possible to authorize input. This may be done through programmed controls.

Data Input

Data input is the process of converting data from non-machine-readable form (such as hard-copy source documents) into a machine-readable form so that the computer can update files with the transactions. Because the data-input process is typically a manual operation, control is needed to ensure that the data input has been performed accurately.

Source-Data Preparation

In many automated systems, conventional source documents are still used and, therefore, no new control problems are presented prior to the conversion of source documents into machine-readable form. Specially designed forms promote the accuracy of the initial recording of the data. A pre-audit of the source documents by knowledgeable personnel to detect misspellings, invalid codes, unreasonable amounts, and other improper data helps to promote the accuracy of input preparation.

In IT systems where the source document is eliminated or is in a form that does not permit human review, control over source-data preparation should be such that access to, and use of, the recording and transmitting equipment is properly controlled to exclude unauthorized or improper use.

Turnaround Documents

Other control techniques to promote the accuracy of input preparation include the use of turnaround documents, which are designed to eliminate all or part of the data to be recorded at the source. A good example of a turnaround document is a bill from an oil company. Normally, the bill has two parts: one part is torn off and included with the remittance you send back to the oil company as payment for your bill; the other you keep for your records. The part you send back normally includes prerecorded data for your account number and the amount billed so that this returned part can be used as the input medium for computer processing of the cash receipts for the oil company.

Prenumbered Forms

Sequential numbering of the input transaction form with full accountability at the point of document origin is another traditional control technique. This can be accomplished either by using prenumbered forms or by having the computer issue sequential numbers.

Input Validation

An important segment of input processing is the validation of the input itself. This is an extremely important process because it is really the last point in the input preparation where errors can be detected before files are updated. The primary control techniques used to validate the data are associated with the editing capabilities of the computer.

Based on the characteristics of the computer, an IT system has unique capabilities to examine or edit each element of information processed by it. This editing involves the ability to inspect and accept (or reject) transactions according to validity or reasonableness of quantities, amounts, codes, and other data contained in input records. The editing ability of the computer can be used to detect errors in input preparation that have not been detected by other control techniques discussed previously.

The editing ability of the computer is achieved by installing checks in the program of instructions—hence, the term "program checks." They include the following:

- **Validity tests.** Validity tests are used to ensure that transactions contain valid transaction codes, characters, and field sizes. For example, in an accounts receivable system, if only PB through PL are valid transaction codes for input, then input with other codes is rejected by the computer. In a labor data collection system, all time transactions and job transactions could be checked by the computer against the random-access file of active job numbers, and non-matches indicated on a report could be brought to the attention of the shop foreman.

- **Completeness tests.** Completeness checks are made to ensure that the input has the prescribed amount of data in all data fields. For example, a payroll application requires that each new employee have data in all the fields in the input screen be valid data. A check may also be included to see that all characters in a field are either numeric or alphabetic.

- **Logical tests.** Logical checks are used in transactions where various portions, or fields, of the record bear some logical relationship to one another. A computer program can check these logical relationships to reject combinations that are erroneous even though the individual values are acceptable.

- **Limit tests.** Limit tests are used to test record fields to see whether certain predetermined limits have been exceeded. Generally, reasonable time, price, and volume conditions can be associated with a business event. For example, on one payroll application, the computer is programmed to reject all payroll rate changes greater than 15 percent of the old rate. The Hours field is checked to see whether the number of hours worked exceeds 44. In another application, an exception report is generated when a customer's balance plus the total of his unfilled orders exceeds his credit limit.

- **Self-checking digits.** Self-checking digits are used to ensure the accuracy of identification numbers such as account numbers. A check digit is determined by performing some arithmetic operation on the identification number itself. The arithmetic operation is formed in such a way that typical errors encountered in transcribing a number (such as transferring two digits) will be detected.

- **Control totals.** Control totals are used to ensure that data is complete and/or correct. For example, a control total could indicate the number of active employees to be paid and the accumulated net pay for a weekly payroll.

File Auto-Updating

The updating phase of the processing cycle is the auto-updating (via computer) of files with the validated transactions. Typically, auto-updating involves sequencing transactions, comparing transaction records with master-file records, performing computations, and manipulating and reformatting data for the purpose of updating master files and producing output data for distribution to user departments for subsequent computerized processing.

The accuracy of file updates depends on controls to ensure the programming, hardware checks designed and built in to the equipment by the manufacturer, and programmed controls included in the computer programs themselves.

Another control technique for the proper updating of files is file maintenance. File maintenance consists of the procedures involved in making changes to the permanent information contained in master files, such as an employee's name, address, employee number, and pay rate. Because these data are so important to the proper computerized processing of files, formalized procedures are required to make changes to this type of permanent information. All master-file changes should be authorized in writing by the department initiating the change. A notice or register of all changes should be furnished to the initiating department to verify that the changes were made.

Processing Controls

As discussed previously, programmed controls are an important part of application control. Programmed controls on the auto-updating of files are also important because they are designed to detect data loss, check mathematical computations, and ensure the proper posting of transactions. Programmed checks to detect data loss or incorrect processing include record counts, control totals, and has totals:

- **Record count.** A *record count* is the number of records a computer processes, which can then be compared with a predetermined count. Typically, a record count is established when the file is assembled, and the record count is carried as a control total at the end of the file and adjusted whenever records are added or deleted. For example, a record count may be established for all new hires or fires processed. This record count can then be compared internally (if a control card is included with the input transactions) or manually to predetermined totals of new hires or fires. Each time the file is processed, the records are recounted and the quantity is balanced to the original or adjusted total. Although the record count is useful as a proof of processing accuracy, it is difficult to determine the cause of error if the counts are out of balance.

- **Control total.** A *control total* is made from amount or quantity fields in a group of records and is used to check against a control established in previous or subsequent manual or computer processing.

- **Has total.** A *has total* is another form of control total made from data in a non-quantity field (such as vendor number or customer number) in a group of records.

Programmed checks of mathematical calculations include limit checks, cross-footing balance checks, and overflow tests.

Some calculations produce illogical results, such as million-dollar payroll checks or negative-amount payroll checks. Such calculations can be highlighted in exception reports with the use of limit checks, which test the results of a calculation against predetermined limits. For example, a payroll system may include limit checks to exclude from machine payroll check preparation all employees with payroll amounts greater than $500 or less than $0.

Cross-footing balance checks can be programmed so that totals can be printed and compared manually or internally during processing. For example, the computer-audit program is used in testing accounts receivable and in selecting accounts for confirmation. Each account is aged according to the following categories: current, 30, 60, and 90 days. The aged amounts for each account are temporarily stored in accumulators in the central processing unit. When all open items for the account have been aged, the aged totals for the account are compared to the account balance stored elsewhere in the central processing unit. Any difference results in an error. The program also includes for all accounts the accumulation and printout of aged amounts for manual comparison with the total accounts receivable balance.

The overflow test is widely used to determine whether the size of a result of a computation exceeds the registered size allocated to hold it. If so, there must be a means of saving the overflow portion of the results that otherwise would be lost. Overflow control may be programmed or may be available as a hardware or software control provided by the equipment manufacturer.

Programmed checks for proper postings may be classified as file checks. Basically, these are controls used to ensure that the correct files and records are processed together. The problem of using the correct file is significant in IT systems because of the absence of visible records and because of the ease with which wrong data can be stored electronically. The increase in the size and complexity of modern data processing systems has resulted in the growth of large system libraries containing data that can cost thousands of dollars to generate. For the purpose of preserving the integrity of data, various labeling techniques have been devised to provide maximum protection for a file to prevent accidental destruction or erasure and to ensure proper posting, updating, and maintenance. Two types of labels are used, external and internal. (External labels are a physical safeguard that properly falls under the category of documentation and operating practices. They are attached to the exterior of data processing media.)

Detective Controls

Detective controls alert individuals involved in a process of a problem so that action can be taken. One example of a detective control is a listing of all paychecks for individuals who worked more than 80 hours in a week. Such a transaction may be correct, or it may be a systems error, or even fraud.

Detective controls will not prevent problems from occurring, but rather will point out a problem once it has occurred. Examples of detective controls include batch control documents, batch serial numbers, clearing accounts, labeling, and so forth.

This section discusses the following detective controls:

- Data transmission
- Control register
- Control totals
- Documentation and testing
- Output checks

Data Transmission

After the source data have been prepared, properly authorized, and converted to machine-processable form, the data usually are transmitted from the source department to the data processing center. Data transmission can be made by conventional means (such as messenger and mail) or by data transmission devices that allow data transmission from remote locations on a timelier basis.

One important control technique in data transmission is batching, the grouping of a large number of transactions into small groups. Batching typically is related more to sequential-processing systems where transactions have to be put into the same order as the master files; however, batching may also apply to many direct-access systems where it may be desirable to batch input for control purposes.

Let us consider a payroll example as an illustration of batching. The source document may include time cards (source-data preparation), which should have been approved by a foreman (data authorization). For batching, these data time cards could be divided into groups of 25, with a control total for hours worked developed for each batch along with the total for all batches. Each batch transaction and its control totals could then be sent (data transmission) to the internal control group in the IT department for reconciliation with the batch control totals. Thus, batching and controls totals are useful techniques for the control of both data conversion and data transmission. These control totals could also be used during the computer processing phase during which the payroll files would be updated (as discussed later in this chapter).

Control totals should be developed on important fields of data on each record to ensure that all records have been transmitted properly from the source to the data processing center. Controls might be developed on the number of records in each batch or could be based on some quantitative field of data such as invoice amount or hours worked, and so on. Such controls serve as a check on the completeness of the transaction being processed and ensure that all transactions have been received in the data processing center.

Control Register

Another technique to ensure the transmission of data is the recording of control totals in a control log so that the input processing control group can reconcile the input controls with any control totals generated in subsequent computer processing.

Control Totals

Control totals are normally obtained from batches of input data. These control totals are prepared manually, prior to processing, and are then incorporated as input to the computer processing phase. The computer can be programmed to accumulate control totals internally and make a comparison with those provided as input. A message confirming the comparison should be printed out, even if the comparison did not disclose an error. These messages are then reviewed by the internal processing control group.

Documenting and Testing

Accuracy of programming is ensured by properly documenting and extensively testing program procedures. Good documentation aids in locating programming errors and facilitates correction even in the absence of the original designer or programmer. Extensive program test procedures under real-life conditions, testing all possible exceptions without actual programmer involvement, minimizes the possibilities of hidden program bugs and facilitates the smooth running of the system.

Output Checks

The output checks consist of procedures and control techniques to do the following:

- Reconcile output data, particularly control totals, with previously established control totals developed in the input phase of the processing cycle
- Review output data for reasonableness and proper format
- Control input data rejected by the computer during processing and distribute the rejected data to appropriate personnel
- Distribute output reports to user departments on a timely basis

Proper input controls and file-updating controls should give a high degree of assurance that the computer output generated by the processing is correct. However, it is still useful to have certain output controls to achieve the control objectives associated with the processing cycle. Basically, the function of output controls is to determine that the processing does not include any unauthorized alterations by the computer operations section and that the data are substantially correct and reasonable. The most basic output control is the comparison of control totals on the final output with original input control totals such as record counts or financial totals. Systematic sampling of individual items affords another output control. The testing can be done by the originating group or the control group.

One of the biggest controls in any system occurs when the originating group reviews reports and output data and takes corrective action. Review normally consists of a search for unusual or abnormal items. The programmed controls discussed previously, coupled with exception reporting, actually enhance the ability of responsible personnel to take necessary corrective action.

Another form of output control in some organizations is the periodic and systematic review of reports and output data by an internal audit staff. This group normally has the responsibility to evaluate operating activities of the company, including computer operations, to determine that internal policies and procedures are being followed.

Corrective Controls

Corrective controls assist in the investigation and correction of causes of exposures that have been detected. These controls primarily collect evidence that can be used to determine why a particular problem has occurred. Corrective action is often a difficult and time-consuming process; however, it is important because it is the prime means of isolating system problems. Many systems improvements are initiated by individuals taking corrective actions on problems.

Note that the corrective process itself is subject to error. Many major problems have occurred in organizations because corrective action was not taken on detected problems. Therefore, detective control should be applied to corrective controls.

Examples of corrective controls are audit trails, discrepancy reports, error statistics, backup and recovery, and so on. This section discusses two corrective controls: error detection and resubmission, and audit trails.

Error Detection and Resubmission

Until now we have talked about data control techniques designed to screen the incoming data to reject any transactions that do not appear valid, reasonable, complete, and so on. We also must deal with these errors upon detection. We must establish specific control techniques to ensure that all corrections are made to the transactions in error and that these corrected transactions are reentered into the system. Such control techniques should include the following:

- Having the control group enter all data rejected from the processing cycle in an error log by marking off corrections in this log when these transactions are reentered; open items should be investigated periodically.

- Preparing an error input record or report explaining the reason for each rejected item. This error report should be returned to the source department for correction and resubmission. This means that the personnel in the originating or source department should have instructions on the handling of any errors that might occur.

- Submitting the corrected transactions through the same error detection and input validation process as the original transaction.

Audit Trails

Another important aspect of the processing cycle is the *audit trail*. The audit trail consists of documents, journals, ledgers, and worksheets that enable an interested party (for example, the auditor) to trail an original transaction forward to a summarized total or from a summarized total backward to the original transaction. Only in this way can he determine whether the summary accurately reflects the business's transactions.

Cost/Benefit Analysis

In information systems, a cost is associated with each control. Because no control should cost more than the potential errors it is established to detect, prevent, or correct, the cost of controls must be evaluated. As part of that evaluation, remember that the extent to which controls are poorly designed or excessive, they become burdensome and may not be used. This failure to use controls is a key element leading to major exposures.

Preventive controls are generally the lowest in cost. Detective controls usually require some moderate operating expense. On the other hand, corrective controls are almost always quite expensive. Prior to installing any control, some cost/benefit analysis should be done.

Controls need to be reviewed continually. This is a prime function of the auditor, who should determine whether controls are effective. As the result of such a review, an auditor will recommend adding, eliminating, or modifying system controls.

Assessing Internal Controls

If software testers perform tests to evaluate the adequacy of a system of internal controls, the work of internal auditors is lessened. The internal auditors would be able to rely on the work performed by the software testers. However, it is recommended that software testers confine their tests to identifying strengths and weaknesses of internal controls. The identified weaknesses can form the basis of improving the system of controls within an application system.

Figure 17-2 illustrates the workbench for assessing internal controls.

Task 1: Understand the System Being Tested

Testing the adequacy of a system of internal controls begins with a tester understanding the objectives and implementation of an application system. When preparing for any type of test of an application system, the tester needs this background information on the application system. The background information can be obtained in two ways:

- **Study the system documentation.** The documentation from the user area about the application system, as well as the documentation prepared by the system development team, provides information on the application system. This documentation will not only help the tester understand the system but will also be an important component in performing Task 3, which is a review of the application system controls.

- **Interview the application system stakeholders.** The tester may want to talk to various individuals/groups that have a stake in the processing of the application system. The types of people interviewed may include the following:

- **Customer personnel.** Those who have requested the info system for their processing purposes.

- **System users.** Those individuals who will use the system to perform their day-to-day responsibilities

- **Control personnel.** Those that have the responsibility to ensure that the application system is under control and, if not, to take appropriate action.

- **Internal auditors.** If the organization's internal auditors have reviewed the application system in the user area, they have knowledge that would help the tester determine the types of tests to perform.

Work Paper 17-1 is an application internal-control questionnaire. Section A of this questionnaire defines a minimum acceptable level of documentation for the tester to understand the application system using system documentation.

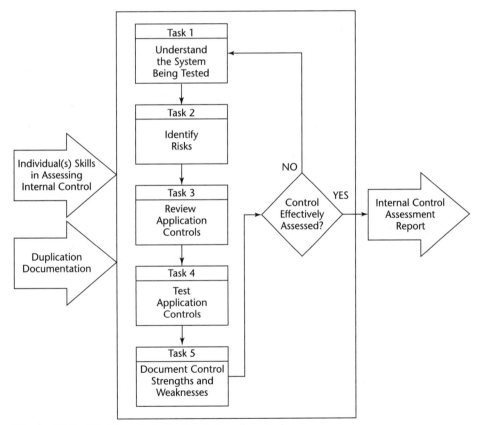

Figure 17-2 Workbench for testing internal controls.

Task 2: Identify Risks

Ideally, system documentation includes the application system risks. This is normally a component of the process system developers use to help define requirements. If the system developers have not done this, those assigned testing responsibilities for the application system should have completed a risk-assessment activity. The seven-step software-testing process presented earlier in this book provides a methodology for identifying application system risks.

These risks become the requirements for designing controls. First the risk must be identified, and then the exposure estimated and the threats identified. When you know the exposure and threats, a decision can be made as to the importance of controlling the risk. For example, if the risk is minor (for example, $100 or less), no controls may be needed. On the other hand, if the risk is high, in the hundreds of thousands of dollars, significant strong controls are needed.

Testers should not make decisions about whether a specific risk requires controls. That is the responsibility of the customer/user of the application system. However, if the customer/users have not determined whether controls are needed, and estimated the strength of controls that might be needed, testers should merely identify this as a weakness in the system of internal controls. It would not be necessary for the testers to estimate the exposure, but rather just indicate a specific risk that has not been controlled through the application system's internal controls.

Task 3: Review Application Controls

A detailed review of the system should encompass an understanding of both the details of the processing and the major controls over the major phases of the application (namely, input, processing, and output). A useful starting point to enable the tester to determine the details of processing is the review of the system's documentation, such as systems flowcharts, narrative description, and record layouts of transactions being processed and the master files being updated. The review of the system's documentation should be followed by interviews with user and system personnel about the specific control aspects of the application. Work Paper 17-1 provides questions that the tester should ask when reviewing a specific application. The tester should be involved in reviewing documentation for the specific application to determine the nature of the input controls, processing controls, output controls, and file controls (types of controls discussed earlier in this chapter).

Task 4: Test Application Controls

After the tester has reviewed the system documentation and has interviewed relevant IT and user personnel, the tester should have a pretty good understanding of the nature of the specific application and the types of controls included. The information obtained through the initial review of the system should then be supplemented by tracing different types of transactions through the system. The tracing of transactions is designed to establish the existence of system procedures and to confirm the tester's understanding of the system obtained through discussions with responsible personnel and through the review of systems documentation.

The tester may be able to test the system in a non–computer-processing way; in other situations, it may be desirable, if not necessary, to test with the use of computer processing.

Testing Without Computer Processing

If the processing application being evaluated is well documented and a visible audit trail exists, the tester may test the existence and effectiveness of the client's controls and processing procedures by checking source data, control reports, error listings, transaction registers, and management reports. The tester, in effect, views the computer program as a black box and makes an inference about what goes on in the program by looking at known input (source documents) and known output (i.e., error listings or transaction registers).

Testing without using computer processing or by using conventional source documents and printed outputs is a process quite familiar to testers and requires no further discussion.

Testing with Computer Processing

When testing the applications system, dynamic testing is used primarily to obtain information about the operation of the application and the programmed controls. Basically, there are two ways to test a system with the computer: the test-data approach and the mini-company approach.

Test-Data Approach

The test-data approach is one of the methods available to the tester to evaluate computer-based systems. This approach is primarily used to obtain information about the operation of the computer program or set of programs in an application and about the program controls.

The test-data method is probably most applicable when:

- A significant part of the system of internal control is embodied in the computer program.

- There are gaps in the audit trail making it difficult or impractical to trace input to output or to verify calculations.

- The volume of records is so large that it may be more economical and more effective to use test-data methods instead of manual testing methods.

Because most accounting and financial processing systems involve the updating of records, the use of test data usually involves the use of master records. So, as Figure 17-3 suggests, the sample transactions processed with master records determine how the computer system and programmed controls update the master files and generate output.

As the diagram indicates, the tester, with an understanding of how the computer program (including the programmed controls) should operate, develops predetermined processing results that he compares to the actual results from his testing process. Based on the comparison of actual results to predetermined results, he makes some conclusions about the effectiveness and existence of the system and programmed controls.

The inherent advantage of creating test transactions over selecting actual transactions is that the tester may include representative types of transactions in his tests with relative ease. Conventionally, to test the system, the tester selects actual accounting transactions previously processed by the client. Typically, this approach calls for tracing several transactions from the recording of the source documents, through whatever intermediate records might exist, to the output reports or records produced. Often this approach is incomplete and inexact, and the transactions do not include the ones requiring exception handling. By creating transactions, the tester can process data that are truly representative and that can include any type of transactions.

By several methods, the tester can determine the types of transactions to be included in his test data. One approach is to analyze the data used to test the computer programs. Much of such test data tests the processing steps and controls that the tester is interested in. Such a method is the most expedient because many transactions can be devised by mere duplication or slight modification of the system test data. This method has the added advantage of reviewing the system procedures in testing. Such a review might prove highly informative and beneficial to user/personnel by uncovering outdated tests and areas in the program not being tested at all. Another and more time-consuming way to determine the types of transactions to include in the test data involves analyzing the input records and creating simulated transactions in accordance with the test objectives. Typically, a combination of the two approaches is necessary to include all the transactions that the tester is interested in processing.

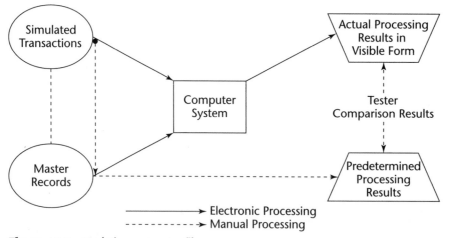

Figure 17-3 Updating computer files.

Regardless of the approach used to determine the types of transactions to be processed, several observations should be made. All possible combinations within all data fields need not be set out as separate transactions. Distinguish between data fields that merely represent identification data (that is, account numbers, social security numbers) and those that involve invariable data. In the case of the former, only a limited number of possibilities needs be included to test the identification routines in the program. For example, to test sequence checking and identification comparison routines, a transaction with a valid transaction code and employee number and containing valid information could be placed out of sequence in the test deck. Additional tests for sequence checking and identification comparison would not be necessary. Not all combinations within variable data fields need testing either.

The tests should include transactions that determine the processing and handling of the following general conditions:

- Valid conditions

- Out-of-sequence conditions

- Out-of-limits conditions

- Routines arising from a major decision point where alternative processing takes place as a result of comparing transaction records with master records (that is, where the transaction identification number can be greater, equal to, or less than the identification number on the master record)

- Units of measure differences (that is, tons instead of pounds)

- Incomplete, invalid, or missing input information

- Wrong master and/or transaction files

- Numeric characters in fields where alphabetic characters belong and vice versa

- Characters in certain fields that exceed prescribed length (an overflow condition)

- Illogical conditions in data fields where programmed consistency checks test the logical relationship between the fields

- Conditions where transaction codes or amounts do not match the codes or amounts established in tables stored in internal memory

Obviously, all these conditions cannot be tested with each type of transaction, but the majority of them may be tested in processing all transactions included in the test data.

- **Obtaining master records.** The tester must obtain master records with which to process the test transactions. The contents of the master records must also be available in visible form to compute the predetermined results for comparison with output resulting from the processing of test data.

  Although actual master records may be readily obtained in many systems, getting the same records in printed form without advance planning is difficult. One method is to time the tests so they are processed with the output master file used to prepare a printed report, such as the accounts receivable aged trial balance or an inventory report. Another method is to have an inquiry program prepared that will print out selected master records from the master file to be used in processing the test transactions.

- **Control of client's program.** One of the important procedures for testing a system is to make sure that the program being tested is the one the company actually uses to process data.

Mini-Company Approach

The mini-company approach appears to have great potential for fast-response systems. This approach overcomes some of the limitations of the test-data approach and enables remote entry of test data, online testing, and surprise testing of systems.

The mini-company approach can be defined as a means of passing fictitious test transactions through a computer system simultaneously with live data, without adversely affecting the live files or outputs. In other words, it is a small subsystem of the regular system. A separate set of outputs, including statistics and reports, are produced for the mini-company.

Consider how the mini-company approach could be used in a payroll system. In the time-recording system, a fictitious department could set up records for fictitious employees included as part of the live master file. The test transactions or mini-company transactions could be entered into the system through the terminals used for time recording and run with normal transactions. Exception reports on clock-in transactions and job transactions could be prepared for the mini-company for unusual or error transactions entered. The valid transactions for the mini-company recorded on the daily transactions tape could be separated from the actual data and then processed in a normal manner, generating daily labor reports and providing input for payroll processing and preparation of payroll reports, including payroll checks. The results of the mini-company's input could be compared with results predetermined to indicate any irregularities in controls or processing.

Transaction Flow Testing

Transaction flow testing is a method used to document controls in computerized applications. This control review method requires the auditor to identify the following:

- The organization's cycles of business activities
- The types of transactions that flow through each cycle (for example, in the payroll cycle are new employee transactions, employee rate increase transactions, hours worked transactions, absences transactions, and so on)
- The functions that are performed within each cycle to recognize, authorize, process, classify, and report transactions (activities performed within each cycle; for example, in a payroll system activities include authorizing a change to pay rates, the classification of absences by type, and the preparation of output such as payroll checks)
- Specific internal control objectives for each cycle
- The internal control techniques used to achieve each stated objective

Transaction flow testing requires the tester to develop a flowchart showing what transactions flow through the business activity being tested. As the tester traces the transaction flow, the tester would indicate the various functions performed on that transaction in the order in which they occur. The control objective at each point is identified, as well as the technique used to achieve that objective.

Using this flowchart of transaction processing, documented in accordance with the transaction flow testing methodology, provides the auditor with the type of information needed to assess the adequacy of internal control.

Objectives of Internal Accounting Controls

Objectives of internal control for an entity's cycles and its financial planning and control function can be developed using a step-down analysis. As shown in Figure 17-4, the analysis begins with the broad objectives of internal control contained in professional accounting literature.

From such an analysis, two levels of objectives can be identified:

- Systems control and financial planning and control objectives
- Cycle control objectives

The systems control and financial planning and control objectives are more specific than the broadly stated objectives of internal control contained in professional accounting literature. Cycle control objectives can be developed from the systems control objectives by refining them for the different categories of transactions found within a cycle.

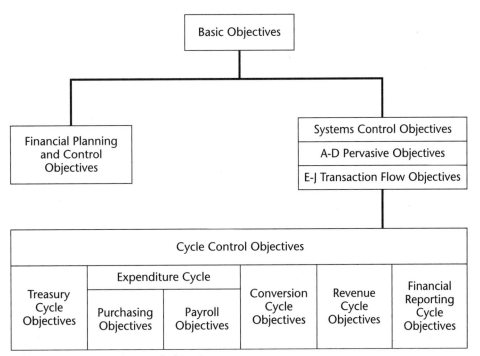

Figure 17-4   Internal control objectives.

Systems Control Objectives

This section identifies ten systems control objectives that apply to all accounting systems in all industries. For convenience in reference, the systems control objectives are identified as A through J. The first four (A through D) are pervasive and deal with authorization, classification, substantiation and evaluation, and physical safeguards. The final six (E through J) address the flow of transactions through a system.

The systems control objectives are as follows:

A. Authorizations should be in accordance with criteria established by the appropriate level of management.

B. Transactions should be classified in a manner that permits the preparation of financial statements in conformity with generally accepted accounting principles and management's plan.

C. Report and database contents should be periodically substantiated and evaluated.

D. Access to assets should be permitted only in accordance with management's authorization.

E. Economic events should be recognized and submitted for acceptance on a timely basis.

F. All, and only, economic events meeting management's criteria should be accurately converted to transactions and accepted for processing on a timely basis.

G. All accepted transactions should be processed accurately, in accordance with management's policies, and on a timely basis.

H. The results of processing should be reported accurately.

I. Database elements should accurately reflect the results of processing.

J. Events affecting more than one system should result in transactions that are reflected by each system in the same accounting period.

Systems control objectives apply to all cycles. They are not intended, however, to be used directly in evaluating an entity's internal control techniques. Rather, they represent a base from which specific cycle control objectives applicable to an individual entity can be developed.

Financial Planning and Control Objectives

In addition to the ten systems control objectives, four financial planning and control objectives may be used to evaluate the techniques employed by management to define and communicate the objectives and business of the entity; the long- and short-range plans for the entity; and the framework for reporting to the designated representatives of stockholders, owners, or members. Figure 17-5 shows the relationship between these control objectives and transaction processing. These financial planning and control objectives are as follows:

- The objectives of the entity and the nature of its business activities should be defined and communicated.

- A strategic (long-range) plan should be maintained and communicated.

- A short-range plan should be developed and communicated.

- Management's plans and the performance of the entity should be regularly reported to the designated representatives of the shareholders, owners, or members

The relationship of these matters to internal accounting controls may seem remote, particularly since the management planning process extends beyond accounting and financial disciplines and embraces marketing, productions, public relations, and legal and legislative considerations. A financial plan is, however, a quantification of an entity's total planning process. A well-developed, properly communicated, and effectively administered financial plan is a powerful tool for controlling economic events.

Cycle Control Objectives

Specific internal control objectives can be derived for each of an entity's recognized cycles from the systems control objectives. Cycle control objectives should address authorization, transaction processing, classification, substantiation and evaluation, and access to assets within each cycle, as follows:

- **Authorization objectives derived from systems control objective A.** These objectives address controls for securing compliance with policies and criteria established by management as part of the financial planning and control function.

- **Transaction processing objectives derived from systems control objectives E through J.** These objectives address the controls over recognition, processing, and reporting of transactions and adjustments.

- **Classification objectives derived from systems control objective B.** These objectives address controls over the source, timeliness, and propriety of journal entries.

- **Substantiation and evaluation objectives derived from systems control objective C.** These objectives address periodic substantiation and evaluation of reported balances and the integrity of processing systems.

- **Physical safeguard objectives derived from systems control objective D.** These objectives address access to assets, records, critical forms, processing areas, and processing procedures.

The illustrative cycle control objectives are oriented toward a manufacturing entity in which the following cycles are recognized:

Treasury

Expenditure (Purchasing)

Expenditure (Payroll)

Conversion

Revenue

Financial Reporting

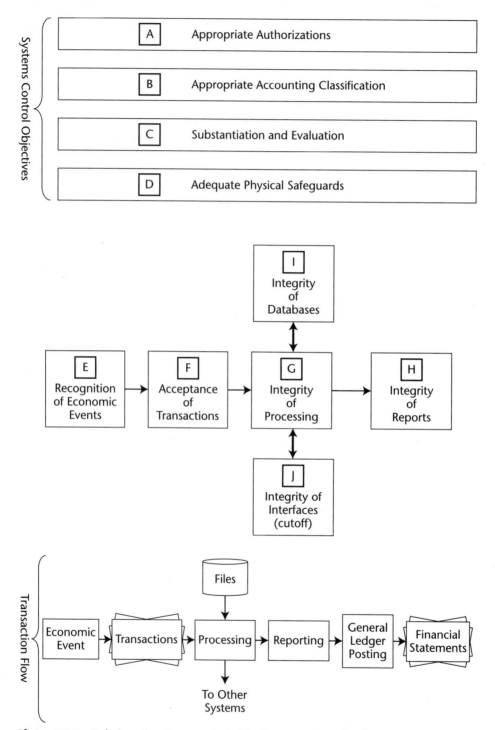

Figure 17-5   Relation of systems control objectives to transaction flow.

The illustrative objectives make certain assumptions about the entity. For example, the functions that are assumed to be part of the expenditure (purchasing) cycle are purchasing, receiving, accounts payable, and cash disbursements. In the conversion cycle, as another example, it is assumed that the entity has a cost accounting system.

Although the illustrative cycle control objectives have a particular industry orientation and are based on a number of assumptions, they probably are usable, with only minor modifications, by many entities in a wide variety of industries.

Modifications should be made to recognize the nature of economic activity in an entity's industry and the terminology and transaction-processing methods that are unique to the industry. For example, objectives identified for a particular retail company that makes only cash sales may address controls over cash registers (which are not much of a problem to most manufacturers) while ignoring customer accounts receivable. Similarly, the objectives for a utility might recognize that services delivered are billed on the basis of meter readings rather than delivery tickets. Whatever modifications are made, however, the internal control objectives for a cycle should derive from the control objectives for a cycle, which should derive from the ten systems control objectives to ensure coverage of each major control within each significant flow of activity.

Results of Testing

At the completion of Tasks 1 through 4, testers have gathered the following information about the test performed on internal controls:

Risks for which there were no controls

Controls for which there were no risks

Controls that were not adequate to control the risk to the level specified by the stakeholders of the application system

Interfaces to other systems that are not adequately controlled (see the material on control cycles)

Risks that appear to be adequately controlled

Task 5: Document Control Strengths and Weaknesses

Most testers do not have sufficient training to determine the adequacy of internal controls, which normally is an audit/management responsibility. What the testers can do is identify strengths and weaknesses that customer management can use to determine whether more controls are needed.

The following guide should prove helpful to testers to determine whether controls are strong, average, weak and or non-effective.

- **Strong controls.** An automated preventive control with an automated corrective action—for example, a control that checks the customers credit limit and denies a purchase if that credit limit is exceeded.

- **An automated detective control with a monitored corrective action.** A detective control might identify a customer ordering more than the normal number of a product, with a message going to marketing personnel that must be responded to.

- **A manual preventive control with a monitored corrective action.** An instructor in a warehouse checks to ensure that the products shipped are those on the invoice, and if not, stops shipment until the correct shipment can be determined.

- **Weak controls.** A manual preventive control with a manual corrective process but not a required process—for example, a guard checks employees' badges manually but does not have to stop an employee from entering if the guard is busy with other actions (for example, a telephone call) or if the guard recognizes that individual as an employee.

- **Non-effective controls.** A detective control with no action required—for example, a computer compiler message does not require the programmer to take action.

If risks have been identified, and exposures estimated, the tester's report of strengths and weaknesses should be based on level of risk. This is consistent with a concept of internal controls. The tester would look at the totality of controls from the initiation of the source information to the use of the output deliverables.

If risks are not identified in the system documentation, testers would use the risks determined in Task 2 of this process to report strengths and weaknesses.

Quality Control Checklist

Testers should use the questionnaire in Work Paper 17-1 as a quality-control checklist for assessing their organization's level of internal control.

Summary

This chapter examined a five-step process to test the adequacy of internal controls in an application system. The chapter also discussed preventive, detective, and corrective control categories to help the tester understand controls and determine control strength and weaknesses. For more information on building and/or testing systems of internal control, visit www.internalcontrolinstitute.com.

WORK PAPER 17-1   Internal Control Questionnaire

QUESTION	YES	NO	COMMENTS

A. Documentation

Documentation consists of work papers and records that describe the system and procedures for performing a processing task. It is the basic means of communicating the essential elements of the data processing system and the logic followed by the computer programs. Preparing adequate documentation is a necessary, although frequently neglected, phase of data processing. A lack of documentation indicates a serious weakness within the management control over a data processing installation.

■ Is the program supported by an adequate documentation file? A minimum acceptable level of documentation should include the following:

   Problem statement
   System flowchart
   Transactions and activity codes
   Record layouts
   Operator instructions
   Program flowchart
   Program listing
   Approval and change sheet
   Description of input and output forms

B. Input Controls

Input controls are designed to authenticate the contents of source documents and to check the conversion of this information into machine-readable formats or media. Typically, these controls will not be designed to detect 100 percent of all input errors because such an effort would be either too costly or physically impractical. Therefore, an economic balance must be maintained between the cost of error detection and the economic impact of an undetected error. This should be considered when evaluating input control. Judgment must be used when identifying essential information, the accuracy of which must be verified.

The following questions can also be used to evaluate internal control practices:

■ Are procedures adequate to verify that all transactions are being received for processing? To accomplish this, there must be some systematic procedure to ensure all batches entered for processing or conversions are returned. Basic control requirements are being met if the answer to one of the following questions is "yes."

(continues)

WORK PAPER 17-1 *(continued)*

QUESTION	YES	NO	COMMENTS
■ Are batch controls (at least an item count) being established before source documents are sent for processing?			
■ If batch controls are established, is there some other form of effective control (such as prenumbered documents) that ensures that all documents have been received?			
■ If no batch control is used, is there some other means of checking the receipt of all transactions? If yes, describe. (For example, in a payroll operation, the computer may match attendance time cards and corresponding job tickets for each employee as the master file is updated.)			
■ Are procedures adequate to verify the recording of input data? Control is being maintained if the answer to one of the following questions is "yes."			
■ Are important data fields subject to verification?			
■ If only some (or none) of the important data fields are verified, is an alternate checking technique employed? Acceptable alternate techniques include the following: Self-checking digits Control totals Has totals Editing for reasonableness			
■ If input data is converted from one form to another prior to processing on the computer system, are controls adequate to verify the conversion? Normal conversion controls include the following: Record counts Has totals Control totals			
■ If data transmission is used to move data between geographic locations, are controls adequate to determine transmission is correct and no messages are lost? Controls would normally include one or more of the following: Message counts Character counts Dual transmission			
■ Is the error correction process and the re-entry of the corrected data subject to the same controls as is applied to original data?			

WORK PAPER 17-1   *(continued)*

QUESTION	YES	NO	COMMENTS
■ Are source documents retained for an adequate period of time in a manner that allows identification with related output records and documents?			

C. Program and Processing Controls

Programs should be written to take the maximum advantage of the computer's ability to perform logical testing operations. In many cases, tests that could be employed are not used because the programmer does not know the logical limits of the data to be processed.

■ Is adequate control exercised to ensure that all transactions received are processed by the computer? Note: The answer to one of the following two questions should be "yes."

■ If predetermined batch control techniques are being used, does the computer accumulate matching batch totals in each run wherein the corresponding transactions are processed, and is there adequate provision for systematic comparison of computer totals with predetermined totals?

(Note: Having the computer internally match totals is more accurate than external visual matching. In addition, note that original batch totals are often internally combined into pyramid summary totals as different types of input transactions are merged during progressive stages. This is acceptable if it does not create a serious problem when attempting to locate errors when the overall totals are compared.)

■ If no batch total process is in use, is there an effective substitute method to verify that all transactions are processed? (Example: Any application where source documents are serially numbered and the computer system checks for missing numbers.)

■ Is adequate use being made of the system's ability to make logical data validity tests on important fields of information? These tests may include the following:

■ Checking code or account numbers against a master file or table

■ Using self-checking numbers

■ Testing for alpha or blanks in a numeric field

(continues)

WORK PAPER 17-1 *(continued)*

QUESTION	YES	NO	COMMENTS
■ Comparing different fields within a record to see whether they represent a valid combination of data			
■ Checking for missing data			
■ Is sequence checking employed to verify sorting accuracy of each of the following:			
■ Transactions that were presorted before entry into the computer (sequence check on the first input run)			
■ Sequenced files (sequence check incorporated within processing logic that detects out-of-sequence condition when files are updated or otherwise processed)			

D. Output Control

Output control is generally a process of checking whether the operation of input control and program and processing controls has produced the proper result. The following questions should be answered regarding all controls in effect:

■ Are all control totals produced by the computer reconciled with predetermined totals? (Basically, control totals on input plus control totals on files to be updated should equal the control totals generated by the output.)			
■ Are control total reconciliations performed by persons independent of the department originating the information and the data processing department?			
■ Are error corrections and adjustments to the master file:			
■ Prepared by the serviced departments' personnel?			
■ Reviewed and approved by a responsible official who is independent of the data processing department?			
■ Are procedures adequate to ensure that all authorized corrections are promptly and properly processed and that the corrections result in a file that matches the control totals?			

WORK PAPER 17-1   *(continued)*

QUESTION	YES	NO	COMMENTS
E. File Control			
Because data files can be destroyed by careless handling or improper processing, proper file control is vital in all data processing installations.			
■ Are control totals maintained on all files and are such totals verified each time the file is processed?			
■ Are all files backed up to permit file re-creation in case files are lost/destroyed during processing?			
■ Are all files physically protected against damage by fire or other accidental damage?			
■ Are there adequate provisions for periodic checking of the contents of master files by printout and review, checking against physical counts, comparison to underlying data, or other procedures?			

CHAPTER 18

Testing COTS and Contracted Software

(Note: Much of the material in this chapter derives from a forthcoming book on testing and supporting COTS applications by William E. Perry, Randall Rice, William Bender, and Christina Laiacona.)

Increasingly, organizations are buying software from stores. This software is sometimes referred to as "shrink-wrap" software or commercial off-the-shelf (COTS) software. The fact that it is commercially available does not mean that it is defect free, or that it will meet the needs of the user. COTS software must be tested.

Contracted software, or outsourced software, is a variation of COTS. The commonality between the two is that an organization other than the one using the software builds and tests the software. In contrast to COTS software, however, software development that is outsourced entails a closer relationship between the organization using the software and the organization building the software. Often, that closer relationship allows the contracting organization access to developers and/or the internal documentation regarding the software under development.

Over time, more organizations will rely on COTS software than software developed in-house. Although organizations will therefore need fewer or no software developers, in-house testing will still need to be performed. This chapter explains the role of testers when their organization acquires COTS software.

Overview

COTS software must be made to look attractive if it is to be sold. Thus, developers of COTS software emphasize its benefits. Unfortunately, there is often a difference between what the user believes the software can accomplish and what it actually does accomplish. Therefore, this chapter recommends both static and dynamic testing. Static testing concentrates on the user manual and other documentation; dynamic testing examines the software in operation. Note that normally you will have to purchase the software to perform these tests (unless the software developer provides a trial version for testing purposes). However the cost to purchase is usually insignificant compared to the problems that can be caused by software that does not meet an organization's needs. The cost of testing is always less than the cost of improper processing.

The testing process in this chapter is designed for COTS software, and for contracted or outsourced software for which a close relationship with the developer does not exist. However, the testing process presented in this chapter can be modified to test contracted software developed according to an organization's specified requirements. This chapter first explains the differences between COTS and contracted software. The chapter then discusses the changes that may need to be made to the testing process when software is custom developed under contract with outside sources.

COTS Software Advantages, Disadvantages, and Risks

This section distinguishes between COTS and contracted software, highlighting not only the differences but also the inherent advantages and disadvantages of COTS software and the testing challenges organizations face with COTS software. The final subsection details the risks organizations face when implementing COTS software.

COTS Versus Contracted Software

The two major differences between COTS and contracted software are as follows:

- **Who writes the requirements.** With COTS software, the developer writes the requirements. With contracted software, the contracting organization writes the requirements. Testers then perform verification testing on the requirements specified in the contract. This type of testing cannot be performed with COTS software.

- **Ability to influence and test during development.** During development, the only limits imposed on testers of contracted software are the contract provisions. In contrast, an organization seeking software cannot usually test COTS software during development at all (unless as part of a beta testing scheme).

Therefore, the main difference between the testing of COTS software and contracted software is that when the development of software is contracted, testing can occur prior to the delivery of the software.

COTS Advantages

Organizations gain multiple potential advantages when deploying COTS products, including the following:

- **They reduce the risks the come with internal software development.** Software projects are inherently risky. With COTS products, the vendor assumes the risks.

- **They reduce the costs of internal software development.** Software development is costly. With COTS products, the vendor spreads the costs over a population of customers.

- **They increase the speed and reliability of delivering applications.** You don't have to wait months or years for a system to become reality. COTS products are available immediately. The time-consuming part is the acquisition, integration, and testing of the products to deliver the right solution.

- **They increase the possible sources of software.** In-house software typically has one or a few sources: in-house developers, contracted developers, and perhaps outsourced development. In contrast, a variety of vendors might offer COTS products to meet a need.

- **They tend to be higher-quality software.** Although COTS products will have defects, COTS products have fewer overall defects as compared to software developed in-house. According to Capers Jones, in his book *Software Assessments, Assessments, Benchmarks, and Best Practices* (Addison-Wesley Professional, 2000), management information systems (MIS) applications have an average defect removal efficiency of about 85 percent. This is compared to 91 percent for commercial (vendor) software. This metric is derived by dividing the defects found by the producer by the total defects found during the life span of the application. The metric does not take into account defect severity.

- **They enable organizations to leverage newer technology.** To stay competitive and thus in business, COTS product vendors are motivated to stay current with technology. As operating systems and other applications progress in technology, COTS products must also evolve to maintain and support their customer base.

- **They enable easier integration with other applications.** Although there are integration issues with COTS products in general, applications developed in-house may have even more integration issues because private, nonstandard interfaces may be developed and used by in-house developers.

COTS Disadvantages

COTS products are not without their disadvantages (challenges), including the following:

- **Selecting the right package.** There may be many alternatives in the marketplace, but getting the best fit may require time to evaluate several alternatives.

- **Finding the right product.** After searching for and evaluating multiple products, you may realize that there are no acceptable products to meet your requirements.

■ **Product changes driven by vendors and other users.** When it comes to COTS products, you are one voice among many in the marketplace. Although you might like to see certain product features implemented, you have little control over a product's direction. The U.S. federal government used to have a lot of control over certain product directions; in the PC era, however, private-sector demand has greatly increased, and as a result, government influence has decreased.

■ **Dealing with vendor licensing and support issues.** A frequent complaint among COTS product customers is that vendors often change their licensing practices with little or no notice to the customers. Many times, the changes favor the vendor.

■ **Integrating with existing and future applications.** Many times, COTS products are used with other products. The integration with some products may be rather seamless, whereas other products may require extensive effort to develop interfaces.

■ **Testing from an external perspective.** As compared to applications developed in-house, COTS products do not allow the tester to have an internal perspective regarding the product for test-case development. Black-box testing (explained in the next section) is almost always the testing approach.

■ **Continual testing for future releases.** COTS testing is never done. The product evolves, and the environment and interfaces evolve (and therefore interfaced applications).

■ **Lack of control over the product's direction or quality.** Perhaps one of the most troubling issues in COTS products is that the customer has no control over certain things, such as the future direction of the product. Sometimes products are sold to other vendors, who then abandon support for a product just to make it noncompetitive with other products they own. Obviously, such practices frustrate organizations when they find a COTS product that meets their needs (but that might not meet their needs in the future).

Implementation Risks

As COTS products are deployed, some of the risks are as follows:

■ **Functional problems.** Some of the product features will not work at all, and some will work in a way that is less than desired. This risk can be mitigated by defining feature requirements before evaluating products.

■ **Security issues.** Currently, we seem to be in a "fix on failure" mode when it comes to COTS security. About the only line of defense is for customer and users to be constantly aware of new security vulnerabilities and stay current with patches.

■ **Compatibility issues.** There is also the risk that the product may work well in some environments but not in others. This risk can be mitigated by evaluating the product in all applicable environments.

- **Integration and interoperability issues.** The product implemented may require extensive efforts to integrate it with other applications. This risk can be mitigated by performing a "proof of concept" in the evaluation phase, as well as talking with other customers who have successfully integrated the same product into their operations.

- **Vendor issues.** There is always a risk that a vendor will go out of business, sell a product to a competitor, or drop support for a product. This risk can be mitigated to a small degree by making vendor stability and support points of evaluation criteria.

- **Procurement and licensing issues.** These are typically contracting concerns, but can also be mitigated to some extent by including such issues as evaluation criteria.

- **Testing issues.** Project sponsors and management often assume that the COTS vendor does most of the testing. Because of this misperception, testing is minimized, and major problems are missed until after deployment. You can minimize this risk with a full understanding of testing as a shared task between vendors and customers, and an understanding that testing is an ongoing job.

It is generally advisable with COTS software to have a repository for user-reported problems, perhaps someone appointed as manager for a specific COTS software package. All problems are reported to that individual. The individual will determine what action needs to be taken, and then notify all the software users.

Testing COTS Software

The testing of COTS products presents a number of challenges, including the following:

- **Unknown structure.** Structure in this case means more than just code—it can extend to interfaces, data stores, add-ins, APIs, and other elements of the architecture.

- **Unknown functional requirements.** COTS products are a good example of testing something without benefit of documented requirements. You may have access to a user manual or training guide, but those are not the same as documented requirements.

- **Requires an external, black-box approach.** Testing is almost always a black-box effort. This means there will be some functional tests that are unnecessary and some structural tests that are missed.

- **Testing integration "glue" with other applications.** Integration glue is what holds one COTS application to other applications (and perhaps to the operating system, too). This glue may be developed by vendors or by in-house developers. The challenge is to understand these points of integration, where they are used, and how to validate them.

- **Compatibility across platforms.** Many organizations have multiple platforms to span when using a particular COTS product. Ideally, the product will be compatible on all the platforms. However, even in operating systems from the same vendor, a product often behaves differently on various platforms. Some COTS products will not work at all on some related operating systems. For this reason, a degree of compatibility testing is often required.

■ **Release schedules.** Just when you think you have one test of a COTS product finished, a new version may be released that totally changes the look and feel of the product. These kinds of changes also affect the test cases, test scripts, and test data you have in place. Most COTS product release schedules are spaced months apart, but there can also be service packs and subreleases to fix problems.

■ **Continual regression testing.** When you consider the number of elements that work together in the COTS environment, nearly everything is in flux. That's why regression testing is needed. You do not have to test everything continuously, but you do need a workable set of test cases you can run as changes are seen in the operational environment.

■ **Technology issues.** The COTS product itself is only one element of the application to be tested. Because technology changes rapidly, the overall technical environment changes rapidly, too. These changes can include standards as well as software and hardware components. This fact reinforces the idea that testing is never really finished for a COTS product.

■ **Test-tool issues.** The test automation issues in COTS are huge. Ideally, you want automated test scripts that do not require extensive maintenance. There are two problems here, at least:

  ■ The COTS products under test will change (probably often) to keep up with new technology.

  ■ Test tools will change to keep up with technology about 6 to 12 months after the technology is introduced.

This means that there is often a window of time when you will not be able to automate the tests you would like to automate, or have been able to automate in the past. This situation is unlikely to improve.

Testing Contracted Software

The major differences between testing COTS software and testing contracted software are as follows:

■ **Importance of vendor reputation.** COTS testing focuses more on the application. With COTS, an organization is buying a specific application. Their concern is the applicability and quality of that application to achieve a specific organizational objective. With contracted software, the application is not developed in-house. In both cases, testers should be involved in the formulation of selection criteria to identify a vendor to build and maintain the software.

■ **Access to software developers.** Rarely does an organization acquiring COTS software have access to the software developers. Normally, they will work with a vendor's marketing group and help desk for answers to questions regarding a

COTS application. With contracted software, the contract can indicate the type of access that the acquiring organization wants with the software developers.

- **Ability to impact development.** With COTS software, the acquiring organization rarely has the ability to influence the development of the application. They may influence changes to the software but rarely the initial release of the software. With contracted software, the contract can indicate that the acquiring organization can meet with developers and propose alternative development methods for building and documenting the software.

- **Requirements definition.** With COTS software, the acquiring organization does not write the requirements for the software package. With contracted software, the acquiring organization writes the requirements. Therefore, with contracted software, if testers are going to be involved prior to acceptance testing they need to focus on the requirements to ensure that they are testable. In addition, testers may want to use verification-testing methods such as participating in reviews throughout the development cycle.

- **The number of vendors involved in software development.** With COTS software, generally only a single vendor develops the software. With contracted software, there may be multiple vendors. For example, some organizations use one vendor to select another vendor that will build the software. Some organizations contract for another vendor to test the software. Some contracted software may involve testers with multiple vendors and the coordination among those vendors.

Objective

The objective of a COTS testing process is to provide the highest possible assurance of correct processing with minimal effort. However, the testing process should be used for noncritical COTS software. If the software is critical to the ongoing operations of the organization, the software should be subject to a full scale of system testing, which is described in Part Three of this book. The testing in the process might be called *80-20 testing* because it will attempt with 20 percent of the testing effort to catch 80 percent of the problems. That 80 percent should include almost all significant problems (if any exist). Later in this chapter, you also learn how to test contracted software.

Concerns

Users of COTS software should also be concerned about the following:

- **Task/items missing.** A variance between what is advertised or included in the manual versus what is actually in the software.

- **Software fails to perform.** The software does not correctly perform the tasks/items it was designed to perform.

■ **Extra features.** Features not specified in the instruction manual may be included in the software. This poses two problems. First, the extra tasks may cause problems during processing; and second, if you discover the extra task and rely on it, it may not be included in future versions.

■ **Does not meet business needs.** The software does not fit with the user's business needs.

■ **Does not meet operational needs.** The system does not operate in the manner, or on the hardware configuration, expected by the user.

■ **Does not meet people needs.** The software does not fit with the skill sets of the users.

Workbench

A workbench for testing COTS software is illustrated in Figure 18-1. The workbench shows three static tasks: test business fit, test system fit, and test people fit. A fourth task is the dynamic test when the software is in an executable mode and the processing is validated. As stated earlier, the tests are designed to identify the *significant* problems, because a tester cannot know *all* the ways in which COTS software might be used (particularly if the software is disseminated to many users within an organization).

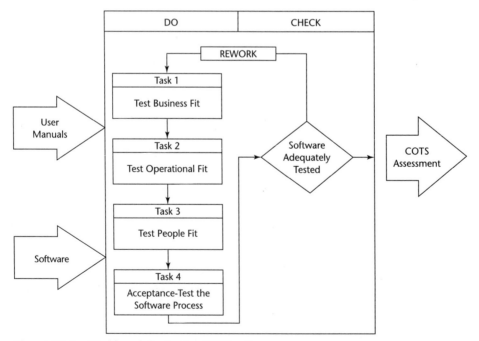

Figure 18-1   Workbench for testing COTS software.

Input

This testing process requires two inputs: the manuals (installation and operation) that accompany the COTS software, and the software itself. The manuals describe what the software is designed to accomplish and how to perform the tasks necessary to accomplish the software functions. Note that in some instances the user instructions are contained within the software. In such cases, the first few screens of the software may explain how to use the software.

Do Procedures

The execution of this process involves four tasks plus the check procedures. The process assumes that those conducting the test know how the software will be used in the organization. If the tester does not know how the software will be used, an additional step is required for the tester to identify the software functionality that users need. The following subsections describe the four tasks.

Task 1: Test Business Fit

The objective of this task is to determine whether the software meets your needs. The task involves carefully defining your business needs and then verifying whether the software in question will accomplish them. The first step of this task is defining business functions in a manner that can be used to evaluate software capabilities. The second step of this task is to match software capabilities against business needs. At the end of this task, you will know whether a specific software package is fit for your business.

Step 1: Testing Needs Specification

This test determines whether you have adequately defined your needs, which should be defined in terms of the following two categories:

- **Products/reports output.** Products/reports output refers to specific documents that you want produced by the computer system. In many instances, the style and format of the output products are important. Consider, for instance, a check/invoice accounting system. The specific location of the check does not have to be defined but, instead, just the categories of information to be included on the check. Computer-produced reports may also be important for tax information (e.g., employee withholding forms), financial statements where specific statements are wanted (e.g., balance sheets or statements of income and expense), or customer invoice and billing forms (which you might want preprinted to include your logo and conditions of payment).

■ **Management information.** This category tries to define the information needed for decision-making purposes. In the output product/report category, you were looking for a document; in this case, you are looking for information. How that information is provided is unimportant. Therefore, the structure of the document and what the documents are (or their size, frequency, or volume) are not significant. All you need is information.

No form is provided for documenting these needs; the method of documentation is unimportant. Writing them on a yellow pad is sufficient. However, it is important to define, document, and have those needs available when you begin your software-selection process.

After documenting your needs, evaluate them using the 10-factor test of completeness of business requirements illustrated in Work Paper 18-1. This evaluation consists of a cause-effect test that attempts to identify the potential causes of poor needs definition. This test indicates the *probability* that you have completely documented your needs. To complete this evaluation, follow these steps:

1. Familiarize yourself with the documented business needs.

2. Consider each of the ten items in Work Paper 18-1 one at a time as they relate to the documented business needs. This review challenges the adequacy of your business needs based on your personal knowledge of the business. Thus, this test must be done by someone knowledgeable in the business. (Note: It can be done by two or more people, if appropriate. In such cases, a consensus can be arrived at by either averaging the assessments or negotiating a common assessment.)

3. Indicate your agreement or disagreement with the statement based on your understanding of each item. Consider, for example, the first item in Work Paper 18-1 (i.e., that the system will experience very few changes over time). For each item assessed with regard to that statement, indicate whether you:

   ■ **SA.** Strongly agree with the statement.

   ■ **A.** Agree with the statement.

   ■ **N.** Neither agree nor disagree with the statement (i.e., are basically neutral and are not sure whether the statement is applicable or inapplicable).

   ■ **D.** Disagree with the statement.

   ■ **SD.** Strongly disagree with the statement.

   Check the appropriate assessment column for each of the ten statements.

4. Calculate an assessment score for each of the ten statements as follows: For each item checked SA, score 5 points; for each S, score 4 points; for each N, score 3 points; for each D, score 2 points; for each SD, score 1 point. Your final score will range between 10 and 50.

   The score can be assessed as follows:

   ■ **10–25 points: Poorly defined requirements.** You are not ready to consider buying a software package; do some additional thinking and discussion about this need.

- **26–37 points: The needs are barely acceptable, particularly at the low end of the range.** Although you have a good start, you may want to do some clarification of the reports or decision-making information.

- **38–50 points: Good requirements.** In this range, you are ready to continue the software testing process.

At the conclusion of this test, you will either go on to the next test or clarify your needs. My experience indicates that it is a mistake to pass this point without well-defined needs.

Step 2: Testing CSFs

This test tells whether the software package will successfully meet your business needs, or critical success factors (CSFs). CSFs are those criteria or factors that must be present in the acquired software for it to be successful. You might ask whether the needs are the same as the CSFs. They are, but they are not defined in a manner that makes them testable, and they may be incomplete. Often the needs do not take into account some of the intangible criteria that make the difference between success and failure. In other words, the needs define what we are looking for, and the critical success factors tell us how we will evaluate that product after we get it. They are closely related and complementary, but different in scope and purpose.

The following list indicates the needs/requirements for an automobile, and is then followed by the CSFs on which the automobile will be evaluated:

- Automobile requirements/needs:
    - Seats six people
    - Four doors
    - Five-year guarantee on motor
    - Gets 20 miles or more per gallon
    - Costs less than $12,000
- Critical success factors:
    - Operates at 20.5 cents or less per mile
    - Experiences no more than one failure per year
    - Maintains its appearance without showing signs of wear for two years

Some of the more common CSFs for COTS applications are as follows:

- **Ease of use.** The software is understandable and usable by the average person.

- **Expandability.** The vendor plans to add additional features in the future.

- **Maintainability.** The vendor will provide support/assistance to help utilize the package in the event of problems.

- **Cost-effectiveness.** The software package makes money for your business by reducing costs and so on.

- **Transferability.** If you change your computer equipment, the vendor indicates that they will support new models or hardware.

- **Reliability.** Software is reliable when it performs its intended function with required precision.

- **Security.** The system has adequate safeguards to protect the data against damage (for example, power failures, operator errors, or other goofs that could cause you to lose your data).

The CSFs should be listed for each business application under consideration. Work Paper 18-2, which is a test of fit, provides space to list those factors. Note that in most applications there are eight or fewer CSFs. Therefore, this test is not as time-consuming as it might appear.

Once Work Paper 18-2 has been considered, it can be used to test the applicability of the software package under evaluation. (Work Paper 18-2 provides space to identify the software package being tested.) When making the evaluation, consider the following factors:

- Thorough understanding of the business application

- Knowledge of the features of the software package

- Ability to conceptualize how the software package will function on a day-to-day basis

- Use of CSFs to indicate whether you believe one of the following:

  - There is a high probability that the software package will meet the CSF. (Mark an X in the Yes column.)

  - The software package does not have a high probability of meeting the CSF. (Mark an X in the No column.)

  - There is more or less than a 50–50 probability of the software package's success. (Mark an X in the appropriate column and then clarify your assessment in the Comments column.)

At the conclusion of this test, you will have matched your business needs against the software capabilities and assessed the probability of the software's success. If the probability of success is low (i.e., there are several No responses or highly qualified Yes responses), you should probably not adopt this software package. Clearly, additional study and analysis is warranted before you move forward and expend the resources to implement a potentially unsuccessful system.

Task 2: Test Operational Fit

The objective of this task is to determine whether the software will work in your business. Within your business, several constraints must be satisfied before you acquire the software, including the following:

- Computer hardware constraints

- Data preparation constraints

- Data entry constraints
- Other automated-processing constraints (e.g., if data from this software package must be fed into another software package, or receive data from another software package, those interface requirements must be defined)

At the end of this task, you will know whether the software fits into the way you do business and whether it will operate on your computer hardware.

This task involves three steps to ensure an appropriate fit between the software being evaluated and your in-house systems.

Step 1: Test Compatibility

This is not a complex test. It involves a simple matching between your processing capabilities and limitations and what the vendor of the software says is necessary to run the software package. The most difficult part of this evaluation is ensuring that the multiple software packages can properly interface.

This test is best performed by preparing a checklist that defines your compatibility needs. Software vendors are generally good about identifying hardware requirements and operating system compatibility. They are generally not good at identifying compatibility with other software packages.

In addition to the hardware on which the software runs, and the operating system with which it must interact, there are two other important compatibilities: compatibility with other software packages and compatibility with available data. If you have no other software packages that you want to have interact with this one, or no data on computer-readable media, you need not worry about these aspects of compatibility. However, as you do more with your computer, these aspects of compatibility will become more important (while the hardware and operating compatibility will become routine and easy to verify).

Finding someone who can tell you whether you have program and/or data compatibility is difficult. That someone must understand data formats, know what data format programs use, and know that those programs or data will work when they are interconnected. In many instances, trial and error is the only method of determination. However, the fact that one program cannot read data created by another program does not mean that the original data cannot be reused. For example, some utility programs can convert data from one format to another.

To prepare a compatibility list for the purpose of testing, use the information listed here:

- **Hardware compatibility.** List the following characteristics for your computer hardware:
  - Vendor
  - Amount of main storage
  - Disk storage unit identifier
  - Disk storage unit capacity
  - Type of printer

- Number of print columns
- Type of terminal
- Maximum terminal display size
- Keyboard restrictions

- **Operating systems compatibility.** List the following for the operating system used by your computer hardware:

  - Name of operating system (e.g., UNIX or Windows)
  - Version of operating system in use

- **Program compatibility.** List all the programs that you expect or would like this specific application to interact with. Be sure that you have the name of the vendor and, if applicable, the version of the program. Note that this linkage may be verifiable only by actually attempting to interact two or more systems using common data.

- **Data compatibility.** In many cases, program compatibility will answer the questions on data compatibility. However, if you created special files, you may need descriptions of the individual data elements and files. Again, as with program compatibility, you may have to actually verify through trial and error whether the data can be read and used by other programs. Note that in Step 3 (demonstration) you will have the opportunity to try to use your own data or programs to see whether you can utilize common data and pass parameters from program to program.

Step 2: Integrate the Software into Existing Work Flows

Each computer business system makes certain assumptions. Unfortunately, these assumptions are rarely stated in the vendor literature. The drawback is that you often must do some manual processing functions that you may not want to do in order to utilize the system. In such cases, you can search for COTS software to automate the manual processes.

The objective of this test is to determine whether you can plug the COTS software into your existing system without disrupting your entire operation. Remember the following:

- Your current system is based on a certain set of assumptions.
- Your current system uses existing forms, existing data, and existing procedures.
- The COTS software is based on a set of assumptions.
- The COTS software uses a predetermined set of forms and procedures.
- Your current system and the new COTS software may be incompatible.
- If they are incompatible, the current business system and the COTS software are not going to change—you will have to.
- You may not want to change—then what?

The process for test of fit of the COTS software into your existing system requires you to prepare a document flow diagram or narrative description. A document flow diagram is a pictorial or narrative description of how your process is performed. That is, you plug the COTS software into your existing system and then determine whether you like what you see. If you do, the COTS software has passed this test. If not, you either have to change your existing method of doing work or search for other software.

The data flow diagram is really more than a test. At the same time that it tests whether you can integrate the COTS software into your existing system, it shows you how to do it. It is both a system test and a system design methodology incorporated into a single process. So, to prepare the document flow narrative or document flow description, these three tasks must be performed:

1. **Prepare a document flow of your existing system.** Through personal experience or inquiry, quickly put down in document flow format the steps required to complete the process as it is now performed. Because there will be 15 or fewer steps in most instances, this should take only a few minutes.

2. **Add the COTS software's responsibility to the data flow diagram.** Use a colored pencil to cross out each of the tasks now being performed manually that will be performed by the computer. Indicate the tasks you will continue to perform manually in a different pencil color. If the computer is going to perform tasks that were not performed before, indicate those with a third color. At the end of this exercise, you will have a clearly marked list of which manual tasks were replaced by the computer, which manual tasks will remain as such, and which new tasks have been added.

3. **Modify the manual tasks as necessary.** Some of the manual tasks can stay as is; others will need to be added or modified. Again, do this in a different color. Difference pencil colors enable you to highlight and illustrate these changes.

The objective of this process is to illustrate the type and frequency of work flow changes that will be occurring. You can see graphically illustrated what will happen when the computer system is brought into your organization. For example, there might be tasks performed now that weren't performed before or tasks that were previously performed but are no longer necessary or tasks that had been performed by people which will now be performed by the computer. Having the computer perform those tasks might mean that the oversight that people had been providing will not be available any more.

At the end of this test, you must decide whether you are pleased with the revised work flow. If you believe the changes can be effectively integrated into your work flow, the potential COTS software integration has passed the test. If you think work-flow changes will be disruptive, you may want to fail the software in this test and either look for other software or continue manual processing.

If the testing is to continue, prepare a clean data flow diagram indicating what actions need to be taken to integrate the computer system into your organization's work flow. This new data flow diagram becomes your installation plan of action. It will tell you what changes need to be made, who is involved in them, what training might be necessary, and areas of potential work flow problems.

Step 3: Demonstrate the Software in Action

This test analyzes the many facets of software. Software developers are always excited when their program goes to what they call "end of job." This means that, among other things, it executes and concludes without abnormally terminating (i.e., stops after doing all the desired tasks). Observing the functioning of software is like taking an automobile for a test drive. The more rigorous the test, the greater the assurance you are getting what you expect.

Demonstrations can be performed in either of the following ways:

- **Computer store, controlled demonstration.** In this mode, the demonstration is conducted at the computer store, by computer store personnel, using their data. The objective is to show you various aspects of the computer software, but not to let you get too involved in the process. This is done primarily to limit the time involved in the demonstration.

- **Customer-site demonstration.** In this mode, the demonstration takes place at your site, under your control, by your personnel, using your information. It is by far the most desirable of all demonstrations, but many computer stores may not permit it unless you first purchase the COTS software.

These aspects of computer software should be observed during the demonstration:

- **Understandability.** As you watch and listen to the demonstration, you need to evaluate the ease with which the operating process can be learned. If the commands and processes appear more like magic than logical steps, you should be concerned about implementation in your organization. If you have trouble figuring out how to do something, think about how difficult it may be for some of your clerical personnel who understand neither the business application nor the computer.

- **Clarity of communication.** Much of the computer process is communication between man and machine. That is, you must learn the language of the computer software programs in order to communicate with the computer. Communication occurs through a series of questions and responses. If you do not understand the communications, you will have difficulty using the routine.

- **Ease of use of instruction manual.** While monitoring the use of the equipment, the tasks being demonstrated should be cross-referenced to the instruction manual. Can you identify the steps performed during the demonstration with the same steps in the manual? In other words, does the operator have to know more than is included in the manual, or are the steps to use the process laid out so clearly in the manual that they appear easy to follow?

- **Functionality of the software.** Ask to observe the more common functions included in the software: Are these functions described in the manual? Are these the functions that the salesperson described to you? Are they the functions that you expected? Concentrate extensively on the applicability of those functions to your business problem.

- **Knowledge to execute.** An earlier test has already determined the extent of the salesperson's knowledge. During the demonstration, evaluate whether a lesser-skilled person could as easily operate the system with some minimal training. Probe the demonstrator about how frequently he runs the demonstration and how knowledgeable he is about the software.

- **Effectiveness of help routines.** Help routines are designed to get you out of trouble. For example, if you are not sure how something works, you can type the word "help" or an equivalent, and the screen should provide you additional information. Even without typing "help," it should be easy to work through the routines from the information displayed onscreen. Examine the instructions and evaluate whether you believe you could have operated the system based on the normal instructions. Then ask the operator periodically to call the help routines to determine their clarity.

- **Evaluate program compatibility.** If you have programs you need to interact with, attempt to have that interaction demonstrated. If you purchased other software from the same store where you are now getting the demonstration, they should be able to show you how data is passed between the programs.

- **Data compatibility.** Take one of your data files with you. Ask the demonstrator to use your file as part of the software demonstration. This will determine the ease with which existing business data can be used with the new software.

- **Smell test.** While watching the demonstration, let part of your mind be a casual overseer of the entire process. Attempt to get a feel for what is happening and how that might affect your business. You want to have a sense of whether you feel good about the software. If you have concerns, attempt to articulate them to the demonstrator as well as possible to determine how the demonstrator responds and addresses those concerns.

To determine whether an individual has the appropriate skill level to use the COTS software, involve one or more typical potential users of the COTS software in the demonstrations (i.e., Task 3) and in the validation of the software processing (i.e., Task 4). If the selected users can perform those dynamic tests with minimal support, it is reasonable to assume that the average user will possess the skills necessary to master the use of the COTS software. On the other hand, if the selected user appears unable to operate the software in a dynamic mode, it is logical to assume that significant training and/or support will be required to use this COTS software.

Task 3: Test People Fit

The objective of this task is to determine whether your employees can use the software. This testing consists of ensuring that your employees have or can be taught the necessary skills.

This test evaluates whether people possess the skills necessary to effectively use computers in their day-to-day work. The evaluation can be of current skills or the program that will be put into place to teach individuals the necessary skills. Note that this includes the owner-president of the organization as well as the lowest-level employee.

First you select a representative sample of the people who will use the software. The sample need not be large. Then this group is given training, which might involve simply handing someone the manuals and software. The users then attempt to use the software for the purpose for which it is intended. The results of this test will show one of the following:

1. The software can be used as is.

2. Additional training/support is necessary.

3. The software is not usable with the skill sets of the proposed users.

Task 4: Acceptance-Test the Software Process

The objective of this task is to validate that the COTS software will, in fact, meet the functional and structural needs of users.

We have divided testing into functional and structural testing, which also could be called correctness and reliability testing. "Correctness" means that the functions produce the desired results. "Reliability" means that the correct results will be produced under actual business conditions.

Step 1: Create Functional Test Conditions

It is important to understand the difference between correctness and reliability because such an understanding affects both testing and operation. Let's look at a test example to verify whether gross pay was properly calculated. This could be done by entering a test condition showing 30 hours of work at $6 per hour. If the program works correctly, it produces $180 gross pay. If this happens, we can say that the program is functionally correct. These are the types of tests that should be prepared under this category.

The types of test conditions that are needed to verify the functional accuracy and completeness of computer processing include the following:

- All transaction types to ensure they are properly processed
- Verification of all totals
- Assurance that all outputs are produced
- Assurance that all processing is complete
- Assurance that controls work (e.g., input can be balanced to an independent control total)
- Reports that are printed on the proper paper, and in the proper number of copies
- Correct field editing (e.g., decimal points are in the appropriate places)
- Logic paths in the system that direct the inputs to the appropriate processing routines
- Employees who can input properly
- Employees who understand the meaning and makeup of the computer outputs they generate

The functional test conditions should be those defined in the test plan. However, because some of the test methods and business functions may be general in nature, the interpretation and creation of specific test conditions may require a significant increase of the test conditions. To help in this effort, a checklist of typical functional test conditions is provided as Work Paper 18-3.

The objective of this checklist is to help ensure that sufficient functional test conditions are used. As test conditions for the types listed on Work Paper 18-3 are completed, place a check mark next to that line. At the completion of the test conditions, those types of functional test conditions that have not been checked should be evaluated to determine whether they are needed. The checklist is designed to help ensure the completeness of functional test conditions.

Step 2: Create Structural Test Conditions

Structural, or reliability, test conditions are challenging to create and execute. Novices to the computer field should not expect to do extensive structural testing. They should limit their structural testing to conditions closely related to functional testing. However, structural testing is easier to perform as computer proficiency increases. This type of testing is quite valuable.

Some of the easier-to-perform structural testing relates to erroneous input. In some definitions of testing, this reliability testing is included in functional testing. It is included here because if the input is correct, the system performs in a functionally correct way; therefore, incorrect input is not a purely functional problem.

Most of the problems that are encountered with computer systems are directly associated with inaccurate or incomplete data. This does not necessarily mean that the data is invalid for the computer system. Consider the following example.

A photographic wholesaler sells film only by the gross. The manufacturer shrink-wrapped film in lots of 144, and the wholesaler limited sales to those quantities. If a store wanted less film, they would have to go to a jobber and buy it at a higher price. A small chain of photo-processing stores ordered film from this manufacturer. Unfortunately, the clerks did not really understand the ordering process. They knew only that they would get 144 rolls of film when they ordered. On the order form submitted to the manufacturer, the clerks indicated a quantity of 144. This resulted in 144 gross of film being loaded onto a truck and shipped to the shopping center. The small photo shop could not store that much film, and 143 gross were returned to the wholesaler. The net result was lost money for the manufacturer. In this case, 144 was a valid quantity, but incorrect for the desired order. This is a structural problem that needs to be addressed in the same manner that entering 144 on the computer when you meant to enter 14 must be addressed.

The second part of structural testing deals with the architecture of the system. Architecture is a data processing term that describes how the system is put together. It is used in the same context that an architect designs a building. Architectural problems that could affect computer processing include the following:

- Internal limits on the number of events that can occur in a transaction (e.g., number of products that can be included on an invoice)

- Maximum size of fields (e.g., quantity only 2 positions in length, making it impossible to enter an order for more than 99 items)

- Disk storage limitations (e.g., you are permitted to have only X customers)

- Performance limitations (e.g., the time to process transactions jumps significantly when you enter more than X transactions)

These are but a few of the potential architectural limitations placed on computer software. You must remember that each software system is finite and has built-in limitations. Sometimes the vendor tells you that you can from time to time find these limitations if you search through the documentation, and occasionally you won't know them until they occur. However, all limits can be determined through structural testing. The questions at hand are these: Do you feel competent to do it? Is it worth doing? The answers to these questions depend on the critical nature of the software and what would happen if your business is unable to continue computer processing because you reach the program limitation.

A final category of potential structural problems relates to file-handling problems. Although these do appear to be a problem, they are frequently found in computer software. Typical problems that occur are incorrect processing when the last record on a file is updated, or adding a record that will become the first record on a file. These types of problems have haunted computer programmers for years. In the PC software market, there are literally hundreds of thousands of people writing software. Some have good ideas but are not experienced programmers; thus, they fall into the age-old traps of file-manipulation problems.

As an aid in developing structural test conditions, Work Paper 18-4 lists the more common structural problem areas. You can use this checklist either to determine which types of structural test conditions you want to prepare or to check the completeness of the structural conditions included in your test matrix. Either way, it may spark you to add some additional test conditions to verify that the structure of your software performs correctly.

Modifying the Testing Process for Contracted Software

The four tasks used to test COTS software equally apply to the testing of contracted software. However, a new task is required, and Task 1 must be modified. The changes to the COTS testing process are made the same way as discussed previously in this book with regard to the seven-step testing process.

A new task must be included, and that task becomes the first task in the test process. The objective of this task is to determine the best vendor to build the contracted software. Testers therefore must evaluate the ability of various vendors to adequately test the software. The testers may actually want to include testing requirements in any requests for a proposal from a vendor. The testers may also want to consider being a part of the vendor's testing to ensure that the interests of the acquiring organization are appropriately represented.

Contracting/outsourcing organizations focus their testing efforts on whether the software meets system specifications. As mentioned many times in this book, there is often a difference between what is specified and what is needed. For example, the specifications may not clearly articulate that ease of use for end users is required. By having the acquiring organization's testers involved in the testing of the software at the vendor location, you can ensure that some of these important "unspecified or inadequately specified" requirements are adjusted during development. The change to Task 1 (test business fit) focuses on the completeness of the requirements. Testers may want to take two actions to ensure that the requirements as included in the proposal are adequate to meet the true needs of the customer/users of the application. These two sub-tasks are as follows:

1. **Organize and participate in a requirements review.** The testers can follow the requirements verification process included in Step 3 of the seven-step testing process to ensure the accuracy and completeness of the requirements.

2. **Certify the requirements as testable.** The testers can evaluate the requirements and make the assessment as to whether a test can validate that the requirements have or have not been correctly implemented.

Check Procedures

At the conclusion of this testing process, the tester should verify that the COTS software test procedure has been conducted effectively. The quality-control checklist for conducting the COTS software review is included as Work Paper 18-5. It is designed for Yes/No responses. Yes indicates a positive response; No responses should be investigated. The Comments column is provided to clarify No responses. The N/A column is provided for items that are not applicable to a specific COTS software test process.

Output

There are three potential outputs as a result of executing the COTS software test process:

- **Fully acceptable.** The software meets the full needs of the organization and is acceptable for use.

- **Unacceptable.** The software has such sufficient deficiencies that it is not acceptable for use.

- **Acceptable with conditions.** The software does not fully meet the needs of the organization, but either lowering those expectations or incorporating alternative procedures to compensate for deficiencies makes the package usable, and thus it will be disseminated for use.

Guidelines

The following guidelines will assist you in testing COTS software:

- Spend one day of your time learning and evaluating software, and you will gain problem-free use of that software.

- Acquire computer software only after you have established the need for that software and can demonstrate how it will be used in your day-to-day work.

- Instinct regarding goodness and badness should be used to help you select software.

- Testing is not done to complicate your life, but rather to simplify it. After testing, you will operate your software from a position of strength. You will know what works, how it works, what doesn't work, and why. After testing, you will not be intimidated by the unknown.

- The cost of throwing away bad software is significantly less than the cost of keeping it. In addition to saving you time and money, testing saves frustration.

- The best testing is that done by individuals who have a stake in the correct functioning of the software. These stakeholders should both prepare the test and evaluate the results.

- If your users can run the acceptance tests successfully from the outset (procedures and training courses), they will be able to run their software successfully in conjunction with their business function.

Summary

The process outlined in this chapter is designed for testing COTS software and contracted software. It assumes that the testers will not have access to the program code; therefore, the test emphasizes usability. The test is similar in approach to acceptance testing.

WORK PAPER 18-1   Test of Completeness of Business Requirements

Assessment Score =

Legend:

SA = Strongly agree

A = Agree

N = Neither agree nor disagree

D = Disagree

SD = Strongly disagree

	ASSESSMENT					COMMENTS
	SA (5)	A (4)	N (3)	D (2)	SD (1)	
1. The system will experience few changes over time.						
2. All involved parties agree the needs are well defined.						
3. The use of the results of the application will require very little judgment on the part of the users of the computer outputs.						
4. The input to the system is well defined.						
5. The outputs from the system and the decision material are well defined.						
6. The users of the system are anxious to have the area automated.						
7. The users want to participate in the selection and implementation of the software.						
8. The users understand data processing principles.						

(continues)

WORK PAPER 18-1   *(continued)*

	ASSESSMENT					COMMENTS
	SA (5)	A (4)	N (3)	D (2)	SD (1)	
9. The application does not involve any novel business approach (i.e., an approach that is not currently being used in your business).						
10. The users do not expect to find other good business ideas in the selected software.						

WORK PAPER 18-2   Test of Fit

Field Requirements

FIELD	INSTRUCTIONS FOR ENTERING DATA
Business Application	Name of business application being tested.
Number	A number which sequentially identifies a CSF.
Critical Success Factors (CSF)	A factor which those responsible for the success of the business application must meet in order for the business application to be successful.
Meets CSF	An assessment as to whether a specific CSF has been met, with a comments column to explain how the assessment was determined.

Business Application

NUMBER	CRITICAL SUCCESS FACTORS	MEETS CSF		
		YES	NO	COMMENTS

WORK PAPER 18-3   Functional Test Condition Checklist

	YES	NO	N/A	COMMENTS
Have tests for the following conditions been prepared?				
1. Test conditions for each input transaction				
2. Variations of each input transaction for each special processing case				
3. Test conditions that will flow through each logical processing path				
4. Each internal mathematical computation				
5. Each total on an output verified				
6. Each functional control (e.g., reconciliation of computer controls to independent control totals)				
7. All the different computer codes				
8. The production of each expected output				
9. Each report/screen heading and column heading				
10. All control breaks				
11. All mathematical punctuation and other editing				
12. Each user's preparation of input				
13. Completeness of prepared input				
14. User's use of output, including the understanding and purpose for each output				
15. A parallel test run to verify computer results against those which were produced manually				
16. Matching of two records				
17. Nonmatching of two records				

WORK PAPER 18-4 **Structural Test Condition Checklist**

	YES	NO	N/A	COMMENTS
Have test conditions for each of these conditions been prepared?				
1. Addition of a record before the first record on a file				
2. Addition of a record after the last record on a file				
3. Deletion of the first record on a file				
4. Deletion of the last record on a file				
5. Change information on the first record on a file				
6. Change information on the last record on a file				
7. Cause the program to terminate by predetermined conditions				
8. Accumulate a field larger than the mathematical accumulators can hold				
9. Verify that page counters work				
10. Verify that page spacing works				
11. Enter invalid transaction types				
12. Enter invalid values in fields (e.g., put alphabetic characters in a numeric field)				
13. Process unusual conditions (of all types)				
14. Test principle error conditions				
15. Test for out-of-control conditions (e.g., the value of records in the batch does not equal the entered batch total)				
16. Simulate a hardware failure forcing recovery procedures to be used				
17. Demonstrate recovery procedures				
18. Enter more records than disk storage can hold				
19. Enter more values than internal tables can hold				
20. Enter incorrect codes and transaction types				
21. Enter unreasonable values for transaction processing				
22. Violate software rules not violated by above structural test conditions				

WORK PAPER 18-5   Off-the-Shelf Software Testing Quality Control Checklist

	YES	NO	N/A	COMMENTS
Have test conditions for each of these conditions been prepared?				
1. Addition of a record before the first record on a file				
2. Addition of a record after the last record on a file				
3. Deletion of the first record on a file				
4. Deletion of the last record on a file				
5. Change information on the first record on a file				
6. Change information on the last record on a file				
7. Cause the program to terminate by predetermined conditions				
8. Accumulate a field larger than the mathematical accumulators can hold				
9. Verify that page counters work				
10. Verify that page spacing works				
11. Enter invalid transaction types				
12. Enter invalid values in fields (e.g., put alphabetic characters in a numeric field)				
13. Process unusual conditions (of all types)				
14. Test principle error conditions				
15. Test for out-of-control conditions (e.g., the value of records in the batch does not equal the entered batch total)				
16. Simulate a hardware failure forcing recovery procedures to be used				
17. Demonstrate recovery procedures				
18. Enter more records than disk storage can hold				
19. Enter more values than internal tables can hold				
20. Enter incorrect codes and transaction types				
21. Enter unreasonable values for transaction processing				
22. Violate software rules not violated by above structural test conditions				

WORK PAPER 18-5   *(continued)*

	YES	NO	N/A	COMMENTS
Task 1: Test Business Fit				
1. Have the business needs been adequately defined?				
2. Does the selected software package meet those needs?				
3. Have the critical success factors for the business application been defined?				
4. Is there a high probability that the software package under consideration will satisfy the critical success factors?				
5. Is the software being evaluated designed to meet this specific business need?				
6. Does the software under consideration push the critical success factors to their limit?				
7. Do you personally believe the software under consideration is the right software for you?				
8. Do you believe this software package will provide your business with one of the four benefits attributable to software (i.e., perform work cheaper, perform work faster, perform work more reliably, or perform tasks not currently being performed)?				
9. Does the business approach, and the software package, fit into your business' long-range business plan?				
10. Is your business system that is being considered for computerization relatively stable in terms of requirements?				
Task 2: Testing System Fit				
1. Will the selected software package operate on your computer hardware?				
2. Will the selected software package operate on your equipment's operating system?				
3. Is the proposed software package compatible with your other computer programs (applicable programs only)?				
4. Can the proposed software package utilize applicable existing data files?				

(continues)

WORK PAPER 18-5 *(continued)*

	YES	NO	N/A	COMMENTS
5. Is the method in which the software operates consistent with your business cycle?				
6. Are you willing to have you and your personnel perform the business steps needed to make the software function correctly?				
7. Is the computer work flow for this area consistent with the general work flow in your business?				
8. Were the software demonstrations satisfactory?				
9. Do you believe that the software has staying power (i.e., the vendor will continue to support it as technological and business conditions change)?				
10. Are you pleased with the fit of this software package into your computer and systems environment?				

Task 3: Testing People Fit

	YES	NO	N/A	COMMENTS
1. Were the workers exposed to or involved in the decision to acquire a computer, and specifically the applications that affect their day-to-day job responsibilities?				
2. Have your and your staff's jobs been adequately restructured after the introduction of the computer?				
3. Have the people involved with the computer been trained (or will they be trained) in the skills needed to perform their new job function?				
4. Has each worker been involved in the establishment of the procedures that he or she will use in performing day-to-day job tasks?				
5. Have the workers been charged with the responsibility for identifying defects in computer processing?				
6. Does each worker have appropriate feedback channels to all of the people involved with his or her work tasks?				
7. Are your people enthusiastic over the prospects of involving a computer in their work?				

WORK PAPER 18-5   *(continued)*

	YES	NO	N/A	COMMENTS
8. Have supervisors been properly instructed in how to supervise computer staff?				
9. Have adequate controls been included within computer processing?				
10. Do you believe your people have a positive attitude about the computer and will work diligently to make it successful?				

Task 4: Validate Acceptance Test Software Process

	YES	NO	N/A	COMMENTS
1. Were test conditions created for all of the test methods included in the test matrix?				
2. Were both static and dynamic tests used as test methods?				
3. Have functional test conditions been prepared which are consistent with the functional requirements and critical success factors?				
4. Have you prepared structural test conditions which address the more common computer architectural problems and incorrect data entry?				
5. Has the sequence in which test conditions will be executed been determined?				
6. Are the test conditions prepared using the most economical source of data?				
7. Have the test conditions been prepared by the appropriate "stakeholder"?				
8. Have the test conditions been prepared in an easy-to-use format?				
9. Has the validity of the test process been adequately challenged?				
10. Do you believe that the test conditions when executed will adequately verify the functioning of the software?				

CHAPTER 19

Testing in a Multiplatform Environment

Software designed to run on more than one platform must undergo two tests. The first test is to validate that the software performs its intended functions. This testing involves the seven-step testing process described in Part Three of this book. The second test is that the software will perform in the same manner regardless of the platform on which it is executed. This chapter focuses on the second test process.

This chapter provides a six-task process for testing in a multiplatform environment. The test process presumes that the platforms for which the software must execute are known. The process also presumes that the software has already been tested and that testers have validated that it performs its intended functions correctly.

Overview

Each platform on which software is designed to execute operationally may have slightly different characteristics. These distinct characteristics include various operating systems, hardware configurations, operating instructions, and supporting software, such as database management systems. These different characteristics may or may not cause the software to perform its intended functions differently. The objective of testing is to determine whether the software will produce the correct results on various platforms.

Objective

The objective of this six-task process is to validate that a single software package executed on different platforms will produce the same results. The test process is basically the same as was used in parallel testing. Software must operate on multiple platforms with the individual results being compared to ensure consistency in output. The testing normally requires a test lab that includes the predetermined platforms.

Concerns

The following are the three major concerns for testing in a multiplatform environment:

1. **The platforms in the test lab will not be representative of the platforms in the real world.** This can happen because the platform in the test lab may not be upgraded to current specifications, or it may be configured in a manner that is not representative of the typical configuration for that platform.

2. **The software will be expected to work on platforms not included in the test labs.** By implication, users may expect the software to work on a platform that has not been included in testing.

3. **The supporting software on various platforms is not comprehensive.** User platforms may contain software that is not the same as that used on the platform in the test lab (for example, a different database management system).

Background on Testing in a Multiplatform Environment

Testers face three major challenges when testing in a multiplatform environment. These challenges are:

1. Determining the type of platform that users operate for the processing

2. Determining which software packages are available to those users

3. Determining the type of processing users will perform in a multiplatform environment

Testing in a multiplatform environment is similar to exhaustive testing—neither is practical nor cost effective. Therefore, testers must make judgments on the most likely platforms to be used, the most likely software packages possessed by the users, and the most likely actions users will perform on a multiplatform environment.

Some of these decisions will be made based on constraints limiting the tester's capabilities. For example, the test lab may have only a limited number of platforms available; therefore, testers cannot test on platforms to which they do not have access. The developers of the system may state that users of the system are required to have X number of software packages, which are named in the software system documentation. Therefore, testers have to be concerned only with that limited number of software packages. Finally, the developers of the software may define the list of uses for which the software can perform and testers only need to test for those defined number of uses.

In developing a test plan for testing in a multiplatform environment, the testers need to make decisions regarding the three challenges previously described. If a test plan is viewed as a contract, then in the test plan the testers can state:

- Testing will occur on these platforms.
- Testing will validate that these software packages are useable in processing in a multiplatform environment.
- Only a defined number of uses will be tested.

Although this test plan definition protects the tester from not testing undefined conditions, it does not necessarily reduce the software application risk. Therefore, testers should in addition to test planning, attempt to identify the risks associated with not testing on certain platforms, certain packages, or certain application processes. This information can be helpful in determining whether additional testing should be performed.

Workbench

Figure 19-1 illustrates the workbench for testing in a multiplatform environment. This figure shows that six tasks are needed to effectively test in a multiplatform environment. Most tasks assume that the platforms will be identified in detail, and that the software to run on the different platforms has been previously validated as being correct. Five of the six tasks are designed to determine what tests are needed to validate the correct functioning of the identified platforms, and the sixth task executes those tests.

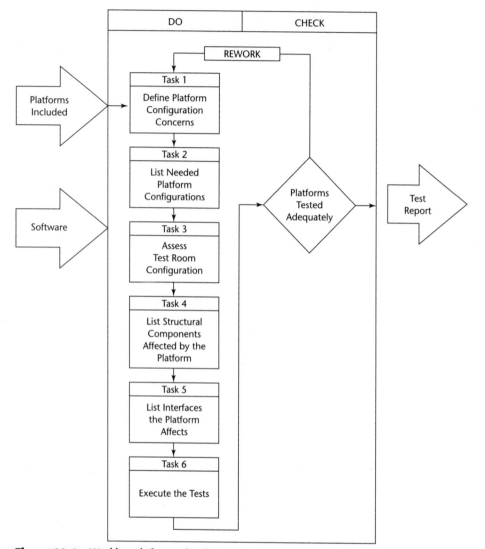

Figure 19-1   Workbench for testing in a multiplatform environment.

Input

The two inputs for testing in a multiplatform environment are as follows:

1. **List of platforms on which software must execute.** The main requirement for multiplatform testing is a list of the platforms. These platforms must be described in detail as input to testing or described in detail prior to commencing testing.

2. **Software to be tested.** The software package(s) to be tested is input to the test process. This software must be validated that it performs its functions correctly prior to multiplatform testing. If this has not been done, then the software should be subject to the seven-step testing process, described in Part Three of this book, prior to commencing multiplatform testing.

Do Procedures

The following six tasks should be performed to validate that software performs consistently in a multiplatform environment:

1. Define platform configuration concerns.
2. List needed platform configurations.
3. Assess test room configurations.
4. List structural components affected by the platform(s).
5. List interfaces platform affects.
6. Execute the tests.

Task 1: Define Platform Configuration Concerns

The first task in testing a multiplatform environment is to develop a list of potential concerns about that environment. The testing that follows will then determine the validity of those concerns. The recommended process for identifying concerns is error guessing.

Error guessing attempts to anticipate problems within the software package and its operation. The proverb "an ounce of prevention is worth a pound of cure" speaks to the error-guessing process. Studies by the IBM Corporation indicate that the same types of software defects occur with the same frequency from project to project. Just as medicine can predict that X percent of the 55-year-old age group will die of a heart attack during the year, so the software test experts can predict the types of defects that will occur in software.

This means that the types of problems that you encounter in one will occur in most other similar tests. The problem may surface in a slightly different way, but it will be the same basic problem. For example, the problem of data exceeding its allocated field size will appear sooner or later in almost all software applications. If you anticipate it and decide what you will do when it happens and how the software will react to the situation, successful use of the software will not be threatened.

Error guessing requires the following two prerequisites:

1. The error-guessing group understands how the platform works.
2. The error-guessing group knows how the software functions.

If the group that tested the software function is the same group doing the error guessing, they will know how the software works. Knowing the platforms may require the addition of platform-knowledgeable people to the error-guessing team.

Although it is possible to perform error guessing with one person, it is basically a brainstorming process. Thus, it is always better when two or more people participate. This is because of the powerful synergistic effect of a group. Synergism means that one individual's comments spark another individual to think about something he or she might not have thought about without the other individual present.

Error guessing requires a recorder to write down the ideas developed by the group. Each member of the group is allowed time to express what he or she believes might go wrong with the software. Until every individual has had an initial opportunity to list problems, there can be no criticism or comment on what other individuals have stated. After the initial go-round, the recorder reads back these items one by one. At this point, open discussion—that is, interactive discussion—commences. One group rule of this discussion is that there can be no criticism of errors raised or the individual who raised them. All comments must be stated positively. If an individual believes that the type of error or condition raised is not realistic, the ensuing discussion should be based on the probability of occurrence rather than the point's validity. If criticism is permitted during brainstorming, communication will cease and much of the value of the process will be lost.

The error-guessing process is normally very brief. In some instances, it lasts no longer than 15 minutes, and only rarely would it exceed 1 hour. However, the process does require total concentration. Therefore, the group should be removed from normal business interruptions during this exercise.

The end product of error guessing is a list of potential error conditions for additional investigation and testing. It is not up to the error-guessing team to determine what happens when these error conditions occur. They need to be familiar enough with the software to know whether there may be a problem, but they do not need to know all of the solutions. This will be done in future testing steps.

Error guessing is meant to be a relatively unstructured, unorganized process. Generally, sufficient ideas are generated to prepare a reasonably comprehensive list of potential problems—particularly when performed by two or more people. The following is a short list of questions to brainstorm during error guessing:

- Does the software have any unusual transactions?
- What are the most common errors that you are now making?
- What would happen to processing if you forgot to perform one of the steps?
- What would happen if you did not enter all of the data in an input transaction?
- Will you be able to determine who performed what computer operation in case questions arise regarding the correctness of operations?
- If a diagnostic message is produced by the computer, how will you know it has been properly corrected?
- How will you know the person operating the computer knows how to operate it correctly?

These questions are designed to spark ideas about what might go wrong within a platform. The questions are not intended to be complete, nor do they need to be answered precisely. Their sole purpose is to steer you into areas for further exploration regarding potential errors.

The concerns should be listed on Work Paper 19-1. Part 1 of the Work Paper provides space for listing multiplatform testing concerns, as well as any recommended test to address those concerns to determine whether they are valid or have already been handled by the software and/or platform.

Task 2: List Needed Platform Configurations

The test must identify the platforms that must be tested. Ideally, this list of platforms and detailed description of the platforms would be input to the test process. If so, this step need only determine if those platforms are available in the test lab.

The needed platforms are either those that will be advertised as acceptable for using the software, or platforms within an organization on which the software will be executed. The platforms need to be described in detail. This information should be recorded on Part 2 of Work Paper 19-1. Note that the description of the Work Paper will list some of the items needed about each platform.

Testers must then determine whether those platforms are available for testing. If the exact platform is not available, the testers need to determine whether an existing platform is acceptable. For example, if an available platform did not contain some feature or configuration, would the existing platform provide a reasonable test? If so, that platform can be used for testing. If the needed platform is not available, the testers must make a determination of whether to obtain such a platform or accept the risk that the software will be released without testing that specific platform.

The determination of whether an available test platform meets the needed test platform should be recorded on Part 2 of Work Paper 19-1. If the platform is not available, testers should record the action they will take.

Task 3: Assess Test Room Configurations

The testers need to determine whether the platforms available in the test room are acceptable for testing. This involves the following two steps:

1. For each needed platform listed on Work Paper 19-1, document the platform to be used for testing, if any is available, on the Work Paper.

2. Make a determination as to whether the available platform is acceptable for testing. Indicate your decision on Work Paper 19-1. If the platform is not acceptable, note any actions to be taken.

Task 4: List Structural Components Affected by the Platform(s)

Structural testing deals with the architecture of the system. Architecture describes how the system is put together. It is used in the same context that an architect designs a building. Some of the architectural problems that could affect computer processing include:

- Internal limits on the number of events that can occur in a transaction (for example, the number of products that can be included on an invoice).

- Maximum size of fields (for example, the quantity is only two positions in length, making it impossible to enter an order for more than 99 items).

- Disk storage limitations (for example, you are permitted to have only X customers).

- Performance limitations (for example, the time to process transactions jumps significantly when you enter more than X transactions).

These are but a few of the potential architectural limitations placed on computer software. You must remember that each software system is finite and has built-in limitations. Sometimes the vendor tells you these limitations, sometimes you can find them if you search through the documentation, and sometimes you won't know them until they occur. However, all limits can be determined through structural testing. The questions at hand are: Do you feel competent to do it? and Is it worth doing? The answers to these questions depend on the critical nature of the software and what would happen if your business was unable to continue computer processing because you reached the program limitation.

Structural testing also relates to file-handling problems. Such file problems include incorrect processing when the last record on file is updated or adding a record that will become the first record on a file. In the personal computer software market, literally thousands of people are writing software. Some have good ideas but are not experienced programmers; thus, they fall into the age-old traps of file manipulation problems.

As an aid in developing structural test conditions, the more common structural problem areas are listed in the following text. You can use this checklist either to determine which types of structural test conditions you want to prepare or to check the completeness of the structural conditions. Either way, it may spark you to add some additional test conditions to verify that the structure of your software performs correctly.

Have test conditions for each of the following transaction processing events been prepared:

- Adding a record before the first record on a file
- Adding a record after the last record on a file.
- Deleting the first record on a file
- Deleting the last record on a file
- Changing information on the first record on a file
- Changing information on the last record on a file
- Causing the program to terminate by predetermined conditions
- Accumulating a field larger than the mathematical accumulators can hold
- Verifying that page counters work
- Verifying that page spacing works
- Entering invalid transaction types

- Entering invalid values in fields (for example, put alphabetic characters in a numeric field)
- Processing unusual conditions (of all types)
- Testing major error conditions
- Testing for out-of-control conditions (for example, whether the value of the records in the batch do not equal the entered batch total)
- Simulating a hardware failure that forces recovery procedures to be used
- Demonstrating recovery procedures
- Entering more records than disk storage can hold
- Entering more values than internal tables can hold
- Entering incorrect codes and transaction types
- Entering unreasonable values for transaction processing
- Violating software rules not violated by preceding structural test conditions

Although some functional processing may be affected by various platforms, it is normally the structural component of the function that is affected. The test team needs to identify the structural components of functions that will be affected by the platform. They may want to use the error-guessing technique described in Task 1 to identify these structural components.

The potentially affected structural component should be documented on Work Paper 19-2. The Work Paper lists the structural component, then each platform that may affect that structural component, as well as how the structural component may be affected by the platform. The testers should then determine which tests are needed to validate that the structural component will or will not be affected by a platform.

Task 5: List Interfaces the Platform Affects

Systems tend to fail at interface points—that is, the points at which control is passed from one processing component to another (for example, when data is retrieved from a database, output reports are printed or transmitted, or a person interrupts processing to make a correction). The purpose of this task is to identify those interfaces so that they can be tested. Note that some of these interfaces will also overlap the software structural components affected by the platform. If the test has been included in the structural component task Work Paper, it need not be duplicated in the test recommended in this task.

This is a two-part task. The first part is to identify the interfaces within the software systems. These interfaces should be readily identifiable in the software's user manual. The second part is to determine whether those interfaces could be affected by the specific platform on which the software executes. This is a judgmental exercise. However, if there is a doubt in the tester's mind, he or she should test that interface on all of the platforms that might affect that interface. The Work Paper should identify the platform on which the interface may be affected, the interface itself, the interface both to and from the potential effect of the platform, and the test(s) that should be undertaken to validate whether the interface is impacted by the platform. Note that this same test for a single interface may have to be performed on multiple platforms. Document the results of this task on Work Paper 19-3.

At the conclusion of this task, the tests that will be needed to validate multiplatform operations will have been determined. The remaining task will be to execute those tests.

Task 6: Execute the Tests

The platform test should be executed in the same manner as other tests are executed in the seven-step software testing process described in Part Three of this book. The only difference may be that the same test would be performed on multiple platforms to determine that consistent processing occurs.

Check Procedures

Prior to completing multiplatform testing, a determination should be made that testing was performed correctly. Work Paper 19-4 provides a series of questions to challenge the correctness of multiplatform testing. A Yes response to those items indicates that multiplatform testing was performed correctly; a No response indicates that it may or may not have been done correctly. Each No response should be clarified in the Comments column. The N/A column is for items that are not applicable to this specific platform test.

Output

The output from this test process is a report indicating the following:

- Structural components that work or don't work by platform
- Interfaces that work or don't work by platform
- Multiplatform operational concerns that have been eliminated or substantiated
- Platforms on which the software should operate but that have not been tested

The report will be used to clarify the software's operating instructions and/or make changes to the software.

Guidelines

Multiplatform testing is a costly, time-consuming, and extensive component of testing. The resources expended on multiplatform testing can be significantly reduced if that testing focuses on predefined multiplatform concerns. Identified structural components that might be affected by the software and interfaces that might be affected by multiple platforms should make up most of the testing. This will focus the testing on what should be the major risks faced in operating a single software package on many different platforms.

Summary

This multiplatform testing process is designed to be used in conjunction with the seven-step testing process in Part Three of this book. It is essential that the software to be tested on multiple platforms be validated prior to multiplatform testing. Combining software validation testing with multiplatform testing normally will slow the test process and increase the cost.

WORK PAPER 19-1   Multiplatform Concerns and Configurations

Field Requirements

FIELD	INSTRUCTIONS FOR ENTERING DATA
Concern	A narrative description of the concerns that need to be addressed in multi-platform testing.
Recommended Test to Address Concern	This field should include any tests that the group developing the concerns believes could be made to determine the validity of that concern.
Needed Test Platform	Detailed description of the platform on which the software will be executed. The description should include at a minimum:
	Hardware vendor
	Memory size
	Hard disk size
	Peripheral equipment
	Operating system
	Supporting software
Available Test Platform	This column should indicate whether the needed test platform is available, and if not, what actions will be taken for test purposes.

Part 1 Multiplatform Testing Concerns

Concern	Recommended Test to Address Concern

Part 2 Needed versus Available Platform Configurations

Needed Test Platform	Available Test Platform	Acceptable	
		Yes	No

WORK PAPER 19-2   Test to Validate Platform-Affected Software Structure

Field Requirements

FIELD	INSTRUCTIONS FOR ENTERING DATA
Structural Component	The name or identifier of the structural component affected by a platform.
Platform	The specific platform or platforms that may affect the correct processing of the identified structural component.
How Affected	A narrative explanation of how the platform may affect the structural component should be documented.
Test(s) to Validate Structural Component	The test group should recommend one or more tests to validate whether the platform affects the structural component. Note that these tests may be different for different platforms.

Software Structure Affected by Platform			Test(s) to Validate Structural Component
Structural Component	**Platform**	**How Affected**	

WORK PAPER 19-3   Test(s) to Validate Platform-Affected Interfaces

Field Requirements

FIELD	INSTRUCTIONS FOR ENTERING DATA
Software Package	The name of the software package that is being tested.
Platform	Description of the platform that may affect an interface.
Interface Affected	A brief narrative name or description of the interface affected, such as "retrieving a product price from the pricing database."
Interface	The interface should be described to indicate the movement of data or processing from one point to another. For example, a product price will be moved from the product price database to the invoice pricing software package.
Effect	This field should explain the potential risk or effect that could be caused by a specific platform. For example, platform X may not have adequate space for over 1,000 product prices.
Test(s) to Validate Interface	This column should describe in detail each task that should be performed to validate interface processing. For example, put 1,001 product prices into the pricing database to validate that the platform can support a pricing database that contains over 999 product prices.

Interfaces Affected by Platform						Test(s) to Validate Interface
Software Package	Platform	Interface Affected	Interface			
			From	To	Effect	

WORK PAPER 19-4 **Multiplatform Quality Control Checklist**

	YES	NO	N/A	COMMENTS
1. Have all of the platforms in which the software is intended to be run been identified?				
2. Has each platform configuration been described?				
3. Have the concerns for correct multiplatform processing been identified?				
4. If so, are those concerns reasonable and complete?				
5. Has a determination been made that the identified platforms will be available for test?				
6. If not, has a decision been made on how to handle the potential risk associated with platforms not being tested?				
7. Have the structural components of the software to be tested been identified?				
8. Are those structural components complete?				
9. Has a determination been made as to how each of the identified platforms may impact those structural components?				
10. Have the interfaces for the software package been identified and documented?				
11. Has a determination been made as to whether any or all of the platforms may affect those interfaces?				
12. Was multiplatform testing conducted under real-world conditions?				

(continues)

WORK PAPER 19-4 *(continued)*

	YES	NO	N/A	COMMENTS
13. Did acceptance testing prove that the procedures were correct and usable?				
14. Did the acceptance test process verify that people are adequately trained to perform their job tasks on multiple platforms?				
15. Did acceptance testing verify that the software performs the functional and structural tasks correctly (i.e., those tested)?				
16. Did acceptance testing verify that the products produced by the computer system are correct and usable?				
17. Did acceptance testing verify that the operations personnel could correctly and effectively operate the software on the multiple platforms?				
18. Did the acceptance test process verify that the operational software system satisfied the predefined critical success factors for the software?				
19. Did the acceptance test process verify that the users/operators of the system can identify problems when they occur, and then correctly and on a timely basis correct and reenter those transactions?				
20. Have all the problems identified during acceptance testing been adequately resolved?				

CHAPTER 20

Testing Software System Security

In today's environment, security is becoming an important organizational strategy. Physical security is effective, but one of the greatest risks organizations now face is software security. This risk occurs both internally (through employees) and externally (through communication lines and Internet processing).

Testing software system security is a complex and costly activity. Performing comprehensive security testing is generally not practical. What is practical is to establish a security baseline to determine the current level of security and to measure improvements.

Effectiveness of security testing can be improved by focusing on the points where security has the highest probability of being compromised. A testing tool that has proved effective in identifying these points is the penetration-point matrix. The security-testing process described in this chapter focuses primarily on developing the penetration-point matrix, as opposed to the detailed testing of those identified points.

Overview

This test process provides two resources: a security baseline and an identification of the points in an information system that have a high risk of being penetrated. Neither resource is statistically perfect, but both have proven to be highly reliable when used by individuals knowledgeable in the area that may be penetrated.

The penetration-point tool involves building a matrix. In one dimension are the activities that may need security controls; in the other dimension are potential points of penetration. Developers of the matrix assess the probability of penetration at various points in the software system at the points of intersection. By identifying the points with the highest probability of penetration, organizations gain insight as to where information systems risk penetration the most.

Objective

The objective of the security baseline is to determine the current level of security. The object of the penetration-point matrix is to enable organizations to focus security measures on the points of highest risk. Although no location or information system can be penetration-proof, focusing the majority of security resources on the high-risk points increases the probability of preventing or detecting penetration.

Concerns

There are two major security concerns: Security risks must be identified, and adequate controls must be installed to minimize these risks.

Workbench

This workbench assumes a team knowledgeable about the information system to be secured. This team must be knowledgeable about the following:

- Communication networks in use
- Who has access to those networks
- Data or processes that require protection
- Value of information or processes that require protection
- Processing flow of the software system (so that points of data movement can be identified)
- Security systems and concepts
- Security-penetration methods

The workbench provides three tasks for building and using a penetration-point matrix (see Figure 20-1). The security-testing techniques used in this workbench are the security baseline and the penetration-point matrix. The prime purpose of the matrix is to focus discussion on high-risk points of potential penetration and to assist in determining which points require the most attention. These techniques can be used by project teams, special teams convened to identify security risks, or by quality assurance/quality-control personnel to assess the adequacy of security systems.

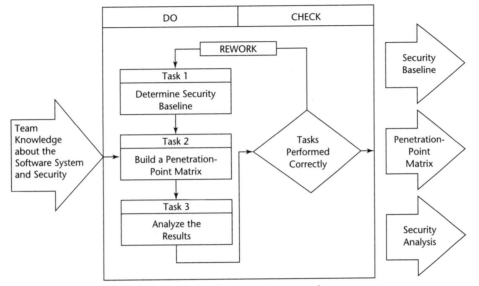

Figure 20-1   Workbench for testing software system security.

Input

The input to this test process is a team that is knowledgeable about the information system to be protected and about how to achieve security for a software system. The reliability of the results will depend heavily on the knowledge of the individuals involved
with the information system and the specific types of individuals who are likely to penetrate the system at risk points. The security-testing techniques presented in this chapter are simple enough that the team should not require prior training in the use of the
security test tools.

Where Vulnerabilities Occur

A vulnerability is a weakness in an information system. It is the point at which software
systems are easiest to penetrate. Understanding the vulnerabilities helps in designing
security for information systems.

   This section describes vulnerabilities that exist in the functional attributes of an
information system. This section identifies the location of those vulnerabilities and distinguishes accidental from intentional losses.

Functional Vulnerabilities

The primary functional vulnerabilities result from weak or nonexistent controls in the following eight categories, listed in order of historic frequency of abuse:

1. **Input/output data.** The greatest vulnerability in this category occurs when access is most open. Data is subject to human interference both *before* it has been entered into a computer and *after* it has been output from the computer. Manual controls offer weaker resistance to people intent on interfering with data than do programs that must be manipulated to achieve unauthorized access. Input/output data controls include separation of data handling and conversion tasks, dual control of tasks, document counts, batch total checking, audit trails, protective storage, access restrictions, and labeling.

2. **Physical access.** When physical access is the primary vulnerability, nonemployees can gain access to computer facilities, and employees can gain access at unauthorized times and in unauthorized areas. Perpetrators' access motives may include political, competitive, and financial gain. Financial gain can accrue through burglary, larceny, and the unauthorized sale of computer services. In some cases, disgruntled employees pose a risk. Physical access controls include door locks, intrusion alarms, physical-access line of sight, secure perimeter identification/establishment, badge systems, guard and automated monitoring functions (e.g., closed-circuit television), inspection of transported equipment and supplies, and staff sensitivity to intrusion. Violations often occur during nonworking hours when safeguards and staff are not present.

3. **IT operations.** In this category of functional vulnerability, losses result from sabotage, espionage, sale of services and data extracted from computer systems, unauthorized use of facilities for personal advantage, and direct financial gain from negotiable instruments in IT areas. Controls in this category include separation of operational staff tasks, dual control over sensitive functions, staff accountability, accounting of resources and services, threat monitoring, close supervision of operating staff, sensitivity briefings of staff, documentation of operational procedures, backup capabilities and resources, and recovery and contingency plans. The most common abuse problem in this functional category is the unauthorized use or sale of services and data. The next most common problem is sabotage perpetrated by disgruntled IT staff.

4. **Test processes.** A weakness or breakdown in a business test process can result in computer abuse perpetrated in the name of a business or government organization. The principal act is related more to corporate test processes or management decisions than to identifiable unauthorized acts of individuals using computers. These test processes and decisions result in deception, intimidation, unauthorized use of services or products, financial fraud, espionage, and sabotage in competitive situations. Controls include review of business test processes by company boards of directors or other senior-level management, audits, and effective regulatory and law enforcement.

5. **Computer programs.** Computer programs are subject to abuse. They can also be used as tools in the perpetration of abuse and are subject to unauthorized

changes to perpetrate abusive acts. The abuses from unauthorized changes are the most common. Controls include labeling programs to identify ownership, formal development methods (including testing and quality assurance), separation of programming responsibilities in large program developments, dual control over sensitive parts of programs, accountability of programmers for the programs they produce, safe storage of programs and documentation, audit comparisons of operational programs with master copies, formal update and maintenance procedures, and establishment of program ownership.

6. **Operating system access and integrity.** These abuses involve the use of time-sharing services. Frauds can occur as a result of discovering design weaknesses or by taking advantage of bugs or shortcuts introduced by programmers in the implementation of operating systems. The acts involve intentional searches for weaknesses in operating systems, unauthorized exploitation of weaknesses in operating systems, or the unauthorized exploitation of weaknesses discovered accidentally. Students committing vandalism, malicious mischief, or attempting to obtain free computer time have perpetrated most of the acts in university-run time-sharing services. Controls to eliminate weaknesses in operating system access include ensuring the integrity and security of the design of operating systems, imposing sufficient implementation methods and discipline, proving the integrity of implemented systems relative to complete and consistent specifications, and adopting rigorous maintenance procedures.

7. **Impersonation.** Unauthorized access to time-sharing services through impersonation can most easily be gained by obtaining secret passwords. Perpetrators learn passwords that are exposed accidentally through carelessness or administrative error, or they learn them by conning people into revealing their passwords or by guessing obvious combinations of characters and digits. It is suspected that this type of abuse is so common that few victims bother to report cases. Controls include effective passwords administration, periodic password changes, user protection of their passwords, policies that require hard-to-guess passwords, threat-monitoring or password-use analysis in time-sharing systems, and rules that forbid the printing/display of passwords.

8. **Media.** Theft and destruction of digital data are acts attributed to weaknesses in the control of computer media. Many other cases, identified as operational procedure problems, involve the manipulation or copying of data. Controls include limited access to data libraries, safe storage of computer media, data labeling, location controls, number accounting, controls of degausser equipment, and backup capabilities.

Vulnerable Areas

The following list ranks the nine functional locations according to vulnerability:

1. **Data- and report-preparation facilities.** Vulnerable areas include key-to-disk, computer job setup, output control and distribution, data collection, and data transportation. Input and output areas associated with online remote terminals are excluded here.

2. **Computer operations.** All locations with computers in the immediate vicinity and rooms housing central computer systems are included in this category. Detached areas that contain peripheral equipment connected to computers by cable and computer hardware maintenance areas or offices are also included. Online remote terminals (connected by telephone circuits to computers) are excluded here.

3. **Non-IT areas.** Security risks also derive from business decisions in such non-IT areas as management, marketing, sales, and business offices; and primary abusive acts may originate from these areas.

4. **Online terminal systems.** The vulnerable functional areas are within online systems, where acts occur by execution of programmed instructions as generated by terminal commands.

5. **Programming offices.** This area includes office areas in which programmers produce and store program listings and documentation.

6. **Handling areas for online data preparation and output reports.** This category includes the same functions described in Chapter 10 for preparing online scripts.

7. **Digital media storage facilities.** This area includes data libraries and any storage place containing usable data.

8. **Online operations.** This category is the equivalent of the computer operations discussed previously, but involves the online terminal areas.

9. **Central processors.** These functional areas are within computer systems themselves, and abusive acts may originate from within the computer operating system (not from terminals).

Accidental Versus Intentional Losses

Errors generally occur during labor-intensive work processes, and errors lead to vulnerabilities. The errors are usually data errors, computer program errors (bugs), and damage to equipment or supplies. Such errors often require jobs to be rerun, errors to be corrected, and equipment to be repaired or replaced.

Nevertheless, it is often difficult to distinguish between accidental loss and intentional loss. In fact, some reported intentional loss results because perpetrators have discovered and made use of errors that result in their favor. When loss occurs, employees and managers tend to blame the computer hardware first (to absolve themselves from blame and to pass the problem along to the vendor to solve). The problem is rarely a hardware error, but proof of this is usually required before searching elsewhere for the cause. The next most common area of suspicion is users or the source of data generation because, again, the IT department can blame another organization. Blame is usually next placed on the computer programming staff. Finally, when all other targets of blame have been exonerated, IT employees suspect their own work.

It is not uncommon to see informal meetings between computer operators, programmers, maintenance engineers, and users arguing over who should start looking for the cause of a loss. The thought that the loss was intentional is remote because they generally assume they function in a benign environment.

In many computer centers, employees do not understand the significant difference between accidental loss from errors and intentionally caused losses. Organizations using computers have been fighting accidental loss for 40 years, since the beginning of automated data processing. Solutions are well known and usually well applied relative to the degree of motivation and cost-effectiveness of controls. They anticipate, however, that the same controls used in similar ways also have an effect on people engaged in intentional acts that result in losses. They frequently fail to understand that they are dealing with an intelligent enemy who is using every skill, experience, and access capability to solve the problem or reach a goal. This presents a different kind of vulnerability, one that is much more challenging and that requires adequate safeguards and controls not yet fully developed or realized, let alone adequately applied.

Do Procedures

This test process involves performing the following three tasks:

1. Establish a security baseline.
2. Build a penetration-point matrix.
3. Analyze the results of security testing.

Task 1: Establish a Security Baseline

A baseline is a snapshot of the organization's security program at a certain time. The baseline is designed to answer two questions:

- What are we doing about computer security?
- How effective is our computer security program?

Baseline information should be collected by an independent assessment team; as much as possible, bias for or against a security program should be removed from the process. The process itself should measure both factual information about the program and the attitudes of the people involved in the program.

Two categories of the baseline information need to be collected. The first is related to the security process and includes the policies, methods, procedures, tools, and techniques used to protect computer resources. The second category of information relates to security acts and includes information about attempted and actual penetrations into computer resources. Wherever possible, actual losses should be quantified.

This task provides a five-step baseline procedure that includes data collection forms and suggested analyses of the data collected. Most organizations will want to customize this procedure based on their in-place security process, which may already have some of the needed information. Therefore, suggestions are offered on customizing the baseline procedure.

Why Baselines Are Necessary

Industrial psychologists tell us that most individuals suffer from cognitive dissonance. This means that an individual is "blinded" by his own background and personal experiences. After surviving life's experiences and performing different jobs and tasks, one comes to believe certain inalienable truths. When the mind becomes hardened with this cognitive dissonance, it is hard to convince an individual that other facts or positions may be more correct than the one held.

One noted security expert defines cognitive dissonance in a slightly different way. He says that there is a 20-year rule in almost all organizations (obviously not in those that have been in business less than 20 years). The rule is that if an unfavorable event has not occurred within the past 20 years, the probability of that even occurring is assumed to be zero by the key officers in the corporation. For example, if the business has not experienced a fire in the past 20 years, the fire procedures will be lax.

We see this 20-year rule vividly applied to the computer security field. Most organizations have not experienced a major computer disaster or fraud within the past 20 years, and thus tend to exclude it as a viable probability. When newspapers report a major computer disaster or problem (for example, hackers intrusions into well-known companies' databases), senior management vicariously substitutes the reported event for a possible event in its organization. This "bends" the 20-year rule slightly, but normally the vicarious experience dissipates quickly and the 20-year rule again dominates management thinking. The net effect of this phenomenon is a widely held "it won't happen here" philosophy.

When senior management adopts this thinking, logical arguments become useless. The only workable solution to cognitive dissonance is a factual presentation. In the area of computer security, this approach is a must.

This approach does not purport to claim to change managerial *attitudes* about the need for computer security. What the factual arguments do is "embarrass" people into changing behavior. The embarrassment results because they cannot intellectually refute the factual data, and thus they accept a position they may not truly believe in but are willing to undertake for the benefit of the organization.

Creating Baselines

The establishment of a security baseline need not be time-consuming. The objective is to collect what is easy to collect, and ignore the information that is difficult to collect. In many instances, the needed information may be already available.

The three key aspects of collecting computer security baseline information are as follows:

- **What to collect.** A determination must be made about what specific pieces of information would be helpful in analyzing the current security program and in building a more effective computer security program.

- **From whom will the information be collected?** Determining the source of information may be a more difficult task than determining what information should be collected. In some instances, the source will be current data collection mechanisms (if used by the organization). In other instances, individuals will be asked to provide information that has not previously been recorded.

- **The precision of the information collected.** There is a tendency to want highly precise information, but in many instances it is not necessary. The desired precision should be both reasonable and economical. If people are being asked to identify past costs, high precision is unreasonable; and if the cost is large, it must be carefully weighed against the benefit of having highly precise information. In many instances, the same decisions would be made regardless of whether the precision was within plus or minus 1 percent, or within plus or minus 50 percent.

The collection of data to create a security baseline should be completed within one week. It may take longer in large organizations or if special programming is needed to gather information from computer logs.

This chapter proposes the following six-step baselining procedure:

1. Establish baseline team.
2. Set baseline requirements and objectives.
3. Design baseline data collection methods.
4. Train baseline participants.
5. Collect baseline data.
6. Analyze and report computer security status.

The baseline procedures described in this chapter are general in nature. They do not take into account any unique features of an organization or the fact that data may already be available. Therefore, the six-step procedure may need to be customized to ensure that the correct information is collected at the least cost.

If customizing the six-step procedure, keep the following in mind:

- **Availability of information.** If data is already available, it should not be collected in the baseline study. Those pieces of information can be excluded from the six-step process and incorporated into the process in Step 5 (data collection step).
- **Need for information.** The baseline team must establish the objectives of the baseline study. The information collected should support these baseline objectives. If recommended information is not needed to support an objective, it should be deleted (and vice versa).
- **Adjust for corporate language and nomenclature.** Generalized terms may have been used in baseline collection forms. If so, these should be adapted to organizational terminology wherever possible. Customized terminology provides the appearance of a baseline process designed specifically for the organization. The more closely people identify with the questions, the greater the reliability of the data collected.

The baseline is presented as a one-time data collection procedure. Nevertheless, the data collected must be updated periodically to measure changes from the baseline. This follow-up data collection should be integrated into the security program, and not separated as a special data collection process in the future.

All processes need to be continually updated as business conditions change. The proper time to change processes depends on the collection and analysis of feedback information. This feedback information is the same information that was collected in the baseline study. Without this continual feedback and analysis, even the most effective security programs will fall into disrepair.

Establish the Team

The selection of the baseline team is a critical step in the baselining process. Team members must exhibit the following characteristics:

- Be representative of the groups involved in computer security
- Believe they are responsible for the performance of the baseline study
- Believe that the baseline study is a worthwhile exercise
- Be responsible for using the results of the baseline study to improve security

The baseline study must belong to the individuals responsible for computer security and not to senior management. This does not mean that senior management does not participate in the baseline study or use the results of the study. It means that as much as possible the baseline will be owned by the people responsible for revising the computer security program.

This principle of ownership cannot be overemphasized in the computer security area. Most computer security programs fail because the employees of the organization do not believe it is their computer security program. They believe it is the program of the security officer, data processing management, senior management, or anybody but themselves. The emphasis in this book is that ownership and responsibility of the computer security belong to all employees of an organization. The concept of ownership begins with the selection of the computer security team. The recommended process for building the computer security team is relatively simple. Senior management convenes a group representative of all parties involved in computer security. In general, these should be the "movers and shakers" in the organization—the people who have the respect of the majority of the employees. These individuals may or may not be supervisors, but all must have the respect of the employees in the area from which they come.

Senior management now describes the importance and objectives of the baseline study. This presentation should be primarily a testimonial by senior management on the importance of computer security in the organization. The baseline study should be presented as a first step in establishing an effective computer security program for the organization. The presentation should not discuss the existing computer security program or identify or imply that the individuals associated with the current program have done less than an admirable job. The emphasis should be on changing requirements and the need to change and update the computer security program.

Senior management should then ask for volunteers to work on the computer security baseline study. Nobody should be appointed to this study group. If the individuals in the group do not believe in computer security, the results of the study will probably reflect that disbelief. On the other hand, if people volunteer, they must have an interest that can be nurtured by senior management to produce the kind of results desired. If senior management's testimonial is believable, there will be sufficient volunteers for the study group. If there are no volunteers, then senior management must seriously reconsider its attitudes and practices on computer security. In that instance it may be better to hire a consultant to perform the study and then begin the new computer security program at the senior management level.

Set Requirements and Objectives

The goal of the initial meeting of the baseline team should be to establish the requirements and objectives of the baseline study. To a large degree, these requirements and objectives will have been established by senior management when the study team was formed. Nevertheless, for the requirements and objectives to be "owned" by the study team, the team must adopt those requirements and objectives as their own and not as orders dictated by management.

The objectives should be twofold: first, to collect information about the computer security process; and second, to collect information about the effectiveness of that process in detecting and preventing intrusions.

These two objectives must be converted into baseline requirements. The requirements should be defined in sufficient detail so that at the end of the baseline study it can be determined whether the baseline requirements have been met. It is these requirements that will motivate the remaining steps of the baseline process.

The baseline requirements must answer the who, what, when, where, why, and how of the baseline study; this information is then supplemented by the precision desired or achieved in the data collection process. The precision can be part of the requirements, or the respondents can be asked to state the level of precision they believe is in their responses.

The baseline requirements worksheet shown in Table 20-1 serves to record information regarding six focuses of concern, as follows:

- **Resources protection.** Whenever possible, place a value on the resource that warrants security measures. The resources can be grouped; for example, the computer media library can be treated as one resource. It is not necessary to identify each reel of tape or each disk.

- **Resources used.** Evaluate the number of people and the amount of computer time, security equipment, and other expenditures made for the sole purpose of providing security over the resources.

- **Methods.** Describe in detail the tools, techniques, and processes used to protect the identified resources so that they are readily understandable by management. For example, a single reference to guards is inadequate; the methods to be described should explain the number of guards and their specific responsibilities.

- **Training.** Define the programs used to train individuals in how to fulfill their security responsibilities, as well as the objectives, the methods used for training, and any procedures used to ensure that the necessary skills have been mastered.

- **Awareness.** Record employee perception regarding the need for security, management's security intent and specific responsibilities, and attitudes about the performance of security responsibilities.

- **Support.** The support received from supervision and peers in performing security responsibilities includes being given adequate time, training, direction, and assistance where necessary.

The security violations should be available through existing reporting systems; if not, information in the following four areas must be collected:

- **Effectiveness.** This involves the judgment of the individuals participating in the security program about the ability of the program to prevent and detect violations.

- **Penetrations prevented.** Automated security systems log attempted violations, thus making this information easy to obtain. Manual security systems such as barriers may prevent a lot of people from penetrating, but unless the suspected offenders actually try and are observed, the information collected may not accurately reflect potential risk and efficacy of prevention.

- **Penetrations detected.** This information should be recorded and reported by the individuals who detected the penetration (either through a formal reporting system or based on the recollection of those involved in the detection).

- **Losses.** These are the losses to the organization that are the result of ineffective security systems. Computer security experts estimate that only about 10 percent of all losses are identified; therefore, this category might be divided into identified and estimated losses.

For all categories in the Baseline Requirements Work Sheet, the baseline team should provide guidance as to the following:

- What should be collected.

- Why the information is necessary.

- Who has the information.

- Where the information is available (For instance, the source of the information might not realize that she has the information within a database.)

- Precision of information wanted.

- How the information is to be provided.

The more complete the information at this point in the data collection process, the easier the remaining steps are to execute.

Design Data Collection Methods

Ideally, the collection of feedback information about computer security should come from the process itself. Feedback information should be a by-product of the process, and not an extra task given to the individuals who perform security-related activities. For example, the scheduling or conducting of training should generate the information about training; forms required to record security violations should provide the information about violations; and job-accounting systems should indicate the amount of resources utilized to provide computer security.

Table 20-1 Baseline Requirements Worksheet

BASELINE REQUIREMENT QUESTION	SECURITY PROCESS						SECURITY VIOLATIONS		
	RESOURCES PROTECTION METHODS	RESOURCES USED FOR SECURITY	TRAIN-ING	AWARE-NESS	SUPPORT	EFFECTIVE-NESS	PREVENTED PENETRATION	DETECTED	LOSSES
What									
Why									
Who									
Where									
When									
How									

The baseline study recognizes that the appropriate feedback mechanisms are not yet in place. The performance of the study is usually a one-time task, and as such, special data collection techniques need to be developed. Even so, these techniques should be commensurate with the value received from collecting the information. Two easy-to-use data collection forms are provided for the baseline study.

This Baseline Factual Data Collection form is designed to collect information that has a factual basis, as opposed to attitudinal information (see Figure 20-2). This does not mean that the factual information is 100 percent accurate, but rather that it is factual in nature as opposed to an individual's opinion. However, both types of information are important because both affect the integrity of the security program.

The factual information represents the areas of information defined in requirements (which are factual in nature). The information is collected according to areas of security. These can be organizational areas or areas of responsibility. The determination of what areas to survey will be based on an analysis of where computer security is conducted. At a minimum, it would include the following:

Central computer site(s)

Remote computer site(s)

Storage areas for computer media and resources

Points of physical protection

Communication lines or networks

Office equipment with security concerns

Origination of security concerns

This data collection form provides general categories of information wanted. The prototype has been designed to assist baseline study teams in developing a customized form for their organization. The end of the form provides space for the respondent to indicate the precision of the information included on the form. This may need to be qualified to indicate which piece of information is being rated. For example, training information may be provided at high precision, but the cost to develop the security measure may be provided at low precision. As stated earlier, the precision can be given by the baseline study team or provided by the respondent. If the baseline study team indicates the desired level of precision, this last item should be omitted from the form.

People's attitudes about security are as important as the factual information gathered. People are the penetrators of security systems, and people are the guardians of the computer resources. If people are dedicated to computer security, it will happen; if they are not, the opportunity for penetration will increase.

The Baseline Attitudinal Data Collection form should be widely distributed throughout the organization (see Figure 20-3). Some organizations allow these forms to be returned anonymously because they think people will be more open if guaranteed anonymity. The baseline study team must make this judgment.

To avoid fence-sitting, the questions on the form must be answered using a Likert scale. This form's six-point scale requires respondents to select a response that is not average: The respondent must decide whether something is better than average or less than average.

Security Area (*where*)_____

Individuals Responsible (*who*)_____

Resources Protected (*why*)_____

_____

_____

Security Methods Used (*what*)_____

Training Provided (*what*)_____

Cost to Develop (*what*)_____

Cost to Use (*how*)_____

Number of Penetrations During Past 12 Months (*why*)_____

   Prevented   _____

   Detected   _____

   Losses   _____

Description (*how*)_____

_____

_____

_____

_____

_____

Accuracy (*precision*)

  +/-5%_____   +/-15%_____   +/-25%_____   +/-50%_____   +/->50%_____

Figure 20-2   Baseline Factual Data Collection form.

The scale for each statement ranges from *completely agree* (a score of 1) to *completely disagree* (a score of 6). The more closely the respondent agrees with the statement, the closer he would score to a 1 (1, 2, and 3 are agreement options). The more he disagrees with the statement, the closer he would come to 6 (the disagree options are 4, 5, and 6).

Train Participants

The individuals administering the baseline study, as well as the individuals involved in providing that data, should be trained in what is expected from them. At a minimum, this training should include the following:

- **Baseline awareness.** All of the individuals who will be participating in the program should be alerted to the fact that there is such a program in place and that they will be involved in it and are an important part of the success of the program.

- **Collection methods.** The participants in the program should be trained in the sources of security information, how to get it, and the attributes of information that are wanted. This primarily will be an explanation of the information recorded on the baseline requirements worksheet (see Table 20-1).

- **Forms completion.** If forms are distributed or used, the respondents to those forms should be instructed in the intent of the request for information, the type and extent of responses desired, and the type of precision needed.

Area of Responsibility (*where*)_____

Individual Responsibility (*who*)_____

1. I am responsible for the computer resources that I use and/or have under my control.

   Completely Agree 1___ 2___ 3___ 4___ 5___ 6___ Complete Disagree

2. I have been adequately trained in the security procedures and policies of the organization, and my supervisor has verified that I have mastered these skills.

   Completely Agree 1___ 2___ 3___ 4___ 5___ 6___ Complete Disagree

3. Security is an important part of my job function.

   Completely Agree 1___ 2___ 3___ 4___ 5___ 6___ Complete Disagree

4. I am evaluated by my supervisor on how well I perform my security-related responsibilities.

   Completely Agree 1___ 2___ 3___ 4___ 5___ 6___ Complete Disagree

5. Computer security is a high priority for senior management.

   Completely Agree 1___ 2___ 3___ 4___ 5___ 6___ Complete Disagree

6. Computer security is a high priority for my supervisor.

   Completely Agree 1___ 2___ 3___ 4___ 5___ 6___ Complete Disagree

7. I receive strong support from my supervisor when I request resources, raise concerns, or make recommendations relating to computer security.

   Completely Agree 1___ 2___ 3___ 4___ 5___ 6___ Complete Disagree

8. The current security program is effective in detecting and/or preventing system penetrations.

   Completely Agree 1___ 2___ 3___ 4___ 5___ 6___ Complete Disagree

9. The organization spends the correct amount of resources on computer security.

   Completely Agree 1___ 2___ 3___ 4___ 5___ 6___ Complete Disagree

10. Management has requested my advice about computer security.

    Completely Agree 1___ 2___ 3___ 4___ 5___ 6___ Complete Disagree

Figure 20-3 Baseline Attitudinal Data Collection form.

The training is the responsibility of the chairman of the baseline study group. That individual should first train the study group, and then the study group should train the other participants.

Collect Data

The collection process should be performed as quickly as possible. When the requests are made, include a response due date on the request (generally, within three to five working days). This provides enough time to work the request into a normal schedule, and yet does not give the appearance that the request is unimportant.

It is recommended, but not required, that the requests be made at a meeting of the participants. This is an opportunity to train the people in the forms and at the same time to make the request to have the data collected. It is the responsibility of the baseline study group to follow up and ensure that the needed data is provided by the prescribed date. In the event that the data is collected from computer files, the baseline team may either personally perform those analyses or contract them out to other parties.

Analyze and Report Security Status

The analysis of the security self-assessment exercise resulted in a profile indicating the elements of security that presented the greatest threat. The analysis of the baseline will result in two more profiles: (1) factual information collected about security practices, and (2) attitudinal information from individuals involved in security. These analyses can be presented individually or as a single report. The approach selected should be based on experience as to how best to influence management decisions.

Let us consider a sample report of an analysis of the computer security baseline (presented in Table 20-2). This analysis shows the individual areas and selected analyses based on both the factual and attitudinal data collection processes. The areas of security listed are general, such as the central computer site. In actual practice, these should be specific organizational units.

The analyses selected show five factual areas (value of computer resources, cost to install security, cost to operate security, number of penetrations, and value of security losses) and two attitudinal areas, (effectiveness of security, and management support for security).

The translation from the data collection work sheets to this report may require some interpretation and further analysis. For example, the report suggests that a value be placed on the computer resources protected so that the cost of security can be shown in relationship to what is being protected. If the individual reports cannot quantify this, the baseline team must do it. The attitudinal analyses, such as effectiveness of security, are taken from the attitudinal data collection work sheets. In our work sheet, we had a rating classification of 1 to 6. These normally would have to be converted to terms that are more easily understandable. For example, if on the Likert scale the rating 1 represented ineffective security and 6 represented very effective security, the numbers might be converted to the following rating system:

Likert scale values of 1 and 2 are rated "poor."

Likert scale values of 3 and 4 are rated "effective."

Likert scale values of 5 and 6 are rated "excellent."

A report of this type obviously requires explanatory material (in writing or orally). The purpose of showing a recommended analysis is to suggest a way of presenting the information. It is expected that the baseline team will use its creativity in putting together a baseline report.

Using Baselines

The baseline is the starting point to a better security program. It both reports the status of the current program and provides a basic standard against which improvements can be measured.

Table 20-2 Report of Analysis of Computer Security Baseline

SECURITY AREA	TOTALS	CENTRAL COMPUTER SITE(S)	REMOTE COMPUTER SITE(S)/ RESOURCES	STORAGE AREA FOR COM- PUTER MEDIA	POINTS OF PHYSICAL PROTECTION	COMMU- NICATION LINES/ NETWORKS	OFFICE EQUIP- MENT	LOCATIONS OF COMPUTER- PRODUCED DATA
Value of computer resources								
Cost to install security								
Cost to operate security								
Number of penetrations prevented								
Number of penetra- tions detected								
Value of security losses								
Effectiveness of security								
Management support for security								

The baseline study serves two primary objectives. First, it reduces computer security discussions from opinion to fact. Even though some of the facts are based on attitude, they are a statistical base of data on which analyses and discussion can be focused, as opposed to people's opinion and prejudices. The baseline helps answer the question of whether the expenditure was worthwhile. For example, if a security software package is acquired but there is no way to determine whether the environment has been improved, management will wonder whether that expenditure was worthwhile. When the next computer security request is made, the uncertainty about the last expenditure may eliminate the probability of a new improvement.

Task 2: Build a Penetration-Point Matrix

A dilemma always exists as to where to place security. Earlier chapters stated that people are the problem, and therefore security should be placed over people. However, watching people is not a practical or desirable way to control people. Therefore, computer security is best achieved through controlling activities. The activities in turn control people.

For example, we want to stop people from removing computer media from the media library unless authorized to do so. This can best be accomplished by placing controls over the computer media in the form of a librarian; we can then exercise our security procedures through the computer media library and librarian.

This task identifies the activities that need control, as well as the data flow points where penetration is most likely to occur. These concepts are used to build a penetration-point matrix that helps identify security vulnerabilities for management action. The creation of the penetration-point matrix answers the question of where security is needed and whether security controls exist at the most likely points of penetration.

Controlling People by Controlling Activities

The computer security challenge in any organization is to control people—not just employees, but also vendors, customers, passers-by, and ex-employees.

The only effective way to control people is to continually monitor their activities. To control an individual, we would have to hire another individual to watch him first, and then hire a third individual to watch the second individual watching the first individual. Not only is this not practical, but it would be resented by a large percentage of employees and customers. Thus, another approach is needed to accomplish the same objective.

The solution to the computer security dilemma is to establish activities that control people. For example, it would be difficult to keep unauthorized individuals out of the computer center, unless a strategy such as card access control were initiated. Control designers refer to this concept as "division of responsibilities." The activities that appropriately divide responsibilities also introduce the controls that monitor people's activities on a continuous basis. The monitoring through activities is not considered objectionable, although constant surveillance would be.

The challenge is the identification of the appropriate activities. This is another critical step in building an effective security program. The number and types of activities selected for control are another aspect of determining the scope or magnitude of the security program in the organization.

Selecting Security Activities

The determination of the magnitude of the security program is based on the following two factors:

- Type and magnitude of risks
- Type and extent of security controls

The greater the risks, the greater the need for control. The two variables of the scope of the security program are directly related. One can measure the magnitude of the risks to determine the strength of the management security controls needed. The amount of management controls to be installed is also a measure of the scope of the security program.

The activities that require management security controls can be divided into the categories discussed in the following three subsections.

Interface Activities

These are the activities and individuals that use computer resources. The specific activities relate to functions either needed by the computer environment or furnished by the computer environment:

- **Program users.** Users are the operational "activities" for which the applications have been developed and for which the processing results are needed. The primary users of computer resources are the operational areas responsible for the application being processed. Secondary users include various staff units in the organization.

- **Technical interfaces.** The operating environment includes many software packages (for example, operating systems, database management systems, and administrative scheduling systems). These individual packages need to be generated and installed; then the interfaces between the packages must be established. Many of the technical interfaces are performed by systems programmers and other specialists, such as database administrators.

- **Application systems.** Application systems are the software packages that process user data to produce the results needed by the users. These application systems can be developed from internally generated specifications, acquired as commercially available software, or developed under contract by vendors. The activity includes testing to ensure that the application functions correctly, and then making any change necessary to ensure the operational efficacy.

- **Privileged users.** Each organization has a group of users who by their stature in the organization are privileged. This means that they may not be subject to the same level of control as nonprivileged users. The two primary categories of privileged users are senior management and auditors.

- **Vendor interfaces.** Organizations contract with a variety of vendors for special services. These include the vendors of hardware, software, and other support services such as maintenance, cleaning, and consulting services. In the performance of vendors' duties, it may be necessary for vendor personnel to interact with computer operations during normal operating periods.

Development Activities

These are the activities that relate to the acquisition, creation, and maintenance of the software needed to accomplish the processing requirements established by users of computer facilities to meet business needs:

- **Policies, procedures, and standards.** The organization develops policies regarding how a function is to be performed. These policies are implemented through procedures, such as system development methods by which work is performed. These standards can apply to both specific professional areas and other users of resources, such as microcomputer users.

- **Training.** Training is key. People should be fully trained in how to perform their job and then supervised (and evaluated) to ensure that they have mastered those skills.

- **Database administration.** Databases are groupings of data that are managed independently of the application programs that utilize the data. The creation of the databases requires a new organization structure to manage and administer the use of this new development. In many organizations, the database also includes the definition of data and the use of the data dictionary software documentation tool.

- **Communications.** This activity encompasses the electronic movement of data between one computer facility and another. Modern communications facilities include the Internet, intranets, local-area networks, virtual private networks, and wireless systems. When common carrier facilities are used, the organization loses control over the security of information from the time it passes into the hands of the common carrier until it is again returned to the organization.

- **Documentation.** Documentation (hard copy or electronic) includes all the narrative information developed and maintained about processing activities. For an application under development, documentation includes record definitions, system specifications, program listings, test conditions and results, operator manuals, user manuals, control documentation, flow charts, and other pictorial representations.

- **Program change control.** The maintenance activity has the responsibility to define, implement, and test changes to application systems. Nevertheless, the control of those changes should be independent of the activity that actually performs the program maintenance. The program change control activity involves logging changes, monitoring their implementation, and verifying that all the changes to programs are appropriately authorized and that all authorized changes are made.

- **Records-retention program.** This activity is designed both to retain needed computer-related documents and to appropriately destroy unneeded documents. Whereas the computer media is designed to physically store the data, the records-retention program relates to the amount of time that the information will be retained. The records-retention program includes both manual and computer media. The time and method by which data will be destroyed is an important part of the records-retention program. Many organizations either shred or burn key hard-copy computer documentation. In addition, some organizations have custodians to retain and control important records.

Operations Activities

These are the procedures and methods used to process data on the computer using the software developed for that purpose as initiated by the activities that interface with the computer center. Activities also include supporting tasks necessary to ensure the integrity of the mainline operations:

- **Computer processing.** This is the activity of processing data to produce desired results. Processing is used in this context to indicate the totality of steps performed between the initiation of a transaction and the final termination of that transaction. Processing includes both manual and automated functions that manipulate data.

- **Media libraries.** Media libraries are repositories for computer media. The media libraries may be on-site, company facilities off-site, or with contractors who hold data at their site. Off-site libraries are used to protect data in the event of a disaster to the on-site media library.

- **Error handling.** This activity begins when data is rejected from normal processing and continues until the time the problem has been resolved and the transaction has been correctly processed. Error handling normally involves a logging of errors and then a monitoring of the correction and reentry process. It is a particularly vulnerable point in many application systems because the reentry may only be subject to minimal control.

- **Production library control.** The production library is the repository for computer programs and program-related parameters. For example, job control language statements are necessary to support programs, but are retained in libraries other than the production library. There are many libraries, but the emphasis in this activity is on control over those libraries that affect the integrity of computer processing.

- **Computer operations.** These are the steps involved in ensuring that the desired results are achieved through computer processing. Operations involve terminal usage, support operations such as offline printers and office systems, and the central computer facility. Operations can also occur at off-site service centers.

- **Disaster planning.** Disaster planning encompasses the retention of data for purposes other than normal operations, and all the procedures and methods needed to restore the integrity of operation in the event that it is lost. Because disasters can occur at any point of activity—for example, at a terminal operation—there may be many different activities included within the disaster plan. It is generally advisable to involve users in the development of the plan affecting their operations.

- **Privileged utilities and commands.** Various aids are employed to assist the technicians, operators, and developers in the performance of their job responsibilities. Many of these utilities and aids are designed to circumvent the normal operation controls.

Organizations may want to divide their activities into different categories, or add other categories of activities subject to control. It is generally advisable to select activities that closely relate to the organizational structure of the company. For example, if the records-retention program and media library are under the same individual, it would not be necessary to break these into two distinct activities. On the other hand, the policies, procedures, and standards may involve several organizational units and therefore should be divided into two or more different activities.

Controlling Business Transactions

The second dimension of the security program concerns controlling application processing. The activities are designed to support transaction processing. The primary objective of the data processing function is to process data (i.e. business transactions).

The security of transaction processing occurs at those points where there is transaction activity. Any time a transaction is originated, moved, stored, retrieved, or processed, it is subject to unauthorized and unintentional manipulation.

When developing security over transaction processing, it is important to identify the point where the transaction could be manipulated. These points are where the risk of manipulation is greatest and thus where control should be established. Most organizations refer to these as control points.

The ten control points in transaction processing are as follows:

- **Transaction origination.** The creation of a business transaction through the normal conduct of business activities is the first opportunity for manipulation. An order received from a customer would originate the business transaction of filling a customer order.

- **Transaction authorization.** It is management's responsibility to ensure that transactions are only processed in accordance with the intent of management. The method by which this is achieved is to require transactions to be authorized prior to processing. In some instances, this requires a special authorization, such as signing a purchase order; in other instances, management has authorized a transaction if it meets predetermined criteria, such as an order from a customer whose credit has been approved by management.

- **Data entry.** This process transcribes transactions onto computer media. In some instances, the transaction is both originated and authorized at the point where it is entered. Nevertheless, these are still three distinct control events to be performed.

- **Transaction communication.** This control point relates to all the movement activities of transactions. Although shown as a single control point, it may be repeated several times during the life of a single transaction. For example, a transaction can be moved between the origination and authorization step, as well as from the output control point to the usage control point.

- **Transaction storage.** This point involves placing transactions in a location to await further processing. Like communication, it is shown as a single control point but may occur several times in the transaction life cycle. For example, the paper document that originates the transaction may be stored in a file cabinet, whereas the electronic image of that transaction is stored in a database.

■ **Transaction processing.** Processing encompasses all mathematical and logical manipulations on data, as well as the updating of information stored in computer files. Processing can be automated (by computer) or manual by (by people).

■ **Transaction retrieval.** This control point involves the removal of transactions from storage. As with the storage function, this can be a manual storage cabinet or a computerized file. The removal can be the electronic image; in this case, the image is retained on file. There is also a form of retrieval in which no document or image is retained after the retrieval action is concluded.

■ **Transaction preparation (output).** This action involves the conversion of electronic media to a format usable by people. It may involve the display of a single transaction on a terminal, or it may involve the consolidation, summarization, and presentation of large volumes of transactions on reports. The content may be altered in this process; for example, state codes may be converted to the formal spelling of the state name.

■ **Transaction usage.** This involves actions taken on computer-produced results by either people or programs to meet user needs. Actions can range from doing nothing, which in many instances is a definitive action, to initiating a whole series of steps, for example, reordering products.

■ **Transaction destruction.** This final action on a transaction is the destruction of the transaction itself. In many instances, organization policy and/or the law specifies the time that a transaction must be retained before it can be destroyed. In other instances, the destruction of a transaction is up to the individual responsible for the transaction processing.

These ten control points represent the points at which transactions are vulnerable to penetration. If security is to be broken, it will be broken at one of these points. Invariably, the system will be penetrated at the weakest point.

There is a close relationship between the processing activities and the control points in transaction processing. The transactions are processed by the previously described activities. These activities either directly contribute to the processing (for example, the communication activity) or support the processes that carry out the transaction (for example, the program change control activity ensures that the programs that perform the processing are current with business requirements).

Characteristics of Security Penetration

Many hundreds of years ago, the Chinese built a great wall around their entire civilization to protect themselves from penetrators. This was a costly and time-consuming exercise and in the end proved futile. The French tried the same tactic by building the Maginot line after World War I, only to find that the Germans went around these great fortifications, which in the end proved to be a useless defense.

A smarter strategy is to locate security defenses at the point where penetration could be the greatest. To select those points, we need to analyze the history of penetrations and develop hypotheses that tell us where our systems are most vulnerable.

We need to explore two premises to understand where penetration will occur. First, penetration will occur at the weakest point in transaction processing. Penetrations aimed at manipulating transaction processing will pick the weakest control point in the processing cycle for penetration. The term *hacking* means a continual probing to identify a weakness. Penetrators invariably hack until they find the weak point and then penetrate at that point. Therefore, if the weakest point in the cycle is strengthened, the effort required to penetrate the system increases. Each time the weak point is strengthened, the ante to play the penetration game goes up.

Second, penetration will occur in the least-controlled activity. The activity in which there is the greatest opportunity to manipulate is the activity that is most subject to manipulation. For example, if it is easiest to manipulate training, then that is the activity that will be used to penetrate the system. In one of the classic computer fraud cases, the head teller in a bank trained new tellers to ignore the warning messages that indicated unauthorized manipulation was occurring.

The two variables described in this chapter, control points and controllable activities, hold the key to determining where security is needed. If either a control point or an activity is weak, it needs to be strengthened; and if activities and control points that are related are both weak, the opportunity for penetration is even greater. By looking at these variables and showing the relationship, we can identify the point where the computer processes are most likely to be penetrated.

Building a Penetration-Point Matrix

The Computer Security Penetration-Point Matrix is directed at data manipulation (see Table 20-3). It is not designed to identify all security threats. For example, natural disasters are a threat, but not a people threat. Disgruntled employees may wish to sabotage the computer center by destroying equipment; this is a threat to computer processing, but not a threat to transaction processing. On the other hand, most of the day-to-day security threats are data related and are identifiable through the use of the Computer Security Penetration-Point Matrix.

This matrix lists the 10 transaction control points in the vertical column and the 19 controllable activities in the horizontal column.

The matrix can be completed for each major business transaction. If the organization has a control design methodology, the insight gained from completing the form for the organization will suffice to identify the major penetration points. If each application is uniquely controlled, the matrix should be prepared for each transaction.

The matrix is completed control point by control point. The processing at each control point is viewed in relation to the activities that are involved in that processing. In most instances, many of the activities will be involved. Several questions need to be asked when looking at each activity. First, is there a high probability that this control point could be penetrated through this activity? For example, the first control point is transaction origination, and the first controllable activity is users of that application. The question then becomes: Do the users have a high probability of penetrating the point where the transaction is originated? If so, three points are allocated and recorded in the intersection of the lines from that control point and controllable activity.

Table 20-3A Computer Security Penetration-Point Matrix

	USERS OF APPLICATION DATA AND PROGRAMS	TECHNICAL INTERFACE TO COMPUTER ENVIRONMENT	DEVELOPMENT AND MAINTENANCE OF APPLICATION SYSTEMS	PRIVILEGED USERS	VENDOR INTERFACES	POLICIES, PROCEDURES, AND STANDARDS	TRAINING	DATABASE ADMINISTRATION	COMMUNICATIONS	DOCUMENTATION
Transaction organization										
Transaction authorization										
Data entry										
Transaction communication										
Transaction storage										
Transaction processing										
Transaction retrieval										
Transaction preparation										
Transaction usage										
Transaction destruction										
Subtotal										

Table 20-3B Computer Security Penetration-Point Matrix

	PROGRAM CHANGE CONTROL	RECORDS RETENTION PROGRAM	COMPUTER PROCESSING	MEDIA LIBRARIES	ERROR HANDLING	PRODUCTION LIBRARY CONTROL	COMPUTER OPERATIONS	DISASTER PLANNING	PRIVILEGED UTILITIES AND COMMANDS
Transaction organization									
Transaction authorization									
Data entry									
Transaction communication									
Transaction storage									
Transaction processing									
Transaction retrieval									
Transaction preparation									
Transaction usage									
Transaction destruction									
Subtotal									
Subtotal Table 20-3a									
Total Score									

If there is not a high probability of penetration, the question must be asked whether there is an average probability. If so, a score of 2 is put in the intersection between the control point and controllable activity. If there is a low probability, but still a probability, of penetration, then a score of 1 should be recorded in the matrix intersection. If there is no probability of penetration, or a minimal probability of penetration, a dash or zero should be put in the intersection. This procedure is continued until all the control points have been evaluated according to each of the 19 controllable activities.

The scores allocated for each intersection should be totaled vertically and horizontally. This will result in a minimum horizontal score of 0, and a maximum score of 57. The vertical scores will total a minimum of 0 and a maximum of 30. Circle the high scores in the vertical and horizontal Total columns. These will indicate the high-risk control points and the high-risk activities. Circle the intersections for which there are high scores for the transaction control point, and a high score for the controllable activity and either a two or three in the intersection between those high total scores.

The most probable penetration points should be listed in this order:

- **First priority** is given to the intersection at which both the controllable activity and the control point represent high probabilities of penetration through high total scores. These are the points where there is the greatest risk of penetration.

- **Second priority** is given to the high-risk controllable activities. The activities are general controls, which usually represent a greater risk than application control points.

- **Third priority** is given to the high-risk control points as indicated by high total scores for the control point.

At the end of this exercise, management will have an indication of where security is needed most. Because security will be placed on activities and at transaction control points through activities, this identification process is important in determining the magnitude of the computer security program.

Task 3: Analyze the Results of Security Testing

Software testers can analyze the results from testing computer security. This analysis provides a baseline and the points at which security most likely could be penetrated. If the testers have identified the controls at the penetration points, they will have most of the information needed to analyze the adequacy of security.

If software testers have a background in security, they will have uncovered a lot of information during their baseline exercise and while developing the penetration-point matrix. This additional information can prove helpful in analyzing.

Analysis of the following proves helpful in determining whether security is adequate for an information system:

- Whether adequate controls exist at the points of highest probability of penetration

- Whether controls exist at the points of most probable penetration

- Adequacy of the controls to protect against penetration at the points of most probable penetration

- Strengths and weaknesses identified in the baseline assessment
- Risks for which there are no controls
- Penetration points for which there are no controls

Because security is a highly specialized topic, software testers may need assistance in evaluating the adequacy of security in high-risk systems. If the data or assets controlled by the system pose minimal risk to the organization, software testers should be able to make a judgment regarding the adequacy of security controls.

Evaluating the Adequacy of Security

To limit the amount of testing that must be done, complete one or all of the following three tests on the points with the highest probability of penetration. Fraud studies indicate that those points with the highest potential to penetrate are the ones where penetration is most likely to occur:

- **Evaluate the adequacy of security controls at identified points.** The objective of this test is to evaluate whether the security controls in place are adequate to prevent or significantly deter penetration. The process is one of evaluating the magnitude of the risk and strength of controls. If the controls are perceived to be stronger than the magnitude of the risk, the probability of penetration at that point is significantly reduced. On the other hand, if the controls appear inadequate, testers could conclude that the identified point is of high risk.

- **Determine whether penetration can occur at identified point(s).** In this test, testers actually try to penetrate the system at the identified point. For example, if it is the payroll system and testers are trying to determine whether invalid overtime can be entered into the payroll system, the testers attempt to do this. In fact, the testers would attempt to break security by actually doing it.

  This type of test requires pre-approval by management. The testers must protect themselves so that they are not improperly accused of actually trying to penetrate the system. Also, if the system is actually penetrated at that point by the technique used by the testers, they stand to be among the potential perpetrators who might be investigated.

- **Determine whether penetration has actually occurred at this point.** This test involves conducting an investigation to determine whether the system has actually been penetrated. For example, if improper overtime is the area of concern and the payroll clerks are the most likely perpetrators, testers investigate paid overtime to determine whether it was in fact properly authorized overtime.

NOTE Software testers can create a penetration-point matrix. The testers may want to work with security experts and/or internal/external auditors when performing any or all of the three tests. The software testers can be helpful in this process, and also learn how auditors perform these types of tests.

Check Procedures

The check procedures for this test process should focus on the completeness and competency of the team using the security baseline process and the penetration-point matrix, as well as the completeness of the list of potential perpetrators and potential points of penetration. The analysis should also be challenged.

Work Paper 20-1 contains questions to help check the completeness and correctness of the security test process. Yes responses indicate good control. No responses should result in challenging the completeness and correctness of the conclusions drawn from the matrix.

Output

The output from this test process is a security baseline, the penetration-point matrix identifying the high-risk points of penetration, and a security assessment.

Guidelines

You can use the penetration-point matrix in one of two ways:

- It can be used to identify the people and the potential points of penetration so that an investigation can be undertaken to determine whether a particular location/information system has been penetrated.

- It can be used to evaluate/build/improve the security system to minimize the risk of penetration at high-risk points.

Summary

This test process is designed to help software testers conduct tests on the adequacy of computer security. The process is built on two premises: First, extensive security testing is impractical; after all, practical security testing involves focusing on specific points of vulnerability. Second, software testers are most effective in identifying points of potential security weakness, but help may be needed in performing the actual security analysis.

WORK PAPER 20-1   Test Security Quality Control Checklist

	YES	NO	N/A	COMMENTS
1. Has a team of three or more people been put together to prepare and use the penetration-point matrix?				
2. Is there a reasonable possibility that the team members can identify all the major potential perpetrators?				
3. Do the team members have knowledge of the location/information system under investigation?				
4. Is there a high probability that the team will identify all the major potential points of penetration?				
5. Will the team use a synergistic tool to facilitate brainstorming/discussion to identify potential perpetrators/penetration points?				
6. Does the prepared penetration-point matrix include the identified potential perpetrators and potential points of penetration?				
7. Has the team used appropriate synergistic tools to rate the probability that a given perpetrator will penetrate a specific point?				
8. Has every perpetrator and penetration point been analyzed?				
9. Has the accumulation of points been performed correctly?				
10. Have the high-risk penetration points been identified?				
11. Has there been a reasonable challenge that the identified high-risk points are in fact the high-risk points of penetration?				

Testing a Data Warehouse

A data warehouse is a central repository of data made available to users. The centralized storage of data provides significant processing advantages but at the same time raises concerns of the data's security, accessibility, and integrity. This chapter focuses on where testing would be most effective in determining the risks associated with those concerns.

Overview

This testing process lists the more common concerns associated with the data warehouse concept. It also explains the more common activities performed as part of a data warehouse. Testing begins by determining the appropriateness of those concerns to the data warehouse process under test. If appropriate, the severity of the concerns must be determined. This is accomplished by relating those high-severity concerns to the data warehouse activity controls. If in place and working, the controls should minimize the concerns.

Concerns

The following are the concerns most commonly associated with a data warehouse:

- **Inadequate assignment of responsibilities.** There is inappropriate segregation of duties or failure to recognize placement of responsibility.

- **Inaccurate or incomplete data in a data warehouse.** The integrity of data entered in the data warehouse is lost because of inadvertent or intentional acts.

- **Losing an update to a single data item.** One or more updates to a single data item can be lost because of inadequate concurrent update procedures.

- **Inadequate audit trail to reconstruct transactions.** The use of data by multiple applications may split the audit trail among those applications and the data warehouse software audit trail.

- **Unauthorized access to data in a data warehouse.** The concentration of data may make sensitive data available to anyone who gains access to the data warehouse.

- **Inadequate service level.** Multiple users vying for the same resources may degrade the service to all because of excessive demand or inadequate resources.

- **Placing data in the wrong calendar period.** Identifying transactions with the proper calendar period is more difficult in some online data warehouse environments than in others.

- **Failure of data warehouse software to function as specified.** Vendors provide most data warehouse software, making the data warehouse administrator dependent on the vendor to ensure the proper functioning of the software.

- **Improper use of data.** Systems that control resources are always subject to misuse and abuse.

- **Lack of skilled independent data warehouse reviewers.** Most reviewers are not skilled in data warehouse technology and, thus, have not evaluated data warehouse installations.

- **Inadequate documentation.** Documentation of data warehouse technology is needed to ensure consistency of understanding and use by multiple users.

- **Loss of continuity of processing.** Many organizations rely heavily on data warehouse technology for the performance of their day-to-day processing.

- **Lack of criteria to evaluate.** Without established performance criteria, an organization cannot be assured that it is achieving its data warehouse goals.

- **Lack of management support.** Without adequate resources and "clout," the advantages of data warehouse technology may not be achieved.

Workbench

Figure 21-1 illustrates the workbench for testing the adequacy of the data warehouse activity. The workbench is a three-task process that measures the magnitude of the concerns, identifies the data warehouse activity processes, and then determines the tests necessary to determine whether the high-magnitude concerns have been adequately addressed. Those performing the test must be familiar with the data warehouse activity processes. The end result of the test is an assessment of the adequacy of those processes to minimize the high-magnitude concerns.

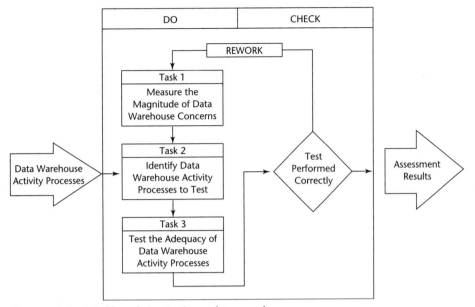

Figure 21-1   Workbench for testing a data warehouse.

Input

Organizations implementing the data warehouse activity need to establish processes to manage, operate, and control that activity. The input to this test process is knowledge of those data warehouse activity processes. If the test team does not have that knowledge, it should be supplemented with one or more individuals who possess a detailed knowledge of the data warehouse activity processes.

Enterprise-wide requirements are data requirements that are applicable to all software systems and their users. Whenever anyone accesses or updates a data warehouse, that process is subject to the enterprise-wide requirements. They are called enterprise-wide requirements because they are defined once for all software systems and users.

Each organization must define its own enterprise-wide controls. However, testers should be aware that many IT organizations do not define enterprise-wide requirements. Therefore, testers need to be aware that there may be inconsistencies between software systems and/or users. For example, if there are no security requirements applicable enterprise-wide, each software system may have different security procedures.

Enterprise-wide requirements applicable to the data warehouse include but are not limited to the following:

- **Data accessibility.** Who has access to the data warehouse, and any constraints or limitations placed on that access.

- **Update controls.** Who can change data within the data warehouse as well as the sequence in which data may be changed in the data warehouse.

- **Date controls.** The date that the data is applicable for different types of processes. For example, with accounting data it is the date that the data is officially recorded on the books of the organization.

- **Usage controls.** How data can be used by the users of the data warehouse, including any restrictions on users forwarding data to other potential users.

- **Documentation controls.** How the data within the data warehouse is to be described to users.

Do Procedures

To test a data warehouse, testers should perform the following three tasks:

1. Measure the magnitude of data warehouse concerns.
2. Identify data warehouse activities to test
3. Test the adequacy of data warehouse activity processes

Task 1: Measure the Magnitude of Data Warehouse Concerns

This task involves two activities. The first activity is to confirm that the 14 data warehouse concerns described earlier are appropriate for the organization. The list of concerns can be expanded or reduced. In addition, it may be advisable to change the wording of the concerns to wording more appropriate for the culture of the organization under test. For example, Concern 1 is inadequate assignment of responsibilities. If it is more appropriate in your organization to talk of job description responsibilities, make the appropriate change.

Once the list of potential data warehouse concerns has been finalized, the magnitude of those concerns must be determined. Work Paper 21-1 should be used to rate the magnitude of the data warehouse concerns. If the list of concerns has been modified, Work Paper 21-1 will also have to be modified.

To use Work Paper 21-1, a team of testers knowledgeable in both testing and the data warehouse activity should be assembled. For each concern, Work Paper 21-1 lists several criteria. The criteria should each be answered with a Yes or No response. The test team should have a consensus on the response. A Yes response means that the criterion has been met. Being met means that it is both in place and used. For example, Criterion 1 for Concern 1 asks whether a charter has been established for a data warehouse administration function. A Yes response means that the charter has been established and is, in fact, in place and used. A No response means that either the criterion has not been established or it is not being used. The Comments column is available to clarify the Yes and No responses.

At the conclusion of rating the criteria for each concern, the percent of No responses should be calculated. For example, the first concern lists seven criteria. If three of the seven criteria have a No response, then approximately 43 percent would have received a No response.

When Work Paper 21-1 has been completed, the results should be posted to Work Paper 21-2. For example, if Concern 1 received 43 percent of No responses, the bar on Work Paper 21-2 would be completed vertically above Concern 1 on Work Paper 21-2 to 43 percent. This would put that concern in the "medium" category. At the conclusion of this task, Work Paper 21-2 will show the magnitude of the data warehouse concerns.

Task 2: Identify Data Warehouse Activity Processes to Test

There are many ways organizations can establish a data warehouse activity. Associated with the data warehouse are a variety of processes. This section describes the more common processes associated with data warehouse activity.

Organizational Process

The data warehouse introduces a new function into the organization, and with that function comes a shifting of responsibilities. Much of this shifting involves a transfer of responsibilities from the application system development areas and the user areas to a centralized data warehouse administration function.

The introduction of the data warehouse is normally associated with the organization of a formal data warehouse administration group. This group usually reports within the data processing function and frequently directly to the data processing manager. The objective of the data warehouse administration function is to oversee and direct the installation and operation of the data warehouse.

The data warehouse administration function normally has line responsibilities for data documentation, system development procedures, and standards for those applications using data warehouse technology. The database administrator (DBA) function also has indirect or dotted-line responsibilities to computer operations and users of data warehouse technology through providing advice and direction. In addition, the data warehouse administrator should be alert to potential problems and actively involved in offering solutions.

Studies on the success of data warehouse technology strongly indicate the need for planning. A key part of this planning is the integration of the data warehouse into the organizational structure. This integration requires some reorganization within both the data processing and user areas.

Data Documentation Process

The transition to data warehouse technology involves the switching of information technology emphasis from processing to data. Many existing systems are process-driven, whereas data warehouse technology involves data-driven systems. This change in emphasis necessitates better data documentation.

If multiple users are using the same data, documentation should be easy-to-use and complete. Misunderstandings regarding the data's content, reliability, consistency, and so on will lead to problems in the data's interpretation and use. Clear, distinct documentation helps reduce this risk.

Many organizations use standardized methods of data documentation. The simplest method is to use forms and written procedures governing the method of defining data. More sophisticated installations use data dictionaries. The data dictionary can be used as a standalone automated documentation tool or integrated into the processing environment.

The data warehouse administrator normally oversees the use of the data dictionary. This involves determining what data elements will be documented, the type and extent of documentation requested, and assurance that the documentation is up-to-date and in compliance with the documentation quality standards.

The documentation requirement for data is a threefold responsibility. First, individuals must be educated in the type of documentation required and provide that documentation. Second, the documentation must be maintained to ensure its accuracy and completeness. Third, the data used in the operating environment must conform to the documentation. If the data in operation is different from the documentation specifications, the entire process collapses.

System Development Process

Data warehouse technology is designed to make system development easier; however, this occurs only when the application system fits into the existing data hierarchy. If the system requirements are outside the data warehouse structure, it may be more difficult and costly to develop that system by using the data warehouse than by using non–data warehouse methods.

One method of ensuring that applications effectively use data warehouse technology is to have data warehouse administration personnel involved in the development process. In other words, more front-end planning and assessment are required to ensure the effective use of data warehouse technology than when the data warehouse is not used. This front-end effort also ensures that the application project team understands the resources available through data warehouse technology.

The data warehouse is a continually changing grouping of data. Part of the data warehouse involvement in system development is to adjust and modify the structure continually to meet the changing needs of application systems. Thus, the development process for the data warehouse is twofold: to ensure that the applications effectively use the data warehouse, and to establish new data warehouse directions in order to keep the data warehouse in step with application needs.

The system development process in the data warehouse technology has the following three objectives:

- To familiarize the system's development people with the resources and capabilities available

- To ensure that the proposed application system can be integrated into the existing data warehouse structure, and if not, to modify the application and/or the data warehouse structure

- To ensure that application processing will preserve the consistency, reliability, and integrity of data in the data warehouse

A problem that often surfaces in the use of data warehouse technology is how to charge for data warehouse usage. Some applications operate more effectively using the data warehouse than others. Experience has shown that moving some applications from non–data warehouse to data warehouse technology substantially reduces the cost of processing, while in other instances the cost increases. The reason for this is that the data warehouse must be optimized toward a specific data usage. Obviously, the data warehouse administrator must attempt to optimize the data warehouse toward the high-usage applications and let the usage be less efficient in the small-volume applications. The costs associated with a data warehouse should not be allowed to discourage its use.

Access Control Process

One of the major concerns for management about the data warehouse is the ready accessibility of information. As more data is placed into a single repository, that repository becomes more valuable to perpetrators.

The access control function has two primary purposes. The first is to identify the resources requiring control and determine who should be given access to those resources. The second is to define and enforce the control specifications identified in the previous responsibility in the operating environment.

The access control function can be performed by the data warehouse administration function or an independent security officer. Obviously, an independent function is stronger than the same function that administers the data warehouse. The method selected will depend on the value of the information in the data warehouse and the size of the organization. The more valuable the data, or the larger the organization, the more likely it is that the function will be implemented through an independent security officer.

The enforcement of the security profile for the data warehouse in online systems is performed by security software. Some data warehouse management systems have security features incorporated in the data warehouse software, whereas others need to be supplemented by security packages. Many of the major hardware vendors, such as IBM, provide security software. In addition, several independent vendors provide general-purpose security software that interfaces with many data warehouse software systems.

The access control function has the additional responsibility of monitoring the effectiveness of security. Detecting and investigating potential access violations are important aspects of data warehouse access control. Unless the access control procedures are monitored, violators will not be detected; and if violators are not reprimanded or prosecuted, there will be little incentive for other involved parties to comply with access control rules.

Data Integrity Process

The integrity of the contents of the data warehouse is the joint responsibility of the users and the data warehouse administrator. The data warehouse administrator is concerned more about the integrity of the structure and the physical records, while the users are concerned about the contents or values contained in the data warehouse.

The integrity of dedicated files is primarily the responsibility of the user. The data processing department has a responsibility to use the correct version of the file and to add features that protect the physical integrity of the records on the file. However, the ultimate responsibility for the integrity resides with the user, and the application systems need to be constructed to ensure that integrity. This is usually accomplished by accumulating the values in one or more control fields and developing an independent control total that can be checked each time the file is used.

In a data warehouse environment, the traditional integrity responsibilities change. No longer does a single user have control over all the uses of data in a data warehouse. Several different application systems may be able to add, delete, or modify any single data element in the data warehouse. For example, in an airline reservation system, any authorized agent can commit or delete a reserved seat for a flight. On the other hand, the data warehouse administrator doesn't have control over the uses of the data in the data warehouse. This means that the data integrity must be ensured through new procedures.

The data integrity process may involve many different groups within an organization. These groups, such as various users and the data warehouse administration function, will share parts of this data integrity responsibility. In fulfilling data integrity responsibility, the following tasks need to be performed:

1. Identify the method of ensuring the completeness of the physical records in the data warehouse.

2. Determine the method of ensuring the completeness of the logical structure of the data warehouse (i.e. schema).

3. Determine which users are responsible for the integrity of which segments of the data warehouse.

4. Develop methods to enable those users to perform their data integrity responsibilities.

5. Determine the times at which the integrity of the data warehouse will be verified.

Operations Process

The normal evolution of data warehouse operations is from the data warehouse administration function to specialized operations personnel and then to regular computer operators. This evolution is necessary so that an organization can develop the appropriate skills and methods needed for training and monitoring regular computer operators. Without taking the appropriate time to develop skills, operators may be placed into a position where their probability of success is minimal.

Data warehouse technology is more complex than non–data warehouse technology. Normally, the data warehouse is coupled with communication technology. This means that two highly technical procedures are coupled, making the resulting technology more complex than either of the contributing technologies.

Most of the day-to-day operations are performed by users. The data warehouse provides the basis for a user-operated technology. One of the advantages of the data warehouse is the powerful utilities associated with the technology that are available to the users. One of the more powerful utilities is the query languages, which provide almost unlimited capabilities for users to prepare analyses and reports using the data within the data warehouse.

Computer operators face the following challenges when operating data warehouse technology:

- Monitoring space allocation to ensure minimal disruptions because of space management problems

- Understanding and using data warehouse software operating procedures and messages

- Monitoring service levels to ensure adequate resources for users

- Maintaining operating statistics so that the data warehouse performance can be monitored

- Reorganizing the data warehouse as necessary (usually under the direction of the data warehouse administrator) to improve performance and add capabilities where necessary

Backup/Recovery Process

One of the most technically complex aspects of data processing is recovering a crashed data warehouse. Recovery can occur only if adequate backup data is maintained. The recovery procedure involves the following four major challenges:

1. Verifying that the integrity of the data warehouse has been lost.

2. Notifying users that the data warehouse is inoperable and providing them with alternate processing means. (Note: These means should be predetermined and may be manual.)

3. Ensuring and having adequate backup data ready.

4. Performing the necessary procedures to recover the integrity of the data warehouse.

Many data warehouses are operational around the clock during business days, and some, seven days a week. It is not uncommon for many thousands of transactions to occur in a single day. Thus, unless recovery operations are well planned, it may take many hours or even days to recover the integrity of the data warehouse. The complexity and planning that must go into data warehouse contingency planning cannot be overemphasized.

The responsibility for data warehouse recovery is normally that of computer operations. However, the users and data warehouse administrators must provide input into the recovery process. The data warehouse administrator usually develops the procedures and acquires the recovery tools and techniques. The user provides the specifications on time span for recovery and determines what alternate procedures are acceptable during this period.

One of the problems encountered is notifying users that the data warehouse is no longer operational. In larger organizations, there may be many users, even hundreds of users, connected to a single data warehouse. It may take longer to notify the users that the data warehouse is not operational than it will take to get the data warehouse back online. The group involved in the recovery may not have adequate resources to inform all of the users. Some of the procedures to inform users of the loss of data warehouse integrity include:

- Sending messages to terminals if facilities to transmit are available

- Having a telephone number that users can call to determine if the data warehouse is down

- Providing users with the service expectations so that when those expectations are not met the users can assume a data warehouse problem has occurred

The backup/recovery process begins with determining what operations must be recovered and in what time frame. This provides the recovery specifications. From these specifications, the procedures are developed and implemented to meet the recovery expectations. Much of the process involves collecting and storing backup data; thus, it is very important for all involved parties to agree on what backup data is needed.

Performing Task 2

Two events are associated with this task. First, use Work Paper 21-3 to determine whether the preceding activities are appropriate to your data warehouse activity, supplementing or reducing the list of data warehouse activities, as necessary. In addition, you should change the process name to the specific vocabulary of your organizational culture.

Task 3: Test the Adequacy of Data Warehouse Activity Processes

This task is to evaluate that each of the seven identified processes contains controls that are adequate to reduce the concerns identified earlier in this chapter. A control is any means used to reduce the probability of a failure. The determination of whether the individual applications enter, store, and use the correct data is made using the seven-step process included in Part Three of this book.

Figure 21-2 indicates which activity processes should be tested. This figure is used by first identifying the significant data warehouse concerns, as determined in Task 1. The check marks in the "Data Warehouse Activity Processes" columns indicate which processes should reduce the concerns so that the probability of failure is minimized. For example, if a significant data warehouse concern is that "there is an inadequate assignment of responsibility," then the three data activity processes of organization, system development, and access control should be tested.

Figure 21-3 shows the types of tests that should be undertaken for each data warehouse activity process for the identified concerns. The tests are those focused on determining that specific controls exist. If those controls exist, then the testers can assume that the process is adequately controlled so that the probability of failure is minimized.

Data Warehouse Activity Processes Data Warehouse Concerns	Organization	Data Documentation	System Development	Access Control	Data Integrity	Operation	Backup/Recovery
Inadequate assignment of responsibility	√		√	√			
Inaccurate or incomplete data in a database	√		√		√	√	√
Losing an update to a single data item			√		√		
Inadequate audit trail	√	√		√		√	
Unauthorized access to a database				√		√	
Inadequate service level		√			√	√	
Placing data in the wrong calendar period		√	√		√		
Failure of data warehouse software to function as specified	√	√	√		√	√	√
Fraud/embezzlement	√		√	√			
Lack of independent database reviews	√		√				
Inadequate documentation	√	√	√		√	√	√
Continuity of processing			√		√	√	
Lack of performance criteria	√		√			√	
Lack of management support	√		√	√			

√ = should be tested

Figure 21-2   Which data warehouse activities should be tested?

ORGANIZATIONAL CONTROL OBJECTIVES		
Concern Number	**Concern**	**Test should determine that a control exists**
1.	Inadequate assignment of responsibilities	1. To assign data warehouse responsibilities to individuals 2. To see that user retains organizational responsibility for the accuracy, completeness, and security of data 3. To perform independent reviews to ensure the adequate assignment of responsibilities
2.	Inaccurate or incomplete data in a data warehouse.	1. To see that the organizational structure is designed to ensure the adequate assignment of responsibilities

Figure 21-3   Organizational control objectives.   *(continues)*

ORGANIZATIONAL CONTROL OBJECTIVES		
Concern Number	**Concern**	**Test should determine that a control exists**
8.	Failure of the data warehouse software to function as specified	1. To see that the organizational structure is designed to ensure prompt detection and correction of data warehouse software errors 2. To document data warehouse expectations
9.	Fraud/embezzlement	1. To divide responsibilities so that an individual cannot perform *and* conceal a single event
10.	Lack of independent data warehouse reviews	1. To see that a data warehouse review group is established that is independent of the data warehouse function 2. To define review responsibilities
11.	Inadequate documentation	1. To document departmental data warehouse organizational responsibilities in the department charter 2. To document individual data warehouse responsibilities in their job description
13.	Lack of performance criteria	1. To define data warehouse expectations in measurable terms
14.	Lack of management support	1. To ensure that senior management defines and enforces data policy 2. To ensure that senior management participates in data warehouse decision making 3. To ensure that senior management supports independent data warehouse review groups
DATA DOCUMENTATION CONTROL OBJECTIVES		
4.	Inadequate audit trail	1. To define data warehouse audit trail requirements 2. To divide requirements between the user and the DBA function 3. To document data warehouse deletions
7.	Placing data in the wrong calendar period	1. To define data accounting requirements
8.	Failure of data warehouse software to function as specified	1. To assign centralized control of external schema 2. To define data independently of the applications that use the data
11.	Inadequate documentation	1. To develop an inventory of data elements 2. To document data in accordance with documentation standards 3. To enforce the use of data as documented

Figure 21-3   (continued)

SECURITY/ACCESS CONTROL OBJECTIVES		
Concern Number	**Concern**	**Test should determine that a control exists**
1.	Inadequate assignment of responsibilities	1. To assign responsibility for security to a function independent of the one requiring security
5.	Unauthorized access in the data warehouse	1. To define access to each data warehouse resource 2. To include all individuals involved in data warehouse in the access control process 3. To ensure prompt punishment of violators 4. To create logs of security-related activities
9.	Fraud/embezzlement	1. To see that security measures address the common methods of fraud
12.	Continuity of processing	1. To ensure that visitors and service personnel are escorted 2. To assess the risks of security problems on disruptions to processing
14.	Lack of management support	1. To see that management establishes the desired level of security 2. To see that management supports punishment for security violations

COMPUTER OPERATIONS ACTIVITY CONTROL OBJECTIVES		
2.	Inaccurate or incomplete data in a data warehouse	1. To ensure that data is not lost or changed due to improper operations
5.	Unauthorized access in a data warehouse	1. To physically protect the data warehouse from unauthorized access
6.	Inadequate service level	1. To minimize both the frequency and the impact of inadequate service level 2. To monitor service-level performance
8.	Failure of the data warehouse software to function as specified	1. To monitor data warehouse software failures to determine responsibility and implement fixes as appropriate
11.	Inadequate documentation	1. To document data warehouse software operating procedures and controls
12.	Continuity of processing	1. To plan for expected capacity requirements 2. To minimize data warehouse software downtime
13.	Lack of performance criteria	1. To establish data warehouse software expectations

Figure 21-3   *(continued)*   *(continues)*

DATA WAREHOUSE BACKUP/RECOVERY CONTROL OBJECTIVES		
Concern Number	**Concern**	**Test should determine that a control exists**
2.	Inaccurate or incomplete	1. To verify controls after recovery to ensure the integrity of the recovered data warehouse
4.	Inadequate audit trail	1. To maintain records on the recovery process
6.	Inadequate service level	1. To include segments of the application in the recovery process 2. To specify assignments 3. To retain adequate backup data
8.	Failure of the data warehouse software to function as specified	1. To test the recovery process
11.	Inadequate documentation	1. To document recovery procedures
12.	Continuity of processing	1. To determine expected failure rates 2. To specify recovery requirements 3. To define alternate processing procedures 4. To inform users about service interruptions
DATA WAREHOUSE INTEGRITY CONTROL OBJECTIVES		
2.	Inaccurate or incomplete data in a data warehouse	1. To verify the integrity of the initial population of the data warehouse 2. To validate conformance to data definition 3. To control access for data modification 4. To provide adequate backup and recovery methods 5. To preserve the integrity of the data warehouse 6. To preserve the consistency of data redundancy 7. To control the placement of data warehouse data on media and devices 8. To maintain independent data warehouse controls 9. To maintain data warehouse segment counts
3.	Losing an update to a single data item	1. To utilize concurrency and lockout controls
4.	Inadequate audit trail	1. To maintain adequate audit trails to permit reconstruction of processing
7.	Placing data in the wrong calendar period	1. To establish accounting controls to ensure that data is recorded in the proper calendar period

Figure 21-3 (continued)

DATA WAREHOUSE INTEGRITY CONTROL OBJECTIVES		
Concern Number	**Concern**	**Test should determine that a control exists**
8.	Failure of data warehouse software to function as specified	1. To verify the proper functioning of the data warehouse software 2. To verify the correctness of the interface to the data warehouse software
11.	Inadequate documentation	1. To document the data definitions for creation of the data warehouse
SYSTEM DEVELOPMENT CONTROL OBJECTIVES		
1.	Inadequate assignment of responsibilities	1. To divide system development responsibilities among the DBA function, the application project team, and the user
14.	Lack of management support	1. To ensure that senior management participates in system planning 2. To ensure that senior management approves data warehouse application proposals
13.	Lack of performance criteria	1. To establish performance criteria for all data warehouse applications
4.	Inadequate audit trail	1. To include the audit trail in the design specifications
2.	Inaccurate or incomplete data in the data warehouse	1. To include the methods of ensuring accurate and complete data in the design specifications
7.	Placing data in the wrong calendar period	1. To include the accounting requirements in the design specifications
11.	Inadequate documentation	1. To ensure that documentation conforms to data warehouse documentation standards 2. To ensure that documentation is up to date
3.	Losing an update to a single data item	1. To implement controls to ensure the proper sequencing of updates
10.	Lack of independent data warehouse reviews group	1. To establish a test plan 2. To have the test plan implemented or monitored by an independent group
9.	Fraud/embezzlement	1. To test the adequacy of of controls
8.	Failure of the data warehouse software to function as specified	1. To test to ensure that the system achieves specified performance criteria
6.	Inadequate service	1. To monitor the installed application to ensure that specified performance criteria are achieved

Figure 21-3 *(continued)*

Check Procedures

Work Paper 21-4 is a quality control checklist for testing a data warehouse. It is designed so that Yes responses indicate good test practices and No responses warrant additional investigation. A Comments column is provided to explain No responses and to record results of investigation. The N/A response is used when the checklist item is not applicable to the test situation.

Output

The output from the data warehouse test process is an assessment of the adequacy of the data warehouse activity processes. The assessment report should indicate the concerns addressed by the test team, the processes in place in the data warehouse activity, and the adequacy of those processes.

Guidelines

The testing of the data warehouse activity as proposed in this chapter is one of risk assessments. It is not designed to ensure that the data warehouse will function properly for each use, but rather to apprise management of the probability that failures will be minimized or that additional management action should be taken. The actual determination of the correct processing of the warehouse should be done in conjunction with the application software that uses the data warehouse.

Summary

This chapter is designed to assist testers in evaluating the work processes associated with a data warehouse activity. It is designed to be used in conjunction with the test of application software that uses the data warehouse. The actual processing of data from the data warehouse should be tested using the seven-step process included in Part Three of this book. However, unless adequate control procedures are in place and working, the testers cannot rely on results of the one application software test to be applicable to other data warehouse applications.

If the data warehouse activity processes are adequate to address the concerns, the testers can assume that the results of testing one application will be similar to testing other applications using the data warehouse. On the other hand, if the processes do not adequately minimize the probability of failure in the data warehouse, more extensive testing may be required of all the individual applications that use the data warehouse.

WORK PAPER 21-1   Rating the Magnitude of Data Warehouse Concerns

Worksheet Concern #1:   Inadequate Assignment of Responsibilities

Description of Concern:

There is inappropriate segregation of duties or failure to recognize placement of responsibility.

		YES	NO	COMMENTS
1.	Has a charter been established for the database administration function outlining the role and responsibilities for the function?			
2.	Have the user responsibilities regarding the integrity of the data warehouse been defined?			
3.	Have job descriptions been modified for all individuals interfacing with the data warehouse to define their data warehouse responsibilities?			
4.	Have job descriptions been developed for full-time data warehouse administration personnel?			
5.	Has a formal method of resolving data warehouse disputes been established?			
6.	Does the organization have a data policy which outlines organizational data responsibility?			
7.	Are the functions being performed by data warehouse administration within that administration's formal role and responsibility?			
	Percent of No responses		%	

(continues)

WORK PAPER 21-1   *(continued)*

Worksheet Concern #2:   Inaccurate or Incomplete Data in a Data Warehouse

Description of Concern:
The integrity of data entered in the data warehouse is lost due to inadvertent or intentional acts.

		YES	NO	COMMENTS
1.	Has each element of data in the data warehouse been identified?			
2.	Have the data validation rules for each data element been documented?			
3.	Have the data validation rules for each data element been implemented?			
4.	Are the data validation rules adequate to ensure the accuracy of data?			
5.	Have procedures been established to ensure the consistence of redundant data elements?			
6.	Have procedures been established for the timely correction of data entry errors?			
7.	Are procedures established to promptly notify all users of the data warehouse when an inaccuracy or incomplete data condition has been identified?			
8.	Are the data warehouse administration tools and techniques adequate to ensure the consistency of redundant data elements?			
	Percent of No responses		%	

WORK PAPER 21-1 *(continued)*

Worksheet Concern #3:   Losing an Update to a Single Data Item

Description of Concern:

One or more updates to a single data item can be lost due to inadequate concurrent update procedures.

		YES	NO	COMMENTS
1.	Does the data warehouse software in use have a lockout feature to prevent concurrent updates to a single data item?			
2.	Does the data warehouse software have a feature to resolve deadlock in accessing data (for example, user A has item 1 and wants item 2, while user B has item 2 and wants item 1)?			
3	Has the sequencing of updates to the data warehouse been defined?			
4.	Are there controls in the data warehouse software to ensure that events can only be recorded in the predetermined sequence?			
5.	Have the parties that can create, update, or delete a data element been identified?			
	Percent of No responses		%	

(continues)

WORK PAPER 21-1   *(continued)*

Worksheet Concern #4:   Inadequate Audit Trail

Description of Concern:
The use of data by multiple applications may split the audit trail among those applications and the data warehouse software audit trail.

		YES	NO	COMMENTS
1.	Has the audit trail for data warehouse applications been identified and documented?			
2.	Has the retention period for each part of the data warehouse audit trail been determined?			
3.	Is a data warehouse software log maintained?			
4.	Does management determine what information will be maintained in the data warehouse software log?			
5.	Can the audit trail trace source transactions to control totals and trace control totals back to the initiating transactions?			
6.	Can the audit trail provide the evidence needed to reconstruct transaction processing?			
7.	Is the audit trail in operation whenever the data warehouse is in operation?			
8.	Are all overrides of normal data warehouse software procedures recorded on the data warehouse software log?			
9.	Can the application audit trail records be cross-referenced to the data warehouse software log audit trail records?			
	Percent of No responses		%	

WORK PAPER 21-1   *(continued)*

Worksheet Concern #5:   Unauthorized Access to Data in a Data Warehouse

Description of Concern:
The concentration of sensitive data may make it available to anyone gaining access to a data warehouse.

		YES	NO	COMMENTS
1.	Have all of the data elements requiring security procedures been identified?			
2.	Have all of the data warehouse users been identified?			
3.	Has a user profile been established indicating which resources can be accessed by which users?			
4.	Has the enforcement of the user profile been automated?			
5.	Is the access mechanism, such as passwords, protected from unauthorized manipulation?			
6.	Has the organization established a data warehouse security officer function (note that this need not be a full-time function)?			
7.	Are security violators promptly punished?			
8.	Are formal records maintained on security violations?			
9.	Are security violation summaries presented to management in regular reports?			
	Percent of No responses		%	

(continues)

WORK PAPER 21-1 *(continued)*

Worksheet Concern #6: <u>Inadequate Service Level</u>

Description of Concern:
Multiple users contesting for the same resources may degrade the service to all due to excessive demand or inadequate resources.

		YES	NO	COMMENTS
1.	Has the level of service that is desired been documented?			
2.	Are procedures established to monitor the desired level of service to users?			
3.	Are users encouraged, by the use of such techniques as varying chargeout rates, to spread out their nonurgent processing?			
4.	Have the identified options to improve service when it degrades been identified?			
5.	Does the data warehouse administrator continually monitor the service level and make adjustments where appropriate?			
6.	Are steps to take established at points where service level degrades?			
7.	Do procedures identify the cause of degradation in service, such as a single user consuming exorbitant amounts of resources, so that action can be taken to eliminate those causes where appropriate?			
	Percent of No responses		%	

WORK PAPER 21-1 *(continued)*

Worksheet Concern #7: Placing Data in the Wrong Calendar Period

Description of Concern:
Identifying transactions with the proper calendar period is more difficult in some on-line data warehouse environments than in others.

		YES	NO	COMMENTS
1.	Do procedures identify the criteria for determining into which accounting period transactions are placed?			
2.	Are all postdated transactions date-stamped to identify the accounting period in which they belong?			
3.	Are procedures established to cut off processing at the end of significant accounting periods, such as at year-end?			
4.	For applications where data must be segregated into accounting periods, are significant transactions entered both immediately before and immediately after the accounting cutoff period manually reviewed to ensure they are in the appropriate accounting period?			
5.	Are formal procedures established to move data from one accounting period to another if appropriate?			
	Percent of No responses		%	

(continues)

WORK PAPER 21-1   *(continued)*

Worksheet Concern #8:   Failure of Data Warehouse Software to Function as Specified

Description of Concern:
Most data warehouse software is provided by vendors, making the data administrator dependent on the vendor to assure the proper functioning of the software.

		YES	NO	COMMENTS
1.	Have the processing expectations been determined?			
2.	Is the data warehouse software evaluated to determine that it performs in accordance with the predetermined requirements?			
3.	Is each new release of data warehouse software thoroughly tested?			
4.	Has a maintenance contract for the data warehouse software been established?			
5.	Are procedures established to identify data warehouse software problems?			
6.	Are operations personnel trained to identify and report data warehouse software problems?			
7.	Have backup procedures been developed for use in the event of a data warehouse software failure?			
8.	Are data warehouse software failures recorded and regularly reported to the data warehouse administrator?			
9.	Are the vendors promptly notified in the event of a data warehouse software problem so that they can take appropriate action?			
	Percent of No responses		%	

WORK PAPER 21-1   *(continued)*

Worksheet Concern #9:   **Fraud/Embezzlement**

Description of Concern:
Systems that control resources are always subject to fraud and embezzlement.

		YES	NO	COMMENTS
1.	Do data warehouse administration personnel have access to the data in the data warehouse?			
2.	Has methodology been established for designing data warehouse controls?			
3.	Has the data warehouse been reviewed within the last year by an independent reviewer?			
4.	Have procedures been established to identify and report errors, omissions, and frauds to senior management?			
5.	Are all data warehouse resources access controlled?			
6.	Are passwords or other access control procedures changed at least every six months?			
7.	Are all error messages acted upon in a timely fashion?			
8.	Are deviations from normal processing investigated?			
9.	Do data validation routines anticipate and report on unusual processing?			
	Percent of No responses		%	

(continues)

WORK PAPER 21-1   *(continued)*

Worksheet Concern #10:   Lack of Independent Data Warehouse Reviews

Description of Concern:

Most reviewers are not skilled in data warehouse technology and thus have not evaluated data warehouse installations; in addition, many auditor software packages cannot access data warehouse software.

		YES	NO	COMMENTS
1.	Is there an internal audit function having jurisdiction over reviewing data warehouse technology?			
2.	Is there an EDP quality assurance group having jurisdiction over reviewing data warehouse technology?			
3.	Does either of these groups have adequate skills to perform such a review?			
4.	Has an independent review of data warehouse technology been performed within the last 12 months?			
5.	Was a report issued describing the findings and recommendations from that review?			
6.	Were the findings and recommendations reasonable based upon the current use of data warehouse technology?			
7.	Is an independent review of data warehouse technology planned during the next 12 months?			
Percent of No responses			%	

WORK PAPER 21-1 *(continued)*

Worksheet Concern #11: Inadequate Documentation

Description of Concern:

Documentation of data warehouse technology is needed to ensure consistency of understanding and use by multiple users.

		YES	NO	COMMENTS
1.	Do data documentation standards exist?			
2.	Are data documentation standards enforced?			
3.	Is a data dictionary used to document the attributes of data elements?			
4.	Is a data dictionary integrated into the data warehouse software operation, so that the only entry into data warehouse software-controlled data is through the data dictionary?			
5.	Does the data warehouse administration group provide counsel in documenting and using data?			
6.	Does the data documentation contain the data validation rules?			
	Percent of No responses		%	

(continues)

WORK PAPER 21-1   *(continued)*

Worksheet Concern #12:   Continuity of Processing

Description of Concern:

Many organizations rely heavily on data warehouse technology for the performance of their day-to-day processing.

		YES	NO	COMMENTS
1.	Have the potential causes of data warehouse failure been identified?			
2.	Has the impact of each of those failures on the organization been assessed?			
3.	Have procedures been developed to continue processing during a data warehouse failure?			
4.	Are procedures established to ensure that the integrity of the data warehouse can be restored after data warehouse failure?			
5.	Has the sequence of actions necessary to restore applications after a data warehouse failure been documented?			
6.	Have computer operations personnel been trained to data warehouse recovery procedures?			
7.	Is sufficient backup data stored off-site to permit reconstruction of processing in the event of a disaster?			
8.	Are records maintained on data warehouse failures so that specific analysis can be performed?			
	Percent of No responses		%	

WORK PAPER 21-1 *(continued)*

Worksheet Concern #13: **Lack of Performance Criteria**

Description of Concern:
Without established performance criteria, an organization cannot be assured that it is achieving data warehouse goals.

		YES	NO	COMMENTS
1.	Have measurable objectives for data warehouse technology been established?			
2.	Are those objectives monitored to determine whether they are achieved?			
3.	Can the cost associated with data warehouse technology be identified?			
4.	Can the benefits associated with data warehouse technology be identified?			
5.	Was a cost/benefit analysis prepared for the installation and operation of data warehouse technology?			
6.	Has the cost/benefit projection been monitored to measure whether those projections have been achieved?			
7.	Is the achievement of the performance criteria evaluated by an independent group, such as EDP quality assurance?			
	Percent of No responses		%	

(continues)

WORK PAPER 21-1 *(continued)*

Worksheet Concern #14: <u>Lack of Management Support</u>

Description of Concern:

Without adequate resources and "clout," the advantages of data warehouse technology may not be achieved.

		YES	NO	COMMENTS
1.	Has a member of senior management been appointed responsible for managing data for the organization?			
2.	Was senior management involved in the selection of the organization's data warehouse technology approach?			
3.	Has a review board been established comprising users, EDP personnel, and senior managers to oversee the use of data warehouse technology?			
4.	Has data processing management attended courses on the use of data warehouse technology?			
5.	Has senior management requested regular briefing and/or reports on the implementation and use of data warehouse technology?			
6.	Has senior management been involved in the preparation of a long-range plan for use of information in the organization?			
7.	Is senior management involved in the settlement of disputes over the attributes or use of information in the organization?			
	Percent of No responses		%	

WORK PAPER 21-2 Magnitude of Data Warehouse Concerns

Field Requirements

FIELD	INSTRUCTIONS FOR ENTERING DATA
% of No Responses	This column divides the percentage of No responses into three categories: low, medium, and high.
Concern Ratings	The rating for the concerns listed on this work paper represents the percentages of No responses calculated for those concerns on Work Paper 21-1.
Data Warehouse Concerns	These are the 14 data warehouse concerns described earlier in this chapter.

1.	2.	3.	4.	5.	6.	7.	8.	9.	10.	11.	12.	13.	14.
Inadequate assignment of responsibilities	Inaccurate or incomplete data in a database	Losing an update to a single database	Inadequate audit trail	Unauthorized access in a database	Inadequate service level	Placing data in the wrong calendar period	Failure of DBMS to function as specified	Fraud/embezzlement	Lack of independent database reviews	Inadequate documentation	Continuity of processing	Lack of performance criteria	Lack of management support

(Continues)

WORK PAPER 21-2 *(continued)*

% OF NO RESPONSES	CONCERN RATINGS												
100%	High											
68%												
67%	Medium											
34%												
33%	Low											
0%												

WORK PAPER 21-3   Data Warehouse Activity Process

	APPROPRIATE			COMMENTS
	YES	NO	N/A	
1. Organizational Process				
2. Data Documentation Process				
3. System Development Process				
4. Access Control Process				
5. Data Integrity Process				
6. Operations Process				
7. Backup/Recovery Process				

WORK PAPER 21-4 Data Warehouse Quality Control Checklist

	YES	NO	N/A	COMMENTS
1. Does someone assigned to the test team have data warehouse skills?				
2. Does the tester understand the generic data warehouse concerns?				
3. Does the final list of data warehouse concerns represent the true concerns of your organization?				
4. Has the vocabulary in all of the work papers and figures been adjusted to the vocabulary in use in your organization?				
5. Does the test team understand the criteria that are used to determine the magnitude of the data warehouse concerns?				
6. Do the ratings of the magnitude of the concerns seem reasonable?				
7. Have the data warehouse activity processes been identified?				
8. Do the identified processes appear to represent the actual processes in use in the data warehouse activity?				
9. Does the test team understand the controls that are needed to minimize failure in each of the data warehouse activities processes?				
10. Does the final assessment of the test team regarding the data warehouse appear reasonable to the test team?				
11. Does the assessment report issued by the test team appear to represent the results of the test?				

CHAPTER 22

Testing
Web-Based Systems

This chapter focuses on the unique characteristics of web-based testing. Testing can use the same seven-step process described in Part Three of this book. This chapter focuses on determining whether web-based risk should be included in the test plan, which types of web-based testing should be used, and selecting the appropriate web-based test tools for the test execution phase.

Web-based systems are those systems that use the Internet, intranets, and extranets. The Internet is a worldwide collection of interconnected networks. An intranet is a private network inside a company using web-based applications, but for use only within an organization. An extranet is a private network that allows external access to customers and suppliers using web-based applications.

Overview

Web-based architecture is an extension of client/server architecture. The following section describes the difference between client/server architecture and web-based architecture.

In a client/server architecture, as discussed in Chapter 15, application software resides on the client workstations. The application server handles processing requests. The back-end processing (typically a mainframe or super-minicomputer) handles processing such as batch transactions that are accumulated and processed together at one time on a regular basis. The important distinction to note is that application software resides on the client workstation.

For web-based systems, the browsers reside on client workstations. These client workstations are networked to a web server, either through a remote connection or through a network such as a local area network (LAN) or wide area network (WAN).

As the web server receives and processes requests from the client workstation, requests may be sent to the application server to perform actions such as data queries, electronic commerce transactions, and so forth.

The back-end processing works in the background to perform batch processing and handle high-volume transactions. The back-end processing can also interface with transactions to other systems in the organization. For example, when an online banking transaction is processed over the Internet, the transaction is eventually updated to the customer's account and shown on a statement in a back-end process.

Concerns

Testers should have the following concerns when conducting web-based testing:

- **Browser compatibility.** Testers should validate consistent application performance on a variety of browser types and configurations.

- **Functional correctness.** Testers should validate that the application functions correctly. This includes validating links, calculations, displays of information, and navigation.

- **Integration.** Testers should validate the integration between browsers and servers, applications and data, and hardware and software.

- **Usability.** Testers should validate the overall usability of a web page or a web application, including appearance, clarity, and navigation.

- **Security.** Testers should validate the adequacy and correctness of security controls, including access control and authorizations.

- **Performance.** Testers should validate the performance of the web application under load.

- **Verification of code.** Testers should validate that the code used in building the web application (HTML, Java, and so on) has been used in a correct manner. For example, no nonstandard coding practices should be used that would cause an application to function incorrectly in some environments.

Workbench

Figure 22-1 illustrates the workbench for web-based testing. The input to the workbench is the hardware and software that will be incorporated in the web-based system to be tested. The first three tasks of the workbench are primarily involved in web-based test planning. The fourth task is traditional software testing. The output from the workbench is to report what works and what does not work, as well as any concerns over the use of web technology.

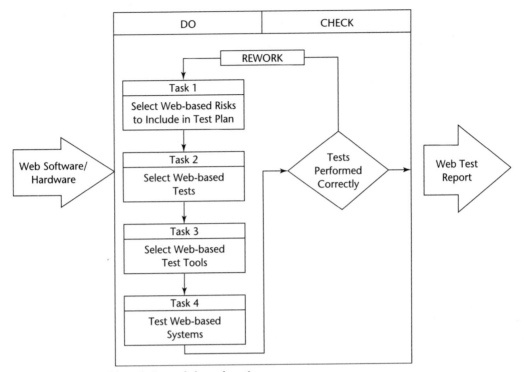

Figure 22-1   Workbench for web-based testing.

Input

The input to this test process is the description of web-based technology used in the systems being tested. The following list shows how web-based systems differ from other technologies. The description of the web-based systems under testing should address these differences:

- **Uncontrolled user interfaces (browsers).** Because of the variety of web browsers available, a web page must be functional on those browsers that you expect to be used in accessing your web applications. Furthermore, as new releases of browsers emerge, your web applications will need to keep up with compatibility issues.

- **Complex distributed systems.** In addition to being complex and distributed, web-based applications are also remotely accessed, which adds even more concerns to the testing effort. While some applications may be less complex than others, it is safe to say that the trend in web applications is to become more complex rather than less.

- **Security issues.** Protection is needed from unauthorized access that can corrupt applications and/or data. Another security risk is that of access to confidential information.

- **Multiple layers in architecture.** These layers of architecture include application servers, web servers, back-end processing, data warehouses, and secure servers for electronic commerce.

- **New terminology and skill sets.** Just as in making the transition to client/server, new skills are needed to develop, test, and use web-based technology effectively.

- **Object-oriented.** Object-oriented languages such as Java are the mainstay of web development.

Do Procedures

This section discusses the four tasks testers should perform when testing a web-based system.

Task 1: Select Web-Based Risks to Include in the Test Plan

Risks are important to understand because they reveal what to test. Each risk points to an entire area of potential tests. In addition, the degree of testing should be based on risk. The risks are briefly listed here, followed by a more detailed description of the concerns associated with each risk:

- **Security.** As we have already seen, one of the major risks of Internet applications is security. It is very important to validate that the application and data are protected from outside intrusion or unauthorized access.

- **Performance.** An Internet application with poor performance will be judged hard to use. Web sites that are slow in response will not retain the visitors they attract and will be frustrating to the people who try to use them.

- **Correctness.** Obviously, correctness is a very important area of risk. It is essential that the functionality and information obtained from web-based applications are correct.

- **Compatibility (configuration).** A web-based application must be able to work correctly on a wide variety of system configurations including browsers, operating systems, and hardware systems. All of these are out of the control of the developer of the application.

- **Reliability.** An Internet application must have a high level of availability and the information provided from the application must be consistent and reliable to the user.

- **Data integrity.** The data entered into an Internet application must be validated to ensure its correctness. In addition, measures must be taken to ensure the data stays correct after it is entered into the application.

- **Usability.** The application must be easy to use. This includes things like navigation, clarity, and understandability of the information provided by the application.

- **Recoverability.** In the event of an outage, the system must be recoverable. This includes recovering lost transactions, recovering from loss of communications, and ensuring that proper backups are made as a part of regular systems maintenance.

Security Concerns

The following are some of the detailed security risks that need to be addressed in an Internet application test plan:

- **External intrusion.** Perhaps the most obvious security concern is that of protecting the system from external intrusion. This can include intrusion from people who are trying to gain access to sensitive information, people who are trying to intentionally sabotage information, and people who are trying to intentionally sabotage applications.

- **Protection of secured transactions.** Another major area of concern is that of protecting transactions over the Internet. This is especially true in dealing with electronic commerce transactions. Many consumers are reluctant to give credit card information over the Internet for fear that information will be intercepted and used for fraudulent purposes.

- **Viruses.** The Internet has become a vehicle for propagating tens of thousands of new viruses. These viruses are contained in downloaded files that can be distributed from web sites and e-mail.

- **Access control.** Access control means that only authorized users have security access to a particular application or portion of an application. This access is typically granted with a user ID and password.

- **Authorization levels.** Authorization levels refer to the ability of the application to restrict certain transactions only to those users who have a certain level of authorization.

Performance Concerns

System performance can make or break an Internet application. Several types of performance testing can be performed to validate an application's performance levels. Performance testing is a very precise kind of testing and requires the use of automated tools for testing to be accomplished with any level of accuracy and efficiency. Unfortunately, manual approaches to performance testing fall short of the accuracy needed to correctly gauge an application's performance and may lead to a false level of confidence in the test.

Typically, the most common kind of performance testing for Internet applications is load testing. Load testing seeks to determine how the application performs under expected and greater-than-expected levels of activity. Application load can be assessed in a variety of ways:

- **Concurrency.** Concurrency testing seeks to validate the performance of an application with a given number of concurrent interactive users.

- **Stress.** Stress testing seeks to validate the performance of an application when certain aspects of the application are stretched to their maximum limits. This can include maximum number of users, and can also include maximizing table values and data values.

- **Throughput.** Throughput testing seeks to validate the number of transactions to be processed by an application during a given period of time. For example, one type of throughput test might be to attempt to process 100,000 transactions in one hour.

Correctness Concerns

Of course, one of the most important areas of concern is that the application functions correctly. This can include not only the functionality of buttons and "behind the scenes" instructions but also calculations and navigation of the application.

- **Functionality.** Functional correctness means that the application performs its intended tasks as defined by a stated set of specifications. The specifications of an application are the benchmark of what the application should do. Functional correctness is determined by performing a functional test. A functional test is performed in a cause-effect manner. In other words, if a particular action is taken, a particular result should be seen.

- **Calculations.** Many web-based applications include calculations. These calculations must be tested to ensure correctness and to find defects.

- **Navigation.** Navigation correctness can include testing links, buttons, and general navigation through a web site or web-based application.

Compatibility Concerns

Compatibility is the capability of the application to perform correctly in a variety of expected environments. Two of the major variables that affect web-based applications are operating systems and browsers.

Currently, operating systems (or platforms) and how they support the browser of your choice will affect the appearance and functionality of a web application. This requires that you test your web-based applications as accessed on a variety of common platforms and browsers. You should be able to define the most commonly used platforms by reviewing the access statistics of your web site.

Browser Configuration

Each browser has configuration options that affect how it displays information. These options vary from browser to browser and are too diverse to address in this text. The most reasonable testing strategy is to define optimal configurations on the most standard kinds of browsers and test based on those configurations.

Some of the main things to consider from a hardware compatibility standpoint are the following:

- **Monitors, video cards, and video RAM.** If you have a web site that requires a high standard of video capability, some users will not be able to view your site, or will not have a positive experience at your site.

- **Audio, video, and multimedia support.** Once again, you need to verify that a web application is designed to provide a level of multimedia support that a typical end-user will need to be able to access your site. If software plug-ins are required, you should provide links on your page to facilitate the user in downloading the plug-in.

- **Memory (RAM) and hard drive space.** RAM is very important for increasing the performance of a browser on a particular platform. Browsers also make heavy use of caching, which is how a browser stores graphics and other information on a user's hard drive. This helps speed the display of web pages the next time the user visits a web site.

- **Bandwidth access.** Many corporate users have high-speed Internet access based on T-1 or T-3 networks, or ISDN telephone lines.

Browser differences can make a web application appear differently to different people. These differences may appear in any of the following areas (this is not intended to be an exhaustive list; these are merely the more common areas of browser differences):

- **Print handling.** To make printing faster and easier, some pages add a link or button to print a browser-friendly version of the page being viewed.

- **Reload.** Some browser configurations will not automatically display updated pages if a version of the page still exists in the cache. Some pages indicate if the user should reload the page.

- **Navigation.** Browsers vary in the ease of navigation, especially when it comes to visiting pages previously visited during a session. A web application developer may need to add navigational aids to the web pages to facilitate ease of navigation.

- **Graphics filters.** Browsers may handle images differently, depending on the graphic filters supported by the browser. In fact, some browsers may not show an image at all. By standardizing on JPG and GIF images you should be able to eliminate this concern.

- **Caching.** How the cache is configured (size, etc.) will have an impact on the performance of a browser to view information.

- **Dynamic page generation.** This includes how a user receives information from pages that change based on input. Examples of dynamic page generation include:
  - Shopping cart applications
  - Data search applications
  - Calculation forms
- **File downloads.** Movement of data from remote data storage for user processing.
- **E-mail functions.** Because e-mail activities can consume excessive processing time, guidelines should be developed.

Each browser has its own interface and functionality for e-mail. Many people use separate e-mail applications outside of a browser, but for those who don't, this can be a concern for users when it comes to compatibility.

Reliability Concerns

Because of the continuous uptime requirements for most Internet applications, reliability is a key concern. However, reliability can be considered in more than system availability; it can also be expressed in terms of the reliability of the information obtained from the application:

Consistently correct results

Server and system availability

Data Integrity Concerns

Not only must the data be validated when it is entered into the web application, but it must also be safeguarded to ensure the data stays correct:

- **Ensuring only correct data is accepted.** This can be achieved by validating the data at the page level when it is entered by a user.
- **Ensuring data stays in a correct state.** This can be achieved by procedures to back up data and ensure that controlled methods are used to update data.

Usability Concerns

If users or customers find an Internet application hard to use, they will likely go to a competitor's site. Usability can be validated and usually involves the following:

- Ensuring the application is easy to use and understand
- Ensuring that users know how to interpret and use the information delivered from the application
- Ensuring that navigation is clear and correct

Recoverability Concerns

Internet applications are more prone to outages than systems that are more centralized or located on reliable, controlled networks. The remote accessibility of Internet applications makes the following recoverability concerns important:

- Lost connections
  - Timeouts
  - Dropped lines
- Client system crashes
- Server system crashes or other application problems

Work Paper 22-1 is designed to determine which web-based risks need to be addressed in the test plan, and how those risks will be included in the test plan. The use of this work paper should be associated with a "brainstorming session" by the web-based test team. The work paper should be completed once the web-based test team has reached consensus regarding inclusion of risks in the test plan.

Task 2: Select Web-Based Tests

Now that you have selected the risks to be addressed in the web-based applications, you must examine the types and phases of testing needed to validate them.

Unit or Component

This includes testing at the object, component, page, or applet level. Unit testing is the lowest level of testing in terms of detail. During unit testing, the structure of languages, such as HTML and Java, can be verified. Edits and calculations can also be tested at the unit level.

Integration

Integration is the passing of data and/or control between units or components, which includes testing navigation (i.e., the paths the test data will follow). In web-based applications, this includes testing links, data exchanges, and flow of control in an application.

System

System testing examines the web application as a whole and with other systems. The classic definition of system testing is that it validates that a computing system functions according to written requirements and specifications. This is also true in web-based applications. The differences apply in how the system is defined. System testing typically includes hardware, software, data, procedures, and people.

In corporate web-based applications, a system might interface with Internet web pages, data warehouses, back-end processing systems, and reporting systems.

User Acceptance

This includes testing that the web application supports business needs and processes. The main idea in user acceptance testing (or business process validation) is to ensure that the end product supports the users' needs. For business applications, this means testing that the system allows the user to conduct business correctly and efficiently. For personal applications, this means that users are able to get the information or service they need from a web site efficiently.

In a corporate web page, the end-user testers may be from end-user groups, management, or an independent test team that takes the role of end users. In public web applications, the end-user testers may be beta testers, who receive a prototype or early release of the new web application, or independent testers who take the role of public web users.

Performance

This includes testing that the system will perform as specified at predetermined levels, including wait times, static processes, dynamic processes, and transaction processes. Performance is also tested at the client/browser and server levels.

Load/Stress

This type of testing checks to see that the server performs as specified at peak concurrent loads or transaction throughput. It includes stressing servers, networks, and databases.

Regression

Regression testing checks that unchanged parts of the application work correctly after a change has been made. Many people mistakenly believe that regression testing means testing everything you ever tested in an application every time you perform a test. However, depending upon the relative risk of the application you are testing, regression testing may not need to be that intense. The main idea is to test a set of specified critical test cases each time you perform the test. Regression testing is an ideal candidate for test automation because of its repetitive nature.

Usability

This type of testing assesses the ease of use of an application. Usability testing may be accomplished in a variety of ways, including direct observation of people using web applications, usability surveys, and beta tests. The main objective of usability testing is to ensure that an application is easy to understand and navigate.

Compatibility

Compatibility testing ensures that the application functions correctly on multiple browsers and system configurations. Compatibility testing may be performed in a test lab that contains a variety of platforms, or may be performed by beta testers. The downside with beta testing is the increased risk of bad publicity, the lack of control, and the lack of good data coming back from the beta testers.

Work Paper 22-2 is designed to assist testers in selecting testing types. The type of testing to be performed should be focused on the web-based risks addressed by the test plan. The test team should determine how the various types of web-based testing selected should be used to assess the various risks. This work paper, like Work Paper 22-1, should be developed through brainstorming and consensus by the web-based test team.

Task 3: Select Web-Based Test Tools

Effective web-based testing necessitates the use of web-based testing tools. A brief description of categories of the more common web-based test tools follows:

- **HTML tools.** Although many web development packages include an HTML checker, there are ways to perform a verification of HTML if you do not use/ have such a feature.

- **Site validation tools.** Site validation tools check your web applications to identify inconsistencies and errors, such as moved or orphaned pages and broken links.

- **Load/stress testing tools.** Load/stress tools evaluate web-based systems when subjected to large volumes of data or transactions.

- **Test case generators.** Test case generators create transactions for use in testing. This tool can tell you what to test, as well as create test cases that can be used in other test tools.

Work Paper 22-3 is designed to document the web-based test tools selected by the test team, as well as how those tools will be used. The work paper should contain all of the specific test tools available to the web-based testing team.

Task 4: Test Web-Based Systems

The tests to be performed for web-based testing will be the types of testing described in the seven-step testing process, which is Part Three of this book. The seven-step process may have to be modified based on the risks associated with web-based testing.

Check Procedures

The web-based test team should use Work Paper 22-4 to verify that the web-based test planning has been conducted effectively. The Comments column is provided to clarify No responses. The N/A column is provided for items that are not applicable to this specific web-based test plan.

Output

The only output from this test process is a report on the web-based system. At a minimum, this report should contain the following:

- A brief description of the web-based system
- The risks addressed and not addressed by the web-based test team
- The types of testing performed, and types of testing not performed
- The tools used
- The web-based functionality and structure tested that performed correctly
- The web-based structure and functionality tested that did not perform correctly
- The test team's opinion regarding the adequacy of the web-based system to be placed into a production status

Guidelines

Successful web-based testing necessitates a portfolio of web-based testing tools. It is important that these test tools are used effectively. These are some common critical success factors for buying, integrating, and using test tools:

- **Get senior management support for buying and integrating test tools.** Top-down support is critical. Management must understand the need for test tools and the risks of not using test tools.
- **Know your requirements.** This will help you avoid costly mistakes. You may not be able to meet all your requirements, but you should be able to find the best fit.
- **Be reasonable in your expectations—start small and grow.** Your first project using any kind of tool is your learning project. Expect to make some mistakes. You can hedge your risk by applying the test tool(s) to simple tasks with high payback.
- **Have a strong testing process that includes tools.** Until this is in place, test tool usage will be seen as optional and the tool may die because of lack of interest. In addition, people need to know how to define what to test.
- **Don't cut the training corner.** People must understand how to use the test tool. Most people will naturally use about 20 to 25 percent of the tool's functionality. If training is not provided and the tool is not effective, don't blame the tool.

Summary

This chapter provides guidelines on how to properly plan for web-based testing. Like other aspects of testing, web-based testing should be risk oriented. The chapter describes the risks, presents the types of testing that can be used to address those risks in testing, and provides guidance in using web-based test tools. The approach for testing web-based systems should be incorporated into a test plan and that plan should be followed during test execution. This chapter does not address the test execution part of web-based testing. Testers should follow the execution components of the seven-step testing process described in Part Three of this book.

WORK PAPER 22-1   Web-Based Risks to Include in the Test Plan

Field Requirements

FIELD	INSTRUCTIONS FOR ENTERING DATA
Web-based Risks	This field lists the eight web-based risks described in this chapter. The description implies that "lack of" is associated with the risk.
Include in Test	The web-based testing should determine whether any or all of the eight identified web-based risks need to be addressed in the test plan. A check in the Yes column indicates that it should be included in the plan, and a check in the No column indicates it is not needed in the plan.
How risk will be included in the web-based test plan	This column is designed to be used in two ways. If the risk is not to be included in test plan, a justification as to why not could be included in this column. The second use is the test team's preliminary thoughts on how this risk will be included in the test plan. The description might involve the types of tests, the types of tools, and/or the approach to be used in testing.

WEB-BASED RISKS (LACK OF)	INCLUDE IN TEST		HOW RISK WILL BE INCLUDED IN WEB-BASED TEST PLAN
	YES	NO	
Security			
Performance			
Correctness			
Compatibility (Configuration)			
Reliability			
Data Integrity			
Usability			
Recoverability			

WORK PAPER 22-2   Types of Web-Based Testing to Perform

Field Requirements

FIELD	INSTRUCTIONS FOR ENTERING DATA
Types of Web-based Testing	This column contains the more common types of web-based testing. The names may need to be modified for your culture. Additional types of testing performed by your test group may need to be added to this column.
Perform	This field is used for the web-based test team to indicate which types of testing will be used during web-based testing. A check mark in the Yes column indicates the type of testing that will be performed, and check mark in the No column indicates that type of testing will not be performed.
Risk Focus	The web-based test team should indicate the risk that this test type will be used to address. The type of risk to be incorporated into the test plan has been identified on Work Paper 22-1. In addition, the column can be used to indicate the justification for not using various types of web-based testing, if appropriate.
How to Be Used	The web-based test team should write a brief narrative description of how they plan to use this test type to address the risks that will be incorporated into the test plan.

TYPES OF WEB-BASED TESTING	PERFORM		RISK FOCUS	HOW TO BE USED
	YES	NO		
Unit/Component				
Integration				
System				
User Acceptance				
Performance				
Load/Stress				
Regression				
Usability				
Compatibility				

WORK PAPER 22-3   Select Web-Based Test Tools

Field Requirements

FIELD	INSTRUCTIONS FOR ENTERING DATA
Web-based Test Tool	All of the test tools available to your web-based test team should be listed in this column. The column contains generic types of test tools, but they should be replaced by specific test tools.
Perform	The web-based test team should identify which web-based test tool will be used during testing. A check in the Yes column indicates that the tool is to be used, and check in the No column indicates that the tool is not to be used.
Test Type Focus	The test team should indicate in this column which type of testing will be performed using this test tool. The test types are those indicated by the check mark in the Yes column on Work Paper 22-3. All of the test types with a Yes check mark on Work Paper 22-2 should be addressed in this column. Note that a single test tool may be used for multiple test types.
How to Be Used	The web-based test team should indicate in this test column how they plan to use a specific test tool during web-based testing. The testers should be as specific as possible in completing this column.

WEB-BASED TEST TOOLS	PERFORM		TEST TYPE FOCUS	HOW TO BE USED
	YES	NO		
HTML text tool				
Site validation test tool				
Java test tool				
Load/stress test tool				
Test case generator				
Other (list tools)				

WORK PAPER 22-4   Web-Based Testing Quality Control Checklist

	YES	NO	N/A	COMMENTS
1. Has a web-based test team been organized?				
2. Does the web-based test team understand the differences between client/server and web-based technology?				
3. Does the web-based test team understand web terminology?				
4. Does the web-based test team understand the risk associated with web technology?				
5. Has the web-based test team reached consensus on which risks are applicable to this specific web-based system?				
6. Has a determination been made as to how the identified risks will be incorporated in the test plan?				
7. Is there a consensus that the web-based risks not included in the test plan are of minimal concern to this web-based system?				
8. Has the web-based test team identified the types of testing required for this system?				
9. If so, how have those testing types been correlated to the web-based risks?				
10. Has the web-based test team reached consensus on how the web-based types of testing will be used for test purposes?				
11. Is there a portfolio of web-based test tools available in the organization?				
12. Are the available test tools adequate for the web-based system being tested?				
13. Has each type of testing that will be included in the test plan been supported by a specific web-based test tool?				
14. Has the test team reached consensus on how the test tools will be used during testing?				
15. Have all of the web-based testing decisions made by the test team been incorporated into the test plan?				

PART

Five

Building Agility into the Testing Process

CHAPTER 23

Using Agile Methods to Improve Software Testing

This chapter introduces a seven-step process to build agility into your software testing process through time compression. Agility not only improves software testing processes; it also adds flexibility and enhances ease of use. Thus, agility leads to a "continuous process enhancement," which significantly increases testing volumes because of satisfaction with the process.

Testers avoid defective and difficult-to-use processes in the worst case; in the best case, they customize the processes, which means that they are not followed as intended. Testers pick and choose those pieces from the process they like, and improvise on those components they do not like, which leads to each testing group having its own testing process. The net result is significant effectiveness and efficiency variability among testing projects. When testers focus on adding agility to the process, the process improves, and all testing groups are likely to follow the agile process.

The Importance of Agility

Agile systems are designed to be quick and easy to use. Much effort has been expended on the development of agile software development processes. Unfortunately, those software development processes have not placed much emphasis on software testing, even though in many systems, testing consumes about one-half the total developmental resources.

Effective agile processes have the following three characteristics:

- Well-defined objectives
- Open information/communication channels
- Task-performance flexibility

The best way to build an agile software testing process is to empower the actual testers to build one. Software testers can build an agile testing process by focusing on the following three goals:

- Eliminating nonproductive aspects of testing
- Identifying and incorporating best testing practices
- Building the process using the practices that offer the greatest payback with the highest probability of successful implementation

Process variability is the enemy of agile software testing. The first step to reduce variability is to identify and measure variability. Variability means the range of resources needed to accomplish a task. For example, if the time to prepare a script of 100 actions takes an average of 100 hours, with the most efficient person doing it in 50 hours, and the least efficient doing it in 150 hours, the process variability is 100 hours for that task.

Flexibility, the desirable attribute of agile software testing, is relatively affected by excessive process variability. For example, if someone prepares a test script using a process with extensive variability, the testing team cannot rely on a task being completed when needed.

As discussed more fully in the following section, common business practices inhibit agility. Remember, therefore, that agility will result only under the following conditions:

- IT management supports and allots resources to building agile systems.
- Testers are empowered to focus on business objectives, rather than just follow test processes.
- Significant emphasis is placed on communication and team building.

Building an Agile Testing Process

To build an agile testing process, you must have a "champion" and an "agile implementation team." Ideally, the champion would be the director of the organization or the Chief Information Officer. It is best that the champion not have direct responsibility for managing or performing software testing.

The agile implementation team can be as few as three or as many as five people, but each person should be a stakeholder in the testing. At a minimum, the team should have these representative members:

- Software manager
- Development representative, particularly, a project leader who respects the importance of testing
- User representative

If more than three individuals are included in the agile implementation team, the additional numbers should be software testers. Although it is not necessary for a member of the process/engineering standards committee to be a member of the agile implementation team, that committee should be kept informed of all activities (and provide input to the process as necessary).

The seven-step process for time compression discussed later in this chapter addresses some of the specific responsibilities and tasks of the agile implementation team. This team does not have to perform all of the tasks involved in building an agile software testing process. For example, if a testing sub-process is to be changed, they might delegate that task to one or two testers knowledgeable in that specific task. However, the agile implementation team should develop a plan, obtain the resources, set work priorities, and oversee the implementation process.

Agility Inhibitors

The following ten factors inhibit agility in software testing processes (and thus contribute to inefficient and ineffective testing):

1. **Test processes are not mature processes, making them prone to defects.**
   Mature test processes have minimal variability. Mature test processes are continuously improved. When testers follow a mature test process, the process itself causes few defects. These characteristics of a mature process rarely exist in today's testing processes.

2. **Test processes are not designed to facilitate changing requirements.** Business requirements change frequently. Opportunities to capitalize on new ideas occur frequently. When creating new information systems, it is difficult to fully define requirements at the start of the project. These factors result in constantly changing requirements. Unfortunately, test processes are not designed to handle these changes.

3. **Quality is not defined in most software testing plans.** Quality is defined as both meeting requirements and satisfying customer needs. However, in most test plans, quality is not an attribute of the plan.

4. **Test processes are not flexible.** No single process is effective in testing all software systems. However, flexibility, to adjust to the challenges individual test teams face, is rarely built in to test processes.

5. **Test processes are not objective-driven.** One of the key principles of agile systems is that everyone understands the objectives. Many testers are mired in the process of creating and executing test conditions and rarely are informed of the business objectives of the system. Therefore, they do not understand how the day-to-day work helps accomplish business objectives and add value.

6. **Lines of communication between testers and developers, users, and IT management are not defined.** Flexibility requires continuous and effective communication. It is important that all stakeholders be involved in the testing process, which means that testers need communication lines to those stakeholders. In most organizations, testers are not encouraged to initiate such communication.

7. **Testers do not get the same respect as developers.** In many organizations, testers are not considered equal to developers. This inequality is expressed in the amount of training provided, the resources expended on tools and processes, and the willingness to send testers to outside seminars and conferences; in many organizations, testers even have a lower pay grade than developers.

8. **Open and honest communication up and down the chain of command does not exist.** In many organizations, testers are viewed as the inhibitors of getting software into production by a scheduled date. Developers don't confide their problems (the errors they believe may exist) in testers; and likewise, testers often keep the type of test they are conducting secret from the developers. This lack of communication can easily increase the cost of development and testing.

9. **Testers are not actively involved, or given the resources to be involved, in determining their own processes.** Experience has shown that the best test processes are those developed by the process users. Unfortunately, most test groups are not provided the time or the training needed to define, upgrade, and continually improve their test processes.

10. **Minimal effort is expended on creating effective and efficient test teams.** One of the most important principles of agile processes is focusing on building and upgrading effective and efficient teams. Most test managers are not trained in team building and team management. Many testers do not view themselves as team members, but merely individuals performing specific tasks.

Is Improvement Necessary?

To decide whether improvement is necessary, you must first ask whether software testing is currently performed efficiently. Then you must ask whether software testing is currently performed effectively. An agile process focuses efficiency (which implies time compression). Experience shows that when testing is efficient, it will also be effective.

From a management perspective, effectiveness is easier to determine than efficiency. You can easily measure effectiveness by using a metric called Defect Removal Efficiency (DRE). DRE refers to the percentage of defects removed through testing. In other words, if software contains 100 defects, and testing finds 75 of those defects, the DRE metric is 75 percent. The higher the DRE metric, the more effective the testing process.

Another way to measure the effectiveness of software testing is to calculate operational measures that relate to availability of software for production purposes. To do so, you must consider the mean time to failure (MTTF), the mean time between failures (MTBF), and the mean time to repair (MTTR). You can readily obtain this information from operational activities (see Figure 23-1).

The MTBF is the amount of time (or number of events) between the last failure and the current failure. Of course, failure must be defined (e.g., incorrect processes and/or non-operational software). As part of your consideration of MTBF, you must factor in the amount of time it takes to make the process/software operational after failure.

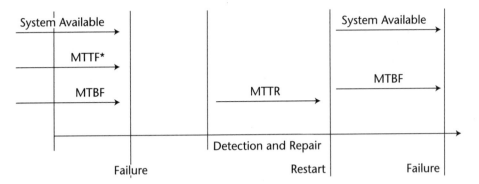

MTTF* = The number of time units the system is operable before the first failure occurs

MTBF = $\dfrac{\text{Sum of the number of time units the system is operable}}{\text{Number of failures during the time period}}$

MTTR = $\dfrac{\text{Sum of the number of time units required to repair the system}}{\text{Number of repairs during the time period}}$

*MTTF applies to non-repairable systems and is not applicable after the first failure. Some experts consider MTTF to be a special case of the MTBF measurement.

Figure 23-1 Measures of MTTF, MTBT, MTTR, and availability.

If you calculate MTBF on a regular basis, you can monitor the number of defects that remain. These types of calculations are beyond the scope of this book; MTFB is used here just to illustrate testing effectiveness. Simplistically, if MTBF is unchanging, it implies a replenishment of defects. In other words, as failures are corrected, new failures are introduced. On the other hand, if MTBF is increasing, you can statistically predict the time when the next failure will be detected.

The bottom-line measure of testing effectiveness is availability of the software, meaning not only available for use, but available for correct processing. If testing is "perfect," the system will be continuously available for correct processing.

An analysis of DRE, MTTF, MTBF, and MTTR provides insight into testing effectiveness. If testing does not appear to be effective, time-compression efforts will improve both testing and effectiveness.

Compressing Time

Many organizations consider software testing an art form rather than an engineering discipline. And although some might think that such an approach to testing is more closely related to an agile process, exactly the opposite is true. The art-form approach, although believed to be highly creative, is inefficient and leads to frustration (among testers and other expecting testing deliverables).

Quality Assurance Institute studies indicate that only about half of software testing groups develop plans for testing. Of those, only about half actually follow the plan in detail. The result is that testers have to spend time developing the testing process, instead of performing actual testing responsibilities.

A software testing process that eliminates most of the rework and communication problems among testers does not eliminate flexibility. A timely (calendar-day efficient) agile process can offer the flexibility testers need to perform their testing tasks.

Challenges

Many testers understand that IT management already tries to save testing time by giving them unreasonable deadlines. If a scheduled implementation date has been established, and dynamic testing can occur only after code is complete, testers feel the pressure of that deadline. Two solutions to this dilemma exist: ask for more time, or complete the process more efficiently. Agile processes facilitate speed.

Many organizations fail to compress testing time because of the following challenges:

- **No time/no resources.** Almost all IT organizations and individual staff members have more work than they can currently handle. The misconception is that if effort is expended on trying to save testing time, then software projects currently needed by customers/users cannot be completed on time. The dilemma is this: Do you spend your time doing the work of the business or do you expend your effort to compress testing time?

- **Long-term process.** Most believe that the time to change a process is in direct relationship to the size of the process. In other words, it requires a massive re-engineering effort to change the software testing process because it is a large process. Software testing is among the most complex process in an IT organization; therefore, changing an extensive and complex process is a long, time-consuming and expensive process.

  Industry models have resulted from efforts to improve quality and productivity. These models include the Software Engineering Institute (SEI) Computer Maturity Model (CMMI), the International Standards Organization Model, and the Malcolm Baldrige National Quality Award Model. Optimistic estimates to fully implement any of these models is three years (usually longer). Because few IT directors have a guaranteed tenure of three or more years, they are reluctant to undertake such an effort.

  No in-house skill sets. Even if IT managers want to compress testing time, many do not believe the current staff possesses the skill sets necessary to do it. Without those skill sets, either a new process needs to be acquired, implemented, and taught, or consultants must be engaged to come in and perform the necessary analysis and changes to compress testing time.

  Poor past experience. Almost since the day the first computer was delivered to an organization, vendors have promised new tools and techniques that will compress testing time and improve productivity. Many of these "vendor miracles" have resulted only in building bad software systems faster. Many of the miracles never really touched the root cause of too much time spent on testing. For example, avoiding test planning is not the way to compress software testing time.

Solutions

Agile approaches to compressing software testing time are needed. Conventional approaches have not worked. Although many have helped, they are long-term solutions in an industry that prefers the short term.

Industrial engineers have used agile methods (known in that sector as time and motion studies) to compress the time required to build manufactured products since the late 1920s. These methods work.

To successfully compress software testing time, organizations must do the following:

1. **Make "compressing" a project.** Asking someone to do a task, but not providing the time, resources, and procedures to do it will not work. Many view unbudgeted tasks as a means by which management can get more work for the same money. In addition, unless compressing testing time is a project, it will not be managed like a project, and therefore the probability of success is diminished.

2. **Focus solely on compressing time.** There are many reasons why an IT organization might want to undertake an improvement effort, of which compressing testing time is but one focus. Objectives might include improving quality and productivity, providing better documentation, and compressing testing time. Unfortunately, when an individual is given many goals, it is difficult to differentiate the important from the unimportant goals.

    Experience shows that if many variables are in play, selecting the most relevant variable will pull the other variables in the same direction. In other words, if process improvement focuses on the correct, single variable, the other desirable variables most likely will also be achieved.

    Manufacturing experience shows that the correct variable to select is "time compression." By focusing on that variable, quality, productivity, and the morale and motivation of the testing staff will be improved.

3. **Use a "time-compression" process.** If you ask someone to do a job, you need to tell them how to do it. Telling someone to compress the time to complete testing without providing a process to perform that "compression" effort has only a minimal probability of success. If you do not provide an individual with a process, they first must develop that process and then execute it.

4. **Use in-house best-of-the-best work practices.** Some software testing projects, when completed, have a high degree of customer satisfaction, whereas others do not. Some software testing projects are performed efficiently; some are not. A quick analysis can readily identify those projects exhibiting high customer satisfaction and those projects that are very efficiently developed. Finding the best practices from the best projects and then having everyone use these best practices is the quickest way to implement time-compression solutions in the software testing process.

Time compression will elicit agility. The following section consolidates time-compression methods into an easy-to-use seven-step process that, when implemented, will result in an agile software testing process.

Measuring Readiness

Wanting to compress software testing time and having the organizational motivation and resources in place to do so are two different things. It is like dieting: You might want to lose weight, but the serious question is whether you are really ready to apply the discipline needed to lose weight. The same applies to readiness for time compression.

The following five criteria are the most significant "time-compression" readiness criteria:

- Management support
- Software testing process in place (The process can have significant variability, but the general activities in the process should exist and be documented.)
- A need for time compression (e.g., an obvious benefit from such for customers, users, and business priorities)
- Surmountable barrier/obstacle identification
- Requisite resources

Testers (in consensus with a small group of key stakeholders in the effort and individuals respected by the teams involved) can use Work Paper 23-1 to evaluate the preceding criteria. If any readiness criterion has fewer than three Yes responses out of the five questions you must ask for each readiness criterion, your organization is not ready for a time-compression process. Any readiness criteria receiving three or four Yes responses should be evaluated to determine whether the items receiving a No response (i.e., not ready for a time-compression improvement process) might warrant more readiness preparatory work before undertaking the time-compression process.

If those key individuals having the responsibility for testing believe, after this analysis, that the organization is ready to compress testing time, begin the seven-step process outlined in the following section. If the individuals responsible for software testing have any reservations about the readiness to proceed, readiness work should be undertaken prior to beginning the seven-step process.

The Seven-Step Process

To compress software testing time/effort, follow these seven steps:

1. **Measure software process variability.** The timeline is the series of activities that must be executed to develop a software system. In this step, you define an activity by documenting a workbench for each activity. The workbench indicates the objective, the standards (for example, exit criteria), as well as the procedures to perform and check the work leading to the completion of that workbench. From this timeline process, you can determine time-compression opportunities.

2. **Maximize best practices.** Identify the software testing projects that are most effective and those that are most efficiently developed (effectiveness meaning high customer satisfaction, and efficiency meaning minimizing resources to complete the testing).

3. **Build on strength, minimize weakness.** An analysis of the testing process will indicate those areas that contain the greatest testing strengths and those where weaknesses exist. Obviously, you must focus your time-compression efforts on the areas of weaknesses.

4. **Identify and address improvement barriers.** Barriers are obstacles to time-compression improvements. The barriers can be budgetary or process oriented (i.e., getting permission to act), or the barrier may come in the form of an obstructionist on the team or in management. You must decide whether you can reduce or eliminate the barriers. If you cannot, you should explore another time-compression activity.

5. **Identify and address cultural and communication barriers.** An IT organization's culture dictates, in many ways, the means by which the organization attempts to achieve results. For example, in a "management-object culture," adherence to process is difficult to achieve. Any time-compression effort must be implemented within the cultural restrictions of an IT organization.

6. **Identify doable improvements.** The totality of the information you gather in Steps 1 through 5 are used in this step to identify those time-compression methods and techniques that have the greatest probability of success.

7. **Develop and execute an implementation plan.** After you have identified the time-compression improvement to seek, you must put a plan needs into place to implement the improvement and make it operational. Resource allocation is part of this step.

Steps 6 and 7 are repeated continuously to achieve shorter and shorter testing cycles. This is a never-ending process. Periodically, probably annually, you should repeat Steps 1 through 5 to identify new opportunities as well new barriers/obstacles.

Summary

It is not good practice to compress a bad software testing process. In other words, to do bad testing faster should not be the objective of time compression. However, industrial engineering experience has shown that if the time-compression effort is focused exclusively on time compression, it will improve both effectiveness and efficiency.

This chapter has described a seven-step process for compressing software testing time. It has also provided a readiness assessment to help determine whether your organization is ready to undertake this process.

WORK PAPER 23-1 Readiness Assessment for Compressing Software Testing Time

Readiness Criteria: Management Support	YES	NO	COMMENTS
Does the IT culture support using work process to test software systems?			
Would IT management support and encourage the more-effective testers to document their best testing practices?			
Would IT management be willing to become personally involved in the efforts to compress software testing time?			
Would IT management reward those who invest time and effort to compress software testing time?			
Do the IT strategic and tactical annual work plans include goals and objectives for compressing software testing time?			
TOTAL			
Readiness Criteria: A Software Testing Process in Place	YES	NO	COMMENTS
Does a software testing process exist?			
Do most of the software testing projects follow the software testing process from, at least, an intent perspective?			
Have the software testers been trained in using the process?			
Is the process divided into self-contained testing activities?			
If so, do each of these self-contained activities contain entrance and exit criteria?			
TOTAL			

WORK PAPER 23-1   *(continued)*

Readiness Criteria: Need for Time Compression	YES	NO	COMMENTS
Do the users/customers of IT software want a shorter testing time?			
Does IT management want a shorter software testing time?			
Do IT project personnel want a shorter software testing time?			
Is there a backlog of software testing projects waiting to be undertaken?			
Is the inability to get software testing projects completed on a timely basis negatively affecting the business?			
TOTAL			

Readiness Criteria: Surmountable Barrier/ Obstacle Identification	YES	NO	COMMENTS
Are the cultural barriers against compliance to work processes surmountable?			
Are political obstacles to time compression surmountable?			
Are organizational barriers to time compression surmountable?			
Are budget and schedule constraint barriers to time compression surmountable?			
Are management hot buttons and red flags related to time compression surmountable?			
TOTAL			

(continues)

WORK PAPER 23-1   *(continued)*

Readiness Criteria: Requisite Resources	YES	NO	COMMENTS
Are the tools needed for time compression available (e.g., consensus techniques)?			
Are the necessary skill sets available?			
Is the staff time needed available?			
Are the resources of the process engineering/standards committee available?			
Because compressing software testing time is achieved through many small efforts, will resources be available over an extended period of time?			
TOTAL			

Building Agility into the Testing Process

To enhance a software testing process, you must follow an improvement plan. Traditional improvement plans focus on identifying a defective component and then minimizing the impact of that defect, thus enhancing the testing process under review. This chapter uses a significantly different approach to improvement: time compression. Time compression drives agility. This process to add agility to software testing has proven in practice to be much more effective than traditional process improvement methods.

This chapter explains in detail each of the seven steps needed to build agility in to your software testing process. Each step is described in a "how-to" format. This chapter assumes that a team of testers has been assigned the responsibility to build agility into the software testing process (as discussed in Chapter 23).

Step 1: Measure Software Process Variability

A process is a method for making or doing something in which there are a number of steps. The steps and the time required to execute those steps comprise a timeline to produce the desired result. This chapter explains how to define and document those steps so that they represent a software testing process timeline. In this chapter, you also learn how to reduce variability.

If the timeline is lengthy, or if some steps are bottlenecks, or if the steps do not permit flexibility in execution, testing cannot be performed in an agile manner. Developing a software testing timeline will help identify those testing components that inhibit agility in software testing.

Timelines

A *timeline* is a graphic representation of the sequence in which the steps are performed and the time needed to execute those steps. The timeline not only shows the time required to execute a process but also the time required for each step. It can also show the time for substeps. Timelines enable someone who is responsible for building an agile testing process to evaluate that process.

A *process* is the means by which a task is performed. Whereas in manufacturing most processes are automated, professional processes rely much more on the competence of the individual performing the process. A professional process consists of two components: the people tasked with completing the process, and the process itself. The process steps normally assume a level of competence for the individual performing the process, and therefore much of the process need not be documented. For example, a programmer coding in a specific language follows a process, which assumes that the programmer following the process is competent in that specific language. Therefore, the process does not attempt to explain the programming language.

A poorly defined process relies much more on the competency of the individual performing that process than does a well-defined process. For example, a poorly defined requirement-gathering process may require only that the defined requirements be easy to understand. A well-defined process may utilize an inspection team of requirement-gathering analysts to determine whether the requirements are easily understandable. In addition, a well-defined process may have a measurement process to measure easy-to-understand requirements.

Normally, as processes mature, more of the process is incorporated into the steps and less depends on the competency of the individual. Therefore, the reliance on people performing the process tends to go down as the process matures.

As the timeline is defined, the variability inherent in the process is also defined. Variability can include the quality of the products produced by the process, as well as the time required to produce those products. A process with extensive variability is considered to be "out of control," whereas a process with acceptable variability is considered to be "in control."

Figure 24-1 illustrates variability in the software testing process. Chart A shows a bell-shaped curve showing extensive variability. For example, to perform a specific task in the software testing process may take an average of 100 hours but have a variability of between 24 and 300 hours to perform that task. Chart B shows that same task in the software testing process with minimal variability. For example, the average time to perform that task, as illustrated in Chart B, may be 100 hours, with a range of between 90 and 110 hours to perform that task. Thus, Chart B shows a process under control, which is more desirable than the out-of-control process illustrated in Chart A.

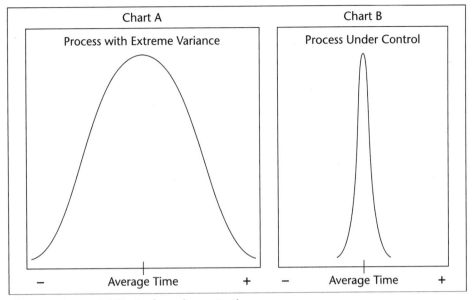

Figure 24-1 Variability in the software testing process.

Process Steps

A process step has the following attributes:

- A self-contained task
- Defined (standards) input and output (i.e., entrance and exit) criteria
- The specific work task(s) necessary to convert the input product(s) to the output product(s)
- The quality control task(s) necessary to determine that specific work tasks have been correctly performed
- The tools required
- A rework procedure in case the output product does not meet exit criteria (standards)

Workbenches

The preferred way to illustrate a process step is to define a "workbench" to perform that step. The components of a workbench for unit testing are as follows:

- **Input products.** The input product is the software to be unit tested.
- **Standards.** The standards for unit testing are the entrance and exit criteria for the workbench. The standards state what those test specifications must include

to be acceptable for unit testing the coding workbench and the attributes of the completed unit test (e.g., one of the exit criteria might be every branch tested both ways).

- **Do procedures.** This would be the task(s) necessary to unit test the code.

- **Toolbox.** One tool in the unit testing toolbox might be the test data generator.

- **Check procedures.** Many check procedures might be used: One might be a routine in the test data generator, which would do a static analysis of the test. If the test data generator indicated an error, rework would occur. In addition, a unit test inspection process may be performed in which peers inspect the unit test data to ensure it meets the appropriate test "standards."

- **Output product.** If the check procedure indicates no errors in the unit test specifications, it becomes an output product from the workbench. The output product, then, would become the input product for integration and/or system testing.

Time-Compression Workbenches

The workbench concept needs to be expanded and used to identify causes of variability. Figure 24-2 shows a time-compression workbench. Added to this workbench are the activities that provide the greatest opportunity to reduce test-time variability. These additional activities are the ones that most commonly cause variability of a software test step.

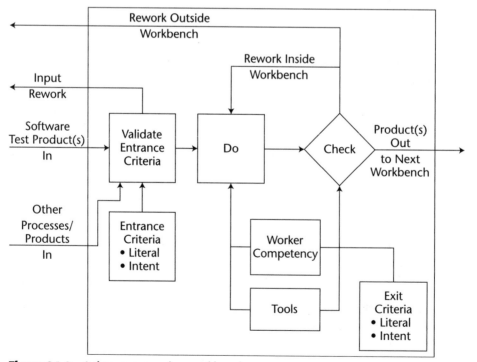

Figure 24-2   A time-compression workbench.

The following four factors cause the most testing variability:

- **Rework associated with not meeting entrance criteria.** The entrance criteria define the criteria the input products must meet to be utilized by the workbench. Failure to meet entrance criteria means that the previous workbench has not met the exit criteria for that workbench.

  A more common scenario is that the entrance criteria for the input are not checked. In other words, the worker for the workbench accepts defective input products. This means that the defects are incorporated into the workbench activities. The net result is that the longer a defect "lives," the more costly it is to correct it. An obvious time-compression strategy is to check entrance criteria.

- **Worker competency.** If the worker is not competent (skill sets or in using the work process), the probability of making defects increases significantly. Note that using the workbench effectively also assumes the worker is competent in using the tools in the toolbox. Therefore, an obvious time-compression strategy is to ensure the competency of the individuals using the workbench step.

- **Internal rework.** Internal rework generally indicates either the worker is incompetent or the processes provided to the worker are defective. In our testing workbench example, if the tester did not prepare tests for all the code specifications and those defects were uncovered by a test inspection process, internal rework would occur. An obvious time-compression strategy is to reduce internal rework.

- **External rework.** External rework refers to a situation in which the worker for a specific workbench cannot complete the workbench without additional input from previous workbench step(s).

Reducing Variability

Measuring testing time variability is a project. It must be recognized as a project and managed as a project. This means that time and resources must be allocated to the time-compression project. You can compress testing time by reducing variability.

Although preparation is needed to compress the testing effort, the actual compressing project will require only minimal staff and resources. The preparation that helps make "compressing" successful includes the following:

1. **Find a "compressing" champion.** Identify someone in the IT organization to be the champion for this effort. It can be the IT director or anyone well-respected in the IT organization.

2. **Teach those having a vested interest in compressing software test time the process to compress testing.** The champion or someone appointed by the champion should learn the seven-step process to compress test time and provide an overview of that process to those who have a vested interest in compressing testing time. Generally, those individuals are project leaders, system designers, systems analysts, system programmers, quality assurance personnel, testers, and standards and/or software engineering personnel. Everyone having

a "stake" in compressing test time should understand the time-compression process.

3. **Find individuals to identify "compressible" components of the testing process.** Identify two to five individuals who want to be involved in compressing the testing process. Generally, it should be at least two individuals, but no more than five. They will become the "agile implementation team."

4. **Assign a budget and timeline to identify implementable time-compression improvements to the testing process.** If the individuals on the team are knowledgeable about the testing process, this should require no more than two to three days for each team member. Generally, these individuals already have an idea about how testing might be compressed. The process that they follow will confirm these ideas and/or identify the probable root causes for excessive test time. Because these individuals are knowledgeable, it is recommended that they spend approximately two to four hours per week over a four to six week period to complete Steps 1 through 6 of the seven-step testing time-compression process. Step 7 deals with selecting these individuals and obtaining resources for the project.

The software testing agile implementation team needs to understand the components of a software testing process for two reasons:

- **To identify testing workbenches.** If your organization has an immature testing process, you may have difficulty identifying specific workbenches because they may be integrated into larger tasks and not easily identifiable.

- **To help define root causes of variability.** As the agile implementation team identifies a specific workbench as one having great variability, they may have difficulty identifying the root cause. By examining their knowledge of specific workbench activity, the agile implementation team may be able to determine that the root cause of variability is a lack of performing a specific activity, or performing it in an ineffective manner.

Developing Timelines

A testing timeline shows the number of workdays needed to complete the testing. The three tasks that need to be followed to develop a software testing timeline are as follows:

1. Identify the workbenches.
2. Measure the time for each workbench via many testing projects.
3. Define the source of major variability in selected workbenches.

Identifying the Workbenches

The workbenches that create the software testing timeline must be defined. These are not all the workbenches in the software test process, just those that might be defined as "the critical path." These workbenches, if lined end to end, determine the time span to complete the software testing.

There may be many other workbenches in software testing that need not be considered in this timeline definition. The types of workbenches that need not be considered include the following:

- Workbenches done in parallel with another workbench, but by themselves do not influence the timeline. For example, there may be a testing estimation workbench that is performed in parallel with defining the testing plan workbench; but it is defining the testing plan workbench that is the one constraining test time, rather than the estimating workbench.

- Report generation workbenches, such as time reporting, status reporting, and so forth.

- Workbenches/tasks normally performed during wait time, such as software testing documentation. Note that as the timeline is "shrunk," some of these workbenches may, at a later time, affect the timeline.

- Estimating changes to the software testing plan.

- Staff training/staff meetings, unless they delay the completion of a critical workbench.

It is important to note that the process for "compressing" software testing time need not be a high-precision exercise. For example, if a critical workbench is left out, or a noncritical one added, it will not significantly affect the process for compressing testing time. Those corrections can be made as the process is repeated over time.

The workbenches defined for the timeline may or may not be the same workbenches/tasks/steps defined in the organization's software testing process. The timeline workbenches may divide a workbench in the organization software testing process, or it may combine one or more steps/tasks in the testing process into a single workbench. What is important is that the workbench be a critical component of software testing (in the opinion of the team responsible for compressing testing).

The workbenches must be identified and defined in a sequence from the beginning to the end of the testing process. For each workbench, the following information is needed:

- **Workbench name.** The name may be one assigned by the software testing agile implementation team or the name given in the organization's software testing process.

- **Input(s).** The entrance criteria that will initiate action for the workbench. The names of the input(s) should be those used in your organization's software testing process.

- **Workbench objective(s).** The specific purpose for performing the workbench. This should be as specific as possible and, ideally, measurable. Note that in compressing the workbench, it is extremely important that those involved clearly understand the objective(s) for performing that workbench.

- **Output(s).** The exit criteria for products produced by the workbench. The output(s) should be identified by the name used in the organization's software testing process.

- **Approximate estimated timeline.** This should be the number of workdays required to execute the workbench. The agile implementation team can determine the unit of measure they desire for the timeline. It can be days, half-days, or hours.

Once defined, this information should be transcribed to Work Paper 24-1. Note that this work paper is representative of what is needed; the actual work paper should be much larger.

The timeline is a completion timeline and not a person-hour timeline. In other words, a three-day timeline is three workdays. It may, in fact, take several individuals all working the three available workdays to complete the task in three days.

Measuring the Time for Each Workbench via Many Testing Projects

The objective of this task is to measure an approximate workbench timeline in workdays for each workbench included in Work Paper 24-1. Note that this would normally be done only for those workbenches that have an extended (that is, large) calendar-day timeline. For each workbench selected to calculate the completion timeline, Work Paper 24-2 should be completed. The objective of this work paper is to measure the completion timeline for a specific workbench for many different projects. If historical data is available, measuring the timeline for 10 to 20 different projects is ideal. However, in practice, most organizations calculate the timeline for fewer projects. If historical data is not available, it should be collected from projects currently being tested.

For each project for which the workbench completion timeline is being calculated, the following information should be collected and recorded on Work Paper 24-2:

- **Workbench name.** The name assigned to the specific workbench on Work Paper 24-1.

- **Project.** The name of the software testing project for which the completion timeline is being documented.

- **Start date.** The calendar date that identifies when the workbench activity commenced.

- **Date "do" procedures completed first time.** This is the date on which the workbench was completed if no rework was required. In other words, if everything was done perfectly, this is the completion date. However, if rework was required, that rework extends the date of completion.

- **Date workbench completed.** This is the date that the work assigned this specific workbench was completed, including any rework.

- **No-rework delivery days.** This is the number of days between the start date for this project and the date the do procedures could have been completed the first time if there was not rework.

- **Actual timeline days.** This is the number of workdays between the start date of this workbench to the date the workbench was completed.

After the workbench completion timeline data has been collected for a reasonable number of projects, the following should be calculated:

- **Average no-rework timeline.** The average days as calculated in the "minimum timeline days" column. The no-rework completion timeline days are totaled for all the projects and divided by the number of projects to get this particular calculation.

- **Variability of no-rework days.** The variability for the average no-rework day timeline is the number of days that the workbench was completed earlier than the average no-rework days and the number of days it was completed later than the average no-rework days. For example, if the average number of days is five and one project is completed in three days and another in eight days, the variability is between plus three days and minus two days.

- **Average actual days timeline.** This is calculated by totaling the days in the "total timeline days" column and dividing by the number of projects.

- **Variability of actual days.** This is calculated by determining which project was completed earliest and which was latest. The number of days early from the average actual days and the number of days late produce the plus and minus variability.

Figure 24-3 shows an example of calculating the delivery timeline for three workbenches that performed testing. Note that to complete a timeline like this, you should use projects of equal size and complexity (perhaps by classifying projects tested as small, medium, or large).

Workbench Name:					
Project Timelines:					
Project(s)	**Start Date**	**Date "Do" Procedures Completed First Time**	**Date Workbench Completed**	**Minimum Timeline Workdays**	**Actual Timeline Workdays**
A	June 1	June 18	June 26	14	20
B	July 30	August 30	September 8	26	33
C	November 3	November 18	December 1	$\dfrac{14}{54}$	$\dfrac{22}{75}$
			÷ 3 =	18	25
Average No Rework Workdays Timeline:18			No Rework Workdays Variability:-4 to +8		
Average Actual Workdays Timeline:25			Actual Workdays Variability:-5 to +8		

Figure 24-3   Workbench completion workday timeline.

As you can see in Figure 24-3, test planning was performed for three projects. For each project, the Minimum Timeline Workdays is the number of workdays between the start date and the date on which the first draft of the test plan was completed. The actual timeline workdays for each project is the number of workdays from the start of test planning until the test plan is complete. This example shows that the minimum average number of workdays for test planning is 18, with a variability of minus 4 and plus 8. The minus 4 means that some test planning projects were completed 4 days earlier than the average, and one was completed 8 days longer than the average. The same basic calculation in the example is performed for the actual timeline workdays.

Defining the Source of Major Variability in Selected Workbenches

For each workbench selected for calculating the workbench completion timeline using Work Paper 24-2, a variability completion timeline analysis should be performed. This analysis should be performed for both the best projects (i.e., completed in less than the average number of workdays) and the least-efficient projects (i.e., required more than the average number of workdays to be completed).

For projects with both the below- and above-average variability, an analysis should be done by the agile implementation team to determine where they believe the major source of variability occurred. For example, if a particular workbench took an average of five workdays and one project completed it in three workdays, the agile implementation team would need to determine the source of the two-day variability. For example, the project team that completed it in three days may have used a tool that none of the other projects used. In this case, the tool would be the source of variability. On the other hand, if a workbench is completed in an average of 5 workdays and one team took 10 workdays to complete it, the source of that variability may be lack of training or competency on the part of the individual performing the workbench. That lack of competency would be the source of the process variability.

The workbench components on Work Paper 24-3 are those previously described in this chapter. For the workbench being analyzed, the agile implementation team would identify one or more of what they believe are the source(s) of variability for that workbench. When they identify the source, they should then attempt to determine the probable cause. To complete Work Paper 24-3, the following needs to be determined:

- **Variability analyzed.** This analysis should be performed both for those projects below the average timeline workdays and again for those projects above the average timeline workdays. (Note: The team may decide only to evaluate the single best and worst performances of the workbench, or it may analyze several of the better and several of the worst performances of the workbench.)

- **Source of variability.** For each of the ten workbench components, the team should determine whether they believe that component is or is not the source of variability.

- **Root cause.** For each workbench component the team believes is the source of variability, they should try to determine the root cause of that variability. Again, it might be the use of a tool by one project, or the lack of training or competence on the part of the worker in another project.

Improvement Shopping List

The objective of performing Step 1 of the seven-step process to compress testing time is to identify some specific components of a testing process in which you can reduce the variability. When Work Papers 24-1 through 24-3 are complete, the agile implementation team should begin to develop a "shopping list" of potential process completion timeline improvements. Work Paper 24-4 is provided for that purpose. Note that this work paper is also used in Steps 2 and 3.

To complete Work Paper 24-4, the agile implementation team needs to provide the following information:

- **Ideas for completion time improvement.** From the analysis performed on the timeline, the team can identify the following types of potential improvements:

  - **Workbench(es) requiring a large number of workdays to complete.** Large workbenches provide opportunities for improvement. Improvements may include dividing one workbench into two or more workbenches, providing a better way to do it, providing a more efficient way to perform the task, and so forth.

  - **Workbench(es) with large negative and/or positive variability.** Workbenches with large variability provide the opportunity to identify the good and bad projects and use the techniques in the good projects to improve the timeline or eliminate the characteristics in the workbench implementation that are less efficiently performed.

  - **Identify the root cause of the variability.** Knowing the potential cause of variability, both positive and negative, provides an opportunity for improvement.

  - **Experience gained from the analysis process.** Sometimes when a team performs an analysis and does impromptu brainstorming, they identify an opportunity for timeline improvement.

- **Reference number.** This column is designed to let the agile implementation team reference other documents that contain more information about improvement suggestions.

- **Priority.** The agile implementation team should give its first impression as to whether this is a good opportunity (higher priority) for timeline compression or an idea that might provide only minimal improvement (lower priority).

Quality Control Checklist

Work Paper 24-5 is a quality control checklist for Step 1 that the agile implementation team can use to minimize the probability of performing this step incorrectly.

If the investigation indicates that a particular aspect of this step was incorrectly performed, it should be repeated. (Note: Some teams prefer to review the quality control checklist before they begin the step to give them a fuller understanding of the intention of this step.)

Conclusion

This step has explained work processes and how an analysis of those work processes can lead to ideas for completion timeline compression. The step has provided a tool, the workbench concept, for analyzing each critical task in the software testing process. The step also provided an expanded workbench for timeline compression. This expanded workbench provides a process to identify ideas to compress the testing timeline. These ideas are used in Step 6 to identify the specific ideas that will be turned into an improvement process. The next step, Step 2, is designed to help the team identify potential causes of weakness in the testing process.

Agile systems maximize flexibility and minimize variability. The primary purpose of this step has been to identify the variability in the software testing process so that the variability in those steps/tasks that would be included in an agile testing process is minimized.

Step 2: Maximize Best Practices

When identifying the best-of-the-best practices, you can begin to move all software testers toward maximum testing competency. Agile software testing needs best practices to be truly "agile." When testers are proficient in the basics, (i.e., best testing practices), they can incorporate agility into those processes to perform software testing more effectively and efficiently.

This step describes how to maximize best practices. To do so, you must consider the skill sets of the individuals involved in testing, the testable attributes of software, and the processes used to test the software. This step will enable you to define any capability barriers in your organization's software testing, determine the best practices available, and continue to develop your list of ideas for compressing time to make your testing process more agile.

Tester Agility

The traditional role of software testers is to validate that the requirements documented by the development team have, in fact, been implemented. This role makes two assumptions. First, that the requirements are, in fact, what the customer/user truly needs. Second, that part of the role of the tester is to identify, for the development team, those requirements that have been incorrectly implemented.

Problems are associated with the testers validating the defined requirements, as follows:

- The belief that the implemented system will satisfy customer needs. This has proven not to be so, and the result is excessive change and maintenance.

- The development team will capture all the needed requirements. The fact is that development teams tend to concentrate on functional requirements, not quality factors.

Quality factors are those attributes of software that relate to how the functional requirements are implemented. For example, ease of use is a quality factor. Requirements can be implemented in a manner that is not easy to use. However, customers/users rarely specify an ease-of-use requirement. The quality factors may be the deciding factors as to whether sales will be made.

Testers must change their role from validating developer-defined requirements to representing customers/users. As this discussion continues, keep in mind these two distinct focuses and how testers (representing users/customers) can eliminate many of the tester capability barriers.

Software Testing Relationships

The interaction of four relationships in software testing helps to determine the agility and the performance of testing. Each party has a perspective concerning the software testing, and that perspective affects test team performance capabilities:

1. **The customer/user.** The perspective of the customer/user focuses on what they need to accomplish, their business objectives (a subjective determination). They may or may not be able to express these business objectives in the detail software testers need. This perspective is often called "quality in perspective."

2. **The software development team.** The development team focuses on how to implement user requirements. They seek to define the requirements to a level that allows the software to be developed (an objective determination). (If they can build that software and meet the requirements, however, they may or may not be concerned as to whether it is the right system for the user/customer.) This is often called the "quality in fact" perspective.

3. **IT management.** The environment established by IT management determines the testing methodology, methodology tools, estimating testing tools, and so forth. The environment determines what testers can do. For example, if they do not have an automated tool to generate test data, testers may be restricted as to the number of test transactions they can deal with.

4. **The testers.** The perspective of the testers focuses on building and executing a test plan to ensure the software meets the true needs of the user.

Operational Software

The testing capability barrier is two dimensional: One dimension is efficiency; the other dimension is effectiveness. However, these two dimensions are affected by software "quality factors." Figure 24-4 shows that these quality factors affect how each party views its role compared to another stakeholder's perspective.

Software Quality Factors

Software quality is judged based on a number of factors, as outlined in Figure 24-5. These factors are frequently referred to as "success factors," in that if you satisfy user desire for each factor, you generally have a successful software system. These should be as much a part of the application specifications as are functional requirements.

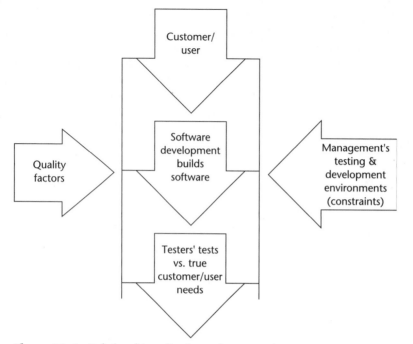

Figure 24-4   Relationships affecting software testing.

Factor	Definition
Correctness	Extent to which a program satisfies its specifications and fulfills the user's mission objectives.
Reliability	Extent to which a program can be expected to perform its intended function with required precision.
Efficiency	The amount of computing resources and code required by a program to perform a function.
Integrity	Extent to which access to software or data by unauthorized persons can be controlled.
Usability	Effort required to learn, operate, prepare input, and interpret output of a program.
Maintainability	Effort required locating and fixing an error in an operational program.
Testability	Effort required testing a program to ensure that it performs its intended function.
Flexibility	Effort required modifying an operational program.
Portability	Effort required to transfer a program from one hardware configuration and/or software system environment to anther.
Reusability	Extent to which a program can be used in other applications related to the packaging and scope of the functions that program performs.
Interoperability	Effort required to couple one system with another.

Figure 24-5   Software attributes (quality factors).

Tradeoffs

It is incorrect to assume that with enough time and resources all quality factors can be maximized. For example, to optimize both integrity and usability is an unrealistic expectation. As the integrity of the system is improved (e.g., through more elaborate security procedures), using the system becomes more difficult (because the user must satisfy the security requirements). Thus, an inherent conflict is built in to these quality factors.

Figure 24-6 shows the relationship between the 11 software quality factors. Note in this figure that a relationship exist between efficiency and most other factors.

Figure 24-7 shows the impact of not specifying or incorporating all the quality factors in software testing. Let's consider one quality factor: maintainability. Figure 24-7 shows that maintainability must be addressed during software test design, code, and testing. However, no significant impact occurs on the system test if maintainability has not been addressed in software testing. Likewise, no impact occurs on operation, initially, if software maintainability has not been addressed in software testing. What is crucial is that there is a high impact, because the software needs to be revised and transitioned into operation. Thus, a high cost is associated with software that is difficult to maintain.

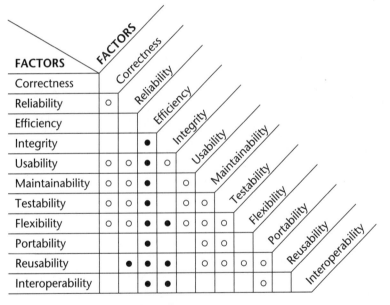

FACTORS	Correctness	Reliability	Efficiency	Integrity	Usability	Maintainability	Testability	Flexibility	Portability	Reusability	Interoperability
Correctness											
Reliability	o										
Efficiency											
Integrity			●								
Usability	o	o	●	o							
Maintainability	o	o	●		o						
Testability	o	o	●		o	o					
Flexibility	o	o	●	●	o	o	o				
Portability			●			o	o				
Reusability		●	●	●	o	o	o	o			
Interoperability			●	●					o		

LEGEND

If a high degree of quality is present for factor,
what degree of quality is expected for the other:

o = High   ● = Low

Blank = No relationship or application dependent

Figure 24-6   Relationships between software quality factors.

Life-Cycle Phases / Factors	Requirements Analysis	Design	Code & Debug	System Test	Operation	Revision	Transition	Expected Cost Saved Vs. Cost to Provide
Correctness	△	△	△	X	X	X		High
Reliability	△	△	△	X	X	X		High
Efficiency	△	△	△		X			Low
Integrity	△	△	△		X			Low
Usability	△	△		X		X		Medium
Maintainability		△	△			X	X	High
Testability		△	△	X		X	X	High
Flexibility		△	△			X	X	Medium
Portability		△	△				X	Medium
Reusability		△	△				X	Medium
Interoperability	△	△		X			X	Low

Legend: X = Quality factors should be measured

△ = Impact of poor quality is realized

Figure 24-7 The impact of not specifying software quality factors.

The objective of discussing quality factors, software testing relationships, and the relationships between quality factors and the tradeoffs of implementing such is to help you understand some of the reasons for performance barriers. Your software testing staffs can only develop software with a predefined effectiveness and a predefined efficiency. If you intend to compress software testing time, you must understand these barriers and incorporate them into the software testing time-compression activities.

Capability Chart

The easiest way to understand the capability barrier is to illustrate that barrier on a capability chart, shown in Figure 24-8. This figure shows the two dimensions of the chart: efficiency and effectiveness. Efficiency is a measure of the productivity of software testing, and effectiveness is a measurement of whether the test objectives are being met.

Figure 24-8 shows ten different projects. At the conclusion of each project, the project is measured for efficiency and effectiveness. The location on the software testing capability chart is determined by that efficiency/effectiveness measurement.

Let's look at two examples. Project A rates very high on efficiency but low on effectiveness. In other words, the test team optimized the resources available to test a project in a very efficient manner. However, the customer of Project A is not satisfied with the test results. Project J is just the opposite. The customer of Project J is extremely pleased with the results, but the test team was very inefficient in testing that project.

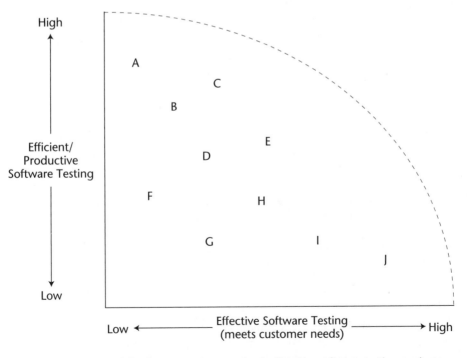

A-J = Assessment scores for testing ten software testing projects

Figure 24-8   Software testing capability chart.

In an effort to compress testing time, an agile implementation team should expect that tested projects on this chart will provide the solutions to compress testing time. For example, the practices used in testing Project A, if they were transferable to the other projects, might result in high test efficiency. Likewise, if the practices used in Project J could be transferred to all tested projects, there might be high customer satisfaction with all projects. Identifying these practices is the key component of this time-compression step.

The capability barrier line illustrated in Figure 24-8 represents the best an IT test team can do given current practices, staff competency, and management support. Agile testers must use new and innovative practices to enable an organization to break through their capability barrier.

A question that people ask about this capability chart is why the capability barrier line does not represent the results of the most efficient and most effective project. Note that if Project A were as effective as Project J, it would be outside the capability barrier line. The reason for this is the relationship between the quality factors. As an organization project becomes more efficient, other quality factors suffer. Likewise, if they become more effective, the efficiency factors deteriorate. Therefore, the best compromise between effectiveness and efficiency will be less than the most effective project or the most efficient project. (Note: This is only true using current best practices. New test practices may enable an organization to break through their testing capability barrier.)

Measuring Effectiveness and Efficiency

Measuring software testing efficiency and effectiveness involves two activities: defining the measurement criteria, and developing a metric for efficiency and a metric for effectiveness. Completed testing projects can then be measured by these two metrics. The result of measuring a specific software testing project is then posted to the software testing capability chart (see Figure 24-8).

There is no single correct way to measure software testing effectiveness and efficiency. The IT industry has not agreed on such a metric. On the other hand, many organizations perform these measurements regularly. The measurement is one of the activities that should be conducted at the conclusion of a software testing project.

The correct metric for efficiency and effectiveness is a metric that is agreed on by the involved parties. In a similar manner, there is no perfect way to measure the movement of the stock market. However, a metric called the Dow Jones Average has been developed and agreed on by the involved parties. Thereby, it becomes an acceptable metric for measuring stock market movement. Does everyone agree that the Dow Jones Average is perfect? No. On the other hand, there is general consensus that it is a good measurement of movement of the stock market.

General rules must be followed to create an acceptable metric, as follows:

- **Easy to understand.** The metric cannot be complex. The recommendation is that the metric range be between 0 and 100, because many measurements are on a scale of 0 to 100.

- **Limited criteria.** If there are too many criteria involved in the metric, it becomes overly complex. The recommendation is that no more than five criteria be included in the metric.

- **Standardized and objective criteria.** There needs to be a general definition of the criteria so that it can be used by different people and, as much as possible, the criteria should be objective (objective meaning that it can be counted as opposed to making a judgment).

- **Weighted criteria.** All criteria are not equal. Therefore, the metric should weight criteria. The most important criteria should get the most weight.

Defining Measurement Criteria

The most common way to measure software testing effectiveness is to determine whether testers can validate the presence or absence of the development team's defined requirements. In this case, four different metrics enable you to measure software testing effectiveness, as follows:

Requirements tested and found correct.

Requirement does not execute as specified.

Requirement is missing.

Requirement found in tested software, but not specified by development team.

Measuring Quality Factors

The quality factor of "correctness" refers to testers validating whether the requirements specified by the development team work. However, the quality factor of correctness does not include all the other quality factors that the test team should be addressing. For example, it does not address whether the software is maintainable. Note that the software can be implemented with all the functional requirements in place and working, but cannot be efficiently or effectively maintained because the software was not built with maintenance in mind. For example, the logic may be so complex that it is difficult for a maintainer to implement a change in the software.

If the tester represents the customer/user, the tester's responsibility may include testing some or all of the quality factors. This is generally determined in the relationship of the tester to the customer/user. If the tester is to evaluate more than the correctness quality factor, additional effectiveness criteria must be determined and used.

The generally accepted criteria used to define software quality are as follow:

- **Traceability.** Those attributes of the software that provide a thread from the requirements to the implementation with respect to the specific testing and operational environment.

- **Completeness.** Those attributes of the software that provide full implementation of the functions required.

- **Consistency.** Those attributes of the software that provide uniform design and implementation techniques and notation.

- **Accuracy.** Those attributes of the software that provide the required precision in calculations and outputs.

- **Error tolerance.** Those attributes of the software that provide continuity of operation under non-nominal conditions.

- **Simplicity.** Those attributes of the software that provide implementation of functions in the most understandable manner (usually avoidance of practices that increase complexity).

- **Modularity.** Those attributes of the software that provide a structure of highly independent modules.

- **Generality.** Those attributes of the software that provide breadth to the functions performed.

- **Expandability.** Those attributes of the software that provide for expansion of data storage requirements or computational functions.

- **Instrumentation.** Those attributes of the software that provide for the measurement of usage or identification of errors.

- **Self-descriptiveness.** Those attributes of the software that provide explanation of the implementation of a function.

- **Execution efficiency.** Those attributes of the software that provide for minimum processing time.

- **Storage efficiency.** Those attributes of the software that provide for minimum storage requirements during operation.

- **Access control.** Those attributes of the software that provide for control of the access of software and data.

- **Access audit.** Those attributes of the software that provide for an audit of the access of software and data.

- **Operability.** Those attributes of the software that determine operation and procedures concerned with the operation of the software.

- **Training.** Those attributes of the software that provide transition from current operation or initial familiarization.

- **Communicativeness.** Those attributes of the software that provide useful inputs and outputs that can be assimilated.

- **Software system independence.** Those attributes of the software that determine its dependency on the software environment (operating systems, utilities, input/output routines, etc.).

- **Machine independent.** Those attributes of the software that determine its dependency on the hardware system.

- **Communications commonality.** Those attributes of the software that provide the use of standard protocols and interface routines.

- **Data commonality.** Those attributes of the software that provide the use of standard data representations.

- **Conciseness.** Those attributes of the software that provide for implementation of a function with a minimum amount of code.

The software criteria listed here relate to the 11 software quality factors previously described. Figure 24-9 shows this relationship. For each of the factors, this figure shows which software criterion should be measured to determine whether the software factor requirements have been accomplished.

Note that some of the software criteria relates to more than one quality factor. For example, the modularity criterion is included in six of the factors, and consistency in three. As a general rule, you could assume that those criteria that appear most frequently have a higher relationship to the overall quality of the application system than do those criteria that appear only once. On the other hand, if the user rated a specific quality factor very high in importance, and that factor had a criterion that appeared only once, that criterion would be important to the success of the application as viewed from a user perspective.

The quality factors and the software criteria relate to the specific application system being developed. The desire for quality is heavily affected by the environment created by management to encourage the creation of quality products. An environment favorable to quality must incorporate those principles that encourage quality.

Factor	Software Criteria	Factor	Software Criteria
• Correctness	Traceability Consistency Completeness	• Testability	Simplicity Modularity Instrumentation Self-descriptiveness
• Reliability	Error Tolerance Consistency Accuracy Simplicity	• Portability	Modularity Self-descriptiveness Machine Independence
• Efficiency	Storage Efficiency Execution Efficiency	• Reusability	Software System Independence
• Integrity	Access Control Access Audit	• Interoperability	Generality Modularity Software System Independence
• Usability	Operability Training Communicativeness		
• Maintainability	Consistency		Modularity Communication Commonality Data Commonality
• Flexibility	Modularity Generality Expandability		

Figure 24-9 Software criteria and related quality factors.

Defining Efficiency and Effectiveness Criteria

Efficiency has sometimes been defined as "doing the job right"; and effectiveness has sometimes been defined as "doing the right job." Because of the lack of standards, IT metrics, and common software testing processes, it is difficult to reach agreement on efficient versus inefficient testing. For example, one would like an efficiency measure, such as X hours to test a requirement. However, because requirements are not equal, a requirement weighting factor would have to be developed and agreed on before this efficiency criteria could be used.

The lack of industry-accepted efficiency metrics should not eliminate the objective to measure testing efficiency.

There are many ways to measure software testing efficiency. One is the efficiency within the testing process. For example, do testers have the appropriate skills to use the testing tools? Does management support early involvement of testers in the development project? Are the testing processes stable and do they produce consistent results? Another way to measure software testing efficiency is the efficiency of the process itself.

Measuring Effectiveness

Measuring effectiveness of software testing normally focuses on the results achieved from testing. The generally acceptable criteria used to define/measure the effectiveness of testing are as follows:

- **Customer satisfaction.** How satisfied are the software customers with the results of software testing.

- **Success criteria.** Customers predefine quantitative success criteria. (If testers meet those criteria, it will be considered a successful project.)

- **Measurable test objectives.** Objectives stated in a manner that can be measured objectively so that it can be determined specifically whether the objectives are achieved.

- **Service-level agreement.** The contract between the customer and the testers as to the expected results of the testing efforts, how it will be measured, responsibilities in completing the testing, and other criteria considered important to the success of the test effort.

- **Inconsistency between the test and customer culture.** If customer and tester cultures are of different types, this can impede the success of the project. For example, if the customer believes in using and complying with a process, but testers do not, conflicts can occur. Step 5 addresses these culture differences.

Measuring Efficiency

Generally acceptable criteria used to define/measure software testing efficiency are as follows:

- **Staff competency.** Train staff members in skills necessary to perform those tasks within the software testing process. (For example, if staff members use a specific automated test tool, the staff members should be trained in the usage of the tool.)

- **Maturity of software testing process.** Usually a commonly accepted maturity level, such as the levels in SEI's CMMI.

- **Toolbox.** The software testing effort contains the tools needed to do the testing efficiently.

- **Management support.** Management support of the use of testing processes and tools, meaning that management requires compliance to process and compliance to the use of specified tools, and rewards based on whether processes are followed and tools are used efficiently.

- **Meets schedule.** The software testing is completed in accordance with the defined schedule for software testing.

- **Meets budget.** The software testing is completed within budget.

- **Software test defects.** The number of defects that software testers make when testing software.

- **Software testing rework.** The percent of the total test effort expended in rework because of defects made by solution testers.

- **Defect-removal efficiency.** The percent of developer defects that were identified in a specific test phase as compared to the total number of defects in that phase. For example, if the developers made 100 requirement defects during the requirement phase, and the testers found 60 of those defects, the defect-removal efficiency for the requirements phase would be .6, or 60 percent.

- **Percent of deliverables inspected.** The criteria transferred from validation to verification, removing defects at a point where they are cheaper to remove.

- **Software testing tool rework.** The amount of resources consumed in using testing tools because of defects in those tools (or defects in how those tools were used).

Building Effectiveness and Efficiency Metrics

The agile implementation team should select the criteria used to measure the effectiveness and efficiency of the testing process. They should select what they believe are reasonable measurement criteria for both efficiency and effectiveness. These can be taken from the criteria examples described in this step or from criteria agreed on by the agile implementation team. They should document the criteria selected.

The measurement criteria should be recorded on Work Paper 24-6 and should include the following:

Criteria name

Description

Efficiency

Effectiveness

Rank

After the agile implementation team has agreed on the criteria used to measure test efficiency and effectiveness, they need to rank those criteria. The ranking should be a two-part process:

1. Rank the criteria high, medium, or low. (Those ranked high are the best criteria for measurement.)

2. Starting with the high criteria, select no more than five criteria for efficiency and five for effectiveness. Note: These do not have to be those ranked high, but those ranked high should be considered before those ranked medium.

Both the efficiency and effectiveness metrics are developed the same way. It is recommended that three to five criteria be used. Then the criteria must be measurable. Use the following method to do that:

1. A method for calculating a criteria score must be determined. It is recommended that the calculated score for individual criteria be a range of 0 to 100. This is not necessary, but it simplifies the measurement process because most individuals are used to scoring a variable using a range of 0 to 100.

2. The criteria used for efficiency or effectiveness must then be weighted. The range should total 100 percent. For example, if there are five criteria and they all weighted equally, they each will be given a 20 percent rating or 20 percent of the total effectiveness or efficiency score.

3. To calculate a specific efficiency or effectiveness score for a project, the criteria score is multiplied by the weighting percentage to produce an efficiency or effectiveness score. The individual scores for efficiency and effectiveness are added to produce a total score.

Work Paper 24-7 is designed to record the criteria score and weighting. You can also use this work paper to calculate a total effectiveness and efficiency score for the selected software testing projects.

Figure 24-10 shows an example of an efficiency and effectiveness metric. For both efficiency and effectiveness, three criteria are defined. For each criterion, a method to calculate the criteria score has been determined. The criteria score is then multiplied by the weighting percentage, and Figure 24-10 shows a project example efficiency score of 76 percent and an effectiveness score of 80 percent.

After Work Paper 24-7 has been developed, the efficiency and effectiveness score for a reasonable number of software testing projects should be calculated. These can be historical projects or projects that will be completed in the near future. Those scores are then posted to Work Paper 24-8. Each project is to be posted to the intersection of the efficiency score and effectiveness score. Figure 24-10 shows an example of this posting. (Note: The circled criteria scores are the ones assigned for this "Project Example.")

Identifying Best Practices from Best Projects

The projects that score best in efficiency and the projects that score best in effectiveness should be selected for analysis. The agile implementation team should analyze those projects to determine the practices that cause some to be most efficient and some to be most effective. If the agile implementation team is knowledgeable in the software testing methodology, and has in-depth discussions with the test teams whose projects are either efficient or effective, the best practices can usually be identified.

Software Project Name:	Project Example		
Measuring Efficiency _____ Efficiency Criteria	Method to Calculate Criteria Score	Weight	Efficiency Score
DRE during requirements and design phases	Defect Removal Efficiency 95% DRE = 100% ⬭ 85-95% DRE = 70% less than 85% DRE=30%	30%	21%
Number of tester defects per function point	Number of Defects ⬭ Less than 2/FP = 100% 3 to 4/FP = 70% 5 6o 6/FP = 40% more than 7/FP = 20%	40%	40%
Percent of Deliverables Inspected	90 to 100% = 70% 75 to 89% = 75% ⬭ 60 to 74% = under 60% = 10%	30%	15%
	Total: 100%		
	Total Efficiency Score:		76%
Measuring Effectiveness	Method to Calculate Criteria Score	Weight	Effectiveness Score
Reliability	System Uptime (first month of operation) 99 to 100% = 100% ⬭ 98 to 99% = 95 to 97% = 50% less than 95% = 10%	20%	16%
Uncorrected detected errors at date of operation	Number of detected errors uncorrected Fewer than 5 = 100% ⬭ 6 to 10 = 11 to 20 = 40% more than 20 = 10%	30%	24%
User satisfaction	User survey in which user rates testing effort 1 to 100%	50%	40%
	Example 80%		
	Total: 100%		
	Total Efficiency Score:		80%

Figure 24-10 Examples of an effectiveness and efficiency metric.

The best practices identified should be posted to Work Paper 24-9. The information posted should include the following:

- **Best practice.** The name of the best practice, which may be named by the project team or it may be a specific commonly used best practice.

- **Description.** The description should clearly state the objective of the best practice.

- **Project used in.** The name of the software testing project that used this practice so that the project team can be consulted if more information is needed.

- **Application efficiency/effectiveness.** Indicate whether this is a best practice that improves efficiency or effectiveness. Check the appropriate column.

By using these practices the software testing process can become more agile.

Improvement Shopping List

The end objective of performing Steps 1 through 3 of the seven-step process is to identify the specific components of a software testing process where the timeline can be reduced.

Work Paper 24-9 has identified the potential best practices for compressing software testing time. The practicality of using these best practices should be investigated. Those that the agile advancement team believes would enhance the agility of the software testing process should be identified as software testing agile best practices and posted to Work Paper 24-10.

To complete Work Paper 24-10, the agile implementation team needs to provide the following information:

- **Best practices for time improvement.** From the analysis performed on the best practices, the team can identify those best practices that, if used in new testing projects, should result in improved agility in testing.

- **Reference #.** This column is designed to let the agile implementation team reference other documents that contain more information about the idea suggested for improvement.

- **Priority.** The agile implementation team should give their first impression as to whether this is a good opportunity for timeline compression or an idea that might provide only minimal improvement.

Quality Control Checklist

Step 2 is an important aspect of compressing software testing time. A misunderstanding of the process or making an error in the performance of Step 2 can lead to missed opportunities to compress software testing time. A quality control checklist is provided for the agile implementation team to use to minimize the probability of performing this step incorrectly.

Work Paper 24-11 is a quality control checklist for Step 2. The investigation should focus on determining whether a specific aspect of the step was performed correctly or incorrectly.

Individuals should first review and answer the questions individually. Then the agile implementation team should review these questions as a team. A consensus Yes or No response should be determined. "No" responses must be explained and investigated. If the investigation indicates that the particular aspect of the step was incorrectly performed, it should be repeated. (Note: Some teams prefer to review the quality control checklist before they begin the step to give them a fuller understanding of the intention of this step.)

Conclusion

The objective of this step is to identify those best practices that, when implemented in new projects, will "compress" software testing time. The method to identify these best practices is to develop a metric that scores the effectiveness and efficiency of completed software testing projects. Those projects that scored high in efficiency are candidates to contain practices that will improve efficiency in future testing efforts. Those projects that scored high in effectiveness are candidates to contain best practices that will improve the effectiveness of future testing projects. By focusing on improving effectiveness and efficiency of the software testing effort, the total completion time should compress. The product of this step is a list of best practices identified as ideas or candidates to use to compress software testing time. The next step focuses on assessing the strengths and weaknesses of the existing software testing process.

Step 3: Build on Strength, Minimize Weakness

After determining the software testing process timeline and determining the testing process best practices, it is time to take an overall look at the software testing process. This will be done by conducting a macro self-assessment of the process. The objective is to identify the major strengths and weaknesses of the process. All projects should capitalize on the strengths and minimize the weaknesses. Doing so can help compress software testing delivery time.

Effective Testing Processes

Software development processes were developed years before much effort was expended on building software testing processes. Even today, many organizations have loosely defined testing processes. In addition, many computer science curricula do not include software testing as a topic. This step defines four criteria for an effective software testing process, and provides you with an assessment to evaluate your software testing process against those criteria.

It is common today to relate effectiveness of a process to the maturity of the process, maturity meaning primarily that variability is removed from the process. This means that each time the process is performed, it produces similar results. For example, if an IT organization desires a defect-removal efficiency of 95 percent in the requirements phase, a process that meets that objective time after time is considered a mature or effective process.

Software testing process characteristics make some more effective than others. In simplistic terms, the answers to these questions will help you determine the effectiveness of a process:

1. Does the software testing process do the right thing?
2. Does the software testing process do the thing right? In other words, is the software testing process efficient?

The five primary components of a software testing process are as follows:

1. Create an environment conducive to software testing.
2. Plan the testing.
3. Execute the task in accordance with the plan.
4. Analyze the result and report the results to software stakeholders.
5. Analyze the test results to improve the testing process based on that analysis.

Efficient test processes perform those five components with minimal resources. They do the work "right the first time." This means that there are minimal defects and minimal rework performed by the software testers.

When software testing is treated as an art form, and depends on the experience and judgment of the testers, it may or may not be effective and efficient. If it is effective and efficient, it is primarily because of the competency of the individual testers. However, when a test process is people dependent, it is not necessarily repeatable or transferable between projects.

Assessing the Process

An inefficient software testing process tends to expand the software testing delivery time. Fine-tuning the process so that it is efficient will compress the testing time. The purpose of an assessment is to identify the strengths and weaknesses of your specific testing process. (Note again that as you focus on efficiency, effectiveness is a by-product of that effort.)

Work Paper 24-12 provides the assessment items that include the three primary components of the software tester's workbench (which represent the process to do work and the process to check work). However, assessment emphasizes those aspects of making processes effective (determining whether testers will do and check work in accordance with the process, and whether those Do and Check procedures are effective). These three components that make processes work are: management commitment to software testing processes, the environment established by management in which software testers perform their work, and management's support and allocation of resources to continuously improve the software testing process.

The time-compression team should use this self-assessment questionnaire to self-assess their software testing process. They should do this as follows:

1. Read each item individually aloud as a team.

2. Have the team discuss the item to ensure a consensus of understanding.

3. Reach consensus on a Yes or No response to the item. If consensus cannot be reached, then a No response should be recorded.

Software testers face many unique challenges. The root cause of these challenges is often the organizational structure and management's attitude toward testing and testers. In many organizations, testers have lower job classifications and pay than developers. Many IT managers consider testing an annoyance and something that will be complete in whatever time is available between the end of development and the commencing of operational status for the software.

Developing and Interpreting the Testing Footprint

At the conclusion of assessing the five criteria in Work Paper 24-12, total the number of Yes responses in each criterion. Then post the number of Yes responses to Work Paper 24-13. This work paper is a software testing process assessment footprint chart. To complete this chart, put a dot in the criteria line that represents the number of Yes responses for that category. For example, if in category 1 (i.e., management commitment to quality software testing), you have two Yes responses, put a dot on the line on the number 2 circle. After posting the number of Yes responses for all five categories, draw a line between the five dots. The connection of the five dots results in a "footprint" that illustrates the assessment results of your software testing process. Explain your No responses in the Comments column.

Three footprint interpretations can be easily made, as follows:

- **Software testing process weaknesses.** The criterion or criteria that score low in the number of Yes responses are areas of weakness in your software testing process. The items checked No indicate how you could strengthen a particular category.

- **Software testing process strengths.** Those criteria that have a high number of Yes responses indicate the strengths of your software testing process. Where your software testing process is strong, you want to ensure that all of your software testing projects benefit from those strengths.

- **Minimal variability of strengths and weaknesses.** Building an effective process involves moving the footprint envelope equally in all five criteria toward the five Yes response levels. The management commitment criterion would push the other four criteria in the right direction. However, there should not be significant variability between the five criteria. Ideally, they will all move outward toward the five Yes response levels one level at a time.

Examples of the type of analysis that you might make looking at this footprint are as follows:

1. If you scored a 5 for management commitment to the process, but the other categories are low in Yes responses, this indicates not "walking the walk" in utilization of an effective software testing process.

2. When there is a wide discrepancy between the numbers of Yes responses in different categories, it indicates a waste of resources. For example, investing a lot in the Do procedures for the process, but not building an effective environment, does not encourage consistency in use.

It is generally desirable to have the time-compression team evaluate their software testing footprint. They need to look at the footprint, draw some conclusions, discuss those conclusions, and then attempt to reach a consensus about them.

Poor Testing Processes

If a worker is given a poor process, that process reduces the probability of the individual being successful at performing the work task. Rather than the work task supporting success, the worker must modify, circumvent, or create new steps to accomplish the work task. In other words, the worker is diverted from doing an effective software testing job because of the time-consuming activity of surviving the use of a poor work process.

The objective of this self-assessment is to emphasize that work processes are much more than just the steps the software tester follows in performing the work task. For a work task to be effective, management must be committed to making that work process successful; management must provide the resources and training necessary to ensure worker competency and motivation in following the process; and management must provide the resources and skills sets needed to keep the software testing process current with the organization's business and technical needs.

If that work process is enhanced using the principles of agile work processes, the workers will have the competency, motivation, empowerment, and flexibility needed to meet today's software testing needs.

Improvement Shopping List

At the conclusion of the self-assessment process, the time-compression team should identify ideas for workday timeline improvements to your software testing process. Consider all category items assessed with a No response as a potential improvement idea. Record these ideas on Work Paper 24-14.

Quality Control Checklist

Work Paper 24-15 is a quality control checklist for Step 3. The quality control investigation should focus on determining whether a specific aspect of the step was performed correctly or incorrectly.

The agile implementation team should review these questions as a team. A consensus Yes or No response should be determined. "No" responses should be explained and investigated. If the investigation indicates that the particular aspect of the step was incorrectly performed, it should be repeated. (Note: Some teams prefer to review the quality control checklist before they begin the step to give them a fuller understanding of its intention.)

Conclusion

This step has proposed a process to self-assess the software testing process to identify ideas to compress testing delivery time. The step provided the criteria associated with effective software testing processes. These effectiveness criteria were converted to a software testing self-assessment work paper. The result of conducting the self-assessment was to develop a software testing process footprint. This footprint, coupled with the results of the self-assessment, should enable the agile implementation team to develop many ideas for compressing software testing delivery time.

Step 4: Identify and Address Improvement Barriers

Many good ideas are never implemented, because barriers and obstacles associated with the ideas cannot be overcome. If the implementation attempt is undertaken without fully understanding the barriers and obstacles, success is less likely. Therefore, it is essential, if software testing time compression is to be effective, that these barriers and obstacles be understood and addressed in the implementation plan.

The software testing agile implementation team will face two types of barriers when attempting to compress testing time: people barriers and organizational/administrative barriers. Both can impede progress. This step identifies a process to identify both barriers, and provides guidance for the agile implementation team on how these barriers and obstacles might be addressed. According to the dictionary, a barrier and an obstacle are approximately the same thing. Both terms are used in this step to highlight the importance of identifying and addressing anything that reduces the probability of effectively reducing delivery time.

Organizations consist of people. The people have different wants and desires, which will surface when change is imminent. People not only normally resist change, they also have many techniques to stop change or turn change in a different direction.

The Stakeholder Perspective

The activity of compressing software testing time involves changing the way people do work. Thus, these individuals have a "stake" in the change happening or not happening. Individuals react differently as they consider what is their stake in the time-compression effort.

An important component in the people barrier concept is the "WIIFM" concept. WIIFM stands for "What's in it for me?" If an individual cannot identify WIIFM in a proposed change, he or she will either not help the change occur, or will openly resist the change. Individuals have four different reactions to change:

- **Make it happen.** An individual having this stake wants to be a driving force in reducing software testing delivery time. This person is willing to assume a leadership role to make change happen.

- **Help it happen.** This individual does not want to lead the change, but will actively support the change. That support is expressed in a willingness to help change happen. In other words, if there is an assignment to help compress software testing time, the individual will work on activities such as data gathering, building solutions, writing new software testing procedures, and so forth to help compress software testing time.

- **Let it happen.** This individual neither supports nor objects to the change. However, this individual will view that there is nothing in the change for them. Whether the change occurs or not, it is not important to them. They will neither support nor resist the change.

- **Stop it from happening.** This individual does not believe that the change is worthwhile, or the individual just objects to the change. This individual may openly object to the change and take whatever action possible to stop the change from happening. Or even worse, some of these individuals outwardly support the change but quietly work hard to stop the change from happening by raising barriers and obstacles.

The agile implementation team must identify the key individuals in the activities for compressing software testing time and determine what stake they have in the change. These individuals usually include the following:

- IT management
- Testers
- User management
- Quality assurance/quality project leaders
- Control personnel
- Software designers
- Administrative support
- Programmers
- Trainers
- Test managers
- Auditors

It may be desirable to identify these individuals by name. For example, list the individual names of IT management. This should be done whenever the individual is considered personally involved in the change or can influence a change. In other instances, the stakeholders can be grouped (for example, testers). If the agile implementation team determines that the testers all have approximately the same stake in the change, they do not need to name them individually.

In viewing which stake an individual has, the agile implementation team must carefully evaluate the individual's motives. For example, some individuals may outwardly support compressing software testing time because it is politically correct to do so. However, behind the scenes, they may believe that the wrong group is doing it or it is being done at the wrong time, and thus will openly support it, but are in fact, in the "Stop It From Happening" stakeholder quadrant.

Stakeholder Involvement

After reading the preceding section, you might have this logical question: "Why are so many stakeholders involved in software testing?" The answer is that the goal of software testing is to identify defects and deficiencies in the software. Because someone is potentially responsible and accountable for those defects, they are concerned about how software testing is performed, what software testing does, and how and to whom the defects will be reported.

Let's just look at a few examples. If developers and programmers are most likely the individuals responsible for those defects, they potentially consider testers as affecting their performance appraisal. Project leaders may consider the testers as "that group" that is delaying the implementation of the software. IT management may consider testers as the group that stops them from meeting their budgets and schedules. While believing that it is important to identify defects and deficiencies before software goes into operation, they may also believe it is more important to get the software into operation than to complete a test plan.

The bottom line is that as testing becomes more effective and efficient, resistance to testing may increase. This is because testers are identifying more defects. What this means is that the stakeholders' involvement in change is an important component in making the software testing process more effective and efficient. Testers should not believe that just because they are testing more effectively and efficiently that their changes will be welcome by those having a stake in the testing.

Performing Stakeholder Analysis

The agile implementation team needs to do the following to analyze the various stakes held by those who have a vested interest in the change. Work Paper 24-16 is designed to document this analysis.

1. **Identify the stakeholder.** This can be the name or the function (for example, the name Pete Programmer or the users of the software).

2. **Identify the current stake.** For that individual or function, determine which of the four stakeholder quadrants that individual is in (for example, the "Make It Happen" stake).

3. **Document the reasons the individual has that stake.** The agile implementation team must carefully analyze and document why they believe an individual has that stake. For example, testers may be in the "Stop It From Happening" stake because they believe that by compressing time, the organization will need fewer testers.

4. **Identify the desired stake for the individual or function.** If the individual/ function does not have what the agile implementation team believes is the correct stake to make change happen, the team must decide which stake is the most desirable for making the change occur. For example, if the software designers are in the "Stop It From Happening" stake, the team may want to move them to the "Let It Happen" stake. In addition, if there are two or more individuals in the

"Make It Happen" stake, to avoid leadership conflict, one of the leaders should be moved to the "Help It Happen" stake.

5. **Develop a plan to address stakeholder barriers.** If an individual or function is not in a desired stake, a plan must be developed to move that individual/ function to the desired stake. For example, moving the software designers from the "Stop It From Happening" stake to the "Let It Happen" stake might occur if the agile implementation team can assure them that the amount of time allocated for software designing will not be reduced.

Red-Flag/Hot-Button Barriers

This people barrier is highly individual. A red flag or hot button is something that causes a negative reaction on the part of a single individual. It is normally associated with someone in a management position, but can be associated with anyone who can exercise influence over the successful completion of a compression project. An individual, for a variety of reasons, may be strongly against a specific proposal. For example, if an improvement approach is assigned to "reduce defects," the word *defect* may raise a red flag with a specific individual. They do not like the word. They prefer words such as *problem* or *incident*. Thus, by changing a word, a red flag can be avoided.

Other examples of red flags/hot buttons include the following:

- Changing a procedure that was developed by an individual who likes that procedure and wants to keep in place.

- People who do not like anything that was not "invented here."

- The individual or group proposing the change is not liked, and someone does not want them to get credit for anything.

- The idea has been tried before. Some people believe that because something was tried before that a variation or additional attempt to do the same thing will result in failure.

- Not the way I like it done. Some individuals want extreme formal approval processes to occur before any change happens. This means rather than taking a "fast track" process to compressing software testing time, they want it carefully analyzed and reviewed by multiple layers of management before anything happens.

Document these red flag/hot button barriers on Work Paper 24-17.

1. **Barrier/obstacle/red flag.** Name the barrier/obstacle/red flag in enough detail so it is understandable.

2. **Source.** The name of the individual or condition creating the barrier/obstacle/ red flag.

3. **Root cause.** What is the reason that the barrier/obstacle/red flag exists.

4. **How to address.** The team's initial idea to overcome the barrier/obstacle/ red flag.

Staff-Competency Barriers

Changes to the software testing process that can compress software testing time may be desirable, but the existing skills must be available if the implementation of the change is to be successful. In some instances, this is judgment; for example, the manual work process needs to be changed, and the agile implementation team believes for that specific process no one in the IT organization has the needed skills. In other instances, missing skills are obvious. For example, a new tool is recommended, but no one in that organization knows how to use that tool.

Document these competency barriers on Work Paper 24-17.

Administrative/Organizational Barriers

In many instances, the administrative procedures are organizational barriers that inhibit change. Many believe that these administrative and organizational barriers are designed to slow change. Some people believe that rapid change is not good, and by imposing barriers they will cause more analysis before a change is made. Also, delaying implementation will enable all individuals to make known any personal concerns about the change.

A partial list of the administrative and organizational barriers that can inhibit compressing software testing time follows:

- **Funding.** Funds are not available to pay for making the change happen. For example, overtime may be needed, new tools may need to be acquired, specialized training contracted for, and so forth. Some of these money constraints are real, and others represent individual priorities. For example, if you invite someone to go to dinner with you, but they decline because they cannot afford it, it may mean they cannot afford it, but it also may mean that they have higher priorities for using their funds.

- **Staff.** The individuals needed to develop and implement a change may have no time available. Staff resources may be committed to current projects, and therefore a request that new projects be undertaken may be declined because no staff is available to implement them.

- **Improvement approvals.** Approval by one or more individuals may be required before work can be performed. Although the approval process is designed to stop unwanted consumption of resources, it can also inhibit activities that are not desired by the individual authorized to approve those activities. The approval process also gives an individual the opportunity to "sit" on this request to delay the activity until involved individuals become discouraged. If the approval process involves two or more people, delays are built in to the process, which can also discourage individuals from taking action.

- **Paperwork.** Sometimes individuals who want to undertake a work activity might be required to complete a proposal form to have the work done. The organization may have a procedure that indicates how to complete a proposal request. Some of these can include developing budgets and schedules, naming involved parties and affected parties, listing the steps to be performed, identifying the controls built in to the process, and so forth. The paperwork itself might discourage an individual from undertaking a voluntary activity; but when the paperwork is coupled with the approval process, which can delay approval because the paperwork is not properly completed, good projects can be stopped from occurring.

■ **Organizational turf.** Questions may arise as to who has the authority to undertake a project. Third parties sometimes become involved in a project because they believe that their "organizational area" is the one that should undertake the project. For example, if a software testing team decides to improve a testing process, but the quality assurance or process engineering group believes that it is their "turn" to improve processes, they might object to the agile development team doing it and thus delay or kill the project.

■ **Value received.** Sometimes individuals must demonstrate the value they expect to receive from undertaking the work activity. This may involve accounting procedures with detailed return on investment calculations. Sometimes the return on investment calculation must be submitted to the accounting department for review. In many instances, it is easier to eliminate seven workdays from the software testing time than it is to demonstrate quantitatively the value that will be received from undertaking the time-compression project.

■ **Priorities.** Individuals and groups have priorities that they believe are the way in which work should be performed. If a time-compression project does not fit into that prioritization scheme, they will want to delay the time-compression project to deal with their priorities. Obviously, work priorities tend to take precedence over process-improvement priorities. This means that there is always enough time to correct that work but never enough time to eliminate the problem that causes bad work.

The organizational and administrative barriers should also be documented on Work Paper 24-17. At this point, it is unimportant whether a specific barrier/obstacle will stop a time-compression project. It is important to list as many barriers and obstacles as the agile implementation team feels might affect any time-compression project. The relationship between a specific barrier/obstacle and a specific time-compression project will be addressed when a plan is developed to implement a specific time-compression idea.

Determining the Root Cause of Barriers/Obstacles

The barrier/obstacle cannot be adequately addressed until the root cause is determined. Likewise, the barrier/obstacle will continue to exist until the root cause of the barrier/obstacle has been addressed. The process of determining the root cause is an analytical process.

Consider an example. Assume the agile implementation team believes that a new software testing estimating tool will create a better estimate for software testing, in that it will allocate the appropriate time needed for defining software testing objectives. The agile implementation team may believe that if the testing objectives are better defined, they will "compress" the remainder of the software testing time. When the idea is presented for approval, the involved manager indicates that no funds are available to acquire the estimation tool. One might assume that the lack of funds is the root cause. However, when an analysis is done, it becomes obvious that the approving manager does not want that specific estimating tool, but prefers the current estimation method. If the agile implementation team focuses on obtaining funding, the tool will never be acquired. If team members identify the root cause as the manager's resistance to the tool, their efforts will focus on convincing the manager that the tool will be beneficial. If they address that root cause, the funds might become available.

Work Paper 24-18 is the recommended analysis method the agile implementation team should undertake to identify the root cause for a specific barrier or obstacle. It is also called the "Why-Why" analysis. One of these work papers should be used for each barrier/obstacle listed on Work Paper 24-17 that the team believes should be analyzed to identify the root cause.

The agile implementation team then begins the "Why-Why" analysis. Let's revisit the previous example. The barrier/obstacle is the inability to obtain management approval because of lack of funding. The agile implementation team then begins to ask the question "Why?" In this example, it would say "Why can't we get management funding for the estimation tool?" The first answer is that no funds are available. They then begin to ask the question "Why are no funds available?" and they arrive at the conclusion that no funds are available because the root manager does not like the estimation tool. If the agile implementation team believes that is the root cause of the barrier/obstacle, they post that root cause to Work Paper 24-17.

This analysis may be simple to conclude, or it may be complex. A complex analysis may involve many primary and secondary contributors. The "Why-Why" analysis should continue until the agile implementation team believes they have found the root cause. If the barrier identified affects a specific compression-improvement plan, the plan should include the approach recommended to overcome the barrier. If that plan does not work, the "Why-Why" work paper should be revisited to look for another potential root cause.

The success of using this analysis depends on the agile implementation team having an in-depth understanding of how the organization works. They also need to know the traits and characteristics of the individual in authority to overcome the barrier. The analysis will not always lead to the root cause, but in most instances it does.

Addressing the Root Cause of Barriers/Obstacles

After the potential root cause of a specific barrier/obstacle has been identified, the agile implementation team needs to identify how they will address that specific root cause. The "how to address component" can be done in this step, or the agile implementation team can wait until they are developing a specific time-compression plan and then determine how to address the root cause.

There are no easy answers to how to address the root cause. Again, the more the agile implementation team knows about the organization and the characteristics of the key individuals in the organization, the easier the solutions become. Some of the solutions as to how to address the root cause of the barrier/obstacle include the following:

- **Education.** Sometimes the individual involved does not have the necessary knowledge to make a good decision for the IT organization. By providing that education to the individual, the individual is in a better position to make the proper decision. In our estimating tool example, if the approving manager had a better knowledge of how the estimation tool works and why it is more reliable in estimating than the current system, the individual might make that approval.

- **Training.** Training provides the specific skills necessary to do a task. Resistance sometimes occurs because individuals feel inadequate in performing a task they will be required to do. For example, in the estimating tool example, they may not want to use the estimating tool because they are unsure they will be able to use it effectively. If they are provided the training on how to use it before the decision is made, that concern will be alleviated.

- **Champion.** Sometimes a highly respected individual in the organization needs to be recruited to champion a specific improvement idea. The individual can be a member of management, someone from a customer/user area, or a highly respected person in the IT department. After that individual makes his/her position known as a champion for a specific idea, other people will normally accept that recommendation and support the idea.

- **Marketing/communicating.** Marketing first must identify an individual's need, and then provide the solution to satisfy that need. For example, if your approving manager for an estimating tool has a need to complete projects on time with high customer satisfaction, marketing the estimation tool to meet that need can help get approval for the idea. Marketing should not be viewed negatively, but rather, should be viewed as a method of getting ideas accepted. Individuals unfamiliar with marketing techniques should read books, such as those by Zig Zigler, that explain the various steps in a marketing program. Although these books are written for the marketing professional, they have proven beneficial for IT staff members in getting ideas accepted.

- **Rewards.** Individuals tend to do what they are rewarded for. If IT management establishes a reward system for software testing time compression, it will greatly encourage individuals to support those efforts. The rewards can be financial, extra time off, or certain benefits such as special parking areas and so forth. Sometimes just a lunch recognizing success, paid for by the IT organization, will encourage people to work harder because they recognize the reward system as something management wants. (Note: It may be important to reward most or all of the stakeholders.)

- **Competitions.** Organizing a competition to compress software testing time has been effective in some organizations. One organization set up a horse race track. The track was divided into ten parts. The parties were then asked to determine ways to compress software testing time. For each day they were able to compress a software testing effort, their horse moved one position. The first horse that completed the ten-day time-compression goal was rewarded. However, it was equally important that there be prizes for second place, third place, and so on.

The determination about how to address a specific root cause of barrier/obstacle should be posted to Work Paper 24-17. Note the previous examples are only a partial list of the solutions for addressing the root cause(s) of barrier/obstacles. The agile implementation team should select specific solutions to address those root causes.

Quality Control Checklist

Work Paper 24-19 is a quality control checklist for Step 4. The investigation should focus on determining whether a specific aspect of the step was performed correctly or incorrectly.

The agile implementation team should review these questions as a team. A consensus Yes or No response should be determined. "No" responses should be explained and investigated. If the investigation indicates that the particular aspect of the step was incorrectly performed, it should be repeated. (Note: Some teams prefer to review the quality control checklist before they begin the step to give them a fuller understanding of the intention of this step.)

Conclusion

Everybody favors compressing software testing time. What they object to is the method proposed to compress software testing time. They might also object to the allocations of resources for compressing software testing time, especially when the IT organization is behind in implementing business software projects. It is important to recognize that individuals may believe that their career is partially dependent on completing a specific project. Anything that might delay that effort would be viewed negatively.

Many organizations establish approval processes designed to delay the quick implementation of projects. These processes ensure that the appropriate safeguards are in place, that only those projects desired by management are, in fact, implemented. These safeguards also become barriers and obstacles to implementing ideas that can compress software testing time.

Individuals who want to compress software testing time must be aware of what these barriers and obstacles are. Some are people related, whereas others are administrative and organizational related. For all of these, they must look for the root cause and then develop a solution to address that root cause. This step has provided a process to do just that.

Step 5: Identify and Address Cultural and Communication Barriers

The "management culture" of an IT organization refers to the approach management uses to manage the IT organization. The Quality Assurance Institute has identified five different IT cultures. These range from a culture that emphasizes managing people by setting objectives to a culture that encourages and supports innovation. Each of the five cultures requires a different type of solution to be used to compress software testing time.

This step describes the five cultures, and then helps the agile implementation team through a process to identify the barriers and constraints imposed by the IT management culture.

The culture affects the way people do work, and the way people work affects their lines of communications. Open and complete communication is a key component of an agile software testing process. Thus, opening communication lines is an important part of building an agile software testing process.

This step explains how organizational cultures go through an evolutionary process. Some believe that the hierarchal organizational structure is patterned after the methods Moses used to organize his people in the desert. Up until the 1950s, most cultures were hierarchical in structure. The newer cultures have flattened organizational structures and emphasize teams and empowerment. Obviously, those cultures that emphasize teams and empowerment are more suited to agile software testing processes.

Management Cultures

There are five common management cultures in IT organizations worldwide (see Figure 24-11), as follows:

- Manage people
- Manage by process
- Manage competencies
- Manage by fact
- Manage business innovation

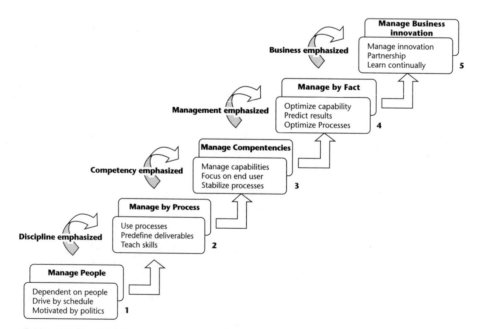

Figure 24-11 The five management cultures.

The five cultures are generally additive. In other words, when an organization moves to a culture of "manage by process," the organization does not stop managing people. When it moves to the "manage by competency" culture, it is addressing the people issue of work processes. Measurement is not effective until the work processes are stabilized at the "manage by competency" level.

Culture 1: Manage People

In this culture, people are managed. This is sometimes called *management by objectives*. The staff is given specific objectives to accomplish. Management's concern is that those objectives be accomplished, but generally they are not concerned about *how* those objectives are accomplished.

The management philosophy for this culture is that good work is accomplished by hiring good people, setting appropriate objectives for those people, setting reasonable constraints, and then managing people to meet those objectives. This is a results-oriented culture. The people performing the work are responsible for determining the means to accomplish the results. Management is more concerned with satisfying constraint objectives than how products are built.

The management environment within this culture has these characteristics:

- **Manage people to produce deliverables.** Results are emphasized and processes de-emphasized when people are given the responsibility to produce the deliverables (i.e., results) on which their performance will be evaluated. How products are built is of little concern to a Culture 1 manager.

- **Control people through budgets, schedules, staffing, and performance appraisals.** Without processes, management cannot directly control or assess interim status of deliverables; thus, management places constraints on the workers and uses those constraints to control the results.

- **Hierarchical organization.** Direction and communication flows from the top of the organization downward. Politically driven personal agendas often take precedence over doing the right thing.

- **Reactionary environment.** Management does not anticipate, but rather reacts to unfavorable situations as they arrive.

- **Emphasis on testing quality into deliverables.** Product testing uses a "fix on failure" (code and fix) approach to eliminate defects from products prior to delivery. This method does not prevent the same type of defect from occurring again in another project.

- **Success depends on who is assigned to a project.** This culture emphasizes assigning the best people to the most important projects because success is primarily based on people's skills and motivation.

- **Objective measures used.** Measurement is based on things that can be counted, such as headcount, workdays, budgets, schedules, etc.

- **Outsourcing.** Outside resources are used to fill competency gaps rather than training existing staff.

Why Organizations Continue with Culture 1

The primary reasons organizations stay at Culture 1 include the following:

- **Inexperience with other cultures.** Management learned this culture prior to becoming management. They were managed using this culture and believe that goals and objectives can be met using this culture. Management is in a comfort zone that is difficult to change.

- **Pressures to meet schedules.** Customers, users, and senior management evaluate IT management on results.

- **Time/resource constraints.** The IT organization thinks it does not have the resources needed to develop and implement disciplined processes.

- **Quality is a discretionary expense.** The actions and resources needed to improve quality are above and beyond current project cost, and thus, come under different budget categories. Many believe that quality costs are not recoverable.

- **The IT staff believes their profession is creative.** Being creative means having the freedom to perform tasks in a manner that is subject to as few constraints as possible, which leads to variability among projects. Management may fear staff turnover if emphasis is placed on disciplined processes.

- **Customers/users control IT budget.** Under charge out systems, IT management may not have the option to fund process improvement processes without concurrence from customers/users.

- **Difficulty.** The change from Culture 1 to Culture 2 is the most difficult change of all the changes to approach.

Why Organizations Might Want to Adopt Culture 2

- Current performance is not acceptable to the customers/users.

- Without improvement, the IT function may be outsourced.

- Without improvement, IT management may be replaced. Outsourcing is fast becoming a viable alternative.

- Response to executive management requests to improve quality, performance, and productivity: executive management finds the IT organization's performance unacceptable and demands improvement.

- Improve staff morale and reduce turnover. IT staff feels overworked and inadequately rewarded and feels the probability of success is low. Thus, the desire to move to another organization.

- Do more with less. Executive management increases the IT workload without corresponding increases in resources to complete the additional work.

- Products delivered by suppliers do not meet the true needs of the IT organization, even though they might meet the purchasing or contractual specifications.

Culture 2: Manage by Process

The second culture manages by work processes. The movement from the "manage people" culture to the "manage by process" culture is significant. In the "manage people" culture, people are held responsible for results. In the "manage by process" culture, management is held responsible for results because they provide the work processes that people follow. If the work processes cannot produce the proper results, management is accountable because they are responsible for those work processes.

The management philosophy behind this culture is that processes increase the probability that the desired results will be achieved. To be successful, this culture requires management to provide the leadership and discipline needed to make technology professionals want to follow the work processes. At Culture 1, the workers are made responsible for success, whereas at Culture 2, management assumes the responsibility for success, while the workers are responsible for effectively executing the work processes. The management environment within the "manage by process" culture has these characteristics:

- **Management provides the means (i.e., processes) for people to perform work with a higher probability of repeatable success than without processes.** Resources (time, people, budget) are allocated to process testing and improvement. Management budgets the funds needed to develop and improve processes.

- **Select staffs/teams are empowered to define and/or improve the processes.** The individuals who use the processes develop processes. Thus, the developers of the processes become the "owners" of the process.

- **Management is proactive in reducing and eliminating the reoccurrence of problems through improved processes.** The IT organization identifies and anticipates problems and then takes action, so that the same problem will not reoccur when the same series of tasks are performed in the future.

- **Cross-functional organizational structures are established.** Teams composed of members of different organizational units are established to resolve cross-functional issues, such as testing of processes and change of management.

- **Subjective measurement is added to objective measurement.** Subjective measures, such as customer surveys, become part of the operational culture.

- **Inputs and outputs are defined.** Detailed definitions reduce misunderstanding and process variability.

Why Organizations Continue with Culture 2

The primary reasons organizations stay at Culture 2 include the following:

- **Management is comfortable with culture.** After investing the time and resources to move to Culture 2, both management and staff have learned to operate at this approach. Management is not anxious to initiate additional significant changes to the way work is performed.

- **Cost/time to move to another culture.** Each move to a different culture has an associated cost—monetary and staff time allocated. Based on current workloads, those resources may not be available.

- **Culture 2 has provided relief from Culture 1 problems.** Many of the problems facing management, such as budget overruns and missed schedules, have been at least partially resolved by moving to Culture 2. Given this, management may follow the "if it isn't broke, don't fix it" philosophy.

- **Project priorities.** Management must devote full effort to meet current project priorities and thus, does not have the time or energy to initiate significant change. These significant changes require moving to another culture.

- **Cross-functional politics.** Timing may not be desirable to change the way the IT organization operates. For example, changing to another culture may put the IT organization out of step with the way its customers and senior management operate.

Why Organizations Might Want to Adopt Culture 3

- **Processes are incomplete.** Culture 2 processes tend to be developed to address a wide variety of needs. For example, one system testing process may be built for implementing any and all projects. These processes tend to be large in order to encompass the many needs the processes have to fill. In addition, some processes may not be defined.

- **Processes are not easily customized.** The organization may not be able to customize a process to meet a specific need of a customer/user.

- **Company needs/goals have changed.** What the company does, and how the IT organization fits into its needs has changed, making the generic process culture (Culture 2) incompatible with the new needs/goals.

- **Processes are not fully integrated.** Culture 2 processes tend to be independently developed and may not take into account the organization's overall mission.

- **There is pressure from executive management and/or customers/user to improve.** The improvements achieved from moving from Culture 1 to Culture 2 may not meet management's current improvement expectation, thus expediting the need to move to another management culture.

- **Suppliers focus on the purchasing and the contractual specifications rather than spending effort on understanding the true business needs of the IT organization.** The IT organization is normally unwilling to invite suppliers into an IT planning session to familiarize suppliers with the strategy and direction of the IT organization.

Culture 3: Manage Competencies

The third culture manages competencies. This means that the hiring and training of people is focused on making them competent in using the organization's work processes. In addition, IT organizations using this cultural approach do not accept work that is outside their areas of competency.

The underlying philosophy for this culture is that an IT organization must identify the needed core competencies and then build an organization that is capable of performing those competencies effectively and efficiently. Requests for work outside those core competencies should be declined; however, IT may assist in obtaining outsourcing assistance in performing those requirements.

At this culture, IT builds trust with its customer base since it is capable of performing as it says it can, within the cost and budget and constraints.

The management environment within the "manage competencies" approach has these characteristics:

- **Processes that support the core competencies.** The IT organization decides which products and services they will support and then builds the competencies (i.e., work processes) to produce and deliver those products and services.

- **Employee hiring based on competencies.** Individuals are hired and trained to perform certain work processes (i.e. competencies).

- **Competencies that support organizational business objectives.** The competencies selected by the IT organization should relate to the information needs incorporated in to the organization's business objectives.

- **High level of process customization.** Processes can be quickly customized and adapted to the specific customer/user needs.

- **Empowered teams.** Teams are organized and empowered to take action and make decisions needed to meet business objectives.

- **Establishment of defect databases.** Defects are recorded and entered into databases for analysis and improvement of core competencies.

- **Continuous learning.** Education and training become an integral part of day-to-day work activities.

Why Organizations Continue with Culture 3

The primary reasons organizations stay at Culture 3 include the following:

- **New skills are required to move to Culture 4.** Management and staff must be convinced that the effort and skill sets needed to move to a statistical approach are worthwhile. The background needed to make that decision may not be available.

- **Rapid changes in technology make it difficult to keep pace.** The effort required to maintain the competencies at this culture is already consuming available resources, making it difficult to institute the changes needed to move to another culture. It may be more effective and economical to outsource.

- **Overcoming learning and unlearning curves is difficult.** Reaching and maintaining competencies involves unlearning old processes and learning new processes. Maintaining learning and unlearning curves, as process changes accelerate, becomes a major activity for the IT staff.

- **Continuous training is expensive.** Incorporating more training in addition to the Culture 3 training will significantly increase the training cost.

Why Organization Might Want to Adopt Culture 4

- **Improvement is needed to remain competitive.** In a global marketplace, organizations are pressured to continually improve productivity and quality, add capabilities, and reduce cost to customers.

- **Need for more reliable data.** Management of Culture 3 produces data about processes, but that data normally does not have the consistency and reliability needed for use in decision making.

- **Reduce judgment factor in decision making.** Without reliable data, managers must make decisions based heavily on judgment. Judgment, although often effective, does not produce the consistency in decisions that encourages confidence from customers/users and senior management.

- **The suppliers not aligned with customer demand.** Suppliers are not positioned to react to customer demand as it occurs so that specialized orders or products and services not previously requested can be obtained quickly enough to satisfy IT customer demand.

Culture 4: Manage by Fact

The fourth culture is "manage by fact." Quantitative results are established and measures are collected and compared against expected results. Based on those measures, management makes whatever changes are needed to ensure that the outcome of the work processes is that needed by IT customers.

The underlying management philosophy of this approach is that decision making should be based on fact (however, those facts will be tempered by judgment and experience). The stability of the Culture 3 work processes produces reliable quantitative data, which management can depend on in decision making. The quantitative feedback data, normally produced as a work process by-product, will be used for managing and adjusting work in progress, as well as identifying defect-prone products and processes as candidates for improvement.

The management environment within the "manage by fact" culture has these characteristics:

- **Making decisions using reliable data.** The more reliable the data, the more it can be incorporated in decision making and the better decisions that can be made.

- **Identifying and improving processes using reliable data.** Having reliable data enables improvement teams to select processes and where within those processes the most productive improvements can be made.

- **Workers measure their own performance.** Workers are provided quantitative data needed to effectively manage their own work processes.

- **Process managed quantitatively.** Project teams and workers have the quantitative data needed to effectively manage their own work processes.

- **Measurement integrated from low levels to high levels.** Quantitative data can be rolled up from low-level data to high-level data showing how low level components affect the goals and objectives of the organization.

■ **Defect rates anticipated and managed.** The defect databases established at Culture 3 can be used to predict defect rates by processes and work products, so that defects can be anticipated and acted upon.

Why Organizations Continue with Culture 4

The primary reasons organizations stay at Culture 4 include the following:

■ **Current processes have been optimized.** The integrated processes and integrated measurement data allows optimization of current work processes.

■ **Allow others to innovate.** It may be cheaper to follow the lead than to be a leader.

■ **Management is comfortable with the culture.** Organizations operate effectively and efficiently at Culture 4. If management is comfortable with that approach, they may not have the desire to initiate changes in the work environment.

■ **Knowledge of business is not required.** It is a major educational effort to train the IT staff in business activities.

■ **Time and effort are required to optimize a measurement program.** Management may wish to use its scarce resources for purposes other than innovating new technological and work approaches.

■ **Unwilling to share processes with other organizations.** Moving to Culture 5 normally involves sharing current work processes with other organizations. IT management may decide that work processes are proprietary and prefer not to share them.

Why Organizations Might Want to Adopt Culture 5

■ **Leapfrog the competition.** Innovative business cultures may provide the organization with a competitive advantage.

■ **Become an industry leader.** Culture 5 produces world-class organizations that tend to be recognized by leading industry associations and peer groups. In turn, this leads to other organizations wanting to share solutions.

■ **Receive pressure from customers/users and senior management to improve.** Even with existing processes optimized, executive management and customer/ user may demand additional improvements in productivity and quality.

■ **Partner with customers in reengineering business solutions.** With current capabilities optimized, IT management and staff can redirect their efforts toward reengineering business solutions and be assured IT has the capabilities and customer trust needed to build these solutions.

■ **Need to develop a business-to-business partnership for reducing supplier cost.** The Internet, coupled with business-to-business partners for jointly ordering supplies and services, can minimize cost, but becomes effective only when cultures support business-to-business activities.

Culture 5: Manage Business Innovation

The fifth culture is one of business innovation. Innovation is possible because at Culture 4, management is confident that they can do what they say they will do with the resources estimated, and the work can be completed within or ahead of schedule. The types of improvements now possible are sometimes called "breakthrough" improvements, meaning significantly new ways to do work. Also in this culture, the focus is on using technology to drive business objectives.

The underlying management philosophy at this culture is using information as a strategic weapon of the business organization. IT is looking at new and innovative technological and system approaches to improve the overall business success of the organization. The culture requires information technology and management to be knowledgeable about the business side of the organization.

The management environment within the "manage business innovation" culture has these characteristics:

- **Supports e-commerce activities.** Integrate e-commerce systems to the "back-office" systems so that they become an integrated network of systems. In many organizations, this involves interfacing with legacy systems.

- **Supports e-business activities.** E-business activities involve rethinking the way organizations conduct their business. It involves developing new relationships with customers, providing customers new ways to acquire products and information regarding product testing and delivery, as well as increasing value of products and services to the customer. For e-business to be successful, IT is normally a major driver of the e-business.

- **Finds innovative solutions to business problems.** Where existing processes are ineffective or cause productivity bottlenecks, innovative solutions may be the only option for productivity breakthroughs.

- **Acquires solution from other industries.** Organizations that share their work processes with other organizations also receive mutual sharing, which can lead to productivity breakthroughs.

- **Enables workforce to become an "alliance" between employees, external customers, suppliers, and other parties having a vested interest in improvement.** After IT organizations have optimized their work processes, they can then build an alliance with all of the parties having a vested interest in the success of the information technology organization.

- **Uses innovative technologies.** New technologies, such as knowledge management and data warehousing, can be incorporated into process-improvement activities (e.g., suppliers, customers, auditors).

- **Strategic business planning and information technology become equal partners in setting business directions.** IT becomes a leader in integrating technology into solving business problems and/or creating new business opportunities.

Cultural Barriers

From the discussion of the five IT management cultures, the agile implementation team must identify their organization's IT culture and the barriers and obstacles associated with that culture. Five tasks are involved in completing this step. The results of the tasks should be recorded on Work Paper 24-20.

Identifying the Current Management Culture

Using the description of the five cultures, the agile implementation team must determine which of the five cultures is representative of their organization's IT management culture. Normally, this is not difficult because at least 90 percent of the IT organizations are in Culture 1 (i.e., manage people) or Culture 2 (i.e., manage process). A Culture 1 organization is one in which IT management focuses more on stating objectives to be accomplished. In Culture 2, IT management expects their staff to follow the software testing process specifically, and if the project team follows it, management must assume responsibility for the results.

Identifying the Barriers Posed by the Culture

The barriers posed by the IT management culture are normally those described as the reasons why the IT organization desires to stay with its existing culture. For example, if the IT organization is a Culture 1 (i.e., manage people), IT management may want to stay with Culture 1. For example, if management likes to set objectives for people to accomplish and manages those objectives, any solution that does not place responsibility on the individual for completing a task would probably not be acceptable to IT management. The agile implementation team should review all the reasons why IT management would want to stay with its current culture and from that extrapolate what they believe are the barriers posed by that culture. These barriers should be transcribed to Work Paper 24-20.

Determining What Can Be Done in the Current Culture

This task is turning the identified barriers into positive statements. For example, in identifying a barrier, we said in the preceding example that any solution that is not focused on establishing and managing objectives for individuals would not be acceptable to IT management. Given this barrier, any solution should include specific objectives for individuals to accomplish.

Determining the Desired Culture for Time Compression

The agile implementation team generally cannot change the IT management culture. However, by this point in the time-compression process, the team members should have some general idea of how they can compress the software testing time. If those solutions would be more effectively implemented in a different culture, the agile implementation team should identify which culture is most conducive to the type of solutions they are thinking about.

Although an agile implementation team cannot change the culture, they may be able to change an aspect of the culture that will enable them to implement one of their time-compression solutions. If that culture would be desirable, the agile implementation team should indicate which is the desired culture and record it on Work Paper 24-20.

Determining How to Address Culture Barriers

Work Paper 24-20 identifies two categories of culture barriers: those imposed by the current IT management culture, and those that exist in a current culture, but could be alleviated if a new culture were in place. Given these two categories of barriers, the agile implementation team should determine how they could address those culture barriers. If the barrier cannot be adequately addressed, any solution inhibited by that barrier should not be attempted. If the barrier can be adequately addressed, the solution must include a plan to address that culture barrier. Those recommendations would be included in Work Paper 24-20. You can use the "Why-Why" analysis to help you identify the root cause of the cultural barrier and then apply the recommended solution to adjust to those cultural barriers.

Open and Effective Communication

Agile processes depend on open and effective communication. Open and effective communication has these three components:

- **Understanding and consensus on objectives.** Those working on an agile software testing project must know the objectives that they are to accomplish and believe they are the right objectives. To accomplish this effectively, the test objectives need to be related to business objectives. In other words, for testing a website, if a business objective is that a website should be easy to use, the test objectives must be related to that business objective. In addition, the testing team must believe as a team these are the proper objectives for them to achieve. Taking time and effort to ensure the testers understand the objectives, and gain their support, is an important component of building an effective software test team.

- **Respect for the individual.** Open and effective communication depends on those communicating having respect for one another. Disagreements are normal, but they must be in an environment of respect. Showing that appropriate respect exists is an important component of team building.

- **Conflict-resolution methods.** Teams need methods to resolve conflict. Individuals may have variant opinions about how to perform a specific task. Those differences must be resolved. The resolution process will not always mean that individuals will change their opinions, but it means they will support the decision made.

For an in-depth discussion of the challenges testers face, refer to Chapter 8, "Step 2: Developing the Test Plan."

Lines of Communication

The first step to improve information flow is to document the current information flow. This should be limited to information obtained and/or needed by a software testing team in the performance of their tasks. However, other information flows can be documented, if needed, such as the flow of information to improve the software testing process.

You can document the lines of communication using the communication graph. To complete this graph, you need to do the following:

1. **Identify the individual/groups involved in communication.** All the stakeholders in the success of the tasks, such as software testing, need to be identified. The agile implementation team can determine whether the graph should show a specific individual, such as the project leader, or the function such as users of the software. Figure 24-12 is an example of a communication graph showing the five different parties involved in communication (in this case, identified as A, B, C, D, and E).

2. **Identify each type of communication going between the individuals/ functions.** Each type of communication, such as reporting the results of a test, is indicated on the graph as a line between the parties. For example, if Party D did the testing and reported the results to Party C, the line going between D and C represents that communication. Each type of communication should be documented. This can be done on the graph or separately.

3. **Determine the importance of the communication.** A decision needs to be made about how important the information communicated is to the overall success of the project. If it is considered very important, it would be given a rating of 3; if it was important, a rating of 2; and if it was merely informative, a rating of 1. For example, if the goal of informing Party C of the results of testing was just to keep that party informed, it would get a rating of 1. A rating of 3 is normally given if not having that information would have a negative impact on the system; a rating of 2 is given if it would have a minor impact on the project, and a rating of 1 is given if it would have little or no impact but would be helpful to the success of the project.

4. **Develop a communication score for each party.** A communication score is developed for each party by adding the importance rating for each line of communication. In the Figure 24-12 example, Party A has a score of 4, and Party C has a score of 9. The objective of developing a party score is to determine which parties are most important to the flow of communication. In Figure 24-12, Party C is the most important individual. This would probably be the software testing manager in the lines of communication for conducting testing for a specific software project.

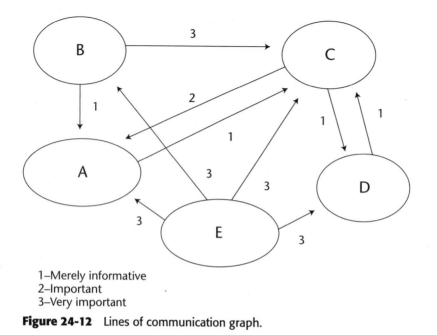

1–Merely informative
2–Important
3–Very important

Figure 24-12 Lines of communication graph.

Information/Communication Barriers

To identify the barriers to effective and open communication, the agile implementation team should analyze their lines of communication graph (see Figure 24-12) to determine whether there is adequate communication, nonexistent communication, communication to the wrong individual, and/or information that is needed by an individual but not provided to that individual. These barriers to effective and open communication should be recorded on Work Paper 24-21. To complete the work paper, you must address the following:

- **Information needed.** Indicate information that is needed but not communicated, or any information that is available but not communicated to the right individual, or from the right individual.

- **Importance.** The importance of the information communicated using the ranking of 3, 2, and 1 should be communicated; indicate the appropriate person to communicate it, and the appropriate person to receive it.

- **Barrier.** The barrier the agile implementation believes is inhibiting the open and effective communication.

- **How to address barrier.** The agile implementation team's recommendation of what they might do to overcome this communication barrier.

Effective Communication

Communication involves dealing with expectations and responsibilities of individuals and groups. Effective communication must occur down, across, and up an organization, and with parties external to the IT organization. Effective communication to manage testing activities requires the following:

- Management is provided with the necessary reports on the tester's performance relative to established objectives. For example, consider whether:

  - Mechanisms are in place to obtain relevant information on project development changes.

  - Internally generated information critical to achievement of the testing objectives, including that relative to critical success factors, is identified and regularly reported.

  - The information that managers need to carry out their responsibilities is reported to them.

- Information is provided to the right people in sufficient detail and on time to enable them to carry out their responsibilities efficiently and effectively. For example, consider whether:

  - Managers receive analytical information that enables them to identify what action needs to be taken.

  - Information is provided at the right level of detail for different levels of the test effort.

  - Information is summarized appropriately, providing pertinent information while permitting closer inspection of details as needed rather than just large amounts of data.

  - Information is available on a timely basis to allow effective monitoring of events and activities—and so that prompt reaction can be taken to business factors and control issues.

- Management's support for the development of necessary information systems is demonstrated by the commitment of appropriate resources (human and financial). For example, consider whether:

  - Sufficient resources (managers, analysts, programmers, all with the requisite technical abilities) are provided as needed to develop new or enhanced information systems.

- Effectiveness with which employees' duties and control responsibilities are communicated. For example, consider whether:

  - Communication vehicles—formal and information training sessions, meetings and on-the-job supervision—are sufficient in effecting such communication.

  - Employees know the objectives of their own activity and how their duties contribute to achieving those objectives.

  - Employees understand how their duties affect, and are affected by, duties of other employees.

- Receptivity of management to employee suggestions of ways to enhance productivity, quality, or other similar improvements. For example, consider whether:

- Realistic mechanisms are in place for employees to provide recommendations for improvement.

- Management acknowledges good employee suggestions by providing cash awards or other meaningful recognition.

- Adequacy of communication across the organization (for example, between testers and users) and the completeness and timeliness of information and its sufficiency to enable people to discharge their responsibilities effectively. For example, consider whether:

  - Salespeople inform engineering, production, and marketing of customer needs.

  - Accounts receivable personnel advise the credit approval function of slow payers.

  - Information on competitors' new products or warranties reaches engineering, marketing, and sales personnel.

- Openness and effectiveness of channels with and among all parties communicating information on changing customer needs. For example, consider whether:

  - Feedback mechanisms with all pertinent parties exist.

  - Suggestions, complaints and other input are captured and communicated to relevant internal parties.

  - Information is reported upstream as necessary and follow-up action taken.

- Timely and appropriate follow-up action by project and user management resulting from communications received from testers. For example, consider whether:

  - Personnel are receptive to reported problems regarding defects or other matters.

  - Errors in software are corrected and the source of the error is investigated and corrected.

  - Appropriate actions are taken and there is follow up communication with the appropriate stakeholders.

  - IT management is aware of the nature and volume of defects.

Quality Control Checklist

Work Paper 24-22 is a quality control checklist for Step 5. The investigation should focus on determining whether a specific aspect of the step was performed correctly or incorrectly.

The agile implementation team should review these questions as a team. A consensus Yes or No response should be determined. "No" responses should be explained and investigated. If the investigation indicates that the particular aspect of the step was incorrectly performed, it should be repeated. (Note: Some teams prefer to review the quality control checklist before they begin the step to give them a fuller understanding of the intention of this step.)

Conclusion

This step, like Step 4, has identified some of the barriers and obstacles that need to be addressed to compress software testing time. Whereas Step 4 identified the root cause of the people and organizational barriers, the root cause of the culture barriers is known; it is the culture itself. It is the culture that primarily determines what information is shared and to whom it is shared. Ineffective and closed communication inhibits the building of an agile software testing process. Knowing these culture and communication barriers, and how to address the barriers, is an important part of the plan to compress software testing time.

Step 6: Identify Implementable Improvements

The best idea for compressing software testing time is one that is "implementable" (that is, "doable"). Implementable means that it will receive appropriate management support, have the needed resources for implementation, and have the acceptance of those who will be using the improved software testing process. This step describes what an implementable is and provides a process on how to identify the most-implementable ideas from the idea list developed from Steps 1 through 3. Those ideas will then be ranked by importance in jumpstarting an agile software testing process.

What Is an Implementable?

An *implementable* refers to something that can actually be realized in an organization. It may not be the most effective or most efficient idea, but it is doable. The implementable is not the idea that is easiest or the quickest to realize, but it is doable. It is not the idea that will compress software testing time by the most workdays, necessarily, but it is doable.

Experience from IT organizations that have been effective in compressing software testing time show there are four criteria for implementables, as follows:

- **User acceptance.** Those individuals who will be required to use the improved process in software testing are willing to use the idea. If the users do not want to use the idea, they will find a way to stop the idea from being effective. An idea can be stopped by blaming problems on the idea, or by taking extra time and then attributing it to the new idea. However, when the users like the idea and want to use it (i.e., it is acceptable to them), they will make the idea work.

- **Barrier free.** The greater the number of obstacles/barriers imposed on an idea, the greater the probability the idea will not be effective. As discussed in the previous two steps, the barriers can be people oriented, cultural, communicational, administrative, or organizational. The more barriers that need to be overcome, the less chance the idea has of being successful. In addition, not all barriers and obstacles are equal. Some barriers and obstacles are almost insurmountable, whereas others are easily overcome. For example, if the senior manager does not like a particular idea, implementing it is almost insurmountable. On the other hand, if the barrier is just paperwork, then by completing the paperwork effectively, the barrier can be overcome.

- **Obtainable.** Ideas that are easy to implement are more obtainable than ideas that are difficult to implement. The difficulty can be lack of competency, the amount of resources and time to implement it, or if the implementation team does not have the motivation to successfully implement the idea.

- **Effective.** Effectiveness is the number of workdays that can be reduced by implementing the idea. If the number of workdays reduced is significant, the implemented idea will be more effective. A less-effective idea is one that might only eliminate a part of a single workday from software testing. Ideas from which no estimate can be made for the number of workdays that can be reduced should not be considered effective.

Obviously, other criteria affect whether an idea is doable. However, the preceding four criteria are most commonly associated with effective ideas.

Identifying Implementables via Time Compression

Ultimately the decision about what is implemented to compress testing time must be based on the judgment of the agile implementation team. The team has knowledge of the software testing process and the IT organization. They should be motivated to do the job, and responsible for the success of the effort. However, many organizations use a process that may help in determining which are the better ideas for implementation.

This process uses the four criteria previously mentioned: user acceptance, barrier free, attainability, and effectiveness. By using a simple scoring system, organizations can score an idea based on these four criteria; that score will help determine how doable an idea is.

The recommended scoring system is to allocate a maximum of three points for each of the four criteria. The agile implementation team evaluates each criterion on a scale of 0 to 3. For a specific idea, 3 is the most desirable state of the criteria, and a 0 is an unacceptable state for the criteria. For each idea, the score for each of the four criteria should be multiplied. Multiplication is used rather than addition because when you multiply by 0 (zero), you eliminate any idea that is awarded a 0 in any of the four criteria.

Listed here is a scoring guide for the four criteria:

- **Criteria 1: User acceptability.** Acceptability will be evaluated on the stakeholder's four quadrants. The most significant stake among the stakeholders must be determined. This does not mean who is in what stake, but the desired stake by the majority of the stakeholders.

SCORE	HOW THE SCORE IS ALLOCATED
0	Stakeholders want to stop it from happening
1	Stakeholders will let it happen
2	Stakeholders will help it happen
3	Stakeholders will make it happen

- **Criteria 2: Barrier free.** Barrier/obstacles need to be classified as major or minor. A major barrier/obstacle is one with little probability of overcoming the barrier, or it would take extensive effort to overcome the barrier/obstacle. A minor barrier is one that can be overcome by the team. The determination of the score for barrier free is as follows:

SCORE	HOW THE SCORE IS ALLOCATED
0	Two or more major barriers
1	One major barrier or three minor barriers
2	One to two minor barriers
3	No barriers

- **Criteria 3: Obtainable.** The agile implementation team has to decide on how obtainable the idea is. The easier it is to obtain or implement, the higher the score. Based on the size of the organization and the skill sets of the implementers, the difficulty to implement should be placed into one of four groups.

SCORE	HOW THE SCORE IS ALLOCATED
0	Very difficult to implement
1	Difficult to implement
2	Some difficulty to implement
3	Easy to implement

- **Criteria 4: Effectiveness.** Effectiveness should be measured on the estimated reduction in workdays needed to test a project. The more "compression" that occurs, the higher the score. The agile implementation team must estimate for each idea how much that idea will compress delivery time. The percent of reduction should be based on the total software testing effort. For example, if it takes 100 workdays to write a test plan, a 2 percent reduction is a two-workday reduction. The scoring for effectiveness is as follows:

SCORE	HOW THE SCORE IS ALLOCATED
0	No known reduction or reduction cannot be estimated
1	Less than 1 workday reduction
2	1 to 3 workday reduction
3	Over 3 day workday reduction

To complete the scoring, the agile implementation team should first list the high-priority improvement ideas developed in Steps 1 through 3 and post them to Work Paper 24-23. For each idea, they should then determine the score for the four criteria used to select an improvement idea for implementation. These four individual criteria scores are multiplied to obtain a doable score. The result will be an overall score between 0 and 81 (zero meaning the idea will be discarded, and 81 is the best possible idea identified through performing Steps 1 through 3).

At the end of this process, the ideas for compressing the software testing process would be ranked from 0 to 81 based on the actual scores. The idea getting the highest overall doable score should be considered the first idea to implement. The idea with the second highest score should be the second idea to implement.

You need to recognize that this selection process is not statistically valid. It includes judgment, but it does help rank the ideas by the probability of success. Obviously, a score of 27 may not be significantly different from a score of 24. However, the score of 24 would be significantly different from a score of 54.

The purpose of this selection process is to help the agile implementation team select the best overall idea for implementation. They should look at the ideas with the highest overall doable score as the ones they should select first for implementation. However, judgment would still apply, and one with a slightly lower score might be determined the better one for implementation even though it has a lower effectiveness score than the idea with the highest score.

After the ideas have been selected, a plan needs to be developed for implementation. It is generally recommended that a single idea be implemented. Then its results are evaluated before the next idea is implemented. This assumes the ideas can be implemented in a relatively short time span. Another advantage to implementing ideas in a series rather than many simultaneously is that it makes it easier for the software testing staff to assimilate the change and support it.

Prioritizing Implementables

A scoring process that ranks implementables is an effective way to select ideas. However, the agile implementation team may want to prioritize the better ideas. Prioritization might prove beneficial in jumpstarting the agile software testing process, by implementing the ideas that could quickly add some agility to the existing test process.

Three sets of guidelines are provided to the agile implementation team to help identify the best doable ideas. These are as follows:

- **The top-six best testing process workbench improvements.** If it is determined that the best approach to achieving agility in a software testing process is to remove variability from the software testing process workbenches, these six ideas should be selected first.

- **The top-six idea categories for use in building an agile testing process.** If the agile implementation team believes that the best approach to add agility to the software testing process is to focus on the environment in which testers perform work, these six categories will help place ideas in the category ranked highest by the agile implementation team (see Table 24-1). To use these guidelines, the categories must be ranked from one through six in a sequence the team believes will best achieve agility in the software testing process. The team should work on the top-ranked categories first. To do this, the ideas scored in sequence of doability need to be cross-referenced to the six categories.

Table 24-1 Top Six for Compressing Software Testing Delivery Time

1	Remove non-essential tasks from the software testing critical plan.
2	Reduce rework if it occurs frequently in a workbench activity.
3	Verify the entrance criteria before starting a workbench activity.
4	Verify the exit criteria before starting a workbench activity.
5	Move testing activities to the front end of software testing.
6	Substitute an in-house best practice for a less effective work practice.

Because these have been discussed throughout this book, they are not described individually.

■ **The top-ten approaches effective for building an agile testing process.** If the majority of the test agility team wants to go back to the basics, these concepts should be their implementation focus (see Table 24-2). To do this, the team needs to rank the ten approaches from 1 to 10 and then focus on the highest-rated approaches first.

Because these approaches are discussed extensively in this book, they are not individually described.

Table 24-2 Top Ten Approaches for Building an Agile Testing Process

	CONCEPT	RANK
1	Eliminate the readiness barriers to building an agile testing process	
2	Minimize process variability	
3	Identify and use the best testing practices	
4	Expand the tester's role to test needs, not just specifications	
5	Restrict test process compliance activities to those activities proven to be effective	
6	Bypass the barriers to building an agile testing process	
7	Incorporate the agile testing process into the existing IT culture	
8	Build the agile testing process by performing the most doable tasks first	
9	Identify and improve the flow of information	
10	Develop and follow a plan to build the agile testing process	

Documenting Approaches

If the agile implementation team determines that it wants to apply judgment to the scored implementables, they should document the basis of that selection process. Work Paper 24-24 can be used for that purpose. To complete this work paper, the following needs to be documented:

- **Implementable improvement idea ranked by doable score.** All of the implementables scored high on Work Paper 24-23 should be transposed to Work Paper 24-24. In the transcription, they should be ranked. Note that the team may decide to eliminate some of the ideas in this transition; they should also eliminate those low-scoring ideas that do not appear to have the probability of making a significant change to the software testing process.

- **Prioritization considerations.** In determining priority beyond the doable score, the team should indicate the basis on which they want to prioritize a specific implementable. This step has provided three categories of guidelines for making this determination. However, the team should feel free to use other methods for prioritization.

- **Prioritization rank.** It is suggested that the team rank ideas for prioritization into these three categories:

  - **High.** Those ideas they will implement first.

  - **Medium.** Those ideas that will be implemented after the high-priority ideas.

  - **Low.** Ideas that may or may not be implemented.

Quality Control Checklist

Work Paper 24-25 is a quality control checklist for Step 6. The investigation should focus on determining whether a specific aspect of the step was performed correctly or incorrectly.

The agile implementation team should review these questions as a team. A consensus Yes or No response should be determined. "No" responses should be explained and investigated. If the investigation indicates that the particular aspect of the step was incorrectly performed, it should be repeated. (Note: Some teams prefer to review the quality control checklist before they begin the step to give them a fuller understanding of the intention of this step.)

Conclusion

Action must be taken if the time required to build software is to be reduced. The action proposed is to select and implement doable ideas to reduce time. This step has provided a process to help the agile implementation team determine which idea to implement first. After that idea has been identified and implemented, the agile implementation team will come back to this process and select another idea for implementation. Thus, the time required for testing software will continue to compress.

Step 7: Develop and Execute an Implementation Plan

A software testing organization can use three approaches to achieve agile software testing. The first is to acquire the agile testing process from a supplier. The second is to build the agile testing process from the bottom up. The third is to convert the current software testing process to an agile process.

I am unaware of any agile testing processes on the market; therefore, that approach won't work. Building an agile testing process from the bottom up is a large, time-consuming, and risky project. Because IT management in general has not been willing to invest large sums of money in the software testing processes, it is unlikely they will support the time and resources needed to build such a process. Experience has shown that it normally costs ten times as much to deploy a new process as it does to build it. Thus, the bottom-up approach would barely get IT management's support or enough support and resources to make it work. The bottom line is that the only realistic and effective approach to acquiring an agile testing process is to go through a continuous change to the current testing process to build more and more agility into that process.

An old but true saying is "If you fail to plan, plan to fail." Having a good idea to compress software testing time is not enough. That idea must be put into action. A good plan will help facilitate action.

The process for planning to compress testing time should be viewed as a project. Thus, the planning process used for software projects is applicable to the planning process to compress software testing time. However, because the compression project is normally a small project, the planning does not have to be nearly as comprehensive. This step provides a simplified, but effective, planning process for implementing an idea to compress software testing time.

Planning

The planning process should start with the assumption that the process of building agility into the software testing process will take time. A pilot project should be used because piloting means there will be an opportunity to evaluate and "kill" the compressing effort. The effort you start should be continuous. Everyone involved in a compressing process must buy in to this concept.

Each idea to be implemented involves all of the four PDCA (Plan, Do, Check, Act) components discussed in detail in Chapter 1. If the implemented idea does not meet its objective, the PDCA cycle may have to be repeated based on the action taken to improve and expand/modify the implemented idea.

Implementing Ideas

In the proposed plan implementation, we use much of the information gathered in Steps 1 through 6. Using this information, the plan will involve modifying the testing environment and the workbench(es) involved in implementing the idea. For example, if the idea relates to the test plan, the implemented idea will modify the test planning workbench. The components of a workbench can be deleted, modified, or expanded (i.e., the input criteria, do procedures, check procedures, skills competency, tools, and exit criteria). Addressing management commitment and overcoming impediments may require changes to the IT management process.

Work Paper 24-26 is used to document the implementation work plan. The work plan should include the following:

- **Improvement idea.** The name of the idea (from the idea list) that is to be implemented.

- **Objective.** The objective to be accomplished by implementing the idea. (Note: This should be stated as a measurable objective.) In most instances, the measurable objective is the number of workdays to be compressed by implementing this idea. (Note: In evaluating the ideas for selection for implementation, an estimate has already been made of the number of workdays that could be compressed by using this idea.) If the objective is focused on the management process, the objective is a prerequisite to implementing an idea.

- **Current results.** This is normally the number of workdays now required to complete the involved workbench (this comes from Step 2). Note that if the software testing process is immature, the current results most likely will be expressed in average days, including the variance associated with that workbench.

- **Expected results.** This is the number of workdays to complete the task after the time-compression idea has been implemented. The variance between current and expected results should be the same as the measurable objective.

- **Method of measurement.** The method is typically workdays. However, if there is a significant variance in the average workdays for the workbench, the method of measurement may need to account for that variance. For example, the method of measurement may measure four or five projects to get the new average and the new variance.

- **Work tasks.** Two types of work tasks are involved. One is to adjust the obstacles/barriers associated with implementing this idea. The other type of work task is the actual tasks to implement the improvement idea. The barriers and obstacles that need to be overcome will be those identified in Steps 4 and 5, which are applicable to this specific improvement idea. (Note: The work papers included in Steps 4 and 5 have also identified how to address the barrier/obstacle. Thus, the task is the process to address the barrier/obstacle from the Step 4 and 5 work papers.)

The task to implement the improvement normally involves modifying a workbench. These may add new Do or Check procedures to the workbench, may change the entrance and exit criteria, which may affect the amount of rework required and may involve additional training for the individuals performing the workbench. It may also add a new tool to the workbench.

The changed workbench should change the work processes used in that segment of the software testing process. Modifications to the organization's work processes must be coordinated with the standards committee/process engineering committee (i.e., the group responsible for defining, implementing, and modifying IT work processes).

- **Resources.** The resources to perform a task will be the people's time and any other resources involved in implementing the work task. Normally, it will just be the people's time, but it may require some test time if automated procedures are modified.

- **Time frame.** The time frame for starting the work task and the target completion date for the work task should also be documented as part of the work plan.

Preparing the Work Plan

The work plan as defined in Work Paper 24-26 should be executed. The plan as written should be followed. If the plan is being executed, the actual start date and the actual completion date should be recorded. If the resources were inadequate or too extensive, a note should be made in the Resources column to indicate the actual resources expended.

Checking the Results

When the work plan is complete, the actual results from the improved workbench should be measured and recorded. The method of measurement in the work plan should be used to record the actual results. If the actual results approximate the expected results, the improvement idea should be considered successful. If the actual results exceeded the expected results, the improvement idea was very successful. However, if the actual results are less than the current results, the implementation idea can be considered unsuccessful. In that instance, an assessment needs to be made as to whether the idea was effectively implemented, whether some modification to the idea can be made to make it successful, or whether the idea should be dropped for now and a new improvement idea be implemented.

Taking Action

If the results are successful, action should be taken to make a permanent modification to the workbench to incorporate the improvement idea. If the improvement idea was not successful, the action can be to modify the plan, re-execute the plan, or not to implement the improvement idea in a workbench. At that point, the team can either re-execute the PDCA cycle using a modified improvement idea, or implement the next improvement idea.

You must identify a leader to implement the plan. Ideally, that leader would be a member of the agile implementation team; however, if the IT organization has a process to change processes, the plan should be led by someone in that improvement process.

Requisite Resources

Time-compression efforts should be considered projects. Therefore, they need to be budgeted and scheduled like any other project. However, the budgetary resources for implementing these projects can derive from any of the following:

1. **Change the current test budget.** The idea implementation costs can be charged to the testing project for which the implementers are currently assigned. The assumption being that if the idea works, that project's workdays will be reduced and that reduction should pay for the time compression project.

2. **Change the resources to an appropriate IT budget category.** IT management can make the decision that time compression projects are worthwhile. They can review their budget and make a decision for an appropriate budgetary account to record the resources. If resources are budgeted for building/improving work processes, that budgetary account is the logical one to record time compression projects. Another potential budgetary account is training.

3. **Establish a special budgetary account for time compression.** IT management can allocate a certain percentage of their budget for time-compression projects. If they do this, they can have project personnel develop a test process work improvement plan and submit it to IT management for approval. Thus, staff members from different projects can become involved in suggesting and implementing ideas to compress software testing delivery time. IT management can control the work by approving the implementation work plan proposals. (Note: Some IT organizations allocate 2 to 5 percent of their testing budget for testing process improvement projects such as building an agile testing process.)

Quality Control Checklist

Work paper 24-27 is a quality control checklist for Step 7. The investigation should focus on determining whether a specific aspect of the step was performed correctly or incorrectly.

The agile implementation team should review these questions as a team. A consensus Yes or No response should be determined. "No" responses should be explained and investigated. If the investigation indicates that the particular aspect of the step was incorrectly performed, it should be repeated. (Note: Some teams prefer to review the quality control checklist before they begin the step to give them a fuller understanding of the intention of this step.)

Conclusion

An idea is not valuable until it is implemented. This step has examined the process for taking the highest-priority recommended idea and developing a plan to implement that idea. The plan needs to involve both modifying the work tasks of the affected workbench, and addressing any obstacles/barriers that might impede the implementation of the improvement idea. The process proposed is the "Plan, Do, Check, Act" cycle. At the end of this cycle, action is taken on whether to make the idea permanent, whether to modify and re-execute a revised plan for the implementation idea, or whether to eliminate the idea and move on to the next high-priority improvement idea.

Summary

Agile processes are more effective than highly structured processes. Because agile processes seem to work best with small teams, and because most software testing projects are performed by small teams, testing is an ideal candidate to incorporate agility into their processes.

The process proposed in this chapter was built on these time-proven concepts:

- It is far better to change the current process than to acquire/build and implement an entirely new process.

- Focusing on time compression (i.e., reducing the time required to perform a task) has, as its by-product, testing effectiveness and process agility.

- The quickest way to compress time in a testing process is to reduce process variability.

- It is more important to determine that ideas are implementable than to select the best idea, which may not be doable.

- Continuous small improvements are superior to a few major improvements.

- Don't make any improvements until you know that the organization, and those involved, will support the improvement (i.e., don't begin a task that you know has a high probability of failure).

WORK PAPER 24-1 Define the Timeline Software Testing Workbenches

	WORKBENCH 1	WORKBENCH 2	WORKBENCH 3	WORKBENCH 4	WORKBENCH 5
Input(s)					
Workbench Name					
Workbench Objective(s)					
Output(s)					
Approximate Estimated Workdays Timeline					

WORK PAPER 24-2 Workbench Completion Calendar Day Timeline

Workbench Name:

Project Timelines:

Project(s)	Start Date	Date "Do" Procedures Completed First Time	Date Workbench Completed	Minimal Timeline Calendar Days	Actual Timeline Calendar Days

Average No Rework Calendar Days Timeline:	No Rework Calendar Days Variability:
Average Actual Calendar Days Timeline:	Actual Calendar Days Variability:

WORK PAPER 24-3   Completion Timeline Variability Analysis

Workbench Name:

Variability Analyzed:	Below Average		Above Average
	Source of Variability		
Workbench Component	**Yes**	**No**	**Root Cause**
Input Criteria			
Checking Input Criteria			
Do Procedures			
Check Procedures			
Toolbox			
Worker Competency			
Internal Rework			
External Rework			
Exit Criteria			
Other (specify)			

WORK PAPER 24-4 Software Testing Completion Timeline Process

	Ideas for Completion Timeline Improvement	Reference Number	Priority	
			High	Low
1				
2				
3				
4				
5				
6				
7				
8				
9				
10				
11				
12				
13				
14				
15				

WORK PAPER 24-5   Quality Control Checklist for Step 1

	YES	NO	COMMENTS
1. Has an agile implementation team been established?			
2. If so, are the members of the team respected individuals in the IT organization?			
3. If so, does the team comprise no less than two members and no more than five members?			
4. Does the agile implementation team understand the relationship of process variability to performing processes effectively?			
5. Does the agile implementation team understand that the skill sets of the individual performing a professional process are assumed and not incorporated into the software testing process?			
6. Does the agile implementation team understand that a process is broken up into steps/tasks?			
7. Does the agile implementation team understand the concept of a process workbench and the various components in the workbench?			
8. Does the agile implementation team understand the time-compression workbench?			
9. Has the agile implementation team identified the key workbenches in the software testing process?			
10. Has the agile implementation team eliminated from consideration those software testing workbenches that do not affect the time to complete the software testing process?			
11. Have the inputs and outputs for each identified workbench been defined?			
12. Have the objectives for each identified workbench been stated in a manner in which the results are measurable?			
13. Is there general consensus on the approximate estimated completion timeline for each of the key workbenches?			
14. Has a reasonable number of workbenches been selected to provide reliable information on the completion timeline for that workbench? (Note: This assumes a reasonable process is used for selecting the workbenches for investigation)			

WORK PAPER 24-5   *(continued)*

	YES	NO	COMMENTS
15. For the workbenches selected for completion time analysis, has a reasonable number of projects been identified and the calendar dates for those projects been documented?			
16. Have the projects for the identified workbenches that are significantly better or significantly worse than the average calendar days been identified?			
17. For each workbench where projects have been identified that were implemented more efficiently than the average timeline, has a variability completion timeline analysis been performed?			
18. For each workbench where projects have been identified that were implemented less efficiently than the average timeline, has a variability completion timeline analysis been performed?			
19. For each of the workbench components for the identified projects, have the source of variability and the probable cause been determined?			
20. Has a reasonable process been followed to identify ideas for completion time improvement?			
21. For those ideas identified for completion timeline improvement, has the agile implementation team assigned a high or low priority to that idea?			
22. Are measurements and analysis performed for testing workbenches executed for software project of equal size and complexity?			

WORK PAPER 24-6   Criteria Recommended to Measure Software Testing Effectiveness and Efficiency

Criteria	Description	Measuring		Rank
		Efficiency	Effectiveness	

WORK PAPER 24-7 Measuring Software Testing Effectiveness/Efficiency

Software Project Name:

Efficiency Criteria	Method to Calculate Criteria Score	Weight	Efficiency Score
		Total 100%	

Total Efficiency Score

Effectiveness Criteria	Method to Calculate Criteria Score	Weight	Effectiveness Score
		Total 100%	

Total Effectiveness Score

WORK PAPER 24-8   Recording Efficiency and Effectiveness Scores

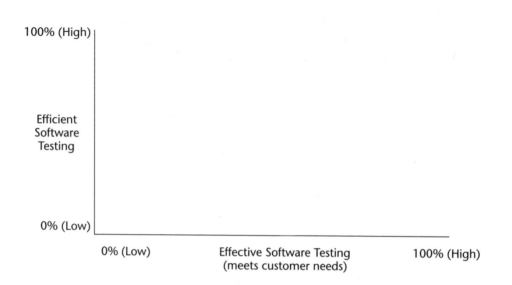

WORK PAPER 24-9   Potential Best Practices for Compressing Software Testing Completion Time

Best Practice	Description	Project Used In	Application Efficiency	Application Effectiveness

WORK PAPER 24-10   Best Practices Shopping List

	Best Practices for Time Improvement	Reference #	Priority High	Low
1				
2				
3				
4				
5				
6				
7				
8				
9				
10				
11				
12				
13				
14				
15				

WORK PAPER 24-11   Quality Control Checklist for Step 2

	YES	NO	COMMENTS
1. Have the roles and responsibilities of the testers been identified?			
2. Does an appropriate relationship exist between the customer/ user, project development team, testers, and IT management to ensure that the project is tested correctly?			
3. Are the quality factors understood by the agile implementation team?			
4. Are the quality factors applicable to the projects being tested in your IT organization?			
5. Are the quality factors complete for assessing the quality of the projects in your IT organization, or are additional factors needed?			
6. Is the concept of trade-offs understood by the agile implementation team?			
7. In each software development project is someone responsible for making trade-offs? (It may be more than one group, depending on the type of trade-off.)			
8. Does the time-compression team understand the type of trade-offs that exist in all software testing projects?			
9. Does the software testing team understand the impact of not making the trade-offs during software testing?			
10. Does the agile implementation team understand the criteria that can be used to evaluate effectiveness and efficiency of a software testing project?			
11. Does the agile implementation team understand the software testing capability barrier chart?			
12. Does the agile implementation team understand why a capability barrier exists, and why it is difficult to break through that barrier?			
13. Has the agile implementation team developed an inventory of criteria they believe will be applicable for measuring testing efficiency and effectiveness?			
14. Has the agile enhancement team selected 3–5 criteria to evaluate projects for efficiency?			

(continues)

WORK PAPER 24-11   *(continued)*

	YES	NO	COMMENTS
15. Has the agile enhancement team selected 3–5 criteria to evaluate projects for effectiveness?			
16. Has the agile implementation team determined how they will create a score for each criterion?			
17. Has the agile implementation team weighted the criteria for both effectiveness and efficiency?			
18. Has the agile implementation team developed efficiency and effectiveness scores for a reasonable number of projects?			
19. Are the projects selected by the agile implementation team representative of the type of testing projects undertaken by the IT organization?			
20. Has the agile implementation team posted the scored projects to the capability barrier chart?			
21. Using the capability barrier chart, has the agile implementation team identified some best practices for both efficiency and effectiveness?			
22. Has the agile implementation team identified which of those best practices they believe has the greatest probability for time compression?			
23. Have the selected best practices been recorded on the improvement shopping list work paper?			

WORK PAPER 24-12   Software Testing Process Self-Assessment

Criteria 1: Management Commitment to Software Testing

	YES	NO	COMMENTS
1. Does management devote as much personal attention and involvement to software testing as it does for software development?			
2. Does management understand the challenges and impediments it will face in moving their IT organization to a quality software testing culture?			
3. Does IT management demonstrate its belief in the software testing process by allocating adequate resources to ensure the testing process is used effectively?			
4. Does management support processes such as management checkpoints, software reviews, inspections, checklists, and other methods that support implementing software testing principles and concepts in day-to-day work?			
5. Does management, on a regular basis, make decisions that reinforce and reward software testing initiatives, such as ensuring that quality will not be compromised for schedule and budget constraints? (Note: This does not mean that requirements and standards will not be negotiated; it means there will be agreement on quality if it conflicts with schedule or budget.)			
Number of Yes Responses			

(continues)

WORK PAPER 24-12   *(continued)*

Criteria 2: Software Testing Environment

	YES	NO	COMMENTS
1. Does the IT organization have a software testing policy that clearly defines the responsibilities and objectives as the software testing function?			
2. Are the software testers organizationally independent from the software developers, except for unit testing?			
3. Does the IT organization allot as many resources for acquisition and development of software testing process and tools as it does for software development processes and tools?			
4. Does the IT organization have a detailed plan to promote and improve software testing throughout the IT organization?			
5. Does the IT organization have an educational plan for all staff members in software testing principles, concepts, and other methods; and is that plan operational?			
Number of Yes Responses			

Criteria 3: Process to Do Work

	YES	NO	COMMENTS
1. Are there formal work processes outlining the detailed step-by-step procedures to perform all software testing projects within the IT organization?			
2. If so, are those work processes comprised of a policy, standards, and procedures to both do and check work?			
3. Does management both enforce compliance to work processes and reward compliance to work processes?			
4. Are the work processes developed and/or approved by those that will use the work processes in their day-to-day work?			
5. Are IT staff members hired to use specific work processes, and then trained sufficiently so that they can perform those work processes to a high level of competence?			
Number of Yes Responses			

WORK PAPER 24-12   *(continued)*

Criteria 4: Processes to Check Work

	YES	NO	COMMENTS
1. Are check procedures developed in a formal manner for each work process?			
2. Is the combination of the work and check procedures integrated so that they are included in the project budget, and executed in a manner so that both become part of the day-to-day work of the IT staff?			
3. Are the check procedures developed commensurate with the degree of risk associated with not performing the "do work procedures" correctly?			
4. Are the results of the check procedures provided to the appropriate decision-makers so they can make any needed changes to the software in order to ensure they will meet the customer's needs?			
5. Are the workers adequately trained in the performance of the check procedures so that they can perform them in a highly competent manner?			
Number of Yes Responses			

Criteria 5: Continuous Improvement to the Software Testing Process

	YES	NO	COMMENTS
1. Is information regarding defects associated with the software testing products and processes regularly gathered, recorded, and summarized?			
2. Is an individual or an organizational unit such as quality assurance charged with the responsibility of maintaining defect information and initiating quality improvement efforts?			
3. Does the IT budget include the money and staff necessary to perform continuous quality improvement?			
4. Is there a process in place that establishes a baseline for the current process, and then measures the variance from that baseline once the processes are improved?			
5. Are resources and programs in place to adequately train workers to effectively use the new and improved work processes?			
Number of Yes Responses			

WORK PAPER 24-13   Software Testing Process Assessment Footprint Chart

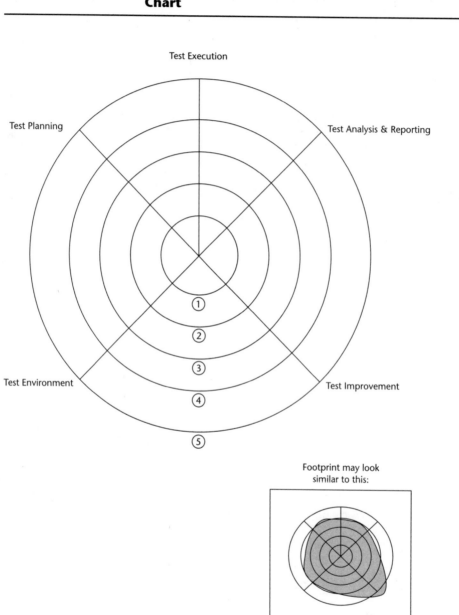

WORK PAPER 24-14   Delivery Timeline Process Improvement Shopping List

	Ideas for Delivery Timeline Improvement	Reference #	Priority High	Priority Low
1				
2				
3				
4				
5				
6				
7				
8				
9				
10				
11				
12				
13				
14				
15				

WORK PAPER 24-15 Quality Control Checklist for Step 3

	YES	NO	COMMENTS
1. Is the software testing process self-assessment being performed by the agile implementation team?			
2. Does the agile implementation team know the software testing process?			
3. Does the agile implementation team know management's attitude about the use of the software testing process (e.g., rewarding for use of the process)?			
4. Does the agile implementation team know the type of support a tester would get if they use the software testing process (e.g., type of training, who can answer the questions, etc.)?			
5. Did the agile implementation team follow the self-assessment process as described in this chapter?			
6. Does the agile implementation team understand the meaning of Yes and No responses?			
7. For items in which the agile implementation team could not arrive at a consensus, was a No response given?			
8. Did the agile implementation team prepare the software testing process footprint and then discuss and draw conclusions about that footprint?			
9. Was each category item that had a No response evaluated as a potential improvement idea to compress the software testing delivery timeline?			

WORK PAPER 24-16   Stakeholder Analysis

Stakeholder (Name of Function)	Current Stake	Reason(s)	Desired Stake	How to Address

WORK PAPER 24-17   Barrier/Obstacles

Barrier/Obstacle	Source	Root Cause	How to Address

WORK PAPER 24-18   Barrier/Obstacle ("Why-Why") Analysis

Job results not known

(why did it occur)

Challanged boss

(why did it occur)

Poor Performance Appraisal   Personal conflict

(Barrier/Obstacle)   (why did it occur)

Different work styles

(why did it occur)

Lack of planning

(why did it occur)

WORK PAPER 24-19 Quality Control Checklist for Step 4

	YES	NO	COMMENTS
1. Does the agile implementation team recognize the impact that a barrier/obstacle can have on implementing a time compression idea?			
2. Does the agile implementation team understand the various views a stakeholder can have on a proposed time compression idea?			
3. Has the agile implementation team identified all of the potential stakeholders in compressing the software testing delivery time?			
4. Has the agile implementation team determined which stakeholders have to be individually identified and which stakeholders can be identified by job position?			
5. Has the current stake for each stakeholder been identified?			
6. Has the agile implementation team defined what they believe is the reason the person holds that specific stake?			
7. Has the desired stake for each individual/job position been determined?			
8. Has the agile implementation team developed a solution on how to address moving an individual from a current stake to a desired stake?			
9. Have the barriers associated with staff competency been identified?			
10. Have the barriers associated with individual's red flags/hot buttons been identified?			
11. Does the agile implementation team understand that the individual looks at an idea from the viewpoint of "What's In It For Me?"			
12. Have the administrative/organizational barriers been identified?			
13. Does the agile implementation team understand how to determine the root cause of each administrative/ organizational barrier?			
14. Has a reasonable solution been developed for each root cause to address that root cause should it become necessary?			
15. Is the agile implementation team in agreement that the important people, administrative, and organizational barriers that can affect time compression projects have been identified?			

WORK PAPER 24-20   Cultural Barrier Work Paper

Current IT management culture

Barrier posed by culture

What can be done in current culture

Desired culture for time compression

How to address cultural barriers

WORK PAPER 24-21   Information and Communication Flow Barrier

Information Flow

Information Needed	Importance	Should Be Communicated		Barrier	How to Address Barrier
		By	To		

WORK PAPER 24-22   Quality Control Checklist for Step 5

	YES	NO	COMMENTS
1. Does the agile implementation team have a good understanding of how an IT management culture affects the operation of the IT organization?			
2. Does the agile implementation team understand the five different cultures that can exist in an IT organization?			
3. Did the agile implementation team reach consensus on the current IT organization's management culture?			
4. Given the discussion of why IT management would want to keep their current culture, can the agile implementation team identify barriers posed by the current IT culture?			
5. Can the agile implementation team convert those barriers into positive statements of how time compression solutions must be implemented?			
6. Has the agile implementation team determined whether or not a different culture would be more advantageous in implementing the proposed time compression solutions?			
7. For each of the barriers identified, has the agile implementation team determined whether those barriers can be adequately addressed in implementing time compression solutions?			
8. For those barriers that the agile implementation team believes can be adequately addressed in the time compression solutions, have they determined a potential solution for addressing those culture barriers?			
9. Does the agile implementation team recognize the importance of information and communication in building an agile software testing process?			
10. Does the agile implementation team understand the three components of effective communication?			
11. Has the team developed a lines of communication graph for software testing?			
12. Has the graph been analyzed to determine: a. Information missing from the graph b. Information not communicated to the right individual			

(continues)

WORK PAPER 24-22 *(continued)*

	YES	NO	COMMENTS
13. Has the team determined the importance of each communication and developed a communication score for each individual/function identified on the communication graph?			
14. Has the team studied and understood the guidelines for information and communication?			
15. Has the team identified the barriers for effective communication in the performance of software testing?			

WORK PAPER 24-23   Software Testing Time Compression Idea

Improvement Idea	User Acceptable	× Barrier Free	× Attainability	× Effectiveness	= Doable Score

WORK PAPER 24-24   Establishing the Priority of Doable Ideas for Jumpstarting an Agile Software Testing Process

Implementable Improvement Idea Ranked by Doable Score	Prioritization Considerations	Prioritization Rank		
		High	Medium	Low

WORK PAPER 24-25   Quality Control Checklist for Step 6

	YES	NO	COMMENTS
1. Has the agile implementation team agreed upon a list of improvement ideas they will consider?			
2. Does the agile implementation team believe that an algorithm to score each idea from best to worst would assist them in selecting the best ideas?			
3. Does the agile implementation team understand the four criteria proposed for the selection for the best idea?			
4. Does the agile implementation team understand and accept the 0 to 3 scoring method for each of the four criteria?			
5. Has the agile implementation team scored each idea using the selection process criteria?			
6. Has the agile implementation team then ranked all the ideas from highest score to lowest score?			
7. Does the agile implementation team believe that the best idea is among the highest scoring ideas?			
8. Has the agile implementation team reviewed the few highest scoring ideas to determine which of those they believe are the best regardless of the final score?			
9. Has the agile implementation team reviewed the top six ideas for compressing software testing time to determine if the idea they selected is consistent with the top six?			
10. Has the agile implementation team agreed upon one idea for implementation?			
11. If the agile implementation team wants to do further prioritization to select doable ideas to implement, have team members determined how they will do that additional prioritization?			

WORK PAPER 24-26 Software Testing Time Compression Tactical Work Plan

Objective to Accomplish:

Improvement Idea:

Objective	Current Results	Expected Results	Actual Results	Method of Measurement

Work Plan

Time Frame

Tasks	Resources	Start Date	Target Completion Date

WORK PAPER 24-27   Quality Control Checklist for Step 7

	YES	NO	COMMENTS
1. Has the agile implementation team gathered all the appropriate information related to a selected improvement idea from Steps 1 through 6?			
2. Does the agile implementation team have a project planning process that it can use to implement the improvement idea?			
3. Does the agile implementation team understand the "Plan-Do-Check-Act" cycle and its relationship to planning and implementing a time compression improvement idea?			
4. Can the agile implementation team express the improvement objective in measurable terms?			
5. Does the agile implementation team know the current results from the workbench that is designated to be improved?			
6. Has the agile implementation team agreed upon a method for measuring the expected results from implementing the time compression idea?			
7. Do the work tasks include both tasks to modify the workbench and tasks to address the obstacle/barrier that may impede implementing the improvement idea?			
8. Has the agile implementation team been authorized the resources needed to implement the improvement idea?			
9. After implementation, have the actual results from implementation been documented?			
10. Was a reasonable process used to record the actual results?			
11. If the actual results indicate a successful implementation of an improvement idea, has the agile implementation team taken the action necessary to make that improvement idea in part of the affected workbench?			

Index

A

acceptance criteria, post-implementation
analysis, 578
acceptance testing
administrative procedures, 498
concerns, 493–494
data components, 492
execution, 499
functionality requirements, 497
input, 495–496
interface quality requirements, 497
objectives, 492–493
overview, 491
people components, 492
performance requirements, 497
plan contents, 498–499
programming testing, 324
project description contents, 498
RAD testing, 637
rules, 492
software quality requirements, 497
structure components, 492
tester roles, 44
use cases, 500–503
user responsibilities, 498
validation, 221
V-concept testing, 158–159

work papers
acceptance criteria, 527
acceptance plan form creation,
544–545
automated application criteria,
566–567
change control forms, 546
checklist, 550–551
data change forms, 547–548
deletion instructions, 538–539
installation phase, 531
inventory material, 552–553
production change instructions,
536–537
program change form completion,
540–541, 549
program change history, 534–535
quality control checklist, 560–563
recovery planning data, 532–533
system boundary diagram, 528
system problem form completion,
542–543
test cases, 530
training checklist form completion,
558–559
training failure notification, 568–569
training module form completion,
556–557

acceptance testing *(continued)*
training plan form completion,
554–555
training quality control checklist,
564–565
use cases, 504–507, 529
workbench concept, 494
access control
best practices, 850
configuration management, 602
data warehouse testing, 770–771, 777
risk assessment, 216
test factors, 41–42
unauthorized, 766
Web-based systems testing, 803
access denied
security testing, 223
verification testing, 301, 319
accidental versus intentional losses,
738–739
accuracy, best practices, 849
acquisition, system processing, 76
activities, Project Status reports, 469
ad hoc process level, client/server
systems testing, 616–617
adequacy evaluation, software security
testing, 761
administration
administrative components
acceptance testing, 498
CM (configuration management),
602–603
test plan development, 250–251
barriers, 865–866
development activities, 753
agile testing process
DRE (Defect Removal Efficiency), 822
flexibility, 820–821
importance of, 819–820
mature processes, 821
MTBF (mean time between failures),
822–823
MTTF (mean time to failure), 822–823

MTTR (mean time to repair), 822–823
objective-driven processes, 821
quality, 821
team representatives, 820–821
tester agility, 842–843
time-compression efforts
best practices, 825
calendar-day efficient, 823–824
challenges, 824
readiness criteria, 826
solutions to, 825
V-concept testing, 826–827
workbench concept, 834
variability and, 820
work papers, 923–927
algebraic specification, 237
alliance, business innovation, 878
allocation of resources, management
support needs, 51
annual report preparation, 120
applications
internal controls testing, 666–669
risks, verification testing, 304–308
system activities, 752
assessment objectives, post-
implementation analysis, 574–575
assessment questionnaires, baseline
development, 10
assessment teams, baseline
development, 10
asset value, post-implementation
analysis, 579
assistant tool managers, 119
audience criteria, documentation, 179
audit trails
corrective controls, 665
inadequate, 766
programming testing, 327
risk assessment, 216
test factors, 40, 42
validation testing, 435
verification testing, 319
auditors, roles and responsibilities, 6

audits, configuration management, 602
authorization
  cycle control objectives, 675
  internal controls testing, 658
  programming testing, 326
  risk assessment, 215
  test factors, 40, 42
  transactions, 755
  validation testing, 434
  verification testing, 301, 318
  Web-based systems testing, 803
authors, inspection process
    responsibilities, 258
automated applications
  operational fit tests, 697
  operational testing, 522–523
  tools, 104, 221
availability, baseline information, 741
Average Age of Uncorrected Defects by
    Type report, 475
average prioritized objectives, 245
awareness concerns, baseline
    information, 743
axiomatic specification, 238

B
back-end processing, 611, 800
background and reference data, test
    plan development, 251
backup data
  data warehouse testing, 773–774, 778
  recovery testing, 223
balance checks, preventive controls,
    662
bandwidth access, Web-based systems
    testing, 805
barrier identification
  communication barriers
    conflict-resolution methods, 880
    effective communication process,
        882–884
    how to address, 882
    lines of communication, 881
    management support solutions, 883

objectives, understanding consensus
    of, 880
  open channel concept, 884
  quality control, 884
  realistic mechanism solutions, 884
  respect for others, 880
cultural barriers
  business innovation management,
      878
  competencies, 874–876
  discussed, 869
  how to address, 879–880
  manage by fact concept, 876–877
  manage by process concept, 873–874
  management cultures, 870
  people management, 871–872
improvement barriers
  administrative/organizational
      barriers, 865–866
  quality control, 869
  red flag/hot button barriers, 864
  root cause, 866–869
  staff-competency barriers, 865
  stakeholder perspective, 861–864
work papers
  communication barriers, 920–922
  cultural barriers, 919
  stakeholder analysis, 915–918
base case, verification testing, 293
baselines
  accurate and precise information, 741
  analysis, 750
  availability, 741
  awareness concerns, 743
  awareness training, 747
  categories, 739
  collection methods training, 747
  configuration management, 604
  corporate language, adjustments for,
      741
  data collection methods, 744–747
  development
    assessment questionnaires, 10
    assessment teams, 10

baselines *(continued)*
  capabilities assessment, 13–14
  cause-effect diagram, 9
  drivers, 8
  environment assessment, 8
  footprint charts, 10
  implementation procedures, 9
  results assessments, 11–12
  tester competency assessment, 14–16
  verification, 13
  forms completion training, 747–748
  methods, 743
  objectives, 751
  one-time data collection procedures,
    741
  reasons for, 740
  resources protected concerns, 743
  security sources, 740
  status, reporting, 749
  support concerns, 744
  team member selection, 742–743
  training concerns, 743
  what to collect, 740
batch jobs, system processing, 76
batch tests, 248
best practices
  access control, 850
  accuracy, 849
  audits, 850
  capability chart, 847
  communication, 850
  completeness, 849
  consistency, 849
  data commonality, 850
  effectiveness and efficiency measures,
    848–849, 852–854
  error tolerance, 849
  execution efficiency, 850
  expandability, 850
  generality, 850
  identifying from best projects, 854–856
  instrumentation, 850
  machine independence, 850
  modularity, 850
  operability, 850
  operational software, 843
  quality control, 856–857
  quality factors, 843–846
  quality in fact perspective, 843
  quality in perspective, 843
  self-descriptiveness, 850
  simplicity, 850
  storage efficiency, 850
  system independence, 850
  tester agility, 842–843
  time-compression efforts, 825
  traceability, 849
  training, 850
  work papers, 906–908
black box testing
  COTS software testing challenges, 689
  discussed, 69
boundary value analysis tools, 105
branch testing, description of, 239
browser compatibility concerns, Web-
  based systems testing, 800, 805–806
budgets
  administrative/organizational
    barriers, 865
  client/server testing readiness, 614
  efficiency measures, 853
  facts, managing, 162
  inadequate, 39
  people management through, 871
  post-implementation analysis, 578
  Project Status reports, 468–469
  Summary Status reports, 467
business innovation management,
  cultural barriers, 878
business logic techniques
  COTS software testing concerns, 692
  testing guidelines, 67–68
business requirements, methodologies,
  592
business transaction control points,
  software security testing, 755–756

C

caching, Web-based systems testing, 805

calculation correctness, Web-based systems testing, 804

capabilities assessment, baseline development, 13–14

capability chart, best practices, 847

Capability Maturing Model Integrated (CMMI), 596–597, 824

capture/playback tools, 105

cause-effect
  diagram, baseline development, 9
  graphing tools, 105

CBOK (Common Body of Knowledge)
  categories, 127–128
  code of ethics, 125
  continuing education, 125
  discussed, 14–15
  tester competency, 125–126
  work papers
    individual competency evaluation, 149
    new information technology, 148
    project management, 135–138
    security procedure assessment, 146–147
    software controls, 146
    test environment, building, 133–135
    test planning, 138–142
    test status and analysis, 143–144
    test team competency evaluation, 150
    testing principles and concepts, 132–133
    user acceptance testing, 144–145

central computer sites, software security testing, 746

central processors, vulnerabilities, 738

Certified Software Tester. *See* CSTE certificate

champion, barrier/obstacle solution, 868

change characteristics, post-implementation analysis, 576

change control
  development activities, 753
  operational testing, 517–518

change estimation, timelines, 837

change in scope criteria, documentation, 174

change recommendation, tester roles, 44

check procedures
  client/server systems testing, 624
  COTS software testing, 705
  data warehouse testing, 780
  edit checks, 414
  multiplatform environment testing, 726
  operational testing, 522
  organization, 200
  post-implementation analysis, 580
  RAD testing, 642
  results analysis, 482
  software security testing, 762
  test plan development, 262
  validation testing, 439
  variability measures, 834
  verification testing, 330
  Web-based systems testing, 809

checklist
  process preparation, 86
  quality control, 207–209
  testing tactics, 100–101
  tools, 105

CI (configuration identification), 601

clarity of communication, COTS software testing, 700

class, classifying defects by, 258

classification objectives, cycle control objectives, 675

clearness, requirements measures, 594

client/server systems testing
  ad hoc process level, 616–617
  back-end processing, 611
  check procedures, 624
  client needs assessment, 622–623
  concerns, 612–613
  consistent process level, 618–619

client/server systems testing *(continued)*
  footprint chart, 621
  guidelines, 624
  installations, 622
  maturity levels, 615–616
  measured process level, 619–620
  optimized process level, 620–621
  output, 624
  readiness assessment, 614–615, 621
  repeatable process level, 617–618
  security, 622
  work papers
    client data, 627–628
    footprint chart, 631
    quality control checklist, 632
    readiness results, 630
    security, 626–627
    standards, 628–629
    system installation, 625
  workbench concept, 613
CM (configuration management)
  administrative activities, 602–603
  audits, 602
  baselines, 604
  basic requirements, 600
  CI (configuration identification), 601
  configuration control, 601
  CSA (configuration-status accounting) system, 601–602
  data distribution and access, 602
  document library, 604
  initial release, 604
  interface requirements, 605
  marking and labeling, 604–605
  planning, 602
  software development library, 604
  technical reviews, 603
  WBS (Work Breakdown Structure), 603
CMMI (Capability Maturity Model Integrated), 596–597, 824
code
  comparison tools, 105
  verification concerns, Web-based systems testing, 800
  walkthrough, program verification, 55

code of ethics, CBOK, 125
coding errors, undetected defects, 66
collection methods training, baseline information, 747
combination teams
  advantages/disadvantages, 171
  communication concerns, 170
commands, operations activities, 754
commercial off-the-shelf software. *See* COTS software testing
Common Body of Knowledge. *See* CBOK
communication
  barriers/obstacle solutions
    conflict-resolution methods, 880
    effective communication process, 882–884
    how to address, 882
    lines of communication, 881
    management support solutions, 883
    objectives, understanding consensus of, 880
    open channel concept, 884
    quality control, 884
    realistic mechanism solutions, 884
    respect for others, 880
  best practices, 850
  combination team concerns, 170
  communication lines and networks, software security testing, 746
  development activities, 753
  failed, application risks, 308–309
compatibility
  COTS implementation risks, 688
  Web-based systems testing, 804–805, 808–809
competency
  barriers, 865
  baseline development, 14–16
  building software skills, 598
  client needs assessment, 623
  competent-programmer hypothesis, 242
  cultural barriers, 874–876
  efficiency measures, 852–853

inadequate, 39
people management skills, 598
process-selection skills, 598
project management skills, 598
testers
 baseline development, 14–16
 CBOK (Common Body of
  Knowledge), 125–128
 competent assessment, 128
 CSTE (Certified Software Tester)
  certificate, 125, 127–128
 fully competent assessment, 128
 job performance roles, 126–127
 negative attitudes, 130
 not competent assessment, 128, 130
 training curriculum development,
  128–130
 work papers, 28–32
 of tests, assessing, 14–16
 variability measures, 835
 work papers, 28–32
competition, barrier/obstacle solutions,
 868
compiler-based analysis tools, 105
completeness evaluation
 best practices, 849
 client needs assessment, 623
 documentation, 179–180
 preventive controls, 660
 requirements measures, 594
complexity measures, structural
 analysis, 238
compliance testing
 examples of, 223
 how to use, 228
 with methodology, 299
 objectives, 227
 parallel testing, 229
 post-implementation analysis, 575
 test factors, 41–42
 validation testing, 434
 when to use, 228
component testing, Web-based systems
 testing, 807

computation faults, error-based testing,
 241
computer operations, vulnerabilities,
 738
computer processing
 operations activities, 754
 testing without, 669
computer programs, vulnerabilities, 736
computer software, system
 processing, 77
computer store demonstration, COTS
 software testing, 700–701
conciseness, best practices, 850
concurrency testing, Web-based systems
 testing, 804
concurrent software development
 criteria, documentation, 175
conditional testing, 240
conditions, validation testing results,
 436, 438–439
configuration identification (CI), 601
configuration management. *See* CM
configuration-status accounting (CSA)
 system, 601–602
confirmation tools, 105
conflict-resolution methods, 880
consensus policies, 46–47
consistency
 best practices, 849
 process advantages, 153
 requirements measures, 594
consistent process level, client/server
 systems testing, 618–619
constraint method, software cost
 estimation, 182–183
constraints
 methodologies, 592
 profile information, 214
content criteria, documentation,
 179–180
contingency planning
 programming testing, 327
 test plan development, 222
 verification testing, 319

continuing education, CBOK, 125
continuity of processing
  risk assessment, 216
  test factors, 41–42
contracted software
  COTS versus, 686
  test tactics, 75
  testing efforts, 704–705
  vendor reputation importance,
    690–691
contracting officers, roles and
    responsibilities, 591
control flow analysis tools, 105
control testing
  examples of, 229
  how to use, 234
  objectives, 234
  when to use, 234
controllability, requirements measures,
    594
controlled demonstration, COTS
    software testing, 700–701
controls
  corrective, 665
  detective
    control totals, 664
    data transmission, 663
    discussed, 662
    documentation, 664
    logs, 663
    output checks, 664–665
  objectives, verification testing, 303
  preventive
    balance checks, 662
    completeness tests, 660
    control data, 661
    control totals, 660
    data input, 659
    file auto-updating, 661
    has totals, 661
    input validation, 659–661
    limit tests, 660
    logical tests, 660

overflow tests, 662
prenumbered forms, 659
project checks, 660
record counts, 661
self-checking digits, 660
source-data, 658–659
turnaround documents, 659
validity tests, 660
project status calculation, 191
risks, 64
conversion, cycle control objectives, 675
core business areas, test plan
    development, 221
corporate language, adjustments for, 741
corrected conditions, undetected
    defects, 66, 155
corrective controls, internal controls
    testing, 665
correctness
  programming testing, 327
  requirements measures, 594
  risk assessment, 217
  software quality factors, 844
  test factors, 40, 42
  tools, 105
  validation testing, 435
  Web-based systems testing, 800, 804
costs
  cost/benefit analysis, 172
  cost-effectiveness of testing, 47–48
  critical success factors, 695
  defects, 67, 154
  internal controls testing, 665
  profile information, 214
  software cost estimation
    inflation, 188
    labor rates, 188
    parametric models, 183–184
    personnel, 187
    prudent person test, 189
    recalculation, 188–189
    resources, 188
    schedules, 187

strategies for, 182–183
validation, 185–189
tools, 114–116
COTS (commercial off-the-shelf)
software testing
advantages, 687
challenges, 689–690
check procedures, 705
clarity of communication, 700
concerns, 691–692
contracted software versus, 686
CSFs (critical success factors), 695–696
data compatibility, 698
demonstrations, 700–701
disadvantages, 687–688
disk storage, 704
ease of use, 700
functional testing, 702–703
guidelines, 706
hardware compatibility, 697–698
help routines, 701
input, 693
knowledge to execute, 701
management information, 694
objectives, 691
operating system compatibility, 698
operational fit tests, 696–697
output, 705
overview, 685
people fit tests, 701–702
probability, 694
products/reports output, 693
program compatibility, 698
risk assessment, 688–689
software functionality, 700
structural testing, 703–704
work flow, 698–699
work papers
completeness tests, 707–708
functional testing, 710
quality control checklist, 712–715
structural testing, 711
test of fit, 709
workbench concept, 692

coupling
coupling-effect hypothesis, 242
programming testing, 328
risk assessment, 218
test factors, 41, 43
validation testing, 434
courses, training curriculum, 128–129
crashes, Web-based systems testing, 807
critical criteria
documentation, 174
requirements measures, 594
critical path definition, timelines, 836
cross-references, inspection process, 260
CSA (configuration-status accounting)
system, 601–602
CSFs (critical success factors), 695–696
CSTE (Certified Software Tester)
certificate
defined, 14–15
tester competency, 125, 127–128
uses for, 127
cultural barriers
business innovation management, 878
competencies, 874–876
discussed, 869
how to address, 879–880
manage by fact concept, 876–877
manage by process concept, 873–874
management cultures, 870
people management, 871–872
culture, client/server testing readiness,
614
curriculum, training, 128–130
customers
profile information, 213
roles of, 6
satisfaction measures, 852
and user involvement, lack of, 210
customer-site demonstration, COTS
software testing, 700–701
customization, V-concept testing,
160–161
cycle control objectives, internal controls
testing, 675

D

data
  accessibility, enterprise-wide
    requirements, 767
  commonality, best practices, 850
  compatibility, COTS software testing,
    698
  components, acceptance testing, 492
  distribution, configuration
    management, 602
  generation aids, test verification, 55
  improper use of, 766
  incomplete, risk factors, 39
  requirements, document development,
    173
data acquisition, system processing, 76
data collection
  baseline information, 744–747
  post-implementation analysis, 577
data dictionary tools, 105, 770
data entry
  errors, undetected defects, 66, 155
  operational fit tests, 697
data exchange issues, test plan
  development, 222
data flow analysis tools, 105, 238–239
data formats, client needs assessment,
  623
data handling areas, vulnerabilities, 738
data input
  preventive controls, 659
  problems, 39
  response time criteria, documentation,
    175
data integrity controls
  data warehouse testing, 771–772,
    778–779
  programming testing, 326
  verification testing, 318
data transmission, detective controls,
  663
data warehouse testing
  access control processes, 770–771, 777

backup/recovery processes,
  773–774, 778
check procedures, 780
concerns, 765–766, 768–769
data integrity processes, 771–772,
  778–779
documentation processes, 769, 771, 776
enterprise-wide requirements, 767–768
front-end planning, 770
guidelines, 780
input, 767–768
operations processes, 772–773, 777
organizational processes, 769, 775–776
output, 780
overview, 765
statistics, 773
system development processes,
  770–771, 779
work papers
  access control, 785
  activity process, 797
  audio trails, 784
  concerns rating, 788, 795–796
  continuity of processing, 792
  data, placing in wrong calendar
    period, 787
  documentation, 791
  fraud, 789
  inadequate responsibility
    assignment, 781
  inadequate service levels, 786
  incomplete data concerns, 782
  management support concerns, 794
  performance criteria, 793
  quality control checklist, 798
  reviews, 790
  update concerns, 783
workbench concept, 766–767
database management
  multiplatform environment testing, 717
  system processing, 76
databases
  built/used, profile information, 214
  sources, validation testing, 413

specifications, document development, 173

tools, 105

date controls

enterprise-wide requirements, 768

Project Status reports, 468

Summary Status reports, 467

debugging

programming testing, 325–326

verification testing, 292

decision and planning aids, system processing, 76

decision tables

as documentation, 180

functional testing, 238

Defect Distribution report, 475–476

Defect Removal Efficiency (DRE), 822

defects

classifying, 258

corrected conditions, 155

costs, 67, 154

data entry errors, 155

efficiency measures, 853

error correction mistakes, 155

extra requirements, 65, 471

failures versus, 65–66

hard to find, 66–67

improperly interpreted requirements, 155

incorrectly recorded requirements, 155

inspection process, 258–259

instructional errors, 155

missing requirements, 65, 471

naming, 471

post-implementation analysis, 576–578, 580

program coding errors, 155

program specification, 155

results analysis, 462

severity levels, 471

testing errors, 155

testing guidelines, 65–67

undetected, 66

wrong specifications, 65, 471

Defects Uncovered versus Correlated Gap Timeline report, 473–474

definition, document development, 172

degree of generality criteria, documentation, 174

deliverables

efficiency measures, 853

inspection process, 256

profile information, 213–214

demonstrations, COTS software testing, 700–701

descriptions, system test plan standards, 81–82

design

bad design problems, 39

changes, regression testing, 55

document development, 172

specifications, undetected defects, 66

verification, SDLC, 53–54

design phase, verification testing, 296–297

design-based functional testing tools, 105

desk checking tools, 106

desk debugging, 325–326

desk reviews, inspection process, 259–260

destruction, transaction, 756

detective controls, internal controls testing

control totals, 664

data transmission, 663

discussed, 662

documentation, 664

logs, 663

output checks, 664–665

developers

functional testing phases, 70

roles and responsibilities, 6

development

document verification, 171–174

documentation development phase, 172

phases, test strategies, 56

development *(continued)*
  process profiles, 212–215
  software security testing, 753–754
  test process improvement, 44
  tester roles and responsibilities, 6
development project types, V-concept
    testing, 75
developmental costs criteria,
    documentation, 174
deviation, validation testing results, 427
diagnostic software, system
    processing, 76
digital storage facilities, vulnerabilities,
    738
disaster planning
  operations activities, 754
  test tools, 106
  validation testing, 436
disk space allocation, stress testing, 223
disk storage
  COTS software testing, 704
  multiplatform environment testing,
    724
document library, configuration
    management, 604
documentation
  audience criteria, 179
  change in scope criteria, 174
  client needs assessment, 623
  combining and expanding documents
    types, 179–180
  completeness evaluation, 179–180
  concurrent software development
    criteria, 175
  content criteria, 179–180
  cost/benefit analysis, 172
  critical criteria, 174
  data dictionaries, 770
  data input response time criteria, 175
  data requirements, 173
  data warehouse testing, 769, 771, 776
  database specifications, 173
  decision tables, 180
  degree of generality criteria, 174

detective controls, 664
development activities, 753
development phases, 171–174
developmental costs criteria, 174
enterprise-wide requirements, 768
equipment complexity criteria, 174
feasibility studies, 172
flexibility criteria, 179
flowcharts, 180
formal publication, 178
format criteria, 180
forms, 180
functional requirements, 173
implementation procedures, 890
inadequate, 766
internal, 177–178
levels, 177–178
minimal, 177
multiple programs/files, 180
need for, 174–175
operations manual, 174
organization, 167
originality required criteria, 174
personnel assigned criteria, 174
problems, 513
program change response time criteria,
    174
program maintenance manuals, 174
program specification, 173
programming language criteria, 175
project requests, 172
redundancy criteria, 179
section titles, 180
size criteria, 179
software summary, 172
span of operation criteria, 174
specification requirements, tester
    roles, 44
standards, 770
stress testing, 223
system/subsystem specifications, 173
test analysis reports, 174
test plans, 174
timelines, 180–181

tool use, 124
user manuals, 174
validation testing, 412
weighted criteria score, 175–177
work papers
  documentation completeness, 202
  estimation, 203–205
  quality control checklist, 207–209
  weighted criteria calculation, 201
working document, 178
domain testing, error-based testing, 241
domino effects, revised testing
  approach, 50
downloads, Web-based systems testing,
  806
DRE (Defect Removal Efficiency), 822
drivers, baseline development, 8
dropped lines, Web-based systems
  testing, 807
dynamic analysis
  program verification, 55
  programming testing, 324
dynamic page generation, Web-based
  systems testing, 806

E
ease of operation
  risk assessment, 218
  test factors, 41, 43
  validation testing, 436
ease of use
  client needs assessment, 623
  COTS software testing, 700
  critical success factors, 695
  programming testing, 327
  risk assessment, 217
  scoring success factors, 317
  test factors, 41, 43
  validation testing, 435
e-commerce activities, 878
edit checks, 414
education, barrier/obstacle solutions,
  868
effect, validation testing results, 436, 438

effectiveness measures
  best practices, 848–849, 852–854
  communication process, 882–884
  testing guidelines, 65
efficiency
  best practices, 848–849
  results analysis, 463
  software quality factors, 844
e-learning courses, QAI, 129
electronic device reliance, revised
  testing approach, 50
e-mail functions, Web-based systems
  testing, 806
end dates, timelines, 838
enterprise-wide requirements
  data warehouse testing, 767–768
  methodologies, 592
environment assessment criteria, 8
environment controls, internal controls
  testing, 656
equipment complexity criteria,
  documentation, 174
equivalence partitioning, 236–237
errors
  accidental versus intentional losses,
    738–739
  application risks, 305–307
  corrective controls, 665
  data entry, 155
  error correction mistakes, 155
  error guessing tools, 106, 721–722
  error handling testing
    examples of, 229
    how to use, 232
    objectives, 231
    operations activities, 754
    when to use, 232
  error tolerance, best practices, 849
  error-based testing, 241–242
  fault estimation, 241
  fault-based testing, 242–243
  instructional, 155
  perturbation testing, 242
  program coding, 155

errors *(continued)*
  statistical testing, 241
  undetected defects, 66
estimation
  parametric models, 183–184
  resources, availability, 181–182, 221
  software cost
    inflation, 188
    labor rates, 188
    parametric models, 183–184
    personnel, 187
    prudent person test, 189
    recalculation, 188–189
    resources, 188
    schedules, 187
    strategies for, 182–183
    validation, 185–189
  troubled project characteristics,
    181–182
evaluation
  policy criteria, 45
  system test plan standards, 81–82
events
  event control, system processing, 76
  test script development, 431
examination tools, 105
executable spec tools, 106
execution
  acceptance testing, 499
  best practices, 850
  execution testing
    examples of, 223
    how to use, 225
    objectives, 225
    when to use, 225
  validation testing, 434–436
expandability
  best practices, 850
  critical success factors, 695
Expected versus Actual Defects
  Uncovered Timeline report, 472–473
expenditure, cycle control objectives,
  675
expenses, Project Status reports, 468

experience evaluation, staffing, 600
expression testing, description of, 240
extensions, project status calculation,
  193–194
external team
  advantages/disadvantages, 170
external/internal work processes,
  variability measures, 835
extra requirements
  COTS software testing concerns, 692
  defects, 65, 471

F
facility requirements, test plan
  development, 222
fact finding tools, 106
fact management, V-concept testing,
  162
failures
  COTS software testing concerns, 691
  defects versus, 65–66
fault design problems, bad design
  decisions, 39
fault estimation, error-based training,
  241
fault-based testing, 242–243
feasibility reviews, 70, 172
file auto-updating, preventive controls,
  661
file design, validation testing, 413–414
file downloads, Web-based systems
  testing, 806
file handling, multiplatform
  environment testing, 724–725
file integrity
  programming testing, 326–327
  risk assessment, 215
  test factors, 40, 42
  validation testing, 435
  verification testing, 301
file reconciliation, control testing, 229
final planning iteration, RAD testing,
  642
final reports, walkthroughs, 314

financial planning objectives, internal controls testing, 674–675

first priority, probable penetration points, 760

flexibility
  agile testing process, 820–821
  documentation criteria, 179
  software quality factors, 844
  test plan development, 262

flowcharts
  as documentation, 180
  tools, 106

follow-ups, inspection process, 261

footprint charts
  baseline development, 10
  client/server systems testing, 621
  work papers, 23

formal publication documentation, 178

format criteria, documentation, 180

forms
  completion training, 747–748
  as documentation, 180

fraud studies, software security testing, 761

front-end planning, data warehouse testing, 770

fully competent assessment, tester competency, 128

functional desk debugging, 326

functional problems, COTS implementation risks, 688

functional requirements, document development, 173

functional testing. *See also* structural testing
  advantages/disadvantages, 69
  algebraic specification, 237
  analysis, 236
  axiomatic specification, 238
  black box testing, 69
  COTS software testing, 702–703
  decision tables, 238
  equivalence partitioning, 236–237
  functional analysis, 236

input domain testing, 236
interface-based, 236–237
output domain coverage, 237
reasons for, 69
special-value testing, 237
state machines, 238
syntax checking, 237
system testing, 70
user acceptance, 70
validation techniques, 69–70
verification techniques, 69–70

functionality requirements, acceptance testing, 497

Functions Working Timeline report, 472

function/test matrix, reporting, 470–472

funding, administrative/organizational barriers, 865

G

generality, best practices, 850

global extent, fault-based testing, 242–243

graphics filters, Web-based systems testing, 805

guidelines, testing
  business logic techniques, 67–68
  defects, uncovering, 65–67
  effective test performance, 65
  functional testing, 69–71
  life-cycle testing, 68
  reasons for, 63–64
  risk reduction, 64–65
  structural testing, 69–71

H

hacking, 757

hardware compatibility
  COTS software testing, 697–698
  Web-based systems testing, 805

hardware configurations, multiplatform environment testing, 717

hardware constraints, operational fit tests, 696

has totals, preventive controls, 661

help it happen concept, stakeholder perspective, 861–862

help routines
    client needs assessment, 623
    COTS software testing, 701

heuristic models, estimation, 183

hierarchical organization, people management, 871

high positive correlation, scoring success factors, 317

high prioritized objectives, 245

high readiness assessment, client/server systems testing, 621

hot button barriers, 864

hotlines, tool manager duties, 119

HTML tools, Web-based systems testing, 809

I

ICS (internal control specialist), 591

IEEE (Institute of Electrical and Electronics Engineers) standards, 595

image processing, 76

impersonation, vulnerabilities, 736

implementation procedures
    baseline development, 9
    discussed, 891
    documentation approaches, 890
    measurability, 892
    methodologies, 592
    objectives, 892
    obtainable ideas, 886
    planning process, 891
    prioritization, 888–889
    profile information, 214
    quality control, 890, 894
    requisite resources, 893–894
    results, 892–893
    test plan development, 251
    time-compression efforts, 886–888
    user acceptance, 885

improperly interpreted requirements, defects, 155

improvement barriers
    administrative/organizational barriers, 865–866
    quality control, 869
    red flag/hot button barriers, 864
    root cause, 866–869
    staff-competency barriers, 865
    stakeholder perspective, 861–864

improvement planning
    criteria, 16
    processes, 154
    self-assessment practices, 17–18

in control processes, variability measures, 832

inadequate assignment concerns, data warehouse testing, 765

inadequate audit trails, 766

inadequate documentation, 766

inadequate service levels, 766

incomplete data
    data warehouse testing, 766
    risk factors, 39

incorrectly recorded requirements, defects, 155

incremental methodology, 588

industry issues, profile information, 214

inefficient testing, 857–860

inflation, software cost estimation, 188

in-house courses, QAI, 129

initial release, configuration management, 604

initiation, documentation development phase, 171

in-phase agreement, RAD testing, 641

input
    acceptance testing, 495–496
    COTS software testing, 693
    data warehouse testing, 767–768
    documentation, 167
    multiplatform environment testing, 720–721
    organization, 167
    post-implementation analysis, 574

RAD (rapid application development) testing, 636

results analysis, 461–463

software security testing, 735

test plan development, 212

timelines, 837

validation testing, 411

verification testing, 296–297

vulnerabilities, 736

Web-based systems testing, 801–802

input component, workbench concept, 71

input domain testing, 236

inspection process

author responsibilities, 258

concerns, 255

cross-references, 260

defect classification, 258–259

design deliverables, 322

desk reviews, 259–260

follow-ups, 261

importance of, 254

individual preparation, 259–260

inspectors responsibilities, 258

meetings, 260–261

moderator responsibilities, 256–257

overview sessions, 259

planning and organizing procedures, 259

products/deliverables, 256

reader responsibilities, 257

recorder responsibilities, 257

tools, 106

validation testing, 436

verification testing, 292

installation phase, operational testing, 508–509

installations

client/server systems testing, 622

verification, SDLC, 53, 55

Institute of Electrical and Electronics Engineers (IEEE), 595

instructional errors, 155

instructions coverage, post-implementation analysis, 578

instrumentation

best practices, 850

tools, 106

integration

COTS implementation risks, 689

revised testing approach, 50

Web-based systems testing, 800

integration scripting, 431

integration testing

as functional tests, 70

RAD testing, 637

tools, 106

validation, 221

Web-based systems testing, 807

integrity, software quality factors, 844

intentional versus accidental losses, 738–739

interfaces

activities, software security testing, 752

design complete factor, verification testing, 320

interface-based functional testing, 236–237

multiplatform environment testing, 725–726

profile information, 214–215

quality, acceptance testing, 497

requirements, configuration management, 605

Interim Test report, 478

internal control specialist (ICS), 591

internal controls testing

application background information, 666–667

application controls, 668–669

corrective controls, 665

cost/benefit analysis, 665

cycle control objectives, 675

detective controls

control totals, 664

data transmission, 663

discussed, 662

internal controls testing *(continued)*
   documentation, 664
   logs, 663
   output checks, 664–665
  environment controls, 656
  financial planning objectives, 674–675
  master records, 671
  mini-company approach, 672
  multiple exposures, 657
  non-effective controls, 678
  objectives, 657
  overview, 655
  password protection, 656
  preventive controls
   balance checks, 662
   completeness tests, 660
   control data, 661
   control totals, 660
   data input, 659
   file auto-updating, 661
   has totals, 661
   input validation, 659–661
   limit tests, 660
   logical tests, 660
   overflow tests, 662
   prenumbered forms, 659
   project checks, 660
   record counts, 661
   self-checking digits, 660
   source-data, 658–659
   turnaround documents, 659
   validity tests, 660
  quality control checklist, 678
  results of, 677
  risk assessment, 668
  strong controls, 677
  system control objectives, 674
  test-data approach, 669–672
  transaction flow testing, 672–673
  weak controls, 678
  without computer processing, 669
  work papers
   documentation, 679
   file control, 683

   input controls, 679–681
   output controls, 682
   program and processing controls, 681–682
   workbench concept, 667
internal documentation, 177–178
internal team
  advantages/disadvantages, 169–170
international standards, 594–595
Internet. *See* Web-based systems testing
interoperability
  implementation risks, 689
  software quality factors, 844
intersystems testing
  examples of, 229
  how to use, 233
  objectives, 233
  when to use, 233
intrusion concerns, Web-based systems testing, 803
invalid data, tests using, 413
inventory process, reporting, 465
IT operations
  management
   policy criteria, managing, 45
   roles and responsibilities, 6, 591
  vulnerabilities, 736
iterative development, test tactics, 75

J

joint policy development, 47
judgment evaluation approach, post-implementation analysis, 575

K

knowledge to execute, COTS software testing, 701

L

labeling and marking, configuration management, 604
labor rates, software cost estimation, 188
lack of training concerns, 210
LAN (local area network), 800

legal/industry issues, profile
    information, 214
legend information
  Project Status reports, 470
  Summary Status reports, 468
let it happen concept, stakeholder
    perspective, 862
licensing issues, COTS implementation
    risks, 689
life cycle phases
  SDLC, 52–53
  tool selection, 109–111
life-cycle testing, testing guidelines, 68
limit tests, preventive controls, 660
limited space, inspection process
    concerns, 255
lines of communication, 881
load testing, Web-based systems testing,
    808
local area network (LAN), 800
local extent, fault-based testing, 242–243
logging tools, 107
logical tests, preventive controls, 660
logs, detective controls, 663
lose-lose situations, test plan
    development, 211
lost connections, Web-based systems
    testing, 807
low prioritized objectives, 245
low readiness assessment, client/server
    systems testing, 621

M
maintainability
  critical success factors, 695
  risk assessment, 217
  software quality factors, 844
  test factors, 41, 43
  validation testing, 436
maintenance
  test tactics, 75
  verification, SDLC, 53, 55
make it happen concept, stakeholder
    perspective, 861

manage by fact concept, cultural
    barriers, 876–877
manage by process concept, cultural
    barriers, 873–874
manageable processes, 154
management
  COTS software testing, 694
  cultural barriers, 870
  IT operations
    policy criteria, managing, 45
    roles and responsibilities, 6, 591
  management support
    communication barrier solutions,
        883
    time-compression readiness criteria,
        826
  risk appetite, 38
  roles and responsibilities, 6–7
  support for testing, 50–51
  test manager responsibilities, 167–168
  tool managers
    assistant, 119
    mentors, 119
    need for, 117
    positions, prerequisites to creating,
        118
    responsibilities of, 117, 119–120
    skill levels, 118–119
    tenure, 120
manual applications, operational
    testing, 523–524
manual support testing
  examples of, 229
  how to use, 232–233
  objectives, 232
  when to use, 233
manual tools, 104
mapping tools, 106
marketing, barrier/obstacle solutions,
    868
marking and labeling, configuration
    management, 604
master records, internal controls
    testing, 671

mathematical models, system
processing, 76
mature test processes, agile testing, 821
maturity levels, client/server systems
testing, 615–616
MBTI (Myers Briggs Type Indicator),
130
mean time between failures (MTBF),
822–823
mean time to failure (MTTF), 822–823
mean time to repair (MTTR), 822–823
measurability
implementation procedures, 892
requirements measures, 594
measured process level, client/server
systems testing, 619–620
measurement first, action second
concept, 581
measurement units, reporting, 464–465
media libraries, 754
media, vulnerabilities, 736
medium readiness assessment,
client/server systems testing, 621
meetings, inspection process, 260–261
memory, Web-based systems testing,
805
mentors, tool managers, 119
message processing, system
processing, 76
methodologies, software development
business requirements, 592
CMMI (Capability Maturity Model
Integrated), 596–597
competencies required, 598–599
compliance with, 299
constraint requirements, 592
enterprise-wide requirements, 592
implementation requirements, 592
incremental methodology, 588
international standards, 594–595
overview, 586
prototyping, 587
RAD (rapid application development)
methodology, 587–588

risk assessment, 215–218
SDLC (software development life
cycle), 588–589
SEI (Software Engineering Institute),
596
self-assessment, 605–606
spiral methodology, 588
sponsor responsibilities, 590
SRS (System Requirements
Specifications), 595
staff experience, 600
state of requirements, 592
systems analyst perspective, 593
user responsibilities, 590
V-concept testing, 588
waterfall methodology, 587
work papers
analysis footprint, 609
self-assessment, 607–608
methods, baseline information, 743
milestones
design verification, 54
project status calculation, 191
test plan development, 251
mini-company approach, internal
controls testing, 672
minimal documentation, 177
misinterpretation, undetected
defects, 66
missing requirements
COTS software testing concerns, 691
defects, 65, 471
modeling tools, 106
moderators, inspection process
responsibilities, 256–257
modifiability, requirements measures,
594
modularity, best practices, 850
monitors, Web-based systems testing,
805
motivation
client/server testing readiness, 614
management support needs, 51
motivation factors, testers, 51

MTBF (mean time between failures), 822–823

MTTF (mean time to failure), 822–823

MTTR (mean time to repair), 822–823

multimedia support, Web-based systems testing, 805

multiplatform environment testing
  challenges, 718–719
  check procedures, 726
  concerns, 718
  disk storage, 724
  error guessing, 721–722
  file handling, 724–725
  guidelines, 726–727
  hardware configurations, 717
  input, 720–721
  interfaces, 725–726
  needed platforms, listing, 723
  objectives, 718
  output, 726
  overview, 717
  structural testing, 723–725
  test room configurations, 723
  transaction processing events, 724
  V-concept testing, 725–726
  work papers
    concerns, 728
    configurations, 728
    quality control checklist, 731–732
    validity, 729–730
  workbench concept, 719–720

multiple exposures, internal controls testing, 657

mutation testing, 242

Myers Briggs Type Indicator (MBTI), 130

N

navigation correctness, Web-based systems testing, 804

needs gap and risks, 38

negative attitudes, tester competency, 130

network and telephone switching equipment, test plan development, 222

new systems development, project scope, 77

non-effective controls, internal controls testing, 678

non-IT teams
  advantages/disadvantages, 170
  vulnerabilities, 738

no-rework day timelines, 839

Normalized Defect Distribution report, 476–477

not competent assessment, tester competency, 128, 130

O

objectives
  acceptance testing, 492–493
  average prioritized, 245
  compliance testing, 227
  control testing, 234
  COTS testing, 691
  error handling testing, 231
  execution testing, 225
  implementation procedures, 892
  internal controls testing, 657
  intersystems testing, 233
  itemizing, 245
  manual support testing, 232
  multiplatform environment testing, 718
  objectives-driven processes, agile testing, 821
  operations testing, 227
  parallel testing, 234
  priority assignment, 245
  profile information, 213
  RAD testing, 634
  recovery testing, 226
  regression testing, 231
  requirements testing, 230
  security testing, 228
  software security testing, 228
  stress testing, 224
  test plan development, 210, 213
  understanding consensus of, 880

objectives *(continued)*
V-concept testing, 159–160
verification testing, 293
object-oriented (OO) system
developments, 500–501, 802
obsolete data, risk factors, 39
obtainable ideas, implementation
procedures, 886
office equipment, software security
testing, 746
online system tests, 248
online terminal systems, vulnerabilities,
738
OO (object-oriented) system
developments, 500–501, 802
open channel concept, communication
barrier solutions, 884
operability, best practices, 850
operating systems
access and integrity, vulnerabilities,
736
compatibility, COTS software testing,
697–698
flaws, application risks, 308
multiplatform environment testing,
717
operational fit tests, COTS software
testing, 696–697
operational needs, COTS software
testing concerns, 692
operational profiles, validation testing,
413
operational software, best practices, 843
operational status, parallel testing, 229
operational testing
automated applications, 522–523
change control, 517–518
check procedures, 522
discussed, 503
guidelines, 525–526
installation phase, 508–509
manual applications, 523–524
output, 522
problems, documenting, 513

production monitoring, 512–513
software version changes, 509–511
test data development, 515–517
test plan development and updates,
514–515
training failures, 524
training materials, 519–522
V-concept testing, 158–159
operations
activities, software security testing,
754–755
documentation development, 172
manuals, document development, 174
operations testing
examples of, 223
how to use, 227
objectives, 227
when to use, 227
processes, data warehouse testing,
772–773, 777
optimized process level, client/server
systems testing, 620–621
organization
check procedures, 200
document verification, 171–175
input, 167
output, 200
project scope, defining, 168
project status calculation, 189–193
software testing model definition, 7
teams, appointing, 168–171
test estimation, 181–185
test managers, appointing, 167–168
V-concept testing, 157
workbench concept, 166
organizational barriers, 865–866
organizational processes, data
warehouse testing, 769, 775–776
origin, classifying defects by, 258
originality required criteria,
documentation, 174
origination, transactions, 755
out of control processes, variability
measures, 832

out-of-phase agreement, RAD testing, 642

output
client/server systems testing, 624
components, workbench concept, 71
COTS software testing, 705
data warehouse testing, 780
multiplatform environment testing, 726
operational testing, 522
organization, 200
output checks, detective controls, 664–665
post-implementation analysis, 580–581
RAD testing, 643
results analysis, 482
software security testing, 762
test plan development, 262
timelines, 837
validation testing, 439
verification testing, 331
vulnerabilities, 736
Web-based systems testing, 810
output domain coverage, 237
outside users, revised testing approach, 50
outsourcing, people management, 871
overflow tests, preventive controls, 662
overlooked details, undetected defects, 66
over-reliance, test plan development, 210
overview sessions, inspection process, 259

P
paperwork, administrative/organizational barriers, 865–866
parallel operation tools, 106
parallel simulation tools, 107
parallel testing
examples of, 229
how to use, 235

objectives, 234
when to use, 235
parametric models
heuristic models, 183
phenomenological models, 183
regression models, 183–184
password protection, internal controls testing, 656
path domains, error-based testing, 241
path testing, 240
paths coverage, post-implementation analysis, 578
pattern processing, 76
payroll application example, validation testing, 416–429
PDCA (plan-do-check-act) cycle, 4–5, 64, 891
peer reviews
programming testing, 328–330
tools, 107
penalties, risk assessment, 58
penetration points, software security testing
business transaction control points, 755–756
characteristics of, 756
development activities, 753–754
first priority, 760
interface activities, 752
operations activities, 754–755
second priority, 760
staff activities, 751
third priority, 760
people components, acceptance testing, 492
people fit tests, COTS software testing, 701–702
people management skills
competencies required, 598
cultural barriers, 871–872
people needs, COTS software testing concerns, 692
percentage-of-hardware method, software cost estimation, 183

performance
  acceptance testing, 497
  inspection process concerns, 255
  methods, project status calculation,
    190–192
  people management through, 871
  programming testing, 328
  RAD testing, 635
  risk assessment, 218
  test factors, 41, 43
  validation testing, 434
  Web-based systems testing, 800,
    803–804, 808
personnel
  design reviews, 321
  software cost estimation, 187
personnel assignment criteria,
  documentation, 174
perturbation testing, error-based testing,
  242
phenomenological models, estimation,
  183
physical access, vulnerabilities, 736
plan-do-check-act (PDCA) cycle, 4–5,
  64, 891
planning
  CM (configuration management), 602
  implementation procedures, 891
platforms. *See* multiplatform
  environment testing
playback tools, 105
point system, project status calculation,
  192–193
policies
  consensus, 46–47
  criteria for, 45
  development activities, 753
  good practices, 45
  joint development, 47
  management directive method, 46
  methods for establishing, 46–47
portability
  programming testing, 328
  risk assessment, 217–218

software quality factors, 844
  test factors, 41, 43
  validation testing, 436
  verification testing, 320
post-implementation analysis
  acceptance criteria, 578
  assessment objectives, 574–575
  asset value, 579
  budgets, 578
  change characteristics, 576
  check procedures, 580
  compliance, 575
  concerns, 572
  data collection, 577
  defects, 576–578, 580
  guidelines, 581
  input, 574
  instructions coverage, 578
  judgment evaluation approach, 575
  measurement assignment
    responsibilities, 575
  measurement first, action second
    concept, 581
  output, 580–581
  overview, 154, 571
  paths coverage, 578
  rerun analysis, 579
  scale of ten, 580
  schedules, 580
  source code analysis, 579
  startup failure, 579
  system complaints, 576
  termination analysis, 579
  test costs, 578
  test to business effectiveness, 578
  testing metrics, 576–579
  user participation, 578
  user reaction evaluation approach, 576
  V-concept testing, 159
  what to measure, 575
  work papers, 582
  workbench concept, 572–573
potential failures, assessing severity of,
  221

pre-implementation, 154
prenumbered forms, preventive
    controls, 659
presentations
  system processing, 76
  walkthroughs, 313–314
preventive controls, internal controls
    testing
  balance checks, 662
  completeness tests, 660
  control data, 661
  control totals, 660
  data input, 659
  file auto-updating, 661
  has totals, 661
  input validation, 659–661
  limit tests, 660
  logical tests, 660
  overflow tests, 662
  prenumbered forms, 659
  project checks, 660
  record counts, 661
  self-checking digits, 660
  source-data, 658–659
  turnaround documents, 659
  validity tests, 660
print handling, 805
priorities
  administrative/organizational
      barriers, 866
  implementation procedures, 888–889
  objectives, 245
privileged users, interface activities,
    752
probability, COTS software testing, 694
problems, documenting, 513
procedures
  development activities, 753
  procedure control, system
      processing, 76
  procedures in place, security testing,
      223
  workbench concept, 71
process control, system processing, 76

process management, V-concept testing,
    161–162
process preparation checklist, 86
process requirements, reporting, 464–466
processes
  advantages of, 153
  improvements, 44, 65, 154
  manageable, 154
  teachable, 154
process-selection skills, 598
procurement, COTS implementation
    risks, 689
production
  installation verification, 55
  validation testing, 413
production library control, operations
    activities, 754
production monitoring, operational
    testing, 512–513
products
  inspection process, 256
  output, COTS software testing, 693
profiles, project, 212–215
program change response time criteria,
    documentation, 174
program coding errors, undetected
    defects, 66, 155
program compatibility, COTS software
    testing, 698
program errors, application risks,
    306–307
program maintenance manuals,
    document development, 174
program specification
  defects, 155
  document development, 173
program users, interface activities, 752
program verification, SDLC, 53, 55
programming, document development,
    172
programming language criteria,
    documentation, 175
programming phase, verification
    testing, 297, 323–324

programming skills, tool selection
considerations, 111–113
programming testing
acceptance testing, 324
complexity of, 323
desk debugging, 325–326
dynamic testing, 324
importance of, 323
peer reviews, 328–330
static analysis, 324
test factor analysis, 326–328
programs, vulnerabilities, 736, 738
project description contents, acceptance
testing, 498
project leader assessment
configuration management plans,
602–603
verification testing, 317
project management
roles and responsibilities, 6–7, 590, 910
skills, competencies required, 598
project phases, V-concept testing, 79
project requests, document
development, 172
project scope
new systems development, 77
organization techniques, 168
V-concept testing, 77
project status calculation
controls, 191
discussed, 189
extensions, 193–194
milestone method, 191
performance methods, 190–192
point system, 192–193
reports, 195
rolling baseline, 195
target dates, 194
tracking systems, 190
project types, V-concept testing, 75
projects
checks, preventive controls, 660
profiling, 212–215

project information
Project Status reports, 468
Summary Status reports, 467
protection points, software security
testing, 746
prototyping
methodology, 587
test tactics, 75
pseudo-concurrency scripting, 431
purchased software, test tactics, 75
pureness, requirements measures, 594

Q

QA specialist roles and responsibilities,
591
QAI (Quality Assurance Institute)
discussed, 5
e-learning courses, 129
in-house courses, 129
management support for testing,
50–51
Web site, 15, 125
QFD (quality function deployment), 292
Quality Assurance Institute. *See* QAI
quality control
agile testing process, 821
best practices, 856–857
checklist, 207–209
communication barriers, 884
implementation procedures, 890, 894
improvement barriers, 869
internal controls testing, 678
unit testing, 244
variability measures, 841
quality factors, best practices, 843–846
quality function deployment (QFD), 292
quality in fact perspective, best
practices, 843
quality in perspective, best practices,
843
questionnaires, baseline development, 10
questions/recommendations,
responding to, 314

R

RAD (rapid application development)
    testing
  acceptance testing, 637
  check procedures, 642
  concerns, 634–635
  defined, 587–588
  discussed, 210
  final planning iteration, 642
  guidelines, 643
  in-phase agreement, 641
  input, 636
  integration testing, 637
  objectives, 634
  out-of-phase agreement, 642
  output, 643
  overview, 633
  performance, 635
  spiral testing, 638
  strengths/weaknesses, 639
  subsequent testing iterations, 640–642
  test planning iterations, 640
  testing components, 635
  work papers
    applicability checklist, 644
    conceptual model development,
        646–647
    logical data model development, 647
    production system development,
        651–652
    production system release, 652
    quality control checklist, 653
    scope and purpose of system
        definition, 645–646
    specifications, revising, 650–651
    system development, 648–649
    test system release, 652
  workbench concept, 635–636
ratio tools, 107
reactionary environment, people
    management, 871
readability, test plan development, 262
readers, inspection process
    responsibilities, 257

readiness assessment
  client/server systems testing, 614–615,
      621
  time-compression efforts, 826
realistic mechanism solutions,
    communication barriers, 884
record counts, preventive controls, 661
recorders, inspection process
    responsibilities, 257
records
  records-retention program, 753
  undetected defects, 66
recoverability concerns, Web-based
    systems testing, 807
recovery testing
  data warehouse testing, 773–774, 778
  examples of, 223
  how to use, 226
  importance of, 225
  objectives, 226
  validation testing, 435
  when to use, 226
red flag/hot button barriers, 864
reduction, variability measures, 835
redundancy criteria, documentation,
    179
regression models, estimation, 183
regression scripting, 431
regression testing
  COTS software testing challenges, 690
  design changes, 55
  examples of, 229
  how to use, 231
  importance of, 230
  maintenance verification, 55
  objectives, 231
  Web-based systems testing, 808
  when to use, 231
relationship tools, 107
relevance, requirements measures, 594
reliability
  risk assessment, 215
  software quality factors, 844
  test factors, 41, 43

reliability *(continued)*
  validation testing, 434
  Web-based systems testing, 806
reliability, critical success factors, 696
reload pages, Web-based systems
  testing, 805
remote computer sites, software security
  testing, 746
repeatable process level, client/server
  systems testing, 617–618
reports. *See also* results
  Average Age of Uncorrected Defects
    by Type, 475
  COTS software testing, 693
  Defects Uncovered versus Correlated
    Gap Timeline, 473–474
  document development, 174
  Expected versus Actual Defects
    Uncovered Timeline, 472–473
  Functions Working Timeline, 472
  function/test matrix, 470–472
  Interim Test, 478
  inventory process, 465
  measurement teams, 465
  measurement units, 464–465
  Normalized Defect Distribution,
    476–477
  preparation, tool manager duties, 120
  process requirements, 464–466
  Project Status, 468–470
  project status calculation, 195
  summaries, 479–480
  Summary Status, 466–468
  system test report example, 480–481
  test verification, 55
  Testing Action, 477
  timeline development, 837
  V-concept testing, 158
  vulnerabilities, 737
  work papers
    defect reporting, 484–485
    quality control, 486–487
    writing guidelines, 488–489
requirement phase, verification testing,
  296

requirements reviews, 70
requirements testing
  examples of, 229
  how to use, 230
  objectives, 230
  when to use, 230
requirements tracing, 292, 314–315
requirements verification, SDLC, 53–54
requisite resources, implementation
  procedures, 893–894
rerun analysis, post-implementation
  analysis, 579
resentment, inspection process concerns,
  255
resources
  allocation for, management support
    needs, 51
  estimation, 181–182, 221
  resources needed, test plan
    development, 221
  resources protected concerns, baseline
    information, 743
  software cost estimation, 188
respect for others, communication
  barriers, 880
responsibilities
  test managers, 167–168
  of tool managers, 119–120
resubmission, corrective controls, 665
results. *See also* reports
  analysis
    check procedures, 482
    concerns, 460
    defects, 462
    efficiency, 463
    guidelines, 482
    input, 461–463
    output, 482
    overview, 459
    test scripts, 433
    workbench concepts, 460
  assessments, baseline development,
    11–12
  implementation procedures, 892
  internal controls testing, 677

managing, V-concept testing, 162
software security testing, 760–761
test verification, 55
validation testing
  conditions, 436, 438–439
  deviation, 437
  effect, 436, 438
retesting activity, maintenance
  verification, 55
retrieval, transaction, 756
reusability, software quality factors, 844
revenue, cycle control objectives, 675
reviews
  feasibility, 70
  method selections, 329–330
  programming testing, 328–330
  requirements, 70
  test plan development, 262
  verification testing, 292
rewards
  barrier/obstacle solutions, 868
  management support needs, 51
rework factors, variability measures,
  835, 839
risks
  application, 304–308
  bad design problems, 39
  controls, 64
  data input problems, 39
  faulty design problems, 39
  identifiable, 303
  incomplete data, 39
  needs gap, 38
  risk appetite, 38
  risk assessment
    access control, 216
    audit trails, 216
    authorization, 215
    continuity of processing, 216
    correctness, 217
    COTS (commercial off-the-shelf)
      software, 688–689
    coupling, 218
    ease of operation, 218

ease of use, 217
file integrity, 215
internal controls testing, 668
maintainability, 217
methodology, 216–217
penalties, 58
performance, 218
portability, 217–218
reliability, 215
service levels, 216
software security testing, 752
test plan development, 27, 215–216
testing guidelines, 64–65
V-concept testing, 77–79
Web-based systems testing, 802–803
work papers, 61
risk matrix
  tools, 107
  verification testing, 293, 302
specifications gap, 38
team member establishment, 302–303
test plan development, 215–218
rolling baseline, project status
  calculation, 195
root cause identification
  improvement barriers, 866–869
  red flag/hot button barriers, 864
  variability measures, 840
rule establishment
  acceptance testing, 492
  programming testing, 329
  walkthroughs, 312–313

S

sampling, scoring success factors, 316
Sarbanes-Oxley Act of 2002, 655
scale of ten, post-implementation
  analysis, 580
schedules
  COTS software testing challenges, 690
  efficiency measures, 853
  facts, managing, 162
  inadequate, 39
  people management through, 871

schedules *(continued)*
    post-implementation analysis, 580
    profile information, 214
    software cost estimation, 187
    test plan development, 222
    tool manager duties, 119
scheduling status
    Project Status reports, 469
    Summary Status reports, 467
scope. *See* project scope
scoring success factors, verification
        testing, 316–318
scoring tools, 107
scripts. *See* test scripts
SDLC (system development life cycle)
    design requirements, 53–54
    economics of testing, 47–49
    installation requirements, 53, 55
    life cycle phases, 52–53
    maintenance requirements, 53, 55
    program requirements, 53, 55
    requirements verification, 53–54
    software development methodologies,
        588–589
    test requirements, 53, 55
second priority, probable penetration
        points, 760
section titles, documentation, 180
security. *See also* software security
        testing
    application risks, 304–305
    client/server systems testing, 622
    COTS implementation risks, 688
    critical success factors, 696
    programming testing, 327
    validation testing, 435
    Web-based systems testing, 800, 803
SEI (Software Engineering Institute),
        596, 824
self-assessment
    improvement planning, 17–18
    software development methodologies,
        605–606
    software testing model definition

    on test processes, 24–27
    work papers, 909–914
self-checking digits, preventive controls,
        660
self-descriptiveness, best practices, 850
senior management roles and
        responsibilities, 6
sensor processing, 76
service levels
    inadequate, 766
    programming testing, 327
    risk assessment, 216
    test factors, 41–42
    validation testing, 435
    verification testing, 319
seven-step software testing process. *See*
        V-concept testing
severity
    classifying defects by, 258
    defect severity levels, 471
signal processing, 76
simplicity, best practices, 850
simulation
    design verification, 54
    software cost estimation, 183
    system processing, 76
site validation tools, Web-based systems
        testing, 809
size criteria, documentation, 179
skill levels
    tool managers, 118–119
    tool selection considerations, 111–114
snapshot tools, 107
Software Certifications Web site, 125
software cost estimation. *See* costs
software development library,
        configuration management, 604
Software Engineering Institute (SEI),
        596, 824
software functionality, COTS software
        testing, 700
software methods, test matrix, 246
software packages, test script
        development, 431

software quality requirements,
  acceptance testing, 497
software security testing. *See also*
  security
  accidental versus intentional losses,
    738–739
  adequacy evaluation, 761
  baseline information
    accurate and precise information, 741
    analysis, 750
    availability, 741
    baseline awareness training, 747
    categories, 739
    collection method training, 747
    corporate language adjustments, 741
    data collection methods, 744–747
    forms completion training, 747–748
    methods, 743
    objectives, 751
    one-time data collection procedures,
      741
    reasons for, 740
    resources protected concerns, 743
    security sources, 740
    status, reporting, 749
    support concerns, 744
    team member selection, 742–743
    training concerns, 743
    what to collect, 740
  central computer sites, 746
  check procedures, 762
  communication lines and networks,
    746
  examples of, 223
  fraud studies, 761
  guidelines, 762
  hacking, 757
  how to use, 228
  input, 735
  objectives, 228, 734
  office equipment, 746
  output, 762
  overview, 733

  penetration points
    business transaction control points,
      755–756
    characteristics of, 756
    developing, 757–760
    development activities, 753–754
    first priority, 760
    interface activities, 752
    operations activities, 754–755
    second priority, 760
    staff activities, 751
    third priority, 760
  protection points, 746
  remote computer sites, 746
  results, 760–761
  risk assessment, 752
  storage areas, 746
  vulnerabilities
    central processors, 738
    computer operations, 738
    computer programs, 736–737
    data and report preparation facilities,
      737
    data handling areas, 738
    digital storage facilities, 738
    discussed, 735
    impersonation, 737
    input data, 736
    IT operations, 736
    media, 737
    non-IT areas, 738
    online terminal systems, 738
    operating system access and integrity,
      737
    output data, 736
    physical access, 736
    programming offices, 738
    test processes, 736
  when to use, 228
  work papers, 763
  workbench concept, 734–735
software summary, document
  development, 172

software systems, V-concept testing, 76–77

software version changes, operational testing, 509–511

source code analysis, post-implementation analysis, 579

source-data, preventive controls, 658–659

space allocation, monitoring, 773

span of operation criteria, documentation, 174

special-value testing, 237

specifications
  implementing, risks associated with, 38–39
  system test plan standards, 81–82
  variance from, 65

spiral testing
  methodology, 588
  RAD testing, 638

sponsor responsibilities, 590

SRS (System Requirements Specifications), 595

SSS (system security specialist), 591

staff
  administrative/organizational barriers, 865
  client/server testing readiness, 615
  competency
    barriers, 865
    efficiency measures, 852–853
    profile information, 214
  experience evaluation, 600
  people management through, 871
  software security testing, 751
  verification testing concerns, 294

stakeholder perspective, improvement barriers, 861–864

standards
  development activities, 753
  documentation process, 770
  policy criteria, 45
  system test plan, 79–82
  unit test plan, 83

start dates
  Project Status reports, 468
  timelines, 838

start time delays, inspection process concerns, 255

starting early, test plan development, 262

startup failure, post-implementation analysis, 579

state machines, functional testing, 238

state of requirements, 592

state of the art technology, tool use, 108

statement testing of, 239

static analysis
  program verification, 55
  programming testing, 324
  verification testing, 293

statistics
  operations process, 773
  profile information, 215
  statistical testing, 241

status. See project status calculation

stop it from happening concept, stakeholder perspective, 862

storage areas, software security testing, 746

storage efficiency, best practices, 850

strategies
  business innovation, 878
  converting to testing tactics, 83–85
  risk assessment, 56–57
  system development phases, identifying, 56
  test factors, selecting and ranking, 56
  V-concept testing, 74–75

strengths, building on, 857–860

stress testing
  examples of, 223
  how to use, 224
  objectives, 224
  test data for, 430
  tools associated with, 104
  validation testing, 435
  Web-based systems testing, 804, 808
  when to use, 224

stress/performance scripting, 431
strong controls, internal controls testing, 677
structural desk debugging, 325
structural testing. *See also* functional testing
  advantages/disadvantages, 69
  branch testing, 239
  conditional testing, 234
  COTS software testing, 703–704
  defined, 69
  expression testing, 240
  feasibility reviews, 70
  multiplatform environment testing, 723–725
  path testing, 240
  reasons for, 69
  requirements reviews, 70
  statement testing, 239
  stress testing
    examples of, 223
    how to use, 224
    objectives, 224
    test data for, 430
    tools associated with, 104
    validation testing, 435
    Web-based systems testing, 804, 808
    when to use, 224
  structural analysis, 238–239
  types of
  validation techniques, 69–70
  verification techniques, 69–70
  work papers, 87–91
structure components, acceptance testing, 492
substantiation objectives, cycle control objectives, 675
success factors
  effectiveness measures, 852
  people management, 871
  verification testing, 293
summaries, report, 479–480
Summary Status reports, 466–468
symbolic execution tools, 107, 239

syntactical desk debugging, 325
system access, application risks, 304
system analyst perspective, software development methodologies, 593
system boundary diagrams, 500–501
system building concepts, workbench concept, 72
system chains, revised testing approach, 50
system component identification, test plan development, 221
system control objectives, internal controls testing, 674
system development life cycle. *See* SDLC
system development processes, data warehouse testing, 770–771, 779
system independence, best practices, 850
system log tools, 107
system maintenance, test tactics, 75
System Requirements Specifications (SRS), 595
system security specialist (SSS), 591
system skills, tool selection considerations, 111, 113–114
system testing
  as functional tests, 70
  validation, 221
  Web-based systems testing, 807
system/subsystem specifications, document development, 173

T

talking the talk, management support, 51
target dates, project status calculation, 194, 468
teachable processes, 154
teams
  agile testing process, 820–821
  appointing, 168–171
  assessment
    baseline development, 10
    verification testing, 317

teams *(continued)*
 baseline information gathering,
  742–743
 combination, 170–171
 composition, 169
 cultural barriers, 875
 design reviews, 321
 external, 170
 internal, 169–170
 non-IT, 170
 report measurement, 465
 risk team establishment, 302–303
 tester agility, 842
 walkthroughs, 313
technical interface activities, 752
technical reviews, configuration
  management, 603
technical risk assessment, work papers,
  93–96
technical skills, tool selection
  considerations, 111, 114
technical status, Summary Status
  reports, 467
techniques versus tools, 103
technological developments, revised
  testing approach, 50
technology issues, COTS software
  testing challenges, 690
telephone and network switching
  equipment, test plan development,
  222
tenure, tool managers, 120
termination analysis, post-
  implementation analysis, 579
test case generators, Web-based systems
  testing, 809
test data generator tools, 107
test factors
 programming testing, 326–328
 selecting and ranking, 56
 verification testing, 299–302
 work papers, 62
test managers, 167–168

test matrix
 batch tests, 248
 defined, 245
 online system test, 248
 risk assessment, 57
 software methods, 246
 structural attributes, 246
 test matrix example, 246
 verification tests, 248–249
test plan development
 administrative components, 250–251
 automated test tools, 221
 check procedures, 262
 constraints, 214
 contingency plans, 222
 core business areas and processes, 221
 cost/schedules, 214
 customer and user involvement, lack
  of, 210
 data exchange issues, 222
 databases built/used, 214
 deliverables, 213
 facility requirements, 222
 flexibility, 262
 implementation, 214, 251
 input, 212
 inspection, 254–258
 interfaces, to other systems, 214
 lack of testing tools, 210
 lack of training concerns, 210
 legal/industry issues, 214
 lose-lose situations, 211
 objectives, 210, 213, 245
 output, 262
 over-reliance, 210
 potential failures, assessing severity of,
  221
 projects, profiling, 212–215
 RAD (rapid application development),
  210
 readability, 262
 resources needed, 221
 reviews, 262

risk assessment, 27, 215–218
schedule issues, 222
staff competency, 214
starting early, 262
statistics, 214
system component identification, 221
telephone and network switching
     equipment, 222
test matrix development, 245–248
testing concerns matrix, 219–220
testing technique selection, 222–223
unit testing and analysis, 235
us versus them mentality, 210
validation strategies, 221
V-concept testing, 157–158
work papers
     administrative checkpoint, 273–274
     batch tests, 267
     general information, 271
     inspection report, 276–280
     milestones, 272
     moderator checklist, 275
     objectives, 264
     online system tests, 268
     quality control, 283–287
     software module, 265
     structural attribute, 266
     test matrix, 270
     verification tests, 269
workbench concept, 211
written example, 252–254
test processes
vulnerabilities, 736
work papers, 24–27
test room configurations, multiplatform
     environment testing, 723
test scripts
developing, 430–432
discussed, 104
execution, 433
integration scripting, 431
maintaining, 434
pseudo-concurrency scripting, 431
regression scripting, 431

results analysis, 433
stress/performance scripting, 431
tools, 107
unit scripting, 431
test to business effectiveness, 578
test verification, SDLC, 53, 55
testability, software quality factors, 844
test-data approach, internal controls
     testing, 669–672
testers
acceptance testing roles, 44
change recommendation roles, 44
competency
     baseline development, 14–16
     CBOK (Common Body of
          Knowledge), 125–128
     competent assessment, 128
     CSTE (Certified Software Tester)
          certificate, 125, 127–128
     fully competent assessment, 128
     job performance roles, 126–127
     negative attitudes, 130
     not competent assessment, 128, 130
     training curriculum development,
          128–130
     work papers, 28–32
developmental improvement roles, 44
documentation specification
     requirement roles, 44
motivation factors, 51
process improvement roles, 44
requirements measures, 594
risk appetite, 38
tester's workbench. *See* workbench
     concept
Testing Action report, 477
testing guidelines. *See* guidelines, testing
testing methodology cube, 83, 85
testing metrics, post-implementation
     analysis, 578
testing strategies. *See* strategies
testing tactical dashboard indicators, 7
third priority, probable penetration
     points, 760

throughput testing, Web-based systems testing, 804

time improvement ideas, variability measures, 841

time-compression efforts
  best practices, 825
  calendar-day efficient, 823–824
  challenges, 824
  implementation procedures, 886–888
  readiness criteria, 826
  solutions to, 825
  V-concept testing, 826–827
  work papers, 828–830
  workbench concept, 834

timelines
  change estimation, 837
  critical path definition, 836
  documentation, 180–181
  end dates, 838
  in control processes, 832
  input, 837
  no-rework days, 839
  out of control processes, 832
  output, 837
  project name, 838
  report generation, 837
  start dates, 838
  work papers, 896–905
  workday, 839

timeouts, Web-based systems testing, 807

tool managers
  assistant, 119
  mentors, 119
  need for, 117
  positions, prerequisites to creating, 118
  responsibilities of, 117, 119–120
  skill levels, 118–119
  tenure, 120

tools
  automatic, 104
  boundary value analysis, 105
  capture, 105

cause-effect graphing, 105
checklist, 105
code comparison, 105
compiler-based analysis, 105
confirmation, 105
control flow analysis, 105
correctness proof, 105
costs, 114–116
data dictionary, 105, 770
data flow analysis, 105, 238–239
database, 105
design reviews, 105
design-based functional testing, 105
desk checking, 106
disaster testing, 106
documentation, 124
error guessing, 106, 721–722
examination, 105
executable specs, 106
fact finding, 106
flowchart, 106
inspection, 106
instrumentation, 106
integrated test facility, 106
lack of, 210
life cycle phase testing, 109–111
logging, 107
manual, 104
mapping, 106
matching to its use, 109
matching to skill levels, 111–114
modeling, 106
most used, 108
parallel operation, 106
parallel simulation, 107
peer review, 107
playback, 105
ratio, 107
relationship, 107
replacements, 120
risk matrix, 107
scoring, 107
selection considerations, 108–109, 121–123

snapshot, 107
specialized use, 108
state of the art technology, 108
stress testing, 104
symbolic execution, 107, 239
system log, 107
techniques versus, 103
test data, 107
test script, 107
tracing, 108
use case, 108
utility program, 108
walkthrough, 108
traceability
  best practices, 849
  requirements measures, 594
tracking systems, project status
    calculation, 190
traditional system development, test
    tactics, 75
training
  barriers/obstacle solutions, 868
  baseline awareness, 747
  best practices, 850
  collection methods, 747
  concerns, baseline information, 743
  curriculum, 128–130
  development activities, 753
  failures, operational testing, 524
  forms completion, 747–748
  lack of, 210
  management support needs, 51
  manual support testing, 229
  material, operational testing, 519–522
  tool usage, 116–117
transaction flow testing, 672–673
transaction processing events, 414, 724
transactions
  authorization, 755
  destruction, 756
  origination, 755
  retrieval, 756
  turnaround time, stress testing, 223
  usage, 756

transferability, critical success factors,
    696
treasury, cycle control objectives, 675
troubled projects, inadequate
    estimation, 181–182
turnaround documents, preventive
    controls, 659

U
unauthorized access, 766
undetected defects, 66
unit scripting, 431
unit testing
  as functional tests, 70
  quality control, 244
  test plan standards, 83
  validation, 221
  Web-based systems testing, 807
unknown conditions
  COTS software testing challenges, 689
  undetected defects, 66
update controls, enterprise-wide
    requirements, 767
upgrades, tool manager duties, 119–120
us versus them mentality, 210
usability
  requirements measures, 594
  software quality factors, 844
  Web-based systems testing,
      800, 806, 808
usage
  enterprise-wide requirements, 768
  training testers in, 116–117
  transaction, 756
use cases
  acceptance testing, 500–503
  tools, 108
  validation testing, 412
user acceptance
  as functional tests, 70
  implementation procedures, 885
  Web-based systems testing, 808
user education, client/server testing
    readiness, 614

user manuals, document development, 174
users
  functional testing phases, 70
  outside users, revised testing approach, 50
  participation, post-implementation analysis, 578
  profile information, 213
  reaction evaluation, 576
  roles and responsibilities, 6, 498, 590
  skills, tool selection considerations, 111–112
utilities and commands, operations activities, 754
utility program tools, 108

V

validation testing
  acceptance testing, 221
  audit trails, 435
  authorization, 434
  check procedures, 439
  compliance, 434
  concerns, 410
  correctness, 435
  coupling, 434
  design goals, defining, 414
  disaster testing, 436
  ease of operation, 436
  ease of use, 435
  execution, 434–436
  file design, 413–414
  file integrity, 435
  functional testing, 69–70
  guidelines, 439–440
  input, 411
  inspections, 436
  integration testing, 221
  maintainability, 436
  objectives, 410
  output, 439
  overview, 408
  payroll application example, 416–429
  performance, 434
  portability, 436
  preventive controls, 659–661
  recovery testing, 435
  reliability, 434
  results, documenting
    conditions, 436, 438–439
    deviation, 437
    effect, 436, 438
  security, 435
  service levels, 435
  stress testing, 435
  structural testing, 69–70
  system testing, 221
  test data
    creating, 415–416
    entering, 414
    sources, 412
    for stress testing, 430
  test plan development, 221
  test scripts
    developing, 430–432
    execution, 433
    levels of, 430
    maintaining, 434
    results analysis, 433
  transaction-processing programs, 414
  unit testing, 221
V-concept testing, 158
work papers
  audit trails, 445
  compliance, 443, 450
  correctness, 451
  coupling, 455
  ease of operations, 456
  ease of use, 452
  file integrity, 444
  functional testing, 442
  maintainability, 453
  performance, 448
  portability, 454
  problem documentation, 457
  quality control, 458
  recovery testing, 446

security, 449
stress testing, 447
test script development, 441
workbench concept, 410–411
value received,
   administrative/organizational
   barriers, 866
variability measures
  agile testing and, 820
  check procedures, 834
  competency measures, 835
  discussed, 831
  external/internal work processes, 835
  quality control, 841
  reduction, 835
  rework factors, 835
  root cause identification, 840
  time improvement ideas, 841
  timelines
    change estimation, 837
    critical path definition, 836
    end dates, 838
    in control processes, 832
    input, 837
    no-rework days, 839
    out of control processes, 832
    output, 837
    project name, 838
    report generation, 837
    start dates, 838
    workday, 839
  workbench concept, 833–834
variance from specifications, 65
V-concept testing
  acceptance testing, 158–159
  analysis, 158
  customization, 160–161
  development project types, 75
  discussed, 72–73
  facts, managing, 162
  importance of, 68
  multiplatform environment testing,
    725–726
  objectives, 159–160

operational testing, 158–159
organization, 157
overview, 156
post-implementation analysis, 159
process management, 161–162
project phases, 79
project scope, 77
reporting, 158
results management, 162
risk identification, 77–79
software system types, 76–77
strategic objectives, determining,
   74–75
strategies, converting to testing tactics,
   83–85
test plan development, 157–158
test plan standards, 79–82
testing methodology cube, 83, 85
time-compression efforts, 826–827
unit test plan standards, 83
validation testing, 158
verification testing, 158
workbench concept with, 162–163
vendors
  COTS implementation risks, 689
  interface activities, 752
  reputation importance, 690–691
  tool manager duties, 119
verification testing
  adequate control assessment, 310
  application risks, 304–308
  base case, 293
  baseline development, 13
  check procedures, 330
  concerns, 294
  control objectives, 303
  debugging, 292
  design deliverables, inspecting, 322
  design phase, 296–297
  design reviews, 320–322
  discussed, 298
  functional testing, 69–70
  guidelines, 331–332
  input, 296–297

verification testing *(continued)*
  inspections, 292
  for large documents, 248–249
  objectives, 293
  output, 331
  programming phase, 297, 323–324
  programming testing
    acceptance testing, 324
    complexity of, 323
    desk debugging, 325–326
    dynamic testing, 324
    importance of, 323
    peer reviews, 328–330
    static analysis, 324
    test factor analysis, 326–328
  project leader assessment, 317
  requirements phase, 296
  requirements tracing, 292, 314–315
  reviews, 292
  risk matrix, 293, 302
  scoring success factors, 316–318
  static analysis, 293
  structural testing, 69–70
  success factors, 293
  team assessment, 317
  test factor analysis, 310–312, 318–319
  test factors, 299–302
  V-concept testing, 158
  walkthroughs, 292, 312
  work papers
    access defined, 347, 366
    audit trails, 363, 394
    authorization rules, 342, 359–360,
      391–392
    business system design review,
      377–380
    computer applications risk scoring
      form, 349–353
    computer processing control
      procedure, 354
    computer systems design review,
      381–385
    contingency planning, 364, 395
    coupling, 404

    data integrity controls, 357–358,
      389–390
    design compliance, 367–371
    design criteria, 374–375
    failure impact, 345
    file integrity, 343, 361–362, 393
    functional specifications, 334
    interface design, 373
    maintenance specifications, 336
    needs communicated, 376
    online processing controls, 355–356
    operation procedure development,
      405
    operational needs, 340
    output control, 355
    performance criteria, 339
    portability needs, 337
    program compliance, 398–402
    quality control, 348, 387–388, 405
    reconstruction requirements, 344
    requirements compliance with
      methodology, 333
    security implementation, 397
    service levels defined, 346, 365, 396
    system interface factors, 338
    tolerances, 341
    usability specifications, 335
  workbench concept, 294–295
verification, validation, and testing
  (VV&T), 589
version changes, operational testing,
  509–511
video cards, Web-based systems testing,
  805
viruses, Web-based systems testing, 803
vulnerabilities
  central processors, 738
  computer operations, 738
  computer programs, 736–737
  data and report preparation facilities,
    737
  data handling areas, 738
  digital storage facilities, 738
  discussed, 735

impersonation, 737
input data, 736
IT operations, 736
media, 737
non-IT areas, 738
online terminal systems, 738
operating system access and integrity,
    737
output data, 736
physical access, 736
programming offices, 738
test processes, 736
VV&T (verification, validation, and
    testing), 589

W

walkthroughs
  of customer/user area, 212–213
  final reports, 314
  presentations, 313–314
  questions/recommendations,
      responding to, 314
  rules, establishing, 312–313
  team selection, 313
  tools, 108
  verification testing, 292, 312
WAN (wide area network), 800
waterfall methodology, 587
WBS (Work Breakdown Structure), 603
weak controls, internal controls testing,
    678
weaknesses, minimizing, 857–860
Web sites
  QAI (Quality Assurance Institute),
      15, 125
  Software Certifications, 125
Web-based systems testing
  access control, 803
  authorization, 803
  back-end processing, 800
  bandwidth access, 805
  browser compatibility concerns, 800,
      805–806
  caching, 805

calculation correctness, 804
check procedures, 809
code verification concerns, 800
compatibility concerns, 804–805,
    808–809
component testing, 807
concurrency testing, 804
correctness concerns, 800, 804
crashes, 807
dropped lines, 807
dynamic page generation, 806
e-mail functions, 806
file downloads, 806
graphics filters, 805
guidelines, 810
hardware compatibility, 805
HTML tools, 809
input, 801–802
integration concerns, 800
integration testing, 807
load testing, 808
lost connections, 807
memory, 805
monitors, 805
multimedia support, 805
navigation correctness, 804
output, 810
overview, 799
performance concerns, 800, 803–804
performance testing, 808
print handling, 805
recoverability concerns, 807
regression testing, 808
reliability concerns, 806
reload pages, 805
risk assessment, 802–803
security concerns, 800, 803
site validation tools, 809
stress testing, 804, 808
system testing, 807
test case generators, 809
throughput testing, 804
timeouts, 807
unit testing, 807

Web-based systems testing *(continued)*
  usability concerns, 800, 806
  usability testing, 808
  user acceptance testing, 808
  video cards, 805
  viruses, 803
  work papers
    quality control checklist, 815
    risk assessment, 812
    testing tool selection, 814
    testing types, 813
  workbench concept, 800–801
weighted criteria score, documentation,
    175–177
wide area network (WAN), 800
Work Breakdown Structure (WBS), 603
work flow, COTS software testing,
    698–699
work papers
  acceptance testing
    acceptance criteria, 527
    acceptance plan form creation,
      544–545
    automated application criteria,
      566–567
    change control forms, 546
    checklist, 550–551
    data change forms, 547–548
    deletion instructions, 538–539
    installation phase, 531
    inventory material, 552–553
    production change instructions,
      536–537
    program change form completion,
      540–541, 549
    program change history, 534–535
    quality control checklist, 560–563
    recovery planning data, 532–533
    system boundary diagram, 528
    system problem form completion,
      542–543
    test cases, 530
    training checklist form completion,
      558–559

    training failure notification, 568–569
    training module form completion,
      556–557
    training plan form completion,
      554–555
    training quality control checklist,
      564–565
    use cases, 504–507, 529
agile testing process, 923–927
barriers
  communication barriers, 920–922
  cultural barriers, 919
  stakeholder analysis, 915–918
best practices, 906–908
CBOK (Common Body of Knowledge)
  individual competency evaluation,
    149
  new information technology, 148
  project management, 135–138
  security procedure assessment,
    146–147
  software controls, 146
  test environment, building, 133–135
  test planning, 138–143
  test status and analysis, 143–144
  test team competency evaluation,
    150
  testing principles and concepts,
    132–133
  user acceptance testing, 144–145
client/server systems testing
  client data, 627–628
  footprint chart, 631
  quality control checklist, 632
  readiness results, 630
  security, 626–627
  standards, 628–629
  system installation, 625
COTS (commercial off-the-shelf)
    software testing
  completeness tests, 707–708
  functional testing, 710
  quality control checklist, 712–715
  structural testing, 711

data warehouse testing
  access control, 785
  activity process, 797
  audio trails, 784
  concerns rating, 788, 795–796
  continuity of processing, 792
  data, placing in wrong calendar
      period, 787
  documentation, 791
  fraud, 789
  inadequate responsibility
      assignment, 781
  inadequate service levels, 786
  incomplete data concerns, 782
  management support concerns, 794
  performance criteria, 793
  quality control checklist, 798
  reviews, 790
  update concerns, 783
documentation
  completeness, 202
  estimation, 203–205
  quality control checklist, 207–209
  weighted criteria calculation, 201
footprint chart, 23
internal controls testing
  documentation, 679
  file control, 683
  input controls, 679–681
  output control, 682
  program and processing controls,
      681–682
methodologies, software development
  analysis footprint, 609
  self-assessment, 607–608
multiplatform environment testing
  concerns, 728
  configurations, 728
  quality control checklist, 731–732
  validity, 729–730
post-implementation analysis, 582
RAD (rapid application development)
      testing
  applicability checklist, 644

  conceptual model development,
      646–647
  logical data model development, 647
  production system development,
      651–652
  production system release, 652
  quality control checklist, 653
  scope and purpose of system
      definition, 645–646
  specifications, revising, 650–651
  system development, 648–649
  test system release, 652
reports
  defect reporting, 484–485
  quality control, 486–487
  writing guidelines, 488–489
risk score analysis, 99
self-assessment, 909–914
size risk assessment, 97–98
software security testing, 763
software testing environment, 19–22
structural testing, 87–91
technical risk assessment, 93–96
test factor ranks, 58–59, 61
test plan development
  administrative checkpoint, 273–274
  batch tests, 267
  general information, 271
  inspection report, 276–280
  milestones, 272
  moderator checklist, 275
  objectives, 264
  online system tests, 268
  quality control, 283–287
  software module, 265
  structural attribute, 266
  test matrix, 270
  verification tests, 269
tester competency assessment, 28–32
time-compression efforts, 828–830
timelines, 896–905
tool use
  documentation, 124
  selection considerations, 121–123

work papers *(continued)*
  validation testing
    audit trails, 445
    compliance, 443, 450
    correctness, 451
    coupling, 455
    ease of operations, 456
    ease of use, 452
    file integrity, 444
    functional testing, 442
    maintainability, 453
    performance, 448
    portability, 454
    problem documentation, 457
    quality control, 458
    recovery testing, 446
    security, 449
    stress testing, 447
    test script development, 441
  verification testing
    access defined, 347, 366
    audit trails, 363, 394
    authorization rules, 342, 359–360,
      391–392
    business system design review,
      377–380
    computer applications risk scoring
      form, 349–353
    computer processing control
      procedure, 354
    computer systems design review,
      381–385
    contingency planning, 364, 395
    coupling, 404
    data integrity controls, 357–358,
      389–390
    design compliance, 367–371
    design criteria, 374–375
    failure impact, 345
    file integrity, 343, 361–362, 393
    functional specifications, 334
    interface design, 373
    maintenance specifications, 336
    need communicated, 376

    online processing controls, 355–356
    operation procedure development,
      405
    operational needs, 340
    output control, 355
    performance criteria, 339
    portability, 337, 372, 403
    program compliance, 398–402
    quality control, 348, 387–388, 405
    reconstruction requirements, 344
    requirements compliance with
      methodology, 333
    security implementation, 397
    service levels defined, 346, 365, 396
    system interface factors, 338
    tolerances, 341
    usability specifications, 335
  Web-based systems testing
    quality control checklist, 815
    risk assessment, 812
    testing tool selection, 814
    testing types, 813
workbench concept
  acceptance testing, 494
  client/server systems testing, 613
  COTS software testing, 692
  data warehouse testing, 766–767
  input component, 71
  internal controls testing, 667
  multiplatform environment testing,
    719–720
  multiple workbenches, 72
  organization, 166
  output components, 71
  post-implementation analysis, 572–573
  procedures to check, 71
  procedures to do, 71
  process advantages, 163
  RAD (rapid application development)
    testing, 635–636
  results analysis, 460
  software security testing, 734–735
  system building concepts, 72
  test plan development, 211

testing tools and, 71
time-compression efforts, 834
validation testing, 410–411
variability measures, 833–834
with V-concept testing, 162–163
verification testing, 294–295
Web-based systems testing, 800–801
workday timelines, 839
working documents, 178
world-class testing organization
  baseline development
    assessment teams, 10
    capabilities assessment, 13–14
    cause-effect diagram, 9
    drivers, 8

environment assessment, 8
footprint charts, 10
implementation procedures, 9
results assessments, 11–12
verification, 13
discussed, 3
improvement planning, 16–18
PDCA (plan-do-check-act) cycle, 4–5
software development process, 4
software testing model definition
  discussed, 5
  organization, 7
  self assessment, 6
wrong specifications, defects, 65, 471